MURDER and MAYHEM:

An Annotated Bibliography of
Gay and Queer Males in Mystery,
1909-2018

by *Matt Lubbers-Moore*

ReQueered Tales
Los Angeles • Toronto
2020

Murder and Mayhem:

An Annotated Bibliography of Gay and Queer Males in Mystery, 1909-2018

by Matt Lubbers-Moore

Copyright © 2020 by Matt Lubbers-Moore.

Cover design: Dawné Dominique, DusktilDawn Designs.

A ReQueered Tales Original Publication, February 2020

ReQueered Tales version 1.50
Kindle edition ASIN: B084DHYF2C
Epub edition ISBN-13: 978-1-951092-14-6
Print edition ISBN-13: 978-1-951092-15-3

For more information about current and future releases, please contact us:
E-mail: requeeredtales@gmail.com
Facebook (Like us!): www.facebook.com/ReQueeredTales/
Twitter: @ReQueered
Instagram: www.instagram.com/requeered/
Web: www.ReQueeredTales.com
Blog: www.ReQueeredTales.com/blog
Mailing list (Subscribe for latest news): http://bit.ly/RQTJoin

ReQueered Tales is a California General Partnership.
All rights reserved. © 2020 ReQueered Tales unless otherwise noted.

MURDER and MAYHEM

An Annotated Bibliography
of Gay and Queer Males in Mystery,
1909-2018

by Matt Lubbers-Moore

Table of Contents

MURDER and MAYHEM
Copyright 2
Acknowledgments 7
   Introduction 8
   How to Use the Bibliography 11
The As 17
The Bs 40
The Cs 122
The Ds 181
The Es 195
The Fs 204
The Gs 230
The Hs 256
The Is 302
The Js 308
The Ks 320
The Ls 352
The Ms 397
The Ns 455
The Os 463
The Ps 469
The Qs 498
The Rs 501
The Ss 536
The Ts 586
The Us 603
The Vs 605
The Ws 608
The Ys 627
The Zs 628
The Man with the Watches 640
References 657

About Matt Lubbers-Moore 659
About ReQueered Tales 660
More ReQueered Tales 662
One Last Word 667

Acknowledgments:

I took on this project as a bit of a hobby in 2014 after interviewing Drewey Wayne Gunn for the Facebook Gay Mysteries-Suspense-Thriller group I co-moderate with Jon Michaelsen. I created an open source bibliography of gay mysteries, but I had a hard time following it because a list of names and authors tells me little about the book itself; plot, how much gay content, what's the mystery genre, and how much is the plot about the mystery. Following Gunn's example, I put together an annotated bibliography. For his encouragement and for leading the way I owe Drewey Wayne Gunn a huge debt. As Gunn passed away in 2018 I will attempt to continue his legacy of writing about gay literary history as much as I can. Although his expertise was far greater than mine I will attempt to build upon the knowledge he left behind.

I owe a great deal to Ty Chadwell, Graeme Cheater, Alexander Inglis, Pekka, and Jon Michaelsen for beta reading and sending me titles that I had not heard of, especially Pekka, who provided me with over three hundred titles as he explored individual publisher websites, Goodreads, Amazon, and a score of other sites more deeply than I had initially. To the authors who assisted me with their entries: Michael Craft, Frank Butterfield, Dean James, Marcia Muller, Neil Plakcy, C. S. Poe, Steven Saylor, Marshall Thornton, and Mark Zubro I am greatly humbled. Thank you to Dawné Dominique for the beautiful cover and my awesome business partners at ReQueered Tales, Justene Adamec and Alexander Inglis for their encouragement and their drive to keep me going. For Jon Michaelsen, for always being there with a piece of advice or encouragement. I also greatly appreciate my good friend Fiona Furlong Plumstead who helped me with the correct transgender terminology.

Most importantly for Doug, my husband, who has tolerated, and somehow slept through, my nighttime typing. I love you more every day and haven't stopped whistling *Walking on Sunshine* yet.

And my mother, Robin Darling, who has been my moral support from day one.

Introduction:

What defines a mystery? What makes a mystery gay? Can a mystery be only a murder investigation, or can it be more than that, involving jewel thefts or arson or kidnapping? Can a mystery take place in outer space, in the future, involve paranormal creatures, or a speculative present? Can thrillers, suspense, horror, westerns be mysteries? Can romances be mysteries? Otto Penzler, author of a great many books about mysteries including *Bibliomysteries: An Annotated Bibliography of First Editions of Mystery Fiction Set in the World of Books, 1849-2000*, writes that romances, as long as they include more mystery than romance, can be counted, but westerns are westerns, science fiction/fantasy are a genre apart, that horrors and paranormal events are excluded from mysteries for being outside the norm of police departments and private eyes unless they involve police departments and private eyes. "Exceptions could be made," he writes. Drewey Wayne Gunn also chose to be narrow in his *The Gay Male Sleuth in Print and Film: A History and Annotated Bibliography*. Only police detectives, private eyes, and amateur sleuths make the cut. I chose to be less narrow and even less rigid in my selections which some argue could make this less useful to completists of gay mysteries, but I disagree. I make sure to state the type of mystery genre of each title and the amount of gay content. One could then make their own mind up if they choose to add that title to their collection or not. Penzler and Gunn chose to exclude e-books from their bibliographies as e-books can be there one day and gone the next, but I chose to include them as they could be an important step in the author's works or be a missing story in a series, but I do make a distinction in the bibliography if they are only available as an e-book. This bibliography is more inclusive than exclusive. There are titles with MTF/FTM transgender characters, bisexual characters, and there are MM romance titles. I chose to include all titles and let the reader decide what they want to exclude than attempting to make that decision for them.

Most of the books in this bibliography have been culled from Gunn's bibliography listed above, from Anthony Slide's *Gay and Lesbian Characters and Themes in Mystery Novels: A Critical Guide to Over 500 Works in English*, and *Murder in the Closet: Essays on Queer Clues in Crime Fiction Before Stonewall* edited by Curtis Evans. Gunn's bibliography had the most updated titles but was last updated in 2012 therefore hundreds of titles were uncollected in any bibliography. Jon Michaelsen and I run a Facebook group that discusses, shares, and collects gay mysteries-suspense-thrillers and I began to mine the titles from the group. I also began searching the Internet for lists of gay mysteries: Neil Plakcy created a list on his website; I used the LAMBDA Literary organization to find gay mysteries; Goodreads, and Amazon have been quite useful. Mark McNease invited me onto his podcast where I discussed my work on this bibliography and a few people began sending me updates and titles that were missing on the open source bibliography I had compiled as a way for more input from readers and authors of the field.

The purpose of my bibliography was to identify mystery novels that include a gay or queer male in whatever role the author assigned him. I started this project after interviewing Drewey Wayne Gunn and he suggested an open source website to accumulate gay mysteries. This required a deep dive into Gunn's own bibliography about gay male sleuths, Anthony Slide's bibliography of gay and lesbians in mystery novels, Curtis Evans' essays on gay and lesbians in mystery novels pre-Stonewall, and Ian Young's non-annotated bibliography of gay men in literature. Gunn's bibliography was the latest published in 2012 and left a six-year gap between the time he stopped and the time I decided to set the end date which required searching publisher websites, Goodreads, Amazon, Facebook groups, Instagram hashtags, Twitter hashtags, and following many different authors.

The bibliography is important for future generations to be able to find works in which gay and queer men appear and how they appear. Early examples of gay and queer men appearances were side characters: usually the bachelor, the quiet male couple in the flat above or below who kept to themselves, or the lady love interest who turns out to be a man. They were always hidden until the 50s and 60s when gay men started becoming the main character, the actual detective. It was an evolution of what publishers and authors believed the general population would be ready for and an evolution of how far gay and queer men have come in society.

I have been working on this bibliography since early 2014 and chose to cut the bibliography off at 2018 primarily because it will be easier for me to update the bibliography over the years rather than adding to it with the possibility of publishing eventually. All bibliographies are a work in progress and this one is no different as I'm positive that there have been books I've missed or wrongly described. I would be more than happy to make corrections as they're presented to me.

How to use the bibliography:

In the bibliography the entries are listed in alphabetical order by author's last name, then in chronological order based on publication dates and in the event of a series the entire series will be listed altogether and then a standalone book, or another series will follow based on the first publication date of the first book in the series. For example, if an author had a series start in 1990 with a last book in the series coming out in 2000 and a standalone book that came out in 1995, the standalone book will follow the 2000 title.

The entries read as follows:
- last name, first name (real name and/or birth/death dates),
- title of the book,
- publisher,
- date first published.
- If part of a series, the name of the series as well as book number in the series is listed next.
- (Mystery Genre)
- Then the book blurb borrowed from Goodreads, Amazon, Gunn, Slide, Evans, or a website description of the book. Some blurbs have been edited for space, grammar, and/or spelling.
- After the blurb I will include information about the book, whether it has been updated, revised, reprinted, any factual information that I believe is important, and if the book has won any major awards such as a LAMBDA or an Edgar. I then conclude this section with who wrote the extra information: Gunn, Slide, me (MLM), or someone else.
- The last aspect of the entry is the valuation of involvement of a gay character:

1 has very little, such as a gay character offering a clue or being a suspect but his homosexuality plays no part in the story other than to add supposed depth to the character,

2 is a gay character who is helpful in solving the mystery

but not the main character,
> **3** is the main character is gay, transgender, or bisexual.

A note about publishing dates. I based the publication dates on when the book was first published. Also, if the title was originally published as an eBook in 2005 but a physical copy came out in 2010, the 2010 publication date is the one I use as the physical copy is the most stable and longer lasting.

This bibliography can follow the acceptance of gay and queer men in mysteries from when they first appeared to the present day and not all authors wrote about gay or queer men in a positive light. Therefore some of the comments below the titles explain how the author may have been homophobic or written their main character to be homophobic/transphobic.

Mystery Genre Definitions:

Amateur Sleuth: The amateur sleuth tries to solve the murder of someone close. Either the police have tried and failed or misread the murder as an accident/suicide. Both the loss and need for a solution is personal. -Definition provided by Stephen D. Rogers.

Bibliomystery: Mystery stories set in the world of books; libraries, bookstores, or those who deal with books; authors, book collectors, book sellers, editors, or publishers.

BDSM: Sexual activity involving such practices as the use of physical restraints, the granting and relinquishing of control, and the infliction of pain –Definition provided by Merriam Webster. BDSM is not a genre of mysteries but I include it as a warning to those who may not want to read sexually explicit and sexually violent titles (MLM).

Caper: A caper is a comic crime story. Instead of suave and calculating, the caper chronicles the efforts of the lovable bungler who either thinks big or ridiculously small. -Definition provided by Stephen D. Rogers.

Classics: Classics are often written by authors in the late 19th and early 20th century, i.e. Agatha Christie, Rex Stout, Raymond Chandler, Daphne du Maurier, Dashiell Hammett, Wilkie Collins, Edgar Allan Poe, and Sir Arthur Conan Doyle. These are the authors that all mystery is built on.

Coming of Age: when a person reaches an important stage of development, growing into adulthood, becoming a mature adult. – Definition provided by Collins Dictionary.

Courtroom Drama/Legal Thriller: Lawyers make effective protagonists since they seem to exist on a plane far above the rest of us. Although popular, these tales are usually penned by actual lawyers due to the demands of the information presented. -Definition provided by Stephen D. Rogers.

Cozies: The cozy, typified by Agatha Christie, contains a bloodless crime and a victim who won't be missed. The solution can be determined using emotional or logical reasoning. There is no sex or swearing, and the detective is traditionally heterosexual or asexual. -Definition provided by Stephen D. Rogers.

- ***Modern Cozies***: Unlike classic cozies, modern cozies include some swearing, discussions of sex, and can have a homosexual detective.

Crime Drama: Suspense in the crime story comes from wondering whether the plan will work. We're rooting for the bad guys because they are smart, organized, and daring. -Definition provided by Stephen D. Rogers.

Domestic Violence: A story that has as its basis violent acts between a couple.

Erotica: A story that is more focused on the sexual lives of the characters than the plot. Closely related to pulps/modern pulps.

Espionage: Spy novels.

Family Drama: A story that focuses on generations of a single family.

Fantasy: Fantasy mysteries involve being transported through time or having super human abilities. Similar but slightly different than paranormal mysteries.

Fictionalized True Crime: Fictionalized true crime novels are based on real events.

Foreign Mysteries: Mysteries that are written by an author in different country and set in that country and then translated into English.

Gothic: Creepy foreboding atmosphere and setting that creates a sense of thrill and terror. Places gothic stories are often located in old castles/mansions, cemeteries, New Orleans, Transylvania, back alleys, or small communities populated by "tribal" religions.

Graphic Novels: Stories that are illustrated rather than pure text.

Historical: Written in contemporary times but the plot is set decades or centuries prior.

Horror: Supernatural beings killing or terrorizing people and those people have to figure out how to stop the supernatural beings. Dark and gritty compared to paranormal.

Jeu D'espirit: a lighthearted display of wit and cleverness, especially in a work of literature. -Definition provided by Dictionary.com.

Journalism: Reporters/journalists are the detectives solving the crime.

Military: An investigation performed by military police or a member of the military.

MM: When these are in front of a genre it means that the romance takes precedence over the genre. MM is the abbreviation for male/male and are known for their explicit sexual encounters.

- *MM Mystery*: The mystery is tertiary to the characters and romance.

Moral Tales: Stories that are written to promote certain morals and ethics among its readers.

Paranormal: Paranormal mysteries involve vampires, ghosts, werewolves, psychics, or other supernatural being. Usually lighter than horror and is similar to fantasy.

Political: Mysteries set around the world of politics; may involve a senator, a president, governor, or other political leader. Often set behind the scenes.

Private Detectives: The Private Eye is as much an American icon as the Western gunslinger. From the hardboiled PIs of the 30s and 40s to the politically correct investigators of today, this subgenre is known for protagonists with a strong code of honor. -Definition provided by Stephen D. Rogers.

- *Hard Boiled Private Eye*: these are serious detective novels that take on serious cases and issues.
- *Soft Boiled Private Eye*: these are often comical detective novels that do not deal with serious cases or issues.

Police Procedurals: The police procedural emphasizes factual police operations. Law enforcement is a team effort where department politics often plays a large role. -Definition provided by Stephen D. Rogers.

Psychological: Psychological mysteries are often more about the main character than the mystery or plot. The main character solves the mystery using the mind, skills, and wit and can involve a psychiatrist as the detective. These are often cerebral mysteries.

Pulp Fiction: Fiction dealing with lurid or sensational subjects, often printed on rough, low-quality paper manufactured from wood pulp. –Definition provided by Merriam Webster.

- Modern Pulp: Fiction that deals with lurid or sensational subjects but is no longer printed on rough, low-quality paper.

Science Fiction: A mystery dealing principally with the impact of actual or imagined science on society or individuals or having a scientific factor as an essential orienting component. –Definition provided by Merriam Webster.

Serial (literature): Anything published, broadcast, etc., in short installments at regular intervals, as a novel appearing in successive issues of a magazine. Very popular way to publish long stories in the Victorian and early 1900s. Dickens, Doyle, Armistead Maupin, and many others published serials in local and national newspapers and magazines, but it is not used very often in contemporary times.

Sherlock Holmes: A mystery novel that has Sherlock Holmes as the central character.

- *Contemporary Sherlock Holmes*: a Sherlock Holmes that lives and takes place in modern times rather than the Victorian age.
- *Futuristic Sherlock Holmes:* a Sherlock Holmes that lives and takes place in a future time or Steam Punk.

Speculative: Similar to Science Fiction, speculative mysteries are set in alternative universes.

Straight Romance (MF): Stories that are focused primarily on a relationship of an opposite sex couple, closely related to Gay Romance (MM) titles.

Suspense: Instead of the sleuth pursuing the criminal, in suspense the protagonist is the one being pursued. You often hear the point of view of both the protagonist and antagonist. –Definition provided by Stephen D. Rogers.

Thriller: Similar to suspense and horror, antagonists hunt the protagonist until the main characters are able to turn the chase around and win the day.

True Crime: A non-fiction literary genre in which an author examines an actual crime and details of real people. –Definition provided by Definitions.com.

Unreliable Narrator: A narrator of the story that gives the reader mistruths, mis-directions, or outright lies to throw the reader off the scent of who committed the crime.

Note: Some titles may use more than one genre or they may cross genres. Titles with multiple viewpoints may fit different genres based on who the character is. A title could be both a crime drama and a police procedural if it follows both the criminal and the police investigating them.

The definitions provided by Stephen D. Rogers are from https://www.writing-world.com/mystery/genres.shtml and are used with his expressed permission.

A

1. **Abbott, Jeff**, *Promises of Home*, Ballantine Books, March 1996. Jordan Poteet Mystery #4 of 4. (Bibliomystery) In a small Texas town, murder brings home the unforgotten past. Twenty years ago, as Hurricane Althea lashed Central Texas, twelve-year-old Jordan Poteet and his friends decided to ride it out in their tree house. But in the still eye of the tempest, they raced for safety–and stumbled over the body of a beautiful girl. Now, the six schoolmates who shared the grisly sight of death so long ago are being coolly murdered, one by one, day by day. By whom? Why? Unless Jordan and Police Chief Junebug Moncrief, another survivor of the storm, can answer those questions fast, it will be their turn to die... –Poteet is surprised to learn of someone's homosexuality (MLM). 1/3

2. **Abramson, Mark**, *Beach Reading*, Lethe Press, 2008. Beach Reading Mysteries #1 of 7. (Amateur Sleuth) Gay tourists are arriving in San Francisco by the planeload for the party of the decade at the Moscone Center, a tribute to a late disco star. On the same night as the dance festival, an infamous evangelist plans to bring his nationwide crusade against gay rights to the Civic Auditorium a few blocks away. Tim Snow finds himself caught in the middle when his activist friends plan a protest. For Tim, the fun and the intrigue are about to begin. 3/3

3. **Abramson, Mark**, *Cold Serial Murder*, Lethe Press, 2009. Beach Reading Mysteries #2 of 7. (Amateur Sleuth) Tim Snow expected to show his visiting Aunt Ruth the wonders of San Francisco, but never expected one of the sights of the city would be the body of his ex-lover. A killer is on the loose in the Castro district. Meanwhile, Tim's cadre of quirky friends and neighbors makes life all the more interesting with their drama of weddings and lost (and found) loves. 3/3

4. **Abramson, Mark**, *Russia River Rat*, Lethe Press, 2009. Beach Reading Mysteries #3 of 7. (Amateur Sleuth) Tim Snow is sure he's finally found the perfect man, a handsome guy with a successful greenhouse business by the Russian River. With his beloved Aunt Ruth now moved to San Francisco, his life should be worry-free. But San Francisco Chronicle's best-selling author Mark Abramson can't stop with telling lively mysteries–Tim starts having troubling dreams; a drowned body haunts his boyfriend, who may be less than perfect; and there are men from both their pasts who might be deadly.

5. **Abramson, Mark**, *Snowman,* Lethe Press, 2010. Beach Reading Mysteries #4 of 7. (Amateur Sleuth) All is not well in the City by the Bay. Tim Snow, recently recovered from a debilitating accident, finds himself aimless and troubled over waning feelings for his boyfriend. And just when he wants to escape all the troubles in his life, new complications arise... three M's worth of trouble: mayhem (a visit from his bigoted and big-haired cousin from Texas), men (a handsome fashion model who's sending mixed signals), and menace (body parts found in the dumpster of Artie's, the restaurant where Tim's works as a waiter). As if the investigations of the police aren't disruptive enough, secrets are soon revealed that affect not only Tim's family by blood but also the treasured souls of the Castro he's made an essential part of his life. 3/3

6. **Abramson, Mark**, *Wedding Season,* Lethe Press, 2011. Beach Reading Mysteries #5 of 7. (Amateur Sleuth) The entire cast of quirky characters is back for Book Seven. Artie's performing career has him traveling more. Aunt Ruth tries to wean herself from San Francisco into married life in Hillsborough. Tim's family–both adopted and blood–are beset by drama amid a rash of armed robberies in the neighborhood. There's a sexy new cop on the Castro beat, and people are getting shot. Nick is in Europe with his grandmother and Tim is left behind to figure out the rules of a 21st century gay relationship. Can–and should–Tim resist Cupid's arrows for such hotties as the sexy cop or the guy he just met at the bar? And what about the teenage British gymnast he's met on the Internet who's asked for an ominous birthday gift? Tim has to decide if honesty is always part of the rules of love. What's love got to do with it? Maybe everything. 3/3

7. **Abramson, Mark**, *California Dreamers,* Lethe Press, 1 January 2012. Beach Reading Mysteries #6 of 7. (Amateur Sleuth) Tim Snow is recruited along with other HIV patients for an experiment with Neutriva, an AIDS drug with the peculiar side effect of enhancing dreams and expanding latent psychic abilities. The team enters a trance-like state ostensibly in order to predict and prevent suicides from the Golden Gate Bridge. But is something sinister going on with these trials? Warnings come from all directions, including from an elderly fortune teller named Malvina who has been plying her trade from a storefront in the Mission District for decades. And who is the mysterious young man who saves the life of Tim's employer? 3/3

8. **Abramson, Mark**, *Love Rules,* Lethe Press, 1 May 2013. Beach Reading Mysteries #7 of 7. (Amateur Sleuth) The entire cast of quirky characters is back. Artie's performing career has him traveling more.

Aunt Ruth tries to wean herself from San Francisco into married life in Hillsborough. Tim's family–both adopted and blood–are beset by drama amid a rash of armed robberies in the neighborhood. There's a sexy new cop on the Castro beat, and people are getting shot. Nick is in Europe with his grandmother and Tim is left behind to figure out the rules of a 21st century gay relationship. Can–and should–Tim resist Cupid's arrows for such hotties as the sexy cop or the guy he just met at the bar? And what about the teenage British gymnast he's met on the Internet who's asked for an ominous birthday gift? Tim has to decide if honesty is always part of the rules of love. What's love got to do with it? Maybe everything. 3/3

9. **Abreu, Caio Fernando**, *Whatever Happened to Dulce Veiga*, trans. from Portuguese by Adria Frizzi, University of Texas Press, 2000. (Journalism) A forty-year-old Brazilian journalist reduced to living in a dilapidated building inhabited by a bizarre human fauna–fortune-tellers, transvestites, tango-loving Argentinean hustlers–is called upon to track down and write the story of Dulce Veiga, a famous singer who disappeared twenty years earlier on the eve of her first big show. Thus, begins a mad race through an underground, nocturnal São Paulo among rock bands with eccentric names, feline reincarnations of Vita Sackville-West, ex-revolutionaries turned junkies, gay Pietas, echoes of Afro-Brazilian religions, and intimations of AIDS ... 3/3

10. **Ackroyd, Dorothy**, *The Case of the Purloined Picasso,* Kindle, 2017. (Cozy) Nick and Norton, SF art gallery owners and men about town, are pulled in to solve the mystery of a purloined Picasso painting. Norton's sister has been accused of stealing the painting from her estranged husband. Nick and Norton know that she couldn't have done it. The suspects range from a jealous painter, to a sleazy art dealer, to a security consultant with a disreputable past. –available as an e-book only (MLM). 3/3

11. **Adams, Derek**, *The Adventures of Miles Diamond and the Case of the Missing Twin,* Badboy, 1993. (Pulp) Miles Diamond Adventures #1 of 3. The erotic adventures of intrepid detective Miles Diamond kick off with The Case of the Missing Twin. Miles is a genius in the bedroom, although he is often at a loss when it comes to solving crimes. Unwilling to let his limitations stand in his way, Miles constantly finds himself in a variety of compromising positions with a cast of randy studs–each of whom harbors a secret of two of his own. Miles diligently sets about uncovering everything within reach as he tracks down the elusive and delectable Daniel Travis. 3/3

12. **Adams, Derek**, *The Adventures of Miles Diamond and the Demon of Death,* Badboy, 1995. Miles Diamond Adventure #2 of 3. (Pulp) Miles stumbles onto an insurance embezzlement scam set up by a

prominent Seattle collector of Mexican artifacts and director of the museum. A small statue is taken, but Miles steals it. When Rudy recognizes it as the demon of death, the trio head for Mexico to see if it is, as rumored, the key to ancient treasures. Rudy realizes the statue is part of a map; Miles sees that it is literally the key to unlock the treasures' doors. 3/3

13. **Adams, Derek**, *The Adventures of Miles Diamond and the Cretan Apollo*, Badboy, 1998. Miles Diamond Adventures #3 of 3. (Pulp) Gay gumshoe Miles Diamond returns for his most perilous case yet! Hired by a wealthy man to track a happy-go-lucky lover, Miles finds himself involved in ways he could never have imagined! When the dangerously jealous Callahan threatens not only Diamond but his lovely boytoy of a sidekick, Miles counters with a little undercover work involving as many horny informants as he can get his hands on! 3/3

14. **Adams, Derek**, *Mark of the Wolf*, Badboy, 1996. (Pulp) Jeffrey Ashford, who thinks he has killed three people, seeks out the aid of police detective Tom Kellerman. 3/3

15. **Aedin, M. Jules**, *Windows in Time*, Frisco, TX, Dreamspinner, 2009. (Amateur Sleuth) Fate added injury to insult when Jonah Sellers's live-in boyfriend left him: while moving out his ex's belongings, Jonah fell down the stairs and broke his leg. Now his house is a prison, and he's working from home while his sister checks up on him. The only diversion in Jonah's routine is catching the odd glimpse of a man in the apartment across the way taking off his clothes in front of the window. But then Jonah is distracted by Liam Brooks, the nurse his sister sends over when she goes on vacation. As they dance around their growing attraction, Jonah and Liam begin to wonder about the man in the window. Why is he always dressed in the same clothes? Why is he there one minute and not the next? How is it that he lives in an old woman's apartment? It's while trying to answer these questions that they stumble across a fifty-year-old missing persons case they can't resist trying to solve. 3/3

16. **Alan, Kage**, *Operation Thunderspell*, Zumaya, 2010. (Espionage Caper) Agents Nicholas Inker and Anthony Hamilton: one's American, the other is Chinese. One has the brains, the other the brawn. And the one thing they share, besides annoying each other, is an arsenal of insults for anyone caught in the crossfire. 3/3

17. **Albanese, Joe**, *Mystery Without Clues*, iUniverse, 2000. Jeremy and Sheraton Mystery #1 of 4. (Amateur Sleuth) They're Not Exactly Nick and Nora! What happens when you take two gay men, one lesbian neighbor, a cross-dresser, a woman on the verge of a nervous breakdown, and assorted other characters and mix in a murder?

A fast and funny murder mystery set in Greenwich Village. Jeremy Baker and Sheraton Rogers, along with their new friend Pris, have quite a time trying to figure out who killed an old college friend. 3/3

18. **Albanese, Joe**, *Textbook Murders,* iUniverse, 2005. Jeremy and Sheraton Mystery #2 of 4. (Amateur Sleuth) Lovers Jeremy Baker and Sheraton Rogers are not having the well-deserved vacation they promised themselves. When bizarre occurrences begin to happen at an isolated all-boys school, Jeremy and Sheraton start investigating-only to discover that everyone involved is in danger. Besides the eerie behavior of the students, the increasingly eccentric staff members, a mix of the supernatural, and a shocking murder prove anything but relaxing for the duo. While meeting all sorts of characters-both funny and dangerous-they remain determined to uncover the identity of the killer. 3/3

19. **Albanese, Joe**, *Our Lady of the Assassins,* Createspace, 2008. Jeremy and Sheraton Mystery #3 of 4. (Amateur Sleuth) When Jeremy, Sheraton and Pris try to defend a friend accused of murder, they are in for nothing short of holy hell. The man says he is innocent. So, who shot the blackmailer? According to the prime suspect, The Blessed Virgin Mother! 3/3

20. **Albanese, Joe**, *Facing Giants,* Createspace, 2012. Jeremy and Sheraton Mystery #4 of 4. (Amateur Sleuth) While rehearsing a play, the death of a young street hustler throws everybody into a panic. It is left to Jeremy and Sheraton to figure out who saw to it that Kid Kidd took his final curtain, and they aim to do so even if it means they'll die trying! 3/3

21. **Alding, Peter (Roderic Jeffries, 1926-)**, *Betrayed by Death,* Walker and Co., 1982. A C.I.D. Room Mystery #13 of 14. (Police Procedural) Inspector Fusil investigates the murders of nine young boys and discovers a relationship between the killings and a series of minor crimes. –gay man, although not defined as one, is suspected of the crimes (MLM). 1/3

22. **Aldyne, Nathan (Michael McDowell 1950-1999 & Dennis Schuetz 1946-1989)**, *Vermillion,* Avon, 1987. (Amateur Sleuth) Valentine and Lovelace Mystery #1 of 4. Driven by differing motives, Clarisse Lovelace, gay bartender Daniel Valentine, and a Boston detective trying to crack down on the gay community search for the murderer of a young hustler found dead with a lipstick-smeared handkerchief in his pocket. 3/3

23. **Aldyne, Nathan**, *Cobalt,* St Martin's Press, 1982. Valentine and Lovelace Mystery #2 of 4. (Amateur Sleuth) Daniel and Clarisse are summering in Provincetown (he is tending bar and she's working at a

gift shop) when Clarisse discovers Jeff's body on a beach. "Cobalt" is the color of Jeff's arresting eyes, and those eyes have made him both a lot of friends and quite a few enemies. Which of these killed him? 3/3

24. **Aldyne, Nathan**, *Slate*, Villard, 1984. Valentine and Lovelace Mystery #3 of 4. (Amateur Sleuth) Slate is set in an exuberantly pre-AIDS world, when to be young, attractive, and the owner of a successful gay bar was a dandy thing indeed. Clarisse has hauled her dainty posterior off to law school, Valentine has opened Boston's grooviest gay boite, Donna Summer is still on the radio, and there's a dead body at the disco: Life doesn't get a whole lot more fun. 3/3

25. **Aldyne, Nathan**, *Canary*, Ballantine Books, 1986. Valentine and Lovelace Mystery #4 of 4. (Amateur Sleuth) Canary finds our two protagonists a bit the worse for wear. Their bar is losing money, largely because someone keeps insisting on leaving dead bodies around. The cops, this is the 1980s, after all, are not wildly interested in the gay community's little problems, so Lovelace and Valentine set up shop as sleuths, determined to stop the killer before he puts them out of business. 3/3

26. **Alexander, Paul (Craig Hintin 1964-2006)**, *Chains of Deceit*, Idol, 1997. Nathan Dexter #1 of 3. (BDSM Pulp) Nathan Dexter's life is turned around when he meets a young student called Scott - someone who offers him the relationship for which he's been searching. then Nathan's best friend becomes the victim of a slavery ring, rumoured to be operating out of London's leather scene. Nathan and Scott go undercover and, as their investigations take them from the leather bars of London and Amsterdam to the backrooms of New York, it becomes clear that they can trust no one, not even each other. 3/3

27. **Alexander, Paul**, *Code of Submission*, Idol, 1998. Nathan Dexter #2 of 3. (BDSM Pulp) After uncovering and defeating a perverted slave ring operating out of London's leather scene, journalist Nathan Dexter had hoped that he and his student boyfriend Scott could start enjoying their life together. However, nothing is that simple. Evidence emerges that the ring is once more in operation, and Nathan and Scott must do everything in their power to shut it down. From the clubs of Munich and Las Vegas to the back streets of Morocco, they must chase down the mysterious figure running this modern-day slave trade. But all too soon they find themselves drawn into the dangerous sexual games of the people they are pursuing. And as the limits of their fantasies and desires are explored, their love for each other faces its ultimate test. 3/3

28. **Alexander, Paul**, *Final Restraint*, Idol, 1999. Nathan Dexter #3 of 3.

(BDSM Pulp) The evil Adrian Delancey has finally outwitted journalist Nathan Dexter in his deadly game of cat-and-mouse, destroying the secretive Elective organisation - and Nathan's relationship with student Scott - into the bargain. Nathan is now all alone and is forced to use all his contacts and all his resources to mount a final assault on Delancey, to stop him and his perverted Syndicate once and for all. From the dungeons and saunas of London to the deepest jungles of South America, Nathan Dexter is forced to play the ultimate chess game, with people as sexual pawns. If he loses, he will pay the ultimate price with his dearest's blood. But if he wins, the cost will be even dearer: his soul. 3/3

29. **Algeo, Donald**, *Steel City Investigations,* Kindle, 2013. (Hard boiled) Eddie Carlyle is a New York City gossip columnist. His brother Nick owns a neighborhood bar in Pittsburgh. The two are also heirs to one of the greatest family fortunes in Pennsylvania. An unlikely pair to form a detective agency? This is how it happened. –e-book only (MLM). 3/3

30. **Allen, Tamara**, *Downtime,* N. P. 2009. (MM Fantasy/Police Procedural) FBI Agent Morgan Nash is on assignment in London when his case goes awry, and he finds himself moments away from a bullet through the heart. But fate has other plans: Morgan gets knocked out pursuing a suspect... and wakes up in 1888. While cataloging ancient manuscripts at the British Museum, Ezra Glacenbie accidentally pulls Morgan out of the twenty-first century-an impromptu vacation that may become permanent for Morgan if they can't locate the spell book Ezra used. Further hampering Morgan's quest to get home is the irresistible temptation to investigate history's most notorious serial killer: Jack the Ripper. But in repressive Victorian London, it's the unexpected romance blossoming between Morgan and Ezra that becomes the most dangerous complication of all. 3/3

31. **Allen, Tamara**, *The Only Gold,* Dreamspinner, 2011. (MM Historical) Jonah Woolner's life is as prudently regulated as the bank where he works. It's a satisfying life until he's passed over for promotion in favor of newcomer Reid Hylliard. Brash and enterprising, Reid beguiles everyone except Jonah, who's convinced Reid's progressive ideas will be the bank's ruin. When the vengeful son of a Union army vet descends upon the bank to steal a government deposit of half a million dollars during the deadliest blizzard to ever sweep New York, Jonah and Reid are trapped, at odds and fighting for their lives. 3/3

32. **Allen, Tamara**, *The Road to Silver Plume,* N.P., 2015. Secret Service #1 of 2. (MM Historical) Secret Service operative Emlyn Strickland may be new to field work, but his talent for identifying counterfeit

bank notes, honed over ten years at the Treasury, has given Sing Sing's population a respectable boost. When counterfeiter August McKee takes illegal advantage of a sinking silver market, his former confederate Darrow Gardiner shares that information with Agent Strickland so they can track down the once-friend who left Darrow to rot in prison. –book two *Playing the Ace* is expected to be published in 2019 (MLM). 3/3

33. **Allin, Lou (1945-2014)**, *Memories are Murder*, RendezVous Crime, 2007. A Belle Palmer Mystery #5 of 5. (Amateur Sleuth) Belle Palmers old high-school boyfriend rents a property on her road, but soon he is found drowned. Did he fall and hit his head, or did a more sinister event occur? Who has been causing havoc in the wilderness and will stop at nothing to cover their crimes? –gay best friend helps solve the crime (MLM). 1/3

34. **Allingham, Margery (1904-1966)**, *Flowers for the Judge*, Doubleday, 1936. Albert Campion Mystery #7 of 19. (Classic Detective) Scandal hits the prestigious publishing house of Barnabas when one of the directors is found dead in a locked cellar. All eyes are on the other partners at the firm–cousins of the dead man with much to gain from his demise–and all rumors hint at a connection to the disappearance of another director decades earlier. Desperate to salvage their reputation, the cousins turn to Albert Campion–but will his investigations clear the Barnabas family name, or besmirch it forever? –gay secondary character tampers with evidence and is described as unsavory and uninterested in women and gets beat up by Campion in a strange gay bashing scene (MLM). 1/3

35. **Allison, Iory (William Iorwerth Allison)**, *Family Jewels*, iUniverse, 2004. (Amateur Sleuth) The young antiquarian from an old Boston family and his sister had just inherited their aunt's Back Bay townhouse. As they walked through the home they felt the sorrow and excitement of new heirs and they reminisce about their childhood days in this antiquated residence where nothing had changed for years. Upstairs in a shuttered bedroom, an ornately enameled chest lured them by its barbaric splendor, and they were compelled to open it. Inside they found a key. 3/3

36. **Ambler, Eric (1909-1998)**, *Light of Day,* Heinemann, 1962. Arthur Abdel Simpson #1 of 2. (Espionage) When Arthur Abdel Simpson first spots Harper in the Athens airport, he recognizes him as a tourist unfamiliar with the city and in need of a private driver. In other words, the perfect mark for Simpson's brand of entrepreneurship. But Harper proves to be more the spider than the fly when he catches Simpson riffling his wallet for traveler's checks. – this book was listed by Anthony Slide for homosexual themes which include rectal exams performed by the Turkish authorities and two accusa-

tions of sodomy as schoolboy hazings (MLM). 1/3

37. **Ames, Jonathon**, *You Were Never Really Here,* Pushkin Vertigo, 2016. (Crime Drama) Joe has witnessed things that cannot be erased. A former FBI agent and Marine, his abusive childhood has left him damaged beyond repair. He has completely withdrawn from the world and earns his living rescuing girls who have been kidnapped into the sex trade. When he's hired to save the daughter of a corrupt New York senator held captive at a Manhattan brothel, he stumbles into a dangerous web of conspiracy, and he pays the price. As Joe's small web of associates are picked off one by one, he realizes that he has no choice but to take the fight to the men who want him dead. 1/3

38. **Amis, Kingsley (1922-1995)**, *The Riverside Villas Murder,* Harcourt Brace Jovanovich, 1973. (Crime Drama) Like all 14-year-olds he is hovering hopefully on the brink between sexual inexperience and initiation, and in this book, under our very eyes, Peter suddenly becomes an adult! A crime, truly murderous, is committed by an unknown and almost unidentifiable assailant. Only Peter begins to guess at the truth–a dangerous truth–which leads him to the river bank by moonlight. –as I have not read this I am unsure of the gay content but may contain elements of homoerotism (MLM). ?/3

39. **Amis, Martin (1949-)**, *Other People: A Mystery,* Viking Press, 1981. (Amateur Sleuth) She wakes in an emergency room in a London hospital, to a voice that tells her: "You're on your own now. Take care. Be good." She has no knowledge of her name, her past, or even her species. It takes her a while to realize that she is human – and that the beings who threaten, befriend, and violate her are other people. Some of whom seem to know all about her. –several of the people around her are gay (MLM). 1/3

40. **Amory, Richard (Richard W. Love 1927-1981)**, *Frost,* Traveler's Companion, 1971. (Political Intrigue) McGraw was great at manipulating people to achieve his ambitions, with scandal, blackmail, and even murder–until he crossed swords with his son Frost, who refused to stay in the closet and mind his own business. Then McGraw found out that some of the pawns in his grim game of power had a weapon of their own, which he could never begin to understand. –this was noted by Gunn as meriting particular attention for its literary or historical importance. 3/3

41. **Anable, Stephen**, *Fisher Boy,* Poisoned Press, 2008. Mark Winslow #1 of 2. (Amateur Sleuth) Boston comic Mark Winslow has arrived this summer with a group of fellow improv actors ready to break into Provincetown's club circuit. It should be a carefree summer,

but currents swirl beneath the sunny surface. Does the tall ship out in the harbor herald an unusually large crowd of Scandinavian tourists? If not, who are the blond and ragged visitors seen everywhere? Then, at a philanthropist's dinner opening the season, Mark gets into a very public fight with the son of local bluebloods – an old school friend. It makes him the prime suspect when the lawyer is later savagely murdered out on the beach. Though he stumbles from the scene, Mark thinks his choice is simple: find the killer or be charged with the crime. 3/3

42. **Anable, Stephen**, *A Pinchbeck Bride*, Poisoned Press, 2011. Mark Winslow #2 of 2. (Amateur Sleuth) A young woman is found strangled in Mingo House, a morbid brownstone museum in Boston's Back Bay. Strangely, she was dressed in Victorian finery as if for high tea. Dubbed the "Victorian Girl" by the media, she becomes the focus of publicity and speculation that reaches back to the Mingoes' roots in England and to the builders of the mansion, a Civil War arms dealer and his séance-holding wife. 3/3

43. **Anderson, Charlotte**, *The Treasure of Pi*, N.P., 2016. (Historical) One hundred and twenty years ago in Boston, MA Charles Robison and William Westerly were robbed of their lives, betrayed by Charles' brother Anthony. The only testament of their love that remains is a journal and a watch with the sign of Pi on its cover. One hundred and twenty years later the watch and the journal will bring two men together once more, will they be to overcome the curse that seems to follow the watch and journal and be free to love each other or will the hatred that destroyed Charles and William threaten their future as well? 3/3

44. **Anderson, Evangeline**, *Assignment*, Loose Id, 2008. (MM Police Procedural) Just as Valenti is coming to grips with his new, unacceptable feelings for his partner, their police chief puts them on a new case that could blow Valenti's cover once and for all. He and O'Brian are going undercover at the country's largest and most infamous gay resort to bust a notorious drug lord and stop the shipments of poison cocaine that are flooding the gay bars all over the city. 3/3

45. **Anderson, John**, *Hot Heads*, Arena, 1984, reprint. (Pulp) California surrogate sleuth Hank Charleston, a television journalist on vacation in New Orleans, with local television journalist Brian Kehoe, discovers the motive to prove importer Cain Losey is behind Cal Ferguson's disappearance. –John Anderson was a house name for pulp publisher Arena (MLM). 3/3

46. **Andress, Lesley (Lawrence Sanders 1920-1998)**, *Caper*, G. P. Putnam's Sons, 1980. Planning out a multimillion-dollar jewel heist as

material for a new novel, which she hopes will restore her flagging career, mystery writer Jannie Shean is horrified when her perfect crime is enacted right in front of her. –two male bisexual friends (MLM). 1/3

47. **Andrews-Katz, Eric,** *The Jesus Injection,* Bold Stroke Books, 2012. Buck 98 #1 of 2. (Comic Espionage) After an assassination attempt ruins his vacation, Agent Buck 98 is given a cryptic message by a dying drag queen: 3-1-4. The numbers match the date of Dr. Timothy Shoulwater's death, the noted scientist rumored to have discovered a potential cure for the AIDS virus before his notes mysteriously disappeared. 3/3

48. **Andrews-Katz, Eric,** *Balls and Chain,* Bold Stroke Books, 2014. Buck 98 #2 of 2. (Comic Espionage) Miguel Reyes is not only the first openly gay governor of Florida, he's also the man behind Referendum 65. If passed, Florida will be the first Southern state in the U.S. to include marriage equality. When the governor's fourteen-year-old son, Alejandro, is kidnapped, the message is clear: Kill the bill or we kill the boy! Agent Buck 98 is given only one week to find and rescue Alejandro. 3/3

49. **Annicelli, Alex,** *Chambers,* Createspace, 2018. A Buried Lies Spy #1 of 1. (MM Japanese Espionage) Grey Nakamura is one of the most brilliant young agents that Japanese Intelligence has ever trained. When Ren Oshira, his mentor and lover, is killed on assignment in London, Grey is determined to seek justice. Grey's recent education positions him perfectly to apply for a pupillage at Upton & Pearce Chambers where his mentor had been investigating barristers Victor Upton and Adrian Pearce shortly before he was found dead. As Grey is thrust into his new role under the supervision of the two men, he finds he must utilize every bit of his training to get close to Victor and Adrian, gain their trust, and uncover the truth in a dangerous game of manipulation and seduction. 3/3

50. **Anonymous,** *Cell Block 69,* Star, 1983. (Pulp) "New York former policeman John McNally, 45, fired because he is gay, is reinstated in a case that stops abruptly without his nailing the drug dealers, or arresting the street kids who are moving into a crime in a pulp procedural (Gunn)." 3/3

51. **Anonymous**, *Low Life Brutes,* Finland, 1985. (Pulp) "New Orleans-based private investigator Christopher Mumm and his assistant Harvey Harris, on vacation in Alabama, easily track down three sexual predators in a pulp inverted mystery (Gunn)." 3/3

52. **Anonymous,** *Bun Gun for Hire,* Star, 1988. (Pulp) "Constance Davenport dies as the result of eating an arsenic-laced apple used for Christmas cheer at an exclusive leather-goods store. The assistant

manager, who has just used New York PI Petrovich's sexual services and in the process found out about his training, hires him to find the murderer (Gunn)." 3/3

53. **Anonymous**, *Cry Uncle!*, Star, 1989. (Pulp) "U. S. undercover agent Henry Foster takes revenge against his own Washington agency (Gunn)." 3/3

54. **Anonymous**, *Beached Bum*, Star, 1990. (Pulp) "Would be actor disappears after he has failed to obtain a thryrsus for collector Rutledge Charrington at an auction selling antique sexual aids. Rutledge hires Shiv to find him and the "Dionysian dildo." The trail takes Shiv to a cultural institute and to Ramon's Roadhouse for a final twist (Gunn)." 3/3

55. **Anonymous**, *Muscling In*, Star, 1996. (Pulp) PI Travis Mccabe, 35, a Marine veteran, former policeman, discovers he is not straight while trying to solve a pulp murder and blackmail case involving Kyle Winthrop, 16 (Gunn)." 3/3

56. **Anthony, Evelyn**, *Janus Imperative*, Coward, McCann, and Geoghehan, 1980. (Historical) After witnessing two political murders more than twenty-five years apart, Max Steiner, a former Hitler Youth, becomes caught up in a mad plot originally planned by Hitler. –Gay lover assassins working for Neo-Nazis (MLM). 2/3

57. **Archman, Bob**, *Clydesdale and Company*, Nazca Plains, 2009. Clydesdale Mystery #1 of 6. (Modern Pulp) The diminutive, but feisty cop, Clydesdale Noland, is unemployed after a witch hunt for gays in the Richmond Police department. Starting his own security firm, Clydesdale & Company, a terrorist bombing makes his first job into crusade to find the bombers. With a gay newspaper office, a women's health clinic and Jewish Temple at Ground Zero, there were too many suspects and too many possible bombers. The well-endowed detective must use his entire bag of tools and tricks to find the perpetrators. 3/3

58. **Archman, Bob**, *Clydesdale Goes to the Hunt*, Nazca Plains, 2009. Clydesdale Mystery #2 of 6. (Modern Pulp) The pony sized, but stallion hung detective Clydesdale goes undercover at an exclusive and conservative Men's club where its members have fallen for a scam combining real sex with fake investments. The combination of older men who have made it and made it big with young men on the make turns deadly. The unhealthy brew of ultra conservative politics and forbidden sex turns ugly. Clydesdale signs on as a locker room attendant and towel boy. This gives him a front row seat watching the young scammers hook and real in their marks. He follows the scam from the locker room to the showers and into the steam rooms. Along the way he meets some misguided, but nice men and intro-

duces them to a new world of man to man pleasure and enjoyment. They discover you can't fool Mother Nature. 3/3

59. **Archman, Bob**, *Clydesdale Goes to a Funeral*, Nazca Plains, 2010. Clydesdale Mystery #3 of 6. (Modern Pulp) Half the residents of Wythetown had considered killing Clydesdale's Aunt Edith at one time or another. She was pompous, sanctimonious and most of all irritating, but when she was murdered, mutilated and burned it was a shock. By the time her murderer was captured, Detective Clydesdale Noland uncovered a complicated scheme involving sadism, drugs and fraud. The pint size, but horse hung detective uses all of his intellectual and physical ability to get to the bottom of complicated scheme. It takes firemen, police, FBI and ATF agents, a Postal Inspector and a dog named Fluffy to catch the perpetrators. 3/3

60. **Archman, Bob**, *Clydesdale Goes to Washington*, Nazca Plains, 2010. Clydesdale Mystery #4 of 6. (Modern Pulp) When they found the up-and-coming naval officer floating face down in Washington's reflecting pool, Clydesdale smelled something fishy. Was the closeted officer driven to suicide by the threat of exposure, or was he killed to keep him quiet? Clydesdale becomes the yardman for an ultra-exclusive Washington club and gets to the bottom of a complicated plot. 3/3

61. **Archman, Bob**, *Clydesdale Moves to Essex Park*, Nazca Plains, 2010. Clydesdale Mystery #5 of 6. (Modern Pulp) No place could be safer than the wealthy, high-security, retirement community of Essex Park. Located on a former plantation in Virginia, the residents felt safe from all the problems of modern America. The residents of Essex Park were afflicted with declining memories as time took its toll, but oddly, inheritances seemed to be vanishing too. Redneck detective, Clydesdale, discovered a clever scam that could relieve the victims of their cash and use the victims' failing memories to avoid detection. 3/3

62. **Archman, Bob**, *Clydesdale and Co.*, Nazca Plains, 2009. Clydesdale Mystery #6 of 6. (Modern Pulp) When a Christmas Eve blizzard left Clydesdale stranded with Santa and seven elves, the resourceful detective makes the best of the situation. Clydesdale, Santa and all the elves hit it off and have a Christmas to remember. Several years later Santa appears at Clydesdale's door with worries about a troubled production of Shakespeare's A Midsummer Night's Dream. Nasty poison pen letters are just the tip of the iceberg of a case that eventually includes hit and run, assault, murder and rape. 3/3

63. **Arnott, Jake**, *The Long Firm*, Soho Crime, 1999. Long Firm #1 of 3. (Crime Drama) Harry Starks, club owner, racketeer and porn king,

is trying to jump the queue into legitimacy. This swinging sixties novel reveals the seedier side of London where the low life met the high life in the city's dark underbelly. –main character is a gay gangster (MLM). 3/3

64. **Arnott, Jake,** *He Kills Coppers,* Sceptre, 2001. Long Firm #2 of 3. (Crime Drama) August 1966 - the long hot summer of World Cup euphoria is abruptly shattered when three policemen are gunned down in a West London street. A bewilderingly senseless crime that shocks a nation seemingly at ease with itself and brings an end to the victory celebrations. 3/3

65. **Arnott, Jake,** *Truecrime,* Sceptre, 2003. Long Firm #3 of 3. (Crime Drama) Harry is rumored to be laying low on Cyprus, the law having given up its pursuit, but someone is looking who isn't concerned with the niceties of extradition, somebody who has as much use for the rules as Harry. 3/3

66. **Asche, Jonathan,** *Mindjacker: an erotic novel,* Starbooks, 2003. (Modern Pulp Fantasy) Just making direct eye contact, Lucas has direct access into a person's mind, turning his wishes into commands. It's a power the government wants to harness for its own means, but Lucas' lust for freedom cannot be contained. Living life on the run, Lucas uses his extraordinary gift to prey upon straight men for their money and to satisfy is own carnal appetites, knowing his embarrassed victims will never report his crimes. Sent to capture him is Joel, a sexy telepath whose own desires were first awakened by Lucas. So far Lucas has eluded Joel, but when he steals a briefcase full of cash, Joel may just be the only one to save Lucas' life. 3/3

67. **Asche, Jonathan,** *Moneyshots: an erotic novel,* Starbooks, 2007. (Modern Pulp) Martin Richter is rapidly sinking into a midlife depression. His longtime lover has left him for a younger man, and the last guy who showed an interest in him was a hustler. Then, Martin meets a sexy, young drifter named Rand, and his outlook, along with his sex life, takes a turn for the better. Then Rand disappears from Martin's life as abruptly as he entered it. Martin is devastated, but when a man claiming to be Rands boyfriend shows up at his door, Martin fears there might be more sinister reasons behind Rand's disappearance. Desperate to find Rand, Martin embarks on a search that puts him in bed with a scheming pornographer and in the cross hairs of a well-endowed hit man. Amidst the naked bodies and flying bullets, Martin discovers his fantasy man just might be his ultimate nightmare. 3/3

68. **Ashe, Gregory,** *Pretty Pretty Boys,* Createspace, 2017. A Hazard and Somerset Mystery #1 of 6. (Police Procedural) After Emery Hazard loses his job as a detective in Saint Louis, he heads back to his

hometown–and to the local police force there. Home, though, brings no happy memories, and the ghosts of old pain are very much alive in Wahredua. Hazard's new partner, John-Henry Somerset, had been one of the worst tormentors, and Hazard still wonders what Somerset's role was in the death of Jeff Langham, Hazard's first boyfriend. When a severely burned body is discovered, Hazard finds himself drawn deeper into the case than he expects. Determining the identity of the dead man proves impossible, and solving the murder grows more and more unlikely. 3/3

69. **Ashe, Gregory**, *Transposition*, Createspace, 2018. A Hazard and Somerset Mystery #2 of 6. (Police Procedural) Hazard finds his life has only grown more complicated as he adjusts to his new home. Living with Somers, whom he has been drawn to since high school, makes 'complicated' the understatement of the year. The turmoil of living together spills over when Hazard and Somers find themselves trapped by the weather in an old mansion and, against Hazard's better judgment, sharing a bed. Strictly as friends, of course. Just when things can't get any more confusing, the next morning brings a worsening storm–and a murder. Cut off from the outside world, Hazard and Somers must face a clever, determined killer who is hiding among the mansion's guests. Without backup, they can only rely on their wits–and on each other–to survive. And as the snow falls and the mansion's guests continue to die one by one, solving the string of murders becomes secondary. First, Hazard and Somers have to survive. 3/3

70. **Ashe, Gregory**, *Paternity Case,* Createspace, 2018. A Hazard and Somerset Mystery #3 of 6. (Police Procedural) It's almost Christmas, and Emery Hazard finds himself face to face with his own personal nightmare: going on a double date with his partner–and boyhood crush–John-Henry Somerset. Hazard brings his boyfriend; Somers brings his estranged wife. Things aren't going to end well. When a strange call interrupts dinner, however, Hazard and his partner become witnesses to a shooting. The victims: Somers's father, and the daughter of a high school friend. The crime is inexplicable. There is no apparent motive, no connection between the victims, and no explanation for how the shooter reached his targets. Determined to get answers, Hazard and Somers move forward with their investigation in spite of mounting pressure to stop. Their search for the truth draws them into a dark web of conspiracy and into an even darker tangle of twisted love and illicit desire. And as the two men come face to face with the passions and madness behind the crime, they must confront their own feelings for each other–and the hard truths that neither man is ready to accept. 3/3

71. **Ashe, Gregory**, *Guilt by Association*, Createspace, 2018. A Hazard and

Somerset Mystery #4 of 6.(Police Procedural) Everything in Emery Hazard's life is finally going well: his boyfriend, Nico, is crazy about him; he has a loyal partner at work; and he has successfully closed a series of difficult murders. By all accounts, he should be happy. What he can't figure out, then, is why he's so damn miserable. After a fight with Nico, Hazard needs work to take his mind off his relationship. And someone in town is happy to oblige by murdering the sheriff. The job won't be easy; the sheriff had enemies, lots of them, and narrowing down the list of suspects will be difficult. Difficult, but routine. The arrival of a special prosecutor, however, throws the case into turmoil, and Hazard and Somers find themselves sidelined. With an agenda of his own, the prosecutor forces the case toward his favorite suspect, while Hazard and Somers scramble to find the real killer. As the people they care about are drawn into the chaos, Hazard and Somers have to fight to keep what they love–and to keep each other. To find the killer, they will have to reveal what each has kept buried for years: their feelings for each other. And for Hazard, that's a hell of a lot scarier than murder. 3/3

72. **Ashe, Gregory,** *Reasonable Doubt,* Createspace, 2018. Hazard and Somerset #5 of 6. (Police Procedural) After almost twenty years, Emery Hazard finally has the man he loves. But things with his boyfriend and fellow detective, John-Henry Somerset, are never easy, and they've been more complicated lately for two reasons: Somers' ex-wife and daughter. No matter what Hazard does, he can't seem to get away from the most important women in his boyfriend's life. While Hazard struggles with his new reality (changing dirty diapers, just to start), a bizarre murder offers a distraction. John Oscar Walden, the leader of a local cult, is found dead by the police, and the case falls to Hazard and Somers. The investigation takes the two detectives into the cult's twisted relationships and the unswerving demands of power and faith. But the deeper Hazard looks into the cult, the deeper he must look into his own past, where belief and reason have already clashed once. And as Hazard struggles to protect the most vulnerable of Walden's victims, he uncovers a deeper, more vicious plot behind Walden's murder, and Hazard finds himself doing what he never expected: racing to save the killer. Only, that is, if Somers doesn't need him to babysit. 3/3

73. **Ashe, Gregory,** *Criminal Past,* Createspace, 2018. Hazard and Somerset #6 of 6. (Police Procedural) It all starts to go wrong at the shooting gallery. Emery Hazard and his boyfriend, John-Henry Somerset, just want to enjoy the day at the Dore County Independence Fair. At the shooting gallery, though, Hazard comes face to face with one of his old bullies: Mikey Grames. Even as a drugged-out wreck, Mikey is a reminder of all the ugliness in Hazard's past. Worse,

Mikey seems to know something Hazard doesn't–something about the fresh tension brewing in town. 3/3

74. **Ashe, Gregory**, *Mr. Big Empty*, Createspace, 2017. A Hollow Folk Mystery #1 of 3. (Paranormal) Vie Eliot arrives in the small town of Vehpese, Wyoming with little more than the clothes–and scars–on his back. Determined to make a new life for himself after escaping his abusive mother, he finds that living with his estranged father brings its own problems. Then Samantha Oates, the girl with blue hair, goes missing, and Vie might be the only one who can find her. His ability to read emotions and gain insight into other people's darkest secrets makes him the perfect investigator, with only one small problem: he wants nothing to do with his gift. When the killer begins contacting Vie through a series of strange cards, though, Vie is forced to hone his ability, because Samantha was not the killer's only target. And, as Vie learns, he is not the only psychic in town. 3/3

75. **Ashe, Gregory**, *All the Inside Howling*, Createspace, 2017. A Hollow Folk Mystery #2 of 3. (Paranormal) Vie Eliot has survived a new high school, an abusive father, and the murderous Mr. Big Empty. Now, as Vie searches for Mr. Big Empty, he also finds himself facing an unexpected complication: how to be a good boyfriend. When a mysterious drifter named River disappears, though, Vie finds himself dragged into finding the missing boy. Vie's psychic abilities have proved useful in the past, and once again they set him on the trail of a gruesome murderer. But the pattern of killings seems to make no sense, and as Vie tries to stop the murderer, he learns that the people he loves most are in terrible danger. 3/3

76. **Ashe, Gregory**, *The Dust Feast*, Createspace, 2017. A Hollow Folk Mystery #3 of 3. (Paranormal) Only days have passed since Vie Eliot's murderous half-brother–a dangerous, out-of-control psychic–was stopped from killing the people Vie loves most but Vie is ready for his life to return to normal. He has plans. Big plans. Make the cross-country team, pick up his grades, and spend a lot of time with his boyfriend. On the day of cross-country tryouts, though, Vie finds one of the teachers dead–and Vie refuses to believe that the death was a suicide. As he searches for the killer, or killers, he discovers that a conspiracy exists in the small town of Vehpese: a conspiracy that might be older and deeper than Vie first suspects, a conspiracy of drugs and human trafficking that might also be tied, in some way Vie can't quite understand, to his own abilities–and to the other psychic abilities in his town. 3/3

77. **Asher, I. Jay**, *Who Shot Jeremy Strange?*, Createspace, 2017. (Suspense) Important social issues and at the same time draws you into Manhattan lifestyles – the stuff of dreams and nightmares. –Jere-

my Strange is a 29-year-old man who is trying to break into acting (MLM). 3/3

78. **Ashford, Jeffrey (Roderic Jeffries 1926-)**, *A Sense of Loyalty*, Walker, 1983. (Amateur Sleuth) How far would you go to protect the ones you love? Mike Sterling is proud to work for HI Motors, a prestigious car manufacturer and, following the death of his wife, he becomes devoted to his work as its PR Manager. When their new engine design, Vulcan, is sold to the competition, internal investigations ensue. All evidence collected by the investigative team point to his department, yet Mike is determined that it's coincidental. All leads run cold, until another betrayal occurs within the company, this time resulting in the murder of a security guard. –only gay "theme" is the use of "Cock and Ball Torture." –Ashford seems fascinated by genital mutilation (Slide). 1/3

79. **Ashford, Jeffrey**, *An Ideal Crime*, Walker, 1985. (Amateur Sleuth) Jim Thorpe is striving for an ordinary life, studying law during the day and working nights at the local Vault. Even pursuing a romance with the daughter of his boss. But all of that changes on one fateful night. A night that he switched shifts to attend dinner with his girlfriend. The vault is robbed, and the night watchman murdered. –only gay "theme" is the use of "Cock and Ball Torture." –Ashford seems fascinated by genital mutilation (Slide). 1/3

80. **Ashworth, Ralph**, *The Killer of Orchids*, State Street, 2009. (Amateur Sleuth) 11-year-old Xander Pooka and middle-aged computer genius Jeff Redwing are friends. When paper headlines announce the news of two men murdered with a mysterious samurai sword, they decided to spend a fun afternoon playing detective. But quickly the game becomes a life and death race for the truth. 3/3

81. **Asprey, Robert (1923-2009)**, *The Panther's Feast*, Putnam, 1959. (Historical Biography) Traces the life and the career of Colonel Alfred Redl, Deputy Chief of Intelligence in the Austro-Hungarian army, explains how he was blackmailed into spying for Russia, and describes the events leading to his suicide. –an "interpretive biography" (MLM). 2/3

82. **Asquith, Roger**, *Selby*, Prestbury Books, 2013. (Hard Boiled) Selby Grant is suspected of embezzling millions of dollars. Awaiting trial in California, he skips bail, dresses in drag and moves to Spain where there is no extradition, hoping to retrieve his wife's briefcase full of legal papers which he suspects are in Brian Townsend's possession, who is on his way to Spain hoping to help his friend, aging movie star, Dixie Lee, write her "unauthorized" biography. –lots of drag and gay men. Available as an e-book only (MLM). 2/3

83. **Asquith, Roger**, *That's Hollywood*, Prestbury Books, 2014. (Caper)

A troupe of talented drag queens from San Francisco go to Hollywood to try their luck on the silver screen...and become entangled in sex, blackmail and murder. –available as an e-book only (MLM). 3/3

84. **Aterovis, Josh**, *Bleeding Hearts*, Regal Crest, 2001. A Killian Kendall Mystery #1 of 5. (Amateur Sleuth) Killian Kendall is used to being overlooked, even in his own family. That's about to change. With the arrival of a new kid at school, Killian's whole world is about to be turned upside down. The new guy is openly gay and, for reasons he can't really understand, Killian finds himself drawn to him. When the boy is killed in a brutal attack, and Killian is injured in the process, Killian begins to question everything around him. The police seem eager to write the attack off as a random mugging, but Killian was there, and he knows better. With the help of the murdered boy's father and his friends, Killian starts his own investigation. His search turns up hatred in small town America, and before it's over, more people will be dead, and Killian's life will be on the line again. –heavily rewritten and re-released by MLR in 2017 (MLM). 3/3

85. **Aterovis, Josh**, *Reap the Whirlwind*, Renaissance Alliance, 2003. A Killian Kendall Mystery #2 of 5. (Amateur Sleuth) Will's life is changing so quickly he can't keep up. He's moving out of his parents' home for the first time, changing careers, making new friends, and falling in love with the person he least expected. In the process, he's also learning a lot about himself. As if he doesn't have enough going on, his life-long best friend dies in what appears to be a drunken accident. But when Will receives a note hinting that it may not have been an accident after all, he finds that he can't rest until he knows the truth. With the help of Killian Kendall and his friends, Will begins an amateur investigation that will result in even more death. Will thought the biggest changes were behind him, but they had only just begun. –Killian takes a backseat to the investigating in this mystery (MM) –updated and re-released by MLR in 2018 (MLM). 3/3

86. **Aterovis, Josh**, *All Lost Things*, P. D., 2009. A Killian Kendall Mystery #3 of 5. (Amateur Sleuth/Hard Boiled PI) Killian Kendall's life is changing faster than he can keep up. He's graduating from high school, breaking up with his boyfriend, and starting a new job with a private investigator. He's barely settled at his new desk when his ex-boyfriend calls with a desperate plea for help. He wants Killian to prove his new boyfriend is innocent in the shockingly violent murder of his abusive father. Killian reluctantly agrees to take the case, little knowing how complicated - and dangerous - things will become before it's over. On the home front, Killian's surrogate par-

ents decide to buy a historic mansion and turn it into a bed and breakfast. The house comes with a rich history... and maybe a ghost or two. Killian doesn't want to believe in such things, but he's quickly becoming convinced that something terrible happened to the home's original owners. The century-old mystery both terrifies and tantalizes Killian. In the end, he may be the only one who can uncover the truth. –updated and re-released by MLR in 2018 (MLM). 3/3

87. **Aterovis, Josh,** *Truth of Yesterday*, P. D., 2011. A Killian Kendall Mystery #4 of 5. (Hard Boiled PI) Killian is thrilled when his first real case takes him on a surveillance trip to Washington D.C. - and with his boyfriend Micah, no less. When Micah takes him out to celebrate the successful resolution of his case, Micah's past comes back to haunt them in a big way. Killian is stunned by what he learns, and even more shocked to hear about the murder of Micah's former lover, Paul. The truth threatens to tear them apart, but at the same time, Killian finds himself drawn to find Paul's killer. Meanwhile, Judy has asked him to investigate an old friend, Jake, whose behavior has changed radically over the last few months. She is worried he may be involved in something dangerous...and she has no idea how right she is. Entering into the perilous and often grim world of male escorts, Killian discovers that things are seldom what they seem, and everyone has a past. The truth of yesterday becomes a lie tomorrow. –heavily rewritten and re-released by MLR in 2018 (MLM). 3/3

88. **Aterovis, Josh,** *A Change of Worlds,* MLR, 2018. Killian Kendall Mystery #5 of 5. (Hard Boiled PI) When Killian takes on an investigation into a series of thefts from a Native American archaeological site as a favor for an old friend, he never dreamed it would escalate into violence and murder. What started out as a seemingly simple case suddenly has much higher stakes than missing artifacts. One person is dead, one injured, and more lives are on the line...including Killian's. Things aren't exactly smooth sailing in Killian's private life either. His boyfriend Micah has given him a huge choice, but his ex-boyfriend Asher's unexpected reappearance has only clouded Killian's decision. He must decide who he wants to be with, and quickly, before time runs out for all of them. –was initially supposed to be published by P. D. in 2011 but was cancelled by the publisher (MLM). 3/3

89. **Aterovis, Josh,** *Never Alone and Other Stories: Killian Kendall Interludes,* MLR, 2018. Killian Kendall #5.5. (Amateur Sleuth) Learn Seth's backstory all the way up until the moment he meets Killian for the first time. Go on vacation with Killian as he finds a mysterious ring on the beach. Experience Kane's first kiss with a guy. Get

haunted by Amalie at Adam and Steve's bed and breakfast. Meet Jacy, a Native American teen struggling to find his place in the present as he tries to uncover his past. 3/3

90. **Attwood, Randy**, *The Fat Cat,* Attwood Consulting, 2016. (Thriller) Five years ago Ellie ran away from a city where she was a TV reporter because two things happened. Now managing a strip club, one of those things is happening again. –have not yet this and unsure of the gay content (MLM). ?/3

91. **Atwill, Douglas**, *Creep around the Corner,* Sunstone, 2010. (Historical Espionage) Europe in the Cold War years was a dangerous place for Harold Bronson and his buddies, draftees commandeered into espionage and counterintelligence. Their low echelon escapades take them to Berlin, Ulm, the South of France, and Zurich. Bronson chooses this time of his life to explore a personal coming out, creating secrets within secrets in a disapproving military. In his off-time, Bronson paints portraits of the other denizens of Schloss Issel, earning money for trips and adventures to Paris and Nice. Always on the edge of life, he taunts the higher-ups with a light-hearted acceptance of life in the spy world of 1957. Real danger is further off from his circle at the Schloss, but it is an insistent melody they can always hear. 3/3

92. **Avocato, Lori**, *Dose of Murder*, Avon, 2004. A Pauline Sokol Cozy Mystery #1 of 7. (Cozy) After years of chasing around sniffly munchkins with a tongue depressor, nurse Pauline Sokol has had it. She's sick of being an "angel of mercy"–she'd like to raise some hell for once! But finding a new career won't be easy for someone who's had no experience beyond thermometers and bedpans. Luckily, the smarmy head of an agency that investigates medical fraud thinks she'd be perfect for the job, since, for him, a potential employee's most important qualification is a killer pair of legs –protagonist has a gay roommate who is dating one of her PI coworkers (MLM). 2/3

93. **Avocato, Lori**, *The Stiff and the Dead*, Avon, 2005. A Pauline Sokol Cozy Mystery #2 of 7. (Cozy) Pauline Sokol has just escaped serious bodily harm during her first investigation, when her second case file is literally thrown into her lap. And this one seems to be a doozie-- with one suspect already dead! Pauline's sleuthing leads her to the Senior Citizen's Clinic, where she realizes that her deceased suspect was part of an illegal Viagra ring! 2/3

94. **Avocato, Lori**, *One Dead Under the Cuckoo's Nest*, Avon, 2005. A Pauline Sokol Cozy Mystery #3 of 7. (Cozy) When Pauline Sokol goes undercover to investigate brokers who match psychiatric patients with treatment facilities for high dollar bounties, she suddenly

finds herself confined against her will in a mental hospital run by nuns! 2/3

95. **Avocato, Lori**, *Deep Sea Dead*, Avon, 2005. A Pauline Sokol Cozy Mystery #4 of 7. (Cozy) A confirmed landlubber, insurance fraud private investigator. Pauline Sokol's never heard the call of the sea. But now the former RN is donning her nurse's whites once more to go undercover as part of the medical team of the *Golden Dolphin* - a lavish luxury liner that's setting sail for Bermuda. 2/3

96. **Avocato, Lori**, *Nip, Tuck, Dead*, Avon, 2006. A Pauline Sokol Cozy Mystery #5 of 7. (Cozy) Ex-nurse-turned-insurance fraud investigator Pauline Sokol's willing to risk *anything* to put a bad doc out of business–even her best friend Goldie's near-perfect proboscis! Her cross-dressing compadre has agreed to get his shnozz bobbed so Pauline can pose as his private nurse and gain entry into Highcliff Manor–a posh plastic surgery "spa" making an illegal killing with their repeat clientele. But when a super-rich "frequent flier" is unexpectedly widowed–and a receptionist who knows too much is given the boot ... off a nearby cliff! –Pauline realizes she's stuck her own nose into something really nasty. 2/3

97. **Avocato, Lori**, *Dead on Arrival*, Avon, 2006. A Pauline Sokol Cozy Mystery #6 of 7. (Cozy) Pauline Sokol is sent undercover to the DaVinci Ambulance company where she finds out that the owner is billing the insurance company fraudulently - however, Mr. DaVinci himself is murdered, sending her investigation into a tailspin - not to mention the fact that someone is sending her riddles - that threaten her life. 2/3

98. **Avocato, Lori**, *Dead Weight*, N. P., 2010. A Pauline Sokol Cozy Mystery #7 of 7. (Cozy) Nothing – not even murder – keeps Pauline Sokol off the case. Pauline Sokol, ex-RN turned medical insurance fraud investigator, finds herself embroiled in a scam at a weight loss clinic in the scenic New Mexico desert. As if being undercover isn't bad enough, she's not allowed to eat chocolate, she lives in a body suit that weighs a ton, and her roommate turns out to be a mysteriously hot guy! –Avocato self-published this 96-page e-book after Avon put her series on hold, however, as of 2015 she states that she may still publish more books for the series under Avon if enough people buy the e-book and audiobooks according to her website (MLM). 2/3

99. **Azevedo, Geno**, *Naked Dick: Cosumnes River Murder*, iUniverse, 2009. A Tony Felice PI Mystery #1 of 3. (Soft Boiled PI) A young, gay Private Investigator, Tony, from San Diego is asked by his boss to go undercover to investigate the mysterious death of a young man in northern California. What Tony didn't realize when he accepted

the challenge was he would be undercover at a gay nudists resort outside of Sacramento. Not being a nudist himself, this presented more of a challenge than just the investigation itself. Tony manages to fit in with the group of gay nudists and starts to question the guests one by one without them becoming suspicious of him and his reason for being there at the resort. 3/3

100. **Azevedo, Geno**, *Naked Innocence, the Bastille Day Murder,* Azevedo Publishing, 2011. A Tony Felice PI Mystery #2 of 3. (Soft Boiled PI) "Tony, I'm glad I caught you. I'm afraid I have some bad news. Your good friend was murdered Saturday night." I could feel the blood drain from my head and I felt faint. I was sick to my stomach to think that someone would deliberately kill this sweet innocent man. "Sorry to be the one to break the news to you, but better that you should hear it from me than to read it in the paper." I had solved my first big murder case last year in northern California and felt good about my skills as a Private Investigator. I never dreamed the next big case for me would be investigating the death of my dear friend. 3/3

101. **Azevedo, Geno**, *Naked Betrayal: The Conspiracy Murder,* Azevedo Publishing, 2014. A Tony Felice PI Mystery #3 of 3. (Soft Boiled PI) Tony and Brad take a vacation that will not soon be forgotten. While cruising on the high seas, Tony finds himself investigating the death of a young man aboard their ship. The storyline takes the reader on a roller coaster of twists and turns as Tony attempts to figure out just what did happen to the young man who appears to have been murdered. 3/3

B

102. **Bacchus, Tom**, *Q-FAQ*, Haworth, 2007. (Modern Pulp) 'Q-FAQ' follows the erotic adventures of Afaik, a gay Arab terrorist. Bombed out of his Manhattan home, Afaik escapes into the arms of Aces Bannon, a surly soldier with a few special replacement parts. Together, the pair discover an underground network of hunky pilots and arms dealers. 3/3

103. **Bacino, Ted**, *Shakespeare Conspiracy*, AuthorHouse, 2010. (Historical) Watch the arguments unfold, showing the actual reasons that many historians believe that it could only have been Christopher Marlowe writing all those great works. It's a tale of murder, mayhem and manhunts in the underbelly of London as the Black Plague scourges the country and the greatest conspiracy plot of all time is hatched. 3/3

104. **Bagby, George (Aaron Marc Stein 1906-1985)**, *Innocent Bystander*, Crime Club/Doubleday, 1977. (Police Procedural) Inspector Schmidt #41 of 48. "Savage attack on a budding piano virtuoso from a poor New York family leads Inspector Schmidt, chief of homicide, NYPD, into the author's vision of gay New York in the mid-1970s (Slide)." 1/3

105. **Baker, James Robert (1946-1997)**, *Anarchy*, Alyson, 2002. (Crime Caper) A potent satire of American culture in an era of media overexposure, where what we are told replaces truth and what we see on television becomes our religion. A logic-defying, plot, encompassing the exploding breasts of a surgically enhanced TV star, Eva Braun's diet pills, a forged O.J. Simpson murder tape, a cult of fundamentalist tech heads, and a profanity-obsessed Russian mafia hit man, leads all the way over the top when a vision of Catherine Deneuve encourages James to take out God. 3/3

106. **Baker, James Robert**, *Testosterone*, Alyson, 2000. (Amateur Sleuth) Dean Seagrave was having an extraordinary day. All his belongings just went up in smoke, and he's tooling around Los Angeles in a rental car with a handheld tape recorder. The police are on his trail for assaulting an old woman outside a grocery store, or so he was just told by the man in a wheelchair he attacked at Venice Beach. "He's an emotional serial killer," he says, explaining his frenzied quest for Pablo Ortega, his lover, who disappeared one night going out for cigarettes. But what bothers Dean more is Pablo's connec-

tion to a cult, all the disappearing animals, and the story about torture in Chile. Problem is, Dean might be crazy. Or everyone might be lying. But now Dean has a machete (because the chainsaw made too much noise), and he just found Pablo. 3/3

107. **Banis, Victor (1937-2019)**, *Deadly Nightshade*, MLR, 2009. Deadly Mystery #1 of 9. (Police Procedural) Straight cop, gay cop, and a woman who "isn't real." Tom and Stanley are on the trail of a drag queen serial killer, and along the way, they find themselves engaged in a more intimate pursuit, trying to resolve another mystery: their unexpected attraction to one another. 3/3

108. **Banis, Victor**, *Deadly Wrong*, MLR, 2009. Deadly Mystery #2 of 9. (Police Procedural) The police say, "involuntary manslaughter," but a tragic accident turns out instead to be murder, plain and simple. And San Francisco Homicide Inspector Stanley Korski, on leave from the force and his unrequited love for fellow detective Tom Danzel, walks right into a murderer's web of treachery. Wrong, Stanley. Deadly wrong. 3/3

109. **Banis, Victor**, *Deadly Dreams*, MLR, 2009. Deadly Mystery #3 of 9. (Police Procedural) A painful past. A mysterious stranger. Footsteps vanishing in the fog. All Stanley wants is just to hear Tom say, "I love you." All Tom wants is Stanley safe. And the stranger? Ah, there's the rub–what exactly is it that he wants? Be careful what you wish for, fellows. You may get it. Dreams can be deadly. 3/3

110. **Banis, Victor**, *Deadly Slumber*, MLR, 2009. Deadly Mystery #4 of 9. (Police Procedural) The House of the Dead: a mortuary whose directors are drop dead gorgeous and terminally horny-and one of them up to mischief. Stanley and Tom try to separate the naturally dead from the murdered dead and find themselves awash with coffins-until they come to the one Stanley's name on it. Deadly Slumber indeed 3/3

111. **Banis, Victor**, *Deadly Silence*, MLR, 2010. Deadly Mystery #5 of 9. (Police Procedural) The hospital says it was an accident. Patience Pendleton says someone is trying to murder her father - but who? Her demented twin, Prudence? Or Farley, the jilted fiancee, who thought he would be marrying money? Or Zack, the queer brother threatened with disinheritance? Or, might it be the ghosts of past evil...? 3/3

112. **Banis, Victor**, *Deadly Kind of Love*, Dreamspinner, 2011. Deadly Mystery #6 of 9. (Police Procedural) Nothing bad is supposed to happen in Palm Springs. At least that's what San Francisco private detective Tom Danzel and his partner Stanley Korski believe. But when their friend Chris finds a dead body in his hotel room bed, Tom and Stanley drive out to help the local police investigate. What

they discover is a gangster's plot, a rather nasty green snake, and an elegant hotel that offers delicacies not usually found on a room service menu. The two detectives are going to have to rely on their skills and each other if they're going to survive this very deadly kind of love. –this is also considered the first book in the Tom and Stanley Mystery Series (MLM). 3/3

113. **Banis, Victor**, *Prayer for the Dead*, Dreamspinner, 2015. Deadly Mystery #7 of 9. (Police Procedural) Does murder follow Tom and Stanley around, or do they follow the murders? After a hospital stay, Stanley is invited by Father Brighton to convalesce at St. Marywood, an isolated monastery on the ocean cliffs of Big Sur. Upon arrival, Stanley finds Father Brighton dead. The order's doctor writes it up as a death by natural causes, but those seem to be quite prevalent at the monastery. The recent demise of a young brother who fell from the cliffs is described as an accident, but Stanley's nose is twitching. Plus the order's finances have taken a sudden, mysterious turn for the better. Is something rotten at St. Marywood? Stanley and Tom can't resist digging around even if it means testing their tumultuous relationship against a gaggle of handsome, young, virginal, and–they are told–gay men. –also #2 of the Tom and Stanley Mystery series (MLM). 3/3

114. **Banis, Victor**, *Dead Men Can't Lie*, MLR, 2018. Deadly Mystery #8 of 9. (Police Procedural) Who was John Bellows and why did he want to see Tom and Stanley dead? A vacation in the Ozarks turns into a cat and mouse game with a killer, who wants to see Tom and Stanley dead. 3/3

115. **Banis, Victor**, *Killing Time in LA*, DSP Publications, 2018. Deadly Mystery #9 of 9. (Police Procedural) No matter how Stanley tries, he and Tom can't seem to get away from bodies. On vacation in LA, Stanley's visit with a friend at a popular Mexican restaurant owned by La Paloma, the flamenco dancer, leads to meeting a couple from Mexico. When the woman is found dead, Tom and Stanley work with LAPD Detective Betts–a recovering alcoholic who lost his son to a child murderer–to find the young man. The bodies pile up as Tom, Stanley, and Betts race to solve the puzzle of a Russian agent, drug smuggling, illegal immigrants, and police corruption. Stanley might hate bodies, but Tom can't resist a mystery. While killing time in LA, will a killer set his sights on Stanley? –also #3 of the Tom and Stanley Mystery series (MLM). 3/3

116. **Bannister, Jo (b. 1951-)**, *Striving with Gods*, Crime Club/Doubleday, 1984. (Amateur Sleuth) Clio Rees and Harry Marsh #1 of 4. Luke Shaw is found dead in a bed sitting room in a small British Midlands city; his death an apparent suicide but his best friend Cleo Rees knows better and begins to investigate. –Shaw is suspected of

being a homosexual which is why he may have committed suicide (MLM). 1/3

117. **Banville, John (b. 1945-)**, *Untouchable*, Knopf, 1997. (Espionage) Elderly Victor Maskell, formerly of British intelligence, for many years art expert to the Queen. Now he has been unmasked as a Russian agent and subjected to a disgrace that is almost a kind of death. But at whose instigation? As Maskell retraces his tortuous path from his recruitment at Cambridge to the airless upper regions of the establishment, we discover a figure of manifold doubleness: Irishman and Englishman; husband, father, and lover of men; betrayer and dupe. –main character is bisexual (MLM) 3/3

118. **Barnard, Robert (1936-2013)**, *Death and the Princess*, Scribner, 1982. (Police Procedural) Perry Trethowan #2 of 5. Princess Helena had only a distant claim to the throne, but when her friends and lovers began turning up dead, Buckingham Palace demanded to know why. And Perry Trethowan of Scotland Yard had to catch a cold-blooded killer intent on causing a scandal that could shake the nation. –a gay secretary in Buckingham Palace is killed (MLM). 1/3

119. **Barnard, Robert**, *Bodies*, Scribner, 1986. Perry Trethowan #3 of 5. (Police Procedural) Police superintendent Percy Trethowan finds London's Soho as colorful and full of life as ever–except for the four corpses he discovers in a seedy photography studio. Shot while doing a layout for a health and fitness magazine, the victims left behind a camera loaded with film, but not clues. –gay pornography explored (MLM). 1/3

120. **Barnard, Robert**, *Scandal in Belgravia*, Bantam, 1991. John Sutcliffe #2 of 2. (Political Intrigue) Murder pays no respect to rank...or the neighborhood. And so, it happened that young aristocrat Timothy Wycliffe was bludgeoned to death in his elegantly furnished flat in Belgravia by a person or persons unknown. Unknown, in fact, for 30 years. Then the dead man's friend Peter Proctor – once a young man on his way up in the diplomatic service, now a retired Member of Parliament – seeks an antidote to boredom by attempting to write his own memoirs. –murdered man was gay (MLM). 3/3

121. **Barnes, Trevor**, *Midsummer Killing*, New English Library, 1989/ *A Midsummer Night's Killing*, William Morrow, 1992. Blanche Hampton #1 of 3. (Police Procedural) Trying to bounce back from being dumped by her husband, Inspector Blanche Hampton reluctantly begins an investigation into a headless corpse discovered on Hampstead Heath and runs into an endless barrage of deceit and trickery. –police detective under the inspector is black, gay, and Catholic (MLM). 2/3

122. **Barnes, Trevor,** *Dead Meat,* New English Library, 1991/ *A Pound of Flesh,* William Morrow, 1993. Blanche Hampton #2 of 3. (Police Procedural) Scotland Yard Detective Superintendent Blanche Hampton investigates the murder of a government minister's daughter and that of another woman, killed in exactly the same manner. 2/3

123. **Barnes, Trevor,** *Taped,* New English Library, 1992. Blanche Hampton #3 of 3. (Police Procedural) When a serious, but unpopular, television reporter is found stabbed to death at TV London, just a few floors below a riotous party, Blanche Hampton, the detective superintendent, is put on the case. 2/3

124. **Bartlett, Neil,** *Skin Lane,* Serpent's Tale, 2007. (Historical) 1960's London. At 47, Mr. F's working life on London's Skin Lane is one governed by calm, precision and routine. So, when he starts to have frightening, recurring nightmares, he does his best to ignore them. The images that appear in his dream are disturbing, Mr. F can't for the life of him think where they have come from. After all, he's a perfectly ordinary middle-aged man. 3/3

125. **Batten, Jack,** *Blood Count,* Macmillan Canada, 1991. Crang #4 of 7. (Hard Boiled) At the height of the AIDS crisis in the early nineties, Crang is enlisted by Alex Corcoran, a close friend who has just lost his lover to the disease, to find the man who infected him. Crang, concerned Corcoran might follow up on his threat to murder the man, tries to find the man to prevent Corcoran from getting himself in trouble. However, when Corcoran himself is killed, Crang owes it to his friends to find their killers. –main character is straight, and the rest of the series do not involve gay men (MLM). 2/3

126. **Battis, Jes,** *Night Child,* Ace, 2008. OSI #1 of 5. (Paranormal Police Procedural) Tess Corday, Occult Special Investigator for Vancouver's Mystical Crime Lab, is used to seeing dead vampires. But there's nothing ordinary about this case. Not the lab results on the cause of death. Not the teenage girl living at the address found in the vamp's pocket, who may well be in thrall to a demon. And certainly not Lucian Agrado, the necromancer who is liaison to the vampire community. Agrado is supposed to be part of the solution, but Tess suspects he might be part of the problem. –gay half-demon assists mc in investigation (MLM). 2/3

127. **Battis, Jes,** *Flash of Hex,* Ace, 2009. OSI #2 of 5. (Paranormal Police Procedural) After a series of brutal murders, Occult Special Investigator Tess Corday is convinced the identity of the killer is locked in her own head. The only question is-how many rules is she willing to break to get to the truth? 2/3

128. **Battis, Jes,** *Inhuman Resources,* Ace, 2010. OSI #3 of 5. (Paranormal

Police Procedural) When a powerful necromancer is killed, Occult Special Investigator Tess Corday must handle the heavy politics in the occult community as carefully as she handles the scant evidence. But with her sometime lover Lucian Agrado representing the necromancers in the grisly matter, things are about to get out of control...fast. 2/3

129. **Battis, Jes**, *Infernal Affairs*, Ace, 2011. OSI #4 of 5. (Paranormal Police Procedural) A dead body on the beach turns out to be a live demon on the run from some of the nastiest bounty hunters in this dimension–or the next. Protecting one demon from another, Tess gets wrapped up in a case that's as dangerous as it is mind-boggling, especially when it begins to involve her own past. 2/3

130. **Battis, Jes**, *Bleeding Out*, Ace, 2012. OSI #5 of 5. (Paranormal Police Procedural) Though she's on leave from the Occult Special Investigations squad, Tess Corday is still grappling with her own personal mysteries. But finding out the truth about her demonic heritage has been more difficult than she expected. Plus, her unauthorized investigation into an addictive new vampire street drug is driving a stake between her and her undead boyfriend. Then Vancouver's premier necromancer turns up dead. Tess suspects that the cases are related. And her suspicions will lead her into a paranormal showdown that can–and will–change the course of her life forever. 2/3

131. **Baty, C. J.**, *Pinkerton Man*, N.P., 2016. Pinkerton Man Romance #1 of 3. (Police Procedural) Stiles Langberry leaves England under the dark cloud of blackmail. He resettles in America with a new name, becoming a Pinkerton Agent. His new employer sends him undercover to a brothel that serves homosexual men, where prostitutes are being murdered. In the course of his investigation, he becomes involved with Paul, one of the prostitutes. Complicating matters, one of the suspects draws Stiles like no man before him. Stiles knows he must stop the killer before he strikes again. –only available as an e-book (MLM). 3/3

132. **Baty, C. J.**, *Home on the Range*, N.P., 2016. Pinkerton Man Romance #2 of 3. (Police Procedural) Pinkerton Agent Stiles Long is sent to the Circle W Ranch to uncover who is killing the ranch's cattle. In order to discover the truth about the goings on at the ranch, Stiles has to prove to the ranchers he's more than a good-looking city slicker. Savage Beare, the head ranch foreman, is far from happy that Stiles is there to check things out. He has secrets of his own. Stiles finds Savage incredibly good-looking, but cold and aloof. He's also a suspect. One of many. When Stiles' best friend and partner, Lizzie Ferguson, is kidnapped things begin to shake apart. Stiles doesn't trust anyone, and he needs to find Lizzie before it's too late. –only

133. **Baty, C. J.**, *Murder in New York*, N.P., 2018. Pinkerton Man Romance #3 of 3. (Police Procedural) Coming back to New York to see her ailing father, Lizzie Ferguson did not expect to find him healthy and newly married to a much younger woman. She, also, didn't expect to connect with an old lover and childhood friend or be accused of killing her father. But, life has a way of knocking you to your knees when you least expect it. Stiles Long had always regretted that the killer, from his first case as a Pinkerton Agent, had got away. Now, in New York it was happening again. The Hotel Astor Bar was a meeting place for men who enjoyed the company of men. And, some of them were being brutally murdered. When one of the suspects from the original case appears at the hotel, Stiles is torn between his desire to stop a killer and kiss the man senseless. Two different cases, but some of the faces overlap from one to the other. Stiles and Lizzie are in a race to discover who the killers are before another body gets added to the count. –only available as an e-book (MLM). 3/3

134. **Baty, C. J.**, *Drifting Sands*, N.P., 2015. Warfield Hotel Romance #1 of 4. (MM Amateur Sleuth) As he approaches his fortieth birthday, Justin Warfield feels alone, drifting like the sand that blows along the beach near his family's hotel. Marcus Drummond once spent a summer with his best friend Peter at the Warfield Hotel and fell hard for Peter's much older brother, Justin. Sparks fly when the two meet again, but there are a few things standing in their way. The closet that Justin has himself buried in and someone on a killing spree, dumping bodies on the Warfield beach ... victims that indicate Justin may be involved in some way. 3/3

135. **Baty, C. J.**, *Crashing Waves*, N.P., 2016. Warfield Hotel Romance #2 of 4. (MM Amateur Sleuth) Justin Warfield ran away to Italy to put the events of last summer and a certain dark-haired private eye behind him, to no avail. If anything, he can't help but rehash what happened over and over. When he finally returns to South Carolina, the hotel he runs with his brother has suffered a series of incidents that are starting to look less accidental after a death threat is received. 3/3

136. **Baty, C. J.**, *Roaring Waters*, N.P., 2017. Warfield Hotel Romance #3 of 4. (MM Amateur Sleuth) Damien Fitzgerald has lived through hell and is determined to never let anyone get close to him again. A fervent reporter, he throws his life into his work and doesn't care whose toes he steps on. But someone else does. He's got a stalker, and the messages are growing increasingly threatening. He turns to his best friend, Justin Warfield and his lover, Private Investigator Marcus Drummond. –only available as an e-book. The fourth book

in the series, *Warfield Christmas* has no mysteries to solve (MLM). 3/3

137. **Bauer, Tal**, *Hush*, N. P., 2017. (MM Thriller) Federal Judge Tom Brewer is finally putting the pieces of his life back together. In the closet for twenty-five long years, he's climbing out slowly, and, with the hope of finding a special relationship with the stunning Mike Lucciano, U.S. Marshal assigned to his DC courthouse. But a devastating terrorist attack in the heart of DC, and the subsequent capture and arrest of the terrorist, leads to a trial that threatens to expose the dark underbelly of America's national security. 3/3

138. **Baumbach, Laura & Josh Lanyon**, *Mexican Heat*, MLR, 2008. Crimes and Cocktails Romance #1 of 3. (MM Police Procedural) SFPD detective Gabriel Sandalini might as well have put a gun to his own head. One red-hot sexual encounter in a bar's back room has put two years of deep undercover work in jeopardy–two years of danger and deception as he worked his way into crime boss Ricco Botelli's inner circle. –Baumbach is owner of MLR Publishing (MLM). 3/3

139. **Baumbach, Laura**, *Tequila Sunrise*, MLR, No Release Date Yet. Crimes and Cocktails Romance #2 of 3. (MM Crime Drama) The only light in Gabriel Sandalini's life is former FBI agent, Antonio Lorenzo. Now Antonio is missing, and no one can – or will – tell Gabriel what's happened to him. –Baumbach has been promising this sequel since 2010 and is supposedly writing it on her own (MLM). 3/3

140. **Baumbach, Laura**, *Sangria White Bull*, MLR, No Release Date Yet. Crimes and Cocktails Romance #3 of 3. (MM Police procedural) It was supposed to be a long-awaited and much deserved romantic getaway: a week in California wine country. Good food, good wine, sunshine and lots of sex. Just what ex-FBI agent Antonio Lorenzo and his lover, ex-SFPD detective Gabriel Sandalini desperately need. But trouble is in the making at the White Bull Vineyard – and Gabriel believes someone in Antonio's family may be getting in too deep with some very dangerous people. Not an attitude that's going to endear him to his newly acquired in-laws – or Antonio. Or some very dangerous people… –no release date yet given (MLM). 3/3

141. **Baumbach, Laura**, *The Lost Temple of Karttikeya*, MLR, 2008. Collector Romance Series #9 of 9. (MM Police procedural) Brandon King is a LA police detective intimately involved with his older male partner. Brandon longs for a stable relationship with his abusive lover, but when a mysterious stranger offers him a chance to have his heart's true desire, he rebuffs the unbelievable offer. Then

circumstances change, and he fears loosing what he thinks he wants the most, he accepts the offer and takes on a deadly assignment that has him traveling to the isolated jungles of India in the company of hunky archeologist Christan Carter, who is intent on achieving his own heart's desire, as well. Combining Brandon's police skills with Christan's knowledge about ancient cultures, the two make an unstoppable pair, but will that winning chemistry carry over into their budding personal relationship and interfere with their quest? 3/3

142. **Baumbach, Laura**, *Burn Card*, MLR, 2008. (MM Police Procedural) A cop struggles to save himself before his lover kills his kidnapper. – reissued from a previous short story anthology (MLM). 3/3

143. **Baumbach, Laura**, *The Dark Side*, MLR, 2016. (MM Police Procedural) Kidnap victim Alex Throne literally drops into the arms of security specialist Reese Holt, pulling Holt into a battle against a ruthless drug cartel, personal betrayal, and a specter from Holt's CIA past. 3/3

144. **Baxt, George (1923-2003)**, *Queer Kind of Death*, Simon and Schuster, 1966. A Pharoah Love Mystery #1 of 5. (Police Procedural/Unreliable Narrator) New York detective Pharoah Love must answer these questions: Was the death of actor-model-hustler Ben, found snuggled up to a transistor radio in his bathtub, an accident – or murder? And if it was murder, who did it? Was it Seth, a writer who was living with Ben most recently before his death and who was, in fact, with Ben just minutes before he was electrocuted? Or maybe Veronica, Seth's estranged wife, who might have held a grudge against the man who took her husband away from her? What about Ella Hurst, Jameson Hurst, Adam Littlestorm, or Ben's sister, Ada? When Seth decides his next book will be about Ben, everyone formerly involved with the dead man is suddenly very interested in Seth's every move – especially the killer. –important as this series is the first gay mystery to be promoted by a main stream publisher (MLM). 3/3

145. **Baxt, George**, *Swing Low, Sweet Chariot*, Simon and Schuster, 1967. A Pharoah Love Mystery #2 of 5. (Police Procedural) Pharoah Love, a New York City detective, investigates a thirty-three-year-old murder that still casts a pall over the life of a middle-aged television actress. 3/3

146. **Baxt, George**, *Topsy and Evil*, Simon and Schuster, 1968. A Pharoah Love Mystery #3 of 5. (Police Procedural) Satan Stagg, a young Black detective, investigates the baffling murder of Guru Raskalnikov, a wealthy tycoon. 3/3

147. **Baxt, George**, *Queer Kind of Love*, Penzler, 1994. A Pharoah Love

Mystery #4 of 5. (Police Procedural) Gay, black and proud–and like no other homicide detective in the history of the NYPD–Pharoah Love finds himself in the middle of a most baffling case. Someone with a serious grudge is knocking off mobsters in unusual ways. In pursuit of clues, Love investigation takes him from a luxurious brothel to a Russian nightclub with a temperamental diva. 3/3

148. **Baxt, George**, *Queer Kind of Umbrella*, Simon and Schuster, 1995. A Pharoah Love Mystery #5 of 5. (Police Procedural) On a foggy New York night, the Green Empress is anchored off the beach at Far Rockaway, waiting to unload its cargo - a cargo nowhere near as exotic as the vessel's regal name suggests. The Empress has 300 aliens crammed into her belly - all are victims of the Asian slave trade, and all are paying very handsome fees for these "luxurious" accommodations to Kao Lee, Chinatown's notorious crime lord and leader of the feared Chi Who gang. But Kao's worried because his astrologer has cautioned him that Jupiter is on the rise, that danger is on its way and will come with the water. What Kao Lee doesn't know is that trouble's already on board and it goes by the name Pharoah Love. 3/3

149. **Baxt, George**, *Tallulah Bankhead Murder Case*, St. Martin's, 1987. A Jacob Singer Mystery #3 of 13. Joe McCarthy is rooting out suspected communists, among them the guests scheduled for Tallulah Bankhead's radio program, "The Big Show," and the situation only worsens when the guests–and Tallulah herself–come under suspicion of murder. –an informer is killed in a bathhouse (MLM). 1/3

150. **Baxt, George**, *Talking Pictures Murder*, St. Martin's, 1990. A Jacob Singer Mystery #4 of 13. The advent of talking pictures causes chaos in Hollywood, and revenge is in the air as Alexander Roland of Diamond Films confronts tyrannical Marie Darling, a mother of fading screen stars. –quite a few gay men appear in this mystery (MLM). 1/3

151. **Baxt, George**, *Greta Garbo Murder Case*, St. Martin's, 1992. A Jacob Singer Mystery #5 of 13. Refusing to be relegated to the status of a Hollywood has-been when World War II interferes with her career, Garbo accepts a role in an independent production. Soon she is at the center of an international imbroglio, where actors are spies, spies are actors, and some actors are simply acting. and humor. –actor William Haynes sleeps with a male producer (MLM). 1/3

152. **Bay, Nathan**, *King of the Sea*, Bay Cove, 2016. Bay Boys #1 of 3. (Paranormal Amateur Sleuth) Carlos Santiago is a man on the edge

of sanity. After battling cancer, he's developed an obsession with death, fearful that it's lurking behind every shadow, waiting to steal his last breath. Then a heart-pounding encounter with a mysterious merman turns his world upside down and gives him new hope for the future. But escaping his vindictive former boyfriend, Dr. Tyson Thorne, won't be so easy. 3/3

153. **Bay, Nathan**, *Invisible Plan*, Bay Cove, 2017. Bay Boys #2 of 3. (Amateur Sleuth) Peter Peartree is a young scientist who could use some stimulation in his life. He's feeling demoted in his job at a prestigious cancer research lab, and his relationship with his boyfriend is hanging on by a thread. But everything is about to change when he and his two best friends, Sabrina and Ernesto, discover a secret box buried in the shadowy bowels of the laboratory basement. Soon Peter finds himself engaged in a lethal game of hide-and-seek with a homophobic scientist who's drunk on power. The entire LGBT community of Nashville is at risk and only Peter can save the day. Will he be able to protect them before it's too late? 3/3

154. **Bay, Nathan**, *Young Forever*, Bay Cove, 2017. Bay Boys #3 of 3. (Amateur Sleuth) Gay men are mysteriously disappearing from the city of Nashville. There are no bodies, no evidence of a crime, and police are turning a blind eye to the pattern. But this is the South, where juicy gossip and sordid rumors spread like wildfire. Is a murderer at large, stealthily slaughtering innocent victims? And if so, who is he, and how can he be stopped? 3/3

155. **Beadle, Jeremy (1956-1995)**, *Death Scene: Thirteen Songs for Guy*, GMP, 1988. (Amateur Sleuth) London banker Michael Hamilton and civil servants Marcus Grey and Dominic Palmer. The three friends discover the body of Guy Latimer outside a London nightclub. Michael and Dominic quickly become suspects. The three commit themselves to discovering the murderer. As a result, the reader gains a fascinating survey of London gay life in the mid-1980s. The final revelation is chilling, designed to leave the reader queasy about any relationship he might be in. 3/3

156. **Beadle, Jeremy**, *Doing Business*, GMP, 1990. (Crime Drama) This quirky, charming little thriller features as its protagonist a most unlikely sleuth for a pop novel–Gordon McKenzie, mathematical genius, diminutive and unattractive, with an especial penchant for London "rent boys" (i.e., male prostitutes). During one of his frequent forays into a sleazy SoHo gay bar, Gordon accidentally stumbles upon the murder of a brewery inspector in progress. He recognizes one of the assailants as a "rent boy" who often hits him up for cash. And the rent boy knows Gordon knows and proceeds to attempt to silence him for good. Gordon is on the run, aided by a handsome male prostitute with whom he has fallen in love. In the

meantime, Gordon is convinced the murder is part of a conspiracy involving drugs and that one of his social-climbing friends is the mastermind behind it. But just which one? And will Gordon live to find out? 3/3

157. **Beakey, Chris**, *Double Abduction*, iBooks, 2007. Mary Bennett and her brother Michael share a close bond, which has grown tighter as they've raised her five-year-old son Justin. But when Justin is abducted, Michael is a prime suspect. Michael was with Mary's older son Benjamin when he was abducted and murdered five years before. He became a suspect in that case as did Scott Brown, Mary's then boyfriend and Justin's father. Michael and Scott are suspects again. But what are their motives? Is Michael trying to hurt Mary? Is Scott seeking revenge for being unable to see his son? What connection does the lead investigator Louis D'Amecourt play, and what secrets do he and Michael share? Policewoman Gloria Towson suspects that D'Amecourt is up to no good and that Michael knows more than he is telling. 1/2

158. **Beakey, Chris**, *Double Bind*, Not Yet Published. This is a 'just finished' copy of a book recently finished by the author and just being sent to his editor. He hopes to have the book published in Fall 2014– and based on the title is probably supposed to be a sequel to Double Abduction (MLM).

159. **Beakey, Chris**, *Fatal Option*, Post Hill Press, 2018. (Thriller) On the coldest night of the year, Stephen Porter is pulled from a restless sleep by a midnight phone call. His 17-year-old daughter Sara is stranded in a blizzard near the top of a mountain beyond their suburban home. She's terrified and unable to stop crying as she begs him to come to her rescue. Unfortunately, Stephen went to bed just an hour before after a night of binge drinking. With his blurred vision and unsteady balance, he knows it's dangerously irresponsible to get behind the wheel. But he heads out into the snowstorm to bring Sara home. High school teacher Kieran O'Shea is also behind the wheel, searching for his autistic younger brother Aidan, who is wandering aimlessly through the storm on that same mountain. –unsure of gay content (MLM). ?/3

160. **Bear, Elizabeth (b. 1971-)**, *Carnival*, Bantam, 2006. (Science Fiction) In Old Earth's clandestine world of ambassador-spies, Michelangelo Kusanagi-Jones and Vincent Katherinessen were once a starring team. But ever since a disastrous mission, they have been living separate lives in a universe dominated by a ruthless Coalition - one that is about to reunite them. The pair are dispatched to New Amazonia as diplomatic agents. Allegedly, they are to return priceless art. Covertly, they seek to tap its energy supply. But in reality, one has his mind set on treason. And among the extraordinary

women of New Amazonia, in a season of festival, betrayal, and disguise, he will find a new ally - and a force beyond any that humans have known.... 3/3

161. **Bear, Elizabeth**, *New Amsterdam*, Subterranean, 2007. New Amsterdam #1 of 5. (Paranormal Speculative Historical) Abigail Irene Garrett drinks too much. She makes scandalous liaisons with inappropriate men, and if in her youth she was a famous beauty, now she is both formidable–and notorious. She is a forensic sorceress, and a dedicated officer of a Crown that does not deserve her loyalty. She has nothing, but obligations. Sebastien de Ulloa is the oldest creature she has ever known. He was no longer young at the Christian millennium, and that was nine hundred years ago. He has forgotten his birth-name, his birth-place, and even the year in which he was born, if he ever knew it. But he still remembers the woman who made him immortal. He has everything, but a reason to live. In a world where the sun never set on the British Empire, where Holland finally ceded New Amsterdam to the English only during the Napoleonic wars, and where the expansion of the American colonies was halted by the war magic of the Iroquois, they are exiles in the new world–and its only hope for justice. –Sebastien de Ulloa is a bisexual wampyr (MLM). 3/3

162. **Bear, Elizabeth**, *Seven for a Secret*, Subterranean, 2009. New Amsterdam #2 of 5. (Paranormal Speculative Historical) The wampyr has walked the dark streets of the world's great cities for a thousand years. In that time, he has worn out many names–and even more compatriots. Now, so that one of those companions may die where she once lived, he has come again to the City of London. In 1938, where the ghosts of centuries of war haunt rain-grey streets and the Prussian Chancellor's army of occupation rules with an iron hand. Here he will meet his own ghosts, the remembrances of loves mortal–and immortal. And here he will face the Chancellor's secret weapon: a human child. 3/3

163. **Bear, Elizabeth**, *White City*, Subterranean, 2010. New Amsterdam #3 of 5. (Paranormal Speculative Historical) For centuries, the White City has graced the banks of the Moskva River. But in the early years of a twentieth century not quite analogous to our own, a creature even more ancient than Moscow's fortress heart has entered its medieval walls. In the wake of political success and personal loss, the immortal detective Don Sebastien de Ulloa has come to Moscow to choose his path amid the embers of war between England and her American colonies. Accompanied by his court–the forensic sorcerer Lady Abigail Irene and the authoress Phoebe Smith–he seeks nothing but healing and rest. But Moscow is both jeweled and corrupt, and when you are old there is no place free of ghosts, and Sebastien

is far from the most ancient thing in Russia.... 3/3

164. **Bear, Elizabeth**, *Ad Eternum*, Subterranean, 2012. New Amsterdam #4 of 5. (Paranormal Speculative Historical) For centuries, the wampyr has drifted from one place to another. From one life to another. It's 1962, and he's returned to New Amsterdam for the first time since he fled it on pain of death some sixty years before. On the eve of social revolution, on the cusp of a new way of life, he's nevertheless surrounded by inescapable reminders of who he used to be. For a thousand years, he's chosen to change rather than to die. Now, at last, he faces a different future.... 3/3

165. **Bear, Elizabeth**, *Garrett Investigates*, Subterranean, 2012. New Amsterdam #5 of 5. (Paranormal Speculative Historical) Five stories that comprise some of the matter surrounding the life of Lady Abigail Irene Garrett, Th.D., sometime Crown Investigator. They are previously uncollected. One is new; the others were only previously available as bonus chapbooks with the limited editions of various novellas.–only available as an e-book (MLM). 3/3

166. **Bear, Elizabeth**, *The Cobbler's Boy*, Sobbing Squonk, 2018. (Historical) Brilliant, bookish Christopher Marlowe is fifteen years old and desperate to qualify for a scholarship to the King's School in order to escape his brutal father. But the only man who could have helped him has been murdered... and now the killers are looking for Kit. 3/3

167. **Beaton, M. C. (Marion Gibbons b. 1936-)**, *Death of an Outsider*, St. Martins, 1988. Hamish Macbeth #3 of 33. (British Cozy) Dreary Cnothan's most hated man is dumped into a tank filled with lobsters which are eaten in Britain's best restaurants. Exiled there with his dog Towser, Hamish Macbeth misses his beloved Highland village Lochdubh, Priscilla, and easy lazy days. His superiors want the business hushed up, a dark-haired lass wants his body, and a killer is out for more blood. –deals with a bigoted clergyman who fears AIDS (MLM). 1/3

168. **Beaton, M. C.**, *Death of a Snob*, St. Martins, 1991. Hamish Macbeth #6 of 33. When health farm owner Jane Wetherby is frightened by an astrologer's prediction of her imminent demise, she offers Police Constable Hamish Wetherby free room in exchange for his protection. Then the prediction proves accurate about the crime, and Wetherby must enliven his distinctively sleepy style of policing to solve the death of a snob. –only gay aspect is Hamish asserts indignantly "I am not a homosexual." to the suggestion that as a single man in his thirties he must be (MLM). 1/3

169. **Beaudet, Marty**, *By a Thread*, N. P., 2010. (Political Intrigue) Air Force One is down. The President is dead. The VP's motorcade

speeds him to the White House, but a rogue delivery truck slams his limo and leaves him in a coma. The work of terrorists is evident, but the sophistication and planning suggest the involvement of a foreign government. The CIA pursues the one loose end the attack's perpetrators left hanging: at the very moment the President's plane was shot down, one of the terrorists placed a call to a mysterious Kuwaiti in Vienna. They find the perfect asset in Kevin "Red" Davis. Through his Mormon missionary work in Vienna, Davis is already on a first-name basis with the Kuwaiti. A bond between the two results. When the moment comes to act, Davis is torn by his many loyalties. 3/3

170. **Beaumont, Sebastian**, *Cruelty of Silence*, Millivres, 1997. (Amateur Sleuth) On the anniversary of the enigmatic disappearance of successful architect Alex Stern, his love Lol has spent a deeply distracted year looking for him – at the cost of both his job and of the comfortable home they shared. After much frustration and an inability to restart his life, Lol discovers that a large sum of money is missing and that a locked computer file may contain the vital clue to what really happened to Alex. 3/3

171. **Beebe, Blair**, *Secret Pestilence,* Archway, 2013. (Thriller) It is 1979, and a young man lying on the ground shivering from septic shock is taken to an emergency room, where doctors discover a rare microbe previously assumed harmless. In the ensuing months, the same disease reappears in other victims, all from the Mission District of San Francisco. The epidemic explodes out of control, taking the lives of countless young men, and overwhelming University Hospital microbiologist Lynn Lucas and her colleagues. –Based in part on real events, this compelling tale shares a glimpse into the early days of the San Francisco AIDS epidemic as young physicians and scientists risk everything to battle one of the most complex diseases in the history of medicine (MLM). 3/3

172. **Beck, Rick**, *Antiques and Homicide/Homocide*, Aventine, 2003. (Police Procedural) Rookie Robert Mann is selected from the Academy for a special taskforce. Commander Brown doesn't trust rookies. Officer Connell believes only a fresh face can get the job done. Mann isn't sure he's cut out for the unique assignment. The "DC Strangler" leaves no clues. Puzzled, Mann sometimes feels the Strangler close, but the murderer isn't the only one with Mann in his sights. Antique dealer and specialist in Native American artifacts, Albert Forrestal, resurrects pieces of Mann's past. With Fran tempting him and Toby depending on him, he wades through DC's gay underground in search of an invisible man. 3/3

173. **Beecham, Rose**, *Introducing Amanda Valentine*, Naiad, 1992. Amanda Valentine #1 of 3. (Police Procedural) Wellington, New

Zealand, is the setting for Detective Inspector Amanda Valentine's escapades, not the least of which is a monster dubbed the "Garbage Dump Killer" and a beautiful TV reporter who has designs on Amanda's living body as well. –this is the first book in a trilogy of lesbian mysteries. This is the only one to include a gay man (MLM). 1/3

174. **Beecroft, Alex**, *Buried with Him,* Createspace, 2016. Unquiet Spirits #0 of 3. (MM Historical) Sentenced to the pillory for the crime of having kissed a man, Jasper Marin has been stripped of his vocation as a priest and seems poised to lose his faith with it. He has always been able to see ghosts but it's just like his luck that the one who's harassing him now seems obsessed with collecting human hearts. –Novella prequel to *Wages of Sin* (MLM). 3/3

175. **Beecroft, Alex**, *Wages of Sin*, MLR, 2010. Unquiet Spirits #1 of 3. (MM Historical) Charles Latham, wastrel younger son of the Earl of Clitheroe, returns home drunk from the theatre to find his father gruesomely dead. He suspects murder. But when the Latham ghosts turn nasty, and Charles finds himself falling in love with the priest brought in to calm them, he has to unearth the skeleton in the family closet before it ends up killing them all. 3/3

176. **Beecroft, Alex**, *Waters of the Deep*, Pronoun, 2017. Unquiet Spirits #2 of 3. (MM Historical) Charles and Jasper are brought in to investigate a fatal stabbing in (the cotton-mill town of) Paradise. But this time the only troublesome ghost in the case is their own adopted child Lily. So what's leaving the glistening trail in the woods? Why did the vicar's daughter suddenly kill herself? And what is happening to the extra cow? 3/3

177. **Beecroft, Robyn (Alex Beecroft)**, *Murder of a Straw Man,* Createspace, 2018. Dancing Detectives #1 of 2. (Cozy) Newly settled in a quaint small town in the English Fens, Rory Cornwell knows no-one and is too shy to go out and make friends. When a local festival is marred by the murder of a morris dancer, his pretty house-mate Haley is distraught–her uncle is the prime suspect. Nervously investigating, and smitten by Zach, the attractive policeman on the case, will Rory uncover the true culprit before the wrong person is jailed? 3/3

178. **Beecroft, Robyn**, *Murder of a Working Ghost,* Createspace, 2018. Dancing Detectives #2 of 2. (Cozy) Halloween approaches and in the ancient capital of the Fens, Haley Thorpe is working as a costumed actor on a ghost tour. When one of the other 'ghosts' is murdered by a cunning device, suspicion falls on Haley–the only one unobserved at the scene. Can she and Rory–her posh house-mate–figure out the real murderer before she gets arrested? And can someone

tell Sean that he's not all that before he starts breaking down the door? 3/3

179. **Beinhart, Larry**, *You Get What You Pay For*, William Morrow, 1988. Tony Cassella PI #2 of 3. (Hard Boiled) Tony Cassella is a private investigator, his assignment here is to expose the shady dealings that lie buried in the past of the present U.S. Attorney General. – Cassella is depicted as incredibly homophobic. The third Tony Cassella novel involves a lesbian love affair, also handled badly (MLM). 1/3

180. **Bell, Robert**, *Final Closure*, Booksmango, 2014. Paul Thai #1 of 2. (Espionage) Paul Swift retires and plans a peaceful life in Thailand. No pressure, no faces from the past, and no more snow. Until he recognizes someone. A face that represents unfinished business; a face that brings his time in Germany back to the fore; a face that makes him reconsider retiring to Pattaya. As he digs deeper, he finds his foes from Germany are back up to their old tricks, and some new ones. It's time to put a spanner in their works. He calls on old friends to help, and in the course of his self-imposed mission, makes new ones. 3/3

181. **Bell, Robert**, *The Fifth Man*, Smashwords, 2013. Paul Thai #2 of 2. (Espionage) Paul and Frank thought with the death of Matthias, they had Final Closure. But they realized they were missing someone, the mastermind. They didn't believe they had everyone, and no one was talking. Paul and Frank look for the puppet master as Chai has his new job and sets up his new undercover team. They find the first cases are not only linked but linked back to the Matthias case. –available as an e-book only (MLM). 3/3

182. **Bell, Sara**, *The Magic in Your Touch*, P. D., 2005. Reed #1 of 2. (MM Amateur Sleuth/Police Procedural) When Dr. Nathan "Nate" Morris moves to Reed, Illinois to open a medical practice, he's looking forward to putting the past–and his homophobic family–behind him. When Nate is attacked outside his office late one night in an apparent gay bashing, he starts to wonder if maybe the good folks of Reed aren't as accepting as he thought. Sheriff Brandon Nash, an openly gay man holding an elected position, finds it hard to believe that Nate's attack is really a hate crime. Brandon, looking into Nate's frightened eyes, knows there's one thing he's absolutely certain of: he'll do whatever it takes to keep Nate safe or die trying. As Nate's assailant steps up his efforts, Nate and Brandon's budding romance is put to the test. Nate decides to leave Reed behind, believing everyone else will be safe once he's gone. 3/3

183. **Bell, Sara**, *The Way You Say My Name*, P. D., 2009. Reed #2 of 2. (Amateur Sleuth) Eighteen-year-old Dillon Carver made the big-

gest mistake of his life when he dumped Jamie Walker two years ago over Jamie's decision to come out of the closet. At the time, he was afraid Jamie's revelation would out him to the world - and his narrow-minded parents. Jamie Walker's heart was ripped to shreds when Dillon walked out on him. With help from his best friend Ben, Jamie was able to pick up the pieces and move on. He still hasn't tried his hand at love again, but for the most part Jamie has been able to put the pain behind him. Now things are different. Dillon wants Jamie back, and he'll do whatever it takes to make that happen. Only one thing stands in his way: Jamie's relationship with bad boy Ben Lewis. When Dillon begins an open campaign to win Jamie back, Jamie's life is once again thrown into chaos. 3/3

184. **Bellew, Don,** *The Return of the Rebel,* Amazon, 2015. Rebel #1 of 2. (Crime Drama) Sam has been living in Dallas for fifteen years and working as a "legal thief" ie. he repossesses cars. A TV news broadcast describes a serial killer rampage in his old home town back in Alabama. Sam's brother is the latest victim. Long estranged from home, his brother was the last of Sam's blood family. Wally was a shy, introverted, closet gay librarian. He'd never hurt anyone. Sam, feeling guilty and remorseful, sets out to avenge his brother. –available as an e-book only (MLM). 3/3

185. **Bellew, Don,** *The Rebel 2,* Amazon, 2015. Rebel #2 of 2. (Crime Drama) Sam begins to settle into his old home town but trouble comes back to send him crashing through the status quo, again, and his cosmic destiny pushes him back into his role of avenging angel. – states that it is the second of three books, but a third book has yet to be published. (MLM). 3/3

186. **Benbow, Dave**, *Daytime Drama,* Kensington, 2003. (Amateur Sleuh) While working on daytime television's hottest soap opera, Sunset Cove, naive newcomer Clay Beasely finds himself immersed in greed, corruption, and lust where he encounters arrogant men, scheming divas, and malicious producers. 3/3

187. **Benbow, Dave**, *Male Model,* Kensington, 2004. (Amateur Sleuth) Blake Jackson is ultra-passionate about designing window displays, but what Blake is more interested in, is renowned designer Cameron Fuller. Does it matter that Cameron is married...to a woman? Cameron Fuller is an icon of chic style, but his marriage isn't nearly as successful. In fact, it is heavily rumored that Cameron's desires lie not with his vicious, drunken, shrew of a wife, Suzette, but with the men he discreetly takes to his bed. Discreetly being the keyword as Cameron and Suzette have a public image to uphold as "America's Couple." When Blake and Cameron engage in a lustful, whirlwind secret affair, Blake couldn't be happier. In need of a fresh look to launch his new cologne, Cameron finds his model in

Blake. But someone is unhappy about Blake's sudden rise to fame and the growing love between the designer and model...someone who knows their secrets...someone determined to make them pay dearly. And as the days tick down until the celebrity-packed party that will make Blake a star, it's clear that the only way Cameron and Blake can hold on to what they have is to let go of everything else. –Clay and Travis from *Daytime Drama* make a cameo appearance (MLM). 3/3

188. **Benbow, Dave**, *Summer Cruising*, Palari, 2006. (Amateur Sleuth) Sweeping romance and steamy sex are the daily activities for the hunky passengers of the RMS Princess Diana, as they set sail on a rollicking all-gay cruise through the sun-drenched Mediterranean and its stunning ports of call...But this idyllic holiday abruptly ends when a calculating psychopath sets in motion a dastardly plan to send the luxurious liner to the bottom of the sea. Soon daring escapes, personal sacrifices, and heart-pounding rescues replace romance and the men of the Diana struggle to survive the sinking ship and each other...–Clay and Travis from *Daytime Drama* make a cameo appearance (MLM). 3/3

189. **Benbow, Dave**, *Jack Colby: Back in Action*, Palari, 2011. (Military) We follow rugged Marine Jack Colby as he is called back into military action for a covert operation in the Middle East. Along the way he is pursued by several "straight" hunks who guard their masculinity with their life. But once they meet Jack and fight side-by-side with him, they develop an attraction that can't be denied. The action moves from Hawaii to the Middle East and back to San Francisco as we follow Jack on his mission to save the world...and find love. 3/3

190. **Benderson, Bruce**, *User*, Dutton, 1994. (Crime Drama) He is the son of a black derelict and a white New Ager, a beautifully toned specimen of urban male beauty, and a New York City street hustler. His special gift is reeling in his customers, who flip to him like spawning salmon. His greatest pleasure is feeling his eyes about to roll back, as the Dilaudid he has just injected races through his veins and begins licking his brain. His name is Apollo, he takes you into his world - a shocking world filled with stark yet hypnotic eroticism, mined with terrors peculiar to the subterranean big city in the hours after midnight. –NY police detective is attracted to the drag queens (MLM). 1/3

191. **Bennet, Nicki & Ariel Tachna**, *Under the Skin*, Dreamspinner, 2011. (MM Police Procedural) Police detective Patrick Flaherty has no illusions about Russian mobster Alexei Boczar, but that doesn't stop his fascination with the bodyguard to one of the most ruthless families in Chicago's growing Eastern European crime community.

From the moment Patrick meets Alexei's eyes over the body of another Russian mobster, Alexei is a thorn in Patrick's side, refusing to cooperate with the police and turning all of Patrick's questions back on him. 3/3

192. **Bentley, Robert**, *Here There be Dragons*, Ontario Press, 1972. (Espionage) Dexter is recruited at the height of the Cold War by the FBI and Naval Intelligence to set himself up for blackmail by the Soviets in order to pass on falsified information about an American espionage operation. What authorities had not anticipated is Dexter's also flushing out a traitor in Navy ranks. 3/3

193. **Berckman, Evelyn**, *Case in Nullity*, Eyre & Spottiswoode, 1967 or *A Hidden Malice*, Belmont Tower Books, 1967. (Psychological) A contemporary novel of divorce on unusual grounds. On one level this is the story of a divorce action based on the non-consummation of a marriage; on another level it is the story of how the alchemy of unfortunate events changes the husband into a man obsessed with revenge. 2/3

194. **Berendt, John**, *Midnight in the Garden of Good and Evil*, Random House, 1994. (Fictionalized True Crime) Shots rang out in Savannah's grandest mansion in the misty, early morning hours of May 2, 1981. Was it murder or self-defense? For nearly a decade, the shooting and its aftermath reverberated throughout this hauntingly beautiful city of moss-hung oaks and shaded squares. –won the seventh LAMBDA Award for Best Gay Mystery (MLM). 2/3

195. **Berliner, Ross (Murray M. Kappelman b. 1931-)**, *The Manhood Ceremony*, Simon and Schuster, 1978. (Thriller) No one knew that 12-year-old Ricky Stern was being lured on a nightmarish journey by a bearded stranger who promised him excitement - excitement that was tinged with the most shocking, shattering, unspeakable terror.... –"This novel reflects the hysteria of the period dominated by Anita Bryant's vicious campaign against gay rights (Gunn)." 2/3

196. **Berman, Steve**, *Vintage: A Ghost Story*, Haworth, 2007. (YA Paranormal) In a small New Jersey town, a lonely boy walking along a highway one autumn evening meets the boy of his dreams, a boy who happens to have died decades ago and haunts the road. Awkward crushes, both bitter and sweet, lead him to face youthful dreams and childish fears. With a cast of offbeat friends, antiques, and Ouija boards. 3/3

197. **Bidulka, Anthony**, *Amuse Bouch*, Insomniac, 2003. A Russell Quaint Mystery #1 of 8. (Hard Boiled) A gay wedding gone bad. A missing groom. An unsullied reputation at risk. Enter Russell Quant; cute, gay, and a rookie private detective. With a nose for good wine and

bad lies, Quant is off to France on his first big case. From the smudgy streets of Paris, he cajoles and sleuths his way to the pastel-colored promenade of Sanary-sur-Mer. 3/3

198. **Bidulka, Anthony**, *Flight of Aquavit*, Insomniac, 2004. A Russell Quaint Mystery #2 of 8. (Hard Boiled) At the dead end of a desolate country road, a late-night meeting suddenly becomes an ambush. Gay private detective Russell Quant is faced with personal threats he can't ignore, a friend who may be a foe, and a cagey client with a treacherous monkey on his back. As Quant trails a menacing blackmailer known only as Loverboy, he finds himself immersed in the midnight world of e-dating and parking lot romance. Lured to New York City, Quant tests his wit, wisdom, and wiles from the Old-World grandeur of Fifth Avenue to the kaleidoscope world of Broadway's electric night-spots. The fast pace continues when Quant returns to Saskatoon where he grapples with decoys and deceit, realizing that no one is as they appear. Threat turns into deadly reality and the need to uncover the identity of Loverboy becomes increasingly desperate. Quant deftly maneuvers through the twists and turns of a perilous case and a personal life rife with its own mystique and mayhem. –won the seventeenth LAMBDA Award (MLM). 3/3

199. **Bidulka, Anthony**, *Tapas on the Ramblas*, Insomniac, 2005. A Russell Quaint Mystery #3 of 8. (Hard Boiled) Charity Wiser, matriarch of the Wiser clan by virtue of her wealth and power, is an indomitable provocateur ... and private detective Russell Quant's newest employer. There is more than a single rotten apple on this family tree, and Quant has been hired to discover which one is intent on murdering his client. To help him sleuth out the evil culprit, Charity Wiser arranges a family reunion aboard the opulent Friends of Dorothy Cruise liner as it tours the most exotic ports of the Mediterranean. But smooth sailing is short-lived as undercurrents of clashes – local and tourist, gay and straight, trendy and traditional – offer Russell insight into the Wisers and reveal a family simmering with rage and greed. He begins to wonder: who doesn't want Charity Wiser dead? 3/3

200. **Bidulka, Anthony**, *Stain on the Berry*, Insomniac, 2006. A Russell Quaint Mystery #4 of 8. (Hard Boiled) Everyone has their Boogeyman. But who-or what-is scaring Saskatoon locals to death? Private detective Russell Quant is roused from sleep only to fall into a nightmare case when the family of a suicide victim hires him to uncover the real cause of death. But what is real and what is imaginary? Quant works to narrow his list of suspects only to find the number of victims growing. Russell is mystified as the trail of fear connects him to a vast landscape of people, including an elegant potash miner, dubious trailer park denizens, reticent farm folk,

the Pink Gopher choir, and a gaseous psychiatrist. Compounding Quant's bewilderment is the complete and perfect disappearance of his once very real friend, Sereena, who has become a ghost he simply can't find. With the Boogeyman always a few paces ahead, Russell struggles to keep the hounds of failure from baying. Travelling from Saskatchewan's summer storms to the menacing Lotus Land of Vancouver, he finally touches down in the Canadian Arctic, where tragic hope resides. Russell returns home to bully attacks, a desperate chase through midnight woods, and a sadistic abduction. As Quant penetrates the truth of the Boogeyman, he finds himself on a perilous suspension bridge between idyllic childhood and grown-up violence. 3/3

201. **Bidulka, Anthony**, *Sundowner Ubuntu*, Insomniac, 2007. A Russell Quaint Mystery #5 of 8. (Hard Boiled) A mother's pain. A million dollars. A missing son. Desperate to right old wrongs, a new client hires Russell Quant to locate her son, Matthew, lost to her for twenty years. But can money relieve remorse? Through good old-fashioned detective work, Russell peels away the layers of a carefully concealed life, grown from the seeds of traumatic childhood violence. Tracking Matthew's life from the schoolyard drug culture of a pleasant prairie city's underbelly to the stunning vistas, vibrant townships, and tinderbox safaris of Africa, Russell finds much more than he was looking for. Ever adept at making both friends and foes, Quant runs a gauntlet of uncharted danger as worlds collide. Thrust into the unfamiliar role of bad guy, stymied by seemingly insurmountable distrust and base fear, Russell cuts a blistering swath through covert threats and overt bullets. But as he searches for his Canadian needle in an African haystack, the brutality escalates. Confronting his own role in the cause and effect of scars and anger, retribution and revenge, Russell Quant faces a difficult question: What happens when the prodigal son resists the return? 3/3

202. **Bidulka, Anthony**, *Aloha, Candy Hearts*, Insomniac, 2009. A Russell Quaint Mystery #6 of 8. (Hard Boiled) Private detective Russell Quant is perplexed. From the middle of the Pacific to the middle of Canada, he's missing clues and proposing answers that only beg questions. The parking lot murder of a passing acquaintance draws Quant to a poem that just might be a treasure map. But is it treasure or extortion he is trailing? Unsure of his commitment to a case he wasn't even hired for, Russell uncovers the hidden history of Saskatoon through an early homestead, a fallen sports hero, and a second-run movie house. As his search progresses, he becomes the quarry being hunted. What exactly did Russell Quant commit to? In this fast-paced mystery, Russell tries to balance his professional life with the demands of a wedding, a memorial, and at least one home-

cooked meal at mom's. While Russell is reluctantly uncovering the past, the present demands his attention. Murder begets blackmail begets murder. And, with the Hawaiian sand barely shaken free from his hair, Russell is confronted, professionally and personally, with the harsh consequences of indecision. 3/3

203. **Bidulka, Anthony**, *Date with a Sheesha*, Insomniac, 2010. A Russell Quaint Mystery #7 of 8. (Hard Boiled) Neil Gupta went to the Middle East looking for antique carpets. He found something equally timeless: murder. When Neil is found stabbed to death in Dubai's spice souk, his distraught father wants revenge. He hires private investigator Russell Quant to catch the killer. In his greatest case to date, Quant goes undercover to match wits with a wily museum curator, shifty souk merchants, corrupt carpet experts, and the denizens of an underground club for "fabulous" men. From the flamboyant glitz of Dubai to the scorching sand dunes of Saudi Arabia, Quant risks his life as he wades further and further into the shadows cast by the desert sun. As Russell's spicy international adventure heats up, he learns a valuable lesson about love, life, and learning to seize the moment...before it's gone. On the verge of making the biggest personal decision of his life, Russell discovers that endings sometimes come before beginnings. 3/3

204. **Bidulka, Anthony**, *Dos Equis*, Insomniac, 2012. A Russell Quaint Mystery #8 of 8. (Hard Boiled) When we left him last, Saskatoon gay PI Russell Quant was a broken man. Dumped by his boyfriend, forced to drive around town in a minivan instead of his beloved sports car, only his dogs still needed him.But, things are looking up. A call for help from an old adversary gives Russell a new purpose in life, and he faces the future with a spring in his step and new highlights in his hair. Set in the beautiful Mexican beach town of Zihuatenengo. 3/3

205. **Billingham, Mark**, *Sleepyhead*, Little Brown, 2001. Tom Thorne #1 of 16. (Police Procedural) Detective Inspector Tom Thorne now knows that three murdered young women were a killer's mistakes – and that Alison was his triumph. And unless Thorne can enter the mind of a brilliant madman – a frighteningly elusive fiend who enjoys toying with the police as much as he savors his sick obsession – Alison Willetts will not be the last victim consigned forever to a hideous waking hell. –gay pathologist is mc's best friend (MLM). 2/3

206. **Billingham, Mark**, *Scaredy Cat*, Little Brown, 2002. Tom Thorne #2 of 16. (Police Procedural) It was a vicious, calculated murder. The killer selected his victim at Euston station, followed her home on the tube and strangled her to death in front of her child. At the same time, killed in the same way, a second body is discovered at

the back of King's Cross station. It is a grisly coincidence that eerily echoes the murder of two other women, stabbed to death months before on the same day... It is DI Tom Thorne who sees the link and comes to the horrifying conclusion. This is not a serial killer the police are up against. This is two of them. Finding the body used to be the worst part of the job. Not anymore. Now each time a body is found, Thorne must live with the knowledge that somewhere out there is a second victim, waiting to be discovered... 2/3

207. **Billingham, Mark**, *Lazy Bones*, Little Brown, 2003. Tom Thorne #3 of 16. (Police Procedural) A MONSTER MURDERED It's only ten days since Douglas Remfry's release from prison, having served seven years for rape, and now he's dead: naked on a bare mattress in a grubby north London hotel room, his head hooded, and his hands tied with a brown leather belt. A DEADLY JUSTICE Someone knew he was coming out. Someone wanted to mete out some punishment of his own. A CASE NO ONE WANTS SOLVED And when a second sex offender is found dead, DI Tom Thorne knows he has a vicious, calculating viliglante on his hands... 2/3

208. **Billingham, Mark**, *Burning Girl*, Little Brown, 2004. Tom Thorne #4 of 16. (Police Procedural) X marks the spot - and when that spot is a corpse's naked back and the X is carved in blood, DI Tom Thorne is in no doubt that the dead man is the latest victim of a particularly vicious contract killer. 2/3

209. **Billingham, Mark**, *Lifeless*, Little Brown, 2005. Tom Thorne #5 of 16. (Police Procedural) It appears that someone is targeting London's homeless community so DI Tom Thorne goes undercover amongst them. The information he gleans is that this is no random killer, it is someone with a specific list of victims. 2/3

210. **Billingham, Mark**, *Buried*, Little Brown, 2006. Tom Thorne #6 of 16. (Police Procedural) Teenager Luke Mullen is missing. He was last seen by schoolmates getting into a car with an older woman, and it is unclear whether he has disappeared voluntarily or been abducted. 2/3

211. **Billingham, Mark**, *Death Message*, Little Brown, 2007. Tom Thorne #7 of 16. (Police Procedural) Thorne looked at the picture, feeling the pulse quicken at the side of his neck. There were times when he couldn't see what was staring him in the face, but this, for better or worse, was his area of expertise. Thorne knew a dead man when he saw him. Delivering the "death message." That's what cops call those harrowing moments when they must tell someone that a loved one has been killed. Now Detective Investigator Tom Thorne is receiving messages of his own: photographs of murder victims sent to his cell phone. Who are the victims? Who is sending the

photographs? And why is he sending them to Tom Thorne? The answer lies in the detective investigator's past, with a man he had once sent to prison for life. But even behind bars, the most dangerous psychopath Thorne has ever faced is still a master at manipulating others to do his dirty work for him. And Thorne must act fast because the photos keep on coming, and the killer's next target is someone the detective investigator knows very well. 2/3

212. **Billingham, Mark**, *Bloodline*, Little Brown, 2009. Tom Thorne #8 of 16. (Police Procedural) It seems like a straightforward domestic murder until a bloodstained sliver of X-ray is found clutched in the dead woman's fist - and it quickly becomes clear that this case is anything but ordinary. Thorne discovers that the victim's mother had herself been murdered fifteen years before by infamous serial killer Raymond Garvey. The hunt to catch Garvey was one of the biggest in the history of the Met and ended with seven women dead. When more bodies and more fragments of X-ray are discovered, Thorne has a macabre jigsaw to piece together until the horrifying picture finally emerges. A killer is targeting the children of Raymond Garvey's victims. Thorne must move quickly to protect those still on the murderer's list, but nothing and nobody are what they seem. Not when Thorne is dealing with one of the most twisted killers he has ever hunted... 2/3

213. **Billingham, Mark**, *From the Dead*, Little Brown, 2011. Tom Thorne #9 of 16. (Police Procedural) It has been a decade since Alan Langford's charred remains were discovered in his burnt-out car. His wife Donna was found guilty of conspiracy to murder her husband and served ten years in prison. But just before she is released, Donna receives a nasty shock: an anonymous letter containing a photo of her husband. The man she hates with every fiber of her being – the man she paid to have murdered – seems very much alive and well. How is it possible that her husband is still alive? Where is he? Who sent the photo, and why? DI Tom Thorne becomes involved in a case where nothing and no one are what they seem. It will take him much further from his London beat than he has ever been before – and closer to a killer who will do anything to protect his new life. 2/3

214. **Billingham, Mark**, *Good as Dead*, Little Brown, 2011. Tom Thorne #10 of 16. (Police Procedural) The Hostage. Police officer Helen Weeks walks into her local newsagents on her way to work. Little does she know that this simple daily ritual will change her life forever. It's the last place she expects to be met with violence, but as she waits innocently at the till, she comes face to face with a gunman. The Demand. The crazed hostage-taker is desperate to know what really happened to his beloved son, who died a year before in youth

custody. By holding a police officer at gunpoint, he will force the one man who knows more about the case than any other to re-investigate his son's death. That man is DI Tom Thorne. The Twist. While Helen fights to stay alive and the body-count rises, Thorne must race against time if he is to bring a killer to justice and save a young mother's life. 2/3

215. **Billingham, Mark,** *The Dying Hours,* Little Brown, 2013. Tom Thorne #11 of 16. (Police Procedural) A fantastic, never-before-published Tom Thorne novel by England's crime king. It's been twenty-five years since Tom Thorne last went to work wearing the "Queen's cloth" but now, having stepped out of line once too often, he's back in uniform. He's no longer a detective, and he hates it. Still struggling to adjust, Thorne becomes convinced that a spate of suicides among the elderly in London are something more sinister. His concerns are dismissed by the Murder Squad he was once part of and he is forced to investigate alone. Now, unable to trust anybody, Thorne risks losing those closest to him as well as endangering those being targeted by a killer unlike any he has hunted before. A man with nothing to lose and a growing list of victims. A man who appears to have the power to make people take their own lives. 2/3

216. **Billingham, Mark,** *The Bones Beneath,* Little Brown, 2014. Tom Thorne #12 of 16. (Police Procedural) Thorne faces perhaps the most dangerous killer he has ever put away, Stuart Nicklin. When Nicklin announces that he wishes to reveal the whereabouts of one of his earliest victims and that he wants the cop who caught him to be there when he does it, it becomes clear that Thorne's life is about to become seriously unpleasant. Thorne is forced to accompany Nicklin to a remote island off the Welsh coast which is cut off from the mainland in every sense. Shrouded in myth and legend, it is said to be the resting place of 20,000 saints and as Thorne and his team search for bones that are somewhat more recent, it becomes clear that Nicklin's motives are far from altruistic. 2/3

217. **Billingham, Mark,** *Time of Death,* Little Brown, 2015. Tom Thorne #13 of 16. (Police Procedural) Two schoolgirls are abducted in the small, dying Warwickshire town of Polesford, driving a knife into the heart of the community where police officer Helen Weeks grew up and from which she long ago escaped. But this is a place full of secrets, where dangerous truths lie buried. When it's splashed all over the press that family man Stephen Bates has been arrested, Helen and her partner Tom Thorne head to the flooded town to support Bates' wife an old school friend of Helen[1]s living under siege with two teenage children and convinced of her husband's innocence. As residents and media bay for Bates' blood, a decomposing

body is found. The police believe they have their murderer in custody, but one man believes otherwise. With a girl still missing, Thorne sets himself on a collision course with local police, townsfolk and a merciless killer. 2/3

218. **Billingham, Mark,** *Love Like Blood,* Little Brown, 2017. Tom Thorne #14 of 16. (Police Procedural) DI Nicola Tanner needs Tom Thorne's help. Her partner, Susan, has been brutally murdered and Tanner is convinced that it was a case of mistaken identity–that she was the real target. The murderer's motive might have something to do with Tanner's recent work on a string of cold-case honor killings she believes to be related. Tanner is now on compassionate leave but insists on pursuing the case off the books and knows Thorne is just the man to jump into the fire with her. 2/3

219. **Billingham, Mark,** *The Killing Habit,* Little Brown, 2018. Tom Thorne #15 of 16. (Police Procedural) While DI Nicola Tanner investigates the deadly spread of a dangerous new drug, Tom Thorne is handed a case that he doesn't take too seriously, until a spate of animal killings points to the work of a serial killer. When the two cases come together in a way that neither could have foreseen, both Thorne and Tanner must risk everything to catch two very different killers. –book sixteen, *Their Little Secret,* will be released in 2019 (MLM). 2/3

220. **Bishop, R. H.,** *Errant Justice,* N. P., 2018. Sanders and Felan #1 of 2. (Court Drama) Brilliant but irascible attorney Lucy Sanders and her stylish gay assistant Armando Felan uncover a dangerous web of personal secrets and international gang warfare as their client's life hangs in the balance. When young immigration attorney Patty Acres is found murdered in her San Diego apartment, her client and lover, Domingo Torres, a Mexican journalist seeking asylum in the U.S., is accused of the crime. 2/3

221. **Bishop, R. H.,** *Cheating Death,* N. P., 2018. Sanders and Felan #2 of 2. (Court Drama) After a young bride falls to her death from the treacherous cliffs of Torrey Pines park, Lucy ventures outside her practice of law to investigate whether the apparent accident was actually murder. 2/3

222. **Bixley, George,** *That First Heady Burn,* Dagmar Miura, 2017. Slater Ibanez #1 of 8. (Hard Boiled) Don't mess with the hothead–or he might just mess with you. Slater Ibanez is only interested in two kinds of guys: the ones he wants to punch, and the ones he sleeps with. Things get interesting when they start to overlap. A freelance investigator, Slater trolls the dark side of Los Angeles, rooting out insurance fraud, not afraid to use whatever means necessary to get things done, and not about to hold back with his fists. A queer anti-

hero for a new age, Slater walks the line between ordinary life and the frayed fringes of society, keeping his balance with the jobs that his employer, Della, throws his way, and the back-channel support he gets from his idiot cop ex-boyfriend, Conrad. 3/3

223. **Bixley, George**, *True Vermilion*, Dagmar Miura, 2018. Slater Ibanez #2 of 8. (Hard Boiled) Hired to look into the theft of an expensive piece of jewelry, Slater soon finds himself entangled with a delusional high-end clothing manufacturer who sees the good in everyone, his snooty socialite wife, described as "damaged," and her book-smart smoking-hot stepson. Which one of them is lying to Slater–and who, exactly, is the slippery con artist in the red miniskirt? From his new digs in the Fashion District, and with the help of a new business partner, Slater stalks wealthy lowlifes and their minions in boutiques and clubs, breaking into places he's not supposed to be, winding up the middle of the desert in the middle of the night–and never hesitating to serve up a beatdown. 3/3

224. **Bixley, George**, *The Dark Shill*, Dagmar Miura, 2018. Slater Ibanez #3 of 8. (Hard Boiled) A routine insurance gig sends Slater after Derek, an accountant who claims to be too debilitated even to meet with him. But why is he never at his crummy little apartment? Rahim, the achingly hot sales manager at Derek's office, doesn't reveal much, except when he and Slater wind up in the sack–an attraction that might be diverting Slater from uncovering the truth. Gwen, the high-style HR director, is definitely concealing her relationship with Derek, just like Dave, the head of the company, caught skulking around dive bars and the back streets of Skid Row. Intensity builds as Slater goes undercover to root out malpractice by a sleazy plastic surgeon, following leads in the case high and low, pausing only to punch out tweakers, grifters, and bullies along the way. 3/3

225. **Bixley, George**, *A Stack of Sawbucks*, Dagmar Miura, 2018. Slater Ibanez #4 of 8. (Hard Boiled) Pulled in on a case by his business partner, Slater investigates reports of a ghost in a faded Miracle Mile apartment, where eerie noises start at the same time every night. But no one believes there's anything supernatural going on, including the tenants–and why is there a sealed-off staircase in the middle of the living room? Using his illicit Russian tech, Slater soon discovers one of the neighbors has some dirty secrets, but the tenant upstairs presents a bigger challenge, with disproportionately sophisticated security measures. Managing his zealous sex life and aided by Andy, a new hookup, Slater tries to weasel out of his obligations to the Russians, finding himself driven to drastic measures when his partner suddenly disappears. Join Slater as he punches out knuckleheads, drinks too much, and muscles his way to the truth. 3/3

226. **Bixley, George,** *The Hillside Roble,* Dagmar Miura, 2018. Slater Ibanez #5 of 8. (Hard Boiled) Investigating a million-dollar heist at a gallery in the Arts District, Slater can't get a face-to-face with the owner, Eli, until he applies a little pressure, which leads to an evening invite to a tony mansion in the hills. Eli turns out to be a minor celebrity, physically flawless but obsessed with his own image, and flaky in that uniquely LA way. Gallery manager Pilar and her girlfriend are hiding something too, but Slater works to uncover the dirt with some surveillance and subterfuge, briefly posing as a straight guy to get some answers. Eli's nephew Ty seems guileless at first, but what is he really up to at his massage-parlor job? Join Slater as he closes in on the truth, never hesitating to use his fists or his libido to cut through the secrets and deception. 3/3

227. **Bixley, George,** *The Peroxide Pomp,* Dagmar Muira, 2018. Slater Ibanez #6 of 8. (Hard Boiled) Interrupted late one night by Marisol, a desperate woman seeking help from his business partner, Slater agrees to go after her husband, Abner, a nebbishy accountant who's making their divorce negotiations a nightmare. But why is Marisol traveling with a bodyguard, and why is she more interested in uncovering Abner's secret assets than just warning him off? With Andy's help, Slater infiltrates Abner's office and befriends staffer Nolan on a quest to figure out where all the money is coming from. Unable to keep his libido in check, Slater winds up in bed with one of the principals and struggles to keep the entanglement from clouding his judgment. –two more books in the series are set to be released in 2019 (MLM). 3/3

228. **Black, Mychael,** *The Duke's Husband,* Phaze, 2008. (MM Paranormal) Jay Wharton and Devon Brooks meet and fall in love in merry ole England. Only everything isn't so merry. Jay is the Duke of Wharton, and his mother doesn't care for his relationship with Devon. The Duchess' schemes drive Devon from England back to the United States. Unwilling to let Devon go, Jay follows him to the States and proposes to him. Devon agrees to marry him, and they are wed in a beautiful ceremony in Canada. What should be the start of a new life together slowly begins to take on a nightmarish quality. Is the love they have for each other strong enough to withstand the trials? 3/3

229. **Black, Sarah,** *Boy Meets Body: Murder at the Heartbreak Hotel,* MLR, 2007. A Partners in Crime Book #1 of 5. (MM Amateur Sleuth) Peter Moon, proprietor of a charming little get-away in the Land of the Midnight Sun, finds himself headed for less comfortable accommodations when he's accused of murder. Then his personal heartbreak showed up, fresh from six months in a Yukon River fish camp, determined to help. –third short story in the Partners in Crime

anthology (MLM). 3/3

230. **Black, Sarah**, *I'll be Dead for Christmas: Death of a Blues Angel*, MLR, 2007. A Partners in Crime Book #2 of 5. (MM Amateur Sleuth) It's Christmas, 1966. Deacon Davis is a veteran black reporter of the Mississippi Civil Rights Movement. But he doesn't know what to expect when three old men, legends of the Blues, bring a new Blues guitar out of Mississippi, and he's so white he glows. Rafael Hurt is hiding a dangerous secret, and the old men are trying to keep him safe. Then a young girl is murdered during Rafe's first gig at the Blues Angel. Rafe and Deke try to find the killer before the secrets around them lead more bloodshed to their door and destroy any chance for the love growing between them. –second short story in the Partners in Crime anthology (MLM). 3/3

231. **Black, Sarah**, *Footsteps in the Dark: Murder at Black Dog Springs*, MLR, 2008. A Partners in Crime Book #3 of 5. (MM Amateur Sleuth) Code-talker Logan Kee returns to his home on the Navajo Reservation from the battlefields of Saipan. But a new battle is waiting for him. Uranium mining has begun within the four sacred mountains. When the old hand-trembler dies at Black Dog Springs, rumors fly that Leetso, the yellow monster, has been set free to walk the land. 3/3

232. **Black, Sarah**, *Fearless*, MLR, 2007. Fearless #1 of 2. (MM Police Procedural) Lt. Colton Wheeler understands the law and the people of the Arizona-Mexico borderlands and his lover, Dr. Diego Del Rio. But a shocking act of violence leaves a battered dead body in their home and Diego charged with murder. Suddenly everything Colton thought he knew turns out to be wrong. What can he still believe in? Who can he trust? He believes in his lover, but Diego is on the run. –short story in the *Fearless* anthology published in print by MLR of Sarah Black books or can be read individually as an e-book (MLM). 3/3

233. **Black, Sarah**, *Lawless*, MLR, 2008. Fearless #2 of 2. (MM Police procedural) Lt. Colton Wheeler is the law in a lawless land. A year after his lover, Dr. Diego Del Rio, lost his eye in a vicious hate crime, trouble from across the border threatens to shatter the life they're building together. An old lover stakes a claim, and Colton suspects he wants more than Diego. Colton's family comes under attack, a missing Apache boy is accused of cattle rustling, and bloody tribal masks from the old rituals are being worn by someone carrying a whip, bent on terrifying the people of the borderlands. Colton only knows one way to protect his people. By walking into trouble, by drawing fire, by putting himself between the people he loves and those who mean them harm. 3/3

234. **Black, Sarah**, *The General and the Elephant Clock of Al-Jazari*, Dreamspinner, 2013. General and the Horselord #2 of 2. (MM Military) Fresh out of the closet, General John Mitchel and Gabriel Sanchez are settling into their new life together when an old army colleague taps them for a rescue mission to Tunisia. Eli and Daniel, two former Rangers working security, have been arrested in Carthage, charged with blasphemy and thrown into prison. With rampant unrest in the ancient city and an old enemy targeting them, John gathers a team to liberate the two captive men. When he discovers Eli s boyhood obsession with Al-Jazari s Elephant Clock, the rescue becomes complicated and strangely beautiful, and John and Gabriel have to risk what they love the most to bring their team home. 3/3

235. **Blankenship, William D.**, *Programmed Man*, Walker, 1973. (Industrial Espionage) When a secret and potentially very valuable invention with its plans and blueprints is stolen, the result can be murder, several murders in fact. -slight gay content (MLM) 1/3

236. **Blake, Victoria**, *Bloodless Shadow*, Orion, 2003. Samantha Falconer #1 of 4. (Hard Boiled) When she left Oxford, Sam Falconer thought she had put the ghosts of her past behind her. But, while working in London as a P.I., she is summoned home by her brother to investigate the disappearance of a young woman-and confront the trauma she's tried so hard to forget. The closer she gets to Oxford, the more uneasy she becomes. Then, out of the blue, Sam receives a letter from a man who's been dead for 28 years-her father. As Sam copes with emotional chaos and investigates her case, she finds that every trail leads back to the university. But academia is stingy with its secrets, and its pursuit of truth is limited by a self-protective instinct that could turn lethal at any moment. –gay ex-policeman teams up with PI Falconer (whose brother is also gay) (MLM). 2/3

237. **Blake, Victoria.**, *Cutting Blades*, Orion, 2005. Samantha Falconer #2 of 4. (Hard Boiled) The year has got off to a bad start for PI Sam Falconer. There's a blizzard in London and Sam has the feeling she's being watched. She's asked to investigate the disappearance of a young rower and he seems to be an elusive figure just beyond reach. Then a body surfaces - but it's not his. 2/3

238. **Blake, Victoria.**, *Skin and Blister*, Orion, 2006. Samantha Falconer #3 of 4. (Hard Boiled) When a student is found hanging in his rooms at St Barnabas College, Oxford, it appears to be suicide. But Sam begins to see a disturbing connection to her brother's recent disappearance. 2/3

239. **Blake, Victoria**, *Jumping the Cracks*, Orion, 2007. Samantha Falconer #4 of 4. (Hard Boiled) Private Investigator Sam Falconer

grew up in an Oxford College and now she's back to set up a branch of her detective agency. When she's asked to guard a collection of strange museum pieces, ranging from shrunken heads to bottled witches, she quickly realizes that being back in Oxford means confronting her own demons, as well as those behind the glass cases. 2/3

240. **Blakeston, Oswell (Henry Joseph Hasslacher 1907-1985)**, *Pass the Poison Separately: A New Mystery*, Catalyst, 1976. (Amateur Sleuth) Film critic, underground experimental filmmaker, novelist. –this is the first title published by Ian Young's Catalyst Press (MLM). 3/3

241. **Blincoe, Nicolas (b. 1965-)**, *Manchester Slingback*, Picador, 1998. Jake is a successful 34-year-old man when DI Davey Green arrives to take him back to Manchester, where 15 years ago, Jake ran wild. In Manchester, Jake's friend, Johnny, had been murdered. Now another corpse has been found, and Jake must finally confront the ghosts of despair that haunt him. –Jake is a gay former snitch (MLM). 1/3

242. **Bloch, Jon P.**, *Best Murder of the Year*, St. Martin's, 2002. Rick Domino #1 of 2. (Journalism) Rick Domino is one of the most sought-after men in Hollywood but he's not an actor, director or even a film producer. He's a popular gossip columnist covering the Hollywood scene and a word from him can be very influential. Normally, Rick loves his job and the scene itself but tonight it's different, but Rick also finds himself in perhaps the most deadly situation in his life. By the time the police arrive, they find Rick standing over a corpse, holding a gun and looking not-so-innocent. 3/3

243. **Bloch, Jon P.**, *Murder by Design*, St. Martin's, 2004. Rick Domino #2 of 2. (Journalism) Rick Domino is at the very top in his world - which is Hollywood - and his stock in trade is celebrity gossip. His finances, however, are the pits and can't begin to pay for his copious good taste. So, when his producer 'suggests' he be a guest on a popular cable decorating/reality program - "My House, Your House" - Rick agrees to appear not only because he's not really given a choice in the matter but it's a chance at a free makeover for his sagging, outdated living room. As if this mess wasn't big enough, one of the designers is savagely-if perhaps understandably. Rick Domino is on a quest to rescue his reputation, salvage his living room, and - if at all possible - find the person responsible for this particularly tasteless act of murder. 3/3

244. **Block, Lawrence**, *Sins of the Father*, Jove, 1976. Matthew Scudder #1 of 17. (Hard Boiled) The pretty young prostitute is dead. Her alleged murderer–a minister's son–hanged himself in his jail cell.

The case is closed. But the dead girl's father has come to Matthew Scudder for answers, sending the unlicensed private investigator in search of terrible truths about a life that was lived and lost in a sordid world of perversion and pleasures. –minister's son is gay (MLM). 2/3

245. **Block, Lawrence**, *Eight Million Ways to Die*, Arbor House, 1982. Matthew Scudder #5 of 17. (Hard Boiled) Nobody knows better than Matthew Scudder how far down a person can sink in this city. A young prostitute named Kim knew it also–and she wanted out. Maybe Kim didn't deserve the life fate had dealt her. She surely didn't deserve her death. The alcoholic ex-cop turned PI was supposed to protect her, but someone slashed her to ribbons on a crumbling New York City waterfront pier. Now finding Kim's killer will be Scudder's penance. –a naked man attacks Scudder (MLM). 1/3

246. **Block, Lawrence**, *Ticket to the Boneyard*, William Morrow, 1982. Matthew Scudder #8 of 17. (Hard Boiled) Matt Scudder put the brilliant and elusive James Leo Motley behind bars - for good, or so he hoped. Because Motley went down swearing revenge on Scudder and anyone who knew him. Twelve years later, Motley is out and giving his psychopathic tendencies free rein. No one is safe, friends, lovers and even strangers unfortunate enough to share the Scudder name. Each step in the resulting grisly dance takes the Big Apple PI one step further away from Al-Anon and one step nearer to death. –Motley loves having anal sex with men and women (MLM). 1/3

247. **Block, Lawrence**, *Dance at the Slaughterhouse*, William Morrow, 1991. Matthew Scudder #9 of 17. (Hard Boiled) In Matt Scudder's mind, money, power, and position elevate nobody above morality and the law. Now the ex-cop and unlicensed PI has been hired to prove that socialite Richard Thurman orchestrated the brutal murder of his beautiful, pregnant wife. During Scudder's hard drinking years, he left a piece of his soul on every seedy corner of the Big Apple. But this case is more depraved and more potentially devastating than anything he experienced while floundering in the urban depths. Because this investigation is leading Scudder on a frightening grand tour of New York's sex-for-sale underworld – where an innocent young life is simply a commodity to be bought and perverted ... and then destroyed. –brother of deceased wife is gay and dying of AIDS and a young male teenager is killed in a bisexual orgy (MLM). 1/3

248. **Blue, Ally**, *Oleandar House*, Samhain, 2006. Bay City Paranormal Investigation #1 of 7. (MM Paranormal) Sam Raintree has never been normal. All his life, he's experienced things he can't explain.

Things that have colored his view of the world and of himself. So, taking a job as a paranormal investigator seems like a perfect fit. His new co-workers, he figures, don't have to know he's gay. When Sam arrives at Oleander House, the site of his first assignment with Bay City Paranormal Investigations, nothing is what he expected. The repetitive yet exciting work, the unusual and violent history of the house, the intensely erotic and terrifying dreams which plague his sleep. But the most unexpected thing is Dr. Bo Broussard, the group's leader. 3/3

249. **Blue, Ally**, *What Hides Inside*, Samhain, 2007. Bay City Paranormal Investigation #2 of 7. (MM Paranormal) Sam Raintree's life changed forever when he started his dream job with Bay City Paranormal Investigations. When his boss hires a new investigator, Dean Delapore, Sam is intrigued in spite of himself. During the intense investigation of South Bay High School, from which three students have mysteriously disappeared, Sam and Dean draw closer together. 3/3

250. **Blue, Ally**, *Twilight*, Samhain, 2008. Bay City Paranormal Investigation #3 of 7. (MM Paranormal) While leading an amateur ghost-hunting expedition in Asheville, NC, Bay City Paranormal is called to investigate Sunset Lodge, a rustic inn situated on a remote Smoky Mountain peak. In recent weeks, employees and guests alike have seen a weird, frightening creature in the forest near the lodge. 3/3

251. **Blue, Ally**, *Closer*, Samhain, 2009. Bay City Paranormal Investigation #4 of 7. (MM Paranormal) After nine months of tumult, Sam Raintree is ready for some peace and quiet. A beach vacation with his boss and lover, Dr. Bo Broussar. Then a new case for the Bay City Paranormal Investigations team puts a crimp in Sam's plans. Fort Medina, a seventeenth-century citadel guarding the mouth of Mobile Bay, is less than five miles from their vacation beach house. Bo invites the group to stay with them while investigating the place, promising Sam he won't get involved. 3/3

252. **Blue, Ally**, *An Inner Darkness*, Samhain, 2009. Bay City Paranormal Investigation #5 of 7. (MM Paranormal) After more than a year as a couple-and plenty of bumps along the road-Sam Raintree and Dr. Bo Broussard are finally settling into life together. Bo has come to terms with his sexuality, their business is thriving, and Sam has begun to accept his role as a step-parent of sorts to Bo's sons, Sean and Adrian. When eleven-year-old Adrian begins exhibiting signs of psychokinesis-the same ability which allows Sam to manipulate interdimensional portals-the friction between Sam, Bo and Janine escalates. Caught in the middle of the conflict and burdened with an ability he can't yet control, Adrian is soon pushed beyond his

limits, Sam and Bo race against time to save both boys and keep an otherworldly horror from breaking free. 3/3

253. **Blue, Ally**, *Where the Heart Is*, Samhain, 2009. Bay City Paranormal Investigation #6 of 7. (MM Paranormal) When Dean Delapore takes a break from Bay City Paranormal Investigations, he doesn't expect his work to follow him to the eclectic town of Carrboro, North Carolina. The chance to investigate a haunting at the Blue Skye Inn and Winery is more than he can resist. As Dean probes the misty secrets of the haunted inn, it's far too late to turn back.If the bones of the past can be laid to rest... 3/3

254. **Blue, Ally**, *Love Likes Ghosts*, Samhain, 2010. Bay City Paranormal Investigation #7 of 7. (MM Paranormal) At age eleven, Adrian Broussard accidentally used his mind to open a portal to another dimension. Now, ten years later, he's successfully harnessed his strong psychokinetic abilities. In the process, he's learned the lessons which have become the guiding principles of his life. Absolute truth. Absolute control. Always. 3/3

255. **Bodeen, Dewitt**, *13 Castle Walk*, Pyramid Books, 1975. (Amateur Sleuth) A fictionalized account of the unsolved murder of William Desmond Taylor in 1922. Set in the present, the gothic mystery novel features a young woman released on parole from prison, where she had been serving time for the mercy killing of her husband. She goes to work for former silent screen star Jennie Jill Jerrard and becomes fascinated with the murder of Jerrard's director, Andrew Riley Rutherford. –Rutherford was bisexual (MLM). 1/3

256. **Bodin, J. S.**, *Orchid of the Night*, Mercury Heartlink, 2017. (Amateur Sleuth/Police Procedural) Kyle's life begins to unravel when a terrible fire consumes his aunt's orchid estate on Maui destroying their livelihood, and killing his only living relative. Realizing that the fire was meant for him, he must flee for his life. He moves to Tempe, Arizona, bringing the only orchid to survive the fire-the Dracula vampira. Finding solace in the gay community of Ixtlan, Kyle begins to heal from his troubled past, but even his new identity as Tom Tanner cannot protect him from his tragic fate. 2/3

257. **Bodner, Hal**, *Bite Club!*, Alyson, 2005. West Hollywood Vampires #1 of 2. (Paranormal Police Procedural) Welcome to the Bite Club–where the only requirement for membership is death. West Hollywood, California. The Creative City. Liberal and welcoming. Free from discrimination and hatred. A safe place to live if you're gay. But West Hollywood isn't safe anymore... Someone in town has a macabre passion for beautiful young men. Healthy, gym-toned male bodies keep turning up–tortured, drained of blood, missing parts and quite, quite dead. WeHo's compulsively overeating City Coro-

ner Becky O'Brien is helpless to stop the accumulation of corpses. At the end of her investigative rope, she calls upon an old college friend, Christopher Driscoll, who is something of an expert on serial killers. Rushing to her aid, Chris arrives in town with his quirky over-the-top boyfriend Troy in tow. Prowling the dark alleys and cruisy bars of WeHo in search of the psychotic fiend, the trio soon realizes that something possibly not human has taken up residence in Boys' Town–something with an insatiable hunger for the flesh and blood of hot young men. 3/3

258. **Bodner, Hal**, *The Trouble with Hairy*, Alyson, 2012. West Hollywood Vampires #2 of 2. (Paranormal Police Procedural) Oh, Bloody Mary – with a twist! Cruel, sharp teeth hunger for a taste of human flesh. Powerful jaws salivate at the thought of innocent victims. And twisted, gnarled claws are just dying for a manicure! Something not-quite-human stalks the city streets under the full moon after the gay bars close. As the ravaged corpses start piling up, coroner Becky O'Brien and her unlikely allies realize they are the only defenders who can protect scores of unsuspecting pretty boys from a grisly, bone crunching Death by Werewolf. Welcome back to West Hollywood, where the drinks aren't the only things that are stiff! Get ready to howl with laughter under a full moon when Becky, her best friend Christopher Driscoll – who happens to be the city's resident vampire! – and his quirky boyfriend Troy battle to save West Hollywood's hottest men from a vicious monster's hunger. 3/3

259. **Bollen, Christopher**, *Orient*, Harper, 2012. (Thriller) Orient is an isolated town on the north fork of Long Island, its future as a historic village newly threatened by the arrival of wealthy transplants from Manhattan–many of them artists. One late summer morning, the body of a local caretaker is found in the open water; the same day, a monstrous animal corpse is found on the beach, presumed a casualty from a nearby research lab. With rumors flying, eyes turn to Mills Chevern–a tumbleweed orphan newly arrived in town from the west with no ties and a hazy history. As the deaths continue and fear in town escalates, Mills is enlisted by Beth, an Orient native in retreat from Manhattan, to help her uncover the truth. With the clock ticking, Mills and Beth struggle to find answers, faced with a killer they may not be able to outsmart. 3/3

260. **Bollen, Christopher**, *The Destroyers*, Harper, 2017. (Thriller) At first Patmos appears to be a dream–long sun-soaked days on Charlie's yacht and the reappearance of a girlfriend from Ian's past–and Charlie readily offers Ian the lifeline he so desperately needs. But, like Charlie himself, this beautiful island conceals a darkness beneath, and it isn't long before the dream begins to fragment. When Charlie suddenly vanishes, Ian finds himself caught up in deception

after deception. As he grapples with the turmoil left in his friend's wake, he is reminded of an imaginary game called Destroyers they played as children–a game, he now realizes, they may have never stopped playing. 3/3

261. **Borton, D. B. (Lynette Carpenter b. 1951-)**, *One for the Money*, Diamond, 1993. Cat Caliban #1 of 8. (Cozy) Life changed for Catherine "Cat" Caliban after thirty-eight years of marriage. She lost a husband, bought an apartment house, got a gun- and decided to become a P.I. And that was "before" she discovered that her upstairs apartment came furnished...with a corpse. –gay bartender assists Cat (MLM). 2/3

262. **Borton, D. B.**, *Two Points for Murder*, Diamond, 1993. Cat Caliban #2 of 8. (Cozy) After raising three kids, Cat Caliban figures she's got exactly what it takes to be a successful P.I. Her latest case begins with a lost kitten and leads to danger when she finds the notebook of a murdered high-school jock. It soon becomes clear that the murder is just the tip of the iceberg. 2/3

263. **Borton, D. B.**, *Three is a Crowd*, Diamond, 1994. Cat Caliban #3 of 8. (Cozy) Cat Caliban, mother of three and Cincinnati's finest amateur sleuth, goes into action when an old friend, Steel, a Vietnam veteran, is accused of the murder of a former peace activist. 2/3

264. **Borton, D. B.**, *Four Elements of Murder*, Diamond, 1995. Cat Caliban #4 of 8. (Cozy) Housewife turned detective Cat Caliban is asked by a friend to investigate the death of her uncle. An environmental activist, the man was killed in a suspicious car accident while on his way to speak to a government official. But when Cat agrees to investigate, she never expects that her discoveries will put millions of dollars, political careers, and her own life on the line. 2/3

265. **Borton, D. B.**, *Five Alarm Fire*, Diamond, 1996. Cat Caliban #5 of 8. (Cozy) Suspicion is second nature to any woman who's raised three kids. So Cat Caliban has what it takes to be a smart snoop. In her fifth adventure in the series, she gets all fired up when she finds the cremated remains of a corpse hidden in the kiln at her pottery class. 2/3

266. **Borton, D. B.**, *Six Feet under*, Diamond, 1997. Cat Caliban #6 of 8. (Cozy) After thirty-eight years of marriage and three kids, Cat Caliban is intent on starting a new life. She buys her apartment building and starts working towards her P.I. license, but she'll be using her investigative skills sooner than she thinks. Cat is truly baffled by her new case-someone is trying to kill Rocky Zacharius, the jump-rope queen of Cincinnati. While on the trail. Cat faces a fate worse than death–caring for Rocky's three kids 2/3

267. **Borton, D. B.**, *Seventh Deadly Sin*, Hillard and Harris, 2004. Cat

Caliban #7 of 8. (Cozy) It's Valentine's Day and in the latest Cat Caliban mystery (7th in the series) love is in the air, especially around the tenants at Cat's apartment building. But things take a more serious turn when a new client, an eccentric old lady in a blue flowered dress, asks Cat to find out why her grandson was murdered. 2/3

268. **Borton, D. B.**, *Eight Miles High*, Hillard and Harris, 2007. Cat Caliban #8 of 8. (cozy) Detective-in-training Cat Caliban meets her latest client when a pilot crash-lands in the middle of a family picnic. Toots Magruder confesses her suspicions that the plane was sabotaged, and tells Cat and her partner, retired cop Moses Fogg, a story that begins during World War II, when young women with a passion for flying traveled from all over the country to Avenger Field in Sweetwater, Texas, for the chance at the best flight training available and a coveted place in the Women Airforce Service Pilots. 2/3

269. **Bosman, Olivier**, *Death Takes a Lover*, Createspace, 2014. DS Billings #.5 of 4. (Historical Police Procedural) The year is 1888. Detective Sergeant John Billings has been sent to a remote house in the Yorkshire Moors to investigate the suspicious death of Roger Thornton, a young man who seemed to have everything to live for. He gets a frosty reception from the lady of the house and her rag-tag collection of domestic staff who try to put him off the scent, but as Billings delves deeper into their lives, he uncovers hidden passions, bitter rivalries and a truth so dark and sinister. 3/3

270. **Bosman, Olivier**, *The Ornamental Hermit*, Createspace, 2015. DS Billings #1 of 4. (Historical Police Procedural) The year is 1890. Detective Sergeant John Billings is a Quaker. He sees God in everyone and takes other people's suffering to heart. He is an honest and hardworking man who has risen swiftly through the ranks to become one of Scotland Yard's youngest detectives. But in his private life he struggles with the demons of loneliness, morphine addiction and homosexuality. While Scotland Yard is in the midst of foiling a Russian counterfeiting operation, Billings is asked to investigate the cold-blooded murder of Lord Palmer. The main suspect is a rough looking vagrant called Brendan Lochrane who was employed by Lord Palmer to live as an 'ornamental hermit' in a grotto in his estate. 3/3

271. **Bosman, Olivier**, *Something Sinister*, Rocket Man Press, 2017. DS Billings #2 of 4. (Historical Police Procedural) On the 21st November 1890, Julius Dunne-Smythe – a wealthy coffee manufacturer – his wife, his sister in law and his butler creep quietly out of their home in the middle of the night, sneak into a carriage and drive off, never to be seen again. When a few weeks later Dunne-Smythe's business partner discovers some discrepancies in the company's

bookkeeping, Dunne-Smythe is suspected of embezzling the company and running away. What initially seems like a simple case of theft, now looks like something far more sinister. 3/3

272. **Bosman, Olivier,** *The Campbell Curse,* Rocket Man Press, 2018. DS Billings #3 of 4. (Historical Police Procedural) The year is 1892. While touring Britain with her production of Macbeth, the famous American actress, Carola LeFevre, receives an anonymous death threat. Detective Sergeant John Billings from Scotland Yard is appointed as her personal security guard. Billings is thrown into a theatrical world of gossip, intrigue and temper tantrums, but things take a darker turn when the tour heads for Edinburgh. A great tragedy befalls Miss LeFevre and Billings becomes embroiled in a horrific crime which appears to be the consequence of an ancient Scottish curse. –*Anarchy,* the fourth book in the series is set to be released in 2019 (MLM). 3/3

273. **Bosman, Olivier,** *Gay Noir,* Rocket Man, 2018. (Noir Short Stories) Inspired by the pulp fiction novels of the 1940's and 50's, the novellas in this anthology emulate the dark, thrilling, sensational and taboo breaking stories of the post war era and gives them a gay twist. The Honeytrap: 1950's London. Felix Stone is an openly gay P.I. He is approached by a mysterious woman who pays him to shadow her husband. What at first seems to be a run of the mill adultery case, soon turns out to be much more serious. When the people involved in the case suddenly start dying around him, Felix finds himself embroiled in the world of cold war espionage and discovers that his own life is in danger. The Deluded: 1949. The East End of London is still recovering from the blitz. Fitzgerald O'Sullivan is a young man with romantic notions of living like an impoverished writer. In an attempt to escape his past, he abandons his life of privilege and rents a room in the East End. There he meets Roy Parker, a chirpy Cockney with a working-class charm. Roy asks Fitz to write a story about how he saved the lives of two Jewish ladies during the war. What follows is a far-fetched tale filled with lies and exaggerations. This is is a noir thriller where nothing is what it seems to be. A dark tale of love, bitterness and vengeance set in the chaotic aftermath of the Second World War Estranged: 1950's L.A. Sixteen-year-old Henry Blomqvist is the son of an aspiring actress and step son of a millionaire businessman. He is an embarrassment to his parents, a useless layabout who is constantly getting arrested for cruising the parks. But his vices pale in comparison with the dark secrets in his parents' lives. The kidnapping of Henry's stepfather triggers a series of events which expose the skeletons in his parents' closets and which finally give Henry the chance to step up to the mark and show what he's really made

of. –reprinted in anthology form from short stories originally published under the pseudonym of Wolf Augustus (MLM). 3/3

274. **Bourgeois, B. Alan**, *God's Army to Purge Homosexuality*, Wizard Consulting, 2007. GAPH #1 of 2. (Hard Boiled) A private investigator and a bodyguard are asked to go undercover to infiltrate a terrorist group. Nothing out of the ordinary here, except that the private investigator is gay, the bodyguard is a lesbian, and the terrorists' sole purpose is to eradicate homosexuals in the United States. Can the pair stop the madman who leads the group before they kill hundreds of thousands of people? 3/3

275. **Bourgeois, B. Alan**, *GAPH 2: The Readers*, Wizard Consulting, 2009. GAPH #2 of 2. (Hard Boiled) Join our two heroes, Brent and Nicole, as they find out that their lives and the lives of hundreds of thousands around the country are at stake once again. They thought they had gotten rid of God's Army to Purge Homosexuality, only to find out that another person has taken the lead in this terrorist desire to rid America of homosexuals. Will they succeed in destroying them, or will Brent and Nicole outwit them once again? 3/3

276. **Bourjaily, Vance**, *The Hound of Earth*, Scribner, 1955. (Psychological) The file on Allerd Pennington, atom bomb scientist, begins with his disappearance from an Army installation in the south after Hiroshima, ends some years later with his arrest in California on a charge of two deaths and several lesser offenses, and in between attempts to resolve the possible political, criminal or insane motivation behind his acts of disloyalty to his country and his family. To Usez, who is assigned to the case, and who follows him intermittently, his is a dissonant personality- and the nihilism of his viewpoint jars with his sense of social mission, his perverse mannerisms with his apparent charm for many people. –unsure of gay content as I have not read it however the term "perverse mannerisms" make it sound like the main character may have an effeminate nature (MLM). ?/3

277. **Bowie, J. P.**, *Portrait of Phillip*, Writer's Group, 2002. Portrait #1 of 6. (MM Paranormal) When Peter Brandon, a gifted young artist awakens from a coma of three years, he learns that his lover, Phillip, was brutally murdered and no one was brought to justice for the crime. With the help of Andrew Connor, his physical therapist, he slowly regains his strength, but it is not until he visits Phllip's graveside and receives an affirmation that his dead lover is somehow guiding him to the truth, that he feels the need to get on with his life. Through mutual friends, he meets Jeff Stevens, an ex-cop now a PI, and together they discover that Phillip was not the victim of a random gay-bashing, but of a deliberate act to silence him. They unravel a web of lies, deceit and a friend's treachery. During their

investigation, Peter and Jeff find a mutual attraction for each other, a situation that is thrown into jeopardy in their final face off with Phillip's killer. 3/3

278. **Bowie, J. P.**, *Portrait of Emily*, iUniverse, 2003. Portrait #2 of 6. (MM Paranormal) When Peter Brandon is commissioned to paint Emily Hastings' portrait, his keen psychic awareness unlocks the dark secret that has haunted her since childhood. Now on the brink of at last finding happiness in the arms of the man she loves, she is faced with her father's resolute desire to destroy her life. When her father, Charles Hastings, is found murdered, Emily is suspected of the crime, and it falls to Jeff Stevens, Peter's lover, to try and clear her name. His investigation turns personal when his ex-lover is also found murdered and he finds himself tracking two killers - at considerable risk to himself. His discovery that Hastings was involved in using the services of a child prostitution ring enrages Jeff and he agrees to be the bait in a police 'sting' operation...but when that goes wrong, Jeff's life is suddenly, once again, in danger. 3/3

279. **Bowie, J. P.**, *Portrait of Andrew*, iUniverse, 2003. Portrait #3 of 6. (MM Paranormal) "A holly jolly Christmas" with friends is all artist Peter Brandon and his private investigator partner Jeff Stevens expect when they visit their buddies, Andrew and David, in New York City. All that changes when a party guest ends up murdered and Andrew is considered to be the prime suspect! The situation worsens when the murdered man's wife accuses Andrew of trying to persuade her husband to have a gay affair with him. It's up to Jeff and a sympathetic NYPD detective, Nick Fallon, to try to clear Andrew's name. They are, at times, aided and then hindered by Peter's erratic psychic abilities (or disabilities, as he calls them) that eventually lead them to a powerful and unexpected showdown when the real killer is exposed. Along the way, new friendships are made and tested and one is irrevocably destroyed by lies and denial. 3/3

280. **Bowie, J. P.**, *Self-Portrait*, iUniverse, 2005. Portrait #4 of 6. (MM Paranormal) Living with a private investigator can bring an element of danger into one's life as Peter Brandon finds out. When his partner Jeff Stevens disappears on a routine trip to meet a friend in LA, Peter's intuition alerts him to the fact that Jeff is somehow being held against his will. Determined to find him, Peter reaches out to his deceased lover, Phillip, through the unbreakable psychic bond that still exists between them. With the certain knowledge that Phillip will aid him in his search, he and his close friends Andrew and David, set out to find Jeff. They enlist the help of Nick Fallon, a NYPD detective, who flies in to help them. 3/3

281. **Bowie, J. P.**, *Portrait of Olivia*, iUniverse, 2006. Portrait #5 of 6. (MM Paranormal) The old axiom of 'What you see is what you get" can-

not be said to apply to Olivia Winters, the seemingly gracious and vivacious daytime television host whom Peter Brandon is commissioned to paint after he and his partner, Jeff Stevens, appear on her popular show. Peter quickly discovers that underneath the veneer of warmth and sophistication, is a bitter and vindictive woman-with an ego bigger than the lavish Beverly Hills penthouse she owns. Her perfect world, however, starts to unravel when she receives threatening letters from a religious fanatic, and when her blackmailing ex-boyfriend attempts to reenter her life. 3/3

282. **Bowie, J. P.**, *Christmas Portrait*, MLR, 2013. Portrait #6 of 6. (MM Paranormal) When Peter and Jeff accept an invitation from their longtime friends Rod and 'A' to spend Christmas in London, they don't expect murder and mayhem to be part of the festivities! A Christmas pantomime a British tradition, when families flock to the theatre for ribald entertainment, gender bending roles and thinly veiled innuendo. But jealousy, hate, murder? Surely that's not part of the entertainment? 3/3

283. **Bowie, J. P.**, *Deadly Game*, iUniverse, 2006. Nick Fallon #1 of 5. (MM Hard Boiled) Nick Fallon, private investigator, living the good life in Laguna Beach, gets a rude awakening when his past life unexpectedly catches up with him. Four years earlier, Nick, then a member of the Pittsburgh Police Department, was instrumental in arresting Fransisco Garcia, a drug dealer and cold-blooded murderer. Garcia breaks out of prison and swears to come after Fallon. 3/3

284. **Bowie, J. P.**, *Deadly Deception*, iUniverse, 2007. Nick Fallon #2 of 5. (MM Hard Boiled) Some things are not always what they appear to be. So Nick Fallon discovers when he is hired to investigate the death of a young man whose body is found buried in a wooded canyon area of Los Angeles. 3/3

285. **Bowie, J. P.**, *Murder above Fourth*, MLR, 2009. Nick Fallon #3 of 5. (MM Hard Boiled) Nick Fallon always knew there would be a day of reckoning between himself and Harold Forsythe, a millionaire who headed a secret group paying big bucks to watch young men and women have sex-sometimes dangerous sex, that had resulted in the deaths of two young men. 3/3

286. **Bowie, J. P.**, *Murder by Proxy*, MLR, 2012. Nick Fallon #4 of 5. (MM Hard Boiled) Nick Fallon and Jeff Stevens take on what they consider an easy case taking photographs of a man cheating on his wife, but they don't expect to see the guy shot down right in front of them. What follows is a bewildering series of events and who can they believe? The dead man's fiancée, her gay brother, her less than loving father, or his wife the woman who hired them in the first place? When the fiancée turns up missing, Nick and Jeff have their

hands full trying to sort the truth from the lies and when Nick is left to face dangerous gunmen alone, who knows what the outcome will be. 3/3

287. **Bowie, J. P.**, *Murder in the Desert*, MLR, 2015. Nick Fallon #5 of 5. (MM Hard Boiled) When Nick Fallon is hired to investigate a series of threatening phone calls and vandalism at a gay resort in Palm Springs, he and his husband, Eric Jamieson, are given first class treatment by the owners... when they first arrive. 3/3

288. **Bowie, J. P.**, *Time after Time*, MLR, 2009. (MM Paranormal) Bewildered by a series of erotic dreams, Michael Ballantyne, a young graphic artist living in Los Angeles is eager to uncover their meaning. When he is informed that he is the sole beneficiary in an unknown man's will and is now the owner of a large estate in Hertfordshire, England, Michael feels that somehow, he has been given a key to unlock the dreams' mysteries. 3/3

289. **Bowie, J. P.**, *Sometimes Life's a Drag*, MLR, 2009. (MM Amateur Sleuth) Peter Farland is over the moon when he lands a solo singing spot in Kenny LaFontaine's new revue at the famous drag star's theatre club. Along with his best friends, Lawrence and Maggie, he looks forward to a long and successful run in the West End of London, when he meets, and is instantly attracted to Ian Bannister, a handsome police detective, Peter feels as though everything in his life is suddenly coming up roses. Ian is investigating an alleged blackmail threat against Kenny, and when the blackmailer is murdered, the drag star becomes the prime suspect. –This short story is also included in the BRAVO! BRAVA! anthology collection (J. P. Bowie). 3/3

290. **Bowie, J. P.**, *The Vampire and the P. I.*, Wilde City Press, 2015. Vampire and PI #1 of 4. (MM Paranormal) When Sean Martin was shot in the hip he thought his days in law enforcement were over. Leaving the force with commendations and a healthy disability agreement he opened up his own private investigative business, and for a while enjoyed success. Master Vampire, Rafael Barrantes, hires him to find the murderer of Julian Hunter, a young male escort. 3/3

291. **Bowie, J. P.**, *The Vampire and the G. I.*, Wilde City Press, 2016. Vampire and the PI #2 of 4. (MM Paranormal) Taking a job as a security guard for a high-tech company, veteran Cole Everett who is trying to build a new life in Los Angeles and reconnect with his cousin, Sean Martin, a private investigator, becomes suspicious when all is not what it seems with so-called 'government contracts'. He can't decide if he should play it safe and call the cops or take a chance on his newfound vampire friends. –the next two books are less mysteries and more good vs evil (MLM). 3/3

292. **Box, Edgar (Gore Vidal 1925-2012)**, *Death in the Fifth Position*, E. P. Dutton, 1952. Peter Sargent #1 of 3. Dashing P.R. man Peter Sargent is hired by a ballet company on the eve of a major upcoming performance. Handling the press seems to be no problem, but when a rising star in the company is killed during the performance - dropped from thirty feet above the stage, crashing to her death in a perfect fifth position - Sargent has a real case on his hands. –the sexuality of the dancers is discussed but is a side issue, and the next two books in the series have no gay content (MLM). 1/3

293. **Boyd, Randy**, *The Devil Inside*, West Beach, 2002. (Science Fiction) A respected businessman must figure out whether the new man in his life is a dream lover or date from hell with strange ties to a bizarre and twisted underworld. 3/3

294. **Boyd, Randy**, *Uprising*, West Beach, 1998. (Espionage/Political Intrigue) Three famous but closeted celebrities plot to assassinate a homophobic US Senator while a straight FBI agent goes undercover to stop them. 3/3

295. **Bozza, Julie**, *The Definitive Albert Sterne*, Manifold, 2012. (MM Crime Drama) Albert Sterne, forensics expert with the FBI, is so obnoxious on the surface that no-one bothers digging deeper. When he's sent to Colorado to investigate what turns out to be the work of a serial killer he encounters Special Agent Fletcher Ash and they end up reluctantly joining forces to unravel the case. It's only a matter of duty, though; it can't be more, because Albert doesn't do friendship - and he certainly doesn't do love! 3/3

296. **Bozza, Julie**, *The Valley of Shadow of Death*, Manifold, 2012. (MM Crime Drama) Joshua Delaney and Carmine Angelo Trezini, cop and mobster, should have absolutely nothing in common. Yet, accidentally brought together, they rapidly became both lovers and allies against organized crime boss Matthew Picano. Of course, taking down a man like that was never going to be easy – but Josh has no idea of the scale of the sacrifice he will eventually be called upon to make. 3/3

297. **Bozza, Julie**, *Mitch Rebecki Gets a Life*, Manifold, 2015. (MM Journalism) Investigative journalist Mitch Rebecki loves his job and loves New York. He doesn't mind making enemies, either. When a crime boss threatens retaliation, Mitch's editor sends him out of harm's way to Sydney. In exile and resentfully working on lifestyle pieces, Mitch is miserable. But he makes a friend or two, meets a man ... and discovers that Australians do organized crime, too, in a small way. Mitch soon finds himself in too deep on all counts and trying to head home again seems the only solution. 3/3

298. **Bradford, Kelly (Lisa Brandt)**, *Footprints*, Crossing Press, 1988.

(Hard Boiled) A three-week-old baby is kidnapped, and San Francisco PI Derek is hired to find the boy. Two adults with previously unknown baby are killed in a car crash, and California special assistant attorney general Torrence Adams is asked to identify the boy. The two cases come together as one. 2/3

299. **Brady, John**, *Unholy Ground*, St. Martin's, 1989. An Inspector Matt Minogue Mystery #2 of 10. (Police procedural) Unholy Ground begins with the murder of 73-year-old Arthur Combs, a terribly ordinary man, in his cottage outside Dublin. He may have surprised a burglar, the Guards believe. But when Detective Sergeant Minogue is assigned to the case, he begins to suspect that Combs may have been a top-level undercover British spy. –Combs is gay, but it is not essential to the plot (MLM). 1/3

300. **Brahms, Caryl**, *Bullet in the Ballet*, Doubleday, 1937. Inspector Quill #1 of 4. (Police Procedural) Two principal characters in the Stroganoff Ballet Company are killed and Inspector Quill is called in to investigate the deaths. 1/3

301. **Bram, Christopher (b. 1952)**, *Hold Tight*, Fine, 1988. (Military/Espionage) Hank Fayette, Seaman Second Class, had enlisted in his Texas hometown, used his shore leave to visit a movie house on 42nd Street, and ended up in a gay brothel near Manhattan's West piers. It was the wrong place to be at the wrong time. When this big, lanky blond with a country boy's drawl–and a country boy's hard muscular body–couldn't fight his way clear of the Shore Patrol who raided the place, he figured he was on his way to the brig or a dishonorable discharge. But in 1942, a few months after Pearl Harbor, the Navy was more interested in capturing spies than in punishing "sex offenders," and Hank was just the kind of sailor they had in mind. Their offer to Hank was simple: go back to the brothel, work undercover as a prostitute, and risk your life to entrap Nazi spies. 3/3

302. **Bram, Christopher**, *Gossip*, Dutton, 1997. (Political Intrigue) Ralph Eckhart meets "Thersites" on the Internet. The manager of a Greenwich Village bookstore and politically to the left, Ralph agrees to an F2F (face-to-face) meeting with Thersites in Washington, D.C., where his friend Nancy writes speeches for a popular woman senator. With his penchant for Shakespearean drama, Ralph should have seen the elements gathering for tragedy...or farce. Thersites proves to be a young, attractive, and enthusiastic lover. He is also Republican, in the closet, right-wing, and the author of a tell-all book that spreads gossip about several Washington women, including a footnote about a lesbian affair between a speechwriter and a "happily married" senator. 3/3

303. **Brandreth, Gyles**, *Oscar Wilde and Candlelight Murders*, John Murray, 2007 or *Oscar Wilde and a Death of No Importance*, Touchstone Books, 2008. Oscar Wilde Mysteries #1 of 7. (Historical) A young artist's model has been murdered, and legendary wit Oscar Wilde enlists his friends Arthur Conan Doyle and Robert Sherard to help him investigate. 3/3

304. **Brandreth, Gyles**, *Oscar Wilde and Ring of Truth*, John Murray, 2008. Oscar Wilde Mysteries #2 of 7. (Historical) It's 1892, and Wilde is the toast of London, riding high on the success of his play *Lady Windermere's Fan*. While celebrating with friends at a dinner party he conjures up a game called "murder" that poses the question: Who would you most like to kill? Wilde and friends – including Arthur Conan Doyle, Bram Stoker, and poet Robert Sherard (the novel's narrator) – write the names of their "victims" on pieces of paper and choose them one by one. The very next day, the game takes an all-too- sinister turn when the first "victim" turns up dead. 3/3

305. **Brandreth, Gyles**, *Oscar Wilde and Dead Man's Smile*, John Murray, 2009. Oscar Wilde #3 of 7. (Historical) Playwright and raconteur Oscar Wilde embarks on another adventure as he sets sail for America in the 1880s on a roller coaster of a lecture tour. But the adventure doesn't truly begin until Oscar boards an ocean liner headed back across the Atlantic and joins a motley crew led by French impresario Edmond La Grange. As Oscar becomes entangled with the La Grange acting dynasty, he suspects that all is not as it seems. What begins with a curious death at sea soon escalates to a series of increasingly macabre tragedies once the troupe arrives in Paris to perform Hamlet. 3/3

306. **Brandreth, Gyles**, *Oscar Wilde and Nest of Vipers*, John Murray, 2010 or *Oscar Wilde and the Vampire Murders*, Touchstone, 2011. Oscar Wilde #4 of 7. (Historical) A glamorous party hosted by the Duke and Duchess of Albemarle with all of London's high society including the Prince of Wales are in attendance at what promises to be the event of the season. Yet Oscar Wilde is more interested in another party guest, Rex LaSalle, a young actor who claims to be a vampire. But the entertaining evening ends in tragedy when the duchess is found murdered with two tiny puncture marks on her throat. 3/3

307. **Brandreth, Gyles**, *Oscar Wilde and Vatican Murders*, John Murray, 2011. Oscar Wilde #5 of 7. (Historical) In 1892 Arthur Conan Doyle, exhausted by his creation Sherlock Holmes, retires to the spa at Bad Homburg. But his rest cure does not go as planned. The first person he encounters is Oscar Wilde, and when the two friends make a series of macabre discoveries amongst the portmanteau of fan mail

Conan Doyle has brought to answer - a severed finger, a lock of hair and finally an entire severed hand - the game is once more afoot. 3/3

308. **Brandreth, Gyles**, *Oscar Wilde and Murders at Reading Gaol*, John Murray, 2012. Oscar Wilde #6 of 7. (Historical) It is 1897, Dieppe. Oscar Wilde, poet, playwright, novelist, raconteur and ex-convict, has fled the country after his release from Reading Gaol. Tonight, he is sharing a drink and the story of his cruel imprisonment with a mysterious stranger. He has endured a harsh regime: the treadmill, solitary confinement, censored letters, no writing materials. Yet even in the midst of such deprivation, Oscar's astonishing detective powers remain undiminished - and when first a brutal warder and then the prison chaplain are found murdered, who else should the governor turn to for help other than Reading Gaol's most celebrated inmate? 3/3

309. **Brandreth, Gyles**, *Jack the Ripper: Case Closed*, Corsair, 2017. Oscar Wilde #7 of 7. (Historical) London. 1894. 'I am not a detective, chief constable.' 'No, but you are a poet, a freemason and a man of the world. All useful qualifications for the business in hand.' So, says Police Chief Macnaghten to Oscar Wilde, in a Chelsea drawing room in the company of Arthur Conan Doyle. The business they are gathered to discuss is none other than the case of Jack the Ripper, the most notorious murderer in England. And thus, the three men set out to solve one of the world's most famous mysteries - the ultimate truth about the identity of Jack the Ripper. 3/3

310. **Branston, Frank**, *Sergeant Ritchie's Conscience*, St. Martin's, 1978. A Tommy Tompkins Mystery #2 of 2. (Police Procedural) An authentic account of the unsentimental world of detectives in a big investigation and, in an unexpected and ironical climax, confronts the thin line that can divide criminality and the law. –a young cop is investigated for possibly being gay (MLM). 1/3

311. **Brass, Perry**, *The Substance of God: Spiritual Thriller*, Belhue, 2004. (Thriller) What would you do with the Substance of God, a constantly regenerating, "self-cloning" material originating from Creation? The Substance can bring the dead back to life but has a willful "mind" of its own. Dr. Leonard Miller, a gay bio-researcher secretly addicted to "kinky" sex, learned this after he was found mysteriously murdered in his laboratory while working alone on the Substance. Once brought back to life, Miller must find out who infiltrated his lab to kill him, how long will he have to live again and, exactly, where does life end and any Hereafter begin? 3/3

312. **Braudy, Susan**, *Who Killed Sal Mineo*, Wyndham Books, 1982. (Fictionalized Biography) A fictional account of newspaper reporter

Sara Martin's investigation into the stabbing death of Sal Mineo, which took place at 8567 Holloway Drive, West Hollywood, on February 12, 1976. 2/3

313. **Brees, C. L.**, *An Unsettled Past*, Brees/Rostveit Media, 2017. Alex Jones #1 of 3. (Amateur Sleuth) In 1998, Alex Jones is enjoying an uneventful senior year of high school in the Denver suburb of Ridgewood Hills with his mother. To the outside world, Alex has such an amazing life – but that amazing life is shattered instantly as a quadruple homicide is just the beginning of the sleepy town's nightmare. As the days pass by Alex finds himself targeted while he tries to delve deeper into his assassinated father's past as an FBI Agent. 3/3

314. **Brees, C. L.**, *Dark Ending*, Brees/Rostveit Media, 2017. Alex Jones #2 of 3. (Police Procedural) Fast-forwarding seven years to find Alex now working as a homicide detective with the NYPD. Only recently promoted from patrol, he is thrust into the spotlight as the lead investigator on a series of grisly murders after several young women are discovered in Prospect Park; strangled and mutilated. –the third book in the series, *The Whole Truth* is expected out in 2019 (MLM). 3/3

315. **Brees, C. L.**, *Among the Ashes,* Brees/Rostveit Media, 2018. (Court Drama) As one of the most up-and-coming criminal defense attorneys in St. John's, Newfoundland, Caleb Winters has virtually everything anybody could hope for: incredible friends, a new lover, and nearly perfect record of crushing his foe, Crown Prosecutor Andrew Murphy, in court. An early morning phone call on the day of his closing submissions dredges up faded memories. Skeletal remains were found north of town and the constabulary believes them to be of his missing husband, Sebastian. 3/3

316. **Brenchley, Chaz,** *The Garden,* Hodder & Stoughton, 1990. (Psychological) At twenty-four, Steph Anderson has been two years a widow, her husband Tom the second victim of a brutal serial murderer terrorizing Newcastle upon Tyne in northern England. The Sherpas, a self-help organization for the bereaved, introduce Steph to Alice Armstrong, a frail elderly woman whose twin brother was violently killed in the kitchen of the remote country cottage they shared. Working to restore the garden Alice's brother loved, Steph discovers renewed life and purpose. ?/3

317. **Brenchley, Chaz,** *Blood Waters,* Flambard, 1996. (Short Stories) All the stories in this book either fed into or grew out of the year I spent as crimewriter-in-residence on the St. Peter's Riverside Sculpture Project in Sunderland, 1993-94. At the time it seemed as though it had to be one of the strangest jobs in the country; retrospect

assures me that I was too cautious in my judgment, and it was in fact the strangest job in the known universe. – The stories are all very firmly set in geographical locations, and all feature death by the water (MLM). ?/3

318. **Brennessel, Barry**, *A Special Kind of Folk*, MLR, 2013. (Horror) Hexes, curses, old family recipes, old family secrets, stolen cars and stolen lives. It's all just another day in the lives (and deaths) of a special kind of folk. Featuring short stories: *Food & Spirits, Visions, Kill Them With Kindness, A Special Kind of Folk, All the Souls on Earth,* and *Commedia dell'Arte*. 3/3

319. **Brennessel, Barry**, *Wellspring*, MLR, 2014. (MM Historical) In the span between the Great War and the Great Depression, Aiden Royce loses both family and fortune. He has nothing left but memories and regrets until a series of letters arrive; incoherent ramblings written by a familiar hand that nevertheless offer Aiden some important clues. 3/3

320. **Brent, Lynton Wright**, *Gay Bunch*, Anchor, 1965. (Hard Boiled Pulp) Bridgeport, CT private investigator Stanley Holby must travel to Hollywood and convince Jason Tate to return home to get married. 3/3

321. **Brett, Simon**, *Not Dead, Only Resting*, Scribner and Sons, 1984. Charles Paris Mystery #10 of 20. (Amateur Sleuth) Tristam Gowers and Yves Lafeu have the flamboyance of stage matinee idols, but currently they are running a very smart restaurant, Tryst, which is much patronized by top people in the theatrical profession. Which means it's not Charles Paris's usual ambience, but this small-part player, who's more successful as an amateur detective than as professional actor, is the guest tonight of another fascinating duo, William Bartlemas and Kevin O'Rourke, wealthy collectors of theatrical memorabilia. –features a number of gay characters (MLM). 1/3

322. **Brett, Simon**, *What Bloody Man is That?*, Scribner and Sons, 1987. Charles Paris Mystery #12 of 20. (Amateur Sleuth) Charles Paris is on his way up again, career-wise. No longer "resting" and no longer just a corpse in a cupboard, he blossoms in the play dreaded by superstitious theatre folk, who will not even speak its name - "the Scottish play" -'Macbeth'. Charles finds himself doubling almost every role in the play that isn't held by the three principals. And as for the principals, they could hardly be more ill-sorted. Macbeth is played by George Birkitt, the TV game-show personality. Lady Macbeth comes straight from Stratford - an intense young woman with method in her madness. And Duncan is that notorious old ham, Warnock Belvedere, who feels that he's in the tradition of great

actor-managers. It's not long before death strikes in the night. And Charles Paris takes on the role of private eye. –Belvedere is gay (MLM). 1/3

323. **Brett, Simon**, *Corporate Bodies*, Scribner and Sons, 1992. Charles Paris Mystery #14 of 20. (Amateur Sleuth) Charles, the often out-of-work actor, is appearing as a forklift operator in a corporate video. It's not prime-time television or a major film, but it seems like easy money–until the forklift is used to murder a sexy secretary with lots of enemies. –gay forklift driver is an unsavory character who seems to like young boys (MLM). 1/3

324. **Brickell, Claude**, *The Napoleon Connection*, BricBooks, 2008. Jewel Trilogy #1 of 3. (Amateur Sleuth) The Napoleon Connection is an art history adventure-mystery set in the French Quarter of present-day New Orleans. Hired by one of that city's prominent citizens, young, accomplished art historian Michael Bennington must discover the whereabouts of a priceless artifact–believed to be a rare jewel–curiously missing from the city's famed Cabildo historical museum. –Bennington is of an unknown sexuality (MLM). ?/3

325. **Brickell, Claude**, *Carlotta's Legacy*, BricBooks, 2008. Jewel Trilogy #2 of 3. (Amateur Sleuth) Bennington traces the whereabouts of a priceless missing diamond and ruby necklace purported to have belonged to Carlota, Empress of Mexico. This is a worldwind adventure from Mexico City to gay St. Petersburg to Paris and then Brussels, captivating and provocative as only Bennington's escapades can be. ?/3

326. **Brickell, Claude**, *Brotherhood Wars*, BricBooks, 2008. Jewel Trilogy #3 of 3. (Amateur Sleuth) Michael Bennington flies to Florence then Heidelberg, Berlin and Amsterdam searching for the missing ceremonial sword of Emperor Charlemagne. The quest takes him at last to Paris and the Louvre for an exciting finale both dangerous and death-defying as only Bennington's escapades can be. ?/3

327. **Brightly, Ki**, *Love it Like You Stole It*, Ninestar Press, 2018. (MM Crime Drama) Michael Levine is backed into a corner. He started tearing apart cars for the local mob with the best of intentions–to save up money to pay for his mechanic certifications and impress his crush and mentor, Ben. But Michael soon finds himself in way over his head. He knows stealing is wrong, but it's only cars, and the insurance will pay to replace them, right? What started out as a small job to make some extra bucks soon turns into a nightmare he's not sure he'll ever be able to find his way out of. –only available as an e-book (MLM). 3/3

328. **Brite, Poppy Z**, *Drawing Blood*, James Cahill, 1993. (Paranormal) Escaping from his North Carolina home after his father murders

their family and commits suicide, Trevor McGee returns to confront the past, and finds himself haunted by the same demons that drove his father to insanity. 3/3

329. **Brite, Poppy Z,** *Exquisite Corpse,* Simon and Schuster, 1996. (Crime Drama) To serial slayer Andrew Compton, murder is an art, the most intimate art. After feigning his own death to escape from prison, Compton makes his way to the United States with the sole ambition of bringing his "art" to new heights. Tortured by his own perverse desires, and drawn to possess and destroy young boys, Compton inadvertently joins forces with Jay Byrne, a dissolute playboy who has pushed his "art" to limits even Compton hadn't previously imagined. 3/3

330. **Brite, Poppy Z,** *The Crow: Lazarus Heart,* HarperPrism, 1998. (Fantasy) The Eternal One At our human limits, when we've gone as far as flesh and imagination can take us, we meet the Eternal One. The Crow. Immemorially old, and inconsolable, he is there only for those who seek both revenge and love and are willing to go all the way–and beyond. The Lazarus Heart Five, four, three, two ... Jared Poe counts the days on Louisiana's Death Row. The controversial S&M photographer has been condemned to die for killing his lover. He doesn't know who did it. –This is part of The Crow series each book written by a different author (MLM). 3/3

331. **Brite, Poppy Z,** *Prime,* Three Rivers, 2005. Ricky and G-Man #3 of 6. (Crime Drama) Two years after the opening of Liquor, New Orleans chefs Rickey and G-man are immersed in the life of their restaurant, enjoying a loyal cast of diners, and cooking great booze-laced food. All's well until a bad review in a local paper not-so-subtle hints that their "silent" backer, celebrity chef Lenny Duveteaux, has ulterior motives. When Lenny is accused of serious criminal activity by eccentric D.A. Placide Treat, Rickey and G-man realize it may be time to end their dependence on him. 3/3

332. **Brite, Poppy Z,** *Soul Kitchen,* Three Rivers, 2006. Ricky and G-Man #4 of 6. (Crime Drama) If you can't stand the heat...Get the hell out of New Orleans! Liquor has become one of the hottest restaurants in town, thanks in part to chefs Rickey and G-man's wildly creative, booze-laced food. At the tail end of a busy Mardi Gras, Milford Goodman walks into their kitchen–he's spent the last ten years in Angola Prison for murdering his boss, a wealthy New Orleans restaurateur, but has recently been exonerated on new evidence and released. Rickey remembers him as an ingenious chef and hires him on the spot. When a pill-pushing doctor and a Carnival scion talk Rickey into consulting at the restaurant they're opening in one of the city's "floating casinos," Rickey recommends Milford for the head chef position and stays on to supervise. But soon Rickey finds himself med-

icating a kitchen injury with the doctor's wares, and G-man grows tired of holding down the fort at Liquor alone. As the new restaurant moves toward its opening, Rickey learns that Milford's past is inextricably linked with one of the project's backers, a man whose intentions begin to seem more and more sinister. 3/3

333. **Britt, K. M.**, *Possessing the Demon*, PublishAmerica, 2007. (Amateur Sleuth) My life with Mary was supposed to be simple. We were going to get married and have kids. That's all I ever wanted, a normal life. But that all changed when I caught her cheating. I got drunk and turned to the new librarian for comfort. He dragged me out of a closet I didn't even know I was in. And worse, Mary was murdered! Of course, everyone in town is blaming me. I need to find out who killed my ex before someone starts poking their nose into my business. The killer isn't the only one with secrets. 3/3

334. **Brockmann, Suzanne**, *The Defiant Hero*, Ballantine, 2001. Troubleshooters #2 of 17. (Military Espionage MF Romance) "The United States refuses to negotiate with terrorists." Meg Moore remembered the warning from her job as a translator in a European embassy. Those same words will spell out a death sentence for her daughter and grandmother who have been kidnapped by a lethal group called the Extremists. Meg will do anything to meet their unspeakable demands; anything–even kill–to save her child. When Navy SEAL Lieutenant, junior grade, John Nilsson is summoned to Washington, D.C., by the FBI to help negotiate a hostage situation, the last person he expects to see holding a foreign ambassador at gunpoint is Meg. He hasn't seen her in years, but he's never forgotten how it feels to hold her in his arms. John could lose his career if he helps her escape. She will lose her life if he doesn't. –FBI Agent Jules Cassidy plays an ever increasing role of importance in the series (MLM). 1/3

335. **Brockmann, Suzanne**, *Over the Edge*, Ballantine, 2001. Troubleshooters #3 of 17. (Military Espionage MF Romance) Her passion is flying. As one of the best helicopter pilots in the naval reserves, Lieutenant Teri Howe is strong, dedicated, and highly skilled-until a past mistake surfaces, jeopardizing everything she's worked for. Rock steady Senior Chief Stan Wolchonok has made a career of tackling difficult challenges. So it's no surprise when he comes to Teri's aid, knowing that his personal code of honor-and perhaps his heart-will be at risk. But when a jet carrying an American senator's daughter is hijacked, Stan's unflinching determination and Teri's steadfast courage are put to the ultimate test. The rescue mission will be daring and dangerous. But somewhere between peril and resolution, the line between friends and lovers begins to blur, pushing both their lives "over the edge." 1/3

336. **Brockmann, Suzanne**, *Out of Control*, Ballantine, 2002. Troubleshooters #4 of 17. (Military Espionage MF Romance) Savannah von Hopf has no choice. To save her uncle's life, she goes in search of Ken "WildCard" Karmody, a guy she barely knew in college who is now a military operative. She must convince him to help her deliver a cache of ransom money into the hands of terrorists halfway around the world. What she doesn't expect is to end up in WildCard's arms before she can even ask for his help. WildCard has always had a soft spot for beautiful women. But when he discovers Savannah's hidden agenda, he is determined to end the affair. But Savannah is bound for Indonesia with or without his protection, and he can't just walk away. When her plan goes horribly wrong, they are trapped in the forsaken jungle of a hostile country, stalked by a lethal enemy. As time is running out, they scramble to escape, risking their lives to stop a nightmare from spinning even further out of control. 1/3

337. **Brockmann, Suzanne**, *Into the Night*, Ballantine, 2002. Troubleshooters #5 of 17. (Military Espionage MF Romance) It was supposed to be a "dog and pony show"–an elaborate demonstration of SEAL rescue techniques–to celebrate a presidential visit to a California naval base. Professional, no-nonsense White House staffer Joan DaCosta arrives early to scope out the area. Assigned to be her SEAL liaison is Lt. (jg) Mike Muldoon, a born leader–strong, decisive, tough, and fearless. Against her better judgment, Joan finds herself drawn to the handsome young officer. Skilled at being "one of the guys" in the mostly male world of politics, she is dismayed when Muldoon breaks through her defenses. While tension mounts between them, fueling their growing attraction, a far more sinister danger is lurking, as terrorists plot a daring attack against the president. To protect their commander in chief, Joan and Muldoon must not only risk their hearts–but their very lives. 1/3

338. **Brockmann, Suzanne**, *Gone Too Far*, Ballantine, 2001. Troubleshooters #6 of 17. (Military Espionage MF Romance) In his career as one of America's elite warriors, Lt. Sam Starrett can do no wrong. In his private life, Sam–the king of one-night stands–has done little right. Now, he's waiting for a divorce and determined to stay active in his young daughter's life. But when Sam shows up at the door of his ex-wife's home in Sarasota, Florida, he makes a grisly discovery. His daughter is gone, and the body of a woman lies brutally murdered on the floor. 1/3

339. **Brockmann, Suzanne**, *Flashpoint*, Ballantine, 2004. Troubleshooters #7 of 17. (Military Espionage MF Romance) Jimmy Nash has already lived two lives–and he can't talk about either of them. Formerly an operative of a top-secret government agency, he has

found a new job with a shadowy company called Troubleshooters Inc. Created by a former Navy SEAL, Troubleshooters Inc. helps anyone in desperate need–which provides a perfect cover for its other, more perilous objective: covert special operations. 1/3

340. **Brockmann, Suzanne**, *Hot Target*, Ballantine, 2004. Troubleshooters #8 of 17. (Military Espionage MF Romance) Like most men of action, Navy SEAL Chief Cosmo Richter never learned how to take a vacation. So, when he finds himself facing a month's leave, he offers his services to Troubleshooters Incorporated. Founded by a former SEAL, the private-sector security firm is a major player in the ongoing war against terrorism, known for carrying out covert missions too volatile for official U.S. military action. But the first case Richter takes on is anything but under the radar. High-profile maverick movie producer Jane Mercedes Chadwick hasn't quite completed her newest film, but she's already courting controversy. The World War II epic frankly portrays the homosexuality of a real-life hero-and the storm of advance media buzz surrounding it has drawn the fury of extremist groups. But despite a relentless campaign of angry E-mails, phone calls, and smear tactics, Chadwick won't be pressured into abandoning the project. Then the harassment turns to death threats. While the FBI appears on the scene, nervous Hollywood associates call in Troubleshooters, and now Chadwick has an army of round-the-clock bodyguards, whether she likes it or not. And she definitely doesn't. But her stubbornness doesn't make FBI agent Jules Cassidy's job any easier. The fiercely independent filmmaker presents yet another emotional obstacle that Cassidy doesn't need-he's already in the midst of a personal tug-of-war with his ex-lover, while fighting a growing attraction to Chadwick's brother. Determined to succeed-and survive-on her own terms, Chadwick will face off with enemies and allies alike. But she doesn't count on the bond she forms with the quiet, capable Cosmo Richter. Yet even as their feelings bring them closer, the noose of deadly terror all around them draws tighter. And when all hell erupts, desire and desperate choices will collide on a killing ground that may trap them both in the crossfire. –Jules plays a larger role in this novel (MLM). 2/3

341. **Brockmann, Suzanne**, *Breaking Point*, Ballantine, 2005. Troubleshooters #9 of 17. (Military Espionage MF Romance) As commander of the nation's most elite FBI counterterrorism unit, agent Max Bhagat leads by hard-driving example: pushing himself to the limit and beyond, taking no excuses, and putting absolutely nothing ahead of his work. That includes his deep feelings for Gina Vitagliano, the woman who won his admiration and his heart with her courage under fire. But when the shocking news reaches him that Gina

has been killed in a terrorist bombing, nothing can keep Max from making a full investigation-and retribution-his top priority. At the scene of the attack, however, Max gets an even bigger shock. Gina is still very much alive-but facing a fate even worse than death. Along with Molly Anderson, a fellow overseas relief worker, Gina has fallen into the hands of a killer who is bent on using both women to bait a deadly trap. His quarry? Grady Morant, a.k.a "Jones," a notorious ex-Special Forces operative turned smuggler who made some very deadly enemies in the jungles of Southeast Asia ... and has been running ever since. But with Molly's life on the line, Jones is willing to forfeit his own to save the woman he loves. Together with Max's top agent Jules Cassidy as their only backup, the unlikely allies plunge into a global hot zone of violence and corruption to make a deal with the devil. Not even Jones knows which ghosts from his past want him dead. But there's one thing he's sure of-there's very little his bloodthirsty enemies aren't willing to do. 2/3

342. **Brockmann, Suzanne**, *Into the Storm*, Ballantine, 2006. Troubleshooters #10 of 17. (Military Espionage MF Romance) In a remote, frozen corner of New Hampshire, a Navy SEAL team and the elite security experts of Troubleshooters, Incorporated are going head-to-head as fierce but friendly rivals in a raid-and-rescue training exercise. Despite the frigid winter temperatures, tension smolders between veteran SEAL Petty Officer Mark "Jenk" Jenkins and former cop turned Troubleshooter Lindsey Fontaine after an impulsive night goes awry. And then, suddenly, Tracy Shapiro, the Troubleshooters' new receptionist, vanishes while playing the role of hostage during a mock rescue operation. 2/3

343. **Brockmann, Suzanne**, *Force of Nature*, Ballantine, 2007. Troubleshooters #11 of 17. (Military Espionage MF Romance) Florida private investigator and ex-cop Ric Alvarado's life is spiraling out of control. His beautiful new girl Friday, Annie Dugan, is far more interested in fieldwork than filing, and despite Ric's best efforts to ignore the attraction, sparks are flying between them. Then one of Ric's clients turns femme fatale and tries to gun down an innocent man. 2/3

344. **Brockmann, Suzanne**, *All Through the Night*, Ballantine, 2007. Troubleshooters #12 of 17. (Military Espionage MF Romance) It's Christmastime in Boston, and this year the silver bells will be wedding bells as FBI agent Jules Cassidy ties the knot with the man of his dreams, Hollywood heartthrob Robin Chadwick. The pair plan a quiet, intimate ceremony, to be witnessed by family and close friends from the FBI, SEAL Team Sixteen, and Troubleshooters, Incorporated, including Sam Starrett and Alyssa Locke. But the holiday season brings more to the happy couple than they expect. A waterfall com-

ing through their kitchen ceiling, a bat colony in the attic, old family tensions ... even an international incident can't dampen their spirits. –sales from this book go to gay charities (MLM). 3/3

345. **Brockmann, Suzanne**, *Into the Fire*, Ballantine, 2008. Troubleshooters #13 of 17. (Military Espionage MF Romance) Vinh Murphy – ex-Marine and onetime operative for the elite security firm Troubleshooters Incorporated – has been MIA ever since his wife, Angelina, was caught in a crossfire and killed during what should have been a routine bodyguard assignment. Overcome with grief, Murphy blames the neo-Nazi group known as the Freedom Network for her death. Now, years later, Freedom Network leader Tim Ebersole has been murdered – and the FBI suspects Murphy may have pulled the trigger. 2/3

346. **Brockmann, Suzanne**, *Dark of Night*, Ballantine, 2009. Troubleshooters #14 of 17. (Military Espionage MF Romance) Danger can be addictive. Badly shaken after the loss of one of their own, the men & women of Troubleshooters Inc. go up against their most deadly opponents yet - the clandestine organization, The Agency. Blackmail, extortion, murder: The Agency's operatives will stop at nothing to achieve their objective. 2/3

347. **Brockmann, Suzanne**, *Hot Pursuit*, Ballantine, 2009. Troubleshooters #15 of 17. (Military Espionage MF Romance) Alyssa Locke is no stranger to dealing with danger. As team leader of the nation's number one personal security company, Troubleshooters Inc., she's seen more than her share of action, survived plenty of close calls, and holds her own with the best of them-and against the worst of them. Guarding lives is her game, and no one plays it better. But her toughest challenge will be protecting herself from a serial killer she's been after for years-known only as The Dentist-who is determined to make her his ultimate trophy. 2/3

348. **Brockmann, Suzanne**, *Breaking the Rules*, Ballantine, 2011. Troubleshooters #16 of 17. (Military Espionage MF Romance) Izzy Zanella wasn't looking for another reason to butt heads with his Navy SEAL teammate, and nemesis, Danny Gillman. But then he met Danny's beautiful younger sister, Eden. When she needed it most, he offered her a place to stay, a shoulder to cry on–and more. And when she got pregnant with another man's child, he offered her marriage. But Eden's devastating miscarriage shattered their life together–and made the intense bad blood between Izzy and Danny even worse. Now Eden's back, and she's on a mission to rescue her teen brother, Ben, from their abusive stepfather. 2/3

349. **Brockmann, Suzanne**, *Some Kind of Hero*, Ballantine, 2017. Troubleshooters #17 of 17. (Military Espionage MF Romance) Navy

men don't come tougher than Lieutenant Peter Greene. Every day he whips hotshot SEAL wannabes into elite fighters. So why can't he handle one fifteen-year-old girl? His ex's death left him a single dad overnight, and very unprepared. Though he can't relate to an angsty teen, he can at least keep Maddie safe–until the day she disappears. 2/3

350. **Brondos, S. Hardy**, *Perfect Trust*, Wayward, 2001. Swedberg and Reilly #1 of 2. (MM Espionage) When Jason Swedborg and Daniel Reilly agree to work as top-secret agents for the US government, they expect to encounter danger and death. What they don't expect is to face a twisted web of conspiracy which includes shadows from Daniel's past and the ominous beat of voodoo drums. Nor do they expect to fall in love with each other. Life is full of surprises. 3/3

351. **Brondos, S. Hardy**, *Perfect Hope*, Wayward, 2001. Swedberg and Reilly #2 of 2. (MM Espionage) Jason Swedborg and Daniel Reilly have been partners and lovers for over a year but working together takes on new meaning and new dangers when Jason is ordered to play the part of a young gay man on the make. Daniel must watch from the sidelines while his partner is used as bait to lure a foreign terrorist who is also a serial killer. But he refuses to watch helplessly and enlists the aid of Jason's family in unravelling a tangled web of intrigue and violence that seems destined to leave both of them alone and without hope. 3/3

352. **Brooke, Anne**, *Maloney's Law*, P. D., 2008. Maloney's Law #1 of 2. (MM Hard Boiled) Paul Maloney, a small-time private investigator from London, reluctantly accepts a case from his married ex-lover, Dominic Allen. Before he knows it, Paul finds himself embroiled in the dark dealings of big business and the sordid world of international crime. The deeper he pushes, the closer he comes to losing everything he holds dear. Can he solve the mystery and protect those he loves before it's too late? 3/3

353. **Brooke, Anne**, *Bones of Summer*, Dreamspinner, 2009. Maloney's Law #2 of 2. (MM Hard Boiled) When Craig Robertson's religious fanatic father disappears, Craig is forced to return to the home he left behind after an underage affair in order to look for answers. He takes with him his new lover, private investigator Paul Maloney, who is more than willing to help solve the mystery. The search soon becomes an investigation into Craig's past, and, because of distressing gaps in his memory, he's terrified of the truths he might find. As Craig's obsession with uncovering clues grows, his fragile relationship with Paul begins to disintegrate. Haunted and stalked, Craig has to face down the horror of his memories if he wants to have any hope of a future at all. 3/3

354. **Brooks, Richard,** *The Brick Foxhole,* Harper and Brothers, 1945. (Historical) Set in the U.S. during the final months of WWII, this story of murder reflects the racism, anti-Semitism, and homophobia of the times. The main characters are a group of soldiers coping with the frustration, boredom, and disgrace of serving stateside while other men are over in Europe and the Pacific, killing the enemy. – gay bashing (MLM). 1/3

355. **Brown, Bethany,** *Picture Perfect,* Dreamspinner, 2009. Lost Boys and Love Letters #2 of 2. (MM Suspense) Perhaps it's a twist of fate when event photographer Cameron Walker runs into veterinarian Jeremy Montgomery at a wedding. Cameron has harbored a crush on the handsome man since high school, and he can't believe his luck. Jeremy asks him to dance, and Cameron's over the moon. Having admired Cameron from afar, Jeremy is just as thrilled to discover Cameron feels the same. After a few dates, Cameron and Jeremy (and their new dog) are ready to embark on a loving journey they both have dreamed of-a new life together. Cameron's best friend, Detective Patrick Hawkins, is very happy for the new couple. But he's equally worried when mysterious gifts with disturbing letters keep appearing, targeting Cameron. When the stalking escalates to a senseless and stunning act of violence, Patrick is there for the two men, both physically and emotionally. Working together, Cameron, Jeremy, and Patrick set out to find the stalker and put a stop to his actions, but will they be able to stop him before it's too late? 3/3

356. **Brown, Dave,** *Bristlecone Peak,* Golden Feather, 1998. Legend of the Golden Feather #1 of 5. (MM Historical) Jake Brady, a farmer from Kentucky, fleeing for his life from his neighbor and four of his sons who have tracked him a thousand miles, ended up in the mining town of Alma, high in the Colorado Rockies. Wiley Deluce, one of the fastest and deadliest draws alive, arrived in Alma to carry out a job he was paid to do. Jake and Wiley met, became partners and blood brothers in the crowded Silver Heels bar, and that's when their love and adventures began. 3/3

357. **Brown, Dave,** *Protectors,* Golden Feather, 1999. Legend of the Golden Feather #2 of 5. (MM Time Traveling) Jake Brady and Wiley Deluce find themselves in the strange Time of 1993 without the golden feather that sent them there. Three factions begin searching for them: the first out of lust, another out of greed and the third from burning hatred. The police are also hunting them. How will the Protectors help Jake and Wiley? And can they ever get back to 1886? 3/3

358. **Brown, Dave,** *Home to Kentucky,* Golden Feather, 2000. Legend of the Golden Feather #3 of 5. (MM Historical) Jake and Wiley return

to 1886 with three men and a dog from 1993. After learning Wiley's true identity and a jolting secret about him, Jake flees. Captured by murderous Harrises, Jake becomes their prisoner on a train to Kentucky. Two days behind Jake, Wiley races after him, fearing what he'll find as he travels east. Will Jake even arrive in Kentucky alive? 3/3

359. **Brown, Dave**, *Pinkerton Partners*, Golden Feathers, 2001. Legend of the Golden Feather #4 of 5. (MM Historical) Wiley is training Jake to be his Pinkerton partner when they're sent to New Orleans on a dangerous case. Trouble arises on the riverboat before they even get there. A hired killer is on board. Is he stalking someone? 3/3

360. **Brown, Dave**, *Alone by the Window*, Golden Feather, 2004. Legend of the Golden Feather #5 of 5. (MM Historical) A man has been asking around Alma for Wiley's whereabouts. Wiley left the Alma telegraph office with a stranger and disappeared. Jake asks the help of Eli and Adam, former Buffalo Soldiers and U.S. Marshals, plus Sheriff Cline and his deputies, to help search for Wiley. Increasingly worried, Jake wonders if Wiley has been kidnapped and killed, or did Wiley leave him for this other man? 3/3

361. **Brown, P. A.**, *LA Heat,* Alyson, 2006. Laine and Bellamere #1 of 5. (MM Police procedural) When LAPD detective David Laine first encounters hunky party boy Chris Bellamere, it is to interrogate him about the murder of one of Chris's many sexual conquests. When Chris's efforts to prove his own innocence mark him as a victim, David steps in to save him, and finds himself falling in love with a man who might be a brutal murderer. 3/3

362. **Brown, P. A.**, *LA Mischief*, Cheyenne, 2009. Laine and Bellamere #2 of 5. (MM Police Procedural) A fast-paced novella that details the early months of their relationship. David – a LAPD Homicide Detective – is stubborn, proud, and barely out of the closet. As the story opens, he is struggling to find the balance between his intense feelings for Chris, the urges of his newly liberated libido, and the demands of a job where bodies pop up on an all too regular basis. Chris-blonde, smart, out and proud-faces his own set of challenges, including helping his best friend cope with his ongoing grief after the brutal murder of his lover. Life events conspire to bring David and Chris together while at the same time keeping them apart – will they be able to push their way through and find a common ground for happiness and their shared love? 3/3

363. **Brown, P. A.**, *LA Boneyard*, MLR, 2009. Laine and Bellamere #3 of 5. (MM Police Procedural) From a shallow grave in Griffith Park, to the bucolic streets of West Hollywood into the dark heart of the

gang-infested streets of East L.A, evil is pursued in this dark story of passion and redemption. Detective David Eric Laine is no stranger to violence and brutality, but even he is taken aback at the sheer viciousness of the murder of two pregnant Ukrainian women. 3/3

364. **Brown, P. A.**, *LA Bytes*, MLR, 2010. Laine and Bellamere #4 of 5. (MM Police Procedural) Los Angeles' Ste. Anne's Medical Center has been hacked by a brilliant, malicious cracker. Christopher Bellamere has been hired to find out who is behind the break in. When tampered medical records nearly kill his lover, Homicide Detective David Eric Laine, the stakes go up and Chris goes after the cracker with all his skills. 3/3

365. **Brown, P. A.**, *Bermuda Heat*, MLR, 2011. Laine and Bellamere #5 of 5. (MM Police Procedural) David Eric Laine always believed his father had died in Vietnam before his birth. His mother remarried, and he was adopted by his stepfather and grew up knowing Graham Laine as his only father. Forty years later, a letter arrives, and David finds out everything he thought was a lie. His father, Joel Cameron, is alive and living in Bermuda where he came from back in 1968 to attend college. He met David's mother, at the time a much more rebellious child of the turbulent sixties. Following David's birth his mother fled back to the safety of her familiar, protected world and the lie was born. Rather than face her shame, David was told his father died a hero in Vietnam. 3/3

366. **Brown, P. A.**, *Geography of Murder*, MLR, 2009. Detective Spider #1 of 2. (MM BDSM Police Procedural) All Jason Zachary wants is to keep the loneliness and despair at bay. He escapes to the clubs where drugs and a warm body for the night offer fleeting comfort. But when he wakes one morning, dazed after another blackout, to find himself in bed with a dead body, his life careens him into the arms of Detective Alexander Spider. For Jason, Spider becomes an addiction, a drug that makes him feel alive and safe; his body craves Spider's control, and Jason falls hard. But Alex Spider sees the darker side of humanity daily, and he isn't looking for connections, only to drown himself in encounters with nameless subs willing to let him play his bondage games. 3/3

367. **Brown, P. A.**, *Forest of Corpses*, MLR, 2010. Detective Spider #2 of 2. (MM BDSM Police Procedural) Santa Barbara Homicide detective Alexander Spider and his lover of seven months, Jason Zachary are still struggling to make their intense but troubled love affair work. To this end Jason talks city boy Alex into a hiking trip in Los Padres National Forest, something Alex has never done. Only his love for Jason makes him agree. Spider is not an outdoor type guy but for Jason he will go. His first introduction to 'roughing it' is fraught

with humorous horrors. Then during an arduous backwoods hike the pair stumble on the decaying bodies of missing hikers, the most recent one barely cold. They were hikers killed for stumbling onto a major grow-op hidden in the vast wilderness. Now Alex and Jason are in a race for their lives. 3/3

368. **Brown, P. A.**, *Memory of Darkness*, AmberQuill, 2009. (MM Thriller) Johnny Wager has been a loser all his life and proud of it. But when a West Hollywood twink ends up dead in a hotel room with Wager literally holding the bag, he knows his life is going to change for the worse. Pursued by the West Hollywood sheriffs for a murder he knows he didn't commit, Wager has to stay one step ahead of them and prove his innocence. 3/3

369. **Brown, P. A.**, *Between Darkness and Light*, MLR, 2010. (MM Police Procedural) Detective Russell Hunter emerges from darkness into fine artist Stephen Fischer, darling of the Los Angeles art world. Can these two unravel the mystery surrounding the death of two of L.A.'s art critics before Stephen becomes the next victim. The downtown Los Angeles financial center is the heart of this thrilling murder mystery and the unwanted love that grows between a cop with a dark secret in his troubled past and an up and coming world class artist. 3/3

370. **Brown, P. A.** *Latin Boyz,* AmberQuill, 2012. (Crime Drama) Gabe's entire world is gang-ridden Cypress Park, in South Central LA. His mother died in a drive-by gang hit on the wrong house. His fourteen-year-old sister was left brain-damaged by the same bullet. He dreams of escaping and rescuing the rest of his family before the gang jumps him or finishes the hit on him. Gabe's life is further complicated when the shooters return, and young LAPD officer Alejandro Carveras answers the 911 call. 3/3

371. **Brown, Rita Mae**, *Wish You Were Here*, Bantam, 1990. Mrs. Murphy #1 of 26. Curiosity just might be the death of Mrs. Murphy–and her human companion, Mary Minor "Harry" Haristeen. Small towns are like families: Everyone lives very close together and everyone keeps secrets. Crozet, Virginia, is a typical small town-until its secrets explode into murder. –gay antiquarian collector (MLM). 1/3

372. **Brown, Russell A.**, *Sherlock Holmes and the Mysterious Friend of Oscar Wilde*, St. Martin's, 1988. (Sherlock Holmes) It's 1895 and deadly games are afoot in London. Against a backdrop of terrorist explosions, a humbled Holmes reluctantly accepts the aid of Oscar Wilde to unravel two tangled plots: the blackmail of an eminent Victorian with a name known all over the world, and the diabolical design of a demented nobleman to inflict 'Death! Or Worse!' upon Holmes himself. Sherlock Holmes and the Mysterious Friend of

Oscar Wilde mingles melodrama and epigram, fact and fiction, as two men with so many differences in common pursue a hellish hound whose actions menace all of England. –includes many gay characters including Oscar Wilde (MLM). 2/3

373. **Bruce, Leo (Rupert Craft-Cooke)** wrote 31 mystery novels between 1936 and 1974. He had two detectives Sergeant Beef of which there were eight from 1936-1952 and Carolus Deene from 1955-1974 of which there were 23 novels. I have not read them nor have I read anywhere that there is gay content however there may be and I'd rather be inclusive and be wrong than exclude him and be wrong. Craft-Cooke was convicted of "acts of indecency" along with two sailors in 1955 and it'd be a shame if there weren't some mention, however brief, in his thirty-one books (MLM).

374. **Bruen, Ken,** *The Hackman Blues,* Do-Not, 1997. (Crime Drama) Brady, our narrator, is fifty, gay, and a manic-depressive professional criminal of Irish descent, strung out on lithium and excessive drinking. Today he has neglected to take his medication, which makes him even more manic, violent, and unpredictable. Brady is hired to find a powerful Irish construction chief's daughter. Known as the "Hackman", the chief believes his daughter is in Brixton, a multi-racial part of London that is predominantly black. Brady recruits his former cellmate, a black thug, and another "associate" to get the girl back. This doesn't please the construction chief, who's an out-and-out racist. The whole thing goes horribly wrong when Brady tries to play her black gangster boyfriend against the "Hackman" and his Irish heavies in a complicated ransom ploy. 3/3

375. **Bruen, Ken**, *Blitz,* Do-Not, 2002. Inspector Brantz #4 of 7. (Police Procedural) The South East London police squad are down and out: Detective Sergeant Brant is in hot water for assaulting a police shrink, Chief Inspector Roberts' wife has died in a horrific car accident, and WPC Falls is still figuring out how to navigate her job as a black female investigator in the notorious unit. When a serial killer takes his show on the road, things get worse for all three. Nicknamed "The Blitz" by the rabid London media, the killer is aiming for tabloid immortality by killing cops in different beats around the city. –Police detective Nash is out in a department of homophobes (MLM). 1/3

376. **Bruen, Ken**, *Vixen,* Do-Not, 2003. Inspector Brantz #5 of 7. (Police Procedural) For the Southeast London police squad, it's rough, tough, dirty business as usual. The Vixen, the most sensuous, crazed female serial killer ever, is masterminding a series of lethal explosions. She is unpredictable, wild, angry–and the cops don't even know she exists. Meanwhile, Inspector Roberts is helpless to stop the explosions and his subordinates aren't doing much better. Brant

is consumed with an even-bigger-than-usual mean streak, and fast-rising Porter Nash finds himself facing serious health problems–everything to do with needles. 2/3

377. **Bruen, Ken**, *Calibre*, St. Martin's, 2006. Inspector Brantz #6 of 7. (Police Procedural) Somewhere in the teeming heart of London is a man on a lethal mission. His cause: a long-overdue lesson on the importance of manners. When a man gives a public tongue-lashing to a misbehaving child, or a parking lot attendant is rude to a series of customers, the "Manners Killer" makes sure that the next thing either sees is the beginning of his own grisly end. When he starts mailing letters to the Southeast London police squad, he'll soon find out just how bad a man's manners can get. 1/3

378. **Bruen, Ken**, *Ammunition*, St. Martin's, 2007. Inspector Brantz #7 of 7. (Police Procedural) Over the many years that Inspector Brant has been bringing his own patented brand of policing to the streets of southeast London, the brilliant but tough cop has made a few enemies. When a crazed gunman, hired by persons unknown, pumps a magazine full of bullets into Brant in a local pub, leaving him in grasping at life (but ornery as ever), his colleagues on the squad are left wondering how to react. 1/3

379. **Bruett, N. J.**, *Dusting*, iUniverse, 2006. (Amateur Sleuth) In a quiet seaside village, an ethereal young wife, a seventy-year-old, adored grandmother, and a cocaine-using, athletic nymphomaniac have been murdered in their homes. They have never met and seemingly share nothing in common, except Stephen Macomber-their hard-bodied, handsome housecleaner. When Stephen becomes a suspect, his lover, Donald Sebastion, and his sixty-year-old friend, Laura English, a modern-day Miss Marple, join forces to clear his name. 3/3

380. **Bruso, Thomas**, *Jay Bird*, JMS, 2018. (YA Coming-Out-Story) Introverted, socially awkward Jay Kirkman, known to his Grams as "Jay Bird," is riding the ups-and-downs of youth while living with overbearing parents and dealing with the pressures of being a senior in high school. A month away from graduation, Jay hopes to flee the small upstate New York town of Milton for a life anywhere but in his dead-end hometown. He wishes for more than he has now: scholarly, eccentric parents, and watching Grams, the closest person to him, slowly dying before his eyes. His equally withdrawn but edgier best friend Rocco has a hearty appetite for drugs, alcohol, and promiscuous sex. When the law comes knocking, asking questions about a crime Rocco may or may not have committed, he finds himself in big trouble and turns to Jay for help. Is Jay and Rocco's friendship strong enough to sustain life's tough obstacles as they navigate the highs and lows of growing up together? 3/3

381. **Bryan, Jed A.**, *Cry in the Desert*, Banned Books, 1987. (Hard Boiled) Las Vegas sleuth Carl Woodsford and his lover work together to defeat a Nevada legislative law that attempts to quarantine gay men. 3/3

382. **Buchanan, James**, *The Good Thief*, MLR, 2008. (MM Crime Drama) What if the wrong guy, turns out to be the right guy for you? Caesar Serrano thought he screwed up when he landed in the bed of LAPD Officer Nathan Reilly. But when Caesar breaks into the wrong house and stumbles upon a heinous crime, implicating a high-ranking LAPD officer, Nate is the only person he knows to turn to. The resulting investigation throws the Blue Brigade into panic. Now he's running for his life and Nate is his only hope for survival. Can two men, on opposite sides of the law, come together to bring a monster to justice? 3/3

383. **Buchanan, James**, *Hard Fall*, MLR, 2009. Deputy Joe #1 of 5. (MM Police Procedural) Deputy Joe Peterson is Mormon and in the closet. Then ex-con Kabe Varghese lands in town on parole. When a tourist falls off the mountain, Joe finds he needs the help of this cliff climbing adrenaline junky to solve the case. Will Kabe tear him apart or does Joe need to fall hard before he can start living? 3/3

384. **Buchanan, James**, *Spin Out*, MLR, 2011. Deputy Joe #2 of 5. (MM Police Procedural) Right guy. Wrong time. Deputy Joe Peterson understood the risks when he got involved with ex-con Kabe Varghese. He didn't, however, see fit to warn Kabe. Now, in the middle of searching for the killer of a local boy, he has to contend with his career and his relationship spinning out of control. Solving the case may be easier than repairing broken trust. 3/3

385. **Buchanan, James**, *Laying Ghosts*, MLR, 2013. Deputy Joe #3 of 5. (MM Police Procedural) Some families are haunted by tragedy. Some people are haunted by their pasts. Some men are haunted by who they are. Joe Peterson is haunted by all three. His parents' return from their mission, combined with a family reunion, forces Joe's kin to deal with his new life: out of the Mormon Church, out of the closet, and living with his lover Kabe. When a decades-old murder of a child lands on Joe's desk, digging into it dredges up long buried truths and festering secrets about folks Joe thought he knew – including Kabe. Joe and Kabe must lay the ghosts of the past and bring closure to a family scarred by loss to move forward in their life together. 3/3

386. **Buchanan, James**, *Requiem in Leather*, MLR, 2015. Joe Deputy #4 of 5. (MM Police Procedural) Kabe's former Dom, the man who protected him in prison, dies and Kabe, along with Jack's other boys, returns to The City to pay their respects. Joe wonders where he fits

in after seeing Kabe at home, with the family and friends he left behind. When he agrees to help track down one of the missing boys he can't understand Kabe's aversion to his getting involved. The emotions dredged up by the search, and Kabe's slipping back into his old out-of-control lifestyle, pitch them along like the rough surf Kabe has so missed riding. If they can find the balance between love, respect and their lifestyle, they may just be able to discover a place Joe thought was closed to him forever. 3/3

387. **Buchanan, James,** *The Family Eternal,* MLR, 2017. Deputy Joe #5 of 5. (MM Police Procedural) Folks will tell you that family is second only to God in Utah. But what brings strength to some can sow sorrow with others. On a bleak winter morning, a young woman's corpse smolders in the remains of a burned rental cabin. Clues to her identity are rarer than frozen chokecherries in the Utah backcountry. Deputy Joe Peterson, assisted by Kabe Varghese in his first case as a fire inspector trainee, doggedly hunts for who she is and why she died. As they sink deeper into the investigation, Joe struggles with how his life is now personally and professionally intertwined with Kabe's. Outed, excommunicated and disciplined because of the man he found love with; the last year of Joe's life has careened like an avalanche toward an abyss. Is doom inevitable? Or is the best chance to live surrendering to the fall? 3/3

388. **Buchanan, James,** *Personal Demons,* MLR, 2009. (MM Police Procedural) Hunting a notorious hit man, FBI Agent Chase Nozick and LAPD Det. Enrique Rios Ocha delve into the inner worlds of Santeria, Voodoo and Palo Mayumbe. A missing informant, her murdered brother and a ghost from Chase's past send them on a hunt through mystics and psychic surgeons to find their witness before it's too late. Can he rely on leads from a child possessed by Orishas? Do cards hold stronger clues than blood? Chase must conquer his own personal demons to bring the killer of his partner to justice and find the strength to take a chance on Enrique. 3/3

389. **Buchanan, James,** *Cheating Chance,* MLR, 2008. Taking the Odds #1 of 3. (MM Police Procedural) Nick O'Mallley is an agent for the Nevada Gaming Commission. He's also a Goth with a hearse he's restoring, and an ex-lover he's only just getting over. Brandon Carr is a cop with the Riverside PD. Lucky for him, he's in Vice where his tattoos and biker boy looks serve him well. The two meet at a Goth convention in San Diego and the sparks fly immediately. Things aren't all sparks and roses though: the two do live a nine hour drive apart, and Brandon's not out. Add to that a murder right in front of them, a company trying to cheat the system and the Mexican Mafia, and Brandon and Nick's relationship will need to overcome a whole slew of obstacles in order to work. 3/3

390. **Buchanan, James**, *Inland Empire,* MLR, 2009. Taking the Odds #2 of 3. (MM Police Procedural) Nicky and Brandon are back, and this time they're on Brandon's turf. Nicky's still on disability when he comes to Riverside to visit Brandon and pick up his 'Querida' from the Bakersfield's impound lot. Brandon loves having Nicky around, but at the same time, he's worried someone might find out that Nicky's more than just a friend. When Nicky becomes involved with the Task Force Brandon's on, the tension ratchets higher as Brandon's paranoia about being outed increases. Will his inability to step out of the closet mean the end of his relationship with Nicky? Or will the danger of the case they're on make it all a moot point? 3/3

391. **Buchanan, James**, *All or Nothing,* MLR, 2010. Taking the Odds #3 of 3. (MM Police Procedural) Blundering his way forward in his relationship with Nevada Agent Nick O'Malley, Riverside Detective Brandon Carr brings his daughter, Shayna, to Las Vegas to meet Nick. Nick has his own reasons for pushing Brandon toward a deeper commitment. But when the unthinkable happens, what every cop knows ends in tragedy, can Brandon hold it together long enough to solve the crime? As Brandon spirals into the hell of being a cop and a distraught parent will his love of Nick, and Nick's love for him, be enough to see them through? It's all or nothing and they can't afford to lose. 3/3

392. **Bujold, Lois McMaster**, *Ethan of Athos*, Baen, 1986. Vorkosigan Saga #3 of 16. (Fantasy) Athos – an all-male planet made possible by the invention of the uterine replicator. Ethan, drawn out of his beloved Athos by a quest, finds himself an alien in more mainstream human society, and cannot help but find women disturbing aliens as well, especially the ultra-competent, ultra-beautiful Elli. 3/3

393. **Bukiet, Melvin Rules**, *Strange Fire*, Norton, 2001. (Political Intrigue) Blind, homosexual, Russian émigré speechwriter Nathan Kazakov has enough problems even before his left ear is obliterated by a bullet presumably meant for the Israeli prime minister. Determined to solve the mystery, Nathan begins exploring a web of conspiracies involving messianic orthodox settlers, Arab terrorists, and the Israeli secret service. Was the bullet intended for Nathan after all? or perhaps for the prime minister's son Gabriel, an archaeologist who shuns his father's politics? One trail leads to Leviticus, another beneath the Temple Mount. 3/3

394. **Bull, Lew**, *Power Buddies,* Nazca Plains, 2008. (Modern Pulp) What happens when a young, muscular and good-looking man stands naked in front of you? Do his looks overpower you with a desire to be subjected to his will, or do you want to control him? These were

the dilemmas facing Mike, a bodybuilder at the City Gym one summer's evening. Power Buddies is a story that has murder, mystery, romance and sexual domination coursing throughout. It is a story of men with beautiful bodies who admire other men with equally beautifully-developed bodies as they intensify their relationships with one another. It encompasses men in varying sexual situations from refined bedroom activities to harsh physical domination in dungeons. The term 'pumping iron' takes on a whole new meaning in the escapades of our heroes as they take their body-building out of the gym and into the bedroom, showers and saunas. 3/3

395. **Bull, Lew**, *The Bonds of Friendship*, Nazca Plains, 2009. PI Clayton #1 of 2. (MM Soft Boiled) What do you get when you mix a match-making Jewish mother with her handsome son, who's in a relationship with an African-American part-time drag artiste, and a masculine private investigator? - A recipe for fun, danger, mystery and sexual antics. Michael Bloomberg and his lover, Selwyn, meet up with hunky Private Investigator, Rob Clayton and between them their lives intertwine through murder, mystery and sexually charged relationships. Thrown into the mix is Michael's mother, Myra who has a penchant for pairing up her son's friends with potential lovers. The story revolves around the relationships between the main characters and how they deal with such issues as interracial love, perceived prejudices, relationships per se, and Myra's persistent matchmaking skills in trying to find a lover for Rob, the P.I. The story climaxes in a murder which forces Rob and Selwyn to go off to Miami to investigate.

396. **Bull, Lew**, *Caribbean Cruising*, Nazca Plains, 2009. PI Clayton #2 of 2. (MM Soft Boiled) The story revolves around the adventures of the masculine P.I and his two best friends Michael and Selwyn as they set off on a gay cruise around the Caribbean, accompanied by Myra, Michael's match-making mother. What more tempting could one ask for than having two thousand muscular, tanned and good-looking men aboard an ocean liner at the same time? In this story, thanks to Myra's match-making skills, Rob finds not one, but two lovers to satisfy his sexual urges while the three young men go about solving some mysterious life-threatening events aboard the ocean liner. The story is filled with humor, intrigue and sexual adventures and adds a new dimension to the word 'cruising'. 3/3

397. **Bulldog, Jack**, *Russian River Murder Case*, Booksforgays.com, 2017. Dick Power #1 of 6. (Hard Boiled) Wealthy, gay, former movie star, and confirmed bachelor, Dick Power, now has a hobby as a very personal investigator. While he and his driver are looking for a summer home in the small Sonoma County community of Guerneville, CA, Dick meets an enchanting straight man whose home he wants to

buy. –only available via e-book (MLM). 3/3

398. **Bulldog, Jack**, *Murder in Cabin 501*, Booksforgays.com, 2017. Dick Power #2 of 6. (Hard Boiled) Dick Power is a wealthy, gay, former movie star known as Thad Austin, and formerly a confirmed bachelor with a promiscuous past. Now Dick has a serious relationship and a hobby as a personal investigator. Dick and his true love, Gopher, are about to embark on a gay "cruise to nowhere" to celebrate their first year together. Because the cruise line has mysteriously offered free cabins to Gopher and his guests, he brings along a crew of friends and acquaintances. –only available in e-book (MLM). 3/3

399. **Bulldog, Jack**, *Tinseltown Massacre*, Booksforgays.com, 2017. Dick Power #3 of 6. (Hard Boiled) Dick and his lover Gopher have been together almost two years. Gopher is now filthy rich himself, and Brad, the Hollywood Megastar that visited Gopher in the hospital after he was shot during the Russian River Murder Case, has sent Gopher 2 screenplays he hopes Gopher will produce and finance. Gopher and Dick decide both screenplays have merit and fly to Hollywood to begin production. Gopher discovers a bullet hole in the side of Brad's limo that wasn't there when they left the airport and soon it becomes clear that someone in the limo has a target on their back. Local police become involved when Dick's name comes up in a missing person investigation of an old acquaintance from Dick's "salad days". Once Dick identifies the intended victim, he devises a plan to draw out the killer. Eventually the Director of the Federal Investigation Bureau takes a personal interest and is there when, with Gopher's help, the killer falls right into Dick's arms. –only available via e-book (MLM). 3/3

400. **Bulldog, Jack**, *Murder in the Big Tomato*, Booksforgays.com, 2018. Dick Power #4 of 6. (Hard Boiled) Mark Harmony, the CEO of Cazzo Cruise Line, which Gopher owns, stumbles onto 320 acres of vacant land close to downtown Sacramento which is sometimes known as "The Big Tomato". There is a small lake on the land, but because of environmentally protected ducks, no developers are interested in the property. Mark pitches the idea of creating a massive gay luxury resort built around the lake. –only available as an e-book (MLM). 3/3

401. **Bulldog, Jack**, *Haunted House Murder*, Booksforgays,com, 2018. Dick Power #5 of 6. (Hard Boiled) with a day trip to Sacramento when Dick and Gopher's Real Estate Brokers, Jake and Bruno, want to borrow the limo to impress a client that has political connections in Sacramento. When Gopher discovers there's a rumor that the house is haunted, he wants to visit the house, too. When Bruno tells Dick that a former porn star acquaintance is accused of murdering

his husband in the house, Dick calls in his top detective, Matt Bonex, and Gopher calls in a Ghost Whisperer. –only available as an e-book (MLM). 3/3

402. **Bulldog, Jack**, *Gopher Davidson Murder*, Booksforgays.com, 2018. Dick Power #6 of 6. (Hard Boiled) Gopher Davidson is killed in a horrific car crash. Following Gopher's death, Dick Power lapses into a deep depression and spends over a year living on fast food and prostitutes in a run-down tract house in West Sacramento. Ace Hold, Dick's pool boy, tires of seeing Dick deteriorating and languishing in self-pity and manages to bring him back to his senses with some harsh tough love but while walking in the rose garden at Capitol Park, Dick and Ace become the target of a pair of drive-by shooters. 3/3

403. **Burford, Steve**, *It's a Sin*, NineStar Press, 2016. Summerskill and Lyon #1 of 2. (Police Procedural) When gay Detective Sergeant Dave Lyon is assigned to Detective Inspector Claire Summerskill's team as part of the Service's 'positive discrimination policy', no-one at Foregate Street Station is happy. And that includes Summerskill and Lyon. Mutual suspicion and mistrust must be shelved however, when a young man's beaten body is found on a canal tow path, and a dead-end case of 'happy slapping' unexpectedly turns into a murder investigation. 3/3

404. **Burford**, *Bodies Beautiful*, NineStar, 2018. Summerskill and Lyons #2 of 2. (Police Procedural) When promising young bodybuilder Paul Best is found gruesomely murdered, DI Claire Summerskill and DS Dave Lyon find themselves deep in the unfamiliar territory of hard-core gyms and weights, supplements and steroids. But when the one thing linking the growing list of murder victims is that they are the last men you'd expect to be victims, Summerskill and Lyon are faced with their toughest case yet. 3/3

405. **Burgess, Anthony**, *A Dead Man in Debtford*, Random House, 1993. (Historical) The whole world of Elizabethan England–from the intrigues of the courtroom, through the violent streets of London, to the glory of the theater–comes alive in this joyous celebration of the life of Christopher Marlowe, murdered in suspicious circumstances in a tavern brawl in Deptford more than four hundred years ago. 1/3

406. **Burgess, Gil**, *Dead of Winter*, AuthorHouse, 2004. (Police Procedural) Pennsylvania policeman Carmine Caputo and Sean Ryan track down a serial killer at a gay resort in the Poconos. 3/3

407. **Burgess, Gil**, *Death and Pride*, AuthorHouse, 2010. (Police Procedural) Death and Pride centers on the frantic search for a serial killer in the weeks prior to the annual Gay Pride Parade in Greenwich

Village, NY. All the victims, attractive, young men were found naked and thrown in dumpsters or in alley-ways in the Village. Police have only one clue to go on; fibers found in the beard stubble of the victims. Lead investigator, Alan Barlow's fears intensify as the body count rises and the date of the parade nears. He is no closer to finding the killer than at the beginning of the investigation. 3/3

408. **Burke, J. F.**, *Kelly Among the Nightingales*, E. P Dutton, 1979. (Hard Boiled/ Bibliography) Samuel Moses Kelly, a native of Harlem, formerly on the New York's finest and now a private investigator on the Big Apples Upper West Side, has a new case that takes him through the high-pressure world of big business publishing. –publisher and ghostwriter were lovers (MLM). 1/3

409. **Burley, W. J.**, *Wycliffe and the Dead Flautist*, St. Martin's, 1992. Wycliffe #17 of 22. (Police Procedural) On the peaceful and secluded estate of Lord and Lady Bottrel, the body of amateur flautist Tony Mills has been found, shot by his own gun. It appears to be suicide, but a closer inspection reveals some sinister inconsistencies, and Chief Superintendent Wycliffe is called in to investigate. As Wycliffe begins to unravel the last days of the dead man, another mystery is revealed: the disappearance of Lizzie Biddick, a pretty young girl who worked for the Bottrell family as a maid. Gradually, bitter family feuds and illicit relationships are uncovered and then another body shatters the pastoral serenity of the Cornish estate forever. –gay love triangle (MLM). 1/3

410. **Burman, Carina**, *Streets of Babylon*, Marion Boyars, 2008. Euthanasia Bondesson #1 of 3. (Historical/Bibliography) The setting is London in 1851, the year of the Great Exhibition. Together with a gay Welsh police inspector, the successful Swedish authoress Euthanasia Bondeson goes in search of her beautiful companion, who has disappeared in the narrow streets and alleyways of London. She meets beggars and whores, artists and society beauties, all actors on the modern city's stage in a drama of dark shadows and ever-changing desires. In this world where gender boundaries are constantly shifting, can we even tell who is a man and who is a woman? –two more books in the series that have yet to be translated into English from Swedish (MLM). 3/3

411. **Burns, Bobby**, *Bone Island*, Homofactus, 2011. (Amateur Sleuth) Identical twin swimwear models Ross and Ryan Blake are inseparable until Ryan goes missing in Key West. Ross drives down from Miami to search for his brother. He finds hustlers, drag queens, pirates, drug barons, and a voodoo priestess who all knew Ryan. 3/3

412. **Bushell, Agnes**, *Days of the Dead*, John Brown, 1995. (Amateur

Sleuth/Military) Guatemala, revolutionaries, death squads, drug cartels, contras, visionaries, and gods wrestle for control. Openly gay American Patrick Day must calculate the odds. Illuminates the tortured souls of Central American revolutionaries and their never-ending struggles. –mc is bisexual (MLM). 3/3

413. *Bushell, Agnes*, *Enumerator*, Serpent's Tail, 1997. (Amateur Sleuth) Lamont Bliss came to San Francisco all right, but when they found him dead the flowers he wore weren't just in his hair – they were spilling out of every wound in his mutilated body. What happened to Lamont should never have been any of Alex's business. She was just back from New Mexico and the main thing on her mind was choosing a new tattoo. Then Sean the enumerator came calling. The enumerators were everywhere that year, sex surveyors tracking the spread of HIV in San Francisco. But when someone told the enumerator a little too much about their sex life – that's when the killing started. Driven by passion and violence, soaked in fear and sex. –Sean is bisexual (MLM). 3/3

414. **Butcher, Amy**, *Paws for Consideration*, Got G'nads, 2012. (Cozy) Daisy-frumpy, wheelchair-bound, self-appointed mayor of her San Francisco neighborhood-likes dogs a little bit more than people. But when she discovers Skittles, a terrified Boston Terrier, still leashed to his very dead owner's arm, she must roll into action. Careening through the Castro and the Mission, past upscale restaurants and low-down dungeons, Daisy and Skittles brave gentrification, gay-bashing, and homelessness to paw and sniff their way deep into that most dangerous of all relationships: neighbor. 1/3

415. **Butler, Gwendoline**, *Coffins in Fashion*, St. Martin's, 1987. John Coffin #19 of 34. A corpse in his new house leads Scotland Yard detective John Coffin on the trail of a murderer that leads him into the world of high fashion and into the arms of a gorgeous designer. –three young men were sexually assaulted and killed yet Coffin determines the murderer was "straight" (MLM). 1/3

416. **Butler, L.**, *Money Gay*, Parisian, 1970. (Pulp) Dave Rogan, a New York–based investments spy, who uses sex for information until he realizes love is more important than money when he meets hustler Steven Birk. 3/3

417. **Butterfield, Frank**, *Unexpected Heiress*, Createspace, 2016. Nick and Carter #1 of 30. (Hard Boiled) The richest homosexual in San Francisco is a private investigator. Nick Williams lives in a modest bungalow with his fireman husband, a sweet fellow from Georgia by the name of Carter Jones. Nick's gem of a secretary, Marnie Wilson, is worried that Nick isn't working enough. She knits a lot. Jeffrey Klein, Esquire, is Nick's friend and lawyer. He represents the guys

and gals who get caught in police raids in the Tenderloin. Lt. Mike Robertson is Nick's first love and best friend. He's a good guy who's one hell of a cop. 3/3

418. **Butterfield, Frank**, *Amorous Attorney*, Createspace, 2016. Nick and Carter #2 of 30. (Hard Boiled) Jeffrey Klein's love affair is heating up and Nick has to chase him down because, frankly, he needs a lawyer to set up his new business. Oh, and Eddie Mannix at Metro is on the warpath and being a general pain in Nick's ass. After finding Jeffrey shacked up in a compromising position, Nick has to deal with his own personal mess when it comes to saying goodbye to an old flame. After receiving a telegram asking for help, Nick and Carter end up flying south of the border, down Mexico way. When they get there, they find a corrupt politician, a flirtatious police captain, and a woman terrified of an uncertain future and what it holds for her. 3/3

419. **Butterfield, Frank**, *Sartorial Senator*, Createspace, 2017. Nick and Carter #3 of 30. (Hard Boiled) Nick and Carter just want to go home to San Francisco after their adventures in Mexico. But, before they can sail into the Golden Gate, Nick receives a subpoena from America's most infamous witch hunter in Washington, D.C. Meanwhile, an old schoolmate from Carter's childhood shows up out of nowhere and revives painful memories. Once they get to the nation's capital, they are plunged into helping yet another flirtatious police detective solves a curious murder that leads to some very dark places. In the end, Nick and Carter set a trap to catch the killer and get much more than they bargained for. 3/3

420. **Butterfield, Frank**, *Laconic Lumberjack*, Createspace, 2017. Nick and Carter #4 of 30. (Hard Boiled) It's just another Thursday morning in July of 1953 when the doorbell rings at 137 Hartford Street and it's bad news. Carter's father has been murdered in Georgia and the local sheriff has no intention of finding out who really did it. So, Nick and Carter borrow the first plane that Marnie, Nick's amazing secretary, can find for them and they zoom off back into the past to see if they can uncover the truth of what really happened before the wrong man is convicted. And, knowing the lay of the land under the moss-covered oaks, Carter is pretty sure that the color of a man's skin will figure heavily in who takes the fall. The best Nick can do is stand by Carter's side as he confronts an awful past, uncovers some surprising secrets, and deals with the unsavory reality of small-town hypocrisy. In the end, Nick and Carter discover more about themselves than they ever expected to find. 3/3

421. **Butterfield, Frank**, *Perplexed Pumpkin*, Createspace, 2017. Nick and Carter #5 of 30. (Hard Boiled) *"Nick! You and Carter have to throw a party for Halloween this year! It's on a Saturday, after all!"*

Grudgingly, Nick agrees to be the less-than-amiable host to what turns out to be a bizarre event that will long be remembered by everyone who attends... When the party is obviously going to be much bigger than Nick & Carter expected, they begin to realize something mysterious is brewing under their very noses. Down in their own basement, as a matter of fact. A two-timing girlfriend, a locked door, and an unexpected visit from the F.B.I. are just some of the clues that begin to add up to a particularly perplexing Halloween. So, come on you ghosts and ghouls, witches and warlocks, put on your Halloween best for you have been invited to a memorable evening at 137 Hartford Street in San Francisco on Saturday, October 31, 1953. Come on in and join the party. If you dare... 3/3

422. **Butterfield, Frank**, *Savage Son*, Createspace, 2017. Nick and Carter #6 of 30. (Hard Boiled) Ivan Kopek is missing and his parents desperately want Nick's help. Ike, as he's known to his friends, is quickly found once Nick, Carter, and their pals are on the case. Unfortunately, Ike's in jail for a murder he didn't commit. And it was only because he didn't get the chance to do it himself. Meanwhile, it's almost Christmas. *Nick's least favorite time of the year.* But, Carter wants a Christmas tree and Dr. Parnell Williams, Nick's evil bastard of a father, has summoned them both to the mansion on Sacramento Street for Christmas day at 12 noon. And they're not to be late. In the end, Christmas brings Nick & Carter a number of unexpected and life-changing packages, both big and small. 3/3

423. **Butterfield, Frank**, *Mangled Mobster*, Createspace, 2017. Nick and Carter #7 of 30. Construction on the new twenty-story building for Consolidated Security at the corner of Market and Montgomery is ahead of schedule, thanks to Henry and Pam. Nick is looking forward to his office on the nineteenth floor. The twentieth floor is designed to be a restaurant. He's hoping for French or Italian. Carter wants something with less garlic. But then an unknown man falls from the top of the steel skeleton and things grind to a halt. When Henry gets a late-night call warning him and Nick to not investigate, Mike takes action to protect them both, but Nick gets a late-night visit from some wise guys and it doesn't end well... For them. That's just the beginning of a tale of mobsters, refugees, and The Old Poodle Dog that twists and turns its way to a thrilling conclusion. In the end, it's an adventure for Nick, Carter, and the whole gang in the City we love the most: Baghdad By the Bay. 3/3

424. **Butterfield, Frank**, *Iniquitous Investigator*, Createspace, 2017. Nick and Carter #8 of 30. (Hard Boiled) Mildred's Diner just isn't the welcoming place it once was. Looking forward to a nice breakfast, including that chewy bacon that Nick and Carter both love, they're asked to leave. Mildred has gone back to Texas and word is

they "ain't welcome." But it's a sunny July day, so Nick puts the top down of the Roadmaster and they head across the Golden Gate to Sausalito for eggs, bacon, toast, and coffee. But it seems like trouble follows them along the way and, before they know it, Nick and Carter are sitting in jail for vagrancy. After making bail, the whole team is on the job figuring what the heck is going on in sleepy Sausalito while also chasing down the missing Mildred, who may have been kidnapped or worse! 3/3

425. **Butterfield, Frank**, *Voluptuous Vixen*, Createspace, 2017. Nick and Carter #9 of 30. (Hard Boiled) Nick and Carter are sailing across the sea to Honolulu on an impromptu holiday. For the sake of propriety and decorum, the ship's captain pairs them off with a "lady couple" who turn out to be much more than they appear at first glance. When one of them turns up dead in Nick and Carter's cabin, the hunt is on to find the other one before it's too late. 3/3

426. **Butterfield, Frank**, *Timid Traitor*, Createspace, 2017. Nick and Carter #10 of 30. (Hard Boiled) It's a cold January morning. As Nick and Carter sip their hot coffee in an attempt to stay warm, passers-by are stopping to gawk at San Francisco's newest skyscraper at 600 Market Street. The grand opening goes off without a hitch (and without the Mayor or anyone else of note, for that matter). Meanwhile, back on Bush Street, Nick has a new client. Her name is Mrs. Anne-Marie Boudier. She's charming. She's chic. She was at Marnie's wedding on the groom's side. And she wants Nick to find her long lost husband. So she can kill him. And so, begins a twisting and turning escapade of old secrets and new betrayals that will eventually take Nick and Carter across the Atlantic Ocean as they finally discover who the real traitor is. 3/3

427. **Butterfield, Frank**, *Sodden Sailor*, Createspace, 2017. Nick and Carter #11 of 30. (Hard Boiled) It's Sunday night and Nick has decided he wants to get back in the kitchen to make a couple of pans of lasagna for dinner, something he hasn't done since he and Carter moved into the big pile of rocks on Nob Hill. Captain Daniel O'Reilly, pilot of *The Flirtatious Captain*, is bringing a friend for dinner. Instead of his latest love interest, the captain introduces Nick and Carter to an old friend, a man who is on his last legs and who has a favor to ask: can Nick and Carter help him get his girl and her son out of Red China? That's where things begin but it's far from where they end... 3/3

428. **Butterfield, Frank**, *Excluded Exile*, Createspace, 2017. Nick and Carter #12 of 30. (Hard Boiled) Nick and Carter are Down Under in Sydney at summer's end and are looking forward to finally having time to spend at the beach so Carter can get in some surfing while Nick works on his tan as a surf widow. Everything is going to plan

until they forget to make it look like they slept in both beds and are asked to leave their hotel. Fortunately, they're able to rent a house in the Eastern Suburbs atop a cliff that is two hundred feet above the Pacific. The house is perfect, with new furniture, an ocean-facing sunroom, and a housekeeper. But then it starts to rain. And a dead body turns up in the kitchen, clobbered with a cast-iron skillet. The questions start piling up. Who cleaned up the blood after the body was removed? Whose car is that parked at the end of the street? Will they ever make it to the beach? In the end, it's another trans-Pacific adventure for Nick and Carter that leads home in a number of unexpected ways. 3/3

429. **Butterfield, Frank**, *Paradoxical Parent*, Createspace, 2017. Nick and Carter #13 of 30. (Hard Boiled) It's been a big year for Nick & Carter and they are finally back home in San Francisco, trying to take it easy after all their globe-trotting adventures. But, there's no rest for the weary, not yet, as Nick learns about the last place his mother lived before she died and is off again, across the country, going from the warm waters of the South Pacific to his first real-life snowstorm in New England. As he and Carter, helped by Frankie & Maria Vasco, meet some of the people who once knew Nick's mother and learn more about who she was and who she loved, they also encounter one of the most disturbing things to come from Nick's own past. After a policeman is murdered and other innocent people are threatened, Nick realizes it's time to put a stop to a killer's madness, even if it means that he has to pull the trigger himself. 3/3

430. **Butterfield, Frank**, *Pitiful Player*, Createspace, 2017. Nick and Carter #14 of 30. (Hard Boiled) Ben White, a movie producer working on Nick's dime, is ready to show off what he's been up to, so Nick and Carter head to Hollywood to see what there is to see and, to be polite, it stinks. Ben's director has an idea and he says it's gonna make Nick even richer than he already is. But, before they can start the cameras rolling, leading man William Fraser is found murdered at the lavish Beverly Hills mansion of seductive silent screen star Juan Zane. Carlo Martinelli, Ben's lover, is arrested and charged with murder even though everyone in town knows he's innocent, including the District Attorney. Meanwhile, the Beverly Hills Police Chief makes sure that Nick knows that his kind of help isn't wanted in the posh village, home to some of Hollywood's most famous stars. The chief is running a good, clean, wholesome town, after all. From Muscle Beach to Mulholland Drive, Nick and Carter begin to piece together the clues that point to who did it and why. Somehow, they manage to do so in the sweltering heat and noxious smog of the Southland. In the end, however, will anyone be brought to justice? It's Hollywood, so you'll have to wait for the final reel to

find out. 3/3

431. **Butterfield, Frank**, *Childish Churl*, Createspace, 2017. Nick and Carter #15 of 30. (Hard Boiled) The Lipstick, Nick's high-rise office building on Market Street, finally has a restaurant on the twentieth floor. The Sky-Brau offers freshly-sliced meats, white linens, and luncheon with a view. It's the new hot-spot in town and, who knows, you might end up sharing a table with the mayor. While trying to get in for some carved roast beef, Nick and Carter run into a daughter with a missing father who's been at work in Africa and hasn't been heard from in a while. Her mother isn't concerned, however. He's been out in the field for months at a time before. But, for the daughter's sake, Nick agrees to look into things. Meanwhile, a real English lord shows up at the office with some disconcerting news and a favor to ask. Nick isn't sure who the man really is but decides to take him at his word. For the time being, at least. Over on Nob Hill, wedding bells are ringing for Carter's mother, the soon-to-be Mrs. Louise Richardson, and Nick and Carter's big pile of rocks is where the celebration will take place. The food, as always, will be delicious. The florist has brought a small army of helpers to deck out the house in the gayest way. The dining table is loaded with gifts for the bride and groom. And, there are a few unexpected guests who show up and bring some surprises of their own. It will be a day that none of the guests will soon forget. 3/3

432. **Butterfield, Frank**, *Rotten Rancher*, Createspace, 2017. Nick and Carter #16 of 30. (Hard Boiled) It's Veteran's Day, and a gorgeous one at that. Parades of flying flags and grizzled old soldiers marching to the tunes of John Philip Souza are definitely in the works. Meanwhile, Nick and Carter are heading south on Highway 1 for a relaxing week down in Big Sur, just south of beautiful Carmel-By-The-Sea. They'll be staying at the home of one Dr. Parnell Williams, Nick's father. It's a modern sort of thing, made of wood and glass, and perched right on the cliff's edge with dramatic views of the ocean and the incoming banks of fog. But when the power goes out late at night and the newly-installed generator kicks on, it's not long before Carter is dragging a bewildered Nick to the front door because, it turns out, someone intentionally disconnected the vent and the house quickly fills up with deadly carbon monoxide. As they search for their would-be murderer, Nick and Carter quickly discover all sorts of secrets, hidden away among the verdant valleys and stands of Monterey pines. Secrets that go back twenty years, or more, and stories of wild times that would deeply shock the gawking tourists from Topeka and Des Moines, if they only knew. Will Nick and Carter uncover the killer before he, or she, strikes again? To find out, jump into the nearest convertible and follow the

narrow, twisting highway that takes you through the land of towering, ancient redwoods and mountains that crash into the bright, blue ocean below. 3/3

433. **Butterfield, Frank**, *Happy Holiday*, Createspace, 2017. Nick and Carter #17 of 30. (Hard Boiled) It's early in the morning and Carter is worried that he and Nick won't be warm enough for their Christmas trip to Vermont. Nick, for his part, is wondering if they will ever be able to return to the big pile of rocks he's finally come to love. An exile in France isn't the worst thing in the world but still... But before they can get much more than halfway from San Francisco to Vermont, they discover that the mob is after them and is on their tails, chasing them across the country as they take planes, trains, and automobiles. They finally get to Vermont, all covered in freshly-fallen white snow, and begin to wonder if it will be their last Christmas, after all. 3/3

434. **Butterfield, Frank**, *Adroit Alien*, Createspace, 2017. Nick and Carter #18 of 30. (Hard Boiled) Nick and Carter have arrived safely in Paris and were even greeted at the airport by a minor government official and a small detachment of the famous Republican Guard. After taking a week to recover from their Christmas adventures in Vermont, they're ready to move into their new house over in the 4th Arrondissement. It takes three cabs to get the whole gang over there from their hotel and, as they stand on the sidewalk outside, none of them can quite believe what they find: a crumbling building, a trash-filled courtyard, several broken windows, and, as Nick tentatively pushes the front door open, the stench of a rotting corpse. The police know that none of them could possibly have committed the crime but what about the mysterious Madame Marika, who has suddenly disappeared? Is she back behind the Iron Curtain? Or has she too been murdered? The entire household gets involved in solving the mystery, dashing around the city that is their new home, and discovering, in the end, the bonds of love and friendship they have brought with them from San Francisco, across the Atlantic Ocean, and to *La Ville-Lumière*–Paris: The City of Light. *And that's only the beginning...* 3/3

435. **Butterfield, Frank**, *Leaping Lord*, Createspace, 2018. Nick and Carter #19 of 30. (Hard Boiled) Life is good. Nick and Carter are living on the French Riviera, having breakfast by the pool every morning with a view of the Mediterranean, and living a quiet life after a busy month. The grand re-opening of Nick's latest acquisition, *l'Hôtel Beau Rivage*, the hottest spot in Nice, has gone off without a hitch. And, best of all, Nick has recovered nicely after taking a bullet in his shoulder. But then, on the same day, they have not one, but two unexpected encounters with the aristocracy. A day of driving down

the coast leads to an amiable but unusual request from the former Grace Kelly, now *Her Serene Highness* The Princess of Monaco. Nick is suspicious of the favor she's asked but he's also smitten with the gorgeous blonde who lives in the Prince's Palace just a few miles down the coast. Carter, of course, can't help but tease Nick about losing his heart to movie-star royalty. Later that evening, Nick and Carter are invited to an impromptu dinner with Her Grace, the Duchess of Boston. She happens to be the mother of the British spy who has been helping Nick and Carter stay out of trouble for the past couple of years. Her son, Lord Gerald Whitcombe, left London for Nice back in July but has since disappeared. The duchess is convinced that the two of them are the only ones who can find him. What follows is a race against time that leads Nick and Carter back to Paris where they find that things are not exactly how they left them. 3/3

436. **Butterfield, Frank**, *Constant Caprese*, Createspace, 2018. Nick and Carter #20 of 30. (Hard Boiled) Nick and Carter have left Nice and, after sailing down the Italian coast, have dropped anchor at the island of Procida, just across the bay from the Naples coast. Nick, as he is wont to do, meets the one homosexual who works at the local post office and, in short order, is invited to dinner along with Carter to meet the entire family. Italians, after all, are so friendly! Meanwhile, Lord Gerald, their friend in British intelligence, has sent a cryptic telegram asking them to take a package over to Capri, an island on the far side of the Bay of Naples. When they dock at Capri the next morning, they find a dying duke, an eccentric earl, and a vigilant viscount all living together in a glorious villa dating back to the turn of the century. These are the final remnants of the once-thriving community of homosexual Englishmen who made the Italian island their sanctuary where they could live in peace as themselves. But is someone haunting this idyllic Mediterranean paradise? Who cut the phone line for no apparent reason? Who opened the locked door and then unlocked it again? Who is playing pranks with the plumbing? Maybe these are all just coincidences... Or maybe there is something more sinister afoot... 3/3

437. **Butterfield, Frank**, *Shameless Sodomite*, Createspace, 2018. Nick and Carter #21 of 30. (Hard Boiled) Nick and Carter are about to witness history! It's an exciting time in Léopoldville, capital of the Belgian Congo and their temporary home on the south side of the Congo River. After living in Africa for nearly two years, they will be on the ground when the colony becomes an independent nation able to govern itself following a tragic history. They've been busy, of course. Nick owns a hotel and a clinic while Carter has opened two gyms on both sides of the river–one in Léopoldville and one in Braz-

zaville in the French colony on the far shore. As they begin to wrap up their lives in Africa and prepare for their next big move, something terrifying and disturbing happens that suddenly accelerates their plan. Before they have time to do much more than pack a few clothes, they're unceremoniously sent down to the docks to wait for the ferry that will take them across the river and back into the safety of the French Congo. Where they go next leads them smack into the biggest challenge the two men have had to face in the 13 years since they first met across a crowded room. 3/3

438. **Butterfield, Frank**, *Harried Husband*, Createspace, 2018. Nick and Carter #22 of 30. (Hard Boiled) It's been three weeks since the case against Nick and Carter was dismissed and life has moved on. They're at home in the big pile of rocks on Nob Hill and doing swell. It's been two weeks since Nick started seeing Dr. Sylvester, an analyst who offices in The Shell Building on Bush Street. And on this particular Monday, at 1 p.m., the good doctor will ask Nick an important question that turns out to be something Nick has never truly considered. As he ponders the answer, he begins to wonder about the nature of his relationship with Carter. *Psychoanalysis can do that, you know.* Meanwhile, a new client wants to see Nick. He claims that only Nick will be able to catch his cheating wife in the act. And it might end up being a good deal for everyone involved. Well, almost everyone. In order to work the case, Nick decides he needs to grow out his beard, so no one will recognize him as he prowls the City. Of course, Carter is along for the ride because beard burn isn't good. So, they're off to the woods for 10 days to rough it. *Or are they?* 3/3

439. **Butterfield, Frank**, *Stymied Star*, Createspace, 2018. Nick and Carter #23 of 30. (Hard Boiled) It's three in the morning when the newly-installed Princess phone (with illuminated dial) next to Carter's side of the bed starts to insistently ring. Raymond Burr from TV's *Perry Mason* is calling and he's in a bit of a pickle. Someone stashed a corpse in his on-studio cottage and he's worried about how this might affect the show. Nick and Carter fly down where they find a handsome stiff. He was a former personal assistant and wanna-be actor who turned to one of the best-paying gigs in town: male companion. And he had a little black book chock full of famous names, home phone numbers, and careers that could easily be ruined. But only one of them is a murderer and it's up to Nick and Carter to find out who it might be... 3/3

440. **Butterfield, Frank**, *The Roving Refugee*, Createspace, 2018. Nick and Carter #24 of 30. (Hard Boiled) Nick and Carter are jetting across the Atlantic to the island of Capri for the funeral of the Dowager Duchess of Boston. On the way, they're dropping off Marnie

and her husband, Alex, so the two can spend a relaxing few days in Paris. When they arrive in Europe, Nick and Carter receive a distressing message. Paul Vermaut, their good friend from the Congo, is sick with a mysterious disease that has the doctors baffled. He's been on the run from the Congolese civil war, traveling thousands of miles over land, and is now hospitalized in Salisbury, the capital of Southern Rhodesia. 3/3

441. **Butterfield, Frank,** *The Perfidious Parolee,* Createspace, 2018. Nick and Carter #25 of 30. (Hard Boiled) It's been 214 days since Nick and Carter promised their friends they would stay home. Los Angeles County still has a warrant out for them both, so they've been good boys and remained within the 49 square miles of the City by the Bay. However, Nick, being Nick, gets carried away with Ben White's idea to build a back lot for Monumental Studios on a few hundred acres in Sonoma County and drives up to have a look around. Unfortunately, they stumble across a decaying corpse. 3/3

442. **Butterfield, Frank,** *The Derelict Dad,* Createspace, 2018. Nick and Carter #26 of 30. (Hard Boiled) It's way too early on a Monday morning, but Nick and Carter are making their way across the country to a clandestine meeting in Miami with Bobby Kennedy at the Attorney General's request. On their last leg into Miami, they receive a radiogram that R.F.K. has had to cancel at the last minute. Determined to get some good poolside time in the hot sun, they continue on to the Sunshine State where they meet a man who turns out to recognize Carter's latest hire. 3/3

443. **Butterfield, Frank,** *The Shifting Scion,* Createspace, 2018. Nick and Carter #27 of 30. (Hard Boiled) Nick is in trouble. He's obstructing justice and might possibly be an accessory to murder, after the fact. The cops are on to him and his lawyer is very concerned. It's all because Sam Halverson, a close friend and an operative for WilliamsJones Security, has murdered a man and is on his way to Mexico to hide out from the law. –as Butterfield is incredibly prolific there were probably be several books released in 2019 (MLM). 3/3

444. **Butterfield, Frank,** *The Sailor Who Washed Ashore,* Createspace, 2018. Daytona Beach #1 of 4. (Hard Boiled) It's June of 1947 and the Spanish moss is twirling in the sea breeze beneath the limbs of a massive live oak somewhere in Daytona Beach, the World's Most Famous... And Tom Jarrell is having a hard time coping with each day. He's recently been made a widower, having lost his wife and daughter (Sarah and Missy) in an accident out on the DeLand Highway back in April. 3/3

445. **Butterfield, Frank,** *The Lawyer who Leapt,* Createspace, 2018.

Daytona Beach #2 of 4. (Hard Boiled) It's Wednesday morning, September 24th to be precise, and Tom Jarrell is in love. He's walking through the tree-covered streets of Daytona Beach, on his way to work, and thinking about the wonderful night he just spent. But, when he gets to the office, he realizes he has a few things that need to be done. For one, he needs to file an affidavit in a murder trial, but he's never done any such thing, so he heads off to his old law school to meet with his favorite professor from before the war to get some much-needed advice. And, while there, he gets much more than he was expecting. 3/3

446. **Butterfield, Frank,** *The Cuban who Paid Dearly,* Createspace, 2018. Daytona Beach #3 of 4. (Hard Boiled) Just when it looks like Tom and Ronnie will finally get some time to themselves, a friend of theirs comes across a dead Cuban and is found holding the gun. He says he didn't do it, but the State's Attorney isn't convinced... –the fourth book, *The Demoiselle Who Departed,* will be released in 2019 (MLM). 3/3

447. **Buttino, Frank,** *A Special Agent: Gay and Inside the FBI,* William Morrow, 1993. (Nonfiction Autobiography) For twenty years he served as one of the nation's top FBI agents. He led investigations into organized crime, narcotics, and foreign counterintelligence - and was praised by every FBI director from J. Edgar Hoover to William Sessions. But Frank Buttino also led a secret life - a life he kept hidden from the FBI, his family, and many of his friends. After years of denial, Frank had finally admitted to himself that he was gay. Extended undercover assignments had prepared him brilliantly for life deep in the closet and enabled him to form a discreet relationship with another man. Then, at forty-three, at the peak of his twenty-year career, an anonymous letter shattered his privacy and revealed his sexual orientation to his parents and to the FBI. 3/3

448. **Byrnes, Rob,** *The Night We Met,* Kensington, 2002. (Crime Caper) A variation on classic screwball comedy: Boy gets gorgeous Mafia boyfriend, boy loses Mafia boyfriend and nearly gets whacked by most of New York, boy gets Mafia boyfriend back – and gets more than he bargained for. Andrew Westlake – gay, 35, and barely scraping by in Manhattan – has two dreams, neither of which has come true. He has yet to become the literary voice of his generation. And he most definitely has not met Mr. Right. 3/3

449. **Byrnes, Rob,** *Straight Lies,* Kensington, 2009. Grant and Chase #1 of 3. (Crime Caper) Grant and Chase are a fun-loving pair of small-time hustlers with no money, little patience, and lots of get-rich-quick schemes. If only they could pull off the perfect crime – "The Big One," as Grant calls it–Chase could finally quit his job at the

supermarket and the two could retire in style. 3/3

450. **Byrnes, Rob**, *Holy Rollers*, Bold Strokes, 2011. Grant and Chase #2 of 3. (Crime Caper) When Grant Lambert and Chase LaMarca–partners in life and crime–learn that $7 million in not-so-petty cash is hidden in the safe of a rightwing mega-church, they assemble a team of gay and lesbian criminals to infiltrate the church and steal the money. 3/3

451. **Byrnes, Rob**, *Strange Bedfellows,* Bold Strokes, 2012. Grant and Chase #3 of 3. (Crime Caper) If politics makes for strange bedfellows, perhaps no bedfellows are stranger than Grant Lambert and Austin Peebles. Austin Peebles is a professional politician with a problem: a prominent rightwing blogger has come into possession of a compromising cell phone photo of the congressional candidate... an image that could derail his campaign. Enter Grant Lambert – a professional criminal who lives so far below society's radar he's never even registered to vote–and his partner in life and crime, Chase LaMarca. If Grant and Chase can make the picture disappear, they'll make a cool $50,000. 3/3

C

452. **Cabell, Robert W.**, *Hair Raising Adventures of Jayms Blonde: Project Popcorn*, iUniverse, 2007. (Espionage Caper) Enter into the salaciously sexy world of "Environmental Espionage" and meet Jayms Blonde. He's gorgeous, he's gay, he makes the bad guys pay! A hairdresser by trade and a secret agent by choice, this former U.S. Navy Seal can handle an Uzi like a teasing comb. Aided by his faithful pedicurist, Precious Needmore, they lead an elite band of Pink Berets to save the planet from bad hair and bad air. Armed with bulletproof mousse, an Uzi blow-dryer, hair curler hand grenades, explosive peel-and-stick plastique nails, and laser teasing combs, they rescue the dude-in-distress and make saving the world look fabulous! 3/3

453. **Cade, Scotty**, *Bounty of Love*, Dreamspinner, 2011. Love #3 of 4. (MM Mystery) The night before his wedding, Zander Walsh, his parents, and his husband-to-be are all shot when they return home and interrupt a mysterious robbery in progress. After three weeks in a coma, Zander wakes up to find out he is the only survivor, and his perfect life falls apart in an instant. Hunky FBI Agent Jake Elliot is investigating the case, and he eventually apprehends the killer-who soon escapes. Following six months of searching, Zander and Jake realize they're being stonewalled by the FBI... 3/3

454. **Cade, Scotty**, *The Royal Street Heist*, Dreamspinner, 2014. Bissonet & Cruz Investigations #1 of 3. (MM Police Procedural) When valuable Civil War era art is stolen from a popular New Orleans gallery, NOPD Lead Detective Montgomery "Beau" Bissonet and his partner set out to solve the crime. When the gallery's insurance company sends Tollison Cruz to the Big Easy to conduct their own independent investigation, personalities clash and battle lines are definitely drawn. The heist quickly becomes a politically driven high-profile case, and Detective Bissonet is furious when he's ordered to work alongside Investigator Cruz to assure a timely arrest. 3/3

455. **Cade, Scotty**, *Veiled Loyalties*, Dreamspinner, 2015. Bissonet & Cruz Investigations #2 of 3. (MM Police Procedural) Halloween is Beau Bissonet's favorite holiday, from carving pumpkins to decorating his yard to donning a costume and scaring the neighborhood kids. But this year his Halloween is about to take a different turn, one that will challenge his skills as a detective and his commitment to his partner in work and love. Tollison's ex, Bastien Andros, shows

up out of the blue. Naturally, Beau's suspicious, but two days after Bastien's arrival, he goes missing, and Tollison worries his past may catch up to him. 3/3

456. **Cade, Scotty**, *A Lethal Mistake*, Dreamspinner, 2016. Bissonet & Cruz Investigations #3 of 3. (MM Police Procedural It's Mardi Gras, and New Orleans is alive and festive, teeming with excited tourists and locals alike. The first few parades go off without a hitch. And then a man is targeted, shot, and killed right in the middle of a crowded street. Auggie and Bruce are called in to investigate, but before they even get started, more deaths occur, one at each of the next two parades. Auggie realizes he's dealing with a serial killer and jumps into action. Beau and Tollison join the investigation and stumble upon some similarities in the murders that are too strong to ignore. 3/3

457. **Cain, James**, *Serenade*, Knopf, 1937. John Sharp had just flopped in Rigoletto, down in Mexico, when he first saw Juana. Somehow, the beautiful Mexican-Indian prostitute offered him a way back, a chance to rebuild his career in New York and Hollywood. But then, like the snake in the garden, Winston Hawes, the prodigiously accomplished conductor, came back in to Sharp's life and an eternal, and lethal, triangle was formed. 1/3

458. **Caldwell, Joseph**, *In Such Dark Places,* Farrar Straus Giroux, 1978. (Journalism) Eugene is a midwesterner living in New York, an erstwhile Catholic and not-quite-openly-gay photographer. When a Holy Week pageant in the gritty Lower East Side erupts into a riot, he is sucked into the city's shadowy depths. While photographing the parade, Eugene has his eye on a handsome teen, but when things turn violent the youth is stabbed and Eugene's camera is stolen. To find the camera and its precious film, which may provide evidence, Eugene has to become acquainted with a seedy, unfamiliar world, and hold on to his sanity in the process. 3/3

459. **Calloway, Kate**, *2nd Fiddle,* Naiad Press, 1997. PI James #2 of 8. (Hard Boiled) At their wits end, two gay men hire private investigator Cassidy Jones to find out who is blackmailing them to leave their home on Cedar Ridge. Cassidy throws herself into the investigation, hoping against hope that it will help her forget the horror of her very first case. –other books do not have gay male characters (MLM). 2/3

460. **Calmes, Mary**, *Timing*, Dreamspinner, 2010. Timing #1 of 3. (MM Amateur Sleuth) Stefan Joss just can't win. Not only does he have to go to Texas in the middle of summer to be the man of honor in his best friend Charlotte's wedding, but he's expected to negotiate a million-dollar business deal at the same time. Stefan's business deal

goes wrong: the owner of the last ranch he needs to secure for the company is murdered. Stefan's in for the surprise of his life as he finds himself in danger as well. 3/3

461. **Cameron, Sam**, *Mystery of the Tempest*, Bold Strokes Books, 2011. Fisher Key #1 of 4. (YA Amateur Sleuths) Twin brothers Denny and Steven Anderson love helping people and fighting crime alongside their sheriff dad on sun-drenched Fisher Key, Florida. Steven likes chasing girls. Denny longs to lose his virginity but doesn't dare tell anyone he's gay. The twins meet the handsome new guy in town, a military veteran with a chiseled body and mysterious past. Meanwhile Brian Vandermark, a gay transfer student from Boston, finds himself falling for closeted Denny but hampered by his shyness. When an antique yacht explodes in Fisher Key harbor, all three boys are caught up in a summer of betrayal, romance, and danger. It's the Mystery of the Tempest–and it just might kill them all. 3/3

462. **Cameron, Sam**, *Secret of Othello*, Bold Strokes Books, 2012. Fisher Key #2 of 4. (YA Amateur Sleuths) A shooting star streaks across Fisher Key's skies. Natural phenomenon or secret military satellite? For Steven Anderson, any mystery is a welcome distraction. As the days get hotter, the twins are drawn into an underwater race against time, tide, and treason. Suddenly, true love is the least of their problems. Under the waves, no one can hear you scream... 3/3

463. **Cameron, Sam**, *If You Like Boys*, Bold Stroke Books, 2014. Fisher Key #4 of 4. (YA Amateur Sleuth) Sean's love life is the pits, at least until cute brothers Rob and Andrew move onto the island. When someone starts leaving cute notes, Sean's drawn into a would-be summer fling hampered by a dark secret the brothers fear to tell. 3/3

464. **Cameron, Sam**, *Kings of Ruin*, Bold Stroke Books, 2013. (MM YA Adventure) Danny Kelly cares only for rock 'n' roll and fast cars. Too bad he's stuck in the capital of country music and he's banned from driving until he turns twenty-one. Plus, he likes other boys, a secret that he's vowed to keep until he graduates high school. When his stepdad's new truck roars off on its own, Danny discovers a secret that is endangering cars and drivers across America. 3/3

465. **Campbell, Michael D.**, *Repercussions: A Murder Mystery*, Reporters, 2002. (Amateur Sleuth) Italian courtier Carlo Cipriani helps trap a triple murderer and discovers his own lover has been up to no good in this romantic mystery (Gunn). 3/3

466. **Campbell, Michael D.**, *Perverted Justice: Childhood Memories to Die For*, Reporters, 2005. (Amateur Sleuth) Twelve-year-old Michael witnesses Norman Morley executing a police officer in a park, but no one believes him. Now in 2004, serving on the jury in Morley's

trial for killing the other two officers who were with him that day, Michael is convinced the case is a setup but feels compelled to discover what was going on in the park and how it tied into the rampant corruption among the police at the time (Gunn).

467. **Campbell, Robert**, *In a Pig's Eye*, Pocket, 1991. Jimmy Flannery #8 of 21. "How's it goin'?".. "Up and down and 'round and 'round. You?" "Sixes and sevens" Plump blue-eyed Italian looking man drops dead right in front of red-haired Irish narrator Jimmy Flannery during their exercise class. Teddy's membership name is "Porky Pig", and his pockets hold no ID, yet old Italian lire "30 pieces of silver". First a police chief asks the newly elected ward rep for help, then says back off. Meanwhile, very pregnant wife Mary counsels pregnant poor teens in their 8th floor walkup. Always curious, Jimmy runs up against Chicago big boys–and an underworld warlord. –this convoluted story has a death in a former bathhouse and there's talk of homosexuals briefly (MLM). 1/3

468. **Cantrell, Rebecca**, *A Trace of Smoke*, Forge, 2009. Hannah Vogel #1 of 4. (Historical) Even though hardened crime reporter Hannah Vogel knows all too well how tough it is to survive in 1931 Berlin, she is devastated when she sees a photograph of her brother's body posted in the Hall of the Unnamed Dead. Ernst, a cross-dressing lounge singer at a seedy nightclub, had many secrets, a never-ending list of lovers, and plenty of opportunities to get into trouble. – Ernst is the gay Nazi who created the SA, the predecessor of the Nazi SS (MLM). 2/3

469. **Cantrall, Rebecca**, *A Night of Long Knives,* Forge, 2010. Hannah Vogel #2 of 4. (Historical) Journalist Hannah Vogel has vowed to never again set foot in her homeland of Germany while the Nazis are still in power. She has good reason: three years ago in 1931, she kidnapped her son, Anton, from the man claiming to be his father–Ernst Rohm, head of the Nazis' SA. A powerful man not to be trifled with, Hannah knows that Rohm will never stop searching for them. 1/3

470. **Cantrell, Rebecca**, *A is for Actress*, MMP, 2015. Malibu #1 of 5. (Cozy) After a decade spent in the glare of the Hollywood spotlight as the star of kids' TV show Half Pint Detective, Sofia Salgado has had enough. Desperate to build a life outside showbiz, she quits acting to do something that everyone around her– including her family – thinks is plain nuts. Get a real job. –gay best friend (MLM). 1/3

471. **Cantrell, Rebecca, & Black, Sean**, *B is for Bad Girls,* Createspace, 2015. Malibu #2 of 5. (Cozy) Maloney Investigation's newest private detective, Sofia Salgado, is back on the case that turns into her

mother's worst nightmare when she ends up undercover in one of Malibu's many rehab clinics. 1/3

472. **Cantrell, Rebecca, & Black, Sean,** *C is for Coochy,* Createspace, 2016. Malibu #3 of 5. (Cozy) Maloney Investigations are drafted in to help thirteen-year-old Daniel find his birth father. There's only one snag. According to Daniel's mom, former Los Angeles party girl, Candy, there's more than one candidate. 1/3

473. **Cantrell, Rebecca, & Black, Sean,** *D is for Drunk,* Createspace, 2016. Malibu #4 of 5. (Cozy) Maloney Investigation's new client? An eccentric vineyard owner convinced his even more eccentric neighbor is siphoning off his precious water. But of course, it's not as simple as that. Or as dignified. 1/3

474. **Cantrell, Rebecca, & Black, Sean,** *E is for Exposed,* Createspace, 2017. Malibu #5 of 5. (Cozy) Sofia Salgado's latest case at Maloney Investigations has some pretty tempting ingredients: blackmail, male strippers, and whipped cream. When a friend of Sofia's mom finds herself the victim of blackmail, stuffy Aidan has to go undercover as an exotic dancer, much to Sofia's delight. *–F is for Fred* is to be released in 2019 (MLM). 1/3

475. **Cape, Tony,** *Cambridge Theorem,* Doubleday, 1989. (Police Procedural) When Simon Bowles commits suicide, no one is surprised. After all, Bowles a graduate student in mathematics at Cambridge University had a long, well-documented history of depression. But as Detective Sergeant Derek Smailes soon discovers, he also had a passion for investigating historical mysteries and an extraordinary knack for solving them. His most recent project: uncovering the identity of the fabled fifth man in the notorious Cambridge spy-ring of the 1930s. Could Bowles possibly have solved that mystery? And could his solution, his theorem have brought about his death? –several gay men populate this book (MLM). 2/3

476. **Cappell, Ian,** *Murder at the Queen's Haven,* Lulu Self-Publishing, 1998 (Unknown due to a lack of copyright or title page). (Pulp) "Police inspector Havealot More conducts his investigation into a double murder at a gay hotel mostly out of sight, while the hotel guests, staff, and his assistants engage in nonstop sex in a whodunit (Gunn)." 3/3

477. **Carey, Kevin,** *Our Little Secret,* 1st Books, 2003. (Espionage) The culmination of all of his efforts is realized as Geoffrey Brooks is sworn in by the Chief Justice of the United States. The journey is far from over as Geoffrey takes us back with him to witness innocence betrayed, childhood violated. He must exorcise twin demons of overpowering Fear and Guilt at the same time he comes to terms with his homosexuality and its implications for a Special Opera-

tions Agent in the National Security Agency. The pain is real...So too is the catharsis...In the end, there is life and love. -Updated in 2010 as Kevin Carey-Infante- As Geoffrey Brooks realizes a dream as an operative for the NSA, he reflects on the winding trail that led him to this place. What is revealed is a dark and dangerous world of child abuse, rape, murder, the loss of childhood innocence, and the ensuing cover up that will forever haunt Geoffrey. With a dream of being something more, Geoffrey must plunge forward into the icy depths of the unknown. 3/3

478. **Carlisle, Kate,** *Homicide in Hardcover,* Obsidian, 2009. Bibliophile #1 of 13. (Cozy/ Bibliomystery) The streets of San Francisco would be lined with hardcovers if rare book expert Brooklyn Wainwright had her way. And her mentor wouldn't be lying in a pool of his own blood on the eve of a celebration for his latest book restoration. With his final breath he leaves Brooklyn a cryptic message and gives her a priceless and supposedly cursed copy of Goethe's *Faust* for safekeeping. Brooklyn suddenly finds herself accused of murder and theft, thanks to the humorless, but attractive, British security officer who finds her kneeling over the body. Now she has to read the clues left behind by her mentor if she is going to restore justice. –Ian McCullough, gay ex-boyfriend of Brooklyn Wainwright plays a small role in this cozy bibliomystery series (MLM). 1/3

479. **Carlisle, Kate,** *If Books Could Kill,* Berkley, 2010. Bibliophile #2 of 13. (Cozy/ Bibliomystery) Book restoration expert Brooklyn Wainwright is attending the world-renowned Edinburgh Book Fair when her ex Kyle shows up with a bombshell. He has an original copy of a scandalous text that could change history–and humiliate the beloved British monarchy. When Kyle turns up dead, the police are convinced Brooklyn's the culprit. But with an entire convention of suspects, Brooklyn's conducting her own investigation to find out if the motive for murder was a 200-year-old secret–or something much more personal. 1/3

480. **Carlisle, Kate,** *The Lies that Bind,* New American Library/Penguin Publishing Group, 2010. Bibliophile #3 of 13. (Cozy/Bibliomystery) Book restoration expert Brooklyn Wainwright returns home to San Francisco to teach a bookbinding class. Unfortunately, the program director Layla Fontaine is a horrendous host who pitches fits and lords over her subordinates. But when Layla is found shot dead, Brooklyn is bound and determined to investigate–even as the killer tries to close the book on her for good. 1/3

481. **Carlisle, Kate,** *Murder Under Cover,* New American Library, 2011. Bibliophile #4 of 13. (Cozy/Bibliomystery) When she receives an exquisite copy of the Kama Sutra from her best friend Robin to appraise and restore, Brooklyn Wainwright anticipates both recreat-

ing a beautiful book *and* spicing up her love life. But then Robin's apartment is ransacked, and the great guy she recently met is murdered in her bed. Now Robin is the #1 suspect. Obviously, exploring the Kama Sutra's bliss will have to wait until after Brooklyn finds the killer... –short story *Pages of Sin*, listed as book #4.5 out of 13 in the series, available as an e-book only published by Penguin Group in 2012 (MLM). 1/3

482. **Carlisle, Kate,** *One Book in the Grave,* New American Library, 2012. Bibliophile #5 of 13. (Cozy/Bibliomystery) There may be grave consequences for bookbinder Brooklyn Wainwright as she attempts to solve two murders tied to one book... Brooklyn's chance to restore a rare first edition of *Beauty and the Beast* seems a fairy tale come true–until she realizes the book belonged to an old friend of hers. Ten years ago, Max Adams, a brawny renowned papermaker, fell in love with a stunning beauty, Emily, and gave her the copy of *Beauty and the Beast* as a symbol of their love. Soon afterward, he died in a car crash, and Brooklyn has always suspected his possessive ex-girlfriend and her jealous beau. Now she decides to find out who sold the book and return it to its rightful owner–Emily. She believes a rare book dealer can assist her, but when she arrives at his shop, she finds him murdered. Is it possible that the same couple who may have killed Max are now after his edition of *Beauty and the Beast*? With the help of her handsome boyfriend, Derek Stone, Brooklyn must unravel the murder plot–before she ends up in a plot herself.... 1/3

483. **Carlisle, Kate,** *Peril in Paperback,* New American Library/Penguin Group, 2012. Bibliophile #6 of 12. (Cozy/Bibliomystery) Rare books and antiquities expert Brooklyn Wainwright is thrilled to be invited to the fiftieth birthday party of her neighbor Suzie's aunt Grace. A retired founder of a major video game corporation, Grace is a larger-than-life character who's turned her Lake Tahoe mansion into a fun house, full of everything from pinball machines and giant props to secret passageways and trap doors. Brooklyn is most excited to catalog Grace's extensive collection of rare paperback pulp fiction. Part of the fun involves a séance, but after the lights flicker, one guest is dead, poisoned by a cocktail intended for Grace. It seems someone is determined to turn Grace's playful palatial estate into a house of horrors. Brooklyn suspects the key to the killer's identity may lie in the *roman á clef* Grace has written about her life. With Grace in great peril, "must-read" takes on a whole new meaning, as Brooklyn tries to stop a murderer who's through playing around... 1/3

484. **Carlisle, Kate,** *A Cookbook Conspiracy,* New American Library, 2013. Bibliophile #7 of 13. (Cozy/Bibliomystery) It's a recipe for

disaster when bookbinder Brooklyn Wainwright is asked to restore an antique cookbook.... Brooklyn has always been a little obsessed with food, but it was her sister Savannah who became a chef, graduating from the prestigious Cordon Bleu culinary school in Paris. She and her classmates all went on to successful careers, but none of them achieved culinary superstardom, like Savannah's ex-boyfriend Baxter Cromwell. When Baxter invites the old gang to participate in his new restaurant's gala opening in San Francisco, Savannah looks forward to seeing her friends, and even asks Brooklyn to restore a tattered cookbook–an old gift from Baxter–as a present for him. But Brooklyn immediately recognizes that the book, which has strange notes and symbols scrawled in the margins, is at least two hundred years old. She thinks that it probably belongs in a museum, but Savannah insists on returning it to Baxter. Shortly after receiving the gift, Baxter is found dead, with Savannah kneeling over him, bloody knife in hand, and the rare cookbook has disappeared. Brooklyn knows her sister didn't kill him, and she suspects the missing cookbook might lead to the real villain. Now Brooklyn will have to turn up the heat on the investigation before Chef Savannah finds herself slinging hash in a prison cafeteria. 1/3

485. **Carlisle, Kate,** *The Book Stops Here,* Obsidian, 2014. Bibliophile #8 of 13. (Cozy/ Bibliomystery) Brooklyn Wainwright is thrilled to be appearing on the San Francisco edition of the hit TV show *This Old Attic* as a rare-book expert and appraiser. Her first subject is a very valuable first-edition copy of the classic children's story *The Secret Garden*, which is owned by a flower vendor named Vera. Once she hears what her book is worth, Vera is eager to have Brooklyn recondition it for resale. But after the episode airs, a furious man viciously accosts Brooklyn, claiming that Vera found the first edition at his garage sale, and he wants it back–or else. Brooklyn is relieved that she's put *The Secret Garden* in a safe place, but Randolph Rayburn, the handsome host of *This Old Attic*, is terrified by the man's threats. He confides in Brooklyn that he fears he is being stalked. He doesn't know who might have targeted him, or why. In the days that follow, several violent incidents occur on the set, and Brooklyn is almost killed, leaving both her and her security expert boyfriend, Derek, shaken. Is someone after Brooklyn and the book? Or has Randolph's stalker become more desperate? And then Brooklyn visits Vera's flower shop...and discovers her dead. Is the murderer one of the two obvious suspects, or is something more sinister–even bizarre–going on? Brooklyn had better find the clever killer soon or more than her chance at prime time may be canceled...permanently. 1/3

486. **Carlisle, Kate,** *Ripped from the Pages,* New American Library, 2015.

Bibliophile #9 of 13. (Cozy/Bibliomystery) Excited to explore the secrets of wine country, Brooklyn attends an excavation of the caves hidden deep under her parents' commune–and the findings are explosive. A room is unearthed, and it contains a treasure trove of artwork, rare books, a chest of jewelry...and a perfectly mummified body. A closer examination of the murdered man's possessions reveals a valuable first edition of Jules Verne's *A Journey to the Center of the Earth*. Hidden in the book is a secret map that unveils an even greater hoard of treasures brought to California by French winemakers fleeing the Nazi invasion with the commune leader's grandfather, Anton, among them. As reporters and art appraisers flock to Sonoma to see the precious bounty, questions begin to rise–did Anton hide these items to protect them, or did he steal them for himself? Who is the mysterious man left for dead inside the cave? But not all crime is buried in the past. When a new presence threatens the town's peace, Brooklyn decides to do a little excavating of her own and solve the mystery of the treasure before anyone else is written off.... 1/3

487. **Carlisle, Kate,** *Books of a Feather,* New American Library, 2016. Bibliophile #10 of 13. (Cozy/Bibliomystery) Brooklyn's friend Ian runs the Covington Library, which is hosting an exhibit featuring John James Audubon's massive masterpiece, *Birds of America*, currently on loan from an Arab sheik. During the gala celebrating the book, she is approached by Jared Mulrooney, the president of the National Birdwatchers Society, who urgently needs Brooklyn's skilled hands to repair a less high-profile book of Audubon drawings that's fallen victim to spilled wine. At the same party, Brooklyn is flying high after she's asked to refurbish and appraise a rare copy of *Poor Richard's Almanac*. But everything runs afoul later that evening when Mulrooney's body is discovered in the library. Rumors fly about a motive for murder. Perhaps Mulrooney wanted to sink his claws into the pricey Audubon book, but Brooklyn believes the man died fighting off a daring thief. Soon more troubles ruffle Brooklyn's feathers. Her parents pop in for a visit with an unsavory friend in tow, and there's a strange man on her tail. With danger beginning to circle Brooklyn's every move, it's clear she must find answers before things really go south ... 1/3

488. **Carlisle, Kate,** *Once Upon a Spine,* Berkley/Penguin Random House, 2017. Bibliophile #11 of 13. (Cozy/Bibliomystery) Brooklyn's future in-laws are traveling from England to meet her, and if that's not enough to set her on edge, rumors abound that the charming Courtyard Shops across the street may be replaced by high-rise apartments. Their trendy neighborhood will be ruined unless Brooklyn and her fiancé, Derek Stone, can persuade the shopkeepers not

to sell. But with a rare edition of *Alice in Wonderland* causing bad blood at the Brothers Bookshop and a string of petty vandalism making everyone nervous, Brooklyn and Derek feel overwhelmed. Then the owner of the Rabbit Hole juice bar is felled by his own heavy shelves, and the local cobbler lies dead beside him. Things get curiouser and curiouser when a second priceless copy of *Alice* is discovered. As the Brits descend, Brooklyn learns they're not so stuffy after all. Derek's dad is won over with chocolate cream pie, and his psychic mum would *kill* to help Brooklyn solve this murder– before another victim takes a tumble. 1/3

489. **Carlisle, Kate,** *Buried in Books,* Berkley, 2018. Bibliophile #12 of 13. (Cozy/ Bibliomystery) Brooklyn has done everything she can to prepare for her nuptials with Derek and simply can't wait to start her new life with him. But things don't go as planned when Brooklyn's former college friends, Heather and Sara, show up at her bridal shower. Brooklyn is touched, however, when each woman gifts her a rare first edition: *The Blue Fairy Book* and *The Three Musketeers*, respectively. When one of them is found murdered and one of the rare books is deemed a forgery, Brooklyn can't help but wonder if the victim played a part in this fraud or if a murderer is still out there scamming and killing. Wedding jitters, counterfeit books, and a killer on the loose could ruin Brooklyn and Derek's big day. Can they make it down the aisle before more bodies start stacking up? – #13 of the Bibliophile Mystery series, *The Book Supremacy,* will be released in June of 2019. 1/3

490. **Carlson, Kim,** *Breakfast in Bedlam,* GMP, 1991. (Scifi Gothic) A surreal landscape of gothic horror and lust; a black comedy with a psychological hard-on. Whatever your fantasy or depravity, from the prosaic to the absurd, this machine will generate the experience, providing life-like data, total sensory attack and full lubrication. 3/3

491. **Carney, T. Lawton,** *Sam Markum and the Palm Springs Predators,* Kindle, 2018. Sam Markum #3 of 3. (Hard Boiled) No description or blurb listed yet and the next two books are set to be released in 2019 (MLM). 3/3

492. **Carney, William,** *Rose Exterminator*, Everest House, 1982. (Pulp) "Museum curator Scotty, attempts to find out why his former lover, plastic surgeon and S/M master Dr. Glenn Symonds is bizarrely castrated and killed which steers him to increasing revelations about Symond's life and involvement in S/M sex (Gunn)." 3/3

493. **Carpenter, Adam,** *Wonderland,* Ravenous, 2009. Wonderland #1 of 3. (Thriller) Prodigal son Rich North and his partner, Marc Anderson, have just relocated to Wonderland after leaving behind

their lives-and a secret scandal-back in New York City. They buy a house on exclusive Eldon Court, where five Victorian homes stand. Three other gay couples lives in the other houses, while Number Two Eldon Court remains mysteriously empty. There they meet Edgar and Jack, the longest-tenured residents of Eldon Court; Aaron and Juan, a couple with their own relationship issues; and Sawyer and Dane, a young, gorgeous couple with too much money and time of their hands. –e-book only. Renamed *Desperate Husbands* and is published by MLR in 2018 (MLM). 3/3

494. **Carpenter, Adam**, *Desperate Lovers*, Ravenous, 2011. Wonderland #2 of 3. (Thriller) Welcome back for another sex-drenched episode in the continuing adventures of Wonderland. The drama on Eldon Court escalates as the "Desperate Husbands" fight for their lives and their loves, all while they indulge passions both desired and forbidden. –e-book only (MLM). 3/3

495. **Carpenter, Adam**, *Desperate Enemies*, Ravenous, 2011. Wonderland #3 of 3. (Thriller) When Rich North and Marc Anderson moved to the idyllic coastal town of Wonderland, they never envisioned they would soon be fighting for their futures. But when the twisted Danvers Converse threatened to take Eldon Court away from them-and their fellow "Desperate Husbands"-they realized they could only fight back by uncovering Wonderland's complex past. –e-book only (MLM). 3/3

496. **Carpenter, Adam**, *Hidden Identity*, MLR, 2014. PI Jimmy McSwain #1 of 6. (Hard Boiled) When Jimmy McSwain is hired to find missing heir Harris Rothschild, he finds that identities can be altered, and lives can be changed–or taken with the simple pull of the trigger. Jimmy McSwain is a New York City private detective, operating out of Hell's Kitchen, the rough and tumble neighborhood he grew up in. At age fourteen, he watched as his NYPD father was gunned down. Now, at age twenty-eight, gay, Jimmy has never given up the pursuit of whoever killed him. But a PI must make a living, and so he's taken on the case of missing heir Harris Rothschild, whose overbearing father doesn't approve of his "alternate" lifestyle. Tracking down Harris is easier than expected, but the carnage that follows isn't. With a shocking murder on his hands, and a threat coming from some unforeseen person. 3/3

497. **Carpenter, Adam**, *Crime Wave*, MLR, 2015. PI Jimmy McSwain #2 of 6. (Hard Boiled) Jimmy McSwain returns to help his sister's boyfriend fight a murder charge–and finds he may just have a lead on a cold case. Hell's Kitchen private investigator Jimmy McSwain returns in a twisting tale of past sins and present-day vengeance. Jimmy McSwain isn't thrilled about taking a case for free but when his sister fears her boyfriend, Rocky, is cheating on her, he has no

choice. But the case takes a deadly turn when Rocky is standing over the body of a man he was just seen kissing, and he's holding the gun. 3/3

498. **Carpenter, Adam**, *Stage Fright*, MLR, 2016. PI Jimmy McSwain #3 of 6. (Hard Boiled) The Harold Calloway Theatre on West 47th Street is home to the new play Triskaidekaphobia, and its playwright has been receiving threatening messages. Theatre owner and lead producer Wellington Calloway has hired Jimmy to investigate, but it's a case not without its complications. 3/3

499. **Carpenter, Adam**, *Guardian Angel*, MLR, 2017. PI Jimmy McSwain #4 of 6. (Hard Boiled) Winter is nearly upon Manhattan, the holidays right around the corner. Jimmy is hired to escort the infamous tabloid favorite Serena Carson to a charity benefit, intent on guarding her from an abusive ex. Yet the job takes a brutal turn as Henderson Carlyle, the privileged, spoiled lothario, is found sliced to death outside of Serena's brownstone. 3/3

500. **Carpenter, Adam**, *Forever Haunt*, MLR, 2018. PI Jimmy McSwain #5 of 6. (Hard Boiled) Hell's Kitchen private detective Jimmy McSwain, his father's death has defined him, defied him, and denied him his chance at happiness. But the shooting death of a young officer named Denson Luke has re-ignited the investigation into the mysterious Blue Death conspiracy. Jimmy still must earn a living, so he cannot ignore a family in distress. –*Fresh Kill*, the sixth installment of the PI Jimmy McSwain series is expected to be released by MLR in 2019 (MLM). 3/3

501. **Carpenter, Adam**, *Scandalous Lies*, MLR, 2018. Canes Inlet #1 of 3. (MM Amateur Sleuth) In a tiny Adirondack village, a secret is about to be exposed. Noah Sanders learns from his mother on her deathbed that he is not who he thought. Suddenly, the unassuming Noah finds his entire life called into question, and only he can separate the truth from the lies. He'd been given one clue: his real name. But what is the reason for his abduction from the family he should have known. The coastal paradise called Cane's Inlet is where Noah finds himself, trying to keep a low profile as he quietly begins his investigation. But Demetri, a sexy diner owner, catches his attention almost immediately, as does the local police chief when Noah stumbles across a corpse on the beach. Cane's Inlet is known for its sunny shores, the lush waves of the ocean. But a deeper mystery lies beneath the surface, and Noah is the unwitting key to unraveling a long-held truth. Insinuating himself into the ways of the locals, Noah learns of the feud between the founding family, the Canes, and to the rich newcomers, the Hatchers. With no one to trust, Noah tries to fight his attraction to Demetri, all while desperately trying to keep secret his reason for coming to town. 3/3

502. **Carpenter, Adam,** *Sinister Motives*, MLR, 2018. Cane's Inlet #2 of 3. (MM Amateur Sleuth) In Cane's Inlet, located on a barrier peninsula along the Jersey Shore, the lucrative summer season is fast-approaching, as is the Opening Night celebration of the Medusa Lounge, where Noah has secured a job. But working alongside the Hatcher's at their exclusive resort is complicated by his own investigation into the scandal that might connect them. With a family secret uncovered during a surreptitious visit to their mansion, Noah's quest to seek the truth behind his mother's deathbed confession takes on sudden credence. With the aid of his new lover, Demetri, as well as Cane's Inlet busybody Cilla Cane, the questions only deepen. When another murder shocks the coastal village, Noah realizes that what's happening no longer concerns only himself, but perhaps all of Cane's Inlet. With a mystery dating back to the village's founding and the raising of the old pirate ship Medusa, no one is safe from being exposed, or from a desperate killer. For Noah, the truth might come at a price higher than he's willing to accept. 3/3

503. **Carpenter, Adam,** *Suspicious Truths,* MLR, 2018. Cane's Inlet #3 of 3. (MM Amateur Sleuth) In Cane's Inlet, located on a barrier peninsula along the Jersey Shore, the lucrative summer season is just two weeks away, with Hatcher's Resort its most-desired attraction, including the newly opened Medusa Lounge. But drama ensued onboard the restored pirate ship, leaving Noah determined to leave Cane's Inlet behind. A killer has another idea, and soon Noah knows there is no escape. Living behind enemy lines, Noah realizes he must finally confront Ginette and Emerson Hatcher about the truth he's been hiding from them all these months. But then the killer strikes again, making Noah's investigation even more personal. 3/3

504. **Carpenter, Carleton**, *Games Murderers Play*, Curtis, 1973. (Amateur Sleuth) New York actor Joseph Cooper discovers the corpse of his murdered female lover. –bisexual main character (MLM). 3/3

505. **Carpenter, Carleton**, *Only Her Hairdresser Knew*, Curtis, 1973. Chet Long #1 of 3. (Amateur Sleuth) Hairdresser Chet Long has a run in with the mafia. 3/3

506. **Carpenter, Carleton**, *Deadhead*, Curtis, 1974. Chet Long #2 of 3. (Amateur Sleuth) Hairdresser Chet Long is working with Broadway show people on a tryout in Boston. 3/3

507. **Carpenter, Carleton**, "The Bum Wrap," (1986), *Silver Screams: Murder Goes Hollywood*, ed. Cynthia Manson and Adam Stern, Longmeadow, 1994. Chet Long #3 of 3. (Amateur Sleuth) Hairdresser Chet Long is now set in Los Angeles. 3/3

508. **Carpenter, Carleton**, *Cat Got Your Tongue?*, Curtis, 1973. (Police Procedural) The house cat didn't like the new boy...it was found the next day with its throat cut. Old Henry made a chance, off-color remark about the boy. He was found hacked to pieces. People were getting suspicious of the new boy–but they were deathly afraid to ask. 3/3

509. **Carpenter, Carleton**, *Sleight of Hand*, Popular Library, 1975. (Amateur Sleuth) Jasper Wild knew all about actor Peter Dooley's meteoric rise in the showbiz heavens. But when he looked into the sensational new superstar's private life, Jasper discovered a hidden hell of compulsive desires and dirty little secrets. Dooley was the leading player in a X-rated drama of sin, blackmail and murder–and Jasper Wild had to find out which of his playmates was performing the role of killer before death rang down the curtain with one last show-stopping bang... –several gay secondary characters (MLM). 2/3

510. **Carr, Caleb**, *Alienist*, Bantam, 1994. Dr. Laszlo Kreizler #1 of 3. (Historical) The year is 1896. The city is New York. Newspaper reporter John Schuyler Moore is summoned by his friend Dr. Laszlo Kreizler–a psychologist, or "alienist"–to view the horribly mutilated body of an adolescent boy abandoned on the unfinished Williamsburg Bridge. From there the two embark on a revolutionary effort in criminology: creating a psychological profile of the perpetrator based on the details of his crimes. Their dangerous quest takes them into the tortured past and twisted mind of a murderer who will kill again before their hunt is over. –no main characters are gay, but the murderer is killing young male prostitutes (MLM). 1/3

511. **Carr, Glyn (Showell Styles 1908-2005)**, *Death of a Weirdy*, Geoffrey Bles, 1965. (Amateur Sleuth) Abercrombie Lewker #13 of 15. An English weirdy is killed while visiting Wales. –the killed man is suspected of being homosexual (MLM). 1/3

512. **Carson, Michael**, *Coming Up Roses*, Victor Gollancz, 1990. (Espionage) King Fadl gazes to the jewel-adorned map of his kingdom on the wall of his royal game cellar. Part of the adjoining Zibda lies on its territory and he wants to have it. King Fadl calls the impoverished Sultan of Zibda and makes him an offer that he cannot refuse. The Secret Service listens and discovers that uranium is in the ground in the controversial area. Charlie Hammond, a disgraced English secret agent, is sent out to collect information. He meets Trevor Armitage, an English teacher, who was attracted to a job in the Arab world after he, 25 years after all the others, had seen Lawrence of Arabia. The Ministry of Suppression of Morality and to promote the virtue decrees of the circumcision of all immigrants. 3/3

513. **Carson, Michael**, *Dying in Style*, Poolbeg, 1998. (Police Procedural) London police inspector Timothy Dyer faces the fact that he may be the final victim if he does not find a murderer who is killing in the same order and manner as in the novel written by Arthur Whitworth. 3/3

514. **Caspary, Vera (1899-1987)**, *A Chosen Sparrow*, Putnam, 1964. (Psychological) Lured by a dazzling facade of opulence into a life of utter decadence. She went to live a fairy tale, certain she would live happily ever after, blind to all the signs she was on the threshold of a monstrous nightmare. –two gay characters are represented as villains (MLM). 2/3

515. **Cassidy, Marsh**, *The Times of the Double Star*, Los Hombres, 1994. (YA Fantasy) Eighteen-year-old Cas' mother has died of leukemia and his father disappeared years earlier. The parents were physicists working on developing time travel. Now Cas is having strong dreams about another self somewhere back in time. His mother's boss tells him he has a twin who is stranded in an 1880's spacetime. Cas also learns his mother and father had gone back to 1950s spacetimes to try to prevent the testing of the atom bomb. Exposure to radiation is what finally led to his mother's death. Cas is determined to find his twin and his father who also may be stranded back in time. However, someone wants Cas to drop his search. If he doesn't, the person says, his life is at stake. 3/3

516. **Caudwell, Sarah (Sarah Cockburn)**, *Thus was Adonis Murdered*, Scribner, 1981. Hilary Timar #1 of 4. (Court Drama) Reduced to near penury by the iniquitous demands of the Inland Revenue, young barrister Julia Larwood spends the last of her savings on an Art Lovers holiday to Venice. But poor, romantic Julia - how could she possibly have guessed that the ravishing fellow Art Lover for whom she conceived a fatal passion was himself an employee of the Inland Revenue? Or that her hard-won night of passion with him would end in murder- with her inscribed copy of the current Finance Act subsequently discovered just a few feet away from the corpse... –gay triangle (MLM). 3/3

517. **Cavale, Tim**, *Nihon Noir*, Xlibris, 2000. (Police Procedural) "Anna Stoupe died of a concussion outside her apartment complex on a college campus near Hiroshima. Was it murder or the result of a fall? Supposedly there had been threatening notes and phone calls. New York PI Vinnie di Napoli arrives in the disguise of an English teacher (Gunn)." 3/3

518. **Chandler, Raymond**, *The Big Sleep*, Knopf, 1939. Philip Marlowe #1 of 7. (Hard Boiled) A dying millionaire hires private eye Philip Marlowe to handle the blackmailer of one of his two troublesome

daughters, and Marlowe finds himself involved with more than extortion. Kidnapping, pornography, seduction, and murder are just a few of the complications he gets caught up in. –several gay elements; suspicion that Marlowe is a closeted homosexual, Carol and Greiger were lovers, and Lundgren is a boytoy (MLM). 1/3

519. **Chandler, Raymond**, *Farewell, My Lovely*, Knopf, 1940. Philip Marlowe #2 of 7. (Hard Boiled) Marlowe's about to give up on a completely routine case when he finds himself in the wrong place at the right time to get caught up in a murder that leads to a ring of jewel thieves, another murder, a fortune-teller, a couple more murders, and more corruption than your average graveyard. –the only gay element is the suspicion that Marlowe is gay (MLM). 1/3

520. **Chandler, Raymond**, *Long Goodbye*, Mifflin, 1954. Philip Marlowe #6 of 7. (Hard Boild) Down-and-out drunk Terry Lennox has a problem: his millionaire wife is dead and he needs to get out of LA fast. So, he turns to the only friend he can trust: private investigator Philip Marlowe. Marlowe is willing to help a man down on his luck, but later Lennox commits suicide in Mexico and things start to turn nasty. Marlowe is drawn into a sordid crowd of adulterers and alcoholics in LA's Idle Valley, where the rich are suffering one big suntanned hangover. Marlowe is sure Lennox didn't kill his wife, but how many stiffs will turn up before he gets to the truth? –according to critic Michael Mason, *The Long Goodbye* is the closest we get to see Marlowe show overt homosexual feelings when he seems to fall in love with the dissolute Terry Lennox (MLM). 1/3

521. **Chaney, David**, *Hot on his Tail*, Surey, 1984. (Pulp) "Los Angeles police detective Brian Carlisle, 29, almost loses his life, as his partner and lover, Kevin Blakely, does to a serial killer because both "think with [their] cock" in a pulp inverted mystery (Gunn)." 3/3

522. **Chapman, Robin**, *Christoferus, or, Tom Kyd's Revenge*, Sinclair-Stevenson, 1993. (Historical Espionage) Set in England during the plague year of 1593. Queen Elizabeth's secret-service agents arrest a well-known playwright, Thomas Kyd, who is detained and tortured at her pleasure. Three days later he denounces his dear friend Christopher Marlowe as an atheist and sodomite. 3/3

523. **Charles, John**, *Scorned and Abandoned*, Manifest Vision, 2014. Aaron Jaycinth #1 of 2. (BDSM Suspense) New to the country, adapting to a personal security guard from Andrews Security, en route to his first UK soccer camp; his life was fantastic! Until a deranged kidnapper decided to sell Ethan as a sex slave. Aaron Jaycynth, an IT specialist for Andrews security, found himself tasked with finding Ethan's captor. His only lead - the email sent to Ethan's father. Desperate for help, Aaron is teamed up with Declan Kinersley, from

MI5. –available as an e-book only (MLM). 3/3

524. **Charles, John,** *One Breath Brings Death,* Manifest Vision, 2015. Aaron Jaycinth #2 of 2. (BDSM Suspense) Someone is systematically targeting the directors of Remedcon Pharmaceuticals. Gillert Taylor's car explodes, Ian Fachan's house bursts into flames, a deadly smoke bomb floods the Remedcon lobby in thick black clouds. While investigating the Remedcon arsons, Aaron finds himself at a crossroad in his personal life, when a former colleague wants to become his submissive. Aaron is dragged into the dark side of the BDSM world of torture, pain and domination as they investigate the fantasy world his sub desires. –available as an e-book only (MLM). 3/3

525. **Charles, John,** *Zero Warning,* Manifest, 2018. Asher Radman: By the Numbers #0 of 1. (MM Police Procedural) It took almost five years, but Mateo not only infiltrated the consortium, he was elevated to the prestigious inner circle. From his vantage point, he provided enough evidence to bring down Demarco Sanchez the head of the Proveedores as well as over a dozen high level members. For decades, Sanchez was the target of every agency in the US. He had his fingers in everything from drugs, to contraband, to counterfeit designer handbags. But they never could gain enough evidence to arrest him. With Mateo's testimony, he received multiple life sentences. He would never see the light of day again. When henchman Abraham Garceau was sentenced for multiple counts of murder, he swore he'd find a way to torture Mateo until he begged to die. Eight years later, Mateo had a new name, new career, and new life. In those eight years, he never stopped looking over his shoulder, never let his defenses slip, and never got close to anyone until he met Isaac Konners. –available as an e-book only (MLM). 3/3

526. **Charles, John,** *11 Seconds,* Manifest, 2018. Asher Radman: By the Numbers #1 of 1. (MM Cyberthriller) He wanted more than revenge. His was a vendetta, a vendetta that he was capable of carrying out. Tenodod was a cyber hacker who knew how to use the skills he developed while working for one of the most powerful systems developers in the world. Only now, he was using those talents to bring down Bertram Lynnworth, Chairman and CEO of ESTG, and would continue until his vendetta was fulfilled, no matter who got hurt in the process.*We Own You* appeared on every monitor in every ESTG facility around the world. *There Is No Escape* voiced the laughing clown as Tenodod took over every system within the company. Tenodod would make Bertram crawl for what he did to all those innocent people. Unfortunately, Marc Lynnworth, Bertram's unsuspecting son, and hundreds of others, would become pawns in Tenodod's evil plot. "I never wanted anyone to die; I only wanted your

father to see the error of his ways." A suspenseful, mind-piercing look into the very real secrets of cyber terrorism. –available as an e-book only (MLM). 3/3

527. **Charles, K. J.,** *The Magpie Lord,* Samhain, 2013. Charm of Magpies #1 of 3. (MM Fantasy) Exiled to China for twenty years, Lucien Vaudrey never planned to return to England. But with the mysterious deaths of his father and brother, it seems the new Lord Crane has inherited an earldom. He's also inherited his family's enemies. He needs magical assistance, fast. He doesn't expect it to turn up angry. 3/3

528. **Charles, K. J.,** *A Case of Possession,* Samhain, 2014. Charm of Magpies #2 of 3. (MM Fantasy) Lord Crane has never had a lover quite as elusive as Stephen Day. He knows Stephen's job as justiciar requires secrecy, but the magician is doing his disappearing act more than seems reasonable–especially since Crane will soon return to his home in China. When a blackmailer threatens to expose their illicit relationship, there's only one thing stopping Crane from leaving the country he loathes: Stephen. 3/3

529. **Charles, K. J.,** *Flight of Magpies,* Samhain, 2014. Charm of Magpies #3 of 3. (MM Fantasy) With the justiciary understaffed, a series of horrifying occult murders to be investigated, and a young student flying off the rails, magical law enforcer Stephen Day is under increasing stress. And the strain is starting to show in his relationship with his aristocratic lover, Lord Crane. 3/3

530. **Charles, K. J.,** *Think of England,* Samhain, 2015. Think of England #1 of 2. (MM Historical) England, 1904. Two years ago, Captain Archie Curtis lost his friends, fingers, and future to a terrible military accident. Alone, purposeless and angry, Curtis is determined to discover if he and his comrades were the victims of fate, or of sabotage. Curtis's search takes him to an isolated, ultra-modern country house, where he meets and instantly clashes with fellow guest Daniel da Silva. Effete, decadent, foreign, and all-too-obviously queer, the sophisticated poet is everything the straightforward British officer fears and distrusts. As the house party's elegant facade cracks to reveal treachery, blackmail and murder, Curtis finds himself needing clever, dark-eyed Daniel. –second book, *Proper English*, is set to be released in 2019 with lesbian main characters (MLM). 3/3

531. **Chrispie, Hagatha,** *Holly Daze @ Home: The Truth Will Out*, Kindle, 2014. Murder's a Drag #1 of 2. (MM Cozy) Hollister Daily has a secret. Weekdays, he's a mild-mannered bookkeeper who keeps up with everybody's business but keeps his own business secret from the small Southern town where he lives. Weekends, he's Holly Daze,

female impersonator extraordinaire, who performs every Saturday night at an exclusive, members-only Cabaret in Atlanta. Hollister had his life neatly separated and well-ordered until the day his dear friend was found murdered on his own front lawn. –available as an e-book only (MLM). 3/3

532. **Chrispie, Hagatha**, *Holly Daze @ the Theater–The Ghost Light's Out*, Kindle, 2015. Murder's a Drag #2 of 2. (MM Cozy) Hollister Daily has a mission. It's been his mission since his best friend's father gave him the task: Keep Fitzie out of trouble! Sometimes, that's easier said than done. When Fitzie gets a bee in her bonnet to turn an old furniture store downtown into a theatre, Hollie, Miss Minnie and the gang are all behind her. Fitzie is the guiding light during the building's renovations and agrees to star in the musical that will open the place to the public. It's all Hollie can do to keep up with her – until she disappears. –available as an e-book only (MLM). 3/3

533. **Christi, B. F.**, *Jerry's First Love*, 5 vols., Star, 1987-1988 (blank title and copyright pages).(Pulp) "Amateur sleuth Jerry Manino, 18, the narrator, high school student, mystery reader, and assistant to Great Detective (Tec), is an enthusiastic apprentice in a pulp series of parodies (Gunn)" based on Doyle's Sherlock Holmes, Edgar Allan Poe's Auguste Dupin, Biggers' Charlie Chan, and Georges Simenon's Maigret (MLM). 3/3

534. **Christi, B. F.**, *Burger Buns*, Star, 1989. (Pulp) "Twin Cities, Minnesota, bakery deliverer Enrico (Rick) Montoy has a lot of sexual fun...to discover who is stealing burger buns from his truck in a pulp crime story (Gunn)." 3/3

535. **Christian, M.**, *The Very Bloody Marys*, Haworth, 2007. (Paranormal) Can San Francisco survive a marauding gang of Vespa-riding vampires? Before it's sucked dry, the city's only hope may be Valentino, who's only a trainee for the supernatural law enforcement agency, Le Counseil Carmin. Swept up in the whole blood-sucking business when his mentor goes missing, Valentino is called upon to deal with the menace of these "Bloody Marys." But Valentino soon realizes that, in order to dispose of the gang, he must go into areas he never dreamed of, deal with some very strange characters and learn the truth about the dark side of town. 3/3

536. **Christian, M.**, *Finger's Breath*, Zumaya, 2011. (Horror) The city is terrified. Someone is haunting the streets of near-future San Francisco, drugging queer men and amputating the tip of their little finger. But worse than this is how the terror transforms the men of the city. For what's worse–a monster, or that something can, all too easily, turn any of us into something even more horrific? 3/3

537. **Christie, Agatha**, *The Moving Finger*, Dodd, Mead, 1942. Miss Marple #3 of 13. (British Cozy) The placid village of Lymstock seems the perfect place for Jerry Burton to recuperate from his accident under the care of his sister, Joanna. But soon a series of vicious poison-pen letters destroys the village's quiet charm, eventually causing one recipient to commit suicide. The vicar, the doctor, the servants–all are on the verge of accusing one another when help arrives from an unexpected quarter. The vicar's houseguest happens to be none other than Jane Marple. –gay element is a retired antiquarian who is a "confirmed bachelor" (MLM). 1/3

538. **Church, Christopher**, *Signs Point to Yes*, Dagmar Muira, 2014. Mason #1 of 10. (Paranormal) After quitting his dead-end job, Mason enacts his dream of becoming a psychic investigator, despite skepticism from his boyfriend. Eluding sketchy Hollywood thugs, surviving his first lap dance, and paying close attention to his dreams, he manages to solve a few mysteries and surprise even himself with his psychic skills. 3/3

539. **Church, Christopher**, *THe Desert Rats*, Dagmar Muira, 2015. Mason #2 of8 10. (Paranormal) Strange things start to happen as soon as psychic investigator Mason and his boyfriend, Ned, and their roommate, Peggy, arrive in the high desert. An old friend sends him on a quest to identify an artifact found hidden among his dead father's possessions, and the journey brings him into contact with a series of odd characters–not least the enigmatic Laura, who's camping out on the desert but seems to be up to something else. 3/3

540. **Church, Christopher**, *Reach for the Sky*, Dagmar Muira, 2016. Mason #3 of 10. (Paranormal) A bougie addict and his wife hire Mason to hunt for buried loot, but he's not even sure it exists. His psychic insights lead him to an old building with a lot to hide, as well as trying to outwit a Freemason, and getting tangled up with a woman who claims to be rooting out corruption in local government–but why does she need a psychic to do that? Working undercover for her at city hall, he runs up against some vicious civil servants who will stop at nothing to protect the status quo. 3/3

541. **Church, Christopher**, *Billy Blood*, Dagmar Muira, 2016. Mason #4 of 10. (Paranormal) A fender-bender on the freeway gets psychic investigator Mason entangled with Catherine, an enigmatic visitor from DC–but who, exactly, does she work for? Trying to track her down, he runs across Billy Blood, a Los Angeles company that markets a stomach-churning "lifestyle drink" made with animal blood, and goes to work for its shady CEO to find out who has been vandalizing the product. 3/3

542. **Church, Christopher**, *Rubber-Band Ball*, Dagmar Muira, 2017.

Mason #5 of 10. (Paranormal) A metallurgist's desire for Mason to locate the earth energy points running under Los Angeles seems straightforward enough, but what is he planning to do with them once he knows where they are? A shady real estate transaction and a bizarre machine hidden in the backyard might reveal some answers. 3/3

543. **Church, Christopher,** *The Invisible Arrow,* Dagmar Muira, 2017. Mason #6 of 10. (Paranormal) When an old client sends psychic investigator Mason on a ghost hunt, he stumbles onto a research lab populated by strangely passive scientists with some remarkably advanced tech. Ingratiating himself with Annette, the director, by participating in the local town's folk festival as the Hunter, Mason scores a gig–to find Qualtrough, a scientist gone missing under mysterious circumstances. Equipped by the researchers with a new suit and a fat wad of cash, and using his burgeoning psychic powers, Mason sets out on his own to hunt for Qualtrough in the shadowy underworld of Los Angeles nightlife, tangling with drag queens, cops, and con artists and finding his voice in an unfamiliar world. 3/3

544. **Church, Christopher,** *Penstock Canyon,* Dagmar Muira, 2018. Mason #7 of 10. (Paranormal) Helping out Gilbert, a friend who's suffering from late-night visitations, psychic investigator Mason is confronted with aliens on the roof, and soon finds himself caught in a whirlwind of paranormal events. Liminal beings contract him to stop a very real land development project in Los Angeles, pitting him against ruthless and powerful forces. 3/3

545. **Church, Christopher,** *The Man from Grapalia,* Dagmar Muira, 2018. Mason #8 of 10. (Paranormal) When Etor shows up on the doorstep of the wealthy Whitby family claiming to be a long-lost relative, Henry, the scion of the Los Angeles dynasty, hires psychic investigator Mason to find out whether the interloper really did come from a parallel universe. 3/3

546. **Church, Christopher,** *The Mythical Blond,* Dagmar Muira, 2018. Mason #9 of 10. (Paranormal) Strange things happen in the desert Southwest. Hired to work a contract job at a remote military base in Nevada, psychic investigator Mason soon finds the Navy's real motivation for luring him there involves an old friend and her ratty jalopy. –a tenth book is set to be released in 2019 (MLM). 3/3

547. **Cicero, Kyle**, *The Case of the Choirboy Killer*, Nazca Plains, 2009. Mark Julian, Vampire PI #1 of 7. (Paranormal Hard Boiled) The city is being hit by a wave of killings where the victims share two things in common: 1) they are gay and, 2) they have been drained of blood. The press is having a field day using a witness' description to label

him as "the choirboy killer" and the gay community is up in arms. 3/3

548. **Cicero, Kyle**, *The Case of the Strega's Touch*, Nazca Plains, 2009. Mark Julian, Vampire PI #2 of 7. (Paranormal Hard Boiled) The crown prince of the werewolf clan has disappeared and Tortego, his vampire enemy on the city's supernatural governing body, is suspected. With a horrific werewolf vs. vampire civil war now looming the crafty Tortego has once more turned to Mark Julian for help in finding the lost prince. But Mark is knee deep in his own problems. After the first rushes of romance his relationship with the very human Detective Vinnie Pasquale is getting tricky. To complicate matters further Vinnie's mother has a personal request: find out who killed and mutilated her best friend's dog. With Jaime's itching to join in the cases will it all come out well in the end or, is war and a breakup on the horizons. 3/3

549. **Cicero, Kyle**, *The Case of the Heavenly Host*, Boner, 2009. Mark Julian, Vampire PI #3 of 7. (Paranormal Hard Boiled) It's a madhouse as Mark and Vinnie prepare for their wedding. Jaime is missing in action consumed with her quest to find "just the right forties' gown" for her own pending nuptials. Vinnie is stuck on a complex "secret" case and has no free time to help with any marriage planning. Mrs. Pasquale, Vinnie's mom, is locked in a battle of wills with an archbishop who won't let her priestly cousin bless, "any such unions". Worse, Tortego is offering to preside over the ceremony in his capacity as, "the leader of our vampire clan who is still an ordained priest you know"! But things really get crazy for Mark when an angelic messenger for the Heavenly Host approaches him. Dark forces are gathering, and Mark is called into action to find the missing sword of the Archangel Michael. As Mark begins his search he encounters two dark angels who take no prisoners. This time Mark Julian will face his worst crises, and, in the end, no one will ever be the same. 3/3

550. **Cicero, Kyle**, *The Case of the Vampire Hunter*, Nazca Plains, 2009. Mark Julian, Vampire PI #4 of 7. (Paranormal Hard Boiled) Vampires from around the globe are gathering in New York City to attend meetings of their worldwide Grand Council. Unfortunately, someone is methodically hunting the delegates and killing them. The undead community has given their host, Tortego, an ultimatum. Find the killer and stop the deaths or face a loss of his power. Despite putting his best vampires on the matter, all efforts have so far failed. In desperation the panicked vampire chief turns once more to Mark Julian for help. But this time that may not solve the problem. Since his last encounter with New York City's Detective Vinnie Pasquale, Mark Julian had become a drunken recluse who

had closed up his private eye offices. When Tortego approaches the newly sober Julian the P.I. agrees to seek out the deadly vampire hunter. The search is on but Jaime, his sex demon secretary, fears that the recently despondent Mark may not be fully up to the task and may wind up as the hunter's next victim. In the face of Mark's possible suicide mission will she step in with her fiancé's reluctant assistance? Will she call on Detective Vincent Pasquale to aid her in saving Mark Julian from a possible death? More importantly, how will he respond to her request? 3/3

551. **Cicero, Kyle**, *The Case No one Foretold,* Nazca Plains, 2010. Mark Julian, Vampire PI #5 of 7. (Paranormal Hard Boiled) Two men engage in an altercation in a movie lobby. Later one of the men turns up dead in a New York City alley. But this is no ordinary murder. The dead man is a sex demon and his fellow combatant was Jean-Claude Roué. Now the werewolf is accused of his murder and faces a trial by before a supernatural tribunal. 3/3

552. **Cicero, Kyle**, *The Case of the Thwarted Lovers,* Nazca Plains, 2010. Mark Julian, Vampire PI #6 of 7. (Paranormal Hard Boiled) It's been a long shift for Detective Vincent Pasquale. Back at his desk at the station he finds a phone message from his vampire spouse, Mark, waiting for him: "Listen our friend Dexter found something about who may have tried to frame Jean-Claude. Turns out that there is a lot more to this thing! It's big. Jean-Claude and Jaime are meeting me here before we all head over to see Tortego at his offices. We should be there in a half hour. If you can join us fine but if not, I'll tell you about it later after your shift is over. Call me." A few moments later a report comes into the station about a possible terrorist bomb explosion at a Midtown office building. No survivors are reported. To his horror Vinnie realizes the bombsite's address is the exact location of Tortego's offices. In a panic Vinnie rushes to the scene where, out of nowhere, he is shot from behind by an unknown assailant. Its' four funerals and a wedding as the newest Julian book unfolds. 3/3

553. **Cicero, Kyle**, *The Case with the Feminine Touch,* Nazca Plains, 2010. Mark Julian, Vampire PI #7 of 7. (Paranormal Hard Boiled) Werewolves assigned to New York City's supernatural security forces are being snatched while on patrols with their new vampire partners. Worse, these vampires are unable to explain to anyone how the events occurred. Jean-Claude, the new chief executive of the supernatural council, is stuck in the middle of this rising tension. He ordered these "mixed" patrols, yet now it seems to be going horribly wrong. 3/3

554. **Cicero, Kyle**, *Bound to Murder and Other Rough Tales,* Nazca Plains, 2007. (MM BDSM) A hot shot quarterback on his way to a feminine

date takes a shortcut through a deserted stadium tunnel to save time but when he interrupts a heavy sex scene between a sub and his master he finds himself unwillingly drafted as the new actor for a ticked off leather master. Two men learn the dangers of the internet as one becomes fascinated then overwhelmed into sexual slavery through a series of email exchanges while another stud revels in his cyber humiliation on cam before a viewer who in the end blows his mind. Straight cops and their submission. In this book we meet two: one a young rookie whose investigation of deviant sex takes its toll; another where an arresting officer gets a lesson in arrests from his prisoner. Join a military doctor as he collects some special military Berets and the studs who wear them or a swaggering homo-hating Olympic gold medal wrestler who loses his smug arrogance and his butt to a crew of weaker gay men on the mat. Take one rising sexy married young star in politics combine with a sexier lawyer and throw in a seductive hustler who loves rough sex. Add a dash of a nasty sex game gone awry and you have one dead, one arrested, and one fighting for a defense against a political establishment that wants to nail this closet door shut. A journey into homicide and politics coupled with hard-edged SM/SD sex that shows all three men that a walk into rough trade can be an experience that is "Bound to Murder!" 3/3

555. **Cicero, Kyle**, *Ace Lewis, International Agent: A hard man for a Hard Job*, Nazca Plains, 2008. (MM Espionage) In today's dangerous world of espionage and counterespionage, one man is known as the 'top' man in his field: Ace Lewis, International Agent. If the mission needs a hard man, he's the one the agency summons. An engagingly seductive lothario, he always gets the job done while getting the woman as well. But this time Ace may have trouble for the elusive arch criminal, the 'fat man', is on the prowl once more with a bizarre sexual scheme that will test the sexy good-looking agent's skills. 3/3

556. **Cicero, Kyle**, *The Rookie Cop and the Leather Master*, Createspace, 2018. (MM BDSM) A rookie cop finds more than he bargained for in a deserted former leather club. –only 39 pages available via ebook only (MLM). 3/3

557. **Clark, Rodd**, *Rubble and the Wreckage,* Driven, 2015. Gabriel Church #1 of 3. (MM Crime Drama) Gabriel Church knows you can't take a life without first understanding just how feeble it is. If you desire murder, you hold a life in your hand. Whether you release it to grant life or grip tighter to end it, it is at your command and discretion. Gabriel is a serial killer with a story to tell. Christian Maxwell studied abnormal psychology in college but chose instead to focus on a career in writing. His background comes in handy when

he thinks of writing about a serial killer. He can't think of anyone more qualified to write the story of Gabriel Lee Church and in the murderer's own words. It's been done before, but never with a killer who has yet to be captured or convicted. With nothing more than a gentleman's understanding between them, Christian records Gabriel's life story. Gabriel doesn't ask for his complicity, nor does he ask for his silence. Christian's interest in the man, though, is fast becoming something more than academic. When Christian and Gabriel become unexpected friends and then lovers, the question remains: What is Gabriel's endgame...and why does he want his story told? 3/3

558. **Clark, Rodd**, *Torn and Frayed*, Driven, 2016. Gabriel Church #2 of 3. (MM Crime Drama) Conscience isn't something all people are born with... Gabriel Church is a portrait in contrast. It would be easy to get lost in his pale-blue eyes, ache with the need to feel the strength of his masculine frame. He appears to be nothing but animal and instinct. The only people who know the full depth of that truth are dead, murdered, or two thousand miles away. Gabe is a serial killer, and for the first time in his life, he has more on his mind than his own survival. This time he is running from Seattle to protect the only person he thinks innocent in his laundry list of crime and murder: Christian Maxwell, his biographer and unexpected lover. Drawn to a place he never thought to return, Gabe finds new and different realities. Realities that insist he let go of his tragic past, those incredible perceptions of God, and his own divinity. He must open his eyes to what the love of a good man can do to heal a broken soul. 3/3

559. **Clark, Rodd**, *Ash and Cinders*, Driven, 2016. Gabriel Church #3 of 3. (MM Crime Drama) Christian Maxwell is resigned when Gabe tells him he's leaving Seattle to protect him, until the truth sinks in, and Chris realizes he may never see Gabe again. Reacting in anger, the two part with cold hostility instead of a warm and loving embrace. Deciding not to fight Chris's obvious disapproval, Gabe leaves anyway, heading south in his faithful Dodge pickup. Gabriel Church is a wanted man, and when he landed in Sonora, California, he believed it would be the first stop in his continuing journey. Road blind and far too weary to continue driving, he has no way of knowing he is about to run out of luck. 3/3

560. **Clark, Rodd**, *Short Ride to Hell*, Createspace, 2015. Brantley Colton #1 of 3. (MM Crime Drama) For Brantley Colton, his crusade was over. There was nothing in the abyss left for him. Whatever he had once believed in had become a lie. There was no light at the end of the tunnel, just a long highway ahead, a dark road without signposts to direct him. Where would he go from here? The finality in his soul

belied some joy in the closing moments. It was over, he could die now...but he couldn't die happy. It had only been a few hours since he had put the Winter Glade Motel in his rear-view, but it seemed longer. Colton drove the desolate highway but felt tired and needed sleep. The air conditioning was on high to fend off the humid Florida evening. The air against his face was the only thing preventing him from drifting into dangerous sleep; even so he contemplated the series of events that had him traveling down 1-75 in the middle of the night...with the blood stains of the murdered man still present on his shirt. He had used an alias to register at the motel, paid in cash but feared something had been left behind which could tie him to the murder. He needed time to finish the job at hand and his sloppy second-guessing had placed him in peril. Colton had never been one for prayer but felt like it was a good time to drop to his knees, to confess his crime and ask for forgiveness. Not that it would have done any good for him. 3/3

561. **Clark, Rodd**, *A Cache of Killers*, Createspace, 2014. Brantley Colton #2 of 3. (MM Crime Drama) Brantley Colton never set out to be anything but normal...but with tragedy came transformation. In his search for peace he is confronted with the darker aspects of men's souls and plagued by horrific murders at every turn. "Why does evil seem drawn to him like a wise virus contaminating his body?" In "A Cache of Killers" Colton runs across a ring of child abductors and killers and sets out to enact his own brand of justice...saving a life because his is so torn and tenuous. 3/3

562. **Clark, Rodd**, *No Place for the Wicked*, Createspace, 2014. Brantley Colton #3 of 3. (Crime Drama) Brantley Colton can't escape being drawn into another series of twisted murders after several naked bodies are unearthed, discarded like garbage. Finding the killer will be tough enough...but when he learns the culprit is a prominent State Senator from Maine, Colton realizes bringing him to justice will become his greatest challenge. He is swept into a sordid, sexual world of bondage and discipline, violence and pain only to discover that the evil in some men's souls is incomprehensible. 3/3

563. **Clary, Julian**, *Murder Most Fab*, Ebury, 2007. (Crime Caper) Hello, I'm Johnny Debonair and this is my book - Murder Most Fab. Buy it. You won't regret it. Everything that has happened so publicly is explained. Of course, I'd prefer it if you remember me as I was at my height, before the past caught up with me so spectacularly - TV's Mr. Friday Night with an enviable lifestyle and the nation at my feet. My fame might have looked easy to you at the time but getting to the top of the celebrity ladder is hard work. It took talent, beauty, commitment and, uniquely in my case, a number of unfortunate deaths. 3/3

564. **Clary, Julian,** *Devil in Disguise,* Ebury, 2009. (Modern Cozy) Simon is Molly's oldest, bitchiest, best friend. Since they high-kicked out of university, keen to taste life, Molly has become a jobbing musical theatre actress, while Simon is on the cusp of fame as his caustic, bitter alter-ego: Genita L'Warts, a drag queen with a talent for abusing audiences. Friendship, fame, and perhaps murder. 3/3

565. **Claxton, Crin,** *Scarlet Thirst,* Red Hot Diva, 2002. (Paranormal) Rani is initiated into the vampire lifestyle by the butch dyke Rob and then embarks on a hedonistic trip through a sex-fuelled underworld to bring more and more women into the life. For once, the lesbian vampire story is not just a metaphor: Scarlet Thirst is as explicit about sex as it is about biting into beautiful young necks. They're butch, they're femme, they're out for blood. –helps a gay, crossdressing vampire find out who killed his lover and who might be after him (MLM). 3/3

566. **Claxton, Crin,** *The Supernatural Detective,* Bold Stroke Books, 2013. Supernatural Detective #1 of 2. (Paranormal) When Tony Carson wakes to a pretty drag queen perched on her chest of drawers, she thinks she's dreaming. But it's Tony's powers that have awoken, and the ghosts just won't leave her alone. Struggling with the mystery surrounding the death of her father, attractive herbalist Maya Silva needs Tony more than she knows, and it's not just for her supernatural detecting. 2/3

567. **Claxton, Crin,** *Death's Doorway,* Bold Stroke Books, 2015. Supernatural Detective #2 of 2. (Paranormal) Death's door is open, as far as supernatural detective Tony Carson is concerned, and ghosts are flooding through it. Tony's got her hands full, but she's obsessed with why the prisoner from Holloway can't rest. Luckily, her trusty drag queen spirit guide is always ready with advice and insults. 2/3

568. **Cleeve, Brian,** *Vote X for Treason,* Random House, 1965. (Espionage) "British undercover agent, Anthony, disguised as a stereotypical hairdresser, does not identify himself to straight counterspy Sean Ryan until the neo-fascist group they have both infiltrated begins taking power in a political thriller (Gunn)." Reprinted as *Counterspy* in 1966 by Lancer (MLM). 1/3

569. **Clement, Blaze (1932-2011),** *Curiosity Killed the Cat Sitter,* Minotaur, 2006. Dixie Hemingway Mystery #1 of 11. (Cozy) Until three years ago, Dixie Hemingway was a deputy with the Sarasota County Sheriff's Department in southwest Florida. Then came a tragic accident. Now Dixie's a pet-sitter on Siesta Key, a lush, exotic barrier island where the people tend to be rich, suntanned, and tolerant of one another's quirks. As Dixie tried to get her life back in order,

pet-sitting is the perfect job. She goes into people's homes while they're gone and takes care of their pets; she likes the animals, they like her, and she doesn't have to deal with people very much. She especially does not have to be afraid that she'll run into a situation that will cause her to lose her hard-won composure. But when Dixie finds a man bizarrely drowned in a cat's water bowl, she is drawn into a tangled web of danger and secrets. Unbeknownst to Lieutenant Guidry, the homicide detective handling the murder, Dixie begins her own investigation into the whereabouts of the cat's owner, who has now vanished. –gay special investigator and husband are related to main character (MLM). 2/3

570. **Clement, Blaze**, *Duplicity Dogged the Dachshund*, Minotaur, 2007. Dixie Hemingway Mystery #2 of 11. (Cozy) Everybody who loves dachshunds knows about their adventurous streak. So when Mame, the elderly dachshund in Dixie Hemingway's care, gets away from her to investigate a mound of mulch, Dixie isn't surprised. What the dachshund digs up, however, is not only a surprise but triggers a set of jolting events that puts Dixie at the center of a hunt for a psychopathic killer, a killer who believes Dixie saw him leaving the scene of a brutal murder.... . 2/3

571. **Clement, Blaze**, *Even Cat Sitters Get the Blues*, Minotaur, 2008. Dixie Hemingway Mystery #3 of 11. (Cozy) Dixie has a knack for being in the wrong place at the wrong time. The day she happens upon the dead body outside a fancy mansion is no different. She's had her fill of homicide investigations, so she leaves the gate-keeper's corpse to be found by somebody else. Unfortunately, that somebody else sees Dixie leaving the scene of the crime, and the fatal bullet might have even come from her own gun! To make matters worse, the owner of the mansion is Dixie's new client–a scientist who is either a genius, insane, or both–whose pet iguana is under her charge. All that, plus a feisty calico kitten that needs some TLC, means that time is running out for Dixie to cat nip this case in the bud... and collar the killer. 2/3

572. **Clement, Blaze**, *Cat Sitter on a Hot Tin Roof*, Minotaur, 2009. Dixie Hemingway Mystery #4 of 11. (Cozy) When Dixie meets Laura Halston, a newcomer to Siesta Key, she recognizes a kindred spirit and believes she's found a new friend. Disarmingly beautiful, Laura confesses that she's in hiding from an abusive husband. Later, when Laura receives threatening phone calls, Dixie is certain the husband is the culprit. But the more Dixie learns about Laura, the less certain she is about anything...and then matters turn deadly. As she tries to understand Laura's past, Dixie is forced to acknowledge things about herself that she has never faced before. 2/3

573. **Clement, Blaze**, *Raining Cat Sitters and Dogs*, Minotaur, 2010. Dixie

Hemingway Mystery #5 of 11. (Cozy) Curiosity is always a killer for former police officer Dixie Hemingway. Even a trip to pick up her parrot at the veterinarian's office is bound to turn up something curious and the teenager Dixie meets in the waiting room is no exception. Jaz, as she calls herself, is inconsolable after her stepfather ran over a rabbit with his car. Really? Dixie's animal-like instinct tells her that something's not quite right about this Jaz–and she's going to make it her purr sonal business to find out more. Even if that means going on a wild-goose chase, from the pampered luxury of Siesta Key's exclusive resorts to the gang wars being fought in the back alleys, to ferret out the truth. And not get caught with her tail between her legs in the process... 2/3

574. **Clement, Blaze**, *Cat Sitter among the Pigeons*, Minotaur, 2011. Dixie Hemingway Mystery #6 of 11. (Cozy) Dixie, no relation to you-know-who, is helping an injured and cantankerous man take care of Cheddar, his orange shorthair cat. Soon Dixie finds herself totally smitten with the man's adorable infant great-granddaughter. But the baby's naive young mother has enough knowledge about certain powerful local big-money honchos to send them to prison for life, and they are willing to do anything, even kill her baby, to shut her up. Caught in the turmoil caused by the grandfather's prickly pride, the granddaughter's misguided plans to regain her young husband's respect by telling the truth in court, and the ruthless determination of wealthy villains to preserve their ill-gotten millions, Dixie is the only person who can rescue the baby. And she has to do it without letting law-enforcement people know – not even Lieutenant Guidry, with whom she has a new romantic relationship. 2/3

575. **Clement, Blaze**, *Cat Sitter's Pajamas*, Minotaur, 2012. Dixie Hemingway Mystery #7 of 11. (Cozy) Dixie Hemingway, no relation to you-know-who, accepts a job taking care of famous linebacker Cupcake Trillin's cats, Elvis and Lucy, while he's away. But what seems like an easy job turns scary when Dixie finds a celebrity fashion model in Cupcake's house. The woman refuses to leave AND she also claims to be Cupcake's wife. But Dixie has met Cupcake's wife, and this woman certainly isn't her. Soon, Dixie is spun into the world of counterfeit high fashion. When a valuable list of fake merchandise sellers goes missing, the criminals go after Dixie. Once again, what started as a simple cat-sitting job has turned into a mess that only Dixie can solve. 2/3

576. **Clement, Blaze**, *The Cat Sitter's Cradle*, Minotaur, 2013. Dixie Hemingway Mystery #8 of 11. (Cozy) No mission is im*paw*sible for pet sitter Dixie Hemingway (no relation to you-know-who). On an early morning walk, she spots an exotic bird rarely seen north of

the equator, much less in the sleepy beach-side town of Siesta Key, Florida. At first, Dixie thinks the bird has been blown off course by a terrible storm, but as she digs deeper into where the bird came from, Dixie becomes increasingly suspicious of its origins. When one client is found dead and a new friend and her baby disappear without warning, Dixie is pulled into a whirlwind of greed, deception, and danger. 2/3

577. **Clement, Blaze**, *The Cat Sitter's Nine Lives*, Minotaur, 2014. Dixie Hemingway Mystery #9 of 11. (Cozy) While driving along the beachside road that runs through the center of her hometown Dixie witnesses a terrible head-on collision. Ever the hero, she springs into action and pulls one of the drivers from his car just before it explodes in flames. A little shaken but none the worse for wear, Dixie proceeds to her local bookstore where she meets Cosmo, a fluffy, orange tomcat, and Mr. Hoskins, the store's kind but strangely befuddled owner. The next day the driver whose life she saved claims that he is Dixie's husband. Meanwhile, both Cosmo and Mr. Hoskins have disappeared without a trace, and a mysterious phone call from a new client lures her to a crumbling, abandoned mansion on the outskirts of town. Soon Dixie finds herself locked in a riddle of deception, revenge, murder, and mystery. 2/3

578. **Clement, Blaze**, *The Cat Sitter's Whiskers*, Minotaur, 2015. Dixie Hemingway Mystery #10 of 11. (Cozy) Her very first client of the morning is Barney Feldman, a Maine coon cat with a reputation for mischief who's guarding his vacationing owner's valuable collection of decidedly creepy antique masks. But someone's hiding in the house when she arrives, and they sneak up and knock her out cold. When the cops arrive at the house, there's just one problem: no one has broken in and nothing is missing. Searching for answers, Dixie soon finds herself hopelessly trapped in a murky world of black-market antiques, dark-hearted secrets, and murderous revenge... a mystery only she can solve. 2/3

579. **Clement, Blaze**, *The Cat Sitter and the Canary*, Minotaur, 2016. Dixie Hemingway Mystery #11 of 11. (Cozy) Despite a couple of bumps in the road (Franklin seems to be hiding in one of his favorite cubby holes, and Charlie scratches up the parlor door trying to get to the other side), everything else is perfectly normal. That is, until the next day, when Dixie discovers a dead body on the other side of that parlor door, along with a note that seems to suggest she had something to do with it. Soon, there's another victim, and then another note, and Dixie quickly finds herself caught in a maze of mystery and danger, where all the clues have her name written all over them, and where she must find the murderer... before he finds her. –Blaize Clement passed away in 2011 and the series had been

carried on by her son John Clement (MLM). 2/3

580. **Clinger, Rob**, *Luke Larkin: Private Detective–4 Gay Cases*, Paxtonian, 2008. (Soft Boiled) "PI Luke Larkin, 33, takes a personal as well as a professional interest in four lighthearted investigations (Gunn)." 3/3

581. **Clinger, R. W.**, *Skin Tour*, Starbooks, 2011. Gay Mafia #1 of 2. (MM Crime Drama) In the gay Mafia, pretty boys are more dangerous than their pistols. Derek Reed is just your average gay guy in Flamingo Cove, Florida. His days consist of running errands for numerous clients and occasionally having sex with the hot architect on the fourth floor in his apartment building. When sexy Rocco Malonni insists on questioning Derek about Fisk Devereaux, the local drug dealer and one of Derek's friends, all hell breaks loose in Derek's so-called average life. 3/3

582. **Clinger, R. W.**, *Skin Artist*, Starbooks, 2013. Gay Mafia #2 of 2. (MM Crime Drama) When Tang Meadow, the owner of the Skin Artist, a tattoo shop in downtown Flamingo Cove, Florida, shows up dead on a private beach, Derek and Rocco begin to unravel many valuable clues. 3/3

583. **Clinger, R. W.**, *Cutie Pie Must Die*, Bold Stroke Books, 2013. Murdock & Ward #1 of 2. (MM Amateur) Things aren't so cute lately in the village, though. When the body of Ben Pieney, the hunky all-star quarterback for the Violators, shows up murdered outside the door of Troy Murdock's hair salon, all hell breaks loose. –the second novel in the Murdock and Ward series, *Mechanics, Men, and Murder*, has yet to be released or have a release date (MLM). 3/3

584. **Clinger, R. W.**, *The Highwaymen*, JMS, 2014. (MM Paranormal Police Procedurals) Damian Truth is an FBI agent who, with the help of his deceased brother Andrew, is able to sketch crime scenes prior to the crimes occurring. 3/3

585. **Clinger, R. W.**, *The Highwaymen 2: Strange Love*, JMS, 2016. (MM Paranormal Police Procedural) What happened to the three fraternity brothers who disappeared from Roth College? Lovers and partners Damian Truth and Ridge Tyson take on the case, searching for two assumed killers associated with the brothers in the hopes of bringing them to justice. –available as an e-book only (MLM). 3/3

586. **Clinger, R. W.**, *Double Coverage*, JMS, 2014. (MM Journalism) Johnny Knight, photojournalist for the Independent, takes on one of the most dangerous jobs and responsibilities he has ever attempted. As he begins to unravel clues about the Helmet Killer murders, he uncovers a gambling ring involving numerous Viper players and a real estate mogul with a town full of secrets. And what about the miss-

ing money from the first victim, a whopping nine hundred thousand dollars? Is a Viper footballer paying off his steep gambling debts by murdering well-to-do officials? –available as an e-book only (MLM). 3/3

587. **Clinger, R. W.,** *Heat,* JMS, 2015. (MM Hard Boiled) Welcome to Hurricane Bay, Florida, where the act of arson isn't uncommon. When a popular gay bar, the Flaming Flamingo, burns to the ground with bartender Rudy inside, fear rocks the Gulf-side community. Bar owner Peter Rotunda wants to learn who destroyed his business and committed murder. Soon after the incident, Rotunda hires adorable and sexy private investigator Axle Dupree to take the case. –available as an e-book only (MLM). 3/3

588. **Cochrane, Charlie**, *Lessons in Love*, Linden Bay Romance, 2008. Cambridge Fellows #1 of 14. (MM Amateur Sleuth) St. Bride's College, Cambridge, England, 1905. When Jonty Stewart takes up a teaching post at the college where he studied, the handsome and outgoing young man acts as a catalyst for change within the archaic institution. He also has a catalytic effect on Orlando Coppersmith. Orlando is a brilliant, introverted mathematician with very little experience of life outside the college walls. He strikes up an alliance with the outgoing Jonty, and soon finds himself having feelings he's never experienced before. Before long their friendship blossoms into more than either man had hoped and they enter into a clandestine relationship. Their romance is complicated when a series of murders is discovered within St. Brides. All of the victims have one thing in common, a penchant for men. While acting as the eyes and ears for the police, a mixture of logic and luck leads them to a confrontation with the murderer can they survive it? 3/3

589. **Cochrane, Charlie**, *Lessons in Desire*, Linden Bay Romance, 2009. Cambridge Fellows #2 of 14. (MM Amateur Sleuth) With the recent series of college murders behind him, Cambridge Fellow Jonty Stewart is in desperate need of a break. A holiday on the beautiful Channel Island of Jersey seems ideal, if only he can persuade Orlando Coppersmith to leave the security of the college and come with him. Orlando is a quiet man who prefers academic life to venturing out into the world. Within the confines of their rooms at the university, it's easy to hide the fact that he and Jonty are far more than friends. But the desire to spend more time alone with the man he loves is an impossible lure to resist. When a brutal murder occurs at the hotel where they're staying, the two young men are once more drawn into the investigation. The race to catch the killer gets complicated by the victim's son, Ainslie, a man who seems to find Orlando too attractive to resist. Can Stewart and Coppersmith keep Ainslie at bay, keep their affair clandestine, and solve the crime? 3/3

590. **Cochrane, Charlie**, *Lessons in Discovery*, Linden Bay Romance, 2009. Cambridge Fellows #3 of 14. (MM Amateur Sleuth) On the very day Jonty Stewart proposes that he and Orlando Coppersmith move in together, Fate trips them up. Rather, it trips Orlando, sending him down a flight of stairs and leaving him with an injury that erases his memory. Instead of taking the next step in their relationship, they're back to square one. It's bad enough that Orlando doesn't remember being intimate with Jonty–he doesn't remember Jonty at all. Back inside the introverted, sexually innocent shell he inhabited before he met Jonty, Orlando is faced with two puzzles. Not only does he need to recover the lost pieces of his past, he's also been tasked by the Master to solve a four-hundred-year-old murder before the end of term. The college's reputation is riding on it. Crushed that his lover doesn't remember him, Jonty puts aside his grief to help decode old documents for clues to the murder. But a greater mystery remains–one involving the human heart. To solve it, Orlando must hear the truth about himself–even if it means he may not fall in love with Jonty the second time around... 3/3

591. **Cochrane, Charlie**, *Lessons in Power*, Samhain, 2009. Cambridge Fellows #4 of 14. (MM Amateur Sleuth) Cambridge, 1907: After settling in their new home, Cambridge dons Orlando Coppersmith and Jonty Stewart are looking forward to nothing more exciting than teaching their students and playing rugby. Their plans change when a friend asks their help to clear an old flame who stands accused of murder. Doing the right thing means Jonty and Orlando must leave the sheltering walls of St. Bride's to enter a labyrinth of suspects and suspicions, lies and anguish. Their investigation raises ghosts from Jonty's past when the murder victim turns out to be one of the men who sexually abused him at school. The trauma forces Jonty to withdraw behind a wall of painful memories. And Orlando fears he may forever lose the intimacy of his best friend and lover. When another one of Jonty's abusers is found dead, police suspicion falls on the Cambridge fellows themselves. Finding this murderer becomes a race to solve the crime...before it destroys Jonty's fragile state of mind. 3/3

592. **Cochrane, Charlie**, *Lessons in Temptation*, Samhain, 2009. Cambridge Fellows #5 of 14. (MM Amateur Sleuth) For friends and lovers Orlando Coppersmith and Jonty Stewart, a visit to Bath starts out full of promise. While Orlando assesses the value of some old manuscripts, Jonty plans to finish his book of sonnets. Nothing exciting...until they are asked to investigate the mysterious death of a prostitute. Then Orlando discovers that the famous curse of Macbeth extends far beyond the stage. It's bad enough that Jonty gets drawn into a local theatre's rehearsals of the play. The producer

is none other than Jimmy Harding, a friend from Jonty's university days who clearly finds his old pal irresistible. Worse, Jimmy makes sure Orlando knows it, posing the greatest threat so far to their happiness. With Jonty involved in the play, Orlando must do his sleuthing alone. Meanwhile, Jonty finds himself sorely tempted by Jimmy's undeniable allure. Even if Orlando solves the murder, his only reward could be burying his and Jonty's love in an early grave... 3/3

593. **Cochrane, Charlie,** *Lessons in Seduction,* Samhain, 2010. Cambridge Fellows #6 of 14. (MM Amateur Sleuth) The suspected murder of the king s ex-mistress is Cambridge dons Orlando Coppersmith and Jonty Stewart s most prestigious case yet. And the most challenging, since clues are as hard to come by as the killer s possible motive. At the hotel where the body was found, Orlando goes undercover as a professional dancing partner while Jonty checks in as a guest. It helps the investigation, but it also means limiting their communication to glances across the dance floor. It's sheer agony. A series of anonymous letters warns the sleuths they'll be sorry if they don't drop the investigation. When another murder follows, Jonty is convinced their involvement might have caused the victim s death. Yet they can't stop, for this second killing brings to light a wealth of hidden secrets. For Orlando, the letters pose a more personal threat. He worries that someone will blow his cover and discover their own deepest secret the intimate relationship he enjoys with Jonty could not only get them thrown out of Cambridge but arrested for indecency. 3/3

594. **Cochrane, Charlie,** *Lessons in Trust,* Samhain, 2010. Cambridge Fellows #7 of 14. (MM Amateur Sleuth) When Jonty Stewart and Orlando Coppersmith witness the suspicious death of a young man at the White City exhibition in London, they're keen to investigate-especially after the cause of death proves to be murder. But Police Inspector Redknapp refuses to let them help, even after they stumble onto clues to the dead man's identity. Orlando's own identity becomes the subject for speculation when, while mourning the death of his beloved grandmother, he learns that she kept secrets about her past. Desperate to discover the truth about his family, Orlando departs suddenly on a solo quest to track down his roots, leaving Jonty distraught. While Jonty frantically tries to locate his lover, Orlando wonders if he'll be able to find his real family before he goes mad. After uncovering more leads to the White City case, they must decide whether to risk further involvement. Because if either of them dares try to solve the murder, Inspector Redknapp could expose their illicit-and illegal-love affair. 3/3

595. **Cochrane, Charlie**, *All Lessons Learned,* Samhain, 2011. Cambridge

Fellows #8 of 14. (MM Amateur Sleuth) The Great War is over. Freed from a prisoner of war camp and back at St. Bride's College, Orlando Coppersmith is discovering what those years have cost. All he holds dear including his beloved Jonty Stewart, lost in combat. A commission to investigate a young officer s disappearance gives Orlando new direction temporarily. The deceptively simple case becomes a maze of conflicting stories is Daniel McNeil a deserter, or a hero? taking Orlando into the world of the shell-shocked and broken. And his sense of Jonty s absence becomes painfully acute. Especially when a brief spark of attraction for a Cambridge historian, instead of offering comfort, triggers overwhelming guilt. As he hovers on the brink of despair, a chance encounter on the French seafront at Cabourg brings new hope and unexpected joy. But the crushing aftereffects of war could destroy his second chance, leaving him more lost and alone than ever. 3/3

596. **Cochrane, Charlie**, *Lessons for Survivors*, Cheyenne, 2012. Cambridge Fellows #9 of 14. (MM Amateur Sleuth) Cambridge, September 1919 Orlando Coppersmith should be happy. WWI is almost a year in the past, he's back at St. Bride's College in Cambridge, he has his lover and best friend Jonty Stewart back at his side and-to top it all-he's about to be made Forsterian Professor of Applied Mathematics. With his inaugural lecture to give and a plagiarism case to adjudicate on, Orlando's hands are full, so can he and Jonty afford to take on an investigative commission surrounding a suspected murder? Especially one which must be solved within a month so that a clergyman can claim what he says is his rightful inheritance? The answer looks like being a resounding "no" when the lecture proves almost impossible to write, the plagiarism case gets turned back on him and Jonty (spiced with a hint of blackmail), and the case surrounding Peter Biggar's death proves to have too many leads and too little evidence. Orlando begins to doubt their ability to solve cases any more, and his mood isn't improved when there seems to be no way of outsmarting the blackmailer. Will this be the first failure for Coppersmith and Stewart? And how will they maintain their reputations-professional, private and as amateur detectives? 3/3

597. **Cochrane, Charlie**, *Lessons for Suspicious Minds*, Cheyenne, 2013. Cambridge Fellows #10 of 14. (MM Amateur Sleuth) An invitation to stay at a friend of the Stewart family's stately home can only mean one thing for Jonty Stewart and Orlando Coppersmith–a new case for the amateur sleuths! With two apparently unrelated suicides, a double chase is on. But things never run smoothly for the Cambridge fellows. In an era when their love dares not speak its name, the chance of discovery (and disgrace) is ever present–how do you

explain yourself when a servant discovers you doing the midnight run along the corridor? The chase stops being a game for Orlando when the case brings back memories of his father's suicide and the search for the identity of his grandfather. And the solution presents them with one of the most difficult moral decisions they've had to make... 3/3

598. **Cochrane, Charlie**, *Lessons for Idle Tongues*, Riptide, 2015. Cambridge Fellows #11 of 14. (MM Amateur Sleuth) Amateur detectives Jonty Stewart and Orlando Coppersmith seem to have nothing more taxing on their plate than locating a missing wooden cat and solving the dilemma of seating thirteen for dinner. But one of the guests brings a conundrum: a young woman has been found dead, and her boyfriend is convinced she was murdered. The trouble is, nobody else agrees. Investigation reveals that several young people in the local area have died in strange circumstances, and rumours abound of poisonings at the hands of Lord Toothill, a local mysterious recluse. Toothill's angry, gun-toting gamekeeper isn't doing anything to quell suspicions, either. But even with a gun to his head, Jonty can tell there's more going on in this surprisingly treacherous village than meets the eye. And even Orlando's vaunted logic is stymied by the baffling inconsistencies they uncover. Together, the Cambridge Fellows must pick their way through gossip and misdirection to discover the truth. 3/3

599. **Cochrane, Charlie**, *Lessons for Sleeping Dogs*, Riptide, 2015. Cambridge Fellows #12 of 14. (MM Amateur Sleuth) When amateur sleuth Jonty Stewart comes home with a new case to investigate, his partner Orlando Coppersmith always feels his day has been made. Although, can there be anything to solve in the apparent mercy killing of a disabled man by a doctor who then kills himself, especially when everything takes place in a locked room? But things are never straightforward where the Cambridge fellows are concerned, so when they discover that more than one person has a motive to kill the dead men–motives linked to another double death–their wits get stretched to the breaking point. And when the case disinters long buried memories for Jonty, memories about a promise he made and hasn't kept, their emotions get pulled apart as well. This time, Jonty and Orlando will have to separate fact from fiction–and truth from emotion–to get to the bottom of things. 3/3

600. **Cochrane, Charlie,** *Lessons in Cracking the Deadly Code*, Right Chair Press, 2018. Cambridge Fellows #12.7 of 14. (MM Amateur Sleuths) St Bride's College is buzzing with excitement at the prospect of reviving the traditional celebration of the saint's day. When events get marred by murder it's natural that Jonty Stewart and Orlando Coppersmith will get called in to help the police with their

inside knowledge. But why has somebody been crawling about on the chapel roof and who's obsessed with searching in the library out of hours?

601. **Cochrane, Charlie,** *Lessons in Loving thy Murderous Neighbor,* Right Chair Press, 2017. Cambridge Fellows #13 of 14. (MM Amateur Sleuth) Jonty Stewart and Orlando Coppersmith like nothing more than being given a mystery to solve. But what happens when you have to defend your greatest enemy on a charge of murder? – novella (MLM). 3/3

602. **Cochrane, Charlie,** *Lessons in Chasing the Wild Goose,* Right Chair Press, 2018. Cambridge Fellows #14 of 14. (MM Amateur Sleuth) Jonty Stewart and Orlando Coppersmith like nothing more than being handed a mystery to solve. But why would anybody murder a man with no enemies? And was it murder in the first place? –novella (MLM). 3/3

603. **Cochrane, Charlie,** *The Best Corpse for the Job,* Riptide, 2014. Lindenshaw #1 of 4. (MM Amateur Sleuth) Schoolteacher Adam Matthews just wants to help select a new headteacher and go home. The governors at Lindenshaw St Crispin's have already failed miserably at finding the right candidate, so it's make or break this second time round. But when one of the applicants is found strangled in the school, what should have been a straightforward decision turns tempestuous as a flash flood in their small English village. 3/3

604. **Cochrane, Charlie,** *Jury of One,* Riptide, 2016. Lindenshaw #2 of 4. (MM Amateur Sleuth) Inspector Robin Bright is enjoying a quiet Saturday with his lover, Adam Matthews, when murder strikes in nearby Abbotson, and he's called in to investigate. He hopes for a quick resolution, but as the case builds, he's drawn into a tangled web of crimes, new and old, that threatens to ensnare him and destroy his fledgling relationship. 3/3

605. **Cochrane, Charlie,** *Two Feet Under,* Riptide, 2018. Lindenshaw #3 of 4. (MM Amateur Sleuth) Things are looking up for Adam Matthews and Robin Bright–their relationship is blossoming, and they've both been promoted. But Robin's a policeman, and that means murder is never far from the scene. –*Old Sin,* book four in the Lindenshaw series will be released in February of 2019 (MLM). 3/3

606. **Cody, Liza,** *Miss Terry,* iUniverse, 2012. (Suspense) Nita Tehri's life seems sorted. She has a good job, she lives in a pretty apartment in a quiet street and she has escaped from the family who endangered her. Yet despite everything she's achieved she still has a problem. She doesn't look like her neighbours. And when a grizzly discovery

is made outside her door all eyes turn towards her. –neighbors include a gay couple (MLM). 1/3

607. **Cody, Liza,** *Lady Bag*, iUniverse, 2013. Lady Bag #1 of 2. (Suspense) Don't judge a book by its cover, or a bag lady by her appearance. 'I didn't always look like this, ' she says. 'Being barmy doesn't mean I'm stupid.' –Lady Bag's friend is a gay man (MLM). 1/3

608. **Cody, Liza,** *Crocodiles & Good Intentions: Further Adventures of Lady Bag*, iUniverse, 2018. Lady Bag #2 of 2. (Suspense) Lady Bag, released at last from prison, is greeted by her friends and reunited with her best-loved companion greyhound, Electra. She has been sober for months, and her friends want to keep her on the straight and narrow. What could possibly go wrong? 1/3

609. **Coe, Tucker (Donald Westlake 1933-2008)**, *Jade in Aries*, Random House, 1970. Mitch Tobin #4 of 5. (Suspense) Disgraced ex-cop Mitch Tobin makes his fourth appearance in a gripping story of terror and suspense. This time out Tobin enters a world as foreign to him as the dark side of the moon: the underworld of the New York City homosexual community. Was Jamie Dearborn – male model and part owner of a men's boutique – murdered by a stranger he'd picked up in a gay bar, as the police maintain? Ronald Cornell, the dead man's partner both in the shop and at home, refuses to believe it. And when Cornell himself becomes the victim of a murder attempt, Tobin reluctantly takes a hand. 2/3

610. **Coggins, Mark**, *The Immortal Game*, Poltroon, 1999. August Riordan #1 of 5. (Hard Boiled) When the world's most innovative computer chess software is stolen, wisecracking, jazz bass-playing PI August Riordan is hired to find it. Sifting through a San Francisco peopled with bruising, ex-NFL henchmen, transvestite techno geeks, and alluring, drug-addicted dominatrices, Riordan has got his work cut out for him. But with a smart-ass attitude like Riordan's, nothing is easy … –gay drag queen helps (MM). 2/3

611. **Coggins, Mark**, *Vulture Capital*, Poltroon, 2002. August Riordan #2 of 5. (Hard Boiled) When venture capitalist Ted Valmont is belatedly informed that the chief scientist of NeuroStimix–a biotech firm in which he has invested–is missing, it's not just business, it's personal. Not only is the scientist an old school chum, but his disappearance jeopardizes the development of NeuroStimix's most important product: a device intended to aid spinal cord injury victims. Since Valmont's twin brother, Tim, was paralyzed in a college driving accident, finding the scientist and getting him back into harness is of utmost importance to both brothers. Valmont engages August Riordan to assist in the search and the men soon discover that the disappearance is part of a larger conspiracy to use NeuroStimix

technology for perverse applications. 2/3

612. **Coggins, Mark**, *Candy from Strangers*, Bleak House, 2006. August Riordan #3 of 5. (Hard Boiled) Caroline Stockwell has a secret: she and her best friend Monica are "cam girls." Soliciting cash donations and gifts via Amazon.com wish lists from anonymous admirers, the young women have put up a web site featuring still photographs, video and web diaries (aka blogs) to help pay their way through art college. But when Caroline goes missing and her mother Ellen engages jazz bass-playing PI August Riordan to find her, Riordan discovers her secret and it appears to everyone that someone she met through the web site is responsible for her disappearance. 2/3

613. **Coggins, Mark**, *Runoff*, Bleak House, 2007. August Riordan #4 of 5. (Hard Boiled) "How much does it cost to fix an election?" August Riordan–private investigator, jazz bass player, smart ass with a foolish heart–is going to find out. He's been hired by Leonora Lee, the all-powerful "Dragon Lady" of San Francisco's Chinatown, to investigate the results of the city's recent mayoral election. 2/3

614. **Coggins, Mark**, *The Big Wake Up*, Bleak House, 2009. August Riordan #5 of 5. (Hard Boiled) The odyssey of María Eva Duarte de Perón–the Argentine first lady made famous in the play and the movie Evita–was as remarkable in death as it was in life. A few years after she succumbed to cervical cancer, her specially preserved body was taken by the military dictatorship that succeeded her deposed husband Juan. Hidden for sixteen years in Italy in a crypt under a false name, she was eventually exhumed and returned to Buenos Aires to be buried in an underground tomb said to be secure enough to withstand a nuclear attack. Or was she? 2/3

615. **Colbert, Curt**, *Queer Street*, Uglytown, 2004. Jake Rossiter & Miss Jenkins #3 of 3. (Hard Boiled) On the night of his birthday, Seattle P.I. Jake Rossiter gets a call from the Garden of Allah, the city's most exclusive gay nightclub. Female impersonator Trixie has been murdered. Never one to refuse a rich client, Jake figures he and junior partner Miss Jenkins will pop into the club before the birthday bash. What he didn't figure on was the cops busting the joint and arresting everyone there - including Jake and Miss Jenkins. 2/3

616. **Colby, Tyler**, *Tosca's Kiss*, Writer's Club, 2000. (Amateur Sleuth/Police Procedural) Mark is a newcomer to gay life, and to the gay summer community of Rehoboth Beach, Delaware, the gay mecca of the mid-Atlantic seaboard. The beautiful, available men, the sudden freedom, and the intense scrutiny of his every asset on the beach draw Mark into this complex world where he learns the rules of beach life, with its exultation, stresses, and, ultimately, mystery.

As prominent gay men die one-by-one throughout the summer, Dr. Mary Fox, the new county Medical Examiner, is pulled into a world she never knew but to which she has surprising connections. 3/3

617. **Coles, GDH (1889-1959) & Margaret (1893-1980)**, *Death of a Millionaire*, Collins, 1925. Superintendent Wilson #2 of 17. (Police Procedural) Superintendent Wilson and Inspector Braikie are very stumped with the case of a millionaire whose secretary seems to have murdered him in his hotel room. No body was found -however, the blood found at the scene, a witness locked in the closet and several eyewitnesses reporting that the secretary left the hotel with a large trunk and the missing millionaire seem to be conclusive evidence. –includes a one-sided homosexual relationship (MLM). 1/3

618. **Collins, James**, *The Saddling*, Createspace, 2017. Saddling #1 of 3. (Paranormal) To inherit his aunt's fortune, Tom Carey must unlock a one-hundred-year-old family mystery. The solution lies on the Romney Marshes where the village of Saddling lives by an ancient Lore. Unknown to Tom, the villagers set in motion a chain of calculated events that will ensure that the winter solstice will witness their last ever 'Saddling' festival. Unaware that his life is in danger, Tom befriends two village youths. 3/3

619. **Collins, James**, *The Witchling*, Createspace, 2017. Saddling #2 of 3. (Paranormal) Saddling is cursed and dying. The village will be lost unless someone burns at the stake on solstice morning. Six months after the life-changing events of The Saddling, Tom Carey must solve the witchling mystery and risk his life to save his lover. 3/3

620. **Collins, James**, *The Eastling*, Createspace, 2018. Saddling #3 of 3. (Paranormal) The spectre of revenge stalks Saddling, and the Eastling is hungry for a victim. At some time on autumn equinox night, someone in the village will die. 3/3

621. **Collins, Max**, *The Broker*, Berkley, 1976. Quarry #1 of 14. Broker deals in murder on the open market with the assistance of a highly paid precise killer named Quarry. –fellow contract killer is gay, republished as *Quarry* (MLM). 2/3

622. **Collins, Max Allan & Terry Beatty**, *Ms. Tree Quarterly: #3, Skeleton in the closet, Midnight & The butcher*, DC, 1991. (Comic) Campus tensions between gays and straights, and a murder in the middle of the tensions. –The main detectives are all straight, but an investigator's muscle turns out to be gay (MLM). 3/3

623. **Colton, James (Joseph Hansen 1923-2004)**, *Lost on Twilight Road*, National Library, 1964. (Pulp) The Lemonade was spiked; the woman was near naked. It was taking unfair advantage of Lonny,

because he hadn't wanted her advances. But it was another of the many episodes which caused him to become lost on twilight road. 3/3

624. **Colton, James**, *Known Homosexual*, Brandon House, 1968. (Pulp) Scorned by his family, defeated by society, Steve was at a major crossroads in his life. His marriage had gone sour, his hopes as a playwright dashed. Confused and friendless, Steve turned to pretty boy Coy Randol for love and support. But then Coy was found brutally murdered and there was only one person the police suspected: Steve. –republished as *Stranger to Himself* in 1977 by Major Books under Hanson's own name, the only Colton book to be reclaimed. It was heavily edited as it removed much of the sex scenes. It was then republished as *Pretty Boy Dead* in 1984 by Gay Sunshine Press. The book is edited to reintroduce some of the items Hansen cut out in *Stranger to Himself* but still left out much of the sex scenes. Steve is an early version of Cecil from Hansen's later Brandstetter books (MLM). 3/3

625. **Colton, James**, *Hang-Up*, Brandon House, 1969. (Pulp) "Accidental sleuth Stone Ransom, 28, a land developer, has to solve several mysteries about himself and his new lover in order to freely embrace his sexuality (Gunn)." 3/3

626. **Colton, James**, *Todd*, Traveler's Companion, 1971. (Pulp) Centers on two lovers - one white, one black - caught up in the militancy of the late 1960s. 3/3

627. **Comer, Curtis Christopher**, *Midnight Whispers: The Blake Danzig Chronicles*, Bold Stroke Books, 2010. (MM Paranormal) Paranormal investigator Blake Danzig, star of the syndicated show Haunted California and owner of Danzig Paranormal Investigations, has been able to see and talk to the dead since he was a small boy. Born into a circus family, Blake eventually made his way to San Francisco where he wrote his first book and opened his paranormal investigation office. Assisted by his best friend and self-proclaimed witch, Melody Adams, Blake helps his ex-lover and San Francisco Police Detective, Brian Cox, solve cold case murders by contacting the spirits of the victims. But, when he gets too close to a psychotic spirit, all hell breaks loose, and Blake ends up risking losing not only his boyfriend, Joe, but his very soul. 3/3

628. **Connor, Robert**, *Cut to the Bone*, Alyson, 2002. (Crime Drama) It was his last job. Santos de la O would make a mint smuggling the most sophisticated weaponry across the Texas-Mexico border for a Mexican drug lord, then retire, take his lover Tony and find the good life for both of them far from the danger and violence of El Paso Ciudad Juarez. But a celebratory night ends in gunfire, Tony dies in

Santos's arms, and things go downhill from there. 3/3

629. **Connelly, Michael**, *The Lincoln Lawyer*, Little, Brown, & Company, 2005. Mickey Haller #1 of 6. (Court Drama) Mickey Haller has spent all his professional life afraid that he wouldn't recognize innocence if it stood right in front of him. But what he should have been on the watch for was evil. Haller is a Lincoln Lawyer, a criminal defense attorney who operates out of the backseat of his Lincoln Town Car, traveling between the far-flung courthouses of Los Angeles to defend clients of every kind. –private investigator is gay (MLM). 1/3

630. **Connolly, John (1968-)**, *Every Dead Thing*, Simon and Schuster, 1999. Charlie Parker #1 of 17. (Thriller) Former NYPD detective Charlie "Bird" Parker, tormented by the brutal, unsolved murders of his wife and young daughter. Driven by visions of the dead, Parker tracks a serial killer from New York City to the American South, and finds his buried instincts – for love, survival, and, ultimately, for killing – awakening as he confronts a monster beyond imagining… –seeks assistance from gay lovers; hitman Louis and thief Angel who appear in varying degrees in the series (MLM). 1/3

631. **Connolly, John**, *Dark Hollow*, Simon and Schuster, 2001. Charlie Parker #2 of 17. (Paranormal) Charlie Bird Parker, returns to uncover a legacy of evil that has haunted Maine citizens for decades. 1/3

632. **Connolly, John**, *The Killing Kind*, Atria Books, 2002. Charlie Parker #3 of 17. (Paranormal) When the discovery of a mass grave in northern Maine reveals the grim truth behind the disappearance of a religious community, private detective Charlie Parker is drawn into a violent conflict with a group of zealots intent on tracking down a relic that could link them to the slaughter. Haunted by the ghost of a small boy and tormented by the demonic killer known as Mr. Pudd, Parker is forced to fight for his lover, his friends…and his very soul. 1/3

633. **Connolly, John**, *The White Road*, Atria Books, 2003. Charlie Parker #4 of 17. (Paranormal) Charlie Parker races to unravel a brutal crime committed in the Deep South. After years of suffering unfathomable pain and guilt over the murders of his wife and daughter, private detective Charlie Parker has finally found some measure of peace. As he and his lover, Rachel, are awaiting the birth of their first child and settling into an old farmhouse in rural Maine, Parker has found the kind of solace often lost to those who have been touched by true evil. 1/3

634. **Connolly, John**, *The Black Angel*, Atria Books, 2005. Charlie Parker #5 of 17. (Paranormal) When a young woman disappears from

the streets of New York City, ties of friendship and blood inevitably draw ingenious, tortured detective Charlie Parker into the search. Soon he discovers links to a church of bones in Eastern Europe, a 1944 slaughter at a French monastery, and to the myth of an object known as the Black Angel – considered by evil men to be beyond priceless. But the Black Angel is not a legend. It is real. It lives. It dreams. And the mystery of its existence may contain the secret of Parker's own origins. 2/3

635. **Connolly, John**, *The Unquiet*, Atria Books, 2007. Charlie Parker #6 of 17. (Paranormal) Daniel Clay, a once-respected psychiatrist, has gone missing. His daughter insists that he killed himself after allegations surfaced that he had betrayed his patients to foul and evil men – but when a killer obsessed with uncovering the truth behind his own daughter's disappearance comes seeking revenge, long-forgotten secrets begin to emerge. Hired by Dr. Clay's daughter to protect her from the predator on the loose, tortured and ingenious private detective Charlie Parker finds himself trapped between those who want the truth to be revealed and those who will go to any length to keep it hidden. 1/3

636. **Connolly, John**, *The Reapers*, Atria Books, 2008. Charlie Parker #7 of 17. (Paranormal) They are the Reapers, the elite among killers. Men so terrifying that their names are mentioned only in whispers. The assassin Louis is one of them. But now Louis and his partner, Angel, are themselves targets - and there is no shortage of suspects. 2/3

637. **Connolly, John**, *The Lovers*, Atria Books, 2009. Charlie Parker #8 of 17. (Paranormal) Charlie Parker is a lost soul. Deprived of his private investigator's license and under scrutiny by the police, Parker takes a job in a Portland bar. But he uses his enforced retirement to begin a different kind of investigation: an examination of his own past and an inquiry into the death of his father, who took his own life after apparently shooting dead two unarmed teenagers. It's a search that will eventually lead Parker to question all that he believed about his beloved parents, and about himself. But there are other forces at work: a troubled young woman who is running from an unseen threat, one that has already taken the life of her boyfriend; and a journalist-turned-writer named Mickey Wallace, who is conducting an investigation of his own. And haunting the shadows, as they have done throughout Parker's life, are two figures: a man and a woman who seem driven to bring an end to Charlie Parker's existence. 1/3

638. **Connolly, John**, *The Whisperers*, Atria Books, 2010. Charlie Parker #9 of 17. (Paranormal) In the vast and porous Great North Woods, that a dangerous smuggling operation is taking place, run

by a group of disenchanted former soldiers, newly returned from Iraq. Illicit goods–drugs, cash, weapons, even people–are changing hands. And something else has changed hands. Something ancient and powerful and evil. The authorities suspect something is amiss, but what they can't know is that it is infinitely stranger and more terrifying than anyone can imagine. Anyone, that is, except private detective Charlie Parker, who has his own intimate knowledge of the darkness in men's hearts. As the smugglers begin to die one after another in apparent suicides, Parker is called in to stop the bloodletting. The soldiers' actions and the objects they have smuggled have attracted the attention of the reclusive Herod, a man with a taste for the strange. And where Herod goes, so too does the shadowy figure that he calls the Captain. To defeat them, Parker must form an uneasy alliance with a man he fears more than any other, the killer known as the Collector. 1/3

639. **Connolly, John**, *The Burning Soul*, Hodder and Stoughton, 2011. Charlie Parker #10 of 17. (Paranormal) When a girl disappears from a small Maine town, her neighbor–a recluse named Randall Haight–starts receiving anonymous letters that contain tormenting references to a different teenage girl, murdered long ago. For many years, Randall has kept a secret: when he was fourteen, he was convicted of killing that girl. Now, his former life has returned to haunt him, and he hires private detective Charlie Parker to make it go away. But in a town built on blood and shadowed by old ghosts, where too many of the living are hiding secrets, the past cannot be dismissed so easily. As Parker unravels a twisted, violent history involving a doomed mobster and his enemies, the police, and the FBI, his search returns again and again to Randall Haight. Because Randall is still telling lies... 1/3

640. **Connolly, John**, *The Wrath of Angels*, Hodder and Stoughton, 2012. Charlie Parker #11 of 17. (Paranormal) In the depths of the Maine woods, the wreckage of an aeroplane is discovered. There are no bodies, and no such plane has ever been reported missing, but men both good and evil have been seeking it for a long, long time. What the wreckage conceals is more important than money: it is power. Hidden in the plane is a list of names, a record of those who have struck a deal with the Devil. Now a battle is about to commence between those who want the list to remain secret and those who believe that it represents a crucial weapon in the struggle against the forces of darkness. 1/3

641. **Connolly, John**, *The Wolf in Winter*, Atria Books, 2014. Charlie Parker #12 of 17. (Paranormal) The community of Prosperous, Maine has always thrived when others have suffered. Its inhabitants are wealthy, its children's future secure. It shuns outsiders.

It guards its own. And at the heart of Prosperous lie the ruins of an ancient church, transported stone by stone from England centuries earlier by the founders of the town... But the death of a homeless man and the disappearance of his daughter draw the haunted, lethal private investigator Charlie Parker to Prosperous. Parker is a dangerous man, driven by compassion, by rage, and by the desire for vengeance. In him the town and its protectors sense a threat graver than any they have faced in their long history, and in the comfortable, sheltered inhabitants of a small Maine town, Parker will encounter his most vicious opponents yet. 1/3

642. **Connolly, John**, *A Song of Shadows*, Hodder and Stoughton, 2015. Charlie Parker #13 of 17. (Paranormal) Grievously wounded, private detective Charlie Parker investigates a case that has its origins in a Nazi concentration camp during the Second World War. Broken, but undeterred, private detective Charlie Parker faces the darkest of dark forces in a case with its roots in the second world war, and a concentration camp unlike any other ... 1/3

643. **Connolly, John**, *A Time of Torment*, Hodder and Stoughton, 2016. Charlie Parker #14 of 17. (Paranormal) Jerome Burnel was once a hero. He intervened to prevent multiple killings and in doing so damned himself. His life was torn apart. He was imprisoned, brutalized. But in his final days, with the hunters circling, he tells his story to private detective Charlie Parker. He speaks of the girl who was marked for death but was saved, of the ones who tormented him, and an entity that hides in a ruined stockade. Parker is not like other men. He died and was reborn. He is ready to wage war. Now he will descend upon a strange, isolated community called the Cut, and face down a force of men who rule by terror, intimidation, and murder. All in the name of the being they serve. All in the name of the Dead King. 1/3

644. **Connolly, John**, *A Game of Ghosts*, Hodder and Stoughton, 2017. Charlie Parker #15 of 17. (Paranormal) It is deep winter. The darkness is unending. The private detective named Jaycob Eklund has vanished, and Charlie Parker is dispatched to track him down. Parker's employer, Edgar Ross, an agent of the Federal Bureau of Investigation, has his own reasons for wanting Eklund found. Eklund is no ordinary investigator. He is obsessively tracking a series of homicides and disappearances, each linked to reports of hauntings. Now Parker will be drawn into Eklund's world, a realm in which the monstrous Mother rules a crumbling criminal empire, in which men strike bargains with angels, and in which the innocent and guilty alike are pawns in a game of ghosts ... 1/3

645. **Connolly, John**, *The Woman in the Woods*, Hodder and Stoughton, 2018. Charlie parker #16 of 17. (Paranormal) Charlie Parker aids

the police when a buried, semi-mummified body of a woman is discovered. She apparently died of childbirth. Parker has to find out who she was and what happened to the child. – #17 of the Charlie Parker series, *A Book of Bones,* will be released in 2019 by Hodder and Stoughton (MM). 1/3

646. **Converse, Matt**, *Behind the Velvet Curtain*, Comet Press, 2015. Stripper Matt #1 of 2. (Suspense) Sex sells, what it attracts can be deadly. People probably have an idea of what being a stripper is like, and they would probably be wrong. It takes swagger to strip for a room full of men, but what's going on in the stripper's head might surprise you. Matt Jaxx was just a scrawny kid from Ohio who moved to San Francisco in hopes of starting a new life. He cut his hair, started working out, his acne cleared, and suddenly he was desirable. But when he was up on stage, he held onto the same insecurities he clung to in his childhood. The stripper façade was complete, but inside, he was still the anxious kid he'd always been. Justin was a young hunk living in the same apartment building. Matt previously would've thought Justin was out of his league. But Matt took a chance and approached, and to his surprise, the attraction was mutual. Over time, the off the charts sex began to turn to love, something Matt hadn't expected. But just when Matt seemed to have everything he desired, a stalker with a twisted obsession appeared with plans to take it all away. –available as an ebook only (MLM). 3/3

647. **Converse, Matt**, *Obsexsion*, Encompass Ink, 2018. Stripper Matt #2 of 2. (Suspense) When sex and a deadly obsession collide, not everyone will survive. Matt fears his nightmares are premonitions that the Creeper will return. Justin comforts him, but they soon face possible separation. Can their love survive? Will Matt return to the stage? And if he does, what–or who–will follow? 3/3

648. **Converse, Matt**, *Leather Head*, Encompass Ink, 2017. (Suspense) Gable is just playing dress up for San Francisco's leather S&M fair, but Leather Head isn't playing. His friend Shawn warns him to be careful what he's advertising for since the community has been rocked by four brutal murders. Gable still thinks it's all in fun, but it isn't. Desire can be deadly. –available via ebook only (MM). 3/3

649. **Cook, Bob**, *Paper Chase*, St. Martin's, 1989. (Espionage) The four old spies are long past their glory days, and now meet up mostly at the funerals of former colleagues, after which they typically enjoy an hour or two of complaining about the relaxation of standards at Britain?s security services. The latest indignity: The Director has recently sent round a most discourteous directive that the four are under no circumstances to consider writing their memoirs. Well,

they are not to be ordered about like some band of errand-boys! They served their country with honor, and the country has the right to know it. In fact, if you think about it, publishing their memoirs is a patriotic duty. Unfortunately, the Director doesn't see it quite that way. –the only gay aspect is one of the funerals were held for a gay colleague (MLM). 1/3

650. **Cook, J. S. (JoAnne Soper-Cook)**, *Because You Despise Me*, MLR, 2009. (MM Historical) Morocco, 1941: a dead German courier, two stolen exit visas, an American drifter, a French policeman, a lot of sand, and a lot of blood. Think you know this story? Think again... 3/3

651. **Cook, J. S.**, *A Cold-Blooded Scoundrel*, Brandon House, 2005. Inspector Devlin #1 of 2. (Historical Police Procedural) In London, with Jack the Ripper's crimes still raw in the great city's memory, a well-known male prostitute is brutally murdered, the head nearly severed, and the body set on fire. Detective Inspector Phillip Devlin of Scotland Yard, mid-thirties and secretly gay, is called to the murder scene by plainclothes constable Freddie Collins, and soon both Collins and Devlin are caught in a web of intrigue as more savage murders occur. 3/3

652. **Cook, J. S.**, *The Paragon of Animals*, Flanker, 2006. Inspector Devlin #2 of 2. (Historical Police Procedural) London finds her streets darkened with the blood of innocents once again. Disfigured bodies with vile, ritualistic markings are turning up at an alarming rate, and the police are at a loss to apprehend the killer, who always seems to be one step ahead of them. Detective Inspector Phillip Devlin of Scotland Yard is having problems of his own. Having fallen for his younger constable, Freddie Collins, Devlin finds that leading his double life is often more complicated than he'd originally thought. But for now, he must set aside his worries, as he is called on once more to catch a killer and expose the perpetrator of this latest threat to his beloved city. He must use every resource at his disposal, both inside the law and out, to halt a string of murders the likes of which London hasn't seen since the days of Saucy Jack. But what Inspector Devlin will soon learn is that murder is not necessarily the greatest of sins ... and some truths are better left undiscovered. 3/3

653. **Cook, J. S.**, *Willing Flesh*, MLR, 2010. Inspector Raft #1 of 3. (MM Police Procedural) When a series of bizarre murders occur in London's notorious East End, Scotland Yard's Inspector Philemon Raft is called on to solve the crimes, but even he is powerless to explain why the victims are displayed in public places – or why the killer insists on drilling burr holes in their skulls. With little to go on except the strange red dust found on the victims' palms, Raft must

scour the city looking for an explanation. Aided only by his newly-appointed constable Freddie Crook, Raft's investigation takes him into London's most dark and dangerous places, where human predators wait to devour and destroy. But Raft has an even bigger problem: a casual acquaintance is blackmailing him, and what she knows about his secrets could tear Raft's life to pieces. 3/3

654. **Cook, J. S.**, *Rag and Bone*, MLR, 2011. Inspector Raft #2 of 3. (MM Police procedural) Scotland Yard Inspector Philemon Raft arrives on the scene of a deadly fire in Whitechapel, only to find a much more sinister force at work, destroying lives with swift abandon - and a lunatic may help Raft capture the master criminal known only as "The Master." 3/3

655. **Cook, J. S.**, *Come to Dust*, Dreamspinner, 2013. Inspector Raft #3 of 3. (MM Police Procedural) In the frigid winter of 1891, with the nation still reeling from the Barings bank crisis, Inspector Philemon Raft returns from an involuntary sabbatical, tasked with solving the kidnapping of highly placed peer Alice Dewberry. Thrust into a sordid underworld where the upper classes indulge in disreputable overseas investments designed to fatten their pocketbooks, Raft finds himself at loose ends without his companion, Constable Freddie Crook. Far from offering their help, the ton use every asset at their disposal to keep Raft from discovering the truth about hapless kidnap victim Alice Dewberry–who may not even exist. Soon Raft discovers that his old nemesis, the workhouse master John Gallant, has returned to London. Gallant doesn't say what he wants–but he knows enough to ruin Raft's career and even his life. Raft tries to solve the case with his usual strange insight, but there are other, darker forces at work. This is a frightened London: the London of Whitechapel, of Jack the Ripper, the London of poverty, dirt and despair, where a right turn down the wrong alley could earn Raft a swift trip to the morgue. 3/3

656. **Cook, J. S.**, *A Little Night Murder,* Dreamspinner, 2013. (MM Historical) In 1942, Pearl Harbor has been bombed and the war is very much in evidence, but it would seem to have little to do with Frank Boyle, a respected Bronx born insurance investigator. He's a man who can keep secrets, and no one suspects that his boyhood friend–local mob boss Nicky Brooks–is his lover. When Brooks accidentally kills Frank's younger brother in a shootout, Frank must choose between his affair with Nicky and revenge for his brother's life. 3/3

657. **Cook, J. S.**, *Famous Last Words,* Dreamspinner, 2014. (MM Historical) When former Indiana farm boy William Henry Rider goes on a bank robbing spree in Benedict Fouts's corner of Depression Era Illinois, it's up to Ben to bring him in. But Rider is no ordinary crim-

inal. Famed for robberies that happen in the blink of an eye, Rider becomes a folk hero who steals from the rich and burns the mortgage papers of poor farmers teetering on the edge of financial ruin. –available as an ebook only (MLM). 3/3

658. **Cook, J. S.**, *Skid Row Serenade*, Dreamspinner, 2015. (MM Mystery) Novelist and war hero Tony Leonard sees private investigator Edwin Malory being mugged outside a seaman's mission in downtown Los Angeles, so he takes him home and gives him clean clothes and access to a hot shower. It doesn't take him long to discover Malory was hired by wealthy industrialist Linton Vanderbilt Stirling, the father of Tony's estranged wife, Janet. The reason for this is simple: Tony's father-in-law suspects him of drinking away his daughter's personal fortune. On a whim, Tony drops in on Janet one night and finds her naked, dead, and tied up, her skull beaten in. 3/3

659. **Cook, Judith**, *The Slicing Edge of Death: Who Killed Christopher Marlowe?*, Simon and Schuster, 1993. (Historical) In the tumultuous world of Elizabethan theater, Shakespeare's contemporary Christopher Marlowe is notorious. Recklessly wayward, the dazzling author of plays both blasphemous and scandalous, he is also a member of Sir Walter Raleigh's secret society, the lover of the powerful Thomas Walsingham, and an occasional agent on the Queen's "most secret business." Marlowe knows too much. For there are men - the Queen's Acting Secretary Robert Cecil and his spymaster among them - who want Marlowe silenced. With the aid of a forgotten manuscript, an unknown, unwitting actor, and a mysterious widow, some of Britain's most powerful will conspire to write Marlowe into a plot more complex, deadly, and artfully engineered than anything seen on the English stage.... 3/3

660. **Cook, Mitchell**, *Boy Orgy*, Star, 1973. (Pulp) "*Herald* reporter Sam is assigned to investigate the death of a wealthy woman (Gunn)." 3/3

661. **Cooke, John Peyton**, *Torsos*, Headline, 1993. (Historical Police Procedural) Arriving in 1935 Cleveland with a determination to clean up the city, Eliot Ness is greeted by a series of grisly murders and is introduced to the local underground that threatens to swallow up his own detectives. 3/3

662. **Cooke, John Peyton**, *Chimney Sweeper*, Mysterious Press, 1995. (Crime Drama) Young Jesse James Colson arrives in Isthmus City, Wisconsin, with some change, a novel, and a stolen .38. By morning, he has shot a transvestite to death and hidden the body. Slowly, he begins to build a life in the town, eventually joining the police force. But when the skeleton of the man he murdered surfaces. things spin out of control. 3/3

663. **Cooke, John Peyton**, *Rape of Ganymede*, Mysterious Press, 1998. Greg Quaintance #1 of 2. (Hard Boiled) Greg Quaintance sports a Desert Storm tattoo, packs a Glock, and drives a Plymouth Barracuda, but only those who know him best see the wounds etched in his heart. As a P.I. in Manhattan's Chelsea neighborhood, he is hired to thwart an extortion attempt aimed at Jimmy Gilbert, a billion-dollar man-child musical superstar accused of having sexual relations with a teenage boy. But when Gilbert's accuser turns up dead and the boy goes on the run, the bodies of the rich and not-so-famous start piling up. From the canyons of Manhattan to the halls of presidential power, Quaintance must now penetrate a minefield fused with greed, depravity, and violence. 3/3

664. **Cooke, John Peyton**, *The Fall of Lucifer*, Cuir Noir, 2008. Greg Quaintance #2 of 2. (Hard Boiled) When a distraught father hires Greg to find his missing son, Greg finds himself up to his neck in the world of the 1990s Goth club scene. But that's the least of his troubles. It's a case so bizarre, it might lead Greg to start believing in vampires.... Greg Quaintance, a Gulf War veteran with a Desert Storm tattoo, is no stranger to blood ... but only those who know him best see the wounds etched in his heart. 3/3

665. **Cooper, Natasha (Daphne Wright b. 1951-)**, *Festering Lilies*, Crown, 1990. Willow King #1 of 7. A murder, a secret identity, and a courageous heroine. –republished as *A Common Death*. –stereotypical gay typist who is prone to burst into tears (MM). 1/3

666. **Cooper, Steven**, *With You in Spirit*, Alyson, 2003. (Amateur Sleuth) "My father's body was found floating face down in the waters off Chappaquiddick. Naturally, everyone assumed a Kennedy did it." Well, perhaps not everyone, as Graydove Hoffenstein, the Native American Jewish heir to a parking meter empire discovers after his mother, Celeste Garrison Hoffenstein, is arrested and sentenced to life in prison for the murder of her husband, Colin Lightfoot Hoffenstein. But Gray believes in his mother's innocence, as does his sister Chaka, who arranges a seance at the family's Martha's Vineyard home with the renowned -psychic Brenda Cloudholder, who arrives in a Yugo driven by her spookily mysterious chauffeur, Derderva. 3/3

667. **Cooper, Steven**, *Saving Valencia*, Alyson, 2004. (Amateur Sleuth) Valencia Brandywine, heiress to a hotel empire, has been kidnapped, and the ransom is $7 million and her brother Rico's denouncement of his homosexuality. Valencia has been kidnapped by a group of zealots determined to convert the world's homosexuals to a life of heterosexuality. Rico, with friend D'vora Wasserman at his side, trots the globe in search of Valencia ... a search that turns out to be a deeply personal and somewhat mystical journey as well.

What follows is a romp through psychotherapy, religion, romance and -several inauspicious erections. 3/3

668. **Cooper, Steven**, *Deadline*, Alyson, 2005. (Journalism) Investigative reporter Damon Fitzgerald is hot on the heels of the story of his career when he is strangled to death in his own apartment. But what kind of reporter lets a little thing like death keep him from a good story? Steven Cooper once again combines thrills, slapstick and the supernatural in the story of a man intent on solving his own murder. 3/3

669. **Copenhaver, John**, *Dodging and Burning*, Pegasus, 2018. (Psychological) A lurid crime scene photo of a beautiful woman arrives on mystery writer Bunny Prescott's doorstep with no return address-and it's not the first time she's seen it. The reemergence of the photo, taken fifty-five years earlier, sets her on a journey to reconstruct the vicious summer that changed her life. -story is focused on a young gay man who is still in love with Bunny's brother who was killed in WWII (MLM). 2/3

670. **Copp, Rick**, *The Actor's Guide to Murder*, Kensington, 2003. Jarrod Jarvis #1 of 3. (Cozy) "Baby, don't even go there!" That was Jarrod Jarvis's catch phrase as the adorable, girl-crazy moppet on the eighty's sitcom, Go to Your Room! It was a great ride until the tabloids caught the popular teen idol kissing another guy at the L.A. gay rodeo. Gay and teen heartthrob not exactly being career-making words at the time, Jarrod's star crashed harder than a Kathie Lee Gifford CD. Flash forward: Now happily living with his cop boyfriend, Charlie, and their dog, Snickers, in the Hollywood Hills, Jarrod's ready to hit the comeback trail–but he never imagines how fame will strike this time. At a reading with his psychic, Jarrod is disturbed to hear that someone close to him will be murdered and even more shocked when it turns out to be his best friend, Willard Ray Hornsby, also a former child star. 3/3

671. **Copp, Rick**, *An Actor's Guide to Adultery*, Kensington, 2004. Jarrod Jarvis #2 of 3. (Cozy) Bad news item #1. Former child actor (and constant comeback candidate) Jarrod Jarvis fails to convince the California parole board not to release Wendell Butterworth, the stalker who has followed him since his first Oscar Meyer commercial. #2. Jarrod's NBC pilot flatlines before it even hits the air. #3. His agent/best friend Laurette decides to marry gorgeous Juan Carlos Barranco, a soap actor more wooden than a Steven Seagal romantic comedy – and shadier than Cher's plastic surgery denials. But things are about to get worse. During Laurette's drive-thru wedding at the Hearst Castle, one of the guests has a heated scene of his own with Juan Carlos–just before he crashes into the three-tier wedding cake, poisoned by a glass of champagne. 3/3

672. **Copp, Rick**, *An Actor's Guide to Greed*, Kensington, 2005. Jarrod Jarvis #3 of 3. (Cozy) Jarrod runs into Wallace Goodwin, one of the former writers on Go to Your Room, the beloved eighties show that made Jarrod a star. He's shocked to discover that the neurotic, egotistical Wallace, whose biggest claim to fame was penning a very special episode of a Marla Gibbs sitcom and marrying leggy sexpot Katrina, has penned a play bound for London's West End, with a scene-stealing part for Jarrod. Like they say, when God closes a door, somewhere, he opens a window seat in coach. Faster than you can say his catchphrase, "Baby, don't even go there!" Jarrod's hitting the boards in London... Jarrod's only friend in the cast is the formidable Claire Richards. The sexy, forty-something, champagne-swilling, Oscar-winning actress is the undisputed star of the show - a lady who can chew scenery and her co-stars with equal abandon. No one can play a death scene like La Claire. Except that this time the diva isn't faking it. She's been poisoned, and the last person to see her alive was Jarrod himself. 3/3

673. **Corbett, Norville**, *Queer Fear*, Publisher's Export, 1970. (Pulp) "San Francisco "hots" Eric Norden attempts to use five spy novelists to figure out who killed his lover, only to realize they are ruthless pawns of the U. S. president out to discredit Norden's brother, a senator (Gunn)." 3/3

674. **Cory, Desmond**, *Deadfall*, Walker, 1965. (Crime Drama) A master jewel thief is hired for a special burglary. –very convoluted, anti-gay writing (MLM). 1/3

675. **Cosentino, Joe**, *Drama Queen*, Lethe, 2015. Nicky and Noah #1 of 6. (Modern Cozy) It could be curtains for college theatre professor Nicky Abbondanza. With dead bodies popping up all over campus, Nicky must use his drama skills to figure out who is playing the role of murderer before it is lights out for Nicky and his colleagues. Complicating matters is Nicky's huge crush on Noah Oliver, a gorgeous assistant professor in his department, who may or may not be involved with a cocky graduate assistant...and is also the top suspect for the murders! –there are scenes in which Nicky discusses the size of his penis which takes this typical cozy to a modern cozy (MLM). 3.3

676. **Cosentino, Joe**, *Drama Muscle*, Lethe, 2016. Nicky and Noah #2 of 6. (Modern Cozy) It could be lights out for college theatre professor Nicky Abbondanza. With dead bodybuilders popping up on campus, Nicky, and his favorite colleague/life partner Noah Oliver, must use their drama skills to figure out who is taking down pumped up musclemen in the Physical Education building before it is curtain down for Nicky and Noah. Complicating matters is a visit from Noah's parents from Wisconsin, and Nicky's suspicion that Noah may

be hiding more than a cut, smooth body. 3/3

677. **Cosentino, Joe**, *Drama Cruise*, Lethe, 2016. Nicky and Noah #3 of 6. (Modern Cozy) Theater professors and couple, Nicky and Noah, are going overboard as usual, but this time on an Alaskan cruise, where dead college theater professors are popping up everywhere from the swimming pool to the captain's table. Further complicating matters are Nicky's and Noah's parents as surprise cruise passengers, and Nicky's assignment to direct a murder mystery dinner theater show onboard ship. Nicky and Noah will need to use their drama skills to figure out who is bringing the curtain down on vacationers before it is lights out for the handsome couple. 3/3

678. **Cosentino, Joe**, *Drama Luau*, Lethe, 2017. Nicky and Noah #4 of 6. (Modern Cozy) Theatre professors and spouses, Nicky and Noah, are on their honeymoon at a Hawaiian resort, where musclemen in grass skirts are keeling over like waterfalls. Things erupt faster than a volcano when Nicky and Noah, along with their best friends Martin and Ruben, try to stage a luau show. Nicky and Noah will need to use their drama skills to figure out who is bringing the grass curtain down on male hula dancers–before things go coconuts for the handsome couple. 3/3

679. **Cosentino, Joe**, *Drama Detective*, Lethe, 2017. Nicky and Noah #5 of 6. (Modern Cozy) Theater professor Nicky Abbondanza is directing a Sherlock Holmes musical in a professional summer stock production at Treemeadow College, co-starring his husband and theatre professor colleague Noah Oliver as Dr. John Watson. When cast members begin toppling over like hammy actors at a curtain call, Nicky dons Holmes' persona on stage and off. Once again Nicky and Noah will need to use their drama skills to figure out who is lowering the street lamps on the actors before the handsome couple get half-baked on Baker Street. 3/3

680. **Cosentino, Joe**, *Drama Fraternity*, Lethe, 2018. Nicky and Noah #6 of 6. (Modern Cozy) Theatre professor Nicky Abbondanza is directing Tight End Scream Queen, a slasher movie filmed at Treemeadow College's football fraternity house, co-starring his husband and theatre professor colleague, Noah Oliver. When young hunky cast members begin fading out with their scenes, Nicky and Noah will once again need to use their drama skills to figure out who is sending the quarterback, jammer, wide receiver, and more to the cutting room floor before Nicky and Noah hit the final reel. –*Drama Castle* is going to be released in 2019 (MLM). 3/3

681. **Craft, Michael**, *Flight Dreams*, Kensington, 1997. Mark Manning #1 of 7. (Journalism) Seven years ago, Chicago socialite Helena Carter disappeared. In three months, she will be declared legally dead and

her fortune will go to Chicago's Catholic Archdiocese. Investigative journalist Mark Manning believes the missing heiress is still alive. To prove his case, he enters a world where religion and politics make uneasy bedfellows – as he confronts the inescapable fact that he is gay. –*Flight Dreams* was the first "gay" book Kensington ever published and the editor of this book, John Scognamiglio, is now the editor-in-chief of Kensington (MLM). 3/3

682. **Craft, Michael,** *Eye Contact*, Kensington, 1998. Mark Manning #2 of 7. (Journalism) A simple assignment for Chicago Journal reporter Mark Manning. He's been hired to replace colleague Cliff Nolan on a top story: renowned astrophysicist Pavo Zarnik claims to have discovered a tenth planet. To the skeptical reporter, there is no story because there is no proof. But soon, Manning makes some startling discoveries. Nolan's body is found with a bullet hole in his back, and the last interview with Zarnik is missing. 3/3

683. **Craft, Michael**, *Body Language*, Kensington, 1999. Mark Manning #3 of 7. (Journalism) An unexpected windfall has given burned-out Chicago journalist Mark Manning the chance to reconnect with his boyhood roots. With the blessing of his lover, Neil, he leaves the Windy City to return to Dumont, Wisconsin, to take over the town paper. His long-awaited family reunion is cut short when his cousin Suzanne is bludgeoned to death just before Christmas dinner. 3/3

684. **Craft, Michael**, *Names Games*, St. Martin's, 2000. Mark Manning #4 of 7. (Journalism) Mark Manning, once a prominent journalist at a major daily newspaper in Chicago, is now the owner and publisher of the Dumont Daily Register, the daily paper in a small Wisconsin city. Here the biggest news is the impending city council report on a proposed new adult bookstore zoning law, the upcoming election for Sheriff and the upcoming annual exhibition of the Midwest Miniatures Society. In a unique coup for the first-ever miniatures exhibition in Dumont, the "king of miniatures", Mr. Carroll Cantrell has agreed to come and judge the show's main event. But the exhibition itself is quickly shoved off the front page of the paper when Cantrell is found murdered in his room. 3/3

685. **Craft, Michael**, *Boy Toy*, St. Martin's, 2001. Mark Manning #5 of 7. (Journalism) At the moment, the biggest news is the forthcoming production of a new play by the local community theater group. Two local teenage boys are alternating in the lead role - one is Jason Thrush, a gregarious and somewhat egotistical athlete, and the other is Thad Quatrain. When Jason and Thad have a verbal clash during rehearsal, it is quickly forgotten by almost everyone involved. But when Jason turns up dead on opening night - leaving Thad to take over the lead role - the local gossip turns against Thad.

Jason's death is soon proved to be murder and, even though he has not been charged, opinion about town has all but convicted Thad of the crime. 3/3

686. **Craft, Michael,** *Hot Spot*, St. Martin's, 2002. Mark Manning #6 of 7. (Journalism) During his distinguished career as a journalist, Mark Manning has seen it all–riots, murder, political corruption, and every manifestation of the dark heart of the human species. But even his proven emotional resources will be stretched when the home he shares with his lover, architect Neil Waite, and his ward and nephew, Thad Quatrain, becomes the site of one of the most daunting, taxing, and potentially dangerous of all human rituals–a wedding. Roxanne Exner, best friend to both Mark and Neil, is having her nuptial ceremony at their house in the normally bucolic Dumont, Wisconsin, partly because Carl Creighton, her husband to be, is in the final weeks of his campaign for lieutenant governor of Illinois. The wedding, despite everyone's fears, comes off with nary a hitch. The reception, however, takes a disastrous turn when a local matron, who happens to be a major donor to the campaign of Creighton's rival, is killed in what appears to be a freak electrical mishap. 3/3

687. **Craft, Michael,** *Bitch Slap*, St. Martin's, 2003. Mark Manning #7 of 7. (Journalism) Journalist Mark Manning has been successfully running his family's newspaper, *The Dumont Daily Register*, for several years now, and he sits on the board of two local companies, Quatro Press and Ashton Mills. So when the respective CEOs of these companies discuss a merger, it is only natural that Manning be interested in the proceedings. What's more, Manning's lover Neil, an architect, is designing a new house for Ashton's CEO, Gillian Reece. Reece is a business friend of Manning but not a friend to many else; she is generally considered overly aggressive and fastidious. When Manning assigns Glee Savage, the newspaper's society reporter, to cover Reece's new home, the subsequent meeting between the two does not end well: Savage huffs off in a fury but not before ferociously bitch slapping Reece in front of everyone. With Reece's cheek still smarting, more bad news comes as the accountant performing due diligence for the merger reports some very questionable items regarding Ashton's books. It seems as though things couldn't go much worse for the unpleasant Reece. That is, until she is murdered. The discovery of her body is greeted with great surprise, but perhaps not much regret on the part of most who knew her. Still, with Manning's friend and employee Glee Savage as the obvious and primary suspect, he cannot resist wading in to this most unsound of business dealings. 3/3

688. **Craft, Michael,** "Carpet Queen," *Inside Dumont: A Novel in Stories,*

Questover Press, 2016. (Cozy) While dressing for dinner on New Year's Eve, the last thing Marson Miles expects is to fall in love that night–with his wife's nephew. But when Brody Norris arrives from California to join his uncle's architectural firm, Marson finds his life turned upside down. And the quirky little town of Dumont, Wisconsin, will never be quite the same. –short story that could work as the prequel to *Flabbergassed* (MLM). 3/3

689. **Craft, Michael**, *FlabberGassed*, Questover Press, 2018. Mister Puss #1 of 1. (Cozy) A weight-loss miracle ... a dashing gay architect ... a talking cat. What could possibly go wrong? In the idyllic little town of Dumont, Wisconsin, wealthy widow Mary Questman adopts an exotic stray cat, Mister Puss, who begins to talk to her. At least she thinks so. Mary's young friend, gay architect Brody Norris, soon finds another reason to worry about Mary's judgment when she decides to help finance a bizarre weight-loss enterprise called FlabberGas, the invention of a flamboyant local dermatologist, Dr. Francis Frumpkin. Brody's skepticism is partially overcome when Dr. Frumpkin commissions him to design the first of a planned chain of FlabberGas clinics. But then, during a public demonstration of Frumpkin's gimmicky new treatment, a volunteer is gassed to death in a hideous mishap that turns out to be no accident. –first book in a new series (MLM). 3/3

690. **Craig, Daniel Edward**, *Murder at the Universe*, Midnight Ink, 2007. Five Star #1 of 3. (Modern Cozy) For thirty-six-year-old Trevor Lambert, life revolves around work. As Director of Rooms at the luxurious and ultra-modern Universe Hotel in New York, he radiates dignified professionalism and high-end hospitality. When Trevor inadvertently escorts VIP guest Brenda Rathberger–the cantankerous executive director of the Victims of Impaired Drivers conference–past the dead body of the hotel's owner, Trevor's perfect world implodes. 3/3

691. **Craig, Daniel Edward**, *Murder at Hotel Cinema*, Midnight Ink, 2008. Five Star #2 of 3. (Modern Cozy) Dedicated hotelier Trevor Lambert takes a job at Hotel Cinema, a multi-million-dollar rejuvenation of an Old Hollywood motor inn. It's a fabulous opening party until Tinseltown's hottest star, Chelsea Fricks, takes a fatal dive from her penthouse balcony. Was it a reckless publicity stunt or did fame drive her to suicide? 3/3

692. **Craig, Daniel Edward**, *Murder at Graverly Manor*, Midnight Ink, 2009. Five Star #3 of 3. (Modern Cozy) Hotelier Trevor Lambert is about to fulfill his ultimate fantasy–managing his own bed and breakfast, a Victorian mansion in Vancouver called Graverly Manor. But there's one caveat: the elderly owner, Lady Graverly, won't sell until Trevor lives and works there for one month. Screams in the

night, foul odors, and the sudden disappearance of a chambermaid have Trevor looking over his shoulder. 3/3

693. **Craig, Jamie**, *Master of Obsidian*, Amber Quill, 2007. Master Chronicles #1 of 11. (Paranormal BDSM) Jesse Madding has been working for Gideon, a vampire fighting to maintain the balance between good and evil, for two years, and has loved him for nearly that long. When Gideon slams him against an alley wall and demands sex, Jesse is too happy to oblige. Jesse's willing submission to Gideon's darker desires-including bondage, pain, and bloodplay-they learn that a new drug is being distributed in the city. Known simply as "obsidian," this drug unleashes a vampire's demon, destroying any sense of self-control. 3/3

694. **Craig, Jamie**, *Unveiled*, Amber Quill, 2007. Master Chronicle #2 of 11. (Paranormal BDSM) Gideon Keel and Jesse Madding have seen dozens of gruesome crime scenes over the years, but nothing compares to the grisly discovery they make in a small apartment above a sporting goods store. The body has clearly been put on display, and clues in the apartment indicate that while the woman was dying, party guests were enjoying rich caviar and expensive champagne. 3/3

695. **Craig, Jamie**, *Mosaic Moon*, Amber Quill, 2007. Master Chronicle #3 of 11. (Paranormal BDSM) Emma Coolidge is accustomed to isolation. Born with the ability to read emotions, Emma reached adulthood without learning how to control her special gift, leading to a life of self-imposed seclusion. Until she meets Gideon Keel and Jesse Madding, a vampire fighting for good and his human lover. Jesse and Gideon are forced to investigate a string of grave desecrations that are somehow siphoning power from the most powerful mage in Chicago. –the continuing series switches from mysteries to battling against evil forces (MLM). 3/3

696. **Craig, Jamie**, *Pas de Deux*, Amber Quill, 2009. (MM Crime Drama) Hotshot defense attorney James Scott isn't afraid of following his gut instinct. Even when his gut tells him that the man everybody knows is guilty is not only innocent, but a victim himself. And all the evidence shows Hector Young is guilty of the cold-blooded murder of a young ballerina. 3/3

697. **Craig, Jeffrey**, *Done Rubbed Out,* Jeffrey Craig, 2016. Reightmen and Bailey #1 of 3. (MM Police Procedural) Things are going well at the Time Out Spa, but the night young proprietor Toby Bailey discovers his former lover naked and dead on a massage table, more things are spoiled than just his white leather shoes. Detective Melba Reightman and partner, Sam Jackson are called in to investigate and soon become embroiled in the most perplexing homicide case seen

in years. 3/3

698. **Craig, Jeffrey,** *Hard Job,* Jeffrey Craig, 2016. Reightman and Bailey #2 of 3. (MM Police Procedural) Detective Melba Reightman is distraught over the murder of her friend and partner, Sam Jackson. The Guzman murder case has been closed, but she knows the real killer is still out there somewhere. Toby Bailey's discovery of a set of incriminating photos proved there were more people involved in Geri Guzman's death than just Dr. Lieberman but getting anyone to listen is more of a challenge than she'd ever imagined. She's going to need help convincing the powers that be that the case needs to be reopened, but she'll find a way to do it. 3/3

699. **Craig, Jeffrey,** *Skin Puppet,* Jeffrey Craig, 2017. Reightman and Bailey #3 of 3. (MM Hard Boiled) It's just two weeks until The Reightman & Bailey Agency officially opens, but Melba Reightman and Toby Bailey have things pretty much under control. After the horrific events of the last six months, things starting to feel almost normal again. They're both happy to just hunker down and do what's needed to make their new business a success. So far, everything looks to be "all systems go and full speed ahead." 3/3

700. **Cranston, Wes,** *Schoolboy into B&D,* Greenleaf, 1984. (Pulp) "Police detective Rex Masters, 30s, married, closeted, arrests teenager Matt preston for the murder of a fellow student, but releases him when Matt insists the death was accidental, to fall victim to the teenager's scatological revenge (Gunn)."

701. **Crombie, Deborah,** *A Share in Death,* Scribner, 1993. Kincaid & James #1 of 18. (Police Procedural) A week's holiday in a luxurious Yorkshire time-share is just what Scotland Yard's Superintendent Duncan Kincaid needs. But the discovery of a body floating in the whirlpool bath ends Kincaid's vacation before it's begun. One of his new acquaintances at Followdale House is dead; another is a killer. –assistant hotel manager was gay and the first one killed (MLM). 1/3

702. **Cross, Amanda (Carolyn Gold Heilbrun)**, *The James Joyce Murder,* E. P. Dutton, 1976. Kate Fansler #2 of 14. (Amateur Sleuth) Kate Fansler is vacationing in the sweet and harmless Berkshires, sorting through the letters of Henry James. But when her next-door neighbor is murdered, and all her houseguests are prime suspects, her idyll turns prosaic, indeed.... –an effeminate gay man assists the main character in cataloging papers (MLM). 1/3

703. **Crow, Kirby,** *Angels of the Deep,* MLR, 2009. (MM Paranormal) Becket Merriday is on the trail of a killer who is murdering beautiful young men in the small town of Irenic. What he discovers an ancient race of immortal beings hunted by an incredibly powerful

adversary: the angel Mastema. Soon, Beck and his partner, Sean Logan, find themselves at the center of a deadly supernatural war. 3/3

704. **Cunningham, Jere**, *Hunter's Moon*, Gold Medal, 1977. (Thriller) "In a plot reminiscent of *Deliverance*, concerns a group of hunters who are tracked by a hillbilly band whose interests include murder and sodomy." -Slide. 1/3

705. **Currier, Jameson**, *A Gathering Storm*, Chelsea Station's Editions, 2014. (Suspense) Inspired by true events, in a small university town in the South when a gay college student is beaten and in the ensuing days as the young man struggles to survive in a hospital, the residents of the town and the university find themselves at the center of a growing media frenzy as the crime reverberates through the local and national consciousness. 3/3

706. **Curzon, Daniel**, *From Violent Men*, IGNA, 1983. (Fictionalized True Crime) An account of an attempt to assassinate a San Francisco Supervisor who is in prison for a short time even though he has killed a gay Supervisor. -Based on the murder of Harvey Milk. 3/3

707. **Cutler, Stan**, *Best Performance of a Patsy*, Dutton, 1991. Goodman/Bradley #1 of 4. (Bibliomystery Hard Boiled) When former Hollywood private eye Rayford Goodman teams up with ghostwriter Mark Bradley, a hip, gay, aspiring novelist, to pen a tell-all autobiography, an old case–called the American Beauty Rose murder–comes back to haunt him. 3/3

708. **Cutler, Stan**, *The Face on the Cutting Room Floor*, Dutton, 1991. Goodman/Bradley #2 of 4. (Bibliomystery Hard Boiled) Hired to guard an Oscar-winning director with mob connections, the pair soon find themselves watching over a bullet-riddled corpse. 3/3

709. **Cutler, Stan**, *Shot on Location*, Dutton, 1993. Goodman/Bradley #3 of 4. (Bibliomystery Hard Boiled) Hired to write a profile of Stacy Jaeger, on trial for killing his sister's boyfriend, gay would-be novelist Mark Bradley must once again team up with sleuth-to-the-stars Rayford Goodman, a juror for the Jaeger trial. 3/3

710. **Cutler, Stan**, *Rough Cut*, Signet, 1994. Goodman/Bradley #4 of 4. (Bibliomystery Hard Boiled) When Rayford Goodman's neighbor turns up dead in her swimming pool, he and Mark Bradley find themselves in the middle of a mystery reaching all the way to the top of the L.A. political machine. 3/3

D

711. **Dabney, J. M., & Davidson King,** *The Hunt,* Hostile Whispers, 2018. (MM Hard Boiled) Disgraced detective turned private investigator, Ray Clancy, left the force with a case unsolved. Finding the killer was no longer his problem, but it still haunted him. How long would he survive the frustration of not knowing before he gave into the compulsion of his nature to solve the crime? 3/3

712. **D'amato, Barbara (b. 1938), Jeanne M Dams (b. 1941), and Mark Zubro (b. 1948),** *Foolproof,* Doherty, 2009. (Political Intrigue) The morning of 9/11 Brenda Grant and Daniel Henderson met for coffee before going to their software firm in the World Trade Center. That casual act saved them from the Twin Towers' collapse, even as their friends and Brenda's fiancé were killed and their company obliterated. Founding their own software security firm, they never forgot that morning of horror. Grant and Henderson then establish a clandestine division inside their company committed to covertly tracking down global terrorists. In a search involving Washington DC, Egypt, Italy and Turkey, they expose a plot to hijack a US presidential election, rig voting machines, and topple democracies worldwide. 3/3

713. **Dale, John,** *Dark Angel,* HarperCollins, 1995. (Crime Drama) Jack Butorov is back from a stretch in Spain and lying low. But the bills are mounting, and he needs money fast. Damian Frick's a model. Well connected, he's into a money-laundering scam and willing to split the dividends. All Jack's got to do is rough him up a little. But things go wrong. 2/3

714. **Dalton, Rick,** *Marco,* Lulu, 2005. Key West Connections #1 of 3. (Hard Boiled) "Jamaica gay resort owner Rick Dalton, 30s, lives in a milieu always beset with crime and mystery (Gunn)." 3/3

715. **Dalton, Rick,** *Alix, Miquel, Kim,* Lulu, 2005. Key West Connections #2 of 3. (Hard Boiled) After Marco, along came Alix. Then Miguel entered Rick's life, and finally Kim. Rick's mystery solving, and adventures continue with his new lover Alix... 3/3

716. **Dalton, Rick,** *Just You and Me,* Lulu, 2006. Key West Connections #3 of 3. (Hard Boiled) Rick and Kim travel to England for a quiet weekend for two and become embroiled in murder, mayhem, and mystery at friend Barry's country estate. 3/3

717. **David, Benjamin,** *Boys Behind Bars,* Surey, 1973. (Pulp) "Illinois reform school inmate Tod Curtis, 16, framed by his father for the murder of his mother and the father's own faked murder, escapes and goes looking for revenge with the help of fellow escapee and lover (Gunn)." 3/3

718. **Davies, David Stuart,** *Brothers in Blood,* Mystery Press, 2013. DI Snow #1 of 3. (Thriller) A brutal game devised by three intelligent but bored teenagers escalate into murder. Led by the charismatic and cunning Laurence, the trio of "brothers" meets once a year to carry out untraceable, motiveless murders–for fun. Until, years later, they must murder in order to protect one of their own, leaving themselves vulnerable to discovery. This killing is investigated by Detective Inspector Paul Snow, a man with a secret of his own which links him to the murder. As Snow grows closer to unmasking the killers, his professional life begins to unravel in a terrifying fashion. 3/3

719. **Davies, David Stuart,** *Innocent Blood,* History Press, 2015. DI Snow #2 of 3. (Thriller) A child's body is found in woodlands, the parents torn apart by grief. But this is only the first victim in a series of apparently motiveless crimes. Detective Inspector Paul Snow, heading the investigation, must discover the pattern and reveal the chilling truth as a cunning and violent murderer becomes desperate and even more unpredictable. Haunted by secrets of his own, the complex DI Snow races against the clock, following a murderous trail. 3/3

720. **Davies, David Stuart,** *Blood Rites,* Urbane, 2018. DI Snow #3 of 3. (Thriller) 1980s Yorkshire. DI Paul Snow has a personal demon. He is a homosexual but is desperate to keep it secret, knowing it would finish his career in the intolerant police force. As this personal drama unfolds, he is involved in investigating a series of violent murders in the town. All the victims appear to be chosen at random and appear to have no connection with each other. 3/3

721. **Davies, Hunter,** *Body Charge,* Weidenfeld and Nicolson, 1972. (Suspense) Thirty-year-old Franko Baxter has an uncomplicated life. He shares a flat with his Gran and works for a shady unlicensed minicab company, a job he likes because it gives him plenty of free time for his true passion: playing football. But things start to get more complicated when Franko gets involved with three of his passengers: Shuggy, a conceited young football star, Zak, a dropout on the dole with a nymphomaniac wife and three kids, and Joff Howard, a bisexual BBC producer. His life begins to get progressively crazier, but the biggest surprise is yet to come. Suddenly Franko finds himself entangled in a police investigation into the murder of a gay man - a mystery that will lead to some shocking revelations about

his new friends ... and himself. 2/3

722. **Davis, Phil**, *The Dancer's Death*, Avon, 1981. (Psychological) New York is under siege by a cross dressing serial killer. New York City police detective Frank Bonomo is on the pursuit. 1/3

723. **Dawson, David**, *The Necessary Deaths*, DSP Publications, 2016. Delingpole Mysteries #1 of 2. (Court Drama) A young journalism student lies unconscious in a hospital bed in Brighton, England. His life hangs in the balance after a drug overdose. But was it attempted suicide or attempted murder? The student's mother persuades British lawyer Dominic Delingpole to investigate, and Dominic enlists the aid of his outspoken opera singer partner, Jonathan McFadden. 3/3

724. **Dawson, David**, *The Deadly Lies*, DSP Publications, 2017. Delingpole Mysteries #2 of 2. (Court Drama) Dominic and Jonathan are on their romantic Spanish honeymoon, and things are perfect... except Dominic has kept a secret from his husband. He's failed to tell Jonathan that he plans to meet his former lover, Bernhardt, who is speeding on his way from Germany to present Dominic with a mysterious gift. 3/3

725. **Dawson, David Laing**, *Double Blind*, Macmillan Canada, 1991. (Thriller) Working the graveyard shift at a Baltimore hospital, Dr. Robert Snow is shocked by a bizarre trend among the patients brought in by the police in the wee hours of the night–they all seem psychotic, and all are infected by the HIV virus. 3/3

726. **De la Croix, Sukie**, "Private Dick," ed. Thomas S. Roche, *Noirotica 3: Stolen Kisses*, Black Books, 2000. (Noir Satire) "Chicago private investigator Dick Fallus, the narrator, finds he can trust no one's word (Gunn), when on the search for missing chocolate-chip cookie tycoon Benjamin Binky-Raffles, who left behind his beloved "Da Vinci's prototype butt-plug. 3/3

727. **Dean, Les**, *Zorro: The Gay Blade*, Leisure, 1981. (Western Satire) A novel by Les Dean based on the Screenplay by Hal Dresner but with added gay details and a reincarnation 150 years after the movie's conclusion. 3/3

728. **Dee Gee, En**, *Murder at "The Post Office,"* Independently Published, 2013. (Police Procedural) In 1989, there was only one bar in Jakarta, Indonesia, which catered exclusively to a certain group of people. Its existence was spread solely through word of mouth to maintain the privacy of its patrons. That bar finally became a true safe haven for its clientele. Its customers called it 'The Post Office'. No one expected their discreet fun at The Post Office would be interrupted; until one of its patrons was found dead there. 3/3

729. **Delacourt, George**, *Cabin Cruiser*, Greenleaf, 1972. (Pulp) Los Angeles temporary government agent Bob Thorpe, a writer, seduces most of the crew of a suspicious yacht that the government is convinced is smuggling in LSD. 3/3

730. **Del Franco, Mark**, *Unfallen Dead*, Ace, 2009. Connor Grey #3 of 6. (Fantasy) For a century since the Convergence of Faerie and modern reality, the Ways between this world and the next have been closed. But now signs point to the chance that the veil may lift again. Connor Grey has enough problems with a vengeful Queen of Faerie and the return of his old Guild partner. Add an occult string of murders, and it's another case that just may kill him. 1/3

731. **DeLand, Gordon**, *Down Cellar*, Createspace, 2018. (Thriller) Jim Worthington is a plumber/handyman with a past. John Green is his best friend with powerful but mysterious political connections. Soon after Jim finds a hidden room in John's basement, someone burns Jim's barn down. Then, one after another, he loses his house, his pets, his truck and his reputation. With his girlfriend in a coma and his best friend suggesting he turn himself into the police, Jim has to find out who is out to ruin him–and more importantly why? –before he loses the one thing he has to left: his life! –MC is straight, but John Green is gay (MLM). 2/3

732. **Delany, Samuel (b. 1942)**, *The Mad Man*, Richard Kasak, 1994. (Psychological) For his thesis, graduate student John Marr researches the life and work of the brilliant Timothy Hassler: philosopher whose career was cut tragically short over a decade earlier. Marr encounters numerous obstacles, as other researchers turn up evidence of Hassler's personal life that is deemed simply too unpleasant and disillusioning for the rarified air of academe. It begins to seem that Hassler's death might hold some key to his own life as a gay man in the age of AIDS. As John Marr learns more about the enigma that was Timothy Hassler, his own increasing sexual debasement leads him to a point where his and the philosopher's lives collide violently.... 3/3

733. **DeMarco, Joseph**, *Study in Scarlet: Queering Sherlock Holmes*, Lethe, 2011. (Sherlock Holmes) What other characters from English literature have captivated hearts and minds as thoroughly as Sherlock Holmes and his loyal companion John Watson? Many fans imagine the relationship between these men is deep and more than platonic. Edited by noted mystery author Joseph R. G. DeMarco, A Study in Lavender queers the Holmes universe; the authors have devised stories in which Holmes and Watson are lovers, or investigate mysteries of inverts hidden from the laws and cultures of the Victorian era; even the indomitable Lestrade has his turn at love; and where strange lights similar to the work of Jules Verne draw the

detectives to infamous Cleveland Street. 3/3

734. **DeMarco, Joseph**, *Murder on Camac*, Lethe, 2009. Marco Fontana #1 of 4. (Hard Boiled) Gunned down in the street, author Helmut Brandt's life ebbs away and puts a chain of events in motion placing P.I. Marco Fontana on a collision course with the Church and local community. Brandt's research into the decades old death of Pope John Paul the First made him serious enemies within the Catholic Church. As Fontana digs into the case, he finds Brandt also had rivals in his work and in his love life. 3/3

735. **DeMarco, Joseph**, *A Body on Pine*, Lethe, 2011. Marco Fontana #2 of 4. (Hard Boiled) When Marco Fontana enters his friend's spa on Pine, he doesn't find the peaceful retreat he expected. Brad, the masseur, is missing. The spa is splattered with blood and a dead client lies sprawled on the floor. 3/3

736. **DeMarco, Joseph**, *Crimes on Latimer*, Lethe, 2011. Marco Fontana #3 of 4. (Hard Boiled) Six of Marco Fontana's early cases show some of the forces that helped shape the young private eye. 3/3

737. **DeMarco, Joseph**, *Death on Delancey*, Lethe, 2014. Marco Fontana #4 of 4. (Hard Boiled) When two popular gay bartenders are found dead in a tony Philadelphia neighborhood the police are ready to close the case as a murder-suicide. Private investigator Marco Fontana has a hunch that there is more to the crime than a domestic dispute gone horribly wrong. 3/3

738. **DeMarco, Joseph**, *Family Bashings*, JMS, 2016. McCann & Verlangen #1 of 2. (MM Police Procedural) Disgraced cop Doyle McCann and former undercover cop Kord Verlangen are forced to partner on a cold case which they must solve or lose their jobs. The case, involving a series of gay bashings two years earlier, takes them through the underbelly of Philadelphia's gay nightlife, and Doyle has reason to believe the Mafia may also be involved. –the second book, *Lethal Attachments*, is set to be released in 2019 (MLM). 3/3

739. **Denby, Ron**, *American Lives*, Knights, 1985. (Journalism/Political Intrigue) Reporter Philip Kristopher investigates a murder when an aide to a front-running presidential candidate is found dead at a gay bath house. 3/3

740. **Devane, Terry (Jeremiah Healy)**, *Uncommon Justice*, Putnam, 2001. Maired O'Clare #1 of 3. (Court Drama) A young female attorney named Maired O'Clare leaves the fast track of corporate law to join ranks with a down-and-almost-out criminal attorney, Sheldon Gold. Her first case is to defend a reclusive homeless man called Alpha who is charged with murdering another homeless man. As the investigation proceeds, the questions of guilt and innocence become more mysterious – and justice, an elusive goal. -gay private

eye working for the straight lawyers (MLM). 2/3

741. **Devane, Terry**, *Juror Number Eleven*, Putnam, 2002. Mairead O'Clare #2 of 3. (Court Drama) The legal team of Mairead O'Clare and Sheldon Gold has just wrapped their successful defense of Gold's childhood friend, Big Ben Friedman. The charge is murder. Now it's the prosecution's turn to move in for the kill. They have a charge of their own–jury tampering. And all bets are on Juror Number Eleven–especially after her lifeless body is discovered in her home strung up by her neck. Her last desperate phone call was to Mairead. That looks bad. The prime suspect, Big Ben, has disappeared. That looks worse. First, they have to bring their client in on a new murder charge. Then they have to do the impossible–they have to defend him. 2/3

742. **Devane, Terry**, *A Stain Upon the Robe*, Putnam, 2003. Mairead O'Clare #3 of 3. (Court Drama) The Honorable Barbara Quincy Pitt is presiding over an explosive new trial–that of a priest who stands accused of a shocking transgression. But the judge's own problems are disturbing her as well. The young law clerk assigned to assist her in the case–who also happens to be her illicit lover–has disappeared 2/3

743. **Deveron, Wyn**, *Weir House,* Createspace, 2011. (Thriller) Col Weir was seven years old when he and his sister Mary saw their father strangle their mother with her long yellow hair and bury her under Weir House. He was sixteen when his father threw him out of the house for dressing up in his dead mother's clothes. Though banished, Col never really leaves. He steals back into Weir House, living a secret life in the tower rooms which are haunted by the ghost of his great Aunt Ibye whose terrible secret had the power to kill two generations later. 3/3

744. **DeWitt, Ben**, *Graveyard Grove*, Oso, 1999. (Police Procedural) Floyd Carter was one of the best homicide detectives in Detroit. Coming out of the closet didn't change his ability, only his beat. He was the Gay Crimes Division. When one of Detroit's best is murdered outside a gay establishment, Detective Carter is assigned the high-profile case, getting stuck with Jefferson Davis Treat, retired wide receiver for the Detroit Lions, as his unofficial partner. 3/3

745. **DeWitt, Ben**, *Nobody Dies in Mexico*, Oso, 2010. (Military) Is it the Russians? The Venezuelans? The Arabs? Or is it the Mexican drug cartels who want Pat Rogers dead? He and his team of old friends are running out of time and luck in their search for answers. A Mexican doctor finds evidence of the senseless murder of young girls in the desert of northern Chihuahua. He brings that problem to Pat Rogers in El Paso and the hunt is on for murderers, assassins, arms dealers

and drug runners. Victory would not be without consequences. – Carter returns in this e-book exclusive (MLM). 1/3

746. **Diamond, Ian**, *Dead White Males*, DC Books, 2000. (Soft Boiled) Who is Vera A. Utall? Why has she entwined celebrity Nick Maggot and legendary literary genius Orville Goner in her sexual web? Hairdresser and private eye David Dennings is hired to track the vanished siren. 3/3

747. **Diamond, Vincent**, "Lions and Tigers and Snares," ed. *Rough Cut: Vincent Diamond Collected,* Lethe, 2008. (Short Stories) Diamonds can be a boy's best friend, too. 3/3

748. **Dickson, Jack**, *Freeform*, Gay Men's Press, 1998. Jas Anderson #1 of 3. (Police Procedural) Set in the criminal underworld of Glasgow, Scotland. Set in the derelict inner-city of Glasgow's Dennistoun. Detective-Sergeant Jas Anderson, a tough gay cop and violent anti-hero, suspended from duty for assault, Jas is the natural suspect when Leigh, his lover and partner in a heavy S/M relationship, is found brutally murdered. Now on the run and struggling to clear his name, Jas uncovers Leigh's involvement in a blackmail ring, and even his lover's identity becomes confused. –will be republished by ReQueered Tales in 2019 (MLM). 3/3

749. **Dickson, Jack**, *Banged Up*, Gay Men's Press, 1999. Jas Anderson #2 of 3. (Police Procedural) Detective-Sergeant Jas Anderson expelled from the Glasgow police force, is being framed by his ex-colleagues, and remanded to Barlinnie prison. He is forced to share a cell with Steve McStay, sentenced for aggravated assault on two gay men. Jas forms an unlikely partnership with Steve in his fight for survival. 3/3

750. **Dickson, Jack**, *Some Kind of Love*, Gay Men's Press, 2002. Jas Anderson #3 of 3. (Hard Boiled) Former Detective Sergeant Jas Anderson, becomes enmeshed in a dangerous web of intrigue and double-dealing. Working as a private investigator on a routine case, he soon finds himself stirring an explosive cocktail of police corruption, sectarianism and murder. 3/3

751. **Dickson, Jack**, *Still Waters*, Prowler, 2001. (Amateur Sleuth) Professor Michael St. Clair and Dr. Richard Rodgers are as much an institution as the university at which they teach. When Richard walks in on Michael's tryst with a security guard, he is told that cruising keeps a relationship fresh. He's not convinced, with two students in tow, they depart for Loch Ness with the agreement that, if they find evidence of the monster, Michael will stop his cheating. However, even in the wilds of the Scottish Highlands, temptation is still to be found. 3/3

752. **Dickson, Jack**, *The Master's File*, Zipper, 2002. (Journalism) Life is

easy for oversexed journalist Gavin Shaw: satisfying work, all his home comforts, a loving boyfriend, and plenty of casual sex to boot. But then an old flame makes him an offer he can't refuse: something Gavin has longed for but repressed all these years. So, what will happen when he gives in to his darkest desires? 3/3

753. **Dickson, Tom**, "Terminal Orgasm" ed. Cecilia Tan, *Wired Hard 2*, Circlet, 1997. (Paranormal) "Pyschic sleuth Joseph (Joe), 20, a hacker, combines sex magic and astral projection to enter cyberspace to figure out how two hundred-twenty users of different computer sex games perished. 3/3

754. **Dietzen, Ryan**, *Murder Most Garlic*, Sauvage Press, 2016. Gardner Lyon #1 of 2. (Cozy) Gardner Lyon's a hot mess but being able to solve a gruesome murder at Havana, NY's annual Garlic Festival might just get his life back on track. Against the wishes of his family and boyfriend, he plunges headlong into his mother's gossipy and insular hometown to prove he can solve the crime–without getting himself killed. 3/3

755. **Dietzen, Ryan**, *The Burnt Man*, N. P., 2017. Gardner Lyon #2 of 2. (Cozy) Freelance writer and erstwhile detective Gardner Lyon is summoned to Burning Man to cover a fashion shoot, but stumbles on what turns out to be his second case. Thrust into the brutal desert north of Reno, he and his boyfriend find themselves in a strange new world, but one not immune to violence. Can he solve the murder of a tech billionaire without suffering the fate of a sparkle pony? 3/3

756. **Dillinger, James (James Robert Baker)**, *Adrenaline*, Signet, 1985. (Crime Drama) It begins as a routine trick: two guys on a beach after midnight. Instant attraction, chemical overload, but in the heat of the moment they are interrupted. Brutalized by police, they fight back, a cop dies, and Nick and Jeff are on the run through Los Angeles at its worst. 3/3

757. **Dobyns, Stephen**, *The Church of Dead Girls*, Metropolitan, 1997. (Thriller) Aurelius is a drowsy bedroom community in upstate New York that is rocked by a vicious, seemingly random killing. A woman is found murdered in her bed, her left hand missing. Just when the grisly details begin to fade, a young girl vanishes. The only clue: a bag with the girl's washed and folded clothes and a mannequin's left hand. Soon two more girls disappear, and when clues remain elusive, conjecture and rumor take over. The town awakens to a nightmare of suspicion and vigilantism. As the killer spirals in to kill again, the town spins out of control, and The Church of Dead Girls heads to a jolting conclusion. It'll give you goosebumps even if you read it at the beach. –narrator is gay as is one of the victims

(MLM). 3/3

758. **Donaghe, Ronald**, *Salvation Mongers*, Writer's Club, 2000. Common Threads in the Life #3 of 4. (Amateur Sleuth) A broken-hearted and enraged Kelly decides to pose as a recruit at Lion's Mouth Christian Ranch to discover why his beloved William committed suicide after experiencing a religious conversion. In the isolated high mountains of the desert, where there is no way out, Kelly soon discovers the awful truth. But can he resist the powerful brainwashing or survive long enough to tell others? Or will he inevitably lose his own self-destiny in this deadly game of religious salvation in The Salvation Mongers? 3/3

759. **Donnelly, Cray**, *Laudanum*, PublishAmerica, 2003. (Amateur Sleuth) After a near-fatal automobile accident, Brandon Keller returns to resume his life in Natchitoches, Louisiana only to confront the unsolved murder of his high school sweetheart. Determined, Brandon investigates the night of his accident and the murder, a night he cannot remember, to uncover the truth. 3/3

760. **Donovan, Dahlia**, *Dead in the Garden*, Hot Tree, 2018. Grasmere Cottage #1 of 3. (MM Cozy) All grown up and graduated, Valor Tarquin Scott, son to Earl and Countess Scott, owns The Ginger's Bread, a biscuit shop, in Grasmere in the Lake District. The love of his life, Bishan Tamboli, has turned his music studies into a successful career playing with the London Symphony Orchestra. It's a perfect life with their cat, spending evenings watching *Poirot* on the television. The nightmare begins with one dead former schoolmate, leading police to believe Bishan is responsible. Valor struggles to solve the cryptic puzzles left behind in a race to prove Bishan's innocence. He can't help wondering how far the body count will rise before they manage to stop the killer. 3/3

761. **Donovan, Dahlia**, *Dead in the Pond*, Hot Tree, 2018. Grasmere Cottage #2 of 3. (MM Cozy) Bishan Tamboli struggles to recover from his false arrest. He worries the police still aren't as convinced about his innocence. With his longtime boyfriend, Valor, at his side, he intends to solve the puzzles and catch the murderer amongst their former schoolmates. He's fought hard for his independence as an autistic and refuses to throw it all away because of a nameless monster. With friends and family in the killer's crosshairs, Bishan fears the mystery will bring the end of everything and everyone he loves. 3/3

762. **Donovan, Dahlia**, *Dead in the Shop*, Hot Tree, 2018. Grasmere Cottage #3 of 3. (MM Cozy) Valor Scott wants nothing more than to enjoy life in his little cottage with his boyfriend. The shadows of a serial killer continue to haunt him, though. He only wants the living

nightmare to end. He battles one catastrophic event after the other, intent on bringing his loved ones through to the other side safely. As their killer finally comes out into the open, Valor finds himself face-to-face with an obsessed murderer intent on destroying everyone in their path. 3/3

763. **Downing, Todd (1902-1974),** author of nine books, is suspected of being gay. There were several books about and by gay men found in his house after he passed away, his lifelong bachelorhood, and his many male close friends. All of his mysteries have strong homoerotic content with no obvious homosexual characters, yet the main characters tend to observe and comment on male forms more than women's, but his sexuality is never confirmed or denied. "Downing's plots cast queer shadows." -Charles J. Rzepka.

764. **Doyle, Arthur Conan (1859-1930),** *Round the Fire Stories*, Doubleday, 1909. (Short Stories) Seventeen tales of suspense and adventure, of the mysterious and the fantastic, meant to be read "round the fire" upon a winter's night. Murder, madness, ghosts, unsolved crimes, diabolical traps, and inexplicable disappearances abound in these exciting accounts narrated by doctors, lawyers, gentlemen, teachers, burglars, dilettantes, and convicted criminals. The titles are inviting "The Pot of Caviare," "The Clubfooted Grocer," "The Brazilian Cat," "The Sealed Room," and "There Fiend of the Coopergate" –in the "Man with the Watches" a young man is killed and is exposed as a transvestite (MLM). 1/3

765. **Drake, Robert,** *Man: A Hero of our Time*, Plume, 1995. (Thriller) One man's fight to conquer hatred in American society. Unable to forget the brutal death of his lover at the hands of a gay-basher, Adam reinvents himself, becoming The Man–America's first gay superhero. -second book has never been published (MLM). 3/3

766. **Drake, Stan, & Leonard Starr,** *The Go-Between,* Dargaud Intl Pub Ltd, 1983. Kelly Green #1 (Crime Drama) Kelly Green; a widowed police officer's wife and her quest to find those responsible for her husband's death. She is assisted by ex-felons that her husband had arrested and been fair to. –drag queens appear in this graphic novel (MLM). 1/3

767. **Drew, Libby,** *State of Mind*, Dreamspinner, 2010. (Science Fiction) Grier Crist works for the Organizationa group of Gifted agents who use their powers to keep peace, help those in need, and combat criminal influence around the globe. When a suspicious bombing drives Grier to break his ties with the group and go into hiding, the head of the Organization sends model agent Alec Devlin after him, claiming Grier is a murderer and traitor to their cause. Grier manages to turn the tables and take Alec hostage long enough to convince

him that the Organization is lying and hiding something sinister. The two strike a bargain: amidst enemies who want them dead, friends with their own agendas, and the growing passion between them, they'll work together to bring down the Organization in order to protect the world and each other. 3/3

768. **Drummond, William,** *Victim,* Corgi/Transworld, 1961. (Court Drama) "London barrister Melville Carr is slightly more active than the film's Melville Farr in seeking out the blackmailers indirectly responsible for the death of a young man to whom he was attracted, adapted from the original screenplay by Janet Green and John McCormick."-Gunn 3/3

769. **Duncan, Sandy Frances**, *Never Sleep with a Suspect on Gabriola Island*, Touchwood, 2009. Islands Investigations International Mystery #1 of 4. (Hard Boiled) On the islands off the coast of British Columbia and Washington State, Noel Franklin and Kyra Rachel team up to form Islands Investigations International. Quickly they come to realize that some crimes respect no boundaries. Their first job takes Noel and Kyra to Gabriola Island and the unsolved murder of an art gallery groundskeeper. The vicious rumors surrounding the case take several sinister turns, leading them into grave personal danger. As each investigator falls prey to those they need to trust, Kyra and Noel discover that even charming island communities can keep deadly secrets. 3/3

770. **Duncan, Sandy Frances**, *Always Kiss the Corpse on Whidbey Island*, Touchwood, 2010. (Hard Boiled) Islands Investigations International Mystery #2 of 4. Sandro Vasiliadis, a nurse at the Whidbey Island General Hospital, has died of an apparent heroin overdose. When his grieving mother bends over to kiss her son's corpse at the viewing, she shrieks, "That's not Sandro!" Convinced that her son must still be alive, Maria Vasiliadis hires Kyra Rachel and Noel Franklin to solve the mystery. With questions of foul play continuing to swirl around the death, the detectives' inquiries lead them deeper into Sandro's life and eventually to a medical clinic that specializes in transgendering. 1/3

771. **Duncan, Sandy Frances**, *Never Hug a Mugger on Quadra Island*, Touchwood, 2011. (Hard Boiled) Islands Investigations International Mystery #3 of 4. Kyra Rachel and Noel Franklin are sleuthing around Quadra Island in the employ of Noel's old high school buddy, Jason Cooper. In a quiet wooded area of the island, Jason, his wife and two younger boys are worried for the oldest son in the family. Derek was discovered badly beaten in the woods by Campbell River and has remained in a deep coma for three weeks. Desperate to find out what happened to his son and why, Jason hires Noel and Kyra. 3/3

772. **Duncan, Sandy Frances**, *Always Love a Villain on San Juan Island*, Touchwood, 2013. (Hard Boiled) Islands Investigations International Mystery #4 of 4. Noel Franklin and Kyra Rachel are called to Moresby University on San Juan Island to investigate a case of possible plagiarism. As they look into the theft, the two get to know the small island's university. They soon discover another, more menacing crime: the daughter of a professor engaged in highly sensitive research has been kidnapped. And her ransom is a piece of intellectual property far greater than any manuscript. While Noel and Kyra navigate the murky waters of university politics and come closer to discovering the origins of the crimes and their perpetrators, their lives are first threatened and then terrorized. 3/3

773. **Dunford, Warren**, *Soon to be a Major Motion Picture*, Riverbank, 1998. Mitchell Draper #1 of 3. (Amateur Sleuth) Mitchell Draper, screenwriter/office temp; Ingrid Iversen, painter/coffeehouse manager; and Ramir Martinez, actor/health-food-store clerk as they come face-to-face with their dreams in the last way they expected. Mitchell's sudden and suspicious opportunity to pen the screenplay of a bad "mafia princess" movie for obnoxious film producer Carmen Denver coincides with the opening of a reluctant Ingrid's first exhibit and Ramir's one-man-show. What goes wrong? 3/3

774. **Dunford, Warren**, *Making a Killing*, Alyson, 2001. Mitchell Draper #2 of 3. (Amateur Sleuth) struggling screenwriter Mitchell Draper was happy to have escaped with his life from his last assignment. But that doesn't stop him from digging into a 20-year-old murder-suicide as meat for a new screenplay that might net him $800,000 from a sexy movie producer who seems just as interested in Mitchell as in his story. Once again, novelist Warren Dunford has created a hilariously satirical study of celebrity culture that pokes good-natured fun both at the insiders and those on the outside desperate to get in. 3/3

775. **Dunford, Warren**, *Scene Stealer*, Cormorant, 2005. Mitchel Draper #3 of 3. (Amateur Sleuth) Screenwriter Mitchell Draper has written a movie about the kidnapping of a famous actress. But, just before the shooting starts, the lead actress is kidnapped in real life" in exactly the same manner as described in Mitchell's script. The only witness, Mitchell is determined to find her. Confusion grows as clues in the kidnapping appear to echo famous kidnapping cases and celebrity disappearances from the Lindbergh baby, Agatha Christie, and Patty Hearst, to Frank Sinatra Junior, Russell Crowe, and Victoria "Posh Spice" Beckham. Among the fans and enemies left behind at the film production, the rumors fly, predominant among them that the actress faked her own kidnapping as a clever publicity stunt a rumor that Mitchell has difficulties in disbelieving.

3/3

7760. **Dunn, Mark**, *Queer Guise*, Publisher's Export, 1967. (Pulp) "Straight detectives, though the narcotics officer is repeatedly drugged and raped by a male nurse (Gunn)." 3/3

777. **Dunn, Mark**, *Gay Sadist*, Publisher's Export, 1970. (Pulp) Possibly a sequel of *Queer Guise*. 3/3

778. **Dunn, Mark**, *Live Bait*, Publisher's Export, 1968. (Pulp) "A sex slavery operation has been uncovered, but the women's destinations have been found. Having penetrated the gang, Bill must accept a passive role in homosexual activities (Gunn)." –Early example of straight for gay love story (MM). 3/3

779. **Dunn, Mark**, *Hard Times*, Greenleaf, 1969. (Pulp) "Industrial spy Mike McClure ferrets out a secret formula but must deal with his feelings for his employer he has used so badly (Gunn)." 3/3

780. **Dunne, Colin (Dianne L Browne b. 1949)**, *Murder in Pastel*, Writer's Club, 2000. (MM Amateur Sleuth) Kyle Bari knows he's in trouble when his ex, Adam, comes back to Steeple Hill. Adam has a new boyfriend named Brett, who seems to have a lot of questions for Kyle and a wandering eye for the other residents of "the colony". When Brett turns up dead, Adam and Kyle are the prime suspects. Add a missing painting and Kyle's reawakened feelings for Adam to the mix, and Kyle knows he has the perfect recipe for trouble. Can he find the missing painting and prove that neither he nor Adam are guilty of anything but love? –there are passages in this book that are identical to Josh Lanyon's *Fatal Shadows*, which led to Josh Lanyon admitting she is Dianne Browne, *Murder in Pastel* may possibly the first MM Mystery/Romance (MLM). 3/3

781. **Dymmoch, Michael Allen**, *The Man Who Understood Cats*, St. Martin's, 1993. Caleb and Thinnes #1 of 5. (Police Procedural) Two unlikely partners join forces to solve a murder disguised as suicide and catch a killer ready to strike again. Gold Coast psychiatrist Jack Caleb is wealthy, cultured, and gay. When one of his clients is found dead in a locked apartment–apparently from a self-inflicted wound– burned-out Chicago detective John Thinnes doesn't believe it was suicide. And Caleb is inclined to agree. But Thinnes regards a shrink who makes house calls suspicious and starts his murder investigation with the doctor himself. 3/3

782. **Dymmoch, Michael Allen**, *The Death of the Blue Mountain Cat*, St. Martin's, 1996. Caleb and Thinnes #2 of 5. (Police Procedural) Chicago detective John Thinnes and psychiatrist Jack Caleb team up once more to face murder on the Magnificent Mile when Native American artist Blue Mountain Cat, whose style is described as Andy Warhol meets Jonathan Swift in Indian country, is murdered at an exclusive

showing in an ultraconservative art museum. 3/3

783. **Dymmoch, Michael Allen**, *Incendiary Designs*, St. Martin's, 1998. Caleb and Thinnes #2 of 5. (Police Procedural) Jogging through Chicago's Lincoln Park, Dr. John Caleb comes upon a group of fanatics setting a police car on fire – with the officer inside. Caleb rescues the man but as Chicago heats up in the most brutal summer on record, it becomes clear that this is the first of a series of deadly arsons.As Detective John Thinnes races to find the culprit and Dr. Caleb sets a trap for a murderer, both men are nearly incinerated in the killer's final act. 3/3

784. **Dymmoch, Michael Allen**, *The Feline Friendship*, St. Martin's, 2003. Caleb and Thinnes #4 of 5. (Police procedural) Unfortunately for John Thinnes, he's got a rape case on his hands. Not only that, he has a new partner--and it's a woman. A tough woman with a make-my-day attitude. As Thinnes learns of his unwelcome assignment, psychiatrist Jack Caleb is in session with a patient who many years before was a victim of rape and still suffers from the experience. When the rapist continues his crimes, and adds killing to rape, Thinnes turns once more to Caleb in the hope that he can point him in the right direction to uncover the killer. 3/3

785. **Dymmoch, Michael Allen**, *The White Tiger*, St. Martin's, 2005. Caleb and Thinnes #5 of 5. (Police Procedural) John Thinnes, a detective on the Chicago police force, and Jack Caleb, a well-known psychiatrist, were friends--unlikely friends, maybe, with very different lives, but men who like and respect each other. And they had one significant experience in common: Both had been "in country" in Vietnam during the war. And now, on a morning shortly into the new millennium, Jack Caleb hears of the shooting death of a Vietnamese immigrant woman in Chicago's "Little Saigon," and a flashback leaves him trembling. Thinnes's reaction to the murder is of a different kind. He had been assigned to the murder case, but when his lieutenant learns that Thinnes had known the dead woman in Saigon, had even attended her marriage to his now-dead buddy, he takes him off the case, leaving Thinnes's partner to use her outstanding talents as a detective under the officer who takes John Thinnes's place. 3/3

E

786. **Eberhart, Mignon G (Mignon Good (1899-1996)**. Her works often featured female heroines, and tended to include exotic locations, wealthy characters, and suspense and romance but "beginning with Eustace Federie in *While the Patient Slept* (1930), Mignon Eberhart included a certain kind of man in thirty-six of her fifty-nine novels. While these men vary in their type, they are all just a bit too...either handsome, foppish, effeminate, high-voiced, pretty, nelly, or something that Eberhart chooses not to label. While some may be interested in women, they are always more interested in themselves. Others may have little to no interest in women. Yet others are too boyish acting. Some even disguise themselves or cross-dress (always with wicked intent). In all cases, something about thee gents just does not quite add up to their being a "real" man... Very often, though not always, it explains their criminal behavior (thirteen of them are murderers). In other instances, it explains why they are not the right mate for the heroine, in spite of their gallant efforts. Afterall, they dance with ease (one suspects better than the female protagonist); walk with grace; converse and behave in charming ways; and dress impeccably. And of course, they are startling handsome or pretty. For Eberhart, that is just plain wrong." – Rick Cypert, "Foppish, Effeminate, or "a little too handsome" Coded Character Descriptions in the Novels of Mignon G Eberhart," *Murder in the Closet* ed. by Curtis Evans, McFarland, 2017.

787. **Edmonson, Roger**, *Silverwolf*, Banned Books, 1990. (Paranormal Hard Boiled) A string of grisly murders is plaguing the gay community in Seattle. The clues point to some kind of wild animal–but Cliff, a PI formerly with the Seattle P.D., is hearing rumors of something very different. Though he doubts it at first, the evidence begins to stack up. Is it possible they're dealing with a werewolf–a gay werewolf. 3/3

788. **Edwards, Hank**, *Fluffers, Inc.*, Alyson, 2002. Fluffers Inc. #1 of 3. (Amateur Sleuth) After leaving his home on an Idaho dairy farm, Charlie Heggensford lands in Los Angeles like a farm fresh egg. He endures a few dead-end jobs until he finds a place to put his particular set of skills to use: Fluffers, Inc. As a fluffer in the gay porn movie business, Charlie bounces between movie sets, the beds of actors and directors, and the backseats of cars. Ride along with Charlie as he navigates the sometimes bitchy, often funny, always smoking hot

waters of the gay porn movie industry with his co-workers Ken, Billy, and Kinitia, sexy and loyal bear actor, Brent Harrington, and hot porn actor Rock Harding, the man that not only gets Charlie hard as he's making Rock hard but has stolen his heart. 3/3

789. **Edwards, Hank**, *A Carnal Cruise*, Lethe, 2009. Fluffers Inc., #2 of 3. (Amateur Sleuth) Charlie and the rest of the gang from Fluffers, Inc. are hitting the high seas. Hired to provide fluffing service on a cruise ship filled with gay porn stars, Charlie soon discovers he is no less clumsy on sea than dry land as he continues to over-stimulate his clients. As the ship steams toward Acapulco, hot, unavailable porn star Rock Harding begins to see ghosts from his past and the shock of his sightings affects his ability to perform. During the cruise, Charlie discovers not only the healing power of vinegar, the trick to running in heels, and the lengths Cedric would stoop to hang onto Rock, but enough secret revelations to make his head swim! 3/3

790. **Edwards, Hank**, *Vancouver Nights*, Lethe, 2010. Fluffers Inc., #3 of 3. (Amateur Sleuth) Hot Fluffer Fun in the Great White North. Charlie gets in so much trouble that his boss, Kinitia Jones, encourages him to take some time off and get out of town. Charlie goes to Vancouver, Canada to visit his good friend and former bear porn star, Brent Harrington, who now owns a pet store, Canadian Critters. A string of pet store break-ins has a hot police inspector keeping his eye on Brent, and when the evidence begins to stack up against his friend, Charlie decides it's time to take matters into his own hands. 3/3

791. **Edwards, Hank**, *Holed Up*, Loose Id, 2009. Up to Trouble #1 of 4. (MM Espionage) FBI Special Agent Aaron Pearce, tall, muscular, a lone wolf with an attitude, is assigned to protect Mark Beecher, a witness to the plans for a terrorist attack. The discovery of an unknown informant within the FBI's ranks, however, forces the two men to hole up in a loft apartment with only one another for company. 3/3

792. **Edwards, Hank**, *Shacked Up*, Loose Id, 2012. Up to Trouble #2 of 4. (MM Espionage) FBI Special Agent Aaron Pearce is recovering from his injuries suffered while on assignment in Detroit, stuck in the offices of the FBI running database searches for agents in the field. He notices a car following him back and forth to work and panics, certain it's the terrorist mole Robert Morgan who escaped them in Detroit. 3/3

793. **Edwards, Hank**, *Roughed Up*, Loose Id, 2013. Up to Trouble #3 of 4. (MM Police Procedural) FBI Special Agent Aaron Pearce and his lover Mark Beecher are taking a well-deserved vacation relaxing on

the beaches of Barbados Island. When Mark sees a young girl in a bar who may be in danger, he begins an informal investigation into her situation, even as Pearce reminds him they are not citizens and have no legal power on the island. Mark is determined, however, and, while investigating on his own, is taken captive by a sex slavery ring. 3/3

794. **Edwards, Hank,** *Choked Up,* Createspace, 2016. Up to Trouble #4 of 4. (MM Police Procedural) When a case in Detroit calls Pearce back to the city where the two met, he grudgingly leaves Mark on his own. The case involves the murders of four gay men, all strangled, and all with a note in one hand. These notes contain clues that point to a case from Pearce's past, and proves what he already fears: Robert Morgan, terrorist mole within the FBI and Pearce's former lover, has invited Pearce back to Detroit to finish things between them. 3/3

795. **Edwards, Hank,** *Repossession is 9/10ths of the Law,* Wilde City Press, 2014. (Amateur Sleuth) Alan Baxter barely scrapes by working as a deejay in suburban Detroit. To make ends meet, he takes a job as an automobile repossession agent, and discovers his very first assignment is a car owned by his drug dealer ex-boyfriend. On top of that, a body is discovered in the trunk...by a cop. Soon Alan's life is completely upturned as he is pulled into a mystery involving more bodies, a highly lethal new street drug, a mysterious man with a top hat and cane, raging dwarves, a house fire, a cranky police detective, and his even crankier cat! 3/3

796. **Edwards, Martin,** *The Coffin Trail,* Allison and Busby, 2004. Lake District #1 of 7. (Police Procedural) What is meant as a fresh start in the English Lakes District begins to reek of buried secrets.... Oxford historian and TV personality Daniel Kind and his new lover, Miranda, both want to escape to a new life. On impulse they buy Tarn Cottage in Brackdale, an idyllic valley in the Lake District that Daniel knew as a boy. He is still fascinated by a place so remote that the dead had to be carried out over the peaks on pack animals along the ancient Coffin Trail. But though the couple hope to live the dream of downsizing, the past has a way of catching up. Tarn Cottage was once home to Barrie Gilpin, an autistic youth suspected of a savage murder-what looks like the ritualistic killing of a young woman visitor to the valley. She was found laid out on the Sacrifice Stone, an ancient pagan site up on the fell. Barrie fell to his death near the crime scene before he could be questioned. All these years later, Daniel retains his belief in Barrie's innocence and questions his own policeman father's handling of the case. When DCI Hannah Scarlett and her squad launch a cold case review, Brackdale's skeletons begin to rattle. The wild geography of the Lakes District

plays against local literary references, all backdrop to the lives of villagers and outsiders drawn to this beautiful spot - but for what reasons? 1/3

797. **Edwards, Martin**, *The Cipher Garden*, Allison and Busby, 2005. Lake District #2 of 7. (Police Procedural) Warren Howe is surprised by a hooded visitor whilst working in a garden in Old Sawrey. Soon he is dead - murdered with his own scythe. As the years pass, the culprit has yet to be found. However, after an anonymous tip-off, DCI Hannah Scarlett is soon on the case. Then there is yet another horrifying death. –Cumbria constabulary detective Nick Lowther, married and closeted, disappears from the series at this point and in a later book reveals that he immigrated to Canada (MLM). 1/3

798. **Ellis, Bret Easton,** *American Psycho,* Vintage, 1991. (Crime Drama) Patrick Bateman is twenty-six and he works on Wall Street, he is handsome, sophisticated, charming and intelligent. He is also a psychopath. Taking us to head-on collision with America's greatest dream–and its worst nightmare. –a few gay secondary characters (MM). 1/3

799. **Ellis, Edward,** *The Pheromone Bomb,* Idol, 2000. (Pulp) A crack army unit - the Special Marine Corps, consisting of five British and five American soldiers - is on a top-secret mission to investigate and, if necessary, eliminate, an illegal private army on a tropical island in the mid-Atlantic. Tony is one of the British soldiers, and this is his first proper action. 3/3

800. **Ellis, Keelan,** *Good Boys,* Createspace, 2018. Solomon #1 of 2. (Police Procedural) Having risen through the ranks of the Baltimore City Police Department to the elite Homicide unit as an out gay man, Paul Solomon has always prided himself on his integrity and self-reliance. As the last vestiges of his failed eight-year-long relationship fall away, Paul finds himself adrift, forced to rely on others to help him find his footing again. When Paul and his partner, Tim Cullen, are called to the scene of a double murder of two high school students on the city's west side, 3/3

801. **Ellis, Keelan,** *High Time,* Createspace, 2018. Solomon #2 of 2. (Police Procedural) When skeletal remains turn up in Baltimore's Leakin Park, Detective Paul Solomon is pessimistic about their chances of solving the case. But a clue discovered near the bones soon leaves his partner, Tim Cullen, in little doubt as to their identity. 3/3

802. **Ellroy, James,** *Big Nowhere*, Mysterious Press, 1988. LA Quartet #2 of 4. (Police Procedural) 1950s Los Angeles: The City of Angels has become the city of the Angel of Death. Communist witch-hunts and insanely violent killings are terrorizing the community. Three men

are plunged into a maelstrom of violence and deceit when their lives become inextricably linked as each one confronts his own personal darkness. 3/3

803. **Ellroy, James**, *L. A. Confidential*, Mysterious Press, 1990. LA Quartet #3 of 4. (Police procedural) Christmas 1951, Los Angeles: a city where the police are as corrupt as the criminals. Six prisoners are beaten senseless in their cells by cops crazed on alcohol. For the three LAPD detectives involved, it will expose the guilty secrets on which they have built their corrupt and violent careers. The novel takes these cops on a sprawling epic of brutal violence and the murderous seedy side of Hollywood. -a murdered male prostitute (MLM). 1/3

804. **Erickson, Alex**, *Death by Coffee*, Kensington, 2015. Bookstore Cafe #1 of 6. (Bibliomystery Cozy) On their very first day of business, Brendon Lawyer huffily takes his coffee...to the grave. It seems he had a severe allergy to peanuts...but how could there have been nuts in his coffee? And who stole his emergency allergy medication? Fortunately, Krissy's love of puzzles and mysteries leads her not only to Officer Paul Dalton, but also to many of her new neighbors, who aren't terribly upset that the book is closed on Brendon. But one of them is a killer, and Krissy needs to read between the lies if she wants to save her new store–and live to see how this story ends... 1/3

805. **Erno, Jeff**, Secrets, Dreamspinner, 2014. Full Nelson #1 of 3. (MM Police Procedural) Chris Nelson is an up-and-coming police detective, new to the force, but his reputation precedes him. Everyone on the force knows he's openly gay and is married to his somewhat flamboyant husband, Ethan. At times Chris is a bit defensive about his sexual orientation, and he's all the more annoyed when his boss assigns him a murder case where the primary suspect is gay. Initially Chris fears he may become overly invested. –available as an ebook only (MLM). 3/3

806. **Erno, Jeff**, *Glitter,* Dreamspinner, 2014. Full Nelson #2 of 3. (MM Police Procedural) When Detective Chris Nelson catches a police call at a gay bar, he finds a murdered drag queen in the alley behind the building. Andrew Brooks, the victim's co-worker at Bambi's, claims he found her. Because she is sprinkled in the same red glitter Andrew uses in his act, Nelson takes him in for questioning. –available as an e-book only (MLM). 3/3

807. **Erno, Jeff**, *Teacher's Pet,* Dreamspinner, 2015. Fell Nelson #3 of 3. (MM Police Procedural) Detective Chris Nelson faces another murder investigation. This time the victims are educators–a college professor and a high school teacher–and both are gay. Jared

Bressman, the first victim, is found strangled in his apartment. A few days later, Stephen Hayes is found in his home, a victim of the same type of assault. Chris must piece together the clues to find a connection–if there is one–between the murders and stop the killer before he strikes again. Once he discovers that the killer also has a link to someone close to him, Chris races to beat the murderer to his final victim. –available as an e-book only (MLM). 3/3

808. **Etienne**, *Bodies of Work*, Dreamspinner, 2011. Avondale #1 of 17. (MM Police Procedural) George Martin and Mike Foster have been best friends since childhood, but recent events have brought them even closer together: Mike has moved into George's house now that George's unfaithful boyfriend has been kicked out. It puts Mike in a pinch, because he's always loved George-maybe more than a best friend should. George doesn't suspect Mike's feelings, being wrapped up in his job as the youngest lieutenant in the Jacksonville sheriff's office and investigating a series of murders. But it will all come to a head when George is stalked by a psycho and Mike steps in front of a bullet meant for George. George then realizes there's much more to their relationship than he thought. 3/3

809. **Etienne**, *Drag and Drop*, Dreamspinner, 2011. Avondale #2 of 17. (MM Police Procedural) After surviving the threat of a murderer and finding love with each other, George Martin and Mike Foster, best friends since childhood, are settling into a happy life. George's new promotion to the youngest captain in the Jacksonville Sheriff's Office keeps him busy, and his current case is no exception. The body of a fifty-year-old drag queen is found in the locked dressing room of a bar. As George delves into the subsequent murder investigation, he uncovers a dangerous trail of murdered drag queens and young gay men that intersects with another case involving porn films, torture, and worse. He struggles to make sense of the murders, but it's Mike who asks the question that leads to a break in the case. 3/3

810. **Etienne**, *Break and Enter*, Dreamspinner, 2011. Avondale #3 of 17. (MM Police Procedural) After surviving the threat of a murderer and finding love with each other, George Martin and Mike Foster, best friends since childhood, are settling into a happy life. George's new promotion to the youngest captain in the Jacksonville Sheriff's Office keeps him busy, and his current case is no exception. The body of a fifty-year-old drag queen is found in the locked dressing room of a bar. As George delves into the subsequent murder investigation, he uncovers a dangerous trail of murdered drag queens and young gay men that intersects with another case involving porn films, torture, and worse. He struggles to make sense of the murders, but it's Mike who asks the question that leads to a break in

the case. 3/3

811. **Etienne**, *Sleuth LLC: Birds of a Feather*, Dreamspinner, 2011. Avondale #4 of 17. (MM Police Procedural) Quentin Quasar has found that being a telepath is a mixed bag: it's great when he's catching an unfaithful spouse or tracking down a thief, but it's horrible when his bedmate is thinking unflattering thoughts during sex. It's no wonder that instead of saying his prayers every night, Quentin sends tendrils of thought out into the world, looking for another telepath to ease the loneliness. Imagine his surprise when he finds one-and the young man needs help! Nate Braddock was plenty panicked at being kidnapped by fanatics who planned to "beat the devil" out of him. With Quentin's help, and then his partnership, Nate finds the courage to take a stand against his mother's religious intolerance and together they'll confront an uncomfortable truth: telepaths may not be devils, but not all of them are angels either. Quentin and Nate will need their combined gifts to tell the difference. 3/3

812. **Etienne**, *The Burdens of Truth*, Dreamspinner, 2011. Avondale #6 of 17. (MM Police Procedural) Professor and secret government analyst Ian Sanderson's bad day gets worse when he arrives home one miserable November evening to find an apparently incriminating photograph in a FedEx envelope in his doorway, followed by increasingly threatening photographs over the next two or three weeks. It isn't just Ian being set up: his partner, Randy, a lieutenant colonel working on a top-secret Pentagon project, is also at risk. Someone obviously wants something, but what? And from whom? Soon, a mysterious caller demands that Randy disclose information about the project he's been working on. When he refuses, Ian's and Randy's sons, David and Paul, are kidnapped from an Amtrak passenger train. Resourceful and intelligent, the boys manage to escape-only to find themselves lost and alone in a remote wilderness. With time running out, can Ian and Randy track down their blackmailers? Or will the man known only as The Broker claim another set of victims? 3/3

813. **Etienne**, *Fold, Do Not Starch*, Dreamspinner, 2014. Avondale #15 of 17. (MM Police Procedural) Captain George Martin has handled many difficult cases during his career in law enforcement. When an employee of one of Mike's clients reaches out to them for help, they find themselves immersed in the complex world of money-laundering. –available via ebook only (MM) 3/3

814. **Etienne**, *Sleuth, LLC: Bring Out Your Dead*, Dreamspinner, 2014. Avondale #16 of 17. (MM Police Procedural) Telepathic private investigator Quentin Q. Quasar and his partner Nate Braddock are back. They accidentally stumble on a series of kidnapping/murders and begin to investigate. –available via e-book only (MM).

815. **Etienne**, *All Fall Down*, Dreamspinner, 2015. Avondale #17 of 17. (MM Police Procedural) Happy birthday to you... now die. Someone is on a murder spree and it's up to Chief George Martin's team to find out who. The murders, which have taken place on the victims' birthdays, have occurred in not just Jacksonville, but also Orlando, and as far away as Asheville. Even when the team finds them, the clues don't seem to lead anywhere, especially when everyone seems to have an alibi. Eleven people have died, and the race is on to catch the killer before he strikes again. –available via e-books only (MLM). 3/3

816. **Evanovich, Janet**, *Four to Score*, St. Martin's, 1998. Stephanie Plum #4 of 26. (Modern Cozy) Nabbing Maxine Nowicki, thief and extortionist, would be the answer to Stephanie's prayers and monetary woes. The only trouble is that Maxine is no where to be found, and her friends have been mysteriously turning up dead. To make matters worse, Stephanie's arch nemesis since grade school is also looking for Nowicki, hoping to cash in first. And Stephanie's Grandma Mazur, sidekick, Lula, and a six-foot-tall transvestite rock musician want to take Stephanie to Atlantic City. –Sally Sweet, the 6' tall transvestite rock musician appears in four of the Plum mysteries (MLM). 1/3

817. **Evanovich, Janet**, *Ten Big Ones*, St. Martin's, 2004. Stephanie Plum #10 of 26. (Modern Cozy) when Stephanie pegs a robber as a member of a vicious Trenton gang, they peg her as dead. Vice cop Joe Morelli fears she's in way too deep - even with the help of crime-solving, cross-dressing, bus driver Sally Sweet, and Stephanie's friend Lula riding shotgun as backup. 1/3

818. **Evanovich, Janet**, *Eleven on Top*, St. Martin's, 2005. Stephanie Plum #11 of 26. (Modern Cozy) Stephanie is stalked by a maniac returned from the grave for the sole purpose of putting her into a burial plot of her own. He's killed before, and he'll kill again if given the chance. Caught between staying far away from the bounty hunter business and staying alive, Stephanie reexamines her life and the possibility that being a bounty hunter is the solution rather than the problem. 1/3

819. **Evanovich, Janet**, *Twelve Sharp*, St. Martin's, 2006. Stephanie Plum #12 of 26. (Modern Cozy) While chasing down the usual cast of miscreants and weirdos Stephanie discovers that a crazed woman is stalking her. 1/3

820. **Evans, Gene**, *Murder on Queer Street*, Cameo Library, 1968. Straight detective, unknown plot as I was unable to find a description for this book (MM). ?/3

821. **Evans, Gene**, *Homo Hunt*, Cameo Library, 1969. (Pulp) Chicago-based bounty hunter Jeffrey Carter teams up with Don Richards, an ex-teacher and unreliable narrator, to track down a homosexual Nazi war criminal last seen in Illinois. -Gunn. 3/3

822. **Evans, Jane**, "Inside Out," ed. Joyce H. Hindman, *Scoundrels & Rascals*, ImPress, 1999. (Police Procedural/Hard Boiled) "San Francisco police inspector Gareth Resnick and private investigator Jim Wolf, Native American, first work independently and then together (Gunn)." 3/3

823. **Evans, Jane**, "A Favor for a Friend," ed. Joyce H. Hindman, *Scoundrels, Rascals, & Rogues*, ImPress, 2001. (Police Procedual/Hard Boiled) "San Francisco police inspector Gareth Resnick and private investigator Jim Wolf, Native American, first work independently and then together to reach [a] solution (Gunn)." 3/3

824. **Eversz, Robert**, *False Profit*, Viking Penguin, 1990. Paul Marston and Angel Cantini #2 of 2. (Hard Boiled/Crime Drama) When a prominent investment broker is found boiled to death in his hot tub, Paul Marston and Angel Cantini track the globe in search of the murderer and $500 million in missing investments. 1/3

F

825. **Fair, Alan**, *Villa of Queens*, Greenleaf, 1968. (Pulp) "Cote d'Azur American resident Glen Andrews, 23, tries to discover what is going on in Jason Wilding's villa (Gunn)." 3/3

826. **Falconer, Jade**, *Murder by Design*, Phaze, 2009. (MM Police Procedural) Sidney has it all: he's a gorgeous, sought-after male model, and he lives with Alan, who worships the ground he walks on. He's surrounded by friends and luxury. His life may not be conventional, but he's happy. Then Alan is murdered, and Sidney is arrested for the crime. All evidence points to Sidney, but the detective assigned to the case is sure they've got the wrong man. Detective Greg Wilson is convinced of Sidney's innocence, but is it because he's falling for him? 3/3

827. **Faraday, Paul**, *The Straight Shooter: A Nate Dainty Manhunt!*, Bold Strokes Books, 2010. (Amateur Sleuth) Fresh from a summer on the beach, West Hollywood Junior Collegiate, Nate Dainty is armed with a syllabus and a hidden agenda: to meet adult film sensation and (somewhat less) dedicated calculus student, Myles Long. Myles returns Dainty's desire, but before their big scene, the Paragon of Porn is snatched out from under Nate by masked men in a van in a parking lot! 3/3

828. **Faraday, Paul**, *The Affair of the Porcelain Dog*, Bold Stroke Books, 2011. Ira Adler #1 of 3. (Historical Crime Drama) London, 1889. For Ira Adler, former rent-boy and present plaything of crime lord Cain Goddard, stealing back the statue from Goddard's blackmailer should have been a doddle. But inside the statue is evidence that could put Goddard away for a long time under the sodomy laws, and everyone's after it, including Ira's bitter ex, Dr. Timothy Lazarus. 3/3

829. **Faraday, Paul**, *Turnbull House*, Bold Stroke Books, 2014. Ira Adler #2 of 3. (Historical Crime Drama) London 1891. Former criminal Ira Adler has built a respectable, if dull, life for himself as a confidential secretary. He even sits on the board of a youth shelter. When the shelter's landlord threatens to sell the building out from under them, Ira turns to his ex-lover, crime lord Cain Goddard, for a loan. But the loan comes with strings, and before he knows it, Ira is tangled up in them and tumbling back into the life of crime he worked so hard to escape. Two old flames come back into Ira's life, along

with a new young man who reminds Ira of his former self. Will Ira hold fast to his principles, or will he succumb to the temptations of easy riches and lost pleasures? 3/3

830. **Faraday, Paul**, *Fool's Gold*, Bold Stroke Books, 2015. Ira Adler #3 of 3. (Historical Crime Drama) For once, Ira Adler has it easy. He has money in his pocket, a comfortable arrangement with an undemanding young man, and no one's punched, chased, or shot at him in years. Suddenly, an explosion turns everything upside down. 3/3

831. **Farley, Jerry**, *After Hours – Life's a Drag*, Kindle, 2015. (Police Procedural) An introverted performer, with no family and few friends to care for her, is found murdered in her dressing room and no one is talking. With no leads, the police have given up on finding the killer. It seems that the case may go unsolved until Richard (Dick) Saunders is brought in on the case. –available as an e-book only (MLM). 3/3

832. **Farnsworth, J. L.**, *Mortal Enemies*, Dreamspinner, 2010. (MM Police Procedural) A simple drug bust–that's all it was supposed to be–but when the targeted dealer turns the tables, ex-Navy SEAL and LAPD narcotics officer Tyler Michaels finds himself the target of an old adversary, a killer who wants Tyler not just to die... but to die a very slow and very painful death. 3/3

833. **Farrell, Derek**, *Death of a Diva*, Createspace, 2016. Danny Bird #1 of 3. (Modern Cozy) Danny Bird is having a very bad day. In the space of just a few hours he lost his job, his partner and his home. Ever the optimist, Danny throws himself headlong into his dream to turn the grimmest pub in London into the coolest nightspot south of the river. Sadly, everything doesn't go quite as planned when his star turn is found strangled hours before opening night. 3/3

834. **Farrell, Derek**, *Death of a Nobody*, Createspace, 2016. Danny Bird #2 of 3. (Modern Cozy) As usual though things don't quite go to plan and it isn't long before the body count starts to mount. Danny and the unflappable Lady Caroline find themselves thrown into a classic murder mystery complete with poison pen letters, family feuds, money, jealousy and a cast of characters that would put the average Agatha Christie country house mystery to shame. 3/3

835. **Farrell, Derek**, *Death of a Devil*, Createspace, 2017. Danny Bird #3 of 3. (Modern Cozy) With local crime-lord Chopper Falzone keeping a watchful eye on his investment, Danny and Lady Caz must unmask a murderer, find some stolen diamonds and thwart a blackmailer – just another day at The Marq. 3/3

836. **Farrell, Kirby**, *The American Satan*, Walker, 1990. (Hard Boiled) Someone with anti-Iranian sentiments has been threatening Dr.

Mehdi Farhat, an Iranian-born Boston Chiropractor. New York based private investigator Duncan Ames, in Boston while his ex-wife Meg recovers from a car accident, is hired by Mehdi's assistant, Dorothy O'Hare...but when he arrives at her house later to get the details, Dorothy is dead-shot in an execution-style murder. –one of the victims is gay (MLM). 1/3

837. **Fearing, Kenneth,** *The Big Clock,* Harcourt & Brace, 1946. (Crime Noir) George Stroud is a hard-drinking, tough-talking, none-too-scrupulous writer for a New York media conglomerate that bears a striking resemblance to Time, Inc. in the heyday of Henry Luce. One day, before heading home to his wife in the suburbs, Stroud has a drink with Pauline, the beautiful girlfriend of his boss, Earl Janoth. Things happen. The next day Stroud escorts Pauline home, leaving her off at the corner just as Janoth returns from a trip. The day after that, Pauline is found murdered in her apartment. – based loosely on the Lonergan murder case (MLM). 1/3

838. **Feeley, F. E.,** *The Haunting of Timber Manor,* Dreamspinner, 2013. Memoirs of the Human Wraiths #1 of 3. (MM Paranormal) While recovering from the recent loss of his parents, Daniel Donnelly receives a phone call from his estranged aunt, who turns over control of the family fortune and estate, Timber Manor. When Daniel arrives to begin repairs, strange things happen. Nightmares haunt his dreams. 3/3

839. **Feeley, F. E.,** *Objects in the Rearview Mirror,* Dreamspinner, 2014. Memoirs of the Human Wraiths #2 of 3. (MM Paranormal) Their new home on Frederick Street in Clay Center, Kansas, was supposed to give writer Jonathan David and his husband, clinical psychologist Dr. Eddie Dorman, an opportunity to enjoy married life. They have barely settled in when the nightmare begins. Noises, disembodied voices, and mysterious apparitions make Jonathan's life hell. 3/3

840. **Feeley, F. E.,** *Still Waters,* Dreamspinner, 2015. Memoirs of the Human Wraiths #3 of 3. (MM Paranormal) Promise, Michigan is very much like every other small town across the state. Built on the edge of a lake, the homes sit in neat little rows in cute little neighborhoods. But Promise holds a terrible secret. In the center of the lake is an abandoned island where a curse is rumored to wait for victims, unabated and deadly. 3/3

841. **Feeley, F. E.,** *Closer,* Beaten Tracks, 2018. (MM Paranormal) Maplewood, Vermont is a picturesque town filled with unique shops, unique homes, and a quaint familiarity all centered around a lake with an unusual history. Legends, old as well as Urban, float around like the mist that hovers above the lake at break of dawn. But

they're just stories, right? However, something underneath the water is stirring. Something rotten wakes underneath the black waters of Lake Veronica so disturbing it haunts the nightmares of the local residents. 3/3

842. **Fennelly, Tony**, *Glory Hole Murders*, Carrol and Graf, 1985. Matt Sinclair #1 of 3. (Amateur Sleuth) The gay New Orleans aristocrat, Matt Sinclair, solves the murder of a supposedly-straight family man in the men's room of a gay bar. 3/3

843. **Fennelly, Tony**, *The Closet Hanging*, Carrol and Graf, 1987. Matt Sinclair #2 of 3. (Amateur Sleuth) Matt Sinclair is in trouble. A real estate developer has been found dead in a building owned by his family. It appears to be a murder disguised as a suicide. And Matt has become the prime suspect. 3/3

844. **Fennelly, Tony**, *Kiss Yourself Goodbye*, Arlington, 1989. Matt Sinclair #3 of 3. (Amateur Sleuth) Matt Sinclair, the gay scion of an old New Orleans family must clear his cousin Sylvia of murder. One Rodger Lloyd, Sylvia's ex-lover, and the sire of one of her sons was murdered in his hotel room. Lloyd's "dying message" seems to accuse Sylvia herself, as his last act was to open a book of Audubon prints to a picture of a Garden Warbler, "Sylvia Borin". 3/3

845. **Fennelly, Tony**, *The Hippie in the Wall*, St. Martin's, 1994. Margo Fortier #1 of 4. (Amateur Sleuth) In the French Quarter of New Orleans, a construction crew happens upon a corpse walled up in a topless bar 20 years prior. Investigation reveals that a prominent socialite–who was once a dancer in the bar and hides her own skeletons–might have knowledge of the murder. –Margo's husband is gay (MM). 2/3

846. **Fennelly, Tony**, *1-900-Dead*, St. Martin's, 1996. Margo Fortier #2 of 4. (Amateur Sleuth) When New Orleans's most famous telephone psychic is stabbed to death in her Lakefront home, Margo Fortier, a stripper-turned-society-columnist, gets on the case. Margo invents her own phony psychic act, pretending to channel her Irish great-grandmother to trap the killer. Or be trapped. 2/3

847. **Fennelly, Tony**, *Don't Blame the Snake*, St. Martin's, 2001. Margo Fortier #3 of 4. (Amateur Sleuth) Down South in stifling New Orleans, a literary celebrity lies dead of a mysterious rattlesnake bite in his penthouse hotel suite, while Margo Fortier, the Bourbon Street stripper-turned-society columnist deals with the heat by stretching out under a ceiling fan covered by a wet towel. Margo's husband Julian invites her to escape the heat and join him at a mystery writers' conference aboard the (blessedly air-conditioned) cruise ship Julep Queen. While sailing down the Mississippi, the Fortiers become acquainted with the arcane world of crime fiction publishing

and the characters who populate it. Margo fends off the advances of the lecherous and conniving publisher, Harvey Gould, who soon afterward is found murdered in his cabin. 2/3

848. **Fennelly, Tony**, *Home Dead for the Holidays*, St. Martin's, 2009. Margo Fortier #4 of 4. (Amateur Sleuth) It's Christmas time in New Orleans when young, handsome, Glen Watley arrives. Watley claims to be the grandson of the richest man in the Garden District, the issue of a weekend fling between a young private on his way to Vietnam and a Bourbon Street stripper. But is he an imposter? Margo Fortier, former showgirl-turned-society columnist is called to investigate. The story shifts between the hippie times of the early seventies and the modern era of the Clinton impeachment. 2/3

849. **Ferrari, Roberto C.**, *Pierce*, Haworth, 2007. (Psychological) Grad student Leo Vasari's life was shattered when his lover Matt died in a car accident. Then exactly one year later, Millie, Matt's mother and Leo's close friend, tries to kill herself. Leo, still mourning his loss, must somehow unravel the mystery that lies at the heart of the troubled Pierce family. Pierce is about grief and rebirth and moving on to love once more. But the only way Leo can do that is by finding out the true reasons for his lover's death. Leo struggles with his sadness and guilt as he searches for answers–and discovers dark family secrets never meant to be revealed. 3/3

850. **Ferrars, Elizabeth**, *Murder Among Friends*, William Collins Sons, 1946. (Amateur Sleuth) "The leading character Alice Church is investigating a murder and meets one of the potential suspects Roger Mace in a London pub during the blackout of the Second World War. Among the customers in the pub are "a group of gentle-faced young men in very pretty clothes who were earnestly interested in one another (Slide).'" 1/3

851. **Ferris, Monica (Mary Monica Pulver)**, *Crewel World*, Berkley, 1999. Needlecraft Cozy #1 of 19. (Cozy) When Betsy's sister is murdered in her own needlecraft store, Betsy takes over the shop and the investigation. But to find the murderer, she'll have to put together a list of motives and suspects to figure out this killer's pattern of crime...Includes a beautiful embroidery pattern! –store manager is gay and assists in solving the crimes (MLM). 2/3

852. **Ferris, Monica**, *Framed in Lace*, Berkley, 1999. Needlecraft Cozy #2 of 19. (Cozy) When the historic Hopkins ferry is raised from the lake, a skeleton is discovered. Unfortunately, the only evidence is a piece of lace-like fabric. But once Betsy Devonshire and the patrons of her needlecraft shop lend a hand, they're sure to stitch together the details of this mystery... 2/3

853. **Ferris, Monica**, *A Stitch in Time*, Berkley, 2000. Needlecraft Cozy

#3 of 19. (Cozy) When a damaged tapestry is discovered in a small-town church closet, needleworkers join to stitch together the clues which lead to a crafty crime. 2/3

854. **Ferris, Monica,** *Unraveled Sleeve,* Berkley, 2001. Needlecraft Cozy #4 of 19. (Cozy) Betsy Devonshire has settled into her new home in Excelsior, Minnesota, as owner of the town's needlecraft shop. So why is she suffering from terrifying nightmares? She hasn't a clue–but she thinks maybe it would help to get away for a while. With her friend Jill in tow, she heads north for a "stitch-in" at a remote, rustic lodge. But her nightmares only get worse–especially after she finds a dead woman no one else had seen. Then the body disappears–and she knows she won't get any rest until she untangles the mysterious threads of the crime.... 2/3

855. **Ferris, Monica,** *A Murderous Yarn,* Berkley, 2002. Needlecraft Cozy #5 of 19. (Cozy) Heavens to Betsy Devonshire! She never intended to get so caught up in this year's antique car race. But as sponsor of one of the entrants, she can't help but keep a close eye on the outcome–and it's not pretty. One of the drivers never makes it to the finish line. His car is found exploded in flames. Now Betsy and her crafty friends must determine if it was an accident or the work of a jealous competitor. The answer may be in a piece of needlework, but pinning down a suspect won't be easy... 2/3

856. **Ferris, Monica,** *Hanging by a Thread,* Berkley, 2003. Needlecraft Cozy #6 of 19. (Cozy) Betsy is still new enough to Excelsior, Minnesota, to not know a scandal when she causes one. So, when she hires Foster Johns to fix her roof, the resulting uproar has her needled. The whole town has pinned a five-year-old unsolved double murder on him. Betsy believes Johns when he says he isn't guilty. But she'll have to use every stitch of her sleuthing skills to tie up all the loose ends that will prove his innocence once and for all. 2/3

857. **Ferris, Monica,** *Cutwork,* Berkley, 2004. Needlecraft Cozy #7 of 19. (Cozy) After an artisan is murdered at the Excelsior, Minnesota, art fair, everyone is on pins and needles. It's up to needlework shop owner Betsy Devonshire to figure out who had designs on the dead designer. 2/3

858. **Ferris, Monica,** *Crewel Yule,* Berkley, 2004. Needlecraft #8 of 19. (Cozy) Betsy prepares for a chilling holiday season filled with mistletoe-and murder. This year's needlework convention is tragically interrupted when one shop owner tumbles nine stories to her untimely death. Now Betsy, Godwin, and other knitting hands must unravel the clues that will put the killer to rest...for a long winter's night. 2/3

859. **Ferris, Monica,** *Embroidered Truths,* Berkley, 2005. Needlecraft

Cozy #9 of 19. (Cozy) After her friend Godwin has a nasty quarrel with his significant other, John, Betsy Devonshire finds herself with a roommate. But heartbreak turns to grief when Betsy and Godwin discover John dead in his home, and Godwin is arrested for the murder. Betsy sets out to prove him innocent and finds that John had some dishonest dealings that made him a lot of money–and a lot of enemies. Now Betsy has to untangle a cat's cradle of lies if she's going to save Godwin... before the murderer decides to cut off all the loose ends for good. 2/3

860. **Ferris, Monica,** *Sins and Needles,* Berkley, 2006. Needlecraft Cozy #10 of 19. (Cozy) Owner of the Crewel World needlework shop and part-time sleuth, Betsy Devonshire must help clear Jan Henderson's name when her wealthy aunt is found dead, courtesy of a double-zero knitting needle. Just like the kind Jan knits with. And an embroidered map of Lake Minnetonka, found among the aunt's effects, could lead Betsy to a buried treasure-or to a secret that someone would kill to keep buried. 2/3

861. **Ferris, Monica,** *Knitting Bones,* Berkley, 2007. Needlecraft Cozy #11 of 19. (Cozy) The stitchers of the Embroiderers Guild are thrilled to have raised over $20,000 for charity-but they're less pleased when the representative who accepts the check disappears with it. After breaking her leg in a fall from a horse, Betsy's confined to her apartment and loopy on pain killers-she can't possibly investigate. But Godwin, her store manager, insists that he can do the legwork. Little do they know that a man across town has a similar injury-and he too is wondering what happened to that check. Betsy and Godwin have got to figure it out first, or it'll be a bad break for everyone. 2/3

862. **Ferris, Monica,** *Thai Die,* Berkley, 2008. Needlecraft Cozy #12 of 19. (Cozy) As full-time owner of the Crewel World needlework shop and part-time sleuth, Betsy Devonshire has become skilled at weaving suspicious threads. But when one of her regulars unwittingly becomes involved in a deadly delivery of exotic antiquities, Betsy fears something is seriously warped. 2/3

863. **Ferris, Monica,** *Blackwork,* Berkley, 2009. Needlecraft Cozy #13 of 19. (Cozy) Part-time sleuth and needlework shop owner Betsy Devonshire works to clear murder suspect Leona Cunningham and find the real killer after the victim was last seen blaming the peaceful Wiccan and microbrewery owner for a series of local accidents 2/3

864. **Ferris, Monica,** *Button and Bones,* Berkley, 2010. Needlecraft Cozy #14 of 19. (Cozy) Owner of the Crewel World needlework shop and part-time sleuth Betsy Devonshire heads for the Minnesota north

woods to renovate an old cabin. But beneath the awful linoleum is something even uglier- the skeleton of a Nazi. Betsy's investigation yields the site of a former German POW camp, a mysterious crocheted rug, and an intricately designed pattern of clues to a decades-old crime. 2/3

865. **Ferris, Monica,** *Threadbare,* Berkley, 2011. Needlecraft Cozy #15 of 19. (Cozy) When an elderly homeless woman is found dead on the shore of Lake Minnetonka, she's wearing something that holds the key to her identity but also opens up a mystery. Embroidered on her blouse is her will, in which she bequeaths everything she owns to her niece-Emily Hame, a member of the Monday Bunch at Betsy Devonshire's Crewel World needlework shop! Emily's aunt turns out to be the second homeless woman to be found dead under mysterious circumstances. 2/3

866. **Ferris, Monica**, *And Then You Dye,* Berkley, 2012. Needlecraft Cozy #16 of 19. (Cozy) Betsy is a natural-born yarnsmith–so it's only fitting that some of her favorite items to stock come from the dyeworks of Hailey Brent. Hailey makes hand-dyed knitting wool, silk, soy, and corn yarns. She uses only natural vegetable dyes, creating soft and beautiful colors. Which means her yarns are expensive, but well worth it. Unfortunately, someone thinks they're worth killing for. When Hailey's body is discovered shot dead in her workshop, Betsy discovers that there was a lot about Hailey she would have never guessed. 2/3

867. **Ferris, Monica,** *The Drowning Spool,* Berkley, 2014. Needlecraft Cozy #17 of 19. (Cozy) Even though running Crewel World keeps Betsy plenty busy, a little extra cash on the side doesn't hurt. So when the local senior complex, Watered Silk, asks her to teach a class on the tricky punch needle technique, Betsy jumps at the opportunity to win over some new customers. Unfortunately, the business that Betsy drums up is not of the needlework variety. A young woman is found floating in Watered Silk's therapy pool, and Betsy's sleuthing skills are immediately called upon to figure out who drowned her. But the list of suspects is more twisted than any Betsy has encountered before. The young woman had three lovers–each with a motive for the murder. 2/3

868. **Ferris, Monica**, *Darned if You Do,* Berkley, 2015. Needlecraft Cozy #18 of 19. (Cozy) After a tree falls on Tom Riordan's house, landing him in the hospital, the police discover a mountain of junk piled high in his home. Locals in Excelsior, Minnesota–including Betsy and her Crewel World Monday Bunch–offer to help with the clean-up while Tom recuperates. But when Tom is found murdered in his hospital bed, the sole heir to his property–his cousin Valentina–becomes the number one suspect. Betsy believes there's more to the

case than meets the eye, but finding clues to the killer's identity in the clutter Tom left behind will be like looking for a needle in a haystack ... 2/3

869. **Ferris, Monica,** *Knit Your Own Murder,* Berkley, 2016. Needlecraft Cozy #19 of 19. (Cozy) The Monday Bunch and other local knitters are participating in a fundraising auction to save a community center, creating a growing pile of stuffed animals and toys right in front of the auctioneers as the audience bids. Among those contributing the most knitted goods is temperamental businesswoman Marsha Hanover–who keels over halfway through the event. After she is pronounced DOA at the hospital, an autopsy reveals that Marsha had been poisoned. But how? And by whom? One of the prime suspects is her ruthless business rival Joe Mickels, who lost a bitterly contested property bid to Marsha. When Mickels pleads his innocence to Betsy, she reluctantly believes him. But if Betsy is going to uncover the real murderer's identity, she must first untangle the knots Marsha made in her relationships throughout her life... 2/3

870. **Fiano, Alex Rian,** *The Hanged Man,* Astrid Fiano, 2012. Gabriel 's World #1 of 5. (MM Mystery) Perry Conway was a man of principle with strong business ethics. He and his former lover, Rick McFadden, had a successful business selling used cars. Together in business, they knew their friendship was stronger than their love ever could be. They had the right staff and a great business model. The company was expanding, their profits were up, and Perry had plans to expand into a high-profile automotive empire that rivaled other dealerships. But all that changed the day they found a body in the trunk of one of the used cars. 3/3

871. **Fiano, Alex Rian,** *Two Faced Woman,* Astrid Fiano, 2013. Gabriel's World #2 of 5. (MM Mystery) New York City private investigator Gabriel Ross immerses himself in the cases of two special women. Sophie Faulkner, a woman with a second self, has been falsely accused of murder. Geneva Lennon, a transgender woman, is searching for her true birth identity. While working to help these women Gabriel also attempts to reclaim his spirituality and deal with his turbulent relationships. 3/3

872. **Fiano, Alex Rian,** *The Book of Joel,* Astrid Fiano, 2014. Gabriel's World #3 of 5. (MM Mystery) For Joel, his initial success as an artist is shadowed by his need to confront his parents, who threw him out at age 15. Joel finds his mother is anxious to reconnect with him, but his father is still hostile. 3/3

873. **Fiano, Alex Rian,** *Dead for Now,* Troublemaker, 2016. Gabriel's World #4 of 5. (MM Mystery) New York City private investigator

Gabriel Ross has a feeling he's being watched. His paranoia is justified–a rogue faction from the sinister Tertullian Society is stalking him. Psyops master Damon Clement has dangerous plans for Gabriel. –ebook only. The fifth book, *Hard Core*, has yet to be released (MM). 3/3

874. **Fielding, Kim**, *Love Can't Conquer*, Dreamspinner, 2016. Love Can't Series #1 of 2. (MM Amateur Sleuth) Bullied as a child in small-town Kansas, Jeremy Cox ultimately escaped to Portland, Oregon. Now in his forties, he's an urban park ranger who does his best to rescue runaways and other street people. His ex-boyfriend, Donny–lost to drinking and drugs six years earlier–appears on his doorstep and inadvertently drags Jeremy into danger. 3/3

875. **Fielding, Kim**, *Love is Heartless*, Dreamspinner, 2017. Love Can't Series #2 of 2. (MM Police procedural) Small but mighty–that could be Detective Nevin Ng's motto. Now a dedicated member of the Portland Police Bureau, he didn't let a tough start in life stop him from protecting those in need. He doesn't take crap from anyone, and he doesn't do relationships. Until he responds to the severe beating of a senior citizen and meets the victim's bow-tied, wealthy landlord. –there is a short story, "No Place Like Home," involving Stephen Walker which is a more edited version than appeared in the anthology, *Snow on the Roof*, which is free on the author's website (MLM). 3/3

876. **Fielding, Kim**, *The Spy's Love Song*, Dreamspinner, 2018. Stars from Peril #1 of 2. (MM Espionage) Jaxon Powers has what most only dream of. Fame. Fortune. Gold records and Grammy awards. Lavish hotel suites and an endless parade of eager bedmates. He's adored all over the world–even in the remote, repressive country of Vasnytsia, where the tyrannical dictator is a big fan. –second book is to be released in 2019 (MLM). 3/3

877. **Fields, L. A.**, *My Dear Watson*, Lethe, 2013. (Sherlock Holmes) One of the most famous partnerships in literature yields, over time, to a peculiar romantic triangle. Sherlock Holmes. Dr. John Watson. And the good doctor's second wife, whom Doyle never named. Mrs. Watson is a clever woman who realizes, through examining all the prior cases her husband shared with the world's greatest consulting detective, that the two men shared more than adventures: they were lovers, as well. In 1919, after the pair has retired, Mrs. Watson invites Holmes to her home to meet him face to face. Thus, begins a recounting of a peculiar affair between extraordinary men. 3/3

878. **Fields, L. A.**, *Homo Superiors*, Lethe, 2016. (Thriller) Two college seniors: Noah, frail like the hollow-boned birds he enjoys watching,

caged by his intellect, and by his sense that the only boy as smart as himself is his best friend; Ray who has spent years aping leading men so that his every gesture is suave, but who has become bored with petty cheats and tricks, and now, during summer break in Chicago, needs something momentous to occupy himself. -based on Leopold and Loeb (MLM). 3/3

879. **Filippi, Thomas,** *Dungeons and Drag Queens,* Writer's Club, 2001. (Fantasy) What happens when a small town drag queen gets sucked into a realm of sword and sorcery and forced to do much more than lip-sync for her life? After a weird wizard transports Sleazella LaRuse to the realm of Houmak, Green Bay's number one diva must battle to save her life and protect the lip-syncing, potty-mouthed persona she's worked so hard to cultivate. Will her bones be devoured by the gnawing nipple-mouths of slavwolves or crushed by the brutal Blada Femma? Worse yet, will she find love amongst the scum sailors and slopulating sky serpents? Will she win this glamorous game of thrones? The answer is clear in the most fierce and fabulous fantasy epic ever. 3/3

880. **Finson, Jon,** *Death on the Drive,* Createspace, 2018. Frank Salino #1 of 3. (Police Procedural) When the body of Steven Powers, author of a modest (by Florida standards) Ponzi scheme, turns up on "The Drive" in the gay village of Warren Beach, the police face a dilemma. Did the old fraudster simply drop dead crossing the street after some late-night kink with a hustler in a back alley? Or did an enraged "investor" place the corpse on dramatically public display? Detective Frank Salino reluctantly accepts the task of determining the cause of death. Aided by his Lesbian partner, Detective Carmen Rodriguez, and young CSI John Lytle, Salino puzzles fruitlessly over the conflicting scenarios leading to Powers' last end–until Frank's former boyfriend, Bureau Agent Mark Barrington, finally provides some crucial evidence. 3/3

881. **Finson, Jon,** *Mortality Watch,* Createspace, 2018. Frank Salino #2 of 3. (Police Procedural) What's killing the muscle-boy bartenders of Warren Beach? Have they overdosed, committed suicide, or run afoul of a conspiracy? Detective Frank Salino, who had ties to many of the young men, takes a keen interest in their untimely deaths (which grieve him personally) and in the fate of their unborn children. Aided by Detective Carmen Rodriguez, CSI John Lytle, and newly minted K9 Officer James Reed (Frank's new husband), Salino must unravel a labyrinth of relationships–gay and lesbian–in the LGBT village. 3/3

882. **Finson, Jon,** *In Death's Shade,* Createspace, 2018. Frank Salino #3 of 3. (Police Procedural) They summoned Detective Frank Salino and his husband, K9 Officer James Reed, from their warm bed to

investigate a "crisper." The immolated corpse, seemingly unidentifiable, marked just the onset of grisly murders committed by spectral figures in the LGBT village of Warren Beach. 3/3

883. **Firth, Anthony**, *Tall, Balding, Thirty-Five*, Harper & Row, 1967. (Espionage) Closeted British spy John Limbo in Bavarian espionage story. 1/3

884. **Fisher, Kit**, *Paper Flowers*, Wayward, 2000. (MM Police Procedural) Seeking vital clues to bring a gang of corrupt police to justice, Peter Duncan finds more pain – and more love – than he ever bargained for. With an enemy on one side and a lover on the other, his life is about to be torn apart, maybe forever. 3/3

885. **Fitzroy, Adam**, *In Deep*, Manifold, 2015. (MM Police Procedural) Arriving on a remote Scottish island to investigate an unexplained death, retired police officer Ted Harris finds himself entangled in the life of the community – and becomes attracted to Athol, his enigmatic landlord. Soon they're working together, depending on each other for survival in perilous circumstances, and slowly unravelling the mystery. Will they ever figure out exactly how and why Kieran Parnes died and who was responsible for his death. 3/3

886. **Fitzroy, Adam**, *Ghost Station*, Manifold, 2016. (MM Espionage) It's 1976, the Cold War is still at its coldest, and retired agent John Dashwood is persuaded to return to supervise one last mission. However, nothing at Ghost Station is quite the way he remembers it and everybody seems to have something to hide – including his two valued colleagues, Rick Wentworth and Harry Tilney, and his enigmatic boss Sir Charles Grandison. When operational necessity requires Dashwood to send Rick and Harry into a dangerous situation, the boundaries between friend and enemy begin to blur and he's left isolated and wondering which of his so-called allies he can really trust. 3/3

887. **Fitzroy, Adam**, *The Bridge on the River Wye*, Manifold, 2016. (MM Mystery) Chef Rupert's picking up the pieces after a catastrophe; he's lost his love, his business, his home and even his dog, and he's trying to make a fresh start. Linking up with Jake almost on a whim he soon finds himself involved in a strange tale of organic farming, migrant workers, greed and even possibly murder. 3/3

8880. **Flewelling, Lynn**, *Luck in the Shadows*, Bantam, 1996. Nightrunner #1 of 7. (MM Fantasy) When young Alec of Kerry is taken prisoner for a crime he didn't commit, he is certain that his life is at an end. But one thing he never expected was his cellmate. Spy, rogue, thief, and noble, Seregil of Rhiminee is many things–none of them predictable. And when he offers to take on Alec as his apprentice, things may never be the same for either of them. Soon Alec is traveling roads he never knew existed, toward a war he never suspected was brewing. Before long he and Seregil are embroiled in a sinister plot that runs deeper than either can imagine, and that may cost them far more than their lives if they fail. But fortune is as unpredictable as Alec's new mentor, and this time there just might be... Luck in the Shadows. –Prequel *By the River* is a short story that introduces Seregil in an e-book exclusive published in 2001 (MLM). 3/3

889. **Flewelling, Lynn**, *Stalking Darkness,* Bantam, 1997. Nightrunner #2 of 7. (MM Fantasy) With the Leran threat laid to rest, Alec and Seregil are now able to turn their attention to the ancient evil which threatens their land. The Plenimarans, at war with Skalans, have decided to defeat their ancient enemy by raising up the Dead God, Seriamaius. The early attempts at this reincarnation–masterminded by the sinister Duke Mardus and his sorcerous minion Vargul Ashnazai–once left Seregil in a sorcerous coma. Now, an ancient prophecy points to his continuing role in the quest to stop Mardus in his dread purpose. Seregil's friend and Mentor, the wizard Nysander, has long been the guardian of a deadly secret. 3/3

890. **Flewelling, Lynn**, *Traitor's Moon,* Bantam, 1999. Nightrunner #3 of 7. (MM Fantasy) Wounded heroes of a cataclysmic battle, Seregil and Alec have spent the past two years in self-imposed exile, far from their adopted homeland, Skala, and the bitter memories there. But as the war rages on, their time of peace is shattered by a desperate summons from Queen Idralain, asking them to aid her daughter on a mission to Aurnen, the very land from which Seregil was exiled in his youth. Here, in this fabled realm of magic and honor, he must at last confront the demons of his dark past, even as Alec discovers an unimagined heritage. And caught between Skala's desperate need and the ancient intrigues of the Aurnfaie, they soon find themselves snared in a growing web of treachery and betrayal. 3/3

891. **Flewelling, Lynn**, *Shadow's Return,* Bantam, 2008. Nightrunner #4 of 7. (MM Fantasy) After their victory in Aurënen, Alec and Seregil have returned home to Rhíminee. But with most of their allies dead or exiled, it is difficult for them to settle in. Hoping for diversion, they accept an assignment that will take them back to Seregil's homeland. En route, however, they are ambushed and separated, and both are sold into slavery. Clinging to life, Seregil is sustained only by the hope that Alec is alive.But it is not Alec's life his strange master wants–it is his blood. For his unique lineage is capable of producing a rare treasure, but only through a harrowing process that will test him body and soul and unwittingly entangle him and Seregil in the realm of alchemists and madmen–and an enigmatic

creature that may hold their very destiny in its inhuman hands.... But will it prove to be savior or monster? 3/3

892. **Flewelling, Lynn,** *The White Road,* Bantam, 2010. Nightrunner #5 of 7. (MM Fantasy) Having escaped death and slavery in Plenimar, Alec and Seregil want nothing more than to go back to their nightrunning life in Rhíminee. Instead they find themselves saddled with Sebrahn, a strange, alchemically created creature–the prophesied "child of no woman." Its moon-white skin and frightening powers make Sebrahn a danger to all whom Alec and Seregil come into contact with, leaving them no choice but to learn more about Sebrahn's true nature. –*Glimpses: A Collection of Nightrunner Short Stories* released in 2010 by Dreamspinner Press and does not contain any mystery (MM). 3/3

893. **Flewelling, Lynn,** *Casket of Souls,* Spectra, 2012. Nightrunner #6 of 7. (MM Fantasy) More than the dissolute noblemen they appear to be, Alec and Seregil are skillful spies, dedicated to serving queen and country. But when they stumble across evidence of a plot pitting Queen Phoria against Princess Klia, the two Nightrunners will find their loyalties torn as never before. Even at the best of times, the royal court at Rhíminee is a serpents' nest of intrigue, but with the war against Plenimar going badly, treason simmers just below the surface. And that's not all that poses a threat: A mysterious plague is spreading through the crowded streets of the city, striking young and old alike. Now, as panic mounts and the body count rises, hidden secrets emerge. And as Seregil and Alec are about to learn, conspiracies and plagues have one thing in common: The cure can be as deadly as the disease. 3/3

894. **Flewelling, Lynn,** *Shards of Time,* Del Rey, 2014. Nightrunner #7 of 7. (MM Fantasy) The governor of the sacred island of Korous and his mistress have been killed inside a locked and guarded room. The sole witnesses to the crime–guards who broke down the doors, hearing the screams from within–have gone mad with terror, babbling about ghosts ... and things worse than ghosts. Dispatched to Korous by the queen, master spies Alec and Seregil find all the excitement and danger they could want–and more. For an ancient evil has been awakened there, a great power that will not rest until it has escaped its otherworldly prison and taken revenge on all that lives. And only those like Alec–who have died and returned to life–can step between the worlds and confront the killer ... even if it means a second and all too permanent death. 3/3

895. **Flinders, Karl,** *The Boy Avengers,* Travellers Companion, 1971. (Crime Drama) You've heard of strange and sensuous practices among schoolboys before–but they pale into insignifance before the fiendish, blackly funny machinations of Grant Lattimer when he

sets out to perpetrate an elaborate sexual revenge on the rapists of his beloved! –based losely on the Lonergan murder case (MLM). 3/3

896. **Floyd, Bill May**, *Saturday Night Fervor,* Blueboy, 1978. (Pulp) The reader becomes the accidental sleuth when your lover John has been murdered in your home while you were away (Gunn). 3/3

897. **Ford, Catt**, *Lily White, Rose Red,* Dreamspinner, 2010. (MM Hard Boiled) Meet Grey Randall, a detective whose sense of humor makes it hard for him to stay strictly noir. It's 1948 in Las Vegas–the newborn Sin City–and he's just landed his first murder case. He's more at ease among the lowlifes, but his new client, a beautiful, wealthy woman, a real femme fatale, moves in the upper crust of society. Grey's hot on the trail of a killer, despite obstructive cops who don't want a private dick sniffing around and digging up secrets. And he starts getting close to the truth, but one of his suspects, Phillip Martin, AKA Mr. Big–AKA Mr. Beautiful–proves to be a man who could force Grey to reveal a dark secret of his own. –states that this is the first in a series but there are no sequels (MLM). 3/3

898. **Ford, Michael Thomas**, *What We Remember,* Kensington, 2009. (Amateur Sleuth) James McCloud, a Seattle district attorney, gets an early morning phone call from his sister, Celeste, announcing that their father's body has been found. Police officer Daniel McCloud disappeared years ago, but a bigger bombshell is in store - evidence from the body proves that he was murdered. –McCloud does not do any sleuthing but ponders back to his childhood which reveals the needed clue, won the twenty-second LAMBDA Award (MLM). 3/3

899. **Ford, Rhys**, *Dirty Kiss,* Dreamspinner, 2011. Cole McGinnis #1 of 6. (MM Hard Boiled) Cole Kenjiro McGinnis, ex-cop and PI, is trying to get over the shooting death of his lover when a supposedly routine investigation lands in his lap. Investigating the apparent suicide of a prominent Korean businessman's son proves to be anything but ordinary, especially when it introduces Cole to the dead man's handsome cousin, Kim Jae-Min. 3/3

900. **Ford, Rhys**, *Dirty Secret,* Dreamspinner, 2012. Cole McGinnis #2 of 6. (MM Hard Boiled) Loving Kim Jae-Min isn't always easy: Jae is gun-shy about being openly homosexual. Ex-cop turned private investigator Cole McGinnis doesn't know any other way to be. When a singer named Scarlet asks him to help find Park Dae-Hoon, a gay Korean man who disappeared nearly two decades ago, Cole finds himself submerged in the tangled world of rich Korean families, where obligation and politics mean sacrificing happiness to preserve corporate empires. 3/3

901. **Ford, Rhys,** *Dirty Laundry,* Dreamspinner, 2013. Cole McGinnis #3 of 6. (MM Hard Boiled) For ex-cop turned private investigator Cole McGinnis, each day brings a new challenge. Too bad most of them involve pain and death. Claudia, his office manager and surrogate mother, is still recovering from a gunshot, and Cole's closeted boyfriend, Kim Jae-Min, suddenly finds his teenaged sister dumped in his lap. Cole is approached by Madame Sun, a fortune-teller whose clients have been dying at an alarming rate. -two short stories follow; *Dirty Sweets* and *Dirty Day* were both published in 2013 (MLM). 3/3

902. **Ford, Rhys**, *Dirty Deeds,* Dreamspinner, 2014. Cole McGinnis #4 of 6. (MM Hard Boiled) Sheila Pinelli needed to be taken out. Former cop turned private investigator Cole McGinnis never considered committing murder. But six months ago, when Jae-Min's blood filled his hands and death came knocking at his lover's door, killing Sheila Pinelli became a definite possibility. Thanks to the Santa Monica police mistakenly releasing Sheila following a loitering arrest, Cole finally gets a lead on Sheila's whereabouts. –short story *Dirty Minds* was published in 2015 (MLM). 3/3

903. **Ford, Rhys,** *Down and Dirty,* Dreamspinner, 2015. Cole McGinnis #5 of 6. (MM Hard Boiled) From the moment former LAPD detective Bobby Dawson spots Ichiro Tokugawa, he knows the man is trouble. 3/3

904. **Ford, Rhys,** *Dirty Heart,* Dreamspinner, 2016. Cole McGinnis #6 of 6. (MM Hard Boiled) Former LAPD detective Cole McGinnis's life nearly ended the day his police partner and best friend Ben Pirelli emptied his service weapon into Cole and his then-lover, Rick. Since Ben turned his gun on himself, Cole thought he'd never find out why Ben tried to destroy him. Years later, Cole has stitched himself back together. Now a private investigator and in love with Jae-Min Kim, a Korean-American photographer he met on a previous case, Cole's life is back on track–until he discovers Jeff Rollins, a disgraced cop and his first partner, has resurfaced and appears to be working on the wrong side of the law–Ford states that this is the final book in the Cole McGinnis series but there was a Christmas short story, *Dirty Bites*, that was published in 2016 (MLM). 3/3

905. **Ford, Rhys**, Cops and Comix, Dreamspinner, 2018. Murder and Mayhem #.5 of 2. (MM Amateur Sleuth/Police Procedural) It's all fun and games until someone leaves a dead body on the floor. Life for comic book store owner Alex Martin usually runs to the mundane. Sure, he has a regular influx of geeks and freaks, but for the most part, it's a familiar weird. That all changes when he opens up Planet X Comics one morning and finds a corpse in the middle of his shop. When Detective James Castillo is called in to investigate,

Alex is torn between wanting to climb the man like a tree and giving him a wide berth. Luckily for Alex, the handsome detective is just as interested in him–as a suspect in the murder. focus on Detective Castillo rather than Dante or Rook (MM). 3/3

906. **Ford, Rhys**, *Murder and Mayhem,* Dreamspinner, 2015. Murder and Mayhem #1 of 2. (MM Amateur Sleuth) Dead women tell no tales. Former cat burglar Rook Stevens stole many a priceless thing in the past, but he's never been accused of taking a life–until now. 3/3

907. **Ford, Rhys**, *Tramps and Thieves,* Dreamspinner, 2017. Murder and Mayhem #2 of 2. (MM Amateur Sleuth/Police Procedural) Whoever said blood was thicker than water never stood in a pool of it. Retiring from stealing priceless treasures seemed like a surefire way for Rook Stevens to stay on the right side of the law. Instead, Rook ends up not only standing in a puddle of his cousin Harold's blood but also being accused of Harold's murder...and sleeping with Harold's wife. 3/3

908. **Ford, Rhys**, *Sinner's Gin,* Dreamspinner, 2012. Sinners #1 of 6. (MM Amateur Sleuth/Police Procedural) There's a dead man in Miki St. John's vintage Pontiac GTO, and he has no idea how it got there. Kane Morgan, the SFPD inspector renting space in the art co-op next door, initially suspects Miki had a hand in the man's murder, but Kane soon realizes Miki is as much a victim as the man splattered inside the GTO.–short story collection *Hair of the Dog* published in 2014 for free by the author as an e-book (MM). 3/3

909. **Ford, Rhys**, *Whiskey and Wry,* Dreamspinner, 2013. Sinners #2 of 6. (MM Amateur Sleuth/Police Procedural) He was dead. And it was murder most foul. If erasing a man's existence could even be called murder. When Damien Mitchell wakes, he finds himself without a life or a name. His chance to escape back to his own life comes when his prison burns, but a gunman is waiting for him, determined that Damien Mitchell will not escape. With the assassin on his tail, Damien flees to the City by the Bay, but keeping a low profile is the only way he'll survive as he searches San Francisco for his best friend, Miki St. John–short story *The Devil's Brew* was published in 2014 as an e-book exclusive (MLM). 3/3

910. **Ford, Rhys**, *Tequila Mockingbird,* Dreamspinner, 2014. Sinners #3 of 6. (MM Amateur Sleuth/Police Procedural) Lieutenant Connor Morgan of SFPD's SWAT division wasn't looking for love. Especially not in a man. His life plan didn't include one Forest Ackerman, a brown-eyed, blond drummer who's as sexy as he is trouble. Instead, he finds a murdered man while on a drug raid and loses his heart comforting the man's adopted son. –four short stories followed;

Wild Turkey (2014), *Rotgut Gin* (2015), *Shot Glass Sin* (2015), and *A Touch of Irish* (2015) all available as e-books only (MLM). 3/3

911. **Ford, Rhys,** *Sloe Ride,* Dreamspinner, 2015. Sinners #4 of 6. (MM Amateur Sleuth/Police Procedural) It isn't easy being a Morgan. Especially when dead bodies start piling up and there's not a damned thing you can do about it. Rafe Andrade returned home to lick his wounds following his ejection from the band he helped form. -short story *Appleshots and Beer* published in 2016 follows as an e-book exclusive (MLM). 3/3

912. **Ford, Rhys,** *Absinthe of Malice,* Dreamspinner, 2016. Sinners #5 of 6. (MM Amateur Sleuth/Police Procedural) *We're getting the band back together.* Those six words send a chill down Miki St. John's spine, especially when they're spoken with a nearly religious fervor by his brother-in-all-but-blood, Damien Mitchell. But those demons and troubles won't leave them alone, and with every mile under their belts, the band faces its greatest challenge–overcoming their deepest flaws and not killing one another along the way. 3/3

913. **Ford, Rhys***, Sin and Tonic,* Dreamspinner, 2018. Sinners #6 of 6. (MM Amateur Sleuth/Police Procedural) Miki St. John believed happy endings only existed in fairy tales until his life took a few unexpected turns… and now he's found his own. It's a pity someone's trying to kill him. Old loyalties and even older grudges emerge from Chinatown's murky, mysterious past, and Miki struggles to deal with his dead mother's abandonment, her secrets, and her brutal murder while he's hunted by an enigmatic killer who may have ties to her. The case lands in Kane's lap, and he and Miki are caught in a deadly game of cat-and-mouse. When Miki is forced to face his personal demons and the horrors of his childhood, only one thing is certain: the rock star and his cop are determined to fight for their future and survive the evils lurking in Miki's past. 3/3

914. **Ford, Rhys***, Fish and Ghosts,* Dreamspinner, 2013. Hellsinger #1 of 2. (MM Paranormal) When his Uncle Mortimer died and left him Hoxne Grange, the family's Gilded Age estate, Tristan Pryce knew he wasn't going to have an easy time of it. He was to be the second generation of Pryces to serve as a caretaker for the estate, a way station for spirits on their final steps to the afterlife. The ghosts were the simple part. He'd been seeing boo-wigglies since he was a child. No, the difficult part was his own family. Determined to establish Tristan's insanity, his loving relatives hire Dr. Wolf Kincaid and his paranormal researchers, Hellsinger Investigations, to prove the Grange is not haunted. Skeptic Wolf Kincaid has made it his life's work to debunk the supernatural. After years of cons and fakes, he

can't wait to reveal the Grange's ghostly activity is just badly leveled floorboards and a drafty old house. The Grange has more than a few surprises for him, including its prickly, reclusive owner. Tristan Pryce is much less insane and much more attractive than Wolf wants to admit and when his Hellsinger team unwittingly release a ghostly serial killer on the Grange, Wolf is torn between his skepticism and protecting the man he'd been sent to discredit. 3/3

915. **Ford, Rhys**, *Duck Duck Ghost,* Dreamspinner, 2014. Hellsinger #2 of 2. (MM Paranormal) Paranormal investigator Wolf Kincaid knows what his foot tastes like. Mostly because he stuck it firmly in his mouth when his lover, Tristan Pryce, accidentally drugged him with a batch of psychotropic baklava. Needing to patch things up between them, Wolf drags Tristan to San Luis Obispo, hoping Tristan's medium ability can help evict a troublesome spirit haunting an old farmhouse. With Wolf's sister handling Hoxne Grange's spectral visitors, Tristan finds himself in the unique position of being able to leave home for the first time in forever, but Wolf's roughshod treatment is the least of his worries. –third book in the series, *Send in the Ghosts* to be published by Dreamspinner in 2019 (MLM). 3/3

916. **Ford, Rhys**, *Dim Sum Asylum,* Dreamspinner, 2017. (MM Paranormal) Welcome to Dim Sum Asylum: a San Francisco where it's a ho-hum kind of case when a cop has to chase down an enchanted two-foot-tall shrine god statue with an impressive Fu Manchu mustache that's running around Chinatown, trolling sex magic and chaos in its wake. Senior Inspector Roku MacCormick of the Chinatown Arcane Crimes Division faces a pile of challenges far beyond his human-faerie heritage, snarling dragons guarding C-Town's multiple gates, and exploding noodle factories. After a case goes sideways, Roku is saddled with Trent Leonard, a new partner he can't trust, to add to the crime syndicate family he doesn't want and a spell-casting serial killer he desperately needs to find. While Roku would rather stay home with Bob the Cat and whiskey himself to sleep, he puts on his badge and gun every day, determined to serve and protect the city he loves. When Chinatown's dark mystical underworld makes his life hell and the case turns deadly, Trent guards Roku's back and, if Trent can be believed, his heart... even if from what Roku can see, Trent is as dangerous as the monsters and criminals they're sworn to bring down. –this is the full-length novelization of a short story printed in *Charmed & Dangerous Anthology* (MLM). 3/3

917. **Ford, Rhys**, *Fish Stick Fridays,* Dreamspinner, 2015. Half Moon Bay #1 of 3. (Crime Drama) Deacon Reid was born bad to the bone with no intention of changing. A lifetime of law-bending and living on the edge suited him just fine–until his baby sister died and he found himself raising her little girl. Staring down a family history of bad

decisions and reaped consequences, Deacon cashes in everything he owns, purchases an auto shop in Half Moon Bay, and takes his niece, Zig, far away from the drug dens and murderous streets they grew up on. Zig deserves a better life than what he had, and Deacon is determined to give it to her. Lang Harris is stunned when Zig, a little girl in combat boots and a purple tutu blows into his bookstore, and then he's left speechless when her uncle, Deacon Reid walks in, hot on her heels. Lang always played it safe but Deacon tempts him to step over the line... just a little bit. More than a little bit. And Lang is willing to be tempted. Unfortunately, Zig isn't the only bit of chaos dropped into Half Moon Bay. Violence and death strikes leaving Deacon scrambling to fight off a killer before he loses not only Zig but Lang too. 3/3

918. **Ford, Rhys**, *Hanging the Stars*, Dreamspinner, 2016. Half Moon Bay #2 of 3. (Crime Drama) Angel Daniels grew up hard, one step ahead of the law and always looking over his shoulder. A grifter's son, he'd learned every con and trick in the book but ached for a normal life. Once out on his own, Angel returns to Half Moon Bay where he once found...and then lost...love. Now, Angel's life is a frantic mess of schedules and chaos. Between running his bakery and raising his troubled eleven-year-old half-brother, Roman, Angel has a hectic but happy life. Then West Harris returns to Half Moon Bay and threatens to break Angel all over again by taking away the only home he and Rome ever had. When they were young, Angel taught West how to love and laugh but when Angel moved on, West locked his heart up and threw away the key. Older and hardened, West returns to Half Moon and finds himself face-to-face with the man he'd lost. Now, West is torn between killing Angel or holding him tight. But rekindling their passionate relationship is jeopardized as someone wants one or both of them dead, and as the terrifying danger mounts, neither man knows if the menace will bring them together or forever tear them apart. –short story *Tutus and Tinsel* follows but is not a mystery (MLM). 3/3

919. **Forrest, Katherine V.**, *Murder by Tradition*, Naiad, 1991. Kate Delafield #4 of 9. (Police Procedural) When a successful gay restaurateur is stabbed to death, Kate Delafield's investigation puts her in conflict with her own fear of being outed as a lesbian. Can Kate testify for the prosecution with her integrity intact, when the killer's attorney, the only man who knows the truth about Kate's -sexuality, prepares a "homosexual panic" defense? 3/3

920. **France, Christiane**, *Missing, Presumed Dead*, Amber Allure, 2011. Amethyst Cove #2 of 7. (MM Hard Boiled) Private investigator and ex-cop, Greg Stewartson, is on his way to bed when his Hollywood-producer brother, Vance, shows up on his doorstep. With

him is the handsome, sexy, and blond Tim Fensham, the brother of Vance's latest girlfriend, movie star Petra Lianne. Vance says Petra went missing more than a month ago after last being seen in Amethyst Cove. He has new information, but the police refuse to follow it up. They've closed the case, declaring the actress "Missing, Presumed Dead." –series written by KC Kendrick as well. 57 pages, available as an e-book only (MLM). 3/3

921. **France, Christiane,** *Missing, But Not Dead,* Amber Allure, 2014. Amethyst Cove #4 of 7. (MM Hard Boiled) When Greg Stewartson, ex-cop, private investigator, and half-owner of Amethyst Cove Security & Investigations, meets Ash Tyler, a handsome and very sexy nurse, their mutual attraction turns Greg's world upside down. Greg begins investigating Ash's biological family, he also starts to wonder, if the missing persons were Ash's real family, what made them vanish almost as effectively as if they'd never existed in the first place? –61 pages, available as an e-book only (MLM). 3/3

922. **France, Christiane,** *Still Missing,* Amber Quill, 2015. Amethyst Cove #7 of 7. (MM Hard Boiled) One night, a half-drowned man is brought into the urgent care clinic where Ash works. He says he's looking for Jack Smith, the man Ash knew as "Grandpa." Suddenly Greg is up to his ears in new information and fresh leads. Will he finally be able to provide Ash with the answers he so desperately wants, or is he being conned by a pair of clever hustlers determined to conceal the truth? –64 pages, available as an e-book only (MLM). 3/3

923. **Francis, Dick,** *Odds Against,* Harper and Row, 1965. Sid Halley #1 of 5. (Hardboiled) Former hotshot jockey Sid Halley landed a position with a detective agency, only to catch a bullet from some penny-ante thug. Now, he has to go up against a field of thoroughbred criminals–and the odds are against him that he'll even survive. –a closeted witness comes forward but begs Halley to remain anonymous (MLM). 1/3

924. **Francis, Manna,** *Mind Fuck,* Casperian, 2007. The Administration #1 of 9. (MM Police Procedural) There are no bad guys or good guys. There are only better guys and worse guys. One of the worse guys is Val Toreth. In a world in which torture is a legitimate part of the investigative process, he works for the Investigation and Interrogation Division, where his colleagues can be more dangerous than the criminals he investigates. One of the better guys is Keir Warrick. His small corporation, SimTech, is developing a "sim" system that places users in a fully immersive virtual reality. Their home is the dark future dystopia of New London. A totalitarian bureaucracy controls the European Administration, sharing political power with the corporations. 3/3

925. **Francis, Manna,** *Quid Pro Quo,* Casperian, 2008. The Administration #2 of 9. (MM Police Procedural) When he agrees to do a favor for his old friend Liz Carey in Corporate Fraud, Para-investigator Val Toreth is hoping for a simple case. After all, kidnapping and dismemberment are all in a day's work for the Investigation and Interrogation Division. But in the European Administration, simplicity is often a dangerous illusion, and anyone who goes looking for trouble in the corporate world is certain to find more than they bargained for. Fraud, sabotage, espionage, blackmail, decades-long vendettas, and murder–the more powerful the corporations, the darker their secrets. 3/3

926. **Francis, Manna,** *Game and Players,* Casperian, 2008. The Administration #3 of 9. (MM Police Procedural) Socioanalysts can read minds and motives at a glance, predict the future, manipulate the smallest actions of their unwitting puppets, and crush careers with a single word...or so the popular rumors say. Their arrival is dreaded everywhere in the European Administration, even the Investigation and Interrogation Division. Para-investigator Val Toreth, accustomed to being feared himself, is about to discover the truth of the rumors at first hand, when he is assigned as personal liaison to Carnac, the socioanalyst seconded to I&I to root out anti-Administration sentiments among its staff. 3/3

927. **Francis, Manna,** *Control,* Casperian, 2009. The Administration #4 of 9. (MM Police Procedural) Gaining it, keeping it, or losing it, control is more than just a game–it's a critical tool for survival. No more so than in the Administration, where the Investigation and Interrogation Division's Val Toreth faces professional and personal hazards every day. And when an attack on one of the most loyal and valued members of his investigative team makes the professional very personal indeed, Toreth finds himself entangled once more in the darker side of corporate life and crime. 3/3

928. **Francis, Manna,** *Quis Custodiet,* Casperian, 2009. The Administration #5 of 9. (MM Police Procedural) No protests, no bombings, no subversion. Is it possible that in one part of the European Administration at least, almost all the citizens are happy with their lot in life? It seems unlikely. When the numbers don't add up at the Athens branch of the Investigation and Interrogation Division, Para-investigator Toreth is sent there from New London to review their procedures. 3/3

929. **Francis, Manna,** *First Against the Wall,* Casperian, 2010. The Administration #6 of 9. (MM Police Procedural) Who is leading the rabble to victory? Toreth shifted against the wall, trying to get comfortable. Between bruises and handcuffs, he didn't have much success. On the first day, in the first cell, the lights had been on, the

water dispenser working, and the prisoner feeding schedule still running. Then the lights went out, and things had gone steadily downhill from there. 3/3

930. **Francis, Manna,** *For Certain Values of Family,* Casperian, 2011. The Administration #7 of 9. (MM Police Procedural) Every silver lining has a cloud. After the revolution, stability returns for most of the citizens of the European Administration. Revolution has delivered a little more freedom, if not as much as its architects hoped. Some, however, are finding that change also brings more complications and fresh dangers. For Para-investigator Val Toreth, the Investigation and Interrogation Division isn't quite the home it used to be. With a reduced investigation team, fractured relationships, and political uncertainty about the future, the last thing he needs is trouble from someone else's family, or unexpected news from his own. 3/3

931. **Francis, Manna,** *Blood and Circuses,* Casperian, 2015. The Administration #8 of 9. (MM Police Procedural) It's set to be a busy autumn in New London and beyond. With the ripples of the revolt still running through the European Administration, Val Toreth is slowly settling into the new flat he shares with Keir Warrick. But on orders from the very highest levels of the Administration, Toreth finds himself leaving his regular beat far behind and heading over the Atlantic to Washington D.C. Without his usual team or his authority as a Para-investigator to back him up, Toreth is caught up in a world of politics, diplomacy, and religion far outside his experience. 3/3

932. **Francis, Manna,** *Corpora Delicti,* Casperian, 2017. The Administration #9 of 9. (MM Police Procedural) Wealth Is the only reality on the surface, stability has returned to Europe. According to all the official metrics released to news feeds, the Administration and the corporations are stronger and more united than ever. Only in the most secret of government surveillance departments and corporate security divisions would anyone suggest otherwise. On the surface, Senior Para-investigator Toreth's year is ending badly. His boss hates him, his junior is looking for a way out, and his new case seems like a dud. But the new year starts him down a trail that will lead him from an unpromising beginning, via an unappetizing corpse, right into the financial heart of the Administration and the highest-stakes investigation of his career. 3/3

933. **Freeman, Brian,** *Stripped,* St. Martin's, 2006. Jonathan Stride #2 of 9. (Police Procedural) They looked like isolated cases: a hit-and-run and a celebrity murdered during a fling with a prostitute. No one could ever imagine they'd be linked to a brutal crime in Las Vegas's steamy past–and that the race against the clock to corner a deter-

mined serial killer would stir up secrets long thought buried with the dead. As detectives Jonathan Stride and Serena Dial are called separately to investigate, they have no idea what they're stepping into: a world where desperate ambition rules and loyalties know no bounds, and where their own uncharted emotions and sexual desires will reach an explosive conclusion. -a transgender female officer is involved in the hunt (MLM). 2/3

934. **Freney, Denis,** *Larry Death,* Mandarin Australia, 1991. (Political Intrigue) For Larry Death, life doesn't begin at 40. His crime novels aren't selling, is on the dole, who drinks too much, and his love life is a shambles. His political commitments are more like memories. But when a union organizer from the Philippines is murdered in Sydney, Larry finds himself entangled in a real-life crime story that involves child prostitution, corrupt police, the seedy side of the Third World and Australian politics and even a short time with the NPA Communist guerrillas in the hills outside Manila. 3/3

935. **Frey, Bob,** *The DVD Murders,* Infinity, 2009. (Police Procedural) Someone is killing the A-List actors of Hollywood and leaving a defaced DVD of one of their films at the crime scene. Who? Who is intent on depriving the movie-going public of their greatest national treasures, and why? 3/3

936. **Frey, Bob,** *Bashful Vampire Murder and Comic Book Murders,* Van Fleet, 2011. (Police Procedural) Frank Callahan is a gay LAPD detective. He and his long-term friend and partner, Detective Barry Jennings, are back. The Bashful Vampire Murder begins where most vampire tales end: in the apprehension of a vampire hunter right after he has driven a stake through his quarry's heart. The defense attempts to prove that vampires exist and the homicide was justified. To Callahan's horror, the trial ends in a hung jury. Only the resourcefulness and savvy of the tough cynical detective stand between justice and the killer being allowed to walk. In the Comic Book Murders, the two flatfoots run the gamut of superhero and villain suspects, from Captain America and the Caped Crusader to the Joker and Firebug until outstanding police work and dogged persistence lead them to the unlikely killer. On the way, we get to visit a kinetic comic book convention, the backstreets of Hollywood, and a firebombing in Westwood on Halloween eve. 3/3

937. **Friedman, Kinky,** *Greenwich Killing Time,* Beechtree/William Morrow, 1986. Kinky Friedman #1 of 18. (Amateur Sleuth) In Greenwich Killing Time, a street-smart country singer, who just happens to be named Kinky, turns detective to help his best friend, Mike McGovern, beat a murder rap. –bisexual man is killed (MLM). 2/3

938. **Friel, James,** *Taking the Veil,* St. Martin's, 1989. (Psychological) A

story about a priest with a grudge, a father with a secret, a red-headed lesbian called Sonny, a blond young lover called Andreas, a woman hanged with her own tights and a girl who thinks she is a car. - the priest is gay and although important in the first half disappears in the second (MLM). 1/3

939. **Fritsch, Ron,** *Elizabeth Daleiden on Trial,* Ron Fritsch, 2016. (Legal Drama) A politically ambitious state's attorney charges Elizabeth Daleiden with the murders of her father and two elderly neighbors in the 1950s. Her trial threatens to blow the lid off her Illinois farming community's darkest secrets. 3/3

940. **Fritsch, Ron,** *His Grandfather's House,* Assymetric, 2017. (Family Drama) The neighbors tell Kurt his grandfather, who has been his guardian since he was four years old, committed a series of crimes to acquire his farm. In this coming-of-age novel, Kurt needs to know if the neighbor's stories are true. The crimes they say his grandfather got away with include fraud, forgery, arson and murder. 3/3

941. **Froscher, Jon (b. 1939),** *The Woodstock Murders,* Overlook, 1998. (Police Procedural) Senior Investigator Thomas Jamison Wilder– very intelligent, very handsome, and very gay. Someone has taken a weedcutter to Lucille Driver, wife and mother of three of the most devious men in town. As someone continues to knock off the entire Driver clan, Tom must juggle a busy love life with solving the case. 3/3

942. **Fuller, Roy,** *Fantasy and Fugue,* Macmillan, 1956. (Psychological) Harry Sinton is a murderer. He knows it. There can be no doubt about it. His mind is filled with fearful knowledge, his trembling hands fouled by invisible blood, his soul reeks of murder. And yet - though murder is the most vivid of crimes - he cannot recall any of the details of the crime he is sure he committed. His killing of a drunken poet is blanketed in a fog of amnesia. Frantically - but with desperate cunning - he seeks to discover the facts surrounding his disastrous act in order to establish an appropriate alibi. His heady investigations take him on a feverish chase through the literary and Bohemian circles of London. With every step he takes, he comes closer to the dreadful truth that lies in wait. –author is homophobic in how he deals with homosexuality within the book (MLM). 1/3

943. **Fury, Jason,** *The Rope Above, The Bed Below,* Badboy, 1994. (Pulp) Jason Fury's memoirs of a wild, sexually free Manhattan of 1980 before the AIDS epidemic became an overnight bestseller-first in America, and then around the world. Although beset with censorship problems, critics and fans quickly hailed the novel for its

"feverish writing," it's breathless plot of a mad killer stalking New York's male strippers, and its hypnotic remembrance of a sex-filled world now vanished. 3/3

G

944. **Gabaldon, Diana**, *Lord John and the Private Matter*, Delacorte, 2003. Lord John #1 of 4. (Historical) The year is 1757. On a clear morning in mid-June, Lord John Grey emerges from London's Beefsteak Club, his mind in turmoil. A nobleman and a high-ranking officer in His Majesty's Army, Grey has just witnessed something shocking. But his efforts to avoid a scandal that might destroy his family are interrupted by something still more urgent: the Crown appoints him to investigate the brutal murder of a comrade in arms, who may have been a traitor. Obliged to pursue two inquiries at once, Major Grey finds himself ensnared in a web of treachery and betrayal that touches every stratum of English society – and threatens all he holds dear. From the bawdy houses of London's night-world to the stately drawing rooms of the nobility, and from the blood of a murdered corpse to the thundering seas ruled by the majestic fleet of the East India Company, Lord John pursues the elusive trails of a vanishing footman and a woman in green velvet, who may hold the key to everything – or nothing. 3/3

945. **Gabaldon, Diana**, *Lord John and the Brotherhood of the Blade*, Delacorte, 2007. Lord John #2 of 4. (Historical) In 1758, in the heart of the Seven Years' War, Britain fights by the side of Prussia in the Rhineland. For Lord John and his titled brother Hal, the battlefield will be a welcome respite from the torturous mystery that burns poisonously in their family's history. Seventeen years earlier, Lord John's late father, the Duke of Pardloe, was found dead, a pistol in his hand and accusations of his role as a Jacobite agent staining forever a family's honor. Now unlaid ghosts from the past are stirring. Lord John's brother has mysteriously received a page of their late father's missing diary. Someone is taunting the Grey family with secrets from the grave, but Hal, with secrets of his own, refuses to pursue the matter and orders his brother to do likewise. Frustrated, John turns to a man who has been both his prisoner and his confessor: the Scottish Jacobite James Fraser. Fraser can tell many secrets and withhold many others. But war, a forbidden affair, and Fraser's own secrets will complicate Lord John's quest. Until James Fraser yields the missing piece of an astounding puzzle, and Lord John, caught between his courage and his conscience, must decide whether his family's honor is worth his life. 3/3

946. **Gabaldon, Diana**, *Lord John and the Hand of Devils*, Delacorte,

2007. Lord John #3 of 4. (Historical Short Stories) In "Lord John and the Hellfire Club," Lord John glimpses a stranger in the doorway of a gentlemen's club–and is stirred by a desperate entreaty to meet in private. The rendezvous forestalled by a sudden murder, Lord John will wade into a maze of political treachery and a dangerous, debauched underground society. In "Lord John and the Succubus," English soldiers fighting in Prussia are rattled by the nocturnal visitations of a deadly woman who sucks life and soul from a man. Called to investigate the night-hag, Lord John finds a murdered soldier and a treacherous Gypsy, and comes to the stark realization that among the spirits that haunt men, none frighten more than the specters conjured by the heart. In "Lord John and the Haunted Soldier," Lord John is thrust into the deadly case of an exploding battlefield cannon. Wounded in the same battle, Lord John is called to testify and soon confronts his own ghost–and the shattering prospect that a traitor is among the ranks of His Majesty's armed forces. –collection of short stories that fall before book one, between book one and book two, and between book two and three (MLM). 3/3

947. **Gabaldon, Diana,** *The Scottish Prisoner,* Delacorte, 2011. Lord John #4 of 4. (Historical) Lord John Grey - soldier, gentleman, and no mean hand with a blade. Set in the heart of the eighteenth century, Lord John's world is one of mystery and menace. The strands of Lord John's secret and public lives; the lonely, tormented, and courageous career of a man who fights for his crown, his honor, and his own secrets. –collected short story volume *Seven Stones to Stand of Fall* published in 2017 by Dell has several stories of Lord John (MLM). 3/3

948. **Gadol, Peter,** *Light at Dusk,* Picador, 2000. (Political Intrigue) Will Law, a rising star in the U.S. Foreign Service, mysteriously walks away from his post and, in Paris, falls into the arms of his onetime lover Pedro. When the child of a mutual friend is kidnapped by a Nationalist gang, Will is reluctantly drawn back to the diplomatic world he abandoned. Fighting against a rising tide of French anti-immigrant hatred, the Americans launch a desperate search across the city. In the process, Will must challenge the moral burdens of his past, and in an attempt to rescue the child, he must also find a way to redeem himself. 3/3

949. **Gala, Lyn,** *Urban Shaman,* Dreamspinner, 2010. (MM Police Procedural) New York City cop Miguel Rassin's life is going downhill fast. He's got a spotty record from the Army, a one-night stand who won't go away, and a flock of reporters trying to crucify him for shooting a civilian waving a toy pistol, and he's partnered with by-the-book Detective Rob Jackson, a man with problems of his own. 3/3

950. **Galloway, David,** *Lamaar Ransom: Private Eye,* Riverrun, 1979. (Pulp) "Los Angeles P. I. assistant Lavender Trevelyan, African American, supports his lesbian boss in multiple ways in a whodunit with a touch of science fiction set in 1943 (Gunn)." 3/3

951. **Gamble, Geoffrey,** *Breakfast with a Cereal Killer,* Decent Exposure, 1997. (Journalism) "A serial killer strikes down his victims and sprinkles breakfast cereals around their bodies–after previously sending a box of cereal to the police as a clue to the next murder (Gunn)." –the author wrote two sequels to *Breakfast with a Cereal Killer; Deadly Outing* and *Forlorn Hope* for the Rainbow Mystery series but they were never published (MLM). 3/3

952. **Garland, Rodney,** *Heart in Exile,* WH Allen, 1953. (Amateur Sleuth) Why did Julian Leclerc commit suicide just as he has become engaged to a rich young woman? As he is forced to dip back into the underground London milieu he has left behind, will Dr Anthony Page, a psychiatrist, discover the answer to that question - and what more will he discover before he is fully satisfied he has resolved the mystery? 3/3

953. **Garland, Rodney,** *Troubled Midnight,* WH Allen, 1954. (Espionage) I read them over and over, the confidential secret-service documents which by a freak of chance had come into my hands. They were all lies, but they were undeniably, brutally official... They were all about me... 3/3

954. **Garris, Robert,** *Murder in the Tiergarten,* Smashwords, 2014. (Historical) William Heath, an American journalist, has been found dead in the Tiergarten in Berlin, in the months just before the outbreak of the First World War. The investigations into his death bring together an American diplomat new to the foreign service, an outspoken young noblewoman, a naive police officer, and a reticent friend of the victim. –victim was gay, available as an e-book only (MLM) 1/3

955. **Gaston, James,** *Bad Planning,* Createspace, 2014. Asher #1 of 2. (Police Procedural) City planner Chris Jensson is trying to preserve the natural landscape on some property near the Asher airport. A local real estate broker, his shady Houston lawyer, and Chris' boss are intent on rezoning the land for industrial development. When a young man dies in an early morning hit-and-run, insurance investigator Kyle Decker and police Detective Ernie Zepeda begin to unravel a criminal conspiracy with far reaching implications. Chris Jensson, who is Kyle's gay lover, may lose more than his career when the violence escalates. 3/3

956. **Gaston, James,** *Hard Lesson,* Createspace, 2017. Asher #2 of 2. (Police Procedural) An arson on the campus of Riverside Christian Col-

lege goes horribly wrong, resulting in the death of popular faculty member. The investigation focuses on the college's unscrupulous leadership and uncovers a connection to the murder of a federal witness in Florida. When suspects begin to die in bizarre attacks, Detective Kyle Decker finds himself in jeopardy. The FBI's involvement gets very personal. Decker is faced with a tough decision when his gay partner, Chris Jensson, forces Decker to examine his career and their relationship. 3/3

957. **Gatiss, Mark**, *The Vesuvius Club*, Scribner, 2004. Lucifer Box #1 of 3. (Espionage) Lucifer has a charming countenance and rapier wit that make him the guest all hostesses must have. And most do. But few of his conquests know that Lucifer is also His Majesty's most daring secret agent, at home in both London's Imperial grandeur and in its underworld of despicable vice. So when Britain's most prominent scientists begin turning up dead, there is only one man his country can turn to for help. Following a dinnertime assassination, Lucifer is dispatched to uncover the whereabouts of missing agent Jocelyn Poop. Along the way he will give art lessons, be attacked by a poisonous centipede, bed a few choice specimens, and travel to Italy on business and pleasure. Aided by his henchwoman Delilah; the beautiful, mysterious, and Dutch Miss Bella Pok; his boss, a dwarf who takes meetings in a lavatory; grizzled vulcanologist Emmanuel Quibble; and the impertinent, delicious, right-hand-boy Charlie Jackpot, Lucifer Box deduces and seduces his way from his elegant townhouse at Number 9 Downing Street (somebody has to live there) to the ruined city of Pompeii, to infiltrate a highly dangerous secret society that may hold the fate of the world in its clawlike grip. 3/3

958. **Gatiss, Mark,** *The Devil in Amber,* Simon and Schuster, 2006. Lucifer Box #2 of 3. (Paranormal Espionage) Lucifer Box – portraitist, dandy and terribly good secret agent – is feeling his age. He's also more than a little anxious about an ambitious younger agent, Percy Flarge, who's snapping at his heels. Assigned to observe the activities of fascist leader Olympus Mons and his fanatical followers, or "Amber Shirts," in F.A.U.S.T. – The Fascist Anglo-United States Trinity (an acronym so tortuous it can only be sinister) – in snowbound 1920s New York, Box finds himself framed for a vicious, mysterious murder. Using all of his native cunning, Box escapes aboard a vessel bound for England armed with only a Broadway midget's suitcase and a string of unanswered questions: What lies hidden in the bleak Norfolk convent of St. Bede? What is "the lamb" that Olympus Mons searches for in his bid for world domination? And what has all this to do with a medieval prayer intended to summon the Devil himself? From the glittering sophistication of Art Deco Manhattan to

the eerie Norfolk coast and the snowcapped peaks of Switzerland, *The Devil in Amber* takes us on a thrilling, delicious ride that pits Lucifer Box against the most lethal adversary of his career: the Prince of Darkness himself. 3/3

959. **Gatiss, Mark,** *Black Butterfly,* Simon and Schuster, 2008. Lucifer Box #3 of 3. (Espionage) With the young Queen Elizabeth newly established on her throne, Lucifer Box Esq. is now 'by Appointment to Her Majesty'. But the secretive Royal Academy seems a very different place and, approaching retirement, Box decides to investigate one last case. 3/3

960. **Gayle, Stephanie,** *Idyll Threats,* Seventh Street, 2015. Thomas Lynch #1 of 3. (Police Procedural) Clean-cut Thomas Lynch is police chief of Idyll, Connecticut, where serious crimes can be counted on one hand –until Cecilia North is found murdered on the town's golf course. The case should be a slam dunk. But there's a problem. If he tells his detectives about meeting the victim, he'll reveal his greatest secret–he's gay. Lynch works angles of the case on his own. Without the aid of fellow detectives, he is forced to seek help from unlikely allies–a Goth teen and a UFO-obsessed conspiracy theorist. 3/3

961. **Gayle, Stephanie,** *Idyll Fears,* Seventh Street, 2017. Thomas Lynch #2 of 3. (Police Procedural) Two weeks before Christmas, Police Chief Thomas Lynch faces a crisis when Cody Forrand, a six-year-old with a life-threatening medical condition, goes missing during a blizzard. Lynch's suspicions about who abducted Cody are met with scorn by his detectives, some of whom can't handle the fact that he's gay. 3/3

962. **Gayle, Stephanie,** *Idyll Hands,* Seventh Street, 2018. Thomas Lynch #3 of 3. (Police Procedural) Charleston, Massachusetts, 1972: Rookie cop Michael Finnegan gets a call from his mother. His youngest sister, Susan, has disappeared, the same sister who ran away two years earlier. Anxious not to waste police resources, Finnegan advises his family to wait and search on their own. But a week turns into two decades, and Susan is never found. Idyll, Connecticut, 1999: In the woods outside of town, a young woman's corpse is discovered, and Detective Finnegan seems unusually disturbed by the case. When Police Chief Thomas Lynch learns about Finnegan's past, he makes a bargain with his officer: He will allow Finnegan to investigate the body found in the woods–if Finnegan lets the bored Lynch secretly look into the disappearance of his sister. Both cases reveal old secrets–about the murder, and about the men inside the Idyll Police Station and what they've been hiding from each other their whole careers. 3/3

963. **Gaynor, Raymond (Gary Martine) & William Maltese,** *Total Meltdown: A Tripler and Clarke Adventure,* Wildside, 2009. (Science Fiction Political Intrigue Satire) When the U.S. President flees the country with a trillion dollars in his back pocket, America is left leaderless while facing an unprecedented economic crisis. President-Elect Jackson must turn to his trusty aides and lovers, Adelphous Tripler and Shawn Clarke, to save the day. 3/3

964. **George, Elizabeth,** *Well-Schooled in Murder,* Bantam Books, 1990. Lynley #3 of 20 (Police Procedural) When thirteen-year-old Matthew Whately goes missing from Bredgar Chambers, a prestigious public school in the heart of West Sussex, aristocratic Inspector Thomas Lynley receives a call for help from the lad's housemaster, who also happens to be an old school chum. –teacher collects nude photos of boys and girls and older boys indulge in sadistic homosexual acts on younger pupils, and some boys have crushes on other boys (MLM). 2/3

965. **Gerard, Gregory,** *In Jupiter's Shadow,* Infinity, 2009. (YA Fictionalized Autobiography) Searching for self-truth, a religious, teenage "detective" confronts Heaven and Hell as he struggles to solve the mysteries of sexuality and faith within a family full of secrets. 3/3

966. **Gilbert, Peter & Tom Holt,** *Adam and the Paradise Garden,* Acolyte, 1992. (YA Amateur Sleuth) "Schoolmate Mark Lee is presumed drowned, but several details do not fit. Adam and Ben, English boy sleuths, 15 and 14 respectively, report their suspicions to best-selling author Simon Spencer, 30s, who encourages them in their sleuthing and their sexuality (Gunn)." –non-mystery sequel *A Boy's Sweet Sorrow and Satisfaction* was published in 1994 (MLM). 3/3

967. **Gilbert, W. Stephen (William S. Gilbert b. 1947),** *Spiked,* Gay Men's Press, 1991. (Political Intrigue) Sam Bone is not the world's most successful journalist, seeing himself instead as a Bogart-style gumshoe. But his wildest fantasies come to life when an American actress is murdered. 3/3

968. **Gill, B. M. (Barbara Margaret Trimble),** *Death Drop,* Scribner's Sons, 1979. (Amateur Sleuth) When twelve-year-old David Fleming dies in what looks like an accident, his father goes to his school seeking an explanation, only to receive the cold shoulder. As he looks deeper he discovers it was murder, but why would anyone want to kill a twelve-year-old? –12-year-old threatened to expose a homosexual relationship between an older boy and a teacher (MLM). 2/3

969. **Gilmartin, Katie,** *Blackmail, My Love,* St. Martin's, 2014. (Historical) Josie O'Conner travels to San Francisco in 1951 to locate her

gay brother, a private eye investigating a blackmail ring targeting lesbians and gay men. Jimmy's friends claim that just before he disappeared he became a rat, informing the cops on the bar community. Josie adopts Jimmy's trousers and wingtips, to clear his name, halt the blackmailers, and exact justice for too many queer corpses. –winner of the 27th LAMBDA Award for Best Gay Mystery (MLM). 2/3

970. **Giroux, E. X.**, *A Death for Adonis*, St. Martin's, 1984. Robert Forsythe #1 of 10. (Court Drama) Barrister Robert Forsythe investigates a 25-year-old murder accompanied by his ever-faithful secretary Miss Sanderson. Sculptor Sebastian Calvert is believed to have killed his beautiful young lover, David Mersey and has been locked in an asylum ever since. But did he really kill the man he loved? 2/3

971. **Giroux, E. X.**, *A Death for a Dreamer*, St. Martin's, 1989. Robert Forsythe #7 of 10. (Court Drama) Should residents be allowed to have pets? That's the burning question agitating the trustees of the Jamie Coralund Home for the Aged. Barrister Robert Forsythe is called on to mediate, but he's no fool and declines the honor. Instead, he sends his formidable secretary, Miss Sanderson, to deal with this tempest in a provincial teapot. – It might have ended there but for two things: a dog is poisoned, and an old lady is smothered. –author is homophobic with the characters often referring to the gay character as "that creature (MLM)." 1/3

972. **Glenn, Stormy**, *Promise Kept*, Torquere, 2009. Promise #1 of 2. (MM Police Procedural) Mason is in love with his brother's best friend, Jack. It's been ten years of secret fantasies, hidden glances, and forbidden yearnings. Just when Mason decides to give up on Jack and move away, his friends step in to get them together. Even with the most determined matchmakers, new love is not always easy. Especially when a serial killer who has his sights set on Mason being his next victim will destroy anyone who gets in his way. Can Jack keep Mason safe, or will their new love be over before it gets going? 3/3

973. **Glenn, Stormy**, *Promise Given*, Torquere, 2010. Promise #2 of 2. (MM Police Procedural) Detective Cooper Thomas was kidnapped and tortured by a psychotic serial killer bent on revenge. If that wasn't bad enough, Alec Whitley, the only man Cooper ever really loved, the man who left him ten years ago without a word, came back just in time to rescue him. But before Cooper can come to terms with Alec being back in his life he has to discover who's killing young gay men before he and Alec become the next victims. Between undercover assignments and startling revelations, Cooper and Alec don't know if their fragile relationship can survive. Can

they solve the case and find a way to be together? 3/3

974. **Godfrey, Wallace,** *Sunfish & Starfish: Tropical Drag Queen Detectives,* Strand Hill, 2011. (Amateur Sleuth) Two unlikely heroes. Two confounding mysteries. How did a $1,000 jewel encrusted Prada shoe end up under a dumpster in a back alley in a deserted part of town? And will we ever find out whether the man hiding in the shadows of a South Florida gay bar is really a conservative South Carolina reverend–who's running for Congress? Two fun-loving drag performers are lured out of the spotlight and into some very dark places: the shady, drug-fueled world of Miami's high-society debutantes, and the cutthroat world of national politics. 3/3

975. **Goldstein, Lisa,** *Strange Devices of the Sun and Moon,* Tor, 1993. (Fantasy) A series of strange events links the lives of an ordinary woman, a bookseller in St. Paul's, and the great writer Christopher Marlowe, as the Faerie Queen and her court invade London in search of the Queen's son, the reborn King Arthur. Marlowe must become in effect a detective, and Alice, strangely favored by the fairies, must become a heroine in a struggle against evil forces. The culmination of this extraordinary fantasy, a battle between the opposing dragons of good and evil. 3/3

976. **Golin, James,** *Philomel Foundation,* McClelland and Stewart, 1980. Alan French #1 of 4. (Espionage) Alan French is a versatile, not-quite-starving musician who's quasi-leader of Manhattan's Antiqua Players–a quintet of Upper West Side types (four guys and beautiful Jackie) devoted to Early Music played on authentic instruments (lute, viola da gamba, harpsichord, recorder, etc.). And when Alan receives an invitation from the Philomel Foundation to play for big bucks in Switzerland and Germany, the quintet eagerly grabs the gig... despite some worries over the Foundation's real motives. Sure enough, once the tiresome has wowed Geneva, the Philomel chief–a slick U.S. millionaire–begs the players to help sneak a famous dissident cellist out of East Germany. The group semi-reluctantly complies, manages the escape during an outdoor concert (through a childishly implausible ruse), and Alan–now engaged to hard-to-get Jackie–finds that he's been the dupe for a convoluted CIA scare. 1/3

977. **Golin, James,** *Eliza's Galiardo,* St. Martin's, 1983. Alan French #2 of 4. (Amateur Sleuths) The Antiqua Players, a group of pre-classical musicians, learn of a musical manuscript which may have belonged to Queen Elizabeth I. 1/3

978. **Golin, James,** *Verona Passamezzo,* Doubleday, 1985. Alan French #3 of 4. (Amateur Sleuth) Alan French and The Antiqua Players are invited by an Italian count to perform at a Verona music festival. In-

stead of getting their big break they end up dealing with blackmail, kidnapping and murder. 1/3

979. **Golin, James,** *Broken Consort,* St. Martin's, 1989. Alan French #4 of 4. (Amateur Sleuth) When Alan French, leader of the brilliant and quirky troupe known as Antiqua Players, accepts the chance to play a private concert for TBG Boyle, he is flattered and intrigued. This leads to an invitation to play aboard Boyle's yacht, Alan is delighted. The troupe watch as Boyle juggles favors and finances leading to shipboard mixture of rage, jealousy, greed, and family pride. 1/3

980. **Gomez-Dossi, Joel,** *Pursued,* Bold Stroke Books, 2012. Pursued #1 of 2. (MM Thriller) Nestled in upstate New York, Stratburgh University has a problem. Three sorority sisters have disappeared, and the police say they simply ran away. The students are outraged. Even openly gay junior Jamie Bradford is concerned, only he has other worries. He doesn't have a boyfriend and is willing to disregard the troublesome news on campus to find one. 3/3

981. **Gomez-Dossi, Joel,** *Deadly Cult,* Bold Stroke Books, 2013. Pursued #2 of 2. (MM Thriller) Jamie Bradford is now the pursuer when he receives a mysterious package containing a class ring from his alma mater, Stratburgh University. Wrapped inside the ring is the address to a Rhodes Petroleum corporate office in Boston and the name of an ultra-conservative religious cult based in the Adirondack Mountains. To solve the mystery, Jamie and his husband, Eddie Delgado, infiltrate the cult and discover a paramilitary-style inner circle hellbent on making the cult's beliefs everyone's beliefs. 3/3

982. **Gomez-Dossi, Joel,** *Lethal Elements,* Bold Stroke Books, 2015. (MM Thriller) In the wilderness, man is the deadliest element. Geologist Tom Burrell's relationship with his husband, Roman, is on rocky ground. So, when a mysterious company asks Tom to perform mineral studies in the Adirondack Mountains, he jumps at the chance. But before he can finish his tests, he finds himself lost in the wilderness and chased by a hired gun. And now it's up to Roman to rescue his husband. 3/3

983. **Gordon, Alison,** *Safe at Home,* St. Martin's, 1990. Kate Henry #2 of 5. (Journalism) A serial killer is stalking the streets of Kate Henry's hometown, claiming one young boy after another as his victim. For Kate Henry, the star baseball reporter for the *Toronto Planet*, the killings are placing a strain on her relationship with her lover, Staff Sgt. Andy Munro, who is deeply involved in the beleaguered murder investigation. In the meantime, Kate is in hot water herself as she prepares to break a news story that will throw the Toronto Titans team – and the game of professional baseball – into turmoil...

984. **Gosling, Paula,** *Death Penalties,* Mysterious Press, 1991. Luke Abbott #2 of 2. (Police Procedural) Following the death of her husband in a suspicious auto accident, Tess Leland begins to receive threatening phone calls from a mysterious blackmailer. –gay interior designer is suspected (MLM). 1/3

985. **Gouda, Michael,** *Crimes of Passion,* MLR, 2011. (MM Hard Boiled) Twelve criminal cases to be solved by British, gay P.I., Tim Silvain, ranging range from finding an errant partner, to a guy who swears he's been abducted by aliens, a cruel poison-pen writer, the mystery of a guy who apparently returns from the dead, and murder most foul. But Tim Silvain has a private life which is often fraught with problems, as he finds it difficult to keep his sexual desires under control even knowing that the real love of his life is Paul Massingham. 3/3

986. **Graeme, Roland,** *Executive Privilege,* Hudson Communication, 1982. (Pulp) "Washington DC, secret service agent Henry Zentner, 30s, is assigned to protect Tom Steffins, 23, the president's gay son (Gunn)." 3/3

987. **Grafton, Sue,** *E is for Evidence,* Henry Holt, 1988. Kinsey Millhone #5 of 25. (Hardboiled) Anyone who knows me will tell you that I cherish my unmarried state. I'm female, twice divorced, no kids and no close family ties. I'm perfectly content to do what I do . . It was two days after Christmas when Kinsey Millhone received the bank slip showing a credit for five thousand dollars. The account number was correct, but Kinsey hadn't made the deposit. Then came the phone call and suddenly everything became clear. The frame-up was working, and Kinsey was trapped ... –ex-husband is outed during the investigation (MLM). 1/3

988. **Grafton, Sue,** *Y is for Yesterday,* Marion Wood/Putnam, 2017. Kinsey Millhone #25 of 25. (Hardboiled) In 1979, four teenage boys from an elite private school sexually assault a fourteen-year-old classmate–and film the attack. Not long after, the tape goes missing and the suspected thief, a fellow classmate, is murdered. In the investigation that follows, one boy turns state's evidence and two of his peers are convicted. But the ringleader escapes without a trace. –antagonist is gay (MLM). 2/3

989. **Graham, Caroline,** *Killing at Badger's Drift,* William Morrow, 1989. Chief Inspector Barnaby #1 of 7. (Police Procedural) Badger's Drift is an ideal English village, complete with vicar, bumbling local doctor, and kindly spinster with a nice line in homemade cookies. But when the spinster dies suddenly, her best friend kicks up an unseemly fuss, loud enough to attract the attention of Detective Chief

Inspector Tom Barnaby. And when Barnaby and his eager-beaver deputy start poking around, they uncover a swamp of ugly scandals and long-suppressed resentments seething below the picture-postcard prettiness. –rude gay man lives down the street and an assistant to Barnaby states that homosexual men should be castrated (MLM). 1/3

990. **Graham, Caroline,** *Death of a Hollow Man,* William Morrow, 1989. Chief Inspector Barnaby #2 of 7. (Police Procedural) Actors do love their dramas, and the members of the Causton Amateur Dramatic Society are no exception. Passionate love scenes, jealous rages? They're better than a paycheck (not that anyone one in this production of Amadeus is getting one). But even the most theatrically minded must admit that murdering the leading man in full view of the audience is a bit over the top. –gay couple in the acting troupe (MLM). 1/3

991. **Grayson, Richard,** *Death en Voyage,* St. Martin's, 1986. Inspector Gautier #6 of 9. (Police Procedural) A fin de siècle Parisian novel, featuring Inspector Gautier, in which a salacious 19th century sexual scandal is linked with the murder of an English milady some years earlier. –gay angle is a red herring (MLM). 1/3

992. **Green, Anthony,** *Bleeding Love,* Independently Published, 2018. (YA Suspense) Evan Graham is a college student struggling with his intersectionality, community and purpose and thus, dreading the upcoming Memphis Black Gay Pride. Pride is a time of celebration and connection, but Evan has never been lucky in love, with a string of misfortunate past relationships to prove it. This year, when each of his ex-lovers begin to fall victim to a local serial killer, Evan is the prime suspect. Evan has a very sexy detective on his heels, two hedonistic best friends trying to show him the weekend of his life and a dating history that leaves more questions than answers. 3/3

993. **Green, R. G.,** *Jumping at Shadows,* Dreamspinner, 2011. (MM Police Procedural) Detective Eric Geller just saw his case against crime boss Victor Kroger thrown out of court. Convinced there's more to the dismissal than contaminated evidence, Eric shifts from investigating Victor to investigating the judge, determined to bring Victor to justice. 3/3

994. **Green, William,** *See How They Run,* Bobbs-Merrill, 1975. (Espionage) "Sewell Crockett and Austin Tobin, who are obviously modeled on J. Edgar Hoover and Clyde Tolson. Crockett is director of the Domestic Security Agency, feared in Washington D.C., for the files he has accumulated on public and political figures. When he is felled by a stroke, his assistant Austin Tobin feels it is imperative to

protect those files from outside examination (Slide)." 1/3

995. **Green, William,** *Rainbow Spies: La Conclusion Francaise,* Outskirts, 2008. Marc and Peg #1 of 2. (Thriller) Nuclear missiles controlled by Neo-Nazis Satellite command and control software is being stolen from National Space Corporation's CIA-funded Project Gamma; software that could be used to take control of orbiting satellites armed with nuclear missiles. The pilfering is being done by gay Neo-Nazi agents. Who would you choose to act against these spies? How about a male-female covert CIA team? Maybe - if the male is gay. Follow Peg O'Ryan and Marc Parker as they track the gay Nazi spies from southern California to Paris, London, back to Paris and to a final confrontation in the south of France. 3/3

996. **Green, William,** *Rainbow Spies 2: La Conclusion Mexicano,* N.P., 2017. Marc and Peg #2 of 2. (Thriller) Marc and Peg, the dynamic CIA duo, are back. They are tasked to infiltrate a bio-terrorist camp in central Mexico and close it down. Their intro into the camp is provided by the son of one of the camp instructors. Marc had "rescued" Ramon from the Guantánamo facility in Cuba. Peg assumes the role of healer or witch as her red hair and freckles will not get her into the camp of all men. Mexican folklore assumes red-headed women are witches. She manages a cantina where the men from the camp relax in the evenings. She fills the role of healer/witch by doing tarot card readings. Marc is attracted to the young Mexican national. This leads to complications as the mutual attraction leads to one- sided strong feelings. 3/3

997. **Green, William,** *When Past comes to Present,* Dreamspinner, 2013. PI Beckett #1 of 3. (MM Hard Boiled) Three years ago, private detective Tyler Beckett gained unwanted fame when he found evidence that sent murderer Miles Trubett to prison. Now, three years later, Tyler enjoys a successful business and a happy home life, even if he can't quite make himself ask his lover, Sean St. Claire, to move in permanently. But when a pushy journalist comes to him with the case of a gay man's apparent suicide, Tyler finds himself stuck between a rock and a hard place. The ultimatum: investigate or risk losing the support of the gay community. 3/3

998. **Green, William,** *Lasting Damage,* Dreamspinner, 2013. PI Beckett #2 of 3. (MM Hard Boiled) The police believe the case is closed– or would be if they could find their suspect. However, the victim's brother, Kyle Overstreet, claims the police are pinning the murder on the wrong man, and he uses The Wheaton Brigade to make his views known. Fearing slander that could butcher the department if Kyle is right, Lieutenant Danny Baxter asks close friend and private investigator Tyler Beckett to look into the case. 3/3

999. **Green, William,** *This Time its Personal,* Dreamspinner, 2013. PI Beckett #3 of 3. (MM Hard Boiled) Feeling the strain of lost business thanks to the vicious articles by The Wheaton City Brigade, the city's most inflammatory newspaper, private investigator Tyler Beckett accepts a cold case from Lt. Danny Baxter to fill the gap. He's less than happy, however, when he learns the case may involve the same man who made him the target for The Brigade to begin with: Jamie Carroway. 3/3

1000. **Greene, David,** *Detonate,* Createspace, 2012. (Espionage) Private Investigator Tyrone King finds himself caught up in a series of terrorist acts, including a plot to blow up a train on the border between Canada and the United States. 3/3

1001. **Greene, David,** *The Winkler Case,* David Greene, 2015. (MM Historical) When insurance salesman Elliot Blake meets a handsome boxer at the home of promoter Walt Winkler, he begins to learn the truth about the boxer's bargain with the promoter, and about his own desires. Exploring the predicaments of two gay men in Chicago in 1948, and the hidden desires that lead to murder. 3/3

1002. **Greene, Harlan,** *Why We Never Danced the Charleston,* Penguin, 1985. (Historical) The scene is Charleston, South Carolina; the time, the 1920s, when old ladies dream of the past and a strange new dance, the Charleston, is seducing the youth of the city. Years later, whispers emerge of something baffling and tragic that happened back then. As an old man confronts those demanding the truth, we catch brilliant flashes of the confrontation between the dark, doomed Hirsch Hess, son of immigrants, and the fantastically ethereal Ned Grimke, a scion of the city. 3/3

1003. **Gregg, L. B.,** *Catch Me if You Can,* Samhain, 2011. Romano and Albright #1 of 3. (MM Amateur Sleuth) Lowly art gallery assistant Caesar Romano is freely out of the closet. Now he'd just like to get out of his Nana's guest room. Everything–his reputation and his financial freedom–is riding on the success of tonight's gallery opening. If only he could shake free of the past so easily. A mysterious gatecrasher, Dan Green, looks like a promising addition to his pending new life–until Caesar's ex shows up and suddenly the opening disintegrates into a half-naked dance melee. When the glitter settles, a missing sculpture of Justin Timberlake has Caesar up to his eyebrows in extortion, intrigue and a wild sexual adventure underneath, inside, and on top of a variety of furnishings. 3/3

1004. **Gregg, L. B.,** *Trust Me if You Dare,* Samhain, 2011. Romano and Albright #2 of 3. (MM Amateur Sleuth) Feisty New Yorker Caesar Romano has a knack for getting into a jam, and this week is no exception. When his pregnancy-hormone-buzzed business partner sweet talks him into working a solo gig for his famous ex, Caesar attracts the worst kind of attention. Hit on by a lusty German, stalked by the paparazzi, victim of an unexpected airbag attack–and desperate for some part-time help–he's running out of time, staff and patience. PI Dan Albright is a man of many gifts: investigation, security, sex talk and driving Caesar nuts in and out of the bedroom. Hired to protect an outrageous soap star from a deranged personal assistant, Dan's got his hands full refereeing rival actors, locating one four-foot-eleven woman. 3/3

1005. **Gregg, L. B.,** *With This Bling,* Riptide, 2015. Romano and Albright #3 of 3. (MM Amateur Sleuth) Caesar Romano's catering career is doing better than he'd ever dreamed. And so is his love life–even if his boyfriend's house in Staten Island is way too far from civilization for his liking. Caesar is almost too busy to notice that something is troubling his PI boyfriend, Dan Albright. Almost. Laid-back, open, charming–that's the impression hunky former NYPD Detective Dan Albright gives everyone, but he also knows that Dan is hiding something–something dark and a little dangerous–and when Dan's silence over his mysterious past threatens to harm them both, it's Caesar's turn to save the day. But then again, a break-in, a gallery party, an heirloom ring, a new suit, and a stalker with bad BO are all just a typical week for Caesar Romano. –book four *Gaydar Love* was supposed to be released in 2016 according to the author (MLM). 3/3

1006. **Gregory, Elin,** *Eleventh Hour,* Manifold, 2016. Carstairs #1 of 2. (Espionage) Borrowed from the Secret Intelligence Service cipher department to assist Briers Allerdale - a field agent returning to 1920s London with news of a dangerous anarchist plot - Miles Siward moves into a 'couples only' boarding house, posing as Allerdale's 'wife'. Miles relishes the opportunity to allow his alter ego, Millie, to spread her wings but if Miles wants the other agent's respect he can never betray how much he enjoys being Millie nor how attractive he finds Allerdale. –book two, *Midnight Flit* expected out in 2019 (MLM). 3/3

1007. **Gregory, Elin,** *The Bones of our Fathers,* Manifold, 2017. (MM Mystery) Malcolm Bright, brand new museum curator in a small Welsh Border town, is a little lonely until – acting as emergency archaeological consultant on a new housing development – he crosses the path of Rob Escley, aka Dirty Rob, who makes Mal's earth move in more ways than one. Together they must combat greedy developers and a treasure hunter determined to get his hands on the find. 3/3

1008. **Gregory, Jonathan,** *Country Life,* Createspace, 2012. Gemini and Flowers #1 of 10. (Cozy) After a series of family tragedies, twenty-five-year-old Mike Ash is left alone, raising his two young nephews and trying to save one of the oldest country estates in England. Tom Flowers, thrown out of the Metropolitan police for striking a superior officer, comes to Rilton Castle to stay with his sister Lucy and lick his wounds. Bob Kettle, the publican, wants to get laid. Ramjap Shastri just wants to get away from reporting local news. And Dax? Well, Dax just wants to have fun. When a modern-day highwayman destroys the calm of Rilton Castle village, all these characters and more try to cope with murder and suspicion. And an ex-policeman finds himself facing his hardest case - solving the mystery of his own future. With a cast that includes a naughty vicar, telepathic twins and a very expressive garden gnome, life, and death, in the countryside will never be the same again. 3/3

1009. **Gregory, Jonathan,** *Family Life,* Createspace, 2013. Gemini and Flowers #2 of 10. (Cozy) When his first client as a private detective gets murdered, Tom Flowers has to help Chief Inspector Stonely with his last case before retirement. With another death and a suicide following swiftly, Gemini, Flowers and Stonely struggle to find the killer before he strikes again. 3/3

1010. **Gregory, Jonathon,** *In Real Life,* Createspace, 2013. Gemini and Flowers #3 of 10. (Cozy) All Hell breaks loose in Rilton Castle…. 'You had sex with me in your dressing room. I was thirteen at the time.' Ronny Hudd, lead singer of heavy metal band Hell's Gate and Britain's favourite hard rocker, is being blackmailed. He calls in Tom Flowers to help him, but first Tom has to decide if Ronny is innocent before trying to find the blackmailer. Then a boy is found mutilated in the quiet woods behind Rilton Castle village, giving newly appointed Chief Inspector Regina Muga her first murder since arriving in Dorset. 3/3

1011. **Gregory, Jonathan,** *After Life,* Createspace, 2014. Gemini and Flowers #4 of 10. (Cozy) Mike Ash's godmother, the Duchess of Bloxworth, asks for his help when things start going bump in the night at her stately home, Hollander Hall. While Mike visits her, Tom Flowers and James Stonely are asked to trace fake antiques by local auctioneer Derek Smee. The appearance of an heir to the Hollander estate complicates matters further for Mike and the Duchess and the discovery of a naked body in Rilton Castle Lake brings Chief Inspector Muga and her team back to the village once more. As the attacks on the Duchess get more serious, and many Ash family secrets are revealed, all the regular local characters get involved as murder and mayhem threaten the calm of the village and the future of the Ash estate. 3/3

1012. **Gregory, Jonathan,** *Unsporting Life,* Createspace, 2015. Gemini and Flowers #5 of 10. (Cozy) Bad things can happen to very nice people. Two elderly people are murdered in Dorchester, one with a boule and one with a cricket bat. Apart from the use of sports equipment, there seems no connection between the two victims. If the deaths are as random as they seem then Chief Inspector Muga and her team have a serial killer to catch before he or she strikes again. Meanwhile, Tom Flowers and his partners set off to try and catch a gang of thieves who have been attacking race courses around the south of England. 3/3

1013. **Gregory, Jonathan,** *Wild Life,* Createspace, 2016. Gemini and Flowers #6 of 10. (Cozy) With autumn approaching and where a new school year has started. The Ash twins have gone to Rilton Castle School, meeting new friends and taking on new roles. The family at the Manor House settles down to hard work, rugby and cross country running, as Tom Flowers and James Stonely take on a new case for Sir Freddie Morgan, who keeps big cats on his estate. Sir Freddie needs to know if his place is safe enough from saboteurs to take on a tiger with an evil reputation. Then the peace of Rilton Castle is shattered by a terrorist attack on a parent at the school. 3/3

1014. **Gregory, Jonathan,** *Private Life,* Createspace, 2016. Gemini and Flowers #7 of 10. (Cozy) Rilton Castle has been peaceful for many months but the discovery of the body of a young Indian man dumped in a ditch near the village shatters the calm. Chief Inspector Muga starts an enquiry into the man's death and discovers he had been digging into the private life of several of the local residents. 3/3

1015. **Gregory, Jonathan,** *High Life,* Createspace, 2017. Gemini and Flowers #8 of 10. (Cozy) There is trouble blowing in the wind. Is it the answer or smoke from another holiday cottage, burnt to the ground by an arsonist? Maybe it is the aroma of Moonshadow Grey's cooking, or the scent from one of her ready-rolled joints? Perhaps it is the noise from the huge loud speakers in the flat next door to Mrs. Julia Fothergill, who is suffering from an outbreak of cuckoos. It's July in Dorset and the peaceful summer is about to be disturbed by violence and mayhem, yet again. With the arrival of Superintendent Pritchard to advise Muga's team about drug dealers, and the Right Honourable Harvey Stroll, MP, begging for help for his beloved mistress, the scene is set for one hell of a party. And the discovery of two decapitated corpses sends all of them searching for the killers. –only available as an e-book (MLM). 3/3

1016. **Gregory, Jonathan,** *Street Life,* Createspace, 2018. Gemini and Flowers #9 of 10. (Cozy) A sadistic killer is on the loose in Bournemouth, preying on young homeless lads. Superintendent Regina Muga is brought in, as the existing team have got nowhere in their investigation. At the same time, Tom Flowers and James Stonely are asked to try and find a boy who disappeared twenty years earlier and find him before his father dies of cancer. As Stonely wants to retire again, this will be his last case. –available as an e-book only and the last book in the series will be released in 2019 (MLM). 3/3

1017. **Gregory, Russ,** *Blue,* Bold Strokes Books, 2011. (Thriller) One-hundred-and-three-year-old nursing home resident Ruth Brookes holds the key to an unsolved series of murders, and what she knows has never been more important. A psychotic killer is once again stalking gay men in the streets of Austin. Meanwhile, Matt Bell has finally decided to break out of the social isolation he's lived in since being shot by the still-at-large killer, and meets the handsome, broody, and shy Thatcher. 3/3

1018. **Gregory, Russ,** *Greg Honey,* Bold Stroke Books, 2013. Honey Agency #1 of 2. (Soft Boiled) Honey Agency: If we can't solve your problem, we're sorry. Greg Honey has bigger issues than a sketchy tagline for his one-man detective agency. To start with, his mother is pressuring him to date debutantes, his stalker keeps leaving threatening messages, his new boyfriend is at least four levels higher up on the gay boy food chain, and his best friend, Willa, has lost her panties. To top it all off, things keep pointing toward trouble at the family estate. Will Greg figure out what's going on in time to help Willa find her panties? Lord knows he wants to because Greg is more than a detective... he's also a Honey. 3/3

1019. **Gregory, Russ,** *Big Hair and a Little Honey,* Bold Stroke Books, 2015. Honey Agency #2 of 2. (Soft Boiled) Honey Agency: When you need a dick, and average will do. The tag line's still dodgy, but Greg's too distracted to notice. His relationship with Matt begins to falter when an old flame shows up in Austin just as Grandmother Honey starts hanging out with drag queens and Willa lands a new beau, who may not survive their courtship. To top it all off, Greg's twenty-ninth birthday is just around the corner and his cat is stalking a neighbor's cockatoo. When Livia Honey tries to engineer her son's abduction, Greg's problems look bigger than the hair in Texas. –the next Honey Agency book, currently untitled is described by the author, "It's Holiday time and everything is merry, until Willa finds out her new boyfriend is lying, and Greg uncovers a plot to steal the Honey oil." No release date listed (MLM). 3/3

1020. **Grey, Andrew,** *Uncorked,* Dreamspinner, 2009. Bottled Up #4 of 5. (YA Amateur Sleuth) Bobby Bielecki is heading home from art school to help run the family wine store, so his adopted father and partner can take a vacation. While filling in, Bobby will have to deal with his once-best friend and lost love, Kenny, who pushed him away from their burgeoning relationship, encouraging him follow his dreams and realize his artistic talents. Despite the tension between them, Bobby and Kenny decide to put their differences aside and work together to figure out what happened to a case of expensive wine. Their investigation leads them to a young runaway and people from Bobby's past and dealing with them reminds Bobby and Kenny of how close they once were. But despite their growing feelings, Bobby is afraid Kenny will do what he's done before and push Bobby away for his own good. –previous books and book five are romance with no mystery plot (MLM). 3/3

1021. **Grey, Dorien (Roger Margason 1933-2015),** *Butcher's Son,* GLB, 2001. Dick Hardesty #1 of 15. (Hard Boiled) Dick Hardesty is pressed into service when someone starts burning down gay bars all over town and the police chief (nicknamed 'the butcher') shrugs the whole thing off. Then drag queens and female impersonators get into the act and Dick is required to sleuth out who is hot and who is not. –these books start out with lots of off-screen sex but as Hardesty starts a relationship they become more mainstream mysteries. 3/3

1022. **Grey, Dorien,** *9th Man,* GLB, 2000. Dick Hardesty #2 of 15. (Hard Boiled) A serial killer is stalking the gay community and the police are largely ignoring them because all the victims are gay. Dick Hardesty takes on the job of bringing the real killer to justice as part of his first experience as a gay detective. 3/3

1023. **Grey, Dorien,** *Bar Watcher,* GLB, 2001. Dick Hardesty #3 of 15. (Hard Boiled) Gay men are being killed by unknown assailant but all are unsavoury characters who have acted out in public. At the same time, Hardesty's brain seems to be controlled by his hormones until he realises that one of his bedroom friends may be under suspicion. 3/3

1024. **Grey, Dorien,** *The Hired Man,* GLB, 2002. Dick Hardesty #4 of 15. (Hard Boiled) Dick Hardesty, gay PI, is hired to protect the interests of a gay/bisexual escort service when a client is murdered. 3/3

1025. **Grey, Dorien,** *The Good Cop,* GLB, 2002. Dick Hardesty #5 of 15. (Hard Boiled) One of the residual spots of conflicts in gay rights is in the police force. This work takes that conflict head-on in the murder of a gay policeman and the investigation by the inimitable Dick Hardesty. It involves the entire police force, which is suspect in this community mystery. 3/3

1026. **Grey, Dorien,** *The Bottle Ghosts,* GLB, 2003. Dick Hardesty #6 of 15. (Hard Boiled) Dick is commissioned to find a missing partner who is an alcoholic and finds that several men with an alcoholic history have disappeared in the last few years. Dick and his young lover join an alcoholic's psychology discussion group to try to solve the mystery. 3/3

1027. **Grey, Dorien,** *The Dirt Peddler,* GLB, 2003. Dick Hardesty #7 of 15. (Hard Boiled) A novel about the scandalous behavior of a governor. 3/3

1028. **Grey, Dorien,** *The Role Players,* GLB, 2004. Dick Hardesty #8 of 15. (Hard Boiled) Dick and his lover, Jonathan, finally manage to take a holiday, and it is, to some extent, a sentimental journey for Dick – it is to New York City, the site of former adventures, and where his former lover is now settled in with a new lover, Max, who happens to be involved in a theatre company. Dick and Jonathan fly in for opening night, but also arrive soon after one of the cast is murdered. 3/3

1029. **Grey, Dorien,** *The Popsicle Tree,* GLB, 2005. Dick Hardesty #9 of 15. (Hard Boiled) Dick and Jonathan are left with Jonathan's nephew to raise when the boy's parents are killed in an accident. This is happening when a woman with a son living in their building is also killed and Dick goes after the villain, after someone cuts his brakes lines. It is a time of conflict between parental instincts and Dick's investigative talents. 3/3

1030. **Grey, Dorien,** *The Paper Mirror,* GLB, 2005. Dick Hardesty #10 of 15. (Hard Boiled) The Hardesty household is still adapting to the presence of Joshua, a four-year old, when a book cataloguer is murdered. The investigation leads to a long-dead, secret gay writer, whose remaining family is determined to conceal his sexual preferences. Homophobia rears its ugly head. 3/3

1031. **Grey, Dorien,** *The Dream Ender,* Zumaya, 2007. Dick Hardesty #11 of 15. (Hard Boiled) When rugged construction worker and biker Cal Hysong is killed, PI Dick Hardesty knows the reason-Cal was widely suspected of deliberately spreading AIDS to other gay men. Like the rest of the gay community, Dick's initial reaction is "good riddance." But when Jake Jacobson and Jared Martinson, two of his closest friends, become suspects, the case turns personal, and Dick sets out to clear them and find the real killer. His search takes him into the unfamiliar world of gay bikers and leathermen, and through a labyrinth of suspects, motivations, blind alleys and memorable characters. 3/3

1032. **Grey, Dorien,** *The Angel Singers,* Zumaya, 2008. Dick Hardesty #12 of 15. (Hard Boiled) Grant Jefferson joins the Gay Men's Chorus as a protege of its biggest supporter and begins causing more discord than harmony. Determined he's going to Broadway, Grant sees the chorus as the means to his end and doesn't care much how many of the other members he uses as his stepping stones–or how hard they get stepped on. So, when a car bomb ends Grant's recitative, there is no shortage of possible suspects, and when the chorus's board of directors hires Dick Hardesty to see what he can find out about the murder he ends up in a case as complicated as a madrigal. 3/3

1033. **Grey, Dorien,** *The Secret Keeper,* Zumaya, 2009. Dick Hardesty #13 of 15. (Hard Boiled) PI Dick Hardesty listens with polite interest to his partner Jonathan's stories of his days working for 90-year-old multimillionaire Clarence Bement, helping the old man tend his garden. But when Bement is found dead, an apparent suicide, Jonathan is adamant that the old man would never have killed himself, a theory also held by Bement's grandson, Mel Fowler. 3/3

1034. **Grey, Dorien,** *The Peripheral Son,* Zumaya, 2011. Dick Hardesty #14 of 15. (Hard Boiled) Investigating the disappearance of a freelance writer doing simultaneous exposes on both the boxing profession and construction unions, PI Dick Hardesty finds himself handed a Gordian Knot, with no sword to cut it. A plethora of motives and suspects, and a dearth of solid evidence sorely test both Dick's skills and his patience. 3/3

1035. **Grey, Dorien,** *The Serpent's Tongue,* Zumaya, 2014. Dick Hardesty #15 of 15. (Hard Boiled) When Dick Hardesty is hired to look into threats against former priest Dan Stabile, possibly from someone whose confession Dan heard while still in the priesthood, it's just another case. Then, on a stormy Sunday, on a rain-slick road, Dan is killed, Dick's partner Jonathan is severely injured, and suddenly, it's personal. Was the accident really an accident...or murder? Dick learns Dan's secret could involve a child murderer, and now it seems the man is stalking Joshua and tormenting Jonathan. The objectivity so vital to Dick's role as a private investigator goes out the window as he pursues one lead after another, and it begins to look like Dan wasn't the target after all. –series left unfinished (MLM). 3/3

1036. **Grey, Dorien,** *Calico,* Zumaya, 2006. (YA Western) It seemed like a simple job - guide Josh and Sarah to Bow Ridge to live with their aunt until they reached their 18th birthday. It was what their aunt Rebecca wanted, and the best choice Calico Ramsey thought he could make. But someone wants them dead, which makes no sense to Calico. Neither do the feelings aroused by the nearness of the handsome young man from Chicago - feelings that seem to be returned, and nothing in his past has prepared him for either. –"rewrite of *Stagecoach to Nowhere* by Roger Margason (1976), a traditional straight western, whose hero is Calico Williams (Gunn)." 3/3

1037. **Grey, Dorien,** *His Name is John,* Zumaya, 2008. Elliott Smith #1 of 4. (Paranormal) Elliott Smith never considered himself to be anything special, if you didn't count having wealthy parents, whom he largely ignores. His profession is buying, restoring and reselling small apartment buildings around Chicago. Gay and contentedly single at 38, he has, in addition to his globetrotting parents, a devoted sister, a police detective brother-in-law, two nieces and a nephew. Everything in his life is going along perfectly fine until he wakes in the hospital after being hit by a car aware of being watched by someone who isn't there. 3/3

1038. **Grey, Dorien,** *Aaron's Wait,* Zumaya, 2009. Elliott Smith #2 of 4. (Paranormal) Elliott Smith's latest restoration project is a beautiful old six-unit apartment building. Unfortunately for Elliott, he discovers that Aaron Stiles, one of the tenants, has been dead for four years and doesn't know it. His partner, Bill Somers, left for work one morning and never returned. Devastated to think that Bill might have left him. Aaron suffered a heart attack and died. But he is still waiting for Bill to come home, and unless Elliott can convince him otherwise, he's not going anywhere until that happens. 3/3

1039. **Grey, Dorien,** *Caesar's Fall,* Zumaya, 2010. Elliott Smith #3 of 4. (Paranormal) With a new building to restore and his relationship with Steve growing more serious, the last thing Elliott needs is someone else's problem, but when lottery millionaire Bruno Caesar moves into his building he can't just ignore the man's pleas for help. Then Bruno's life ends abruptly when he falls from his balcony. There's only one problem-he was terrified of heights...and never went onto the balcony. Bruno can't rest until the puzzle of his sudden death is solved, and Elliott and John are once again searching for answers. 3/3

1040. **Grey, Dorien,** *Dante's Circle,* Zumaya, 2012. Elliott Smith #4 of 4. (Paranormal) Dante Benevetti is the darling of the music world... and why not? He's handsome, talented–and arrogant as only a man convinced of his own brilliance can be. As far as he's concerned, the rest of the world exists for his benefit. So, when he hears Dane is dead, a victim of murder, Elliott isn't really surprised. Nor is he surprised when Dante comes for a post-mortem visit, demanding Elliott find out who killed him. Was it the well-known lyricist who was the only one in the house at the time? The talented young musician whose work Dante plagiarized? Or some unknown the great pianist had mortally offended? 3/3

1041. **Greyson, Dirk,** *Day and Knight,* Dreamspinner, 2015. Day and Knight #1 of 3. (MM Espionage) As former NSA, Dayton (Day) Ingram has national security chops and now works as a technical analyst for Scorpion. He longs for fieldwork, and scuttling an attack gives him his chance. He's smart, multilingual, and a technological wizard. But his opportunity comes with a hitch–a partner, Knighton (Knight), who is a real mystery. Despite countless hours of research, Day can find nothing on the agent, including his first name! 3/3

1042. **Greyson, Dirk,** *Sun and Shadow,* Dreamspinner, 2015. Day and Knight #2 of 3. (MM Espionage) Dayton "Day" Ingram is recovering from an injury suffered in Mexico–and from his failed relationship with fellow Scorpion agent, Knight. While researching an old government document, Day realizes he might be holding the key to finding an artistic masterpiece lost since WWII. 3/3

1043. **Greyson, Dirk,** *Dawn and Dusk,* Dreamspinner, 2016. Day and Knight #3 of 3. (MM Espionage) For Scorpion agents Day and Knight, their relationship is slow to develop, and trust is hard to build. Then Day's brother, Stephen, goes missing, and Day finds out more about him than he ever dreamed. Day's first reaction to Stephen's disappearance is to try to get to him as fast as possible. 3/3

1044. **Griffin, Max,** *Flatland,* Loveyoudivine, 2010. (Crime Drama) Where a fortune in mob money, a stone-cold serial killer, and a crooked FBI agent collide with two gay guys looking for love. Danny and Skip are just getting to know each other when organized crime invades their boring trailer park in rural Kansas. Before long, they've acquired a hit man's dog and uncovered clues to his hidden stash of stolen loot. A crooked FBI agent and a vicious professional killer pursue them across Kansas as they follow the trail to wealth beyond their dreams. Murder and mayhem weave with intricate double-crosses while the two struggles to untangle the clues. At the end, they must choose between love and money, for they can't have both. 3/3

1045. **Griffin, Max,** *Hounds of Hollenbeck,* Purple Sword, 2015. Shadowlands of Desire #2 of 3. (Procedural) Allen and Sam are unlikely lovers. Both are graduate students at Browning College in the small Pacific Northwest town of Lagrange. Allen works with hyper-intelligent dogs on a secret Army project, while Sam is a detective on the police force who is also pursuing his master's degree in criminology. Everything changes when one of Allen's professors finds dismembered human bodies in her research habitat. -expanded to full length novel after being published in 2009 as a novella and the other two books in the series are romantic fantasy (MLM). 3/3

1046. **Griffin, Max,** *Seeking Hyde,* Dreamspinner, 2012. (MM Journalism) When Brent Hyde arrives home from college to find his parents missing from their dairy farm, he feels a creeping sense of dread, but the inept local police won't take him seriously. Determined to find them, Brent drags his boyfriend, Gary, into the search. When Jason Killeen, a senior journalism student from Brent's college, shows up to investigate a twenty-year-old research project involving Brent's mother–and Brent's current employer–the situation gets sticky. Jason insists they're all in danger, and a sudden body count proves him right. 3/3

1047. **Griffin, Max,** *Murder me Tender,* Purple Sword, 2013. (MM Amateur Sleuth) Rick's brooding over his missing wife doesn't stop him from inviting Brandon to move into his mansion in the hills of southwest Wisconsin. When the sheriff finds bodies at the estate, it's a race against time to save Rick from accusations of murder. Brandon struggles with poverty and longs to be a doctor. He falls in with Rick, an older, closeted, banker whose wealthy wife Victoria is mysteriously missing. Romance blooms between the two men and all seems well, until the sheriff discovers Victoria's body at the family estate, Lindermont Manor. 3/3

1048. **Griffon, David,** *Jocksucker,* Surrey, 1972. (Pulp) "U. S. secret agent Tom Brawley, 20s, prepares for possible death in a nuclear showdown between the United States and the Soviet Union by relieving his sexual tension with Army lieutenant Carl Djugashlivi, 20s, and his commander's son, Jeff Pike, 17 (Gunn)." 3/3

1049. **Grimes, Martha,** *The Man with a Load of Mischief,* Little Brown, 1981. Richard Jury #1 of 24. (Police Procedural) At the Man with a Load of Mischief, they found the dead body stuck in a keg of beer. At the Jack and Hammer, another body was stuck out on the beam of the pub's sign, replacing the mechanical man who kept the time. Two pubs. Two murders. Detective Chief Inspector Richard Jury arrives in Long Piddleton and finds everyone in the postcard village looking outside of town for the killer. Except for one Melrose Plant. A keen observer of human nature, he points Jury in the right direction: into the darkest parts of his neighbors' hearts... –an effete antiques dealer is most prominent in this novel but does make appearances throughout the series (MLM). 1/3

1050. **Grobeson, Mitchell,** *Outside the Badge,* Vantage, 1999. (Police Procedural) A serial killer is loose on the streets of Los Angeles, targeting young male hustlers. Indifferent to crimes against gays, the police department has categorized the killings as NHI–No Humans Involved. No one gives a damn, except for a gay cop whose fellow officers consider him as expendable as the young men being tortured and murdered. 3/3

1051. **Gronowski, Paul,** *Doomsday Machinery,* Blueboy Library, 1977. (Pulp) One minute in a loving embrace, the next, Jeff and Nick find themselves on a mission to save the lives of an entire city from destruction by terrorists. Having planted one nuclear device in the desert that cost the lives of three soldiers, the Weathermen II strike out in a reign of terror; holding the populace of Los Angeles as hostages with still another bomb. The two young CIA agents find themselves first in the middle of a nuclear blast, then under fire by terrorists, and finally sitting right on top of a bomb powerful enough to wipe out an entire city. – reprinted by Arena as *Under Cover Gays* by Mitch Stone (MLM). 3/3

1052. **Gronowski, Paul,** *Power Play,* Blueboy Library, 1977. (Pulp) "IRS undercover agent Greig Hallman and U. S. Department of Justice agent Rick Unforth work together in a pulp suspense thriller (Gunn)." 3/3

1053. **Gronowski, Paul,** *Secret in the Argentine Jungle,* Blueboy Library, 1977. (Pulp) "Buenos Aires-based U. S. undercover agent Jack Hoover and Jeff Moore, a graduate of Georgetown University with an M. S. in human genetics, go on an assignment together in a pulp action thriller (Gunn)." 3/3

1054. **Gronowski, Paul,** *Behind the Badge,* Blueboy, 1978. (Pulp) "Los Angeles physical therapist Jack Morrison, 28, the narrator, is in on the seizure of two snipers targeting LAPD officers...in a pulp procedural (Gunn)." 3/3

1055. **Gronowski, Paul,** *Dangerous Trade,* Surree, 1978. (Pulp) "Two CIA agents, Boston-based Jack Blanchard and Washington/Los Angeles-based Greg Hennesey, come together...two bodies turn up in Martinique on the eve of the U. S. president's meeting with Arab oil countries' ministers, both killed by a new type of pneumonia...in a pulp action thriller (Gunn)." 3/3

1056. **Gronowski, Paul,** *Bizarre Triangle,* Surree, 1978. (Pulp) "Los Angeles police detective Nick Gettering, a former fireman, works to protect his lover in a pulp procedural (Gunn)." 3/3

1057. **Gronowski, Paul,** *Double Play,* Surree, 1978. (Pulp) "U. S. journalist Rainer (Rain) von Skoltz, a German American assigned to Moscow, becomes intrigued with dissident Erick Nemunaitus, 22, a Lithuanian engineering student, in a pulp suspense thriller (Gunn)." 3/3

1058. **Guillone, Sedonia,** *His Beautiful Samurai,* Torquere, 2006. Genjin/Holmes #1 of 2. (MM Paranormal) John Holmes comes to Tokyo to help stop a killer. Through the use of his psychic abilities, he can help find out things that no one else sees. Toshi is a policeman who reluctantly accepts John's help. The modern killer, a historical murder of two samurai, and the fear that someone very close to Toshi betraying him combine to make the blooming love between John and Toshi difficult. And dangerous. – "Publisher's note: *His Beauti-*

ful Samurai has been extensively revised for release with Ai Press (2014). It is a VASTLY different story from the 2006 edition from Torquere Press." 3/3

1059. **Guillone, Sedonia,** *Beautiful Samurai, White Tiger,* Torquere, 2007. Genjin/Holmes #2 of 2. (MM Paranormal) Toshi and John are still reeling from their last adventure, dealing with family issues and trying to get ready for Toshi's uncle's funeral. During the funeral preparations, Toshi realizes that his uncle's dear friend Tokuma was more than a friend, and that Tokuma needs his help. Fearing his nephew Yuzo has been kidnapped by the Yakuza, Tokuma asks Toshi and John to look into the young man's disappearance. –no mention of revising although it was re-published by Ai Press in 2013 (MLM). 3/3

1060. **Guilone, Sedonia,** *Acts of Passion: A Jack Cade/Michael di Santo Novel of Suspense,* Ellora's Cave, 2010. (MM Police Procedural) When a man is found in his apartment, appearing to have committed hara kiri with a samurai sword, Boston Homicide Detective Jack Cade suspects more is going on than what it appears. The department's criminal profiler has left, and a new guy is taking his place. At first, Cade is skeptical of Dr. Michael Di Santo. Di Santo seems so absent-minded and too neurotic to be effective, but he is brilliant as they close in on a killer, another brilliant, wily person whose sights are now set on Michael. 3/3

1061. **Gummerson, Drew,** *The Lodger: Sharing Can be Murder,* Gay Men's Press, 2002. (Amateur Sleuth) Honza takes in a lodger, Andy, who seems like his opposite - a coarse straight guy who comes home drunk every night to fart happily in front of the TV. But when, in a drunken stupor, Andy confesses to murder, Honza refuses to believe him. Then one weekend Andy disappears, only to return with his face rearranged. 3/3

1062. **Gundy, Bud,** *Somewhere over Lorain Road,* Bold Strokes, 2018. (MM Amateur Sleuth) For more than forty years, the stain of horrific allegations against their father has haunted the Esker sons. When three little boys were murdered in 1975, their dad was suspected of the crimes. The immense strain of the unsolved case shattered the family, sending the brothers reeling into destinies of death, flight, and, in the case of Don Esker, shame-filled silence. Years later, Don returns to the family home in North Homestead, Ohio, to help care for his dying father in his final months. His dad longs for the peace that will only come with clearing his name. 3/3

1063. **Gunn, Rufus,** *Friendship of Convenience: Being a Discourse on Poussin's Landscape with a Man Killed by a Snake,* Gay Men's Press, 1997. (Political Intrigue) The place and time: London 1956. The friends in question: Sir Anthony Blunt, Surveyor of the Queen's Pictures, and Joe Losey, film director and refugee from McCarthyism. Their meeting: the National Gallery, in front of Poussin's disturbing metaphor. Into this landscape, Rufus Gunn introduces a cast of celebrities: Vita Sackville-West, Arthur Miller, Anthony Eden, Ben Nicholson, in a plot where fiction blends effortlessly with fact, as the US intelligence services press the British government to take action against the homosexual peril. Brilliantly evoking the political and intellectual life of the high Cold War, A Friendship of Convenience recreates a world where the appearance of politeness and civility covered up a reality of cynicism and betrayal. 3/3

H

1064. **Habu,** *Death on the Rhine,* eXcessica, 2008. Clint Folsom #1 of 7. (Police Procedural/ Modern Pulp) When his partner and lover is murdered in an investigation of an international crime syndicate, New York police detective Clint Folsom takes leave from his job and flies to Europe in pursuit of the killer. Folsom finds his quarry on the Rhine River gay male-oriented cruise ship, the MS River God, murdered in the same sadomasochistic manner his partner had been killed. As the cruise glides down the Rhine toward Amsterdam, stopping at German cities along the way to add flavor and twists to the increasingly complex plot, Folsom is thwarted at every turn in his inquiries. He slowly unravels not only what is at stake but also who is involved while finding sexual release among the crew and passengers of the River God. When the German police inspector Sigmund Frist enters the scene, Folsom himself becomes the pursued in more ways than one. 3/3

1065. **Habu,** *Death in Eden,* eXcessica, 2008. Clint Folsom #2 of 7. (Police Procedural/ Modern Pulp) Unapologetically promiscuous bottom NYPD detective Folsom finds himself flying to a wealthy hunt country suburb of Washington, D.C., at the request of a former lover, Peter Blair, who is now the Loudon County, Virginia, police chief. He has been summoned to whitewash the murder of a former Mafia sex-torture assassin, Johnny -The Club- Wallace, who had once assaulted Folsom himself. Wallace has been salted away in the unlikely rich hunt country location with the witness protection program but, at the time of his death, was close to being charged in the molestation of the Loudon County Commonwealth Attorney's luscious blond hunk son, Jason. Blair himself was known to have threatened the life of Wallace. Although obviously meant to finger the Mafia for the hit on Wallace, the Loudon County authorities haven't counted on the dedication, honesty, and tenaciousness of Clint Folsom. 3/3

1066. **Habu,** *Death in Key West,* eXcessica, 2009. Clint Folsom #3 of 7. (Police Procedural/ Modern Pulp) Folsom takes a vacation to the "everything goes" paradise of Key West, Florida, to visit the movie producer who had been his first lover. Folsom is still en route when his memories begin to catch up with him and he becomes embroiled in murder and big-ticket crime. Once having fallen into his movie world past and only in channeling back to the summer of his sexual initiation to dredge up his first lover's advice to always look for the connections and question whether everything is what it seems can Folsom begin to unravel the crimes blossoming around him and bring closure to his prior life. –available as an e-book only (MLM). 3/3

1067. **Habu**, *Death in the Rockies,* eXcessica, 2011. Clint Folsom #4 of 7. (Police Procedural/ Modern Pulp) The promiscuous gay male NYPD homicide detective goes West on an assignment that he's one of a very few detectives specializing in. In a soon-to-be released book, prominent crime novel writer Jason Jenks has fingered, not by name, but by clear identification, Giacomo Arcardi, son of one prominent New York crime family, with the sex murder of Lorenzo Rapino, son of another prominent New York crime family. The details of the murder and case that he builds in the book make Jason Jenks appear to be the best living prosecution witness, and the NYPD is tagged with protecting him. –available as an e-book only (MLM). 3/3

1068. **Habu**, Death to Innocence, eXcessica, 2011. Clint Folsom #5 of 7. (Police Procedural/ Modern Pulp) Clint Folsom was no stranger to murder even before he lost his innocence to other men. The distinction of the NYPD homicide detective is his celebratory gay male promiscuity, which the police department frequently finds helps it close cases and thus makes Folsom a valuable investigative asset. This precursor to the Clint Folsom mystery series illuminates the elements of slow but relentless death of young Folsom's adolescent innocence under highly unusual circumstances in narcissistic and hedonist Hollywood. The events that not only developed and sharpened Folsom's sexual proclivities are revealed, but it also illustrates why men gravitate to him like bees to honey. The murder mystery folded into the plot of a young man's journey to manhood illustrates reasons why Folsom is haunted by his past and driven by his profession. –available as an e-book only (MLM). 3/3

1069. **Habu**, *Death in Hollywood,* eXcessica, 2011. Clint Folsom #6 of 7. (Police Procedural/ Modern Pulp) The possibility that the death of Clint Folsom's movie star parents twenty years ago brings the promiscuous NYPD homicide detective back to his L.A. hometown. Here, while trying desperately to discern the real events and meaning of his parents' last moments on the treacherous curves of the Pacific coast highway and what part they played in twenty-year-old murder and suicide cases, Folsom faces ghosts, both recent and past, of his own. A lover who Folsom has tried to give up when the other man married is the L.A. detective who brings Folsom back to California. And the convoluted network of his parents' own lovers awaits their renewed chance at Folsom as well. –available as an e-book only (MLM). 3/3

1070. **Habu,** *Death to Blonds: Stolen Judgment,* Barbarian Spy, 2014. Clint Folsom #7 of 7. (Police Procedural/ Modern Pulp) New York gay Homicide detective Clint Folsom, to the consternation of his partner and current lover, Danny Thompson, appears to be sinking ever deeper into his fetish for almost-constant, on-the-edge rough sex. Danny doesn't know half the danger Clint is in, though, when they are put on two cases, one the murder of a key witness in a mobster trial and the other a serial killer on a spree on the docks in lower Manhattan, and the victims all fall into Clint's demographic: sexually active, insatiable, and edgy bottoms who are in their late twenties or early thirties and blond, who have movie-star looks, and who cruise the gay bars of Chelsea and Christopher Street. – available as an ebook only and unsure where and what books seven and eight are in the series. *Death to Blonds* was listed as "the ninth detective mystery in the Clint Folsom series and is set, chronological, right behind the fourth book, Death in Eden." Not sure how it is the ninth book in the series but falls between books four and five (MLM). 3/3

1071. **Habu,** *Gotta Keep Trying,* Barbarian Spy, 2012. Hardesty Vice #1 of 4. (Crime Drama) Hardesty cruises the gay male clubs of Washington, D.C., where his interest is in checking out the ages of the young men dancing the poles. One night he focuses on a lithe young-looking dancer with a blond Mohawk and a provocatively placed gecko tattoo who looks far too innocent yet also very sexy. Hardesty is so lost to his desires that he takes him away from the club. In the motel he goes far beyond what he knows he should do, but is Hardesty's almost obsessive desire for Todd going to be dangerous or does it actually mean something more is on Hardesty's mind? The world of underground sex in a big city can be dangerous, even fatal, for a young man who is alone and naive. –available as an e-book only (MLM). 3/3

1072. **Habu,** *Snitches: Cleaning up for the Elections,* Barbarian Spy, 2016. Hardesty Vice #2 of 4. (MM Police Procedural) When a U.S. senator is named as a possible vice-presidential running mate, all hell breaks out in his attempt to hide that he has a weakness for sadistic sex with rent-boys. When his thugs mess up an attempt to silence one in a D.C. hotel, snitches descend on D.C. vice cop Hardesty, not a stranger to vice himself, particularly with snitch rent-boys. –available as an e-book only (MM). 3/3

1073. **Habu,** *Retribution: Christmas in DC with the Russian Mob,* Barbarian Spy, 2016. Hardesty Vice #3 of 4. (MM Police Procedural) Christmas Day isn't being kind to D.C. Homicide Vice detective Hardesty. Called to a crime scene at the Georgetown University boathouse on the Potomac River, he is taken aback at seeing the face under the ice of a man he only hours earlier was partying with at an exclusive, full-service gay male brothel. Immediately thereafter identifying a body in a Mercedes in the boathouse's parking lot as a rent-boy from the previous evening, who Hardesty has known (biblically) himself, the plot thickens as the Secret Service descends on the boathouse looking for someone else altogether. –available as an e-book only (MLM). 3/3

1074. **Habu,** *Political Abuse: Politicians' Answer to Me Too,* Barbarian Spy, 2018. Hardesty Vice #4 of 4. (MM Police Procedural) A whistle-blowing former U.S. Senate page entices Washington, D.C., vice unit detective Hardesty, who is an addict to the sex vices he fights, to his apartment with information to impart on a congressional gay male pimping ring. But when he gets offed before he can confide in Hardesty, the detective gets embroiled in the highly sensitive and political sex ring case. –available as an e-book only (MLM). 3/3

1075. **Habu,** *Death on a Ping Pong Table: A Knife, a Book, and a Dead Body,* Barbarian Spy, 2014. (Police Procedural/Modern Pulp) The unusual thing about Hilton Head homicide detective Quinn Fawker isn't just that he is promiscuous and actively bisexual but that he has the looks and equipment to get away with it. When he is called to the Sea Pines compound of South Carolina U.S. Senator Bradford Braxton to investigate the finding of a body draped over the senator's ping pong table, he gets dropped into a cast of characters also accustomed to getting away with sexual shenanigans. –available as an e-book only (MLM). 3/3

1076. **Haig, Brian,** *Mortal Allies,* Warner, 2002. Sean Drummond #2 of 7. (Military) Don't Ask. Don't Tell. Especially when it comes to murder. But Major Sean Drummond never plays it safe. Even when the young son of a South Korean war hero is found dead under dark circumstances and the Army orders Drummond to defend the American officer accused. Even when Drummond must work with his ruthless-and beautiful-old law school rival. Even when what begins as a simple case explodes into a war of secret international agendas...with Drummond in the crosshairs. 2/3

1077. **Hale, Ginn,** *Wicked Gentlemen,* Blind Eye, 2007. (Paranormal) Belimai Sykes is many things: a Prodigal, the descendant of ancient demons, a creature of dark temptations and rare powers. He is also a man with a brutal past and a dangerous addiction. And Belimai Sykes is the only man Captain William Harper can turn to when faced with a series of grisly murders. But Mr. Sykes does not work for free and the price of Belimai's company will cost Captain Harper far more than his reputation. From the ornate mansions of noblemen, where vivisection and sorcery are hidden beneath a veneer of gold, to the steaming slums of Hells Below, Captain Harper must fight for justice and for his life. His enemies are many and his only ally is a devil he knows too well. Such are the dangers of dealing with the wicked. –translated into English by *Arrate Hidalgo* (MLM). 3/3

1078. **Hall, Richard (Richard Hirshfeld 1926-1992)**, *The Butterscotch Prince*, Pyramid, 1975. (Amateur Sleuth) When Cordell's best friend and ex-lover is murdered, the only clue is one that the police seem to consider too kinky to follow up on. Cordell decides to track down the killer himself. –expanded in 1983 by Alyson Press (MLM). 3/3

1079. **Halliday, Fred**, *A Case of Indelicate Champagne: A Gourmet's Guide to Dying Out*, Pinnacle, 1977. (Amateur Sleuth) "Features the world's number one gastronome, Stanley Delphond, dealing with a rash of murders perpetrated by poisoned champagne (Slide)." –a newspaper man and his kept boy are traveling on the cruise (MLM). 1/3

1080. **Hamill, Pete**, *Dirty Laundry*, Bantam, 1978. (Journalism) Former crack columnist for a New York City paper, Sam Brisco gets a terrified phone call from an old flame. Before he can get to her, she is murdered and Sam is plunged into a strange case involving a couple of corpses, a guy who stole a bank and a surprising pay-off.... –gay CIA agent (MLM). 1/3

1081. **Hamilton, R. J.**, *Who framed Lorenzo Garcia*, AlyCat, 1995. Pride Pack #1 of 3. (YA Amatuer Sleuths) Just as 16-year-old Ramon Torres thinks he has found a safe haven, someone sets up his foster father, police officer Sergeant Lorenzo Garcia, for arrest. His homophobic caseworker effectively cuts off communication between the two. So Ramon realizes it is up to him to find out who framed Lorenzo Garcia? Luckily, he has the support of the Pride Pack, his friends from the local gay and lesbian community center! But before they expose the perpetrators more than one of their lives will be in danger. 3/3

1082. **Hamilton, R. J.**, *The Case of the Missing Mother*, AlyCat, 1995. Pride Pack #2 of 3. (YA Amateur Sleuths) Small-town peer pressure and a virulent religious right group at work do not make 16-year-old Rebecca Staley's life easy. She loves both her lesbian mothers, but she is not sure how open she wants to be about them. Then one of them disappears. Once again the Pride Pack springs into action, risking their lives. As a result, Rebecca discovers what is really valuable in her world. 3/3

1083. **Hamilton, R. J.**, *The Quarterback's Secret*, Cheyenne, 2011. Pride

Pack #3 of 3. (YA Amateur Sleuths) Athletics remain largely homophobic environments. How will his teammates react if 16-year-old baseball pitching star Ben Reis admits he is gay? He mostly lies about his sexuality even when he is with the Pride Pack at the local gay and lesbian community center. All that may change however as the result of his falling through a sinkhole into an unknown cavern. 3/3

1084. **Hamlin, L. J.**, *Murder at the Second Chance Ranch,* Less than Three, 2018. (MM Amateur Sleuth) Tommy is an ex con starting fresh at the Second Chance Ranch, where he fervently hopes to live a quiet life. That hope is shaken a bit when he meets Cash and Red, two closeted ranch hands who've been resisting mutual feelings. Tommy doesn't quite know what to do with his own feelings for both of them. As if that's not enough, his hopes for peace and quiet are completely dashed in the aftermath of a murder... 3/3

1085. **Hammett, Dashiell,** *The Maltese Falcon,* Knopf, 1930. (Hard Boiled) Sam Spade is hired by the fragrant Miss Wonderley to track down her sister, who has eloped with a louse called Floyd Thursby. But Miss Wonderley is in fact the beautiful and treacherous Brigid O'Shaughnessy, and when Spade's partner Miles Archer is shot while on Thursby's trail, Spade finds himself both hunter and hunted: can he track down the jewel-encrusted bird, a treasure worth killing for, before the Fat Man finds him? –three gay men appear in this novel, unfortunately all as villains (MLM). 1/3

1086. **Hansen, Joseph,** *Fadeout,* Harper and Row, 1970. Dave Brandstetter #1 of 12. (Hard Boiled) Rugged Dave Brandstetter, an insurance investigator who is contentedly gay. When entertainer Fox Olson's car plunges off a bridge in a storm, a death claim is filed, but where is Olson's body? As Brandstetter questions family, fans, and detractors, he grows certain Olson is still alive and that Dave must find him before the would-be killer does. 3/3

1087. **Hansen, Joseph,** *Death Claims,* Harper and Row, 1973. Dave Brandstetter #2 of 12. (Hard Boiled) When John Oats's body is found washed up on a beach, his young lover April Stannard is sure it was no accident. Brandstetter agrees: Oats's college-age son, the beneficiary of the life insurance policy, has gone missing. 3/3

1088. **Hansen, Joseph,** *Troublemaker,* Harper and Row, 1975. Dave Brandstetter #3 of 12. (Hard Boiled) Who killed gay bar owner and all-around nice guy Rick Wendell? Was it Larry Johns, the attractive young man found wiping his prints off the still-smoking gun mere moments after the murder? If so, why was Johns naked? And what happened to the large sum of money Wendell had just withdrawn from the bar's bank account? Hard-boiled, openly gay insurance

1089. **Hansen, Joseph,** *The Man Everybody was Afraid Of,* Holt, Rinehart, Winston, 1978. Dave Brandstetter #4 of 12. (Hard Boiled) When Ben Orton's head is found bludgeoned by a heavy flower pot, the people of La Caleta are stunned–not because their police chief has been murdered, but because no one thought to do it sooner. A bruising, violent man, Ben had a commitment to order that did not always take the law into account. But as insurance investigator Dave Brandstetter is about to find out, the corruption in Ben's police force did not die with him. By the time Dave arrives in the fading fishing town, a young activist has already been arrested for the murder. Only Dave seems to care that the evidence against the accused is laughably thin. As the people of La Caleta try their best to thwart his investigation, Dave must do whatever it takes to catch Ben's killer. 3/3

1090. **Hansen, Joseph,** *Skinflick,* Holt, Rinehart, Winston, 1979. Dave Brandstetter #5 of 12. (Hard Boiled) Insurance investigator, Dave Brandstetter, who finds too many loose ends to tie up when he investigates a murder. The investigation takes him from an evangelical church to the seedy world of teenage drugs and prostitution. 3/3

1091. **Hansen, Joseph,** *Gravedigger,* Holt, Rinehart, Winston, 1982. Dave Brandstetter #6 of 12. (Hard Boiled) Charles Westover, a disbarred lawyer, alleges that his runaway teenage daughter has been murdered and he files an insurance claim. And then he disappears, leaving claims investigator, Dave Brandstetter to sort through the pieces of the puzzle. Young women have been murdered by the crazed guru of a bizarre sex cult - is this what happened to Serenity Westover? 3/3

1092. **Hansen, Joseph,** *Nightwork,* Holt, Rinehart, Winston, 1984. Dave Brandstetter #7 of 12. (Hard Boiled) In a remote spot outside L.A, a giant truck suddenly plunges in flames off a mountain road at midnight. It looks like an accident, but it isn't. Someone had fastened a bomb under the truck, killing owner-driver, Paul Myers who was insured for $100,000. Crack insurance investigator, Dave Brandstetter is called in to find out what happened and why. Why was Myers hauling in that secluded spot at that hour and for whom? No one wants to answer Dave's questions but then another trucker's death arouses suspicions and a pattern begins to emerge. *–Brandstetter and Others* short stories by Joseph Hansen published in 1984 by Countryman Press. 3/3

1093. **Hansen, Joseph,** *The Little Dog Laughed,* Henry Holt, 1986. Dave Brandstetter #8 of 12. (Hard Boiled) Celebrated foreign correspondent Adam Streeter is found shot dead in his elegant LA condo. The cops say suicide, but the company that insured his life thinks otherwise and sends in crack death-claims investigator Dave Brandstetter. As he pushes deeper into the case, he unearths three more deaths seemingly linked to Streeter's. Little by little, Brandstetter narrows the hunt for the killer - only to find he himself has become the hunted, his enemy more powerful and ruthless than any he has faced before. 3/3

1094. **Hansen, Joseph,** *Early Graves,* Mysterious Press, 1987. Dave Brandstetter #9 of 12. (Hard Boiled) Dave Brandstetter, is called upon to track down a serial killer operating in and around Los Angeles who has been killing gay men who have AIDS. 3/3

1095. **Hansen, Joseph,** *Obedience,* Mysterious Press, 1988. Dave Brandstetter #10 of 12. (Hard Boiled) Dave ventures into Los Angeles' Vietnamese subculture to prevent an innocent man from taking a murder rap. 3/3

1096. **Hansen, Joseph,** *The Boy who was Buried this Morning,* Viking, 1990. Dave Brandstetter #11 of 12. (Hard Boiled) Brandstetter is called out of semi-retirement to investigate the apparently accidental shotgun death of his lover's co-worker. What unfolds is a gripping tale of blackmail and murder set in a sleepy California town, where nothing is as innocent as it appears. 3/3

1097. **Hansen, Joseph,** *A County of Old Men,* Viking, 1991. Dave Brandstetter #12 of 12. (Hard Boiled) After twenty-one years on the detective beat, aging veteran P.I. Dave Brandstetter is finally going to get some rest–that is, after one last case. Even though he is no longer able to sprint after the bad guys like he used to, Brandstetter is not stopped from investigating this wild tale of kidnapping and murder told by a bruised and grubby little boy found wandering the beach alone. The police don't even believe the kid–just as they don't believe that the drug-related shooting death of a pop guitarist in anything out of the ordinary. So, Dave is lured out of retirement to confront street drugs, powerful politicians, sleazy record executives, child abuse, and to unravel as snarled a tangle of carnage and deception as he's ever faced. –won the fourth LAMBDA Award (MLM). 3/3

1098. **Hansen, Joseph,** *A Smile in His Lifetime,* Holt, Rinehart, Winston, 1981. (Psychological) Whit Miller was a struggling writer and a solidly married man. Then came success - and destruction. Of his marriage. And almost of himself. For Whit was gay and now there was nothing to repress who he was and what he wanted: a man to love, among so many men to love. And in an odyssey of desperate need and obsessive desire he journeyed to the heights and to the depths of the heart - and of the flesh... 3/3

1099. **Hansen, Joseph,** *Backtrack,* Foul Play Press, 1982. (Amateur Sleuth) Alan Tarr refuses to accept a police explanation of the death of his father, a small-time actor, and decides to investigate. 3/3

1100. **Hansen, Joseph,** *Job's Year,* Holt, Rinehart, Winston, 1983. (Family Drama) "[Meandering] backwards and forwards in time from the 1940s to the present as actor Oliver Jewett reviews his life as his sister lies dying (Slide)." –very similar to the Brandstetter series with an aloof protagonist and ex-longtime lover interior decorator (MLM). 3/3

1101. **Hansen, Joseph,** *Steps Going Down,* Foul Play Press, 1985. (Crime Drama) Darryl Cutler knows a good thing when he sees it – and old Stewart Moody's fortune is the best thing he's ever seen. So, Darryl takes care of the dying old man, knowing the promised inheritance is well worth the wait. Or so Darryl believes, until something even better comes along. When Chick Pelletier, a young sunny-haired would-be actor appears on the scene Darryl is obsessed: he'll do anything to please Chick. But Darryl has finally met the hustler who can out-hustle him, and the stakes are getting higher all the time. 3/3

11023. **Harden, Eric,** *Motorcycle Cops,* Star, 1977. (Pulp) "Three motorcycle officers were deliberately struck by a speeding car; a fourth officer was killed, and attempts are made upon others' lives. Long Island policeman Abel Ames, Ph.D. in psychology, a loner who grew up in California (Gunn)." 3/3

1103. **Hardwick, Michael (1924-1991) & Mollie Hardwick,** *The Private Life of Sherlock Holmes,* Mayflower, 1970. (Sherlock Holmes) At last revealed–some adventures of Sherlock Holmes that even Dr. Watson did not dare to publish during his lifetime! 3/3

1104. **Hardy, Tom (Gordon Hoban 1941-1993),** *Cock Stealers,* Surree, 1978. (Pulp) Los Angeles gas meter reader and gentleman thief Humphrey Dalton. Humph is no hunk, but the handsome, younger Zoomer fell in love with him at first sight and induced him to leave his family. Now posing as a gas meter reader so as to thwart his bitter wife from getting too much of his money, Humph is actually using his superb analytical skills to rob large conglomerates. Hired to scam an insurance company by stealing a valuable African carving of an ebony penis, the pair find themselves instead being double-crossed and blackmailed. –*Cock Stealers* written by Gordon Hoban, an actor for whom the author Christopher Isherwood lusted, after he appeared in the dramatization of *A Meeting by the River* (MLM). 3/3

1105. **Harnisch, Marco,** *Dead Hustler's Don't Lie,* Self-published, 2018. (MM Amateur Sleuth/Police Procedural) The independent graphic designer Nicolas Zeal finds the body of a naked man in the forest. This gruesome find and the chief investigator, criminal inspector Andreas Bahr, completely turn his quiet and carefree life upside down. Nick also suddenly finds himself as the main suspect. How does he know the names of the victims? Maybe he's the killer himself? After all, he has other sites and events of crime precisely in mind! How can he convince Andreas Bahr of his innocence if he doesn't trust his own memories? –the author is German who translated the book into English himself and begs readers to take pity on him, "As I have written and now translated the story on my own, please do not expect a plain US-American or perfect British English pronunciation...and do not vote it with bad book reviews because of a not flawless English!" (MLM) 3/3

1106. **Harper, Kaje,** *Life Lessons,* MLR, 2011. Life Lessons #1 of 4. (MM Police Procedural) Jared MacLean is a homicide detective, a widowed father, and deeply in the closet. But from the moment he meets Tony's blue eyes in that high school hallway, Mac can't help wanting this man in his life. However, Mac isn't the only one with his eyes on Tony. As the murderer tries to cover his tracks, Mac has to work fast or lose Tony, permanently. 3/3

1107. **Harper, Kaje,** *Breaking Cover,* MLR, 2011. Life Lessons #2 of 4. (MM Police Procedural) For homicide detective Mac, it's been a good year. Having Tony to go home to makes him a better cop and a better person. For Tony, it's been hard being in love with a man he can't touch in public. Evasions and outright lying to friends and family take a little of the shine off his relationship with Mac, but Tony is determined to make it work. As the Minneapolis Police Department moves into a hot, humid summer, Mac is faced with a different challenge. A killer has murdered two blond women, and the police have no real clues. Mac hates to think that another murder may be the only way they'll make progress with the case. But when that murder happens, it hits close to home for Tony. And suddenly Mac faces an ultimatum: come out into the sunlight and stand beside Tony as his lover or walk away and live without a piece of his heart. 3/3

1108. **Harper, Kaje,** *Home Work,* MLR, 2012. Life Lessons #3 of 4. (MM Police Procedural) Mac and Tony thought the hard part was over. They're together openly as a couple, sharing a home and building a life with their two children. It's what they dreamed of. But daughter Anna struggles with the changes, Ben is haunted by old secrets, Mac's job in Homicide still demands too much of his time, and Tony is caught in the middle. It's going to take everything these men can give to create a viable balance between home and work. Especially when the outside world seems determined to throw obstacles in their way. 3/3

1109. **Harper, Kaje,** *Learning Curve,* MLR, 2013. Life Lessons #4 of 4. (MM Police Procedural) Three months after being shot, Detective Jared MacLean is healing, but he's afraid it may not be enough to go back on the job. He won't give up, though. Being a cop is written deep in Mac's bones, and he'll do whatever it takes to carry his badge again. 3/3

1110. **Harper, Lou,** *Dead in L. A.,* Createspace, 2012. LA Paranormal #1 of 3. (MM Paranormal) Jon's beliefs are challenged when Leander has to track down a missing teenager and he ropes Jon into assisting him. Soon the two of them are knee-deep in a decades-old murder case. The hills and valleys of the City of Angels hold many buried secrets, and Leander has a knack for finding them. 3/3

1111. **Harper, Lou,** *Dead in the Desert,* Createspace, 2013. LA Paranormal #2 of 3. (MM Paranormal) Unsolved crimes, missing people and bodies buried in the Mojave Desert make Jon's and Leander's lives anything but uncomplicated. Jon is forced to dig into his soul and find a way to let go of his past if he wants to keep Leander. 3/3

1112. **Harper, Lou,** *Dead and Lost,* Createspace, 2016. LA Paranormal #3 of 3. (MM Paranormal) Leander Thorne makes his living as a psychic pet detective and moonlights as an unofficial police consultant. In his latter role he has agreed to help Detective Cora Bennet from the LAPD with a decades-old murder. Unfortunately, the victim's bones refuse to talk to him. 3/3

1113. **Harper, Lou,** *Secrets and Ink,* Samhain, 2013. Secrets #1 of 4. (MM Thriller) If life was like the movies, Jem Mitchell's wouldn't be such a mess. In LA's glittering world of dreams, he works an unglamorous job at a gourmet grocery store. His past is so deep and dark, the details are lost even to him. All he knows is he was once cursed by a meter maid, and ever since, his love life has sucked. 3/3

1114. **Harper, Lou,** *Secrets and Charms,* Samhain, 2014. Secrets #2 of 4. (MM Thriller) After losing his disapproving father, his job, his girlfriend, and pretty much all his money, Rich packed up his secrets and moved to his actress sister s house to regroup and help her renovate. He doesn't like the curmudgeon he's become, but something about the perpetually cheerful Olly rubs him in a way that should be wrong yet feels pretty damned right. 3/3

1115. **Harper, Lou,** *Secrets and Bowties,* Samhain, 2015. Secrets #3 of 4. (MM Thriller) Dylan, however, isn't made of stone. Coincidence, an obscene candle, even Simon's dorky cardigan compel him to give the shy academic a very special birthday gift, which Dylan files away as a one-night stand. But when Dylan's quest lands him in hot water, he runs to Simon to hide. 3/3

1116. **Harper, Lou,** *Secrets and High Spirits,* Samhain, 2015. Secrets #4 of 4. (MM Paranormal) Between renovation pitfalls, meddling friends, and miles of police tape, Teag and Bruce struggle to keep their venture–and their budding relationship–from going up in flames. And not the good kind. More like the one on the top of a B52 shot. 3/3

1117. **Harper, Steven,** *Dreamer,* Roc, 2001. Silent Empire #1 of 4. (Science Fiction) It is through first contact with an alien species that humanity learns of the Dream. It is a plane of mental existence where people are able to communicate with one another by their thoughts alone – over distances of thousands of light-years. To ensure that future generations will have this ability, human genetic engineering produces newborns capable of finding and navigating the Dream. 3/3

1118. **Harper, Steven,** *Nightmare,* Roc, 2002. Silent Empire #2 of 4. (Science Fiction) Before Kendi learned to use his talent of navigating the plane of mental existence known as the Dream, he had to escape his physical existence as a slave. 3/3

1119. **Harper, Steven,** *Trickster,* Roc, 2003. Silent Empire #3 of 4. (Science Fiction) The telepathic communications net, known as "The Dream," has been shattered. And the majority of the Silent who used it are unable to reenter. But Kendi Weaver has more pressing concerns: finding the family that slavers tore from him more than a decade before... 3/3

1120. **Harper, Steven,** *Offspring,* Roc, 2004. Silent Empire #4 of 4. (Science Fiction) The Dream was a telepathic place of existence where a psychic race known as the Silent could twist the laws of reality. But a madman's lust for power has torn the Dream asunder. Now, only a handful of the Silent can enter it. Kendi Weaver is one of them. And it is up to him to protect it as political and personal enemies line up against him. 3/3

1121. **Harper, Sydney,** *Two, the Hard Way,* Blueboy, 1976. (Pulp) "A businessman and a teenager are killed while having sex. Former sexual partners, an associate, and his wife are suspects. Denver police detective Larry Baldwin, 32, a law student, accepts he's gay (Gunn)." 3/3

1122. **Harper, Sydney,** *Murder One,* Blueboy, 1977. (Pulp) A man had been murdered, then hours later mutilated. The only clues, a missing pornographic photo-album and an underaged boy. Starting at an exclusive men's club, Bert Sonderson, detective, begins learning the facts of the case - and about himself! (MLM). 3/3

1123. **Harrington, William,** *Trial,* David McKay, 1970. (Political Intrigue) Large cast of memorable characters and real, powerful issues, including destroyed careers, political upheaval, racial clashes, and a major scandal. –Cleveland police detective is bisexual (MLM). 3/3

1124. **Harris, Gregory,** *The Arnifour Affair,* Kensington, 2014. Colin Pendragon #1 of 6. (Historical) When a carriage bearing the Arnifour family crest–a vulture devouring a slaughtered lamb–arrives at the Kensington home of Colin Pendragon, it is an ominous beginning to a perplexing new case. Lady Arnifour's husband has been beaten to death and her niece, Elsbeth, left in a coma. Is the motive passion, revenge, or something even more sinister? Police suspicions have fallen on the groundskeeper and his son, yet the Earl's widow is convinced of their innocence. –based on Sherlock Holmes (MLM). 3/3

1125. **Harris, Gregory,** *The Bellingham Bloodbath,* Kensington, 2014. Colin Pendragon #2 of 6. (Historical) After a captain in Her Majesty's Guard and his young wife are brutally murdered in their flat, master sleuth Colin Pendragon and his partner Ethan Pruitt are summoned to Buckingham Palace. Major Hampstead demands discretion at all costs to preserve the repuration of the Guard and insists Pendragon participate in the cover-up by misleading the press. In response, Pendragon makes the bold claim that he will solve the case in no more than three days' time or he will oblige the major and compromise himself. 3/3

1126. **Harris, Gregory,** *The Connicle Curse,* Kensington, 2015. Colin Pendragon #3 of 6. (Historical) When wealthy Edmond Connicle suddenly disappears, his distraught wife enlists the services of master sleuth Colin Pendragon and his loyal partner, Ethan Pruitt. Already on the case, however, is Scotland Yard's Inspector Varcoe. He suspects the Connicles' West African scullery maid of doing in her employer, especially when a badly burned body is discovered on the estate grounds with a sack of Voodoo fetishes buried beneath it. 3/3

1127. **Harris, Gregory,** *The Dalwich Desecration,* Kensington, 2016. Colin Pendragon #4 of 6. (Historical) Master sleuth Colin Pendragon and his trusted partner, Ethan Pruitt, leave their familiar cosmopolitan London for rural Sussex County, where the bucolic peace has been shattered by the murder of a monk. 3/3

1128. **Harris, Gregory,** *The Endicott Evil,* Kensington, 2017. Colin Pendragon #5 of 6. (Historical) Adelaide Endicott–elderly sister of Lord Thomas Endicott, a senior member of Parliament–has plummeted to her death from the third-floor window of her bedroom at Layton Manor. Did she take her own life–or was she pushed? Although Scotland Yard believes it is a clear case of suicide, Adelaide's sister Eugenia is convinced otherwise. 3/3

1129. **Harris, Gregory**, *The Framingham Fiend*, Kensington, 2018. Colin Pendragon #6 of 6. (Historical) The murder scene is chillingly familiar. A young prostitute has been slaughtered in her flat on Framingham Street in the East End. It's not the first time Scotland Yard has seen a murder like this. But with the help of Colin Pendragon and his loyal partner Ethan Pruit, they hope it will be the last. 3/3

1130. **Harris, L. J.**, *Revival*, SA: SASSPA, 2006. (Police Procedural) Rain Godart, South Africa's first gay detective. Rain is not defined by his sexuality; he's a man and he's gay. That's all there is to it. All, that is, except that when he faces the fear of love he is simply human. 3/3

1131. **Harris, Robert**, *Fatherland*, Random House, 1992. (Speculative) It is twenty years after Nazi Germany's triumphant victory in World War II and the entire country is preparing for the grand celebration of the Führer's seventy-fifth birthday, as well as the imminent peacemaking visit from President Kennedy. –a gay army recruit in a country that where being gay is a capital offence (MLM). 1/3

1132. **Harris, Skot**, *Neon Darkness*, First, 2018. (Cold Case) In 1994, high school seniors Oliver and Grant defied the odds and fell in love. But after a shocking murder shattered their sleepy small town, Grant disappeared without a trace. Now, ten years later, Oliver attends their class reunion, desperate to see him again. But Oliver soon discovers the past brings more than happy memories... It brings secrets too. 3/3

1133. **Hartinger, Brent**, *Shadow Walkers*, Flux, 2011. (Paranormal) Zach lives with his grandparents on a remote island in Puget Sound in Washington State. With only his little brother, Gilbert, to keep him company, Zach feels cut off from the world. But when Gilbert is kidnapped, Zach tries the only thing he can think of to find him: astral projection. Soon, his spirit is soaring through the strange and boundless astral realm–a shadow place. While searching for his brother, Zach meets a boy named Emory, another astral traveler who's intriguing (and cute). 3/3

1134. **Hartinger, Brett**, *Three Truths and a Lie*, Simon Pulse, 2016. (Psychological) A weekend retreat in the woods and an innocent game of three truths and a lie go horribly wrong. 3/3

1135. **Hartman, Keith**, *The Gumshoe, The Witch, and the Virtual Corpse*, Meisha Merlin, 1999. Gumshoe #1 of 2. (Hard Boiled) Welcome to

21st century Atlanta. During your stay, depending on your tastes, you can cruise gay midtown or check out the Reverend-Senator Stonewall's headquarters at Freedom Plaza or attend a sky-clad Wiccan sabbat. Avoid the courthouse, where the Cherokee have turned out in full war-paint to renegotiate a nineteenth-century land deal. Also stay away from all cemeteries, at least until the police find out why someone is disinterring and crucifying corpses. 3/3

1136. **Hartman, Keith,** *Gumshoe Guerilla,* Meisha Merlin, 2001. Gumshoe #2 of 2. (Hard Boiled) 2024 was a rough year for Drew Parker. His car broke down, his rent went up, and his partner was kidnapped by a revenge-crazed performance artist with a grant from the NEA. Worse, one of his clients had been tossed off a sky scraper-after being stripped naked, smeared in human fat, and painted with occult symbols. 3/3

1137. **Harvey, John (b. 1938),** *Cutting Edge,* Henry Holt, 1991. Charles Resnick #3 of 12. (Police Procedural) There's a slasher loose in the corridors of a large urban hospital. His knowledge of anatomy is matched by his skill with a surgical blade, and his attacks are fast, furtive, and fatal. Among a welter of suspects, it's Resnick's job to keep him from killing again. –Carl Vincent a gay police detective appears in three of the Resnick procedurals (MLM). 2/3

1138. **Harvey, John,** *Easy Meat,* Heinemann, 1996. Charles Resnick #8 of 12. (Police Procedural) Fifteen-year-old Nicky Snape, a long-time petty juvenile offender, is picked up for killing Eric Netherfield, only to turn up dead himself two days later where he is being held. 2/3

1139. **Harvey, John,** *Still Waters,* Henry Holt, 1997. Charles Resnick #9 of 12. (Police Procedural) The battered body of a young woman is found floating in the still waters of a city canal. Police suspect a serial killer, which makes it a case for the newly formed Serious Crime Squad. Not Charlie Resnick's case, then; not his worry. But soon another body is found, and this time Charlie has a personal interest. 3/3

1140. **Hastings, Banner,** *Blackmailed!,* Blueboy, 1977. (Pulp) "Accidental sleuth Clint Maxson avenges his lover's death (Gunn)." 3/3

1141. **Hauser, G. A.,** *Naked Dragon,* Linden Bay Romance, 2007. (MM Police Procedural) Police Officer Dave Harris has just been assigned to one of the worst serial murder cases in Seattle history: The Dragon is hunting young Asian men. 3/3

1142. **Hauser, G. A.,** *Love You, Loveday,* Linden Bay Romance, 2008. (MM Amateur Sleuth/Police Procedural) Angel Loveday thought he had put his life as a gay soft-porn star of the 1980's behind him. For seventeen years he's hidden his sexuality and sordid past from his teenage son. But when someone threatens Angel's secret and Detective Billy Sharpe is assigned to his case, he finds himself having to once again face them both. 3/3

1143. **Havtikess, Hugh (Michael Yachnik b. 1957),** *Lavender Teasers: Fifteen Gay and Lesbian Mystery-Puzzles,* Xlibris, 2000. (Short Stories) Ready for a challenge? Finger the hit man in a gang that sings show tunes and wears rouge as its 'colors.' Solve the gruesome mystery of the disappearing hunks. Investigate the murder of beautiful Fiona, brutally attacked in her bed. Track survivors on a fantasy island whose choices result in sexual ecstasy or sudden death. These fifteen stories of police investigations, cunning intrigues and dark, exotic fantasies will keep you spellbound and guessing to the end. Come meet a cast of hilarious, sexy and appallingly wicked characters. Party with the rich, drop into a dungeon, or shop your way into the past ... but always, always keep your eyes open and your sleuthing skills sharp. It's a dangerous world out there! 3/3

1144. **Hawk, Jordan,** *Widdershins,* Createspace, 2013. Whyborne & Griffin #1 of 11. (MM Paranormal) When handsome ex-Pinkerton Griffin Flaherty approaches Whyborne to translate a mysterious book, Whyborne wants to finish the job and get rid of the detective as quickly as possible. Griffin left the Pinkertons following the death of his partner, hoping to start a new life. But the powerful cult which murdered Glenn has taken root in Widdershins, and only the spells in the book can stop them. Spells the intellectual Whyborne doesn't believe are real. – short story *Eidolon* released in 2014 falls between book one and two and is available as an e-book only (MLM). 3/3

1145. **Hawk, Jordan,** *Threshold,* Createspace, 2013. Whyborne & Griffin #2 of 11. (MM Paranormal) Introverted scholar Percival Endicott Whyborne wants nothing more than to live quietly with his lover, ex-Pinkerton detective Griffin Flaherty. Unfortunately, Whyborne's railroad tycoon father has other ideas, namely hiring Griffin to investigate mysterious events at a coal mine. 3/3

1146. **Hawk, Jordan,** *Stormhaven,* Createspace, 2013. Whyborne & Griffin #3 of 11. (MM Paranormal) Mysterious happenings are nothing new to reclusive scholar Percival Endicott Whyborne, but finding one of his colleagues screaming for help in the street is rather unusual. Allan Tambling claims he can't remember any of the last hour–but someone murdered his uncle, and Allan is covered in blood. –three short stories, *Carousel* (2015), *Another Place in Time* (2014), *and Remnant* (2014) fall between books three and four and are available as e-books only (MLM). 3/3

1147. **Hawk, Jordan,** *Necropolis,* Createspace, 2014. Whyborne & Griffin #4 of 11. (MM Paranormal) Introverted scholar Percival Endicott Whyborne has spent the last few months watching his lover, Griffin Flaherty, come to terms with the rejection of his adoptive family. So, when an urgent telegram from Christine summons them to Egypt, Whyborne is reluctant to risk the fragile peace they've established. Until, that is, a man who seems as much animal as human tries to murder Whyborne in the museum. 3/3

1148. **Hawk, Jordan,** *Bloodline,* Createspace, 2014. Whyborne & Griffin #5 of 11. (MM Paranormal) Between his bullying father and dissolute brother, Percival Endicott Whyborne has quite enough problematic family members to deal with. So when his sister returns to Widdershins asking for help solving the mystery of a derelict ship, Whyborne is reluctant to get involved. Until, that is, a brutal murderer strikes, leaving Whyborne and his lover Griffin no choice but to take the case. –short story *Harmony* (2014) available as an e-book (MLM). 3/3

1149. **Hawk, Jordan,** *Hoarfrost,* Createspace, 2015. Whyborne & Griffin #6 of 11. (MM Paranormal) Sorcerer Percival Endicott Whyborne and his husband Griffin Flaherty have enjoyed an unprecedented stretch of peace and quiet. Unfortunately, the calm is shattered by the arrival of a package from Griffin's brother Jack, who has uncovered a strange artifact while digging for gold in Alaska. The discovery of a previously unknown civilization could revive the career of their friend Dr. Christine Putnam–or it might kill them all, if the hints of dark sorcery surrounding the find are true. 3/3

1150. **Hawk, Jordan,** *Maelstrom,* Createspace, 2015. Whyborne & Griffin #7 of 11. (MM Paranormal) Between his father's sudden–and rather suspicious–generosity, and his own rash promise to help Christine plan her wedding, Percival Endicott Whyborne has quite enough to worry about. But when the donation of a mysterious codex to the Ladysmith Museum draws the attention of a murderous cult, Whyborne finds himself in a race against time to unlock its secrets first. 3/3

1151. **Hawk, Jordan,** *Fallow,* Createspace, 2016. Whyborne & Griffin #8 of 11. (MM Paranormal) When a man from Griffin's past murders a sorcerer, the situation grows even more dire. Once a simple farmer from Griffin's hometown of Fallow, the assassin now bears a terrifying magical corruption, one whose nature even Whyborne can't explain. –short story *Undertow* (2017) falls between books eight and nine (MLM). 3/3

1152. **Hawk, Jordan,** *Draakenwood,* Createspace, 2017. Whyborne & Griffin #9 of 11. (MM Paranormal) Widdershins has been unusually quiet for months. But now a mysterious creature from the Outside is on the loose, assassinating members of the town's old families by draining their blood. Whyborne and Griffin set out to solve the mystery–but as the evidence piles up, the police begin to suspect Whyborne himself is the murderer. 3/3

1153. **Hawk, Jordan,** *Balefire,* Createspace, 2018. Whyborne & Griffin #10 of 11. (MM Paranormal) Whyborne's Endicott relatives have returned to collect on the promise he made to help them take back their ancestral manor from an evil cult. In exchange, they'll give him the key to deciphering the Wisborg Codex, which Whyborne needs to learn how to stop the masters. –book eleven, *Deosil,* is expected later in 2019 (MLM). 3/3

1154. **Hayes, Julie Lynn,** *Bad Dogs and Drag Queens,* Dreamspinner, 2016. Rose and Thorne #1 of 3. (MM Police procedural) Vinnie Delarosa and Ethan Thorne are partners–on and off the clock. Federal undercover detectives, they're part of a covert task force designed to promote goodwill between the feds and local authorities. They lend an unobtrusive helping hand wherever it's needed. No credit required. Vinnie and Ethan work primarily in the Southeast region of the United States and live together in Richmond, Virginia. A mugger problem brings them to Roanoke, where Vinnie is thrown out as bait to catch the man who's been snatching purses in a city park, but they end up with more than they bargained for. –available as an e-book only (MLM). 3/3

1155. **Hayes, Julie Lynn,** *Civil War and Broken Hearts,* Dreamspinner, 2016. Rose and Thorne #2 of 3. (MM Police Procedural) Hollywood comes to Roanoke when a major film studio announces they're shooting part of their Civil War film at a local plantation. Vinnie is dismayed to discover the lead actress is none other than the beautiful Caroline St. Clair. Ethan and Vinnie met her in LA the previous Halloween, and Vinnie still hates her for hitting on his man. Ethan reassures his partner that Roanoke is big enough for all of them to coexist without running into one another. But Fate has it in for Vinnie and Ethan, and they're assigned to a new case involving the actress. –available as an e-book only (MLM). 3/3

1156. **Hayes, Julie Lynn,** *Family Ties and Family Lies,* Dreamspinner, 2016. Rose and Thorne #3 of 3. (MM Police Procedural) After almost five years together, Vinnie and Ethan have a policy of don't ask, don't tell. But unspoken questions between them are a ticking time bomb, waiting to explode. An innocent remark by a friend starts an insecure Vinnie wondering about things he never considered before... such as why he hasn't met Ethan's family. Is he the love of Ethan's life or just his dirty little secret? And what hasn't he told Ethan about his own past? An emergency phone call from Ethan's twin sister sends them rushing to Georgia. –available as an e-book only (MLM). 3/3

1157. **Hayes, Lee,** *Passion Marks,* AuthorHouse, 2002. Passion #1 of 2. (Psychological) From the outside, Kevin Davis' world leaves nothing to be desired. It is a life of luxury, comfort, and money, but never judge a book by its cover. His pretend world hides the verbal, physical, and sexual abuse he endures at the hands of his lover, James Lancaster, the ambitious CEO of a rising Houston software firm. 3/3

1158. **Hayes, Lee,** *A Deeper Blue,* Strebor, 2006. Passion #2 of 2. (Psychological) Kevin Davis finds his tumultuous relationship with his lover Daryl Harris in serious jeopardy. Pulled in different directions, Daryl must choose between the lover he's dreamed about and a new temptation; both of whom have female lovers–past and present–who are angry about being betrayed. 3/3

1159. **Hayes, Lee,** *The Messiah,* Strebor, 2007. (Journalism) Gabriel Kaine is working furiously to revive his stalled reporting career. Years ago, he got his first big break by investigating murders committed by a killer known as the Messiah. But when the Messiah vanished from the public six months ago, Gabriel's success hit a downward slope. 3/3

1160. **Hayes, Lee,** *The Bad Seed,* Strebor, 2011. (Short Stories) "Why they Call it the Blues" is about a cosmetically beautiful but emotionally damaged young man who marries a wealthy older man to go from rags to riches but as he begins an illicit affair he decides to plan his husband's untimely demise. "Crazy in Love" is about a hypersexual seventeen-year-old who develops a crush on his English teacher but when the teacher rebuffs his advances, Hell hath no fury like a teen wronged, rightly or not. 3/3

1161. **Haymon, S. T.,** *Death of a God,* St. Martin's, 1987. Benjamin Jurnet #4 of 8. (Police Procedural) It is with a minimum of enthusiasm that Inspector Ben Jurnet agrees to attend a concert of the rock group Second Coming with his fiancee, Miriam, who has miraculously obtained tickets. If nothing else, he will find out what all the fuss is about. But to the inspector's surprise, he is caught up in the music, and especially in the charisma of the lead singer, Loy Tanner, a hometown boy who's made good. Still entranced, he is shocked the next morning when the body of Tanner is found hanging from a cross in Angelby Market Place Garden. –Tanner's manager is gay (MLM). 1/3

1162. **Haynes, W. Randy,** *Cajun Snuff,* PublishAmerica, 2005. (Police Procedural) Loner. Free spirit. Rebel. Not words normally associated with an agent of the ultra-conservative FBI Counterterrorism

Division. When the mutilated body of a black U.S. Congressman and Christian minister was found in the steamy bayous of southwestern Louisiana, Special Agent Adam Stephen had the perfect qualities needed to be the lead investigator. Adam discovers that the Congressman may have appeared respectable but finds muddy surprises and vicious enemies instead. From a New Orleans Garden District widow to a bizarre Neo-Nazi group, the suspect list reads like a recipe for a spicy bowl of swamp snake gumbo, and Adam appears to be the next ingredient. 3/3

1163. **Hayward, L. J.,** *Where Death Meets the Devil,* Riptide, 2018. Death and the Devil #1 of 2. (MM Mystery) Jack Reardon, former SAS soldier and current Australian Meta-State asset, has seen some messy battles. But "messy" takes on a whole new meaning when he finds himself tied to a chair in a torture shack, his cover blown wide open, all thanks to notorious killer-for-hire Ethan Blade. –four novellas fall in between book one and book two; *Where Death Meets the Devil: Coda, Bargaining with the Devil, When the Devil Drives,* and *Devil in the Details* all available as e-books only (MLM). 3/3

1164. **Hayward, L. J.,** *Why the Devil Stalks Death,* Self-Published, 2018. Death and the Devil #2 of 2. (MM Mystery) Jack Reardon uncovers secrets for a living, and the Meta-State spy is pretty good at it. Or rather he thought so until he met Ethan Blade–assassin, warrior, enigma. The unlikely pair have decided to give living together a shot, but Jack's not entirely certain what he's gotten himself into–or exactly who he's in it with. –e-book only (MLM). 3/3

1165. **Haze, Raf,** *The Next,* Wilde City Press, 2014. (Amateur Sleuth) A romance springs to life as two strangers merge with a common goal: to catch a killer they suspect occupies one of the apartments across the courtyard. But their romance must hurdle the main protagonist's suffocating, unresolved demons as well as encroaching, life threatening danger. But if they make it through, they can both bring life back to their lives.

1166. **Heald, Tim,** *Blue Blood Will Out,* Stein and Day, 1974. (Amateur Sleuth) A country-house mystery with a zany cast of characters such as Lord Maidenhead and his nympho wife, gay eccentric Cosmo Green, and black eccentric Honeysuckle Johnson. 2/3

1167. **Heald, Tim,** *Deadline,* Stein and Day, 1975. Simon Bognor #3 of 11. (Amateur Sleuth) When St John Derby, the editor of the Samuel Pepys column of the Daily Globe, is found slumped over his desk, both very drunk and extremely dead, it's up to Simon Bognor, special investigator for the Board of Trade, to investigate. But will he be able to make a deadline for murder? –Derby is gay (MLM). 1/3

1168. **Heim, Scott,** *Mysterious Skin,* HarperCollins, 1995. (Psychological) At the age of eight Brian Lackey is found bleeding under the crawl space of his house, having endured something so traumatic that he cannot remember an entire five–hour period of time. 3/3

1169. **Henderson, Bob,** *Hard-core Murder,* Acolyte, 1985. (Hard Boiled) Spiros - 23 and looking younger, ex-hustler, gay and glad of it - and now starting his career as a private eye. Ursula - sexy transvestite from Sweden. Big Billy Paris - 500-pound Athenian producer of films legitimate and otherwise. Vangelis - Billy's kept boy, as quick on his bike as he is with a knife. A brutal murder is committed on the slopes of the Acropolis and Spiros is hired to find the killer. – listed as a first book in a brand-new series but this is the only book published (MLM). 3/3

1170. **Henry, Chester,** *The Margarita Solution,* Dagmar Miura, 2018. Truman and Celeste #1 of 1. (Hard Boiled) Truman stumbles into a detective gig while trying to imbibe a margarita, and soon finds himself hunting for a guy named Jaime in a rough neighborhood, getting embroiled with a series of increasingly troublesome low-lifes, none of whom ever seem to tell him the truth. 3/3

1171. **Henry, Jarad,** *Pink Tide,* Australian Scholarly Publishing, 2012. Rubens #3 of 3. (Police Procedural) DS Rubens McCauley is burnt out and on the edge. Addicted to prescription medication, running away from too many years on the front line, he finds himself wandering the shores of Jutt Rock–a small town on Victoria's south-western coastline–in search for the quiet life. Every day, as the sun sets over the ocean, the brilliant wash of color reflects on the shoreline–a Pink Tide. A picture-perfect respite; no crime, no stress. But after McCauley's nephew and his mate are brutally bashed while walking home from a party, McCauley realizes that the Pink Tide has another meaning. 3/3

1172. **Henry, Lisa, & J. A. Rock,** *The Two Gentlemen of Altona,* Riptide, 2014. Playing the Fool #1 of 3. (MM Police Procedural) Special Agent Ryan "Mac" McGuinness is having a rough week. Not only is he on a new diet, but he's also been tasked with keeping Henry Page – the world's most irritating witness – alive. Con man Henry Page prefers to keep his distance from the law ... though he wouldn't mind getting a little closer to uptight, handsome Agent McGuinness. 3/3

1173. **Henry, Lisa, & J. A. Rock,** *The Merchant of Death,* Riptide, 2015. Playing the Fool #2 of 3. (MM Police Procedural) There's something rotten in the state of Indiana. When con man Henry Page takes it upon himself to investigate the death of an elderly patient at a care facility, he does so in true Shakespearean tradition: dressed as a girl. 3/3

1174. **Henry, Lisa, & J. A. Rock,** *Tempest,* Riptide, 2015. Playing the Fool #3 of 3. (MM Police Procedural) FBI Agent Ryan "Mac" McGuinness and con man Henry Page are on the run again. This time they're headed back to where it all began: Altona, Indiana. Population: some goats. Henry's not happy about lying low at the McGuinness family farm, but they've got nowhere else to go. 3/3

1175. **Hentoff, Nat,** *Blues for Charlie Darwin,* Morrow, 1982. (Police Procedural) Noah Gree, a hard-edged, middle-aged, Jewish cop, and his laconic black partner, Sam McKibbon, are called to the scene of a grisly knife murder. Their investigation leads them to confront an assortment of pimps, professors, musicians, bartenders, and a very nasty dog named Merle Haggard. –police informer is a gay pimp (MLM). 1/3

1176. **Herren, Greg,** *Murder in the Rue Dauphin,* Alyson, 2002. Chanse MacLeod #1 of 7. (Hard Boiled) For gay New Orleans private eye Chanse MacLeod, it seemed like a simple case: find out who was blackmailing his pretty-boy client's rich, closeted boyfriend, collect a nice check, and take some time off. But then the pretty boy turns up dead in what looks like a hate crime and the gay community of New Orleans is up in arms, demanding justice. In the stifling heat of a New Orleans summer, Chanse searches for an extremely clever killer on a trail leading to a gay rights organization, boys for hire, and New Orleans society, knowing he has to find the killer before the entire city explodes. 3/3

1177. **Herren, Greg,** *Murder in the Rue St. Ann,* Alyson, 2004. Chanse MacLeod #2 of 7. (Hard Boiled) When sexy gay private eye Chanse MacLeod investigates the financial shenanigans of club promoter Mark Williams, he discovers that not only does Williams have ties to the New Orleans judiciary, he also has ties to Chanse's lover, Paul–a connection that reveals secrets about Paul's past that Chanse had never guessed and now wishes he didn't know. When Paul disappears, it seems his past has caught up with him in a terrifying way. 3/3

1178. **Herren, Greg,** *Murder in the Rue Chartres,* Alyson, 2007. Chanse MacLeod #3 of 7. (Hard Boiled) In the wake of Hurricane Katrina, Chanse MacLeod returns to a different, shattered New Orleans in an attempt to rebuild his own life and face his own future. When he discovers that his last client before the storm was murdered the very night she hired him to find her long-missing father, he is drawn into a web of intrigue and evil that surrounds the Verlaine family. –won the twentieth LAMBDA Award (MLM). 3/3

1179. **Herren, Greg,** *Murder in the Rue Ursulines,* Alyson, 2008. Chanse

MacLeod #4 of 7. (Hard Boiled) As New Orleans continues to rebuild in the wake of Hurricane Katrina, Chanse MacLeod becomes involved in a high-profile case involving a golden couple of Hollywood who have committed themselves to helping New Orleans recover. 3/3

1180. **Herren, Greg,** *Murder in the Garden District,* Alyson, 2009. Chanse MacLeod #5 of 7. (Hard Boiled) A leading candidate for the upcoming senatorial race and a scion of a Louisiana political dynasty is shot to death in his Garden District mansion, and the prime suspect is his much younger second wife with a checkered past. Detective Chanse MacLeod enters a world where nothing is as it seems and uncovers the dark secrets of the state's first family–secrets someone is willing to kill to keep. 3/3

1181. **Herren, Greg,** *Murder in the Irish Channel,* Bold Stroke Books, 2011. Chanse MacLeod #6 of 7. (Hard Boiled) It begins as a simple missing persons case-a young MMA fighter's mother has mysteriously disappeared. But as New Orleans private eye Chanse MacLeod starts digging around, he discovers that she is the leader of a group fighting the powerful Archdiocese of New Orleans over the closing of two churches. As the trail leads from corrupt church officials to powerful real estate developers to the world of cage fighting, Chanse soon realizes there are a lot of powerful people who want to make sure she stays gone-and don't have a problem with getting rid of a pesky gay private eye. 3/3

1182. **Herren, Greg,** *Murder in the Arts District,* Bold Stroke Books, 2014. Chanse MacLeod #7 of 7. (Hard Boiled) When neither the cops nor their insurance company believes a wealthy gay couple's valuable art collection was stolen, they hire Chanse MacLeod to track down the thieves and the missing art. –Herren has announced he's at work on an eighth MacLeod mystery (MLM). 3/3

1183. **Herren, Greg,** *Bourbon Street Blues,* Kensington, 2003. Scotty Bradley #1 of 7. (Amateur Sleuth/Paranormal) New Orleans native boy Scotty Bradley knows how to bend his hometown's every unwritten rule. it doesn't hurt that he's buff, boyish, and completely irresistible, with a job by day as a personal trainer...and the occasional night gig dancing on the bar for rent money. Scotty has visions as a former trick left a disc in his boot as he was dancing, and another man is shot in front of his apartment. 3/3

1184. **Herren, Greg,** *Jackson Square Jazz,* Kensington, 2006. Scotty Bradley #2 of 7. (Amateur Sleuth/Paranormal) Scott Bradley is nobody's idea of a saint, but when you live in New Orleans it's a bit hard to be monogamous. Unfortunately, Scott's straight-arrow, FBI agent, sort-of-boyfriend Frank has other ideas - which leads Scott to wake up in a hotel room with cutie Bryce Bell, the hottest young figure skater in the country. But when Scott finds a dead body in Bryce's hotel room, he is thrust into a world of lost ancient artefacts, thieves and prophecies. As Scott races to unravel the mystery, he soon feels himself chilled by a foreboding unlike anything he has felt before. 3/3

1185. **Herren, Greg,** *Mardi Gras Mambo,* Kensington, 2006. Scotty Bradley #3 of 7. (Hard Boiled/Paranormal) It's Carnival time in New Orleans, and Scotty Bradley, ex go-go boy turned private eye, is looking forward to relaxing with his boyfriends, Frank and Colin, and partying it up right. Scotty's dealer, Misha, delivers the goods. After a night of partying, they come home to find the cops waiting for them. Misha has apparently been murdered and guess who was the last person to see him alive? 3/3

1186. **Herren, Greg,** *Vieux Carre Voodoo,* Bold Stroke Books, 2010. Scotty Bradley #4 of 7. (Hard Boiled/Paranormal) When an old family friend apparently commits suicide from his French Quarter balcony, Scotty's life accelerates from boring to exciting again in a nanosecond. Why would anyone want the old man dead, and what were they looking for in his ransacked apartment? It's up to Scotty, Frank, his crazy family, and friends to get to the bottom of this bizarre mystery–and when an old, all-too-familiar face turns up, it's not just Scotty's life that's in danger, but his heart. 3/3

1187. **Herren, Greg,** *Who dat Whodunit,* Bold Stroke Books, 2011. Scotty Bradley #5 of 7. (Hard Boiled/Paranormal) The Saints' victory in the Super Bowl just prior to the start of Carnival season has everyone in New Orleans floating on Cloud Nine. But for Scotty Bradley, Carnival looks like it's going to be grim yet again when his estranged cousin Jared–who plays for the Saints–becomes the number one suspect in the murder of his girlfriend, dethroned former Miss Louisiana Tara Bourgeois. 3/3

1188. **Herren, Greg,** *Baton Rouge Bingo,* Bold Stroke Books, 2013. Scotty Bradley #6 of 7. (Hard Boiled/Paranormal) A simple trip up to Baton Rouge to bail his mother out of jail takes a dire turn when her best friend from college, animal rights activist Veronica Porterie, turns up murdered–and Mom hires the boys to find out who killed her! But nothing is as it seems in Veronica's life and past, and soon the boys are involved in a treasure hunt like no other–because Scotty's mom's life hangs in the balance! 3/3

1189. **Herren, Greg,** *Garden District Gothic,* Bold Stroke Books, 2016. Scotty Bradley #7 of 7. (Hard Boiled/Paranormal) The city of New Orleans was rocked to its very shaky foundations when the body of six-year-old beauty queen Delilah Metoyer was found, strangled, in the carriage house behind her family's Garden District mansion. The crime was never solved, and the Metoyer family shattered in the aftermath of the crime. Thirty years later, Delilah's brother asks Scotty to finally find his sister's killer…putting Scotty and his friends and family into the crosshairs of a vicious killer. –according to Greg Herren the eighth book in the Scotty Bradley series will be released in 2019 (MLM). 3/3

1190. **Hetherington, G. N.**, *Un Homme Qui Attend*, Createspace, 2015. Duchamp #1 of 6. (MM Police Procedural) Hugo Duchamp, a Frenchman living and working as a policeman in London is about to have his world turned upside down. Called upon to return to France he finds himself embroiled in the murder of a child and a town embroiled in corruption. 3/3

1191. **Hetherington, G. N.**, *Les Fantomes du Chateau*, GNH, 2016. Duchamp #2 of 6. (MM Police Procedural) Ducham is back in Montgenoux still reeling and haunted by guilt but he is called upon to investigate the brutal murder of a maid and finds himself in the middle of a family at war. 3/3

1192. **Hetherington, G. N.**, *Les Noms Sur les Tombes*, GNH, 2016. Duchamp #3 of 6. (MM Police Procedural) Montgenoux is in turmoil as Dr. Irene Chapeau finds her career at stake, the race for mayor heralds the return of shady characters, and Duchamp is embroiled in a series of shocking murders that seem to originate in Mintgenoux's ancient graveyard. 3/3

1193. **Hetherington, G. N.**, *L'ombre de L'ile*, GNH, 2017. Duchamp #4 of 6. (MM Police Procedural) Duchamp throws himself into a brand-new investigation, far away from his native France as he faces a race against time to free someone he loves from prison. 3/3

1194. **Hetherington, G. N.**, *L'assassiner de Sebastian Dubois*, GNH, 2017. Duchamp #5 of 6. (MM Police Procedural) Duchamp is faced with a riot at the new Montgenoux Prison as well as having to solve a vicious murder. 3/3

1195. **Hetherington, G. N.**, *L'imponderable*, GNH, 2018. Duchamp #6 of 6. (MM Police Procedural) Montgenoux is rocked by the discovery of a thirty year skeleton at the Beaupin vineyard as it triggers a series of events which pits Duchamp against an evil murderer. 3/3

1196. **Higgins, George**, *Kennedy for the Defense*, Knopf, 1980. Jerry Kennedy #1 of 4. (Court Drama) Keen to take some time off, Jerry Kennedy plans a short holiday en famille at Green Harbor, his eclectic clients don't get the memo however. His drive-by clientele, the car thieves, pimps, drug dealers and boatyard mechanics are diverse in all respects but one, persistence. Matters come to a head when a midnight intruder breaks into Kennedy's home, knife drawn and determination blaring in his eyes. In deciphering the imposter's intentions, Jerry's qualities of honesty, responsibility and downright hard work are seriously put to the test. –Kennedy and the author have very little sympathy for the gay character (MLM). 1/3

1197. **Highsmith, Patricia,** *Strangers on a Train,* Harper and Bros., 1949. (Crime Drama) Guy Haines and Charles Anthony Bruno, passengers on the same train. But while Guy is a successful architect in the midst of a divorce, Bruno turns out to be a sadistic psychopath who manipulates Guy into swapping murders with him. "Some people are better off dead," Bruno remarks, "like your wife and my father, for instance." As Bruno carries out his twisted plan, Guy is trapped in the perilous world, where, under the right circumstances, anybody is capable of murder. –the two men are attracted to one another but do not act on it, very understated (MLM). 1/3

1198. **Highsmith, Patricia,** *The Tremor of Forgery,* Doubleday, 1969. (Amateur Sleuth) Under the hot desert sun nothing is quite as it seems. Howard Ingham, an American writer, is sent to Tunisia to gather material for a movie, a love story too sordid to be set in America. But his director fails to arrive as scheduled and the erratic mails bring news of infidelities and suicide. –Ingham is friends with a gay Scandinavian and even contemplates picking up a male Arab prostitute (MLM). 2/3

1199. **Highsmith, Patricia,** *Found in the Street,* Atlantic, 1987. (Psychological) When Ralph Linderman returns a stranger's wallet he found during a morning stroll through Greenwich Village, he is entirely unprepared for the complex maze of sexual obsession and disturbing psychological intrigue he is about to be drawn into. –gay art gallery owner and his lover are side characters (MLM). 1/3

1200. **Highsmith, Patricia,** *The Talented Mr. Ripley,* Coward, 1955. Ripley #1 of 5. (Psychological) Suave, handsome Tom Ripley: a young striver, newly arrived in the heady world of Manhattan in the 1950s. A product of a broken home, branded a "sissy" by his dismissive Aunt Dottie, Ripley becomes enamored of the moneyed world of his new friend, Dickie Greenleaf. This fondness turns obsessive when Ripley is sent to Italy to bring back his libertine pal but grows enraged by Dickie's ambivalent feelings for Marge, a charming American dilettante. 2/3

1201. **Highsmith, Patricia,** *The Boy Who Followed Ripley,* Lippencourt, 1980. Ripley #4 of 5. (Psychological) Tom Ripley meets a young American runaway who has a dark secret that he is desperate to hide. Soon this unlikely pair is drawn into the seamy underworld of Berlin and a shocking kidnapping. In this masterful thriller,

Highsmith shatters our perceptions of her most famous creation by letting us glimpse a more compassionate side of this amoral charmer. 2/3

1202. **Hill, Owen,** *The Chandler Apartments,* Creative Arts, 2002. (Hard Boiled) Clay Blackburn has two jobs. Most of the time he's a book scout in Berkeley. Some of the time he's ... not quite a private detective. He doesn't have a license, he doesn't have a gun, he doesn't have a business card – but people come to him for help and in helping them he comes across more than his fair share of trouble. And all the time he's a poet. When fellow poet and old flame Peggy Denby asks him to help clear up some details about her husband's death, details that include lots of missing money and rare Etruscan artifacts, he's willing to oblige her. After she's murdered, he keeps looking – and comes across a good-looking banker, Peggy's hostile stepson, her strangely attractive stepdaughter, and more than a few Berkeley crazies. 3/3

1203. **Hill, Peter,** *The Savages,* Scribner, 1980. Staunton Wyndsor #4 of 4. (Police Procedural) When Colonel Bannister-Coates, an experienced Intelligence officer, fails to return to his Oxfordshire village home and his immaculate clothes are discovered dressing a scarecrow in a roadside field, there is a flurry of anxious activity in Whitehall. –gay man seeks revenge (MLM). 2/3

1204. **Hill, Reginald (1936-2012),** *Fell of Dark,* Collins Crime, 1971. A friendship renewed; a marriage going sour; Harry Bentick heads for the Lake District not knowing if he's going in search of something or running away. Then two girls are found murdered in the high fells, and suddenly there's no doubt about it. He's running. –Harry seeks help from his college friend Peter who is gay (MLM). 2/3

1205. **Hill, Reginald,** *Another Death in Venice,* Collins Crime, 1976. (Crime Drama) "Two gay men–the older Englishman Sydney Dunkerley and his young French friend Aristide–dramatically affect the lives of a young vacationing English couple, Sarah and Michael Masson (Slide)." 3/3

1206. **Hill, Reginald,** *Pinch of Snuff,* Harper and Row, 1978. Dalziel and Pascoe #5 of 24. (Police Procedural) Love, or at least pornography, are for sale at the arty Calliope Kinema Club on posh, proper Wilkinson Square. According to Yorkshire police superintendent Dalziel, it's all legal. Detective Peter Pascoe, however, doesn't believe it. His dentist, who knows real broken teeth and blood when he sees them, insists that the pretty actress wasn't playing a part when it happened. But the action that puts Pascoe into the picture is homicide. The sudden death of the Calliope's proprietor soon turns a sleazy sex flick into serious police business. And now Dalziel and

Pascoe are looking into the all-too-human desire for pain, pleasure...and murder. –Sergeant Wield is introduced in the fifth book of the series and does not appear in all and in some he appears only slightly (MLM). 2/3

1207. **Hill, Reginald,** *A Killing Kindness,* Pantheon, 1980. Dalziel and Pascoe #6 of 24. (Police Procedural) When Mary Dinwoodie is found choked in a ditch following a night out with her boyfriend, a mysterious caller phones the local paper with a quotation from Hamlet. The career of the Yorkshire Choker is underway. If Superintendent Dalziel is unimpressed by the literary phone calls, he is downright angry when Sergeant Wield calls in a clairvoyant. Linguists, psychiatrists, mediums – it's all a load of nonsense as far as he is concerned, designed to make a fool of him. And meanwhile the Choker strikes again – and again! 2/3

1208. **Hill, Reginald,** *Deadheads,* Macmillan, 1983. Dalziel and Pascoe #7 of 24. (Police Procedural) Patrick Aldermann, an accountant with a company that makes toilets, is passionate about his roses, which he prunes ruthlessly, 'deadheading' any blossoms a minute past their prime so as to make space for the younger blooms. Not much of a gardener, Dalziel views Patrick as a strong contender for the title of Most Boring Man in Yorkshire. Pascoe, though, has noticed that senior executives at the toilet company 'gentlemen, you might say, just a minute past their prime' have an unlucky habit of dying. And when they do, it's all but inevitably Patrick who, like a lucky young bloom, is poised to take their place. 2/3

1209. **Hill, Reginald,** *Exit Lines,* Collins Crime, 1984. Dalziel and Pascoe #8 of 24. (Police Procedural) Three old men die on a stormy November night: one by deliberate violence, one in a road accident and one by an unknown cause. 2/3

1210. **Hill, Reginald,** *Child's Play,* Macmillan, 1987. Dalziel and Pascoe #9 of 24. (Police Procedural) Geraldine Lomas's son went missing in Italy during World War Two, but the eccentric old lady never accepted his death. 2/3

1211. **Hill, Reginald,** *Under World,* Collins Crime, 1988. Dalziel and Pascoe #10 of 24. (Police Procedural) When young Tracey Pedley vanished in the woods around Burrthorpe, the close-knit community had their own ideas about what had happened, but Deputy Chief Constable Watmough has it down as the work of a child-killer who has since committed suicide - though others wondered about the last man to see her alive and his fatal plunge into the disused mine shaft. 2/3

1212. **Hill, Reginald,** *Bones and Silence,* Delacorte, 1990. Dalziel and Pascoe #11 of 24. (Police Procedural) One woman dead and one threatening to die set Yorkshire's police superintendent Dalziel and Inspector Pascoe on a chilling hunt for a killer and a potential suicide. A drunken Dalziel witnesses the murder that others insist is a tragic accident. Meanwhile the letters of an anonymous woman say she plans to kill herself in a spectacular way...unless Pascoe can find her first. Dalziel has been picked to play God in a local Mystery Play, but can he live up to his role by solving this puzzling psychological thriller...or unveiling the passions and perversions that lie hidden in the human heart? 2/3

1213. **Hill, Reginald,** *Recalled to Life,* Collins Crime, 1992. Dalziel and Pascoe #13 of 24. (Police Procedural) It was a crime of passion in one of England's great houses, an open-and-shut case. But thirty years later, when the convicted nanny is freed, then spirited off to America before she can talk, Yorkshire's Superintendent Dalziel returns to the scene of the crime with Inspector Pascoe, determined to dig up the corpus delecti he investigated a generation before. Did the wrong aristocrat hang? Dalziel and Pascoe find decades-old clues that implicate a member of the royal family. When one of their prime leads is found dead, Dalziel is put "on leave"–and heads for New York to learn what the Nanny knows. Back home, Pascoe walks a thin line, quietly pursuing a case someone is trying to bury. Stiff upper lips do telltale, but Dalziel and Pascoe discover on both sides of the Atlantic that it's hell on those trying to unearth the truth. 2/3

1214. **Hill, Reginald,** *Pictures of Perfection,* Collins Crime, 1993. Dalziel and Pascoe #14 of 24. (Police Procedural) The incomparable Dalziel and Pascoe, find themselves in the pretty village of Enscombe, which is steadfastly trying – though somewhat in vain – to repel the advances of both tourists and developers. When a policeman is discovered missing, Pascoe is immediately worried, but Dalziel thinks he's overreacting... until the normally phlegmatic Sergeant Wield also shows signs of changing his first impressions of picture-perfect village life. 2/3

1215. **Hill, Reginald,** *The Wood Beyond,* Collins Crime, 1996. Dalziel and Pascoe #15 of 24. (Police Procedural) Pascoe digging up some old bones and family secrets from his own past. 2/3

1216. **Hill, Reginald,** *On Beulah Height,* Collins Crime, 1998. Dalziel and Pascoe #17 of 24. (Police Procedural) Three little girls, one by one, had vanished from the farming village of Dendale. And Superintendent Andy Dalziel, a young detective in those days, never found their bodies–or the person who snatched them. Then the valley where Dendale stood was flooded to create a reservoir, and the town itself ceased to be ... except in Dalziel's memory. 2/3

1217. **Hill, Reginald,** *Arms and the Women,* Collins Crime, 1999. Dalziel and Pascoe #18 of 24. (Police Procedural) Deeply shaken by her 9-year-old daughter's close encounter with death, Peter's wife Ellie has taken to writing a novel for comfort. It's about the Greeks and the Trojans, but the odd thing is that her Odysseus looks and sounds a lot like Andy Dalziel. Still, her happy days spent writing are soon cut short when she narrowly avoids being kidnapped by a slick couple who show up in a white Mercedes. Then her neighbor, Daphne Aldermann, has her stiff upper lip split when she goes after an intruder outside the Pascoe house and is badly beaten. 2/3

1218. **Hill, Reginald,** *Dialogues of the Dead,* Collins Crime, 2001. Dalziel and Pascoe #19 of 24. (Police Procedural) Yorkshire investigators Dalziel and Pascoe find themselves embroiled in a deadly duel of wits against a killer known only as the Wordman - a brilliant sociopath who leaves literary clues and dead bodies in his wake. 2/3

1219. **Hill, Reginald,** *Death's Jest-Book,* Collins Crime, 2002. Dalziel and Pascoe #20 of 24. (Police Procedural) Ex-convict and aspiring academic, Franny Roote, has started writing enigmatic letters to DCI Peter Pascoe who immediately smells a rat. DS Edgar Wield, intervening in a suspected kidnapping, takes a vulnerable rent boy under his wing, one who is hiding an earth-shattering secret. And young DC Bowler is looking forward to a weekend away with his girlfriend – but her dreams are filled with a horror too terrifying to share. 2/3

1220. **Hill, Reginald,** *Good Morning, Midnight,* Collins Crime, 2004. Dalziel and Pascoe #21 of 24. (Police Procedural) Like father like son... But heredity seems to have gone a gene too far when Pal Maciver's suicide in a locked room exactly mirrors that of his father ten years earlier. 2/3

1221. **Hill, Reginald,** *Death Comes for the Fat Man,* HarperCollins, 2007. Dalziel and Pascoe #22 of 24. (Police Procedural) There was no sign of life. But not for a second did Pascoe admit the possibility of death. Dalziel was indestructible. Dalziel is, and was, and forever shall be, world without end, amen. Everybody knew that. Therein lay half his power. Chief constables might come, and chief constables might go, but Fat Andy went on forever. 2/3

1222. **Hill, Reginald,** *A Cure for All Diseases,* HarperCollins, 2008. Dalziel and Pascoe #23 of 24. (Police Procedural) He may have been in a coma, but it would take an act of God to put Superintendent 'Fat' Andy Dalziel down for good. In the meantime, he'll settle for a few weeks' bed-rest. Sandytown, a pleasant seaside resort devoted to healing, seems just the ticket. And when a fellow newcomer appears in the shapely form of psychologist Charlotte Heywood, Dalziel develops an unexpected passion for alternative therapy. But Sandytown's warring landowners have grandiose plans for the resort. One of them has to go and when one of them does, in spectacularly gruesome fashion, DCI Peter Pascoe is called in to investigate - with Dalziel and Charlotte providing unwelcome support. And Pascoe soon finds dark forces at work in a place where holistic remedies are no match for the oldest cure of all! –renamed *The Price of Butcher's Meat* in the United States (MLM). 1/3

1223. **Hill, Reginald,** *Midnight Fugue,* HarperCollins, 2009. Dalziel and Pascoe #24 of 24. (Police Procedural) It starts with a phone call to Superintendent Dalziel from an old friend asking for help. But where it ends is a very different story. 2/3

1224. **Himes, Chester,** *All Shot Up,* Avon, 1960. Harlem Cycle #5 of 9. (Police Procedural) From murderers to prostitutes, corrupt politicians and racist white detectives, Coffin Ed Johnson and Gravedigger Jones, Harlem's toughest detective duo, must carry the day against an absurdist world of racism and class warfare. –cops raid a black gay bar located near a murder scene (MLM). 1/3

1225. **Hoag, Tami,** *Dust to Dust,* Bantam, 2000. Kovac and Liska #2 of 5. (Police Procedural) The death of internal affairs investigator Andy Paxton is a potential political bomb for the Minneapolis Police Department... Andy Paxton was gay, and he was investigating a possible cop connection in the brutal murder of another gay officer. But Andy's death looks like suicide, or an unfortunate and embarrassing accident, and the pressure is on from the top brass to close the case as soon as possible. But the investigation's lead detective Sam Kovac is not convinced the case is as straightforward as it appears. As he digs deeper, it is looking very much like Paxton discovered something that got him killed. And he might not be the final victim. 1/3

1226. **Hobson, Hank,** *Death Makes a Claim,* Cassell, 1958. (Crime Drama) "It is all blondes, coshing, murders in TV studios, impossible homosexuals, and magnates (Slide)." 1/3

1227. **Hoffman, Cara,** *Running,* Simon and Schuster, 2017. (Thriller) Bridey Sullivan, a young American woman who has fled a peculiar and traumatic upbringing in Washington State, takes up with a queer British couple, the poet Milo Rollack and Eton drop-out Jasper Lethe. Slipping in and out of homelessness, addiction, and under-the-table jobs, they create their own kind of family as they struggle to survive. Jasper's madness and consequent death frame a narrative of emotional intensity. In its midst this trio become linked to an act of terrorism. The group then splinters, taking us from Athens to the cliffs of the Mediterranean, and to modern-day New York. 3/3

1228. **Hoffman, Mark**, *Orgy Slaves*, Greenleaf, 1980. (Pulp) "Virginia-coast policeman Jerome (Jerry) Crawford, 30, a Vietnam veteran, works to protect vulnerable (Gunn)." 3/3

1229. **Holden, J. T.**, *Apple-Polisher*, Kuro, 2016. (Amateur Sleuth) Jack McGregor, an idealistic young high school teacher, who stumbles upon a mystery when he agrees to take on the task of sorting through the personal effects of his recently deceased mentor, the enigmatic and formidable art teacher Gordon Powell. In Gordon's gloomy one-bedroom apartment, Jack discovers the painting of a naked teenage boy–an artistic rendering that hauntingly resembles a former student: senior class golden boy, and apple-polisher extraordinaire, Mickey Greenleaf, who disappeared shortly after graduation five years ago and hasn't been heard from since. 3/3

1230. **Holden, William**, *Secret Societies*, Bold Stroke Books, 2012. Newton #1 of 3. (MM Historical) In 1724, Thomas Newton is cast out of his home by his aristocratic father. Desperate to make a new life for himself, he heads to London. Through a string of intimate encounters, he enters the underground world of male-male desire. The Society for the Reformation of Manners, a group of Christian zealots, begins raiding the Molly houses. They plan to force the arrest, conviction, and execution of any man guilty of "crimes against nature." 3/3

1231. **Holden, William**, *The Thief Taker*, Bold Stroke Books, 2014. Newton #2 of 3. (MM Historical) Fleeing London, Thomas Newton reaches Paris full of hopes for a new life with Pierre Baptiste. The hopes are quickly shattered. There are unsettling rumors about Pierre's past and very real threats in the present. Arrested on false charges, thrown into a dank prison, Thomas must decide whether he can trust Pierre's help to winning back his freedom. But freedom will bring other risks, especially if it requires a return to London and all that he fled. The men from his past whom he betrayed–and who might well want revenge. 3/3

1232. **Holden, William**, *Den of Thieves*, Createspace, 2018. Newton #3 of 3. (MM Historical) It seems like the right time for Thomas Newton to close the door on his past. The hypocritical crusaders of the Society for the Reformation of Manners have stopped their raids and scattered. The arrogant aristocrat who tried to kill Christopher and Pierre, Thomas's lovers, has been executed for treason. The old threats have vanished. But in 18th Century London, nothing is ever quite what it seems. When a series of murders begin plaguing the city, Thomas and Pierre are called to solve them. The crimes may conceal a plot against the king. 3/3

1233. **Holland, Marc,** *Mark Stone: Secret Agent,* Starbooks, 2006. (Espionage) In the shadowy world of international espionage, there exists one man who stands between western civilization and the dark forces that threaten to destroy it. A man with drop-dead looks and come-to-bed eyes, whose weapon is always loaded and who knows exactly where and when to use it. A man whose existence is denied by British Intelligence, but who is always called upon first wherever trouble looms. A man who secretly protects his Queen and country from disaster, and whose services are immediately enlisted when the famous German chemist, Heinz Kriechbaum, is kidnapped by the revolutionary "Crimson Army," threatening the entire world with chemical annihilation. 3/3

1234. **Holliday, Don,** *The Man from C. A. M. P.,* Greenleaf, 1966. Man From C. A. M. P. #1 of 10. (Pulp) Resourceful as James Bond, flamboyant as Austin Powers, and gay as a Christmas goose, there's never been a secret agent quite like Jackie Holmes, the Man from C.A.M.P. Armed with a cache of secret weapons, a body that just won't quit, and a white poodle called Sophie who's trained to kill with her razor-sharp teeth, the blonde bombshell with a license to thrill known as Jackie Holmes will blow you away! 3/3

1235. **Holliday, Don,** *Color him Gay Color Him Gay: The Further Adventures of the Man from C.A.M.P.,* Greenleaf, 1966. Man from C. A. M. P. #2 of 10. (Pulp) Steve thought to cut in on the source of blackmail money that Dingo Stark was paying the boys who wanted to COLOR HIM GAY but his hatred took him too far. As his screams drift through the still air, it's up to the debonair secret agent, Jackie Holmes, that Man from C.A.M.P., to arrive in time to save the day! 3/3

1236. **Holliday, Don,** *The Watercress File: Being the Further Adventures of That Man from C.A.M.P.,* Greenleaf, 1966. Man from C. A. M. P. #3 of 10. (Pulp) The crusader for gay justice is thrown into the most fracturingly funny escapade of his career, being joined by an unbelievably incompetent household of characters, who go by the code name of WATERCRESS, and who insist on helping him with his (barely) dangerous mission. And in process we encounter the antics of such individuals as the straight-laced CIA agent, Craig Mathews, Aunt Lily, Aunt Nasturtia, Aunt Marigold, Honeysuckle the pianist, the gigantic Gladiola, and the very strange Nick. Of course, Jackie always winds up on top in the end. 3/3

1237. **Holliday, Don,** *The Son Goes Down,* Greenleaf, 1966. Man from C. A. M. P. #4 of 10. (Pulp) Working with Irish agent Jerry Shannon to stop a ring kidnapping blond teenage American boys who are fans of the dead actor Dean James, Jackie heads to Tijuana and Lisbon, accompanied by the adopted son of an old friend, a male-to-female transsexual. 3/3

1238. **Holliday, Don,** *Gothic Gaye,* Greenleaf, 1966. Man from C. A. M. P. #5 of 10. (Pulp) After Jackie falls in love with Baron Max von der Gout and leaves C.A.M.P. in order to live with him in the supposedly haunted Castle Gaye, B.U.T.C.H. makes various attempts on his life; at Rich's instigation Summers, Stark, Matthews, and Shannon show up to help. 3/3

1239. **Holliday, Don,** *Rally Round the Fag,* Greenleaf, 1967. Man from C. A. M. P. #6 of 10. Jackie is called upon to impersonate a female double-agent who has become part of a plot to begin World War III; the case leads him to Stockholm, where he dallies with Swedish agent Sven and Russian agent Boris, and for a brief moment to Spain, where he has to put his bullfighting skills to test. 3/3

1240. **Holliday, Don,** *The Gay Dogs: The Further Adventures of That Man from C.A.M.P.,* Greenleaf, 1967. Man from C. A. M. P. #7 of 10. (Pulp) Jackie Holmes, the Man from C.A.M.P., is at it again, this time surrounding himself with the most outrageous crime-fighting team ever assembled: Queens, hustlers, and strippers help out, with many coffee breaks scattered along the way to pursue their favorite sports. Will the purloined pooches bite the dust? It's C.A.M.P. versus B.U.T.C.H., as Jackie Holmes and his furry friends race to a bone-gnawing climax! 3/3

1241. **Holliday, Don,** *Holiday Gay,* Greenleaf, 1967. Man from C. A. M. P. #8 of 10. (Pulp) Would you believe a lavender Santa swishing down the chimney? Well how about Jackie Holmes in little girl drag, chasing the jewels to the tune of the Pearly Freecock as played by Birdie Wing and the Swallow Children? Cruise in for a while... 'tis the season to be gay and jolly... 3/3

1242. **Holliday, Don,** *Blow the Man Down,* Greenleaf, 1968. Man from C. A. M. P. #9 of 10. (Pulp) When Atlantic ships start disappearing just before a Summit Cruise, Lou Upton calls on Jackie and U.S. Agent Andy Parks for help; they are sucked into the domed city of Atlantis, ruled by the emperor Machas Fruche, a.k.a. Mother Schmucker, where Jackie's musical skills save the day. 3/3

1243. **Holliday, Don,** *Gay-Safe,* Greenleaf, 1971. Man from C. A. M. P. #10 of 10. (Pulp) Jackie suspects B.U.T.C.H. is behind the death of Dr. Perry Robert, a founder of the Church of the Homosexual Community; LAPD Detective Tom Lattimer and Agent Andy Parks show up to help. 3/3

1244. **Holly, David,** *The Moon's Deep Circles,* Bold Stroke Books, 2013. (MM YA) Tip Trencher is an eighteen-year-old high school senior and captain of his swim team. He lives on an Oregon farm with his evangelical parents and a deep mystery. His long-departed brother's room is always kept locked until the day Tip's mother forgets her key and Tip discovers that his brother Thad left a series of journals about his initiation into gay pagan rituals. 3/3

1245. **Holmen, Martin,** *Clinch,* Albert Bonniers Förlag, 2015. Harry Kvist #1 of 3. (Swedish Crime Drama) The writing's on the wall for Harry Kvist. Once a notorious boxer, he now spends his days drinking, and his nights chasing debts amongst the pimps, prostitutes and petty thieves of 1930s Stockholm. When women can't satisfy him, men can. But one biting winter's night he pays a threatening visit to a debtor named Zetterberg, and when the man is found dead shortly afterwards, all eyes are on Kvist. 3/3

1246. **Holmen, Martin,** *Down for the Count,* Albert Bonniers Forlag, 2016. Harry Kvist #2 of 3. (Swedish Crime Drama) Harry Kvist walks out of the gates of Langholmen jail into the biting Stockholm winter of 1935. He has nothing to his name but a fiercely burning hope: that he can leave behind his old existence of gutter brawls, bruised fists and broken bones. 3/3

1247. **Holmen, Martin,** *Slugger,* Albert Bonniers Forlag, 2017. Harry Kvist #3 of 3. (Swedish Crime Drama) It's summer in Stockholm, and the city is sweltering in the grip of a rare heatwave while fascists and communists beat each other bloody in the streets. Harry Kvist has had enough. It's time for him to leave. But first he has some business to take care of. His old friend and ex-lover, Reverend Gabrielsson, has been murdered, and the police are more interested in anti-Semitic rumors than finding the truth. But the city has other ideas. Nazis are spreading their poison on the freezing streets, and one of Kvist's oldest friends has been murdered. 3/3

1248. **Holmes, A. V.,** *Death in Twos,* PublishAmerica, 2011. Brantley #1 of 2. (Police Procedural) "Pennsylvania police detective Brantley Noir, the narrator, a divorced father with a son and a longtime partner, fights homophobia (Gunn)." 3/3

1249. **Holmes, A. V.,** *Death Vote,* America Star, 2012. Brantley #2 of 2. (Police Procedural) When the chairman of the Whetherington Park Planning Commission is found dead in his home, Detective Brantley finds himself in the midst of an investigation that seems unsolvable. 3/3

1250. **Holt, Hazel,** *The Cruelest Month,* St. Martin's, 1991. Mrs. Mallory #2 of 21. (Cozy) Sheila Malloy finds herself once again in idyllic Oxford doing research at the Bodleian Library–and once again thrust into an investigation, when an unfortunate accident kills a particularly loathsome woman who was probably also a blackmailer. – "hint of negativism towards its homosexual characters (Slide)." 2/3

1251. **Hooper, Susan,** *Belle Harbor Skeletons,* 1st Books, 2004. Moss and Kotkin #1 of 7. (MM Amateur Sleuth) Barnaby Moss and Arnie Kotkin, have been friends since their boyhood days of schoolyard squabbles and Catholic choirboy impersonations. Their families are as different as their financial backgrounds. As domestic partners, Barnaby and Arnie find themselves trying to lead ordinary lives... but family members are becoming strangers, and their quiet existence is turned upside down when they discover long-hidden secrets and very present dangers. With no previous experience in the field of crime solving, they wonder if they can find the truth in time... 3/3

1252. **Hooper, Susan,** *Murder Junction,* AuthorHouse, 2004. Moss and Kotkin #2 of 7. (MM Amateur Sleuth) Domestic partners for over a year now, they have struggled to get through events that would have torn many couples apart–everything from attempted murder to the real thing. Taking what should have been an enjoyable trip to Vermont in October, they find that red is not only the color of the leaves on the trees.it is also the color of blood on the ground. 3/3

1253. **Hooper, Susan,** *Another Day, Another Murder,* AuthorHouse, 2004. Moss and Kotkin #3 of 7. (MM Amateur Sleuth)) With another summer behind them, they have been called down to Connecticut by Arnie's natural parents after the brutal slaying of their elderly neighbor, and the reluctant sleuths have one deadlier puzzle to piece together. 3/3

1254. **Hooper, Susan,** *Silent Alarm,* AuthorHouse, 2005. Moss and Kotkin #4 of 7. (MM Amateur Sleuth) When their brand-new security system fails the test, Helene and Jack Fentnor are awakened by their daughter's screams, instead of the alarm systems' bells and whistles. Calling on their grown son, Arnie Kotkin, and his partner, Barnaby Moss, for assistance the next day, the Fentnors once again entangle the two young men in solving a crime that turns out to be anything but ordinary. 3/3

1255. **Hooper, Susan,** *Puzzles,* AuthorHouse, 2005. Moss and Kotkin #5 of 7. (MM Amateur Sleuth) Barnaby Moss and Arnie Kotkin, lifelong best friends and now a civilly united couple, cannot stay away from murder. or at least mayhem. When a hauntingly realistic dream forces Arnie to recall a long-ago trip to the shore, he looks to his natural mother, Helene Fentnor, to help him fill in the missing details. What Helene remembers is puzzling–perhaps more puzzling than the dream. Recalling the death of Gladys Frickette some 20 years earlier, Helene begins to wonder why everyone, even the police, accepted the theory that a woman who was hated by all, was killed by none. Maybe she really did cheat everyone one last time, but maybe not. With Barnaby and Arnie unexpectedly called into service as baby-sitters for Arnie's young nephew, Helene is left to puzzle this mystery out for herself. 3/3

1256. **Hooper, Susan,** *Murder, and other Bad Habits,* AuthorHouse, 2006. Moss and Kotkin #6 of 7. (MM Amateur Sleuth) Arnie Kotkin has finally gotten his doctorate in science, but his dream of teaching at the college level eludes him when a private prep school in Vermont makes a far better offer. To add to the changes in his life, his parents have announced that they can no longer care for Todd–the child of his late brother–so he and his partner, Barnaby Moss, are tapped for the honor of raising the boy. Northward bound again, the pair stop to look at a house; it will be a wonderful place to raise a child, but it might also be a great place to share with someone else, someone who should have left 145 years ago. 3/3

1257. **Hooper, Susan,** *Time and Again,* AuthorHouse, 2007. Moss and Kotkin #7 of 7. (MM Amateur Sleuth) It was never any secret that Stars of Tomorrow, a TV talent show, was linked to Legend Studios; contest winners could not be awarded singles' deals there otherwise. When Bob Knox, a producer of some repute, left Legend over a year ago, he was not the first man out the door. Barnaby Moss, the talented engineer he was often teamed with on the Stars' projects, may have been the last man in, but he was the first man out. 3/3

1258. **Horne, David**, *A Love Worth Saving,* Kindle, 2018. (MM Amateur Sleuth) Perry Conway was a man of principle with strong business ethics. He and his former lover, Rick McFadden, had a successful business selling used cars. Together in business, they knew their friendship was stronger than their love ever could be. They had the right staff and a great business model. The company was expanding, their profits were up, and Perry had plans to expand into a high-profile automotive empire that rivaled other dealerships. But all that changed the day they found a body in the trunk of one of the used cars. 3/3

1259. **Hornsby, Wendy,** *Half a Mind,* Dodd, Mead, 1987. Kate Teague #2 of 2. (Amateur Sleuth) A severed head washes ashore, drawing Kate into a bizarre murder case. A head has washed ashore, with semen in its mouth and an armed-forces haircut. It was found just down the shore from Kate's mansion, meaning that she and Tejeda are involved–whether his doctors like it or not. –concerns a gay serial killer and copycats (MLM). 2/3

1260. **Horowitz, Anthony,** *Magpie Murders,* Orion, 2016. (Bibliomystery) When editor Susan Ryeland is given the manuscript of Alan Conway's latest novel, she has no reason to think it will be much different from any of his others. After working with the bestselling crime writer for years, she's intimately familiar with his detective, Atticus Pünd, who solves mysteries disturbing sleepy English villages. An homage to queens of classic British crime such as Agatha Christie and Dorothy Sayers, Alan's traditional formula has proved hugely successful. So successful that Susan must continue to put up with his troubling behavior if she wants to keep her job. –author killed was gay (MM). 2/3

1261. **Hudson, John Paul (1929-2002) & Warren Wexler,** *Superstar? Murder? A Prose Flick: What Happened to Good Queen Bess Her Last Night at the Cosmopolitan Baths?,* Insider, 1976. (Amateur Sleuth) "Spot, while stoned, glimpses the body of entertainer Bess Mittman (based on Bette Midler) in the star's dressing room. It disappears. Spot sets out to discover what has happened (Gunn)." –provides a rich spectrum of gay life in New York in the 1970s (Gunn). 3/3

1262. **Huff, A. M. (James M McCracken),** *Stumptown,* Jamarque, 2017. Andrews #2 of 2. (Amateur Sleuth) Harrison Andrew's fun-loving, carefree boarder, Justus Reynolds is about to get a reality check. One of his friends has gone missing from a gay nightclub in downtown Portland. The police hit a dead end when their investigation fails to uncover any leads. After learning that three other men have disappeared, Justus becomes more determined to find his friends even if he has to become the bait. –the first book in this series, *Ellensburg,* was originally published under his real name (MLM). 3/3

1263. **Huff, Tanya,** *Gate of Darkness, Circle of Light,* Daw, 1989. (Paranormal) Toronto had no idea what was in store for it–an Adept of Darkness had broken the barriers and arrived in this 20th-century city. And in an age when only fools and innocents still believed in magic, who was there to fight against this invasion by evil? 3/3

1264. **Huff, Tanya,** *The Fire's Stone,* Daw, 1990. (Fantasy) AARON. Clan Heir, he has fled his people when his beloved was slain by his own father's command, abandoning his training, duty and beliefs to become a thief. A master of his trade, he now dared the odds in Ischia, city of the volcano, where the price of being caught was death. 3/3

1265. **Huff, Tanya,** *Blood Price,* Daw, 1991. Nelson and Fitzroy #1 of 5. (Paranormal Police Procedural) Vicki Nelson, formerly of Toronto's homicide unit and now a private detective, witnesses the first of many vicious attacks that are now plaguing the city of Toronto. As death follows unspeakable death, Vicki is forced to renew her tempestuous relationship with her former partner, Mike Celluci, to stop these forces of dark magic–along with another, unexpected ally... 3/3

1266. **Huff, Tanya,** *Blood Trail,* Daw, 1992. Nelson and Fitzroy #2 of 5. (Paranormal Police Procedural) For centuries, the werewolves of Toronto have managed to live in peace and tranquility, hidden quietly away on their London, Ontario farm. But now, someone has learned their secret–and is systematically massacring this ancient race. 3/3

1267. **Huff, Tanya,** *Blood Lines,* Daw, 1993. Nelson and Fitzroy #3 of 5. (Paranormal Police Procedural) Sealed away through unending centuries in a sarcophagus never meant to be opened, he had patiently waited for the opportunity to live again, for the chance to feed on the unwary and grow strong. 3/3

1268. **Huff, Tanya,** *Blood Pact,* Daw, 1993. Nelson and Fitzroy #4 of 5. (Paranormal Police Procedural) It began with the call no daughter ever wants to get, the call that told private investigator Vicki Nelson her mother had died. Mrs. Nelson's coworker at the Queen's University Life Science Department told Vicki that the cause of death was a heart attack, and that they'd be waiting for her to arrive in Kingston to make the funeral arrangements. But what started as an all too normal personal tragedy soon became the most terrifying case of Vicki's career. 3/3

1269. **Huff, Tanya,** *Blood Debt,* Daw, 1997. Nelson and Fitzroy #5 of 5. (Paranormal Police Procedural) It began with a ghost in his bedroom. A tormented soul hungry for vengeance, the sort of nocturnal visitation that even a five-hundred-year-old vampire like Henry Fitzroy found tiresome. It would lead Vicki Nelson, PI, into her most deadly investigation yet. –*Blood Bank* by Tanya Huff released in 2008 by Daw of short stories around three main characters: Vicki Nelson, a homicide cop turned private detective, her former partner Mike Celluci, who is still on the force, and vampire Henry Fitzroy, who is the illegitimate son of Henry VIII and makes his living as a writer of bodice rippers (MLM). 3/3

1270. **Huff, Tanya,** *Smoke and Shadows,* Daw, 2004. Tony Foster #1 of 3. (Paranormal Amateur Sleuth) When Tony Foster relocated to Vancouver with his vampire Henry Fitzroy, he knew it was his chance to get his act together. In an example of art echoing life, Tony landed a job as production assistant for the syndicated TV show Darkest Night, a series about a vampire detective. And except for his unrequited crush on the show's handsome costar, Lee Nicholas, Tony was pretty content. 3/3

1271. **Huff, Tanya,** *Smoke and Mirrors,* Daw, 2005. Tony Foster #2 of 3. (Paranormal Amateur Sleuth) When Tony and his TV crew find themselves shooting in an actual haunted house, all hell threatens to break loose. Locked into the house overnight, can Tony keep the diabolical controlling spirit from turning the crew against one another in an orgy of blood? 3/3

1272. **Huff, Tanya,** *Smoke and Ashes,* Daw, 2006. Tony Foster #3 of 3. (Paranormal Amateur Sleuth) Tony Foster and the crew of "Darkest Night," a TV series about a vampire detective. This time they find themselves facing another supernatural menace, a Demonic Convergence. Tony-with the help of vampire Henry Fitzroy and Leah, a stuntwoman who is the last surviving priestess of a sex demon, plus a tabloid reporter and a Canadian Mountie-must keep the key to the convergence alive to prevent a demonic invasion so large scale that it could be the finale-for the whole world. 3/3

1273. **Hughart, Barry,** *The Story of the Stone,* Blueboy, 1977. (Pulp) "Chinese sound-master Moon Boy aids Master Li Kao to discover what lies behind the mysterious theft of a manuscript, two deaths, a weird sound, and destruction of part of the Valley of Sorrows in an Oriental fantasy narrated by Number Ten Ox (Gunn)." 3/3

1274. **Hughes, Peter Tuesday,** *Gay Nights at Maldelangue,* Greenleaf, 1969. (Pulp) "New York tutor Brian Glendon, 23, the narrator, on his first job in Marblehead, Massachusetts, does little real sleuthing to understand the strange things happening set in 1875 (Gunn)." 3/3

1275. **Hughes, Peter Tuesday,** *Groping,* Greenleaf, 1969. (Pulp) "American travel guide Guido (Steve) Stephans, 25, a Vietnam veteran, becomes instrumental in the CIA's unmasking of a Venetian drug-smuggling operation but causes unnecessary deaths because of his own self-deception (Gunn)." 3/3

1276. **Hughes, Peter Tuesday,** *Good Boy,* Blueboy, 1970. (Pulp) "Northeastern accidental sleuths Chris Muthers, 22, and Chester (Chet) Miller, MD, 30s, are two of several narrators (Gunn)." 3/3

1277. **Hughes, Peter Tuesday,** *Tangier 6-6969,* Greenleaf, 1970. (Pulp) "New York travel agent Hugh Randall, 34, part-Jewish, becomes caught in the Arab-Israeli struggle when he acts as a courier on a mission to Tangier and is betrayed by his anti-Semitic lover (Gunn)." 3/3

1278. **Hughes, Peter Tuesday,** *Remake,* Greenleaf, 1971. (Pulp) "San Francisco death-row prisoner Rex Raines, 23, receives an implant of the mind of Lieutenant-Commander Robert (Robin) Wake, 33, so he can infiltrate gay groups under Robin's direction, but the designers forgot to factor in mental feedback or the possibility that sinister forces might have gotten to Robin while he was a North Vietnam prisoner of war (Gunn)." 3/3

1279. **Hughes, Peter Tuesday,** *Strangers, Can You See My Face,* Blueboy, 1971. (Pulp) A crime case. 3/3

1280. **Hughes, Peter Tuesday,** *Third Secret,* Blueboy, 1971. (Pulp) A crime case. 3/3

1281. **Hughes, Peter Tuesday,** *Something in the Blood,* Greenleaf, 1972. (Pulp) "U. S. State Department Greek expert Kenneth Hillier, the narrator, identifies who died in a fiery car crash and who is behind the mask of Apollo in a pulp mystery mostly interested in suggesting the power of the Greek gods in the modern world (Gunn)." 3/3

1282. **Hughes, Peter Tuesday,** *The Phallic Worshippers,* Blueboy, 1977. (Pulp) "Anthropologist and "DOA" undercover agent Gary Dayton, 27, the narrator, is on assignment in the American Southwest (Gunn)." –republished as *Gary's Gay Odyssey* by Gary Dayton in 1983 by Arena (MLM). 3/3

1283. **Hughes, Peter Tuesday,** *The Daemon,* Blueboy, 1977. (Pulp) "London historian Aubrey Portland, 27, acknowledges that, even with the help of Inspector Peter Tyke, "it may be improbable I'll ever solve the puzzle" whether Kyle Owen, 23, is possessed by demonic spirits or what becomes of him set in 1905 (Gunn)." 3/3

1284. **Hughes, Peter Tuesday,** *The Master of Monfortin,* Blueboy, 1977. (Pulp) "Maine accidental sleuth Simon Monfortin, 24, the narrator, an heir to a shipping fortune, reared in England, does not know whom to trust set in 1882 (Gunn)." 3/3

1285. **Hughes, Peter Tuesday,** *The Bright Young Men,* Blueboy, 1976. Bruce Doe #1 of 6. (Pulp) "Cliff Anders, after enticing Bruce to join him and the man who keeps him in Kashmir, disappears with Krishna Rau. Bruce pursues them to Calcutta and then to Hong Kong, where he discovers Cliff has been turned into an opium zombie designed to be used for Rau's international conspiracy to bring Chinese communism to the world. Bruce is captured, but singer Tad Jugger rescues him. The theme that no one is quite who he seems to be is launched an idea developed throughout the series (Gunn)." 6/6

1286. **Hughes, Peter Tuesday,** *Three Got Away,* Blueboy, 1976. Bruce Doe #2 of 6. (Pulp) "After Bruce is recruited for the Desk and trained in Taiwan, Krishna Rau kidnaps him and flies him to San Juan, Puerto Rico. He disables the brain implant the Desk has places in Bruce but misses the cornea implant that transmits pictures. In a shootout in which double agent Joe Foreman plays a curious role, Rau escapes, as do Ruth Hydra and Pauline Ashkanasi. Bruce's immediate boss, Adam Bludger and the Desk's head, Algernon Cloutman, are introduced (Gunn)." 3/3

1287. **Hughes, Peter Tuesday,** *The Eyes of the Basilisk,* Blueboy, 1977. Bruce Doe #3 of 6. (Pulp) Crossdressing communist scientist Rudolph Hidrana, aka Ruth Hydra, tries to wrest control of the Organization for the Suppression of World Capitalism from Rau, whom Hydra thinks has lost sight of his mission and become more interested in power (Gunn)." 3/3

1288. **Hughes, Peter Tuesday,** *The Executioner,* Blueboy, 1977. Bruce Doe #4 of 6. (Pulp) "Nazi Eric Hass, aka Yanick Assousam is in Mallorca with $13 million in Nazi gold and stolen paintings. Several factions converge on him; the Desk, in the persons of Bruce and Adam; Israel's Mossad, in the persons of Shmuel Lanholtz, aka Jerry Stone, and double agent David Klein; the Egyptian executioner Hyppolyte and his sister Om Faroud; and Rau and his Nazi henchman Rudolph Neimbauer, aka General Peregrine, who schemes to destroy Israel (Gunn)." 3/3

1289. **Hughes, Peter Tuesday,** *The Monte Carlo Caper,* Blueboy, 1977. Bruce Doe #5 of 6. (Pulp) "The French SDECE is too interested in a over struggle going on for the head of the Desk; Adam sends Bruce to Paris to investigate. The Russian KGB and a French anti-African nationalist group are also mixed up in the affair (Gunn)." 3/3

1290. **Hughes, Peter Tuesday,** *Hard to Shoot,* Surree, 1978. Bruce Doe #6 of 6. (Pulp) Faryia is murdered in Washington as two factions within the Desk vie for policy control (Gunn)." –reprinted by Pete McBride entitled as Secret Agent Stud by Arena in 1984 (MM). 3/3

1291. **Hull, Richard (1896-1973),** *The Murder of my Aunt,* Faber and Faber, 1934. (Crime Drama) Edward is an effete, poor young man who has something in store for his only relative, his wealthy aunt. –this is the first mystery with a gay narrator however, Edward is an unattractive, devoid of redeeming features, fat and greasy, and entirely self-interested (MLM). 3/3

1292. **Hunsicker, Harry,** *Still River,* St. Martin's, 2005. Oswald #1 of 3. (Hard Boiled) He bears a killer's name... Lee H. "Hank" Oswald inherited more from his bull-headed father than just a name. It's not that he looks for trouble; he just can't seem to keep out of its way. Fortunately, being named Oswald in Dallas makes a man tough enough to get the job done, no matter what side of the law he's forced to walk... –good friend is gay and occasionally provides backup (MLM). 1/3

1293. **Hunsicker, Harry,** *The Next Time You Die,* St. Martin's, 2006.

Oswald #2 of 3. (Hard Boiled) When a bourbon-swilling Baptist preacher hires private detective Lee Henry Oswald to recover a stolen file, Oswald figures the job for a quick and painless infusion of cash. 1/3

1294. **Hunsicker, Harry,** *Crosshairs,* St. Martin's, 2007. Oswald #3 of 3. (Hard Boiled) All he wants is to be left alone, a normal existence away from the assorted creeps and lowlifes inherent to his former profession as a private investigator. Unfortunately, peace and solitude are hard to find for Lee Oswald, a battle-hardened veteran of the first Gulf War, now weary after a decade as the fix-it man of last resort on the back streets of Dallas. 1/3

1295. **Hunt, David,** *The Magician's Tale,* Putnam, 1997. Kay Farrow #1 of 2. (Thriller) When the police find the decapitated head of a young man with the body nowhere to be found, they are stunned. They begin to piece together the clues and soon find out that the head belongs to Tim Lovesey, a handsome prostitute who worked in the seedy section of San Francisco called Polk Gulch. In this sexually charged neverworld, the police prefer to look the other way and chalk this up as another bizarre crime in an equally bizarre area of town. –won the tenth LAMBDA Award for Best Gay Mystery, may have gay secondary characters in the second book, *Trick of Light* (MLM). 2/3

1296. **Hunt, E. Howard,** *The Violent Ones,* Fawcett Gold, 1950. (Crime Drama) It was a red fury that drove Paul Cameron to Paris, into a maelstrom of intrigue and violence. In the center of that whirlpool he found a flaming night-club singer, a fortune in illegal gold - and quick death on every side. –Cameron likes to fight and beats up at least one gay man in this mystery (MLM). 1/3

1297. **Hunt, J. Timothy,** *Killing Time in Taos,* Adhemar, 2011. (Amateur Sleuth) An artist colony in Taos, New Mexico, has an unexpected vacancy to fill, and a young painter is offered the first major residency of his career. A few days after his arrival, this shy, closeted young man discovers the reason such an opportunity became available – when he stumbles upon the corpse of the artist who preceded him. 3/3

1298. **Hunter, Fred (1954-2006),** *Government Gays,* St. Martin's, 1997. Alex Reynolds #1 of 5. (Amateur Sleuth) With Peter, his longtime lover, busy for the evening, Alex Reynolds decides to stop in for a quick beer at a local Chicago gay bar and survey the nightlife scene he left behind for "married" life years before. Quickly unamused, Alex decides to call it an early evening, stopping off in the men's room before going home. But there he is assaulted by two men who demand of him, "Where is it?" 3/3

1299. **Hunter, Fred,** *Federal Fags,* St. Martin's, 1998. Alex Reynolds #2 of 5. (Amateur Sleuth) After spotting an old college flame starring in a rented porn film, Alex Reynolds tracks him down to an L.A. address-only to find him murdered on his apartment floor. Suddenly, his occasional CIA contact is very interested, and the odd spy team of Alex, his lover, and his mother, Jean, must scour the gay porn industry to find the murderer. 3/3

1300. **Hunter, Fred,** *Capital Queers,* St. Martin's, 1999. Alex Reynolds #3 of 5. (Amateur Sleuth) Alex Reynolds and his lover Peter Livesay discover that a mysterious cult has killed friends of theirs over their friends' accidental possession of a stolen religious artifact. Now, Alex, Peter, and Alex's mother have inherited their friends' annoying dog Muffin as well as the unwanted and deadly attention of the killers. 3/3

1301. **Hunter, Fred,** *National Nancys,* St. Martin's, 2000. Alex Reynolds #4 of 5. (Amateur Sleuth) Alex Reynolds and his lover Peter Livesay are campaign volunteers for a liberal senatorial candidate when someone makes good on the daily phoned-in bomb threats, apparently killing the campaign's office manager. Alex, Peter, and Alex's mother reluctantly agree to help uncover the truth about the bombing, but soon find their own lives on the line. 3/3

1302. **Hunter, Fred,** *Chicken Asylum,* St. Martin's, 2001. Alex Reynolds #5 of 5. (Amateur Sleuth) When Alex Reynolds, his lover Peter Livesay, and his mother Jean-occasional freelance operatives for the CIA-are asked to stash an Iraqi military defector in their home, all three are less than thrilled. It turns out the defector is an 18-year-old soldier who has ties to a terrorist organization and, to further complicate matters, is gay. But the real trouble begins when the young man mysteriously disappears, and suddenly Alex, Peter and Jean find themselves in the middle of a very dangerous game. 3/3

1303. **Hunter, Susan,** *Dangerous Habits,* Createspace, 2014. Leah Nash #1 of 5. (Thriller) Reporter Leah Nash returns to her Wisconsin hometown after 10 years away–unfortunately, not in triumph. When she goes out on a limb–her natural habitat–and connects the drowning death of a young nun with a shocking scandal, the story she uncovers could be her comeback–or her last byline. –gay colleague Miguel Santos helps Nash throughout the series (MLM). 1/3

1304. **Hunter, Susan,** *Dangerous Mistakes,* Createspace, 2015. Leah Nash #2 of 5. (Thriller) Murder or suicide? Journalist Leah Nash chases down clues in the death of a local physician and discovers a dangerous web of secrets and lies. Breaking through to the truth, Leah puts herself in harm's way in this fast-paced mystery with an unexpected twist. 1/3

1305. **Hunter, Susan,** *Dangerous Places,* Createspace, 2016. Leah Nash #3 of 5. (Thriller) A person can't just vanish. Can she? Journalist Leah Nash investigates the decades-old disappearance of a teenage girl, and the answer she finds brings her face-to-face with a shattering secret from her own past–and someone determined to keep it there. 1/3

1306. **Hunter, Susan,** *Dangerous Secrets,* Createspace, 2017. Leah Nash #4 of 5. (Thriller) A week that starts out with a woman's dead body in the living room is not going to end well. Writer Leah Nash learns this truth when her friend Miguel arrives home on a Sunday night, only to discover that his weekend renter has failed to checkout–at least in the usual sense of the word. By Wednesday, Miguel's uncle is arrested for murder. 2/3

1307. **Hunter, Susan,** *Dangerous Flaws,* Createspace, 2018. Leah Nash #5 of 5. (Thriller) True crime writer Leah Nash is stunned when police investigating the murder of a beautiful young college professor focus on her ex-husband Nick. Leah has no illusions about her ex, but despite his flaws, she just can't see him as a killer. Reluctantly, she agrees to help Nick's attorney prove that he isn't. –e-book only (MLM). 1/3

1308. **Hutson, Garrett,** *In a Safe Town,* Warfleigh, 2016. (Police Procedural) Who could have wanted to kill Tom Stafford, the most popular kid in school, and the best quarterback in town history? Sheriff Mark Bennett can't fathom a reason. Everyone knows everything about everyone in their small southern Indiana town...or do they? –gay character actively assists the main character (MLM). 3/3

1309. **Hutson, Garrett,** *The Jade Dragon,* Warfleigh, 2017. (Historical Espionage) In 1935, Shanghai is the place to be. Glittering nightlife, bustling business, and a diverse international community are just some of the appeals of the "Paris of the Orient." Douglas Bainbridge, Office of Naval Intelligence, is beginning a two-year immersion in Shanghai when he runs into Tim McIntyre, a childhood friend from San Francisco. Tim is a reporter for the Shanghai office of the Associated Press, and he offers to show Doug the local nightlife. Enjoying a show at the Jade Dragon, Tim steps out at intermission, but never returns. Doug finds Tim's body in an alley. –main character's sexuality is questionable (MLM). 3/3

1310. **Hutson, Garrett,** *Hidden Among Us,* Warfleigh, 2018. (Historical Espionage) As the threat of war looms in Europe, the shadow game of espionage has come to America, and Martin Schuller knows it. While most Americans go about their daily lives oblivious to any threat from abroad, Martin's work at the State Department's counterintelligence office keeps them safe, sometimes going undercover to catch a Nazi spy hidden among them, using a fake American passport. But then an anticipated bust at the rally of the German American Bund in February 1939 results in Martin's mistaken arrest by the FBI, frustrating his efforts to identify the head of a Nazi cell in the United States, code-named Der Skilaufer. –gay character actively assists the main character (MLM). 3/3

1311. **Hyttinen, Roger,** *A Clash of Fangs,* Writer's Club, 2001. (Paranormal) Steve Mitchell falls in love with an exciting and mysterious man. Little does he know, that his new boyfriend is a vampire. Soon, bodies drained of blood begin showing up in Chicago dumsters. Is Steve's new boyfriend responsible? 3/3

I

1312. **Ilett, Paul,** *Expose',* Createspace, 2014. (Crime Drama) For years Gay superstar Adam Jaymes has been the victim of press intrusion. The reporters of The Daily Ear, the world's top selling and most salacious tabloid, have been ruthless in their exploitation of his private life and that of his friends and co-stars. Now with near limitless resources at his fingertips, Jaymes can finally plan his vengeance. And what better way than to publicly expose the lies and private shames of the paper's own staff? After all, reporters have secrets too. –unsure of gay content (MLM). ?/3

1313. **Inman, John,** *Payback,* Dreamspinner, 2015. (MM Crime Drama) When Tyler Powell's life is torn apart by an unspeakable crime, the need for vengeance takes over. Every moment of every day, as he tries to pull his shattered existence together again, it's all he can think about–revenge. 3/3

1314. **Inman, John,** Sunset Lake, Dreamspinner, 2015. (MM Mystery) Reverend Brian Lucas has a secret his congregation in the Nine Mile Methodist Church knows nothing about, and he'd really like to keep it that way. Brian's "close friend," Sam, is urging a resolution to their little problem, but Brian's brother, Boyd, the County Sheriff, is more caught up in chasing down a homicidal maniac who is slaughtering little old ladies. 3/3

1315. **Inman, John,** *Two Pet Dicks,* Dreamspinner, 2016. (MM Soft Boiled) Old friends and business partners, Maitland Carter and Lenny Fritz, may not be the two sharpest pickle forks in the picnic basket, but they have big hearts. And they are just now coming around to the fact that maybe their hearts are caught in a bit of turmoil. 3/3

1316. **Innes, Michael,** *Man from the Sea,* Dodd, Mead, 1955. (Espionage) When a man swims to shore from a freighter off the Scottish coast, he interrupts a midnight rendezvous between Richard Cranston and Lady Blair. Richard sees an obscure opportunity to regain his honour with the Blair family after he hears the swimmer's incredible tale of espionage, treason and looming death. But this mysterious man is not all he seems, and Richard is propelled into life threatening danger. 1/3

1317. **Innes, Michael,** *The Case of Sonia Wayward,* Dodd, Mead, 1960. (Crime Drama) Colonel Ffolliot Petticate's predicament begins when his novelist wife, Sonia, drowns during a sailing trip in the English Channel. 1/3

1318. **Innes, Robert,** *Untouchable,* Createspace, 2016. Blake Hart #1 of 8. (Police Procedural) Harrison Baxter lives on a farm with his parents, on the outskirts of the village of Harmschapel. It's picturesque, idyllic and tranquil – but Harrison is far from happy. His parent's marriage is strained to say the least and on top of that, his boyfriend, Daniel, has been mentally and physically abusing him for years. Detective Sergeant Blake Harte has moved to Harmschapel after his own relationship ended in tatters. But when he is called upon to investigate the mysterious and impossible murder at Halfmile Farm, Blake finds himself facing the most challenging case of his career. How can Daniel have been shot in a locked shed that nobody could possibly have escaped from? 3/3

1319. **Innes, Robert,** *Confessional,* Createspace, 2017. Blake Hart #2 of 8. (Police Procedural) St Abra's church is harbouring a dark secret. Several elderly parishioners have been found dead in the church's confessions booth, all appearing to have suffered fatal heart attacks. 3/3

1320. **Innes, Robert,** *Ripples,* Createspace, 2018. Blake Hart #3 of 8. (Police Procedural) When Detective Sergeant Blake Harte is given the opportunity of a relaxing week away at a spa manor, he jumps at the opportunity. He can take one person with him - and who more than Harrison Baxter deserves time away from Harmschapel after everything he has been through? But once at the Manor of the Lakes, the rest and relaxation they both crave is quickly brought to an end, when Blake and Harrison witness a man being murdered, by a mysterious hooded figure who appears to have the ability to walk on water. 3/3

1321. **Innes, Robert,** *Reach,* Createspace, 2017. Blake Hart #4 of 8. (Police Procedural) Seven years ago Thomas Frost was arrested for the murders of five women in the Manchester area and Detective Sergeant Blake Harte was the officer in charge of his arrest, saving the life of Kerry Nightingale in the process. Now, Frost has promised that Kerry was never safe, and she'll be dead within a few days. Somehow, Kerry is found dead in her top floor apartment - a place that was being guarded by Blake and the apartment's security. How is it possible for Kerry to have been murdered in her apartment when nobody could have gotten in or out? 3/3

1322. **Innes, Robert,** *Spotlight,* Createspace, 2017. Blake Hart #5 of 8. (Police Procedural) Life is stressful for Detective Sergeant Blake Harte. Not only must he come to terms with his difficult new inspector at the station, but then his parents suddenly turn up on his doorstep – and his mother does not approve of his new boyfriend, and his relationship with Harrison soon begins to suffer. Meanwhile, Harmschapel police station is in pursuit of two drug dealers. These two men have proven difficult to apprehend before, but then the case takes a sudden and inexplicable turn. One night, during a high-speed car chase, the two suspects completely vanish into thin air, before Blake's eyes. 3/3

1323. **Innes, Robert,** *Flatline,* Createspace, 2018. Blake Hart #6 of 8. (Police Procedural) When Detective Sergeant Blake Harte finds himself in hospital for a minor operation to have his appendix removed, he is restless and itching to return to work. For Blake, the thought of being stuck on Ward 7A with no work to distract him is akin to torture, and when he finds out that his duties are being overseen by his work rival, Sergeant Gardiner, the situation only seems to worsen. But then, Blake finds himself in the epicenter of the most bizarre case he has seen yet. Doctor Joe Tilsley is alone and stuck in an elevator. When the lift is finally fixed, and the doors open onto Ward 7A, Doctor Tilsley is dead, and most bizarrely of all, he appears to have been drowned. 3/3

1324. **Innes, Robert,** *Skeletons,* Createspace, 2018. Blake Hart #7 of 8. (Police Procedural) Is it possible for someone to rise from the dead? Before meeting Harmschapel's undertaker Patrick Coopland, Detective Sergeant Blake Harte would most certainly have thought not. However, when Coopland is killed in a car crash on the way home with his wife, Angela, she becomes convinced that her mentally abusive husband is still haunting her from beyond the grave. The day after Coopland's funeral, Angela reports her most terrifying encounter yet, forcing Blake and the rest of Harmschapel police to open the grave of Patrick Coopland to prove once and for all that he has been laid to rest. 3/3

1325. **Innes, Robert,** *Touch,* Createspace, 2018. Blake Hart #8 of 8. (Police Procedural) Football fever has Harmschapel in its grip. Detective Sergeant Blake Harte finds himself forced to sit through the tense final in case of any trouble. Though the last thing he expects is to be thrown into the midst of another impossible crime, he and the rest of Harmschapel Police are left baffled when football hero Scott is murdered in the middle of the match. 3/3

1326. **Innes, Roy,** *Murder in the Monashees,* NeWest, 2005. Coswell #1 of 4. (Police Procedural) RCMP Corporal Paul Blakemore is jolted from his mundane policing duties in the small Monashee Mountain village of Bear Creek by the discovery of a frozen corpse on a snowy slope just outside of town. There are no signs indicating how the body got there–no footprints or drag marks–nothing. It's as if the victim has fallen from the sky. 3/3

1327. **Innes, Roy,** *West End Murders,* NeWest, 2008. Coswell #2 of 4. (Police Procedural) When a series of murders threatens the lives of an entire community in Vancouver, RCMP Corporal Paul Blakemore and Inspector Coswell team up once again to solve the case. What begins as an array of hate crimes suddenly culminates into a conspiracy against an American politician, and the lines between Canada and the United States are blurred as suspicions rise from both sides. To solve this case, both detectives must look beyond the powers of one culprit and instead focus on the ventures of an entire underground organization, all while protecting members of their own city. 3/3

1328. **Innes, Roy,** *Murder in the Chilcotin,* NeWest, 2010. Coswell #3 of 4. (Police Procedural) RCMP Inspector Coswell and the newly promoted Sergeant Blakemore are sent to the district of West Caribou in British Columbia, where the murder of a neophyte Mountie, the son of a local rancher, threatens to ignite racial conflicts that have been simmering in the region ever since 1885, when five First Nations men were hanged for treason. 3/3

1329. **Innes, Roy,** *The Extra Cadaver Murders,* NeWest, 2016. Coswell #4 of 4. (Police Procedural) A university professor is murdered, and his corpse is revealed to a first-year anatomy class in spectacular fashion–nude on a slab alongside shrouded medical cadavers. He begins his investigation with Corporal James, his longtime assistant, but is abruptly assigned a new partner, a female officer who arrives under a political cloud. 3/3

1330. **Ironrod, Alex,** *Leather Nights,* Nazca Plains, 2011. (MM BDSM) Kink. Cops. Detectives. Murder in Los Angeles of a former porn star. More leather that you can strip from a stockyard, and enough spunk to coat a condominium. Fast cars and expensive bikes. A privately-run underground sex-slave auction. 3/3

1331. **Ironrod, Alex,** *Leather Days,* MLR, 2013. (MM BDSM) Murderous porn king, gay criminal lawyer, sadistic gang of wealthy businessmen - two LAPD detectives face challenges in finding a killer as well as their own leather relationship. 3/3

1332. **Ironrod, Alex,** *Deception,* MLR, 2014. Palm Springs #1 of 2. (MM BDSM) A US Marine creates tensions by coming back into his gay father's life in Palm Springs, only to disappear again. Is he for real? Can PI Mark find the man behind the name? Deception takes many forms, especially when man-sex is involved, as young Palm Springs PIs, Mark and Dan, find out. 3/3

1333. **Ironrod, Alex,** *Cages: Cathedral City,* MLR, 2015. Palm Springs #2 of 2. (MM BDSM) Dan's BDSM past as a Marine threatens his relationship with Mark, his professional and leather sex partner as the two hunky young Palm Springs private eyes wrestle with the cages, real and imaginary, in the violence of mixed martial arts and in the human mind. 3/3

1334. **Ironstone, John,** *Disco Danger,* Encounter, 1978. (Pulp) "Amateur sleuths Charles (Chaz) Hornay, analytical, mathematical, and James (Jazz) Hornay, 18, intuitive, musical, capable of entering the mind of his identical twin and lover, university students, pair in what was intended to be a series. *Campus Caper,* the first case in the series was never published, but chapters 1 and 12 of *Disco Danger* are from the earlier manuscript (Gunn)." 3/3

1335. **Irving, Jan,** *Wylde,* Dreamspinner, 2009. Wylde #1 of 2. (MM Police Procedural) Noah Matthews brought his son Josh to the pristine woods of Washington State to make a fresh start. The first night in their new home, Noah meets Kell Farraday the police chief who shows up on his doorstep searching for two people lost in the forest. –book #2 of 2 *Born to be Wylde* is an MM romance with no mystery (MLM). 3/3

1336. **Irving, Jan,** *Sahara Blue,* Createspace, 2010. Mastering Toby #2 of 2. (MM Thriller) Seth Hollis lives his passions online under the pseudonym "Lotus" and attracts ex-Navy SEAL Sahara Blue, who avidly follows the erotic tales of passionate submission Seth posts. Seth's writings have also attracted an unwanted and dangerous admirer, and when the glass window of Seth's shop is shattered one night, fate sends Sahara Blue to his rescue. Seth's deranged stalker won't let up, and Seth and Sahara will have to give up their secrets and learn to trust if they're going to keep each other safe. 3/3

1337. **Ison, Graham,** *Confirm or Deny,* St. Martin's, 1989. Gaffney and Tipper #2 of 4. (Police Procedural) There's a traitor in the ranks of MI5. The Director General is forced to find an outside investigator to conduct a search into his teams. Detective Chief Superintendent John Gaffney is in Special Branch, and with his previous experience and highly qualified mind, he is perfect for the job. With a small but select team, Gaffney is put in charge of the operation. –gay men are referred to as queers, poofs, and fags (MLM). 1/3

1338. **Iwanski, Shannon,** *A Body to Die For,* Shannon\Bozarth, 2015. (Modern Cozy) Max has returned from a trip that was supposed to help him get his head and heart together following a break up. Unfortunately, it didn't work, and now Max has to face his ex, Bobby, who also happens to be his business partner. It was bad enough to find out Bobby had already moved on, but it gets worse when the new boyfriend, Skylar, is murdered. Now, Bobby is the primary suspect, and Max takes it upon himself to find the real killer.

3/3

J

1339. **J., Sean**, *The Street Justice Series: Ten to Midnight/The Comfort of Strangers*, iUniverse, 2004. (Police Procedural) "Ten to Midnight," the story of two men hell bent on revenge. When the dust clears one will be dead and the other wishing he was! "The Comfort of Strangers." Who is killing the gay men in Jackson Park, can Detective Jones solve a riddle, and save his badge at the same time? 3/3

1340. **Jackson, John**, *Deadly Orgasm*, Parisian, 1972. (Pulp) Los Angeles accidental sleuth Erik Austin's lover is murdered in San Francisco when he stumbles onto a drug ring operation with police protection. San Francisco policeman Rick Webster sets up a scheme for Erik to identify the murderers, but Erik's life is put in jeopardy, and Rick himself is almost killed (Gunn). 3/3

1341. **James, Bill (James Tucker)**, *Halo Parade*, Foul Press, 1987. Harpur and Iles #3 of 32. (Police Procedural) When Detective Chief Superintendent Colin Harpur places young policeman Ray Street undercover in a vicious drug gang, the entire department knows the risks. If Street is found out, he will take his place in "the halo parade." Then the killing of a fellow officer will have to be avenged, by whatever means ... –Street has to infiltrate a gang led by a gay man and sleeps with him as well (MLM). 1/3

1342. **James, Byron**, *Wild Boys of the Commune*, Guild, 1971. (Pulp) "Sullivan, Washington police chief Kell Faraday works to discover who killed and gutted a local pot farmer, to protect his new lover, Noah Matthews, and his son from a Seattle stalker, and to solve the mystery of the forest ghost (Gunn). 3/3

1343. **James, David (David Stukas)**, *Three Bedrooms, Two Baths, One Very Dead Corpse*, Kensington, 2010. Amanda Thorne #1 of 2. (Cozy) Location, location, location. Like any realtor worth her designer sling-backs, Amanda Thorne knows the golden rule of selling homes. Unless, of course, the prime property includes one very dead corpse... –Amanda has a gay ex-husband who helps with the investigation (MLM). 2/3

1344. **James, David**, *A Not so Model Home*, Kensington, 2012. Amanda Thorne #2 of 2. (Cozy) Times are tough and the real estate market is tanking, even in posh Palm Springs. So when former client Ian Forbes, the eccentric head of an international hair care empire, offers Amanda a chance to list his palatial Spanish style pad, she reluctantly takes him up on it. All she has to do is appear on the bizarre reality dating show he's filming–and starring in–at his estate. The competition quickly grows fierce, and it's almost no surprise when two of Ian's prospective lovers turn up dead. 2/3

1345. **James, Dean,** *Death by Dissertation,* Silver Dagger, 2004. (Amateur Sleuth) For Andy Carpenter, graduate school is stressful enough without adding romantic complications and dead bodies to the mix. First, Andy has to contend with the presence of Rob Hayward, a new student in the history PhD program. He thought Rob was out of his life for good, but now he has to confront his unresolved feelings and not let his work suffer. When Andy discovers the body of fellow graduate student Charlie Harper in the university library, Rob looks like the chief suspect in the murder. Just what was the relationship between Rob and Charlie? Andy and his best friend, Maggie McLendon, agree that Rob isn't a murderer, and they decide the best way to exonerate him is to figure out who really killed Charlie. Who else might have had a motive for murder? When a second murder occurs, Andy, Maggie, and Rob must work quickly to find the killer before Rob ends up charged with two murders he didn't commit. 3/3

1346. **James, Dean,** *Posted to Death,* Kensington, 2002. Simon Kirby-Jones #1 of 4. (Bibliomystery Paranormal Cozy) England has found itself a new sleuth to call its own, but Simon Kirby-Jones is not only a vampire, he's an American to boot. He's pulled up stakes in the States to settle in the quaint English village of Snupperton Mumsley, where his southern charm will be put to work uncovering the deadly secrets of his neighbors. 3/3

1347. **James, Dean,** *Faked to Death,* Kensington, 2003. Simon Kirby-Jones #2 of 4. (Bibliomystery Paranormal Cozy) Simon Kirby-Jones, amateur sleuth, gay American vampire living in the cozy British village of Snupperton Mumsley, is a respected historian and also, under a well-guarded pseudonym, a bestselling crime writer. When he's invited to an exclusive writer's conference he's astonished –and outraged–to see that "Dorina Darlington" is the featured speaker. Clearly the woman is an imposter, because Simon is the real Dorina Darlington! And when the fake Dorina turns up dead, Simon suspects he's next on the killer's list... 3/3

1348. **James, Dean,** *Decorated to Death,* Kensington, 2004. Simon Kirby-Jones #3 of 4. (Bibliomystery Paranormal Cozy) Hardly one to become star-struck, Simon nevertheless deigns to attend a tea at Blitherington Hall in honor of celebrity interior designer Zeke Harwood, star of the popular television show, "Tres Zeke." The self-acclaimed King of Home Decorating makes it immediately obvious that he's there to give the drawing room a makeover–not make friends. So, it's little shock to Simon when the drama-queen decorator meets his demise; he's only surprised it hasn't happened sooner. Now, in a locked-room puzzle worthy of Agatha Christie, Simon must peel away layers of lies to reveal who killed the decorator in the drawing room with a blunt instrument. 3/3

1349. **James, Dean,** *Baked to Death,* Kensington, 2005. Simon Kirby-Jones #4 of 4. (Bibliomystery Paranormal Cozy) With the help of some dandy little pills, Simon can get through his first summer in Snupperton-Mumsley with only a mild aversion to the sun. On the other hand, his assistant, Giles Blitherington, is bemoaning the beginning of the season. A Medieval faire is coming to town–and setting up tent practically in Blitherington Hall's backyard. It doesn't take Simon long to don tunic and tights and gambol straight into controversy. The group putting on the faire is in the midst of a power struggle. Their "king" is about to be dethroned by a charismatic and popular duke. But when the usurper is poisoned by way of a fig pastry, Simon is confronted with enough suspects to fill a royal court. Now Simon must infiltrate the players to uncover a murderer most medieval. –short story "It Came Upon a Midnight Dead," published in the anthology *Kudzo Christmas* ed. By Jim Gilbert and Gail Waller published in 2005 by River City (MLM). 3/3

1350. **James, Hayley B.,** *Undercover Sins,* Dreamspinner, 2011. Secret Sins #1 of 2. (MM Police Procedural) Police officer Gabriel Carter refuses to walk away from an assignment without seeing it through. So, when he goes into deep cover as a male prostitute named Ty, he intends to do everything in his power to see his case to an arrest. He seduces his mark, Demetrius Prado, the second most powerful man in Las Vegas and a human trafficker, but the man is nothing like he expected. 3/3

1351. **James, Hayley B.,** *Undercover Addiction,* Dreamspinner, 2014. Secret Sins #2 of 2. (MM Police Procedural) Working Vice for the Seattle PD, Connor Bishop's favorite part of the job is going undercover. His current assignment is to get close to Riley Drapeau, a human trafficker backed into a corner by the FBI and turned informant. Connor needs to milk him for information on his organization, but while doing so, sees an entirely different Riley than he expected. 3/3

1352. **James, Miranda (Dean James),** *Classified as Murder,* Berkley, 2011. Cat in the Stacks #2 of 11. (Bibliomystery Cozy) Aging eccentric James Delacorte asks Charlie the librarian to do an inventory of his rare book collection–but the job goes from tedious to terrifying when James turns up dead. Relying on his cat Diesel to paw around for clues, Charlie has to catch the killer before another victim checks out. –introduces Stewart Delacorte, a gay chemistry teacher at the university (MLM). 1/3

1353. **James, Miranda,** *File M for Murder,* Berkley, 2012. Cat in the Stacks #3 of 11. (Bibliomystery Cozy) Athena College's new writer in residence is native son and playwright Connor Lawton, known for his sharp writing–and sharper tongue. After an unpleasant encounter, librarian Charlie Harris heads home to a nice surprise: his daughter Laura is subbing for another Athena professor this fall semester. It's great news until he hears who got her the job: her old flame, Connor Lawton… –Stewart Delacorte starts dating the sheriff's deputy (MLM). 1/3

1354. **James, Miranda,** *Out of Circulation,* Berkley, 2013. Cat in the Stacks #4 of 11. (Bibliomystery Cozy) The Ducote sisters are in a tiff with Vera Cassity over the location of this year's library fundraising gala, and Charlie would rather curl up in a corner than get into the fray. It seems everyone–even his housekeeper Azalea–has it in for Vera. And at the gala, she gives them good reason, with a public display of rancor aimed at anyone who gets in her way. 1/3

1355. **James, Miranda,** *The Silence of the Library,* Berkley, 2014. Cat in the Stacks #5 of 11. (Bibliomystery Cozy) It's National Library Week, and the Athena Public Library is planning an exhibit to honor the centenary of famous novelist Electra Barnes Cartwright–creator of the beloved Veronica Thane series. After all, it's rumored that Cartwright penned Veronica Thane stories that remain under wraps, and one rabid fan will stop at nothing–not even murder–to get hold of the rare books. 1/3

1356. **James, Miranda,** *Arsenic and Old Books,* Berkley, 2015. Cat in the Stacks #6 of 11. (Bibliomystery Cozy) In Athena, Mississippi, librarian Charlie Harris is known for his good nature–and for his Maine coon cat Diesel that he walks on a leash. Charlie returned to his hometown to immerse himself in books, but taking the plunge into a recent acquisition will have him in over his head… 1/3

1357. **James, Miranda,** *No Cats Allowed,* Berkley, 2016. Cat in the Stacks #7 of 11. (Bibliomystery Cozy) Springtime in Mississippi is abloom with beauty, but the library's employees are too busy worrying to stop and smell the flowers. The new library director, Oscar Reilly, is a brash, unfriendly Yankee who's on a mission to cut costs–and his first targets are the archive and the rare book collection. 1/3

1358. **James, Miranda,** *Twelve Angry Librarians,* Berkley, 2017. Cat in the Stacks #8 of 11. (Bibliomystery Cozy) Lighthearted librarian Charlie Harris is known around his hometown of Athena, Mississippi, for walking his cat, a rescued Maine Coon named Diesel. But he may soon be taken for a walk himself in handcuffs… 1/3

1359. **James, Miranda,** *Claws for Concern,* Berkley, 2018. Cat in the Stacks #9 of 11. (Bibliomystery Cozy) Charlie Harris has been enjoying some peace and quiet with his new grandson when a mysterious man with a connection to an unsolved murder starts visiting the library... 1/3

1360. **James, Miranda,** *Six Cats a Slayin',* Berkley, 2018. Cat in the Stacks #10 of 11. (Bibliomystery Cozy) December twenty-fifth is right around the corner, and Charlie is making his list and checking it twice. He is doing his best to show some peace and goodwill toward his nosy neighbor Gerry Arbitron, a real estate agent who seems to have designs on his house (and maybe on him, as well), while preparing for a very important role, indeed–his first Christmas as a grandfather. –James' new contract is for two books per year starting in 2018, book eleven in the series, *The Pawful Truth* will be released in 2019 (MLM). 1/3

1361. **James, P. D.,** *An Unsuitable Job for a Woman,* Faber and Faber, 1972. Cordelia Gray #1 of 2. (Hard Boiled) Handsome Cambridge dropout Mark Callender died hanging by the neck with a faint trace of lipstick on his mouth. When the official verdict is suicide, his wealthy father hires fledgling private investigator Cordelia Gray to find out what led him to self-destruction. What she discovers instead is a twisting trail of secrets and sins, and the strong scent of murder. –Gray's assistant, Bevis, a would-be actor, is an unlabeled gay man (MLM). 1/3

1362. **James, P. D.,** *The Skull Beneath the Skin,* Faber and Faber, 1982. Cordelia Gray #2 of 2. (Hard Boiled) Private detective Cordelia Gray is invited to the sunlit island of Courcy to protect the vainly beautiful actress Clarissa Lisle from veiled threats on her life. Within the rose red walls of a fairy-tale castle, she finds the stage is set for death. –Bevis returns to assist Gray (MLM). 1/3

1363. **James, P. D.,** *The Black Tower,* Scribner, 1975. Adam Dalgliesh #5 of 14. (Police Procedural) Commander Dalgliesh is recuperating from a life-threatening illness when he receives a call for advice from an elderly friend who works as a chaplain in a home for the disabled on the Dorset coast. Dalgliesh arrives to discover that Father Baddeley has recently and mysteriously died, as has one of the patients at Toynton Grange. Evidently the home is not quite the caring community it purports to be. Dalgliesh is determined to discover the truth of his friend's death, but further fatalities follow, and his own life is in danger as he unmasks the evil at the heart of Toynton Grange. –the gay character "bears no label; he is only gay to those who perceive him (Slide)." There is however, a beautifully written passage about a physically handicapped man finding love in another physically handicapped man (MLM). 1/3

1364. **James, P. D.**, *Devices and Desires,* Faber and Faber, 1989. Adam Dalgliesh #8 of 14. (Police Procedural) Commander Dalgliesh of Scotland Yard vacations on the remote Larksoken headland in a converted windmill left to him by his aunt. But a psychotic strangler of young women is at large. Dalgliesh finds a body on the beach, head of nearby nuclear power company. He is caught up in dangerous secrets of the headland community and a baffling case. –gay character recounts a night of passion with a straight co-worker who later commits suicide unrelated to the night of passion (MM). 1/3

1365. **Jamison, D. J.**, *Full Disclosure,* Createspace, 2017. Real Estate Relations #1 of 2. (MM Mystery) Can a new real estate agent negotiate a happy ending with his mysterious client? Camden is desperately trying to make a fresh start as a real estate agent. Then things go sideways. His apartment is burglarized and getting caught half-naked while squatting in his own listing is a low point. Reid is a washed-up US marshal turned bodyguard, and even that's lost its appeal. A leave of absence to deal with a house he inherited in Kansas seems like a good opportunity to get his head straight – but when his boss asks him to help a witness being targeted by a gang, he decides to take him with him. The guy is a criminal, but he's young and gay, so we set up a cover as a couple. And then there's still those gang members to think about ... 3/3

1366. **Jamison, D. J.**, *Buyer's Remorse,* Createspace, 2018, Real Estate Relations #2 of 2. (MM Mystery) Will love persevere when the truth comes out? Lee changed his name and spent three years in witness protection. Miguel's been trying to curb his habit of leaping into bad relationships, but when Lee comes back to town, he's hard to resist. Kids are dying, and life's too short to shy away from a good thing. But will Lee's mysterious past come back to bite him? 3/3

1367. **Jane, Alex**, *Gazes into You,* Createspace, 2017. Mr. and Mr. Detective #1 of 2. (MM Mystery) Ex-detective John Right likes to watch. There's no harm in it. The latest object of his obsession–a twenty-something stranger who chains his bike outside John's office–doesn't feel the weight of John's eyes on him, doesn't know about the secret recordings or what John does with them in the dead of night. Except when the kid disappears, John finds himself doing far more than just watching. –book 2 is coming out in 2019 (MLM). 3/3

1368. **Jay, G.**, *Summer Spirit,* Createspace, 2013. Ryan Kinkaid #1 of 5. Ryan Kinkaid, a successful gay Manhattan antique dealer has had it with life in New York City, especially his random love life. Ryan has what most New Yorker's want – his own successful business, and a mortgage-free brownstone on West 71st Street. However, at age forty-one he discovers he is lacking one very important thing in his life ... a meaningful and loving relationship. With summer just around the corner, the approaching heat and his restlessness are reasons for his escape from the city. A four-month rental in historic and picturesque Portsmouth, New Hampshire, with his best friend Lauren was the answer. The stark contrast of the past collides with the present in this tale of lost and betrayed love, and irrational and undying prejudice. 3/3

1369. **Jay, G.**, *Autumn Reveal*, Createspace, 2013. Ryan Kinkaid #2 of 5. (MM Mystery) Gay antique dealer, Ryan Kinkaid, as he settles into his new life with his partner, Ty, in Portsmouth, New Hampshire. Purchasing a desk at a local estate sale, Ryan gets more with his purchase than just another antique to sell in his new shop. He finds an old diary sealed in a hidden drawer. A diary that has blood stains on the page of the last written entry. 3/3

1370. **Jay, G.**, *Winter Justice*, Createspace, 2013. Ryan Kinkaid #3 of 5. (MM Mystery) For gay antique dealer, Ryan Kinkaid, winter starts off much colder than the low temperatures affecting his happy new life with Ty in Portsmouth, New Hampshire. Ryan can't remain idle when his best friend, Jason Norkowski, is a suspect in the death of Grumman Myers, a wealthy art collector and philanthropist. 3/3

1371. **Jay, G.**, *Spring Rite*, Createspace, 2014. Ryan Kinkaid #4 of 5. (MM Mystery) A peaceful Sunday morning is transformed for gay antique dealer, Ryan Kinkaid, when he reads a report in the local newspaper of a teenage boy found dead in a field a few miles away from the Portsmouth, New Hampshire home where he lives with his partner, Ty. It's not where the body was found that concerns Ryan. It was the boy's mother's fear that her son had been killed by a bully. 3/3

1372. **Jay, G.**, *An Unwanted Request*, Createspace, 2015. Ryan Kinkaid #5 of 5. (MM Mystery) Ryan Kinkaid and his husband, Timothy York, witness a crime that others are quick to write off as an accident. Not surprisingly, Ryan can't dismiss it so easily, even though the victim is someone he despises. 3/3

1373. **Jay, Victor (Victor J. Banis)**, *Homo Farm*, Brandon House, 1968. (Pulp) "Midwest farmhand Ingemar (Mar) Olsen, 26, the narrator, questions whether Kenny Baler, 23, who returns to the farm after being gone for five years, really is Kenny (Gunn)." 3/3

1374. **Jeffers, H. Paul**, *Rubout at the Onyx*, Ticknor and Fields, 1981. Harry MacNeil #1 of 3. (Hard Boiled) LaGuardia is the mayor of New York City, Paul Whiteman is the King of Jazz, and, up in his apartment on Riverside Drive, George Gershwin is asking his friends in to hear his newest composition, "Summertime". On Fifty-second Street is the Onyx Club, a famous jazz club owned by ex-bootlegger Joe Helbock. Harry MacNeil, an ex-cop now working as a private eye, lives and works above the Onyx. But he hadn't been in the club on the New Year's Eve when, while Art Tatum was playing the piano, two of Owney Madden's boys came into the club and gunned down a two-bit mobster named Joey Seldes. –the man killed was bisexual (MM). 1/3

1375. **Jeffers, H. Paul,** *Portrait in Murder and Gay Colors,* Knights, 1985. (Police Procedural) "New York police detective Sheldon Lyman, 50s, because he cannot self-identify as gay, becomes destructively obsessed with a gay man (Gunn)." 3/3

1376. **Jeffries, William,** *Mr. Queen,* Greenleaf, 1966. (Pulp) "College student Royall Swan, 18, does not try too hard to discover who is attempting to kill him and the whole ordeal turns out to be a preparation for his role in his father's homophile organization L. A. V. E. N. D. E. R (Gunn)." 3/3

1377. **Jensen, Michael,** *Frontiers,* Pocket, 1999. Savage Land #1 of 2. (Historical) The year is 1797. John Chapman, an impulsive young man and a sexual outlaw, forsaken in the bitter winter of the Allegheny Plateau, clings to his one tenuous dream: to claim a future in the Western outpost. Unarmed and near death, Chapman is on the brink of giving up when an unexpected rescue changes his course in life forever, and he discovers the true meaning of survival. The mysterious savior is Daniel McQuay, a loner whose overpowering bond with Chapman is as shifting as a shadow, as dark as the prairie tale he spins for the impressionable young man. For Chapman, McQuay's story of a deranged killer clings to his transient soul like a nightmare, tracking him further south and into the safe haven of a gentle Indian woman named Gwennie. –renamed and re-edited as *Man and Beast* published by Buddha Kitty in 2016 as an e-book (MLM). 3/3

1378. **Jensen, Michael,** *Firelands,* Alyson, 2004. Savage Land #2 of 2. (Historical) The winter of 1799 is falling fast on the small Ohio Territory settlement of Hugh's Lick. Food is scarce, and relations with the Delaware tribe are strained; but things are about to get much worse. In the midst of a storm, frontiersman Cole Seavey is attacked by a creature that is neither man nor beast but something burst forth from the bowels of hell and reeking of the grave. –renamed and re-edited as *Man and Monster* by Buddha Kitty in 2017 as an e-book (MLM). 3/3

1379. **Jillette, Penn,** *Sock,* St. Martin's, 2004. (Police Procedural) Twisting the buddy cop story upside down and inside out, Penn Jillette has created the most distinctive narrator to come along in fiction in many years: a sock monkey called Dickie. The sock monkey belongs to a New York City police diver who discovers the body of an old lover in the murky waters of the Hudson River and sets off with her best friend to find her killer. The story of their quest swerves and veers, takes off into philosophical riffs, occasionally stops to tell a side story, and references a treasure trove of 1970's and 1980's pop culture. –gay friend assists the main character (MM). 2/3

1380. **Johnson, Connie,** *Confessions of a Corporate Spy,* Surey, 1989. (Pulp) "Texas-based unnamed undercover investigator, the narrator, declares that his mission is to stop corporate leaks in a Memphis department store is a success but recounts only his sexual activities –reprinted as *Spy Stud* by Star in 1996 (Gunn)." 3/3

1381. **Johnson, Steve,** *Final Atonement,* Onyx, 1992. Doug Orlando #1 of 2. (Police Procedural) Ruff, weary, gay Brooklyn Homicide cop Doug Orlando is facing his most shocking case: Rabbi Avraham Rabowitz lay in a pool of his own blood, a prayer shawl stuffed down his throat, and his beard shaved off. The question for Detective Orlando is who hated the right-wing religious sect leader-Rabowitz whom had been the open enemy of blacks, gays, pro-choice women, and even fellow Jews enough to kill him. 3/3

1382. **Johnson, Steve,** *False Confessions,* Signet, 1993. Doug Orlando #2 of 2. (Police Procedural) No one needed this: a serial killer who left his victims naked but for dozens of long, murderous needles. Doug Orlando, the New York cop who had the guts to come out of the closet, was desperately trying to crack the case when another murder came his way. A priest had been found before his altar, bludgeoned with a bat. Were the two cases connected? Orlando's search led him through the underside of modern, urban Catholicism to New York's S & M playgrounds, and a tattoo parlor that left its own unique mark on its patrons. But the closer Orlando got to the truth, the more he came face-to-face with something far more dangerous: a cop with murder in his soul. 3/3

1383. **Johnson, Steve,** *Raising Kane,* Clutching Hands, 2011. (YA Amateur Sleuth) When 16-year-old Spence Williams goes to live with his grandparents in a small farming town, the last thing he expects to find is a world of fear, grave robbing and murder. 3/3

1384. **Johnson, Steve,** *Yellow Canary,* Clutching Hands, 2012. LA after Midnight #1 of 4. (Court Drama) Los Angeles, 1956. It's a dangerous time to be gay. Nobody knows that better than closeted prosecutor Paul Winters, the rising star in the L.A. District Attorney's office. But when the police insist a gay man arrested for soliciting committed suicide in custody–and Paul knows it was murder–he risks everything to uncover the truth. Thrown together with a strikingly handsome vice cop with a dark past, the two men race to expose a conspiracy at the highest levels of government that threatens to tear the city apart. 3/3

1385. **Johnson, Steve,** *The Black Cat,* Clutching Hands, 2014. LA after Midnight #2 of 4. (Court Drama) Los Angeles, 1966. Crusading prosecutor Paul Winters is on the cusp of attaining his dream to become the next District Attorney of L.A. But a mysterious death and the troubled, dangerously handsome cop from his past, Jim Blake, may derail everything he has worked his whole life for. As the two men race to unravel a string of murders against the backdrop of racial strife and political turmoil in mid-sixties Los Angeles, they uncover a terrifying conspiracy that could destroy them both...and Paul is forced to choose between pursuing his dreams...and justice. 3/3

1386. **Johnson, Steve,** *The Blue Parrot,* Clutching Hands, 2016. LA after Midnight #3 of 4. (Court Drama) Los Angeles, 1975. Crusading attorney Paul Winters is drawn into a web of fear and peril when Jim Blake, the dangerously handsome cop from his past, is framed for murder. As they follow clues left by the killer, their search leads them through the freewheeling world of sex and drugs and gay bathhouses in mid-seventies Los Angeles, and into the dark and chilling history of psychiatric abuse in California's most notorious state mental hospital. And Paul is forced to choose between two very different men...and face the truth that he loves them both. –the fourth book in the quartet has not yet been published (MLM). 3/3

1387. **Jones, Dick,** *Man Eater,* F. S., 1971. (Pulp) Jake Gold knows who he is: He's gay, American and a Vietnam-war veteran with PTSD who lost the love of his life in country. Jake subsequently hitched his star to the multinational United Nations Crime Control Commission, but nothing prepared him for his search for the "man eater," a killer cruising Europe for homosexual men who don't meet his exacting standards of masculinity in this gripping crime thriller that's as relevant as today's war on terror. –republished by 120 Days in 2017 (MLM). 3/3

1388. **Jones, John,** *When Divas get Ready,* EbonyWorld, 2017. (Psychological) Set in Chicago in 1994, a mysterious Black gay man is murdered in the parking lot of a crowded nightclub. The investigation into his death uncovers a twisted labyrinth of secrets far more devastating than the identity of those responsible for his death. A community ruptures around everybody and the ghost of a serial killer haunts them all. A Black gay detective. His Partner. His Lover. The Comedian. The Boyfriend. The Retired Female Illusionist. The Manservant. The Heiress. The Lawyer. The Cook. The Magnate. The Witness. The Cops. A divided gay community. A segregated city. They all had something to hide. Not all of them were secrets. –e-book only (MLM). 3/3

1389. **Jordan, R. T.,** *Remains to be Scene,* Kensington, 2007. Polly Pepper #1 of 4. (Cozy) Polly Pepper is a living legend, straight from television's golden age, complete with the star on Hollywood's Walk of Fame. But these days, it seems her only time in the spotlight is accepting some yes-your-career-is-over Lifetime Achievement Award. Really, would it kill someone to offer her a decent role? –son of the main character is gay and assists his mother in solving the crime (MLM). 2/3

1390. **Jordan, R. T.,** *Final Curtain,* Kensington, 2008. Polly Pepper #2 of 4. (Cozy) Polly Pepper, the legendary superstar of television's golden age, is finally back in the entertainment headlines. She's landed the title role in a new production of the musical Mame, and though it's off-off-off-off Broadway (Glendale, California, actually), Polly's bank account–and her ego–need the job. There's one minor detour, though: on the second day of rehearsals, wunderkind director Karen Richards turns up dead. –Tim Pepper assists his mother again in this cozy mystery (MLM). 2/3

1391. **Jordan, R. T.,** *A Talent for Murder,* Kensington, 2009. Polly Pepper #3 of 4. (Cozy) Polly Pepper's been hired to be the "nice" judge on "I'll Do Anything to Become Famous," the latest reality T.V. show to hit the airwaves, in which contestants have to prove that they'll go for another's jugular in order to get their names in the headlines. But someone takes the show's theme literally when Thane Cornwall, the relentlessly critical and universally hated British judge on the panel, is found dead with a ten-inch knife in his back... 2/3

1392. **Jordan, R. T.,** *Set Sail for Murder,* Kensington, 2010. Polly Pepper #4 of 4. (Cozy) The iconic Polly Pepper, musical comedy superstar of yesteryear, is experiencing a bit of a professional dry spell– she can barely keep her bank account afloat, let alone her career. So, when the nefarious Laura Crawford, scene-stealing former cast mate and perpetual diva, proposes a Polly Pepper Playhouse reunion cruise, Polly is on board, full-steam ahead. But she soon realizes that Hollywood on the high-seas will be nothing short of a shipwreck... Unfortunately, Laura is found dead the next morning, slain by Season Six of "The Polly Pepper Playhouse" box set–the collectors DVD ruthlessly sharpened to a razor's edge. –novella going to be released focusing on the gay son, Tim Pepper (MLM). 2/3

1393. **Junot, Dan,** *The Case of "Weehawken's Haunted House,"* Createspace, 2016. Kaspers of Denning Place #1 of 2. (Journalism) On

July 6th, 1989, Isaac Ruhdel, an eccentric, recluse, multi-millionaire, was reportedly killed by an aberrant lightning bolt during a Nor'easter. He willed all his liquid assets and properties to a robustly handsome, young chemist, named Chris A. Laude. Well, all but one property–Ruhdel's home–a mansion at 55 King Street, which, for the next ten years, went unclaimed, and fell into such a state of disrepair, that the Weehawken City Council moved to have the dwelling demolished. During the demolition, 25 skeletons–all of young men between the ages of 12 and 18–were discovered. According to the coroner, Doctor C. Malcolm Gibbs, some had been there only a few months; others for the better part of a decade. 3/3

1394. **Junot, Dan,** *The Case of the Opera Season Serial Killer,* Createspace, 2017. Kaspers of Denning Place #2 of 2. (Journalism) Only days before her opening night performance of Puccini's Suor Angelica at the Weehawken Grand Opera House, soprano Katherine Hanson, scheduled to sing the title role, is found dead in her apartment. While the circumstances of her death are suspicious, no one realizes that hers will be the first in a serious of murders–each corresponding to the scheduled operas of the current season. 3/3

K

1395. **Karjel, Robert,** *The Swede,* Harper, 2015. Ernst Grip #1 of 2. (Espionage/Crime Drama) A Swedish security agent is summoned to interrogate a terror suspect held by the FBI –but the prisoner isn't the only one with something to hide. 3/3

1396. **Karjel, Robert,** *After the Monsoon,* Harper, 2018. Ernst Grip #2 of 2. (Police Procedural) A Swedish army lieutenant drops dead on a shooting range in the desert. Was it an unfortunate accident–or something more nefarious? Ernst Grip, an agent of the Swedish security police, is sent to the Horn of Africa to find out. Once he's on the ground, however, he quickly discovers he's on his own. No one wants him snooping around–especially not the U.S. Embassy's CIA station. Which is no surprise, given that military transport planes are leaving from the base carrying untraceable pallets loaded with cash. 3/3

1397. **Karol, Michael,** *Kiss Me, Kill Me,* Writer's Club, 2003. (Paranormal Police Procedural) New York writer Ray Abreu could deal with getting fired from his job. He could even accept the fact that after looking longer than he was willing to admit, he still hadn't found Mr. Right. 3/3

1398. **Kasey, Lissa,** *Model Citizen,* Dreamspinner, 2015. Haven #1 of 4. (MM Hard Boiled) Oliver "Ollie" Petroskovic's life as an international supermodel was heading in the right direction. He worked part-time for his brother at his detective agency–Petroskovic Haven Investigations–and had just bought his dream house. But all that changed when he found his brother dead, a victim of PTSD-induced suicide. 3/3

1399. **Kaey, Lissa,** *Model Bodyguard,* Dreamspinner, 2016. Haven #2 of 4. (MM Hard Boiled) Things are going well for androgynous model Ollie Petroskovic, ex-Marine Kade Alme, and their business, Haven Investigations, until rock star Jacob Elias shows up in need of their services... and trouble follows. 3/3

1400. **Kasey, Lissa,** *Model Investigator,* Dreamspinner, 2016. Haven #3 of 4. (MM Hard Boiled) With his lover, Kade, missing, androgynous former model turned private investigator Ollie Petroskovic is ready to kick some ass to bring him home. 3/3

1401. **Kasey, Lissa,** *Model Exposure,* Dreamspinner, 2017. Haven #4 of

4. (MM Hard Boiled) After being rescued by Ollie, Kade continues to suffer the aftermath of his ordeal, both physically and psychologically. Not knowing how else to clear his head, he pours his energy into Ollie–the love of his life–and Haven Investigations, but neither Ollie nor Kade can continue to ignore what they learned from their last case: Ollie's brother, Nathan, might have betrayed Kade. 3/3

1402. **Kavanagh, Dan (Julian Barnes b. 1946),** *Duffy,* Cape, 1980. Duffy #1 of 4. (Hard Boiled) Things aren't going so well for Brian McKechnie. His wife was attacked in their home, his cat was brutally killed and now a man with a suspiciously erratic accent is blackmailing him. When the police fail spectacularly at finding out who's after him, McKechnie engages the services of London's most unusual private eye. 3/3

1403. **Kavanagh, Dan,** *Fiddle City,* Cape, 1981. Duffy #2 of 4. (Hard Boiled) Duffy explores shading dealings at London's Heathrow Airport. 3/3

1404. **Kavanagh, Dan,** *Putting the Boot In,* Cape, 1985. Duffy #3 of 4. (Hard Boiled) Duffy investigates the troubled world of England's Third Division football while also facing questions of his possible encounter with AIDS. 3/3

1405. **Kavanagh, Dan,** *Going to the Dogs,* Viking, 1987. Duffy #4 of 4. (Hard Boiled) Duffy finds himself investigating a mysterious death in a country mansion. 3/3

1406. **Kavanagh, Maggie,** *Double Indemnity,* Dreamspinner, 2015. Stonebridge #1 of 3. (MM Journalism) Sam Flynn dreamed of being a journalist until a car accident killed his parents and put his brother into a long-term coma. Now Sam spends his days as a landscaper toiling in the New England sun and his nights drunk in bed with the closest warm body. In his limited spare time, he writes about Stonebridge's local crime and politics on his blog "Under the Bridge." 3/3

1407. **Kavanagh, Maggie,** *Inner Sanctum,* Dreamspinner, 2015. Stonebridge #2 of 3. (MM Journalism) Six months into a relationship, things have heated up between political blogger Sam Flynn and FBI Special Agent Nathan Walker. Though Sam is happy with Nathan and proud of his own sobriety, he's anxious about what their future holds. Things are heating up in Stonebridge, Connecticut, as a series of deadly fires puts the community on edge and eventually threatens Sam's comatose brother. As Halloween approaches, fears rise that the arsonist will strike again. 3/3

1408. **Kavanagh, Maggie,** *Blind Spot,* Dreamspinner, 2016. Stonebridge #3 of 3. (MM Journalism) Living together is bliss for Sam Flynn and

Nathan Walker, but things never stay quiet for long in Stonebridge. On the night of Sam's twenty-ninth birthday, the much-hated mayor of Stonebridge is found dead at his home. Sam suspects foul play, but just as he starts investigating the list of possible culprits, Nathan gets word of a new undercover assignment–one that includes a mysterious, sexy new partner. Though Sam struggles to trust Nathan and control his jealousy during Nathan's absence, the stress makes a return to the bottle seem not only tempting, but inevitable–especially when Nathan starts avoiding his calls. 3/3

1409. **Kaye, H. R.**, *Two Gay Sleuths*, Brandon House, 1969. (Pulp) "Paris amateur sleuths C. Chaudlance and Edgar July, an American, set in 1895, a bizarre transformation of Poe's "murders in the Rue Morgue" (Gunn)." 3/3

1410. **Keating, Henry (H. R. F. 1926-2011)**, *Murder by Death*, Warner, 1976. (Hard Boiled) Various "famous sleuths" (or their somewhat thinly disguised copies) are invited by a mysterious millionaire to stay at his house and solve a who-dun-it, with the winner getting millions. –one of the detectives is in a relationship with his male assistant (MLM). 2/3

1411. **Keegan, Mel**, *Ice, Wind, and Fire*, GMP, 1990. (Journalism) Alex Connor and Greg Farris are investigative journalists on holiday in Jamaica for a romantic break. Their tranquility is shattered by their discovery of a skeleton in the wreck of a light aircraft. From then on, this confident and raunchy thriller never lets up, combining car chases, drug smuggling, hurricanes and plenty of sex. 3/3

1412. **Keegan, Mel**, *Storm Tide*, GMP, 1996. (Thriller) A troubled relationship, a drug smuggling gang, a lucky escape, begin an action-packed adventure. 3/3

1413. **Keegan, Mel**, *Death's Head*, GMP, 1991. NARC #1 of 5. (Science Fiction) On the high-tech worlds of the 23rd century, the lethal designer drug Angel has become an epidemic disease. Kevin Jarrat and Jerry Stone are joint captains in the paramilitary NARC force sent in to combat the Death's Head drug syndicate that controls the vast spaceport of Chell. Under the NARC code of non-involvement, each of the two friends hides his deeper desire for the other. When Stone is kidnapped and forced onto Angel, Jarrat's love for him is his only chance of survival, but the price is that their minds remain permanently linked. 3/3

1414. **Keegan, Mel**, *Equinox*, Dreamcraft, 1993. NARC #2 of 5. (Science Fiction) Angel – a lethal synthetic drug so pervasive and deadly, it has built empires and torn down worlds. 3/3

1415. **Keegan, Mel**, *Scorpio*, Dreamcraft, 2004. NARC #3 of 5. (Science Fiction) A super-city is at war with itself - and NARC is in the crossfire. In the colony of Aurora, the city of Thule is rife with Angel. Tactical has accumulated vast evidence on a syndicate, Scorpio. Col. Janssen just buried the officers who attempted to investigate - NARC's time has come. Young Marcus Brand has been in cryogen since early in the war. Now 80, his senator father is eager for Harry to perform his healing miracles on Marc. The tank must be shipped to NARC's labs, but it's tampered with and Jarrat and Stone realize the truth. Someone tried to murder Marc - to guard ancient secrets that doom Scorpio? The investigation takes Jarrat and Stone into cities where the street is a warzone ... but the seeds of rot lie far away, in surprising places. 3/3

1416. **Keegan, Mel,** *Stopover,* Createspace, 2004. NARC #3.5 of 5. (Science Fiction) Downtime becomes an explosive excursion into an industrial hell-zone. With Scorpio shut down, Kevin Jarrat and Jerry Stone are on furlough, headed for a resort in Rethan's tropics. But when the clipper detours to the halfway station of Sheckley for repairs, the vacation dissolves into unexpected, unpredictable hazard. Stone is fascinated to see the 'gas can with lights' where Jarrat spent his youth, but the tour turns deadly when they run into Scorpio escapees who recognize Jarrat, and the NARC captains find themselves on a flight right into Hades. Cut off from the carrier, backup and weapons, they're surviving on their wits; furlough looks like an impossible fantasy. 3/3

1417. **Keegan, Mel,** *Aphelion,* Dreamcraft, 2007. NARC #4 of 5. (Science Fiction) All roads lead to the homeworlds, to the timeless cities of ancient worlds - dark, corrupt. For the outsider - stranger, colonial, mutoid - it's alien and dangerous. For the 'Earther' headed back after many years, it's not what you expected, nor where you want to be. Chicago, Marsport, Sequoia ... the skycities of the Jupiter system are the new worlds on the old high frontier, new battlefields where Death wears the same old face. Aerosports, Angelwar - politics gone mad - the launch of a supercarrier - the death of a friend. Nothing is as it seems; enemies and allies trade places. Trust only those you know, believe only what you see. 3/3

1418. **Keegan, Mel,** *Endgame Omnibus: Scimitar, Basilisk, and Endgame,* Dreamcast, 2018. NARC #5 of 5. (Science Fiction) *SCIMITAR (NARC #5)* After NARC destroyed DEATH'S HEAD Jarrat and Stone did not expect to return to the colony of Rethan. Chance took them back in STOPOVER, when they were lucky to survive a lethal brush with elements of Death's Head which had evaded the syndicate war. Tactical Colonel Pete Stacy knew full well, at least one key player from Death's Head remained at liberty. BASILISK (NARC #6) Straddling the frontier, the hellish system belonging to an industrial corporation, the Montserrat Lode, is harassed by marauders from the wilderness beyond. Freespacers prey on Montserrat while the system is a perilous chaos better known as Tartarus. ENDGAME (NARC #7) Drawing every thread together from across the whole series, ENDGAME weaves a tapestry from Darwin's World to Aurora. Jarrat and Stone stand at the crux of events which will be written into history. 3/3

1419. **Keegan, Mel,** *Ground Zero,* Dreamcraft, 2009. (Science Fiction) 2048: the city of Adelaide – the capital of South Australia – has grown, developed, changed. The population has doubled, and the city's livelihood is high technology. A new university has grown up since the Twenties – Franklin University, in the hills above the city. It's the home to Doctor Robert Strachan's Paranormal Studies department, where Lee Ronson and Brendan Scott head the data analysis team. They're the best in a difficult business, and they'll be tested to their limits in an assignment handed to Strachan by Metro's most senior criminologist, DCS Maggie Jarmin. It's winter when the city suffers a series of bizarre murders, robberies at high-tech labs – and a virus which sprang from nowhere. 3/3

1420. **Keehnen, Owen,** *Doorway unto Darkness,* Dancing Moon Press, 2012. (Psychological Horror) A grisly tale of possession, murder, and vengeance that transcends time in an ultimate tale of identity theft. 3/3

1421. **Keehnen, Owen,** *Love Underground,* OutTales, 2017. (Historical) A discovered diary... handsome forty-something retail worker Joseph meets young physical culture aficionado Clint at a Chicago department store in 1962. Both men soon discover they are living at the Lawson YMCA. Despite the mutual attraction, each is hesitant to make the first move. Though love eventually blooms, their story is not one of happily ever after. The legal and social consequences of homosexuality during the Cold War era are brutal, but the stakes for these two men are even higher. Soon after Joseph meets Clint's powerful parents, a series of unsettling events begin to unfold. Desperate and afraid, the couple flees the YMCA and Chicago. Going underground they traverse the country, falling deeper in love while eluding an unknown enemy intent on their capture and return. 3/3

1422. **Keith, W.,** *Meat Force,* Eros, 1974. (Pulp) "Chicago police detective Glen Murray, 40s, divorced, and Raymond (Ray) Jones, 30s, a divorced father, work together (Gunn)." 3/3

1423. **Kelleher, Dharma,** *Chaser,* Pariah, 2017. Jinx Ballou #1 of 2. (Hardboiled) When Holly Schwartz, a children's charity poster girl, jumps bail after being charged with her mother's murder, Jinx Ballou is hired to return the young fugitive to custody after a veteran bounty hunter fails to locate her. –Jinx is a transgender female and she has a gay brother as well (MLM). 3/3

1424. **Kelleher, Dharma,** *Extreme Prejudice,* Pariah, 2018. Jinx Ballou #2 of 2. (Hardboiled) Bounty hunter Jinx Ballou is hot on the heels of an accused murderer. Her investigation reveals her fugitive is involved with White Nation, a militant organization stoking the fires of prejudice and violence in Phoenix, Arizona. 3/3

1425. **Kellerman, Jonathan,** *When the Bough Breaks,* New York: Atheneum, 1985/*Shrunken Heads,* London: Macmillan, 1985. Alex Delaware #1 of 33. (Psychological/Police Procedural) Dr. Morton Handler practiced a strange brand of psychiatry. Among his specialties were fraud, extortion, and sexual manipulation. Handler paid for his sins when he was brutally murdered in his luxurious Pacific Palisades apartment. –in the Alex Delaware series, Delaware's best friend Detective Milo Sturgis, who assists Delaware in solving the crimes, is gay (MLM). 2/3

1426. **Kellerman, Jonathan,** *Blood Test,* Atheneum, 1986. Alex Delaware #2 of 33. (Psychological/Police Procedural) When the parents of deathly ill five-year-old Woody Swope vanish with their child, psychologist Dr. Alex Delaware and his friend, homicide detective Milo Sturgis, begin an investigation into their disappearance. Their search, however, leads them into an amoral underworld, where drugs, dreams, and sex are all for sale and where fantasies are fulfilled – even at the cost of a young boy's life. 2/3

1427. **Kellerman, Jonathan,** *Over the Edge,* Atheneum, 1987. Alex Delaware #3 of 33. (Psychological/Police Procedural) When the phone rings in the middle of the night, child psychologist Alex Delaware does not hesitate. Driving through the dream-lit San Fernando Valley, Alex rushes to Jamey Cadmus, the patient he had failed five years before–and who now calls with a bizarre cry for help. But by the time Alex reaches Canyon Oaks Psychiatric Hospital, Jamey is gone, surfacing a day later in the hands of the police, who believe Jamey is the infamous Lavender Slasher, a psychotic serial killer. 2/3

1428. **Kellerman, Jonathan,** *Silent Partner,* Bantam, 1989. Alex Delaware #4 of 33. (Psychological/Police Procedural) At a party for a controversial Los Angeles sex therapist, Alex encounters a face from his own past–Sharon Ransom, an exquisite, alluring lover who left him abruptly more than a decade earlier. Sharon now hints that he desperately needs help, but Alex evades her. The next day she is dead, an apparent suicide. Driven by guilt and sadness, Alex plunges into the maze of Sharon's life–a journey that will take him through the pleasure palaces of California's ultra-rich, into the dark closets of a family's disturbing past, and finally into the alleyways of the mind, where childhood terrors still hold sway. 2/3

1429. **Kellerman, Jonathan,** *Time Bomb,* Bantam, 1990. Alex Delaware #5 of 33. (Psychological/Police Procedural) By the time psychologist Dr. Alex Delaware reached the school the damage was done: A sniper had opened fire on a crowded playground but was gunned down before any children were hurt. 2/3

1430. **Kellerman, Jonathan,** *Private Eyes,* Warner, 1991. Alex Delaware #6 of 33. (Psychological/Police Procedural) It's been 11 years since seven-year-old Melissa Dickinson found help in therapy with Alex Delaware. Now the young heiress desperately calls for help once more. Only this time it looks like her deepest childhood nightmare is coming true. 2/3

1431. **Kellerman, Jonathan,** *Devil's Waltz,* Little Brown, 1992. Alex Delaware #7 of 33. (Psychological/Police Procedural) The doctors call it Munchausen by proxy, the terrifying disease that causes parents to induce illness in their own children. Now, in his most frightening case, Dr. Alex Delaware may have to prove that a child's own mother or father is making her sick. 2/3

1432. **Kellerman, Jonathan,** *Bad Love,* Little Brown, 1993. Alex Delaware #8 of 33. (Psychological/Police Procedural) It came in a plain brown wrapper, no return address - an audiocassette recording of a horrifying, soul-lacerating scream, followed by the sound of a childlike voice delivering the enigmatic and haunting message: "Bad love. Bad love. Don't give me the bad love..." For Alex Delaware, the chant, repeated over and over like a twisted nursery rhyme, is the first intimation that he is about to enter a living nightmare. Others soon follow: disquieting laughter echoing over a phone line that suddenly goes dead, a chilling trespass outside his home in the middle of the night, a sickening act of vandalism. He has become the target of a carefully orchestrated campaign of vague threats and intimidation rapidly building to a crescendo as harassment turns to terror, mischief to madness. 2/3

1433. **Kellerman, Jonathan,** *Self-Defense,* Little Brown, 1996. Alex Delaware #9 of 33. (Psychological/Police Procedural) A session of hypnotic regression is the start of a journey to frightening truth, as Alex finds a link between a young woman's recurring dream, her famous, reclusive father–and the threat of murder. 2/3

1434. **Kellerman, Jonathan,** *The Web,* Bantam, 1995. Alex Delaware #10 of 33. (Psychological/Police Procedural) Dr. Woodrew Moreland, a respected scientist, has invited Alex Delaware, psychologist/detective, to his home on a tiny Pacific island to help him organize his papers for publication. It's a light workload leaving plenty of time for Alex and his girlfriend, Robin, to relax. –Milo plays a very minor role (MLM). 1/3

1435. **Kellerman, Jonathan,** *The Clinic,* Little Brown, 1996. Alex Delaware #11 of 33. (Psychological/Police Procedural) Upon his return to Los Angeles from a harrowing adventure in the South Pacific, Alex is called upon by his friend Milo Sturgis to help solve the murder of a celebrity author. 2/3

1436. **Kellerman, Jonathan,** *Survival of the Fittest,* Bantam, 1997. Alex Delaware #12 of 33. (Psychological/Police Procedural) The daughter of a diplomat disappears on a school field trip–lured into the Santa Monica mountains and killed in cold blood. Her father denies the possibility of a political motive. There are no signs of struggle, no evidence of sexual assault, leaving psychologist Alex Delaware and his friend LAPD homicide detective Milo Sturgis to pose the disturbing question: Why? 2/3

1437. **Kellerman, Jonathan,** *Monster,* Random House, 1999. Alex Delaware #13 of 33. (Psychological/Police Procedural) A second-rate actor is found mutilated in a car trunk. Then a psychologist at a Los Angeles hospital for the criminally insane is murdered in a similar grisly fashion. Suddenly the incoherent ramblings of an inmate at the presumably secure institution begin to make chilling sense– they are, in fact, horrifying predictions. Yet how can a barely functional psychotic locked behind asylum walls possibly know such vivid details of crimes committed in the outside world? Drawn into a labyrinth of secrets, revenge, sex, and manipulation, Dr. Alex Delaware and Detective Milo Sturgis set out to unlock this enigma and put an end to the brutal killings– before the madman predicts their own demise.. 2/3

1438. **Kellerman, Jonathan,** *Dr. Death,* Random House, 2000. Alex Delaware #14 of 33. (Psychological/Police Procedural) A brutalized corpse discovered in a remote region of the Hollywood Hills plunges psychologist-detective Alex Delaware into a landscape of rage and madness as he struggles to solve this most baffling of homicides. 2/3

1439. **Kellerman, Jonathan,** *Flesh and Blood,* Random House 2001. Alex Delaware #15 of 33. (Psychological/Police Procedural) Psychologist Alex Delaware hasn't been in private practice for a long time, but when the mother of a former patient calls and asks for his help, he can't turn her down. He couldn't help Lauren Teague when she was alive, but something about his failure with the beautiful, sullen teenager who grew up to be a high-priced call girl won't let him walk away after her bullet-ridden body turns up in an L.A. dumpster. When she wasn't turning tricks, she was a straight-A student;

despite his detective pal Milo's demurral, Alex is convinced there's a connection between Lauren's death and another beautiful UCLA psych major who disappeared a year earlier. 2/3

1440. **Kellerman, Jonathan,** *The Murder Book,* Ballantine, 2002. Alex Delaware #16 of 33. (Psychological/Police Procedural) L.A. psychologist-detective Alex Delaware confronts a long-unsolved murder of unspeakable brutality – an ice-cold case whose resolution threatens his survival, and that of longtime friend, homicide detective, Milo Sturgis. 2/3

1441. **Kellerman, Jonathan,** *A Cold Heart,* Ballantine, 2003. Alex Delaware #17 of 33. (Psychological/Police Procedural) LAPD homicide detective Milo Sturgis summons his friend, psychologist-sleuth Alex Delaware, to a trendy gallery where a promising young artist has been brutally garroted on the night of her first major showing. The details of the murder scene immediately suggest to Alex not an impulsive crime of passion, but the meticulous and taunting modus operandi of a serial killer. –Milo plays a minor role (MLM). 1/3

1442. **Kellerman, Jonathan,** *Therapy,* Ballantine, 2004. Alex Delaware #18 of 33. (Psychological/Police Procedural) "Been a while since I had me a nice little whodunit," homicide detective Milo Sturgis tells Alex Delaware. But there's definitely nothing nice about the brutal tableau behind the yellow crime-scene tape. On a lonely lover's lane in the hills of Los Angeles, a young couple lies murdered in a car. Each bears a single gunshot wound to the head. The female victim has also been impaled by a metal spike. And that savage stroke of psychopathic fury tells Milo this case will call for more than standard police procedure. As he explains to Delaware, "Now we're veering into your territory." 2/3

1443. **Kellerman, Jonathan,** *Rage,* Ballantine, 2005. Alex Delaware #19 of 33. (Psychological/Police Procedural) Delaware and LAPD homicide detective Milo Sturgis revisit a horrifying crime from the past that has taken on shocking and deadly new dimensions. 2/3

1444. **Kellerman, Jonathan,** *Gone,* Ballantine, 2006. Alex Delaware #20 of 33. (Psychological/Police Procedural) It's a story tailor-made for the nightly news: Dylan Meserve and Michaela Brand, young lovers and fellow acting students, vanish on the way home from a rehearsal. Three days later, the two of them are found in the remote mountains of Malibu -battered and terrified after a harrowing ordeal at the hands of a sadistic abductor. The details of the nightmarish event are shocking and brutal: The couple was carjacked at gunpoint by a masked assailant and subjected to a horrific regimen of confinement, starvation and assault. 2/3

1445. **Kellerman, Jonathan,** *Obsession,* Ballantine, 2007. Alex Delaware #21 of 33. (Psychological/Police Procedural) Tanya Bigelow was a solemn little girl when Dr. Alex Delaware successfully treated her obsessive-compulsive symptoms. Now, at nineteen, she still seems older than her years–but her problems go beyond hyper-maturity. Patty Bigelow, Tanya's aunt and adoptive mother, has made a deathbed confession of murder and urged the young woman to seek Delaware's help. The doctor recalls Patty as a selfless E.R. nurse struggling to raise a child on her own–a woman seemingly incapable of the "terrible thing" she has admitted. But for Tanya's peace of mind, Delaware agrees to investigate, and he enlists LAPD detective Milo Sturgis in the search for the phantom victim of a crime that may never have occurred. 2/3

1446. **Kellerman, Jonathan,** *Compulsion,* Ballantine, 2008. Alex Delaware #22 of 33. (Psychological/Police Procedural) A tipsy young woman seeking aid on a desolate highway disappears into the inky black night. A retired schoolteacher is stabbed to death in broad daylight. Two women are butchered after closing time in a small-town beauty parlor. These and other bizarre acts of cruelty and psychopathology are linked only by the killer's use of luxury vehicles and a baffling lack of motive. The ultimate whodunits, these crimes demand the attention of LAPD detective Milo Sturgis and his collaborator on the crime beat, psychologist Alex Delaware. 2/3

1447. **Kellerman, Jonathan,** *Bones,* Ballantine, 2008. Alex Delaware #23 of 33. (Psychological/Police Procedural) The anonymous caller has an ominous tone and an unnerving message about something "real dead ... buried in your marsh." The eco-volunteer on the other end of the phone thinks it's a prank, but when a young woman's body turns up in L.A.'s Bird Marsh preserve no one's laughing. And when the bones of more victims surface, homicide detective Milo Sturgis realizes the city's under siege to an insidious killer. Milo's first move: calling in psychologist Alex Delaware. 2/3

1448. **Kellerman, Jonathan,** *Evidence,* Ballantine, 2009. Alex Delaware #24 of 33. (Psychological/Police Procedural) In a half-built mansion in Los Angeles, a watchman stumbles onto the bodies of a young couple–murdered and left in a gruesome postmortem embrace. 2/3

1449. **Kellerman, Jonathan,** *Deception,* Ballantine, 2010. Alex Delaware #25 of 33. (Psychological/Police Procedural) Her name is Elise Freeman, and her chilling cry for help comes too late to save her. On a DVD found near her lifeless body, the emotionally and physically battered woman chronicles a long ordeal of abuse at the hands of three sadistic tormentors. But even more shocking is the revelation that the offenders, like their victim, are teachers at one of L.A.'s most prestigious prep schools. Homicide detective Milo Sturgis is assigned to probe the hallowed halls of Windsor Prep Academy, and if ever he could use Dr. Alex Delaware's psychological prowess, it's now. As the scandal-conscious elite close ranks around Windsor Prep, Alex and Milo push to expose the dirty secrets festering among society's manor-born. But while searching for predators among the privileged, Alex and Milo may be walking into a highly polished death trap. 2/3

1450. **Kellerman, Jonathan,** *Mystery,* Ballantine, 2011. Alex Delaware #26 of 33. (Psychological/Police Procedural) The closing of their favorite romantic rendezvous, the Fauborg Hotel in Beverly Hills, is a sad occasion for longtime patrons Alex Delaware and Robin Castagna. And gathering one last time with their fellow faithful habitués for cocktails in the gracious old venue makes for a bittersweet evening. But even more poignant is a striking young woman–alone and enigmatic among the revelers–waiting in vain in elegant attire and dark glasses that do nothing to conceal her melancholy. Alex can't help wondering what her story is, and whether she's connected to the silent, black-suited bodyguard lingering outside the hotel. 2/3

1451. **Kellerman, Jonathan,** *Victims,* Ballantine, 2012. Alex Delaware #27 of 33. (Psychological/Police Procedural) Unraveling the madness behind L.A.'s most baffling and brutal homicides is what sleuthing psychologist Alex Delaware does best. Not since Jack the Ripper terrorized the London slums has there been such a gruesome crime scene. By all accounts, acid-tongued Vita Berlin hadn't a friend in the world, but whom did she cross so badly as to end up arranged in such a grotesque tableau? One look at her apartment-turned–charnel house prompts hard-bitten LAPD detective Milo Sturgis to summon his go-to expert in hunting homicidal maniacs, Alex Delaware. But despite his finely-honed skills, even Alex is stymied when more slayings occur in the same ghastly fashion ... yet with no apparent connection among the victims. And the only clue left behind–a blank page bearing a question mark–seems to be both a menacing taunt and a cry for help from a killer baffled by his own lethal urges. 2/3

1452. **Kellerman, Jonathan,** *Guilt,* Ballantine, 2013. Alex Delaware #28 of 33. (Psychological/Police Procedural) In an upscale L.A. neighborhood, a backyard renovation unearths an infant's body, buried sixty years ago. Soon thereafter, in a nearby park, another disturbingly bizarre discovery is made not far from the body of a young woman shot in the head. Helping LAPD homicide detective Milo

Sturgis to link these eerie incidents is brilliant psychologist Alex Delaware. But even the good doctor's vast experience with matters both clinical and criminal might not be enough to cut down to the bone of this chilling case. Backtracking six decades into the past stirs up tales of a beautiful nurse with a mystery lover, a handsome, wealthy doctor who seems too good to be true, and a hospital with a notorious reputation–all of them long gone, along with any records of a newborn, and destined for anonymity. But the specter of fame rears its head when the case unexpectedly twists in the direction of the highest echelons of celebrity privilege. Entering this sheltered world, Alex little imagines the macabre layer just below the surface–a decadent quagmire of unholy rituals and grisly sacrifice. 2/3

1453. **Kellerman, Jonathan,** *Killer,* Ballantine, 2014. Alex Delaware #29 of 33. (Psychological/Police Procedural) The City of Angels has more than its share of psychopaths, and no one recognizes that more acutely than the brilliant psychologist and police consultant Dr. Alex Delaware. Despite that, Constance Sykes, a sophisticated, successful physician, hardly seems like someone Alex needs to fear. Then, at the behest of the court, he becomes embroiled in a bizarre child custody dispute initiated by Connie against her sister and begins to realize that there is much about the siblings he has failed to comprehend. And when the court battle between the Sykes sisters erupts into cold, calculating murder and a rapidly growing number of victims, Alex knows he's been snared in a toxic web of pathology. 2/3

1454. **Kellerman, Jonathan,** *Motive,* Ballantine, 2015. Alex Delaware #30 of 33. (Psychological/Police Procedural) Even hundreds of closed cases to his credit can't keep LAPD police lieutenant Milo Sturgis from agonizing over the crimes that don't get solved - and the victims who go without justice. Victims like Katherine Hennepin, a young woman strangled and stabbed in her home. A single suspect with a solid alibi leads to a dead end - one even psychologist Alex Delaware's expert insight can't explain. The only thing to do is move on to the next murder case - because there is always a next one. 2/3

1455. **Kellerman, Jonathan,** *Breakdown,* Ballantine, 2016. Alex Delaware #31 of 33. (Psychological/Police Procedural) Psychologist sleuth Alex Delaware is surprised to get the call when well-known TV actress Zelda Chase turns up half-naked, half-mad in the LA's rural Westside. He has little connection to the starlet, save a psychiatric evaluation he performed on her adopted son several years ago, a child who has since vanished without a trace and whom Zelda refuses to talk about. When the actress turns up dead a few weeks later without a scratch on her, Delaware calls in police lieutenant Milo Sturgis to help him crack the case–or at least the wall of silence surrounding it. When the body of a second actress turns up with the same mysterious cause of death, Delaware and Sturgis start to wonder–is this a copycat case or a coincidence? When they uncover the death of another actress, a star from another era who vanished decades ago, never to be found, they realize they're facing one of their most baffling, mind-bending cases yet. 2/3

1456. **Kellerman, Jonathan,** *Heartbreak Hotel,* Ballantine, 2017. Alex Delaware #32 of 33. (Psychological/Police Procedural) At nearly one hundred years old, Thalia Mars is a far cry from the patients that child psychologist Alex Delaware normally treats. But the charming, witty woman convinces Alex to meet with her in a suite at the Aventura, a luxury hotel with a checkered history. 2/3

1457. **Kellerman, Jonathan,** *Night Moves,* Ballantine, 2018. Alex Delaware #33 of 33. (Psychological/Police Procedural) A brilliant criminal psychologist, Alex works with the police to help solve the most complex of crimes in Los Angeles, city of illusions, glamour and infamy. –#34 of the Alex Delaware series, *The Wedding Guest,* to be published by Ballantine in 2019 (MLM). 2/3

1458. **Kellerman, Jonathan,** *True Detectives,* Ballantine, 2009. (Police Procedural/Hard Boiled) Moses Reed and Aaron Fox have the same mother; their respective fathers were cops, friends, and partners. And despite their shared calling, their turbulent family history has set them at odds. Moses is a no-frills LAPD detective; Aaron is a smooth-talking private eye. Usually they go their separate ways, but the disappearance of straight-A student Caitlin Frostig isn't usual. Reluctantly tag-teaming to crack a cold case that won't die, Moses and Aaron descend into the sinister underside of the City of Angels. –Milo Sturgis appears briefly (MLM). 1/3

1459. **Kelly, Daniel W.,** *Combustion,* Bold Stroke Books, 2012. Comfort Cove #1 of 4. (Erotic Fantasy) Burly bearded bear Deck Waxer is a private dick with an attraction to cases of the supernatural. He comes to the city as it is transforming from a ghetto into a gay mecca–and power struggles between the various sub-groups in the community are turning violent. Most horrific is the rash of gay men who are bursting into flames in broad daylight! 3/3

1460. **Kelly, Daniel W.,** *No Place for Little Ones,* Bold Stroke Books, 2013. Comfort Cove #2 of 4. (Erotic Fantasy) Steve, Deck, and friends expose Jude to all the fun and crazy sexual adventures Comfort Cove has to offer. But despite the happiness Jude is finding, he has a setback in his occult recovery and inadvertently releases something heinous that has been hidden away in the basement of the Overpass for years. Something that is hungry for flesh...and not in the good way. 3/3

1461. **Kelly, Daniel W.**, *Rise of the Thing Below,* Bold Stroke Books, 2014. Comfort Cove #3 of 4. (Erotic Fantasy) The boys and bears of Comfort Cove are counting the days until the opening of the sexually charged boardwalk attraction SandMen Strip. But before the naked fun in the sun can begin, the mutilated bodies of a few burly dockworkers wash up on the sand. 3/3

1462. **Kelly, Daniel W.**, *Wet Screams,* Createspace, 2015. Comfort Cove #4 of 4. (Erotic Fantasy) Jeff, an employee at their occult shop, has the ability to astral project. He begins to believe he is being drawn into the body of a vile beast at night–a monster that looks like a man just long enough to have sex with tricks...and then treat them to a fatal mauling. But there are no bodies to be found in the morning. Is Jeff just getting his astral and dream worlds mixed up? 3/3

1463. **Kelly, James,** *Music from Another Room,* Dorchester, 1980. (Crime Drama) Blackmail, violence and greed turn a Mexican fiesta into a murderous masquerade. –as I have not read this I am unsure of the gay content (MLM). ?/3

1464. **Kendrick, Edward,** *The Element Case,* Fireborn, 2015. Quint and Clay Art Crimes #1 of 5. (MM Police Procedural) Clay Richardson is a well-known artist who owns his own gallery. Quint Hawk, a police detective, makes contact with Clay when he sees a portrait Clay has painted in the window of the gallery–a portrait of a homeless young man who was murdered just days before. Unfortunately, Clay has no idea who the subject was. –e-book only (MLM). 3/3

1465. **Kendrick,Edward,** *It Takes an Artist,* Fireborn, 2016. Quint and Clay Art Crimes #2 of 5. (MM Police Procedural) What do you do when someone attempts to frame you for the murder of your roommate? That's the problem facing kinetic artist Trev Eldridge. Although Detective Quint Hawk determines Trev is innocent, it does nothing to assuage Trev's fears. –e-book only (MLM). 3/3

1466. **Kendrick, Edward,** *It Takes a Forger,* Fireborn, 2016. Quint and Clay Art Crimes #3 of 5. (MM Police Procedural) Officer Lou Hernandez is surprised when he's asked to help Gideon Monahan catch an art forger. He's not too happy, though, when he meets the man he'll be working with. Lou thinks Rory Kinley is a supercilious pain in the ass. Rory, on the other hand, sees no reason why Lou has been brought into this. After all, he's just a cop, albeit one who is good at going undercover. –e-book only (MM). 3/3

1467. **Kendrick, Edward,** *It Takes an Archaeologist,* Fireborn, 2016. Quint and Clay Art Crimes #4 of 5. (MM Police procedural) Gideon Monahan is a man dedicated to what he does–recovering stolen art–to the exclusion of anything else, including a personal life. There's a reason for that, something that happened in his past that he can't forget. –e-book only (MLM). 3/3

1468. **Kendrick, Edward,** *It Takes a Photographer,* Fireborn, 2016. Quint and Clay Art Crimes #5 of 5. (MM Police Procedural) Olivia is a photographer working at Rory and Lou's art gallery. While taking pictures at the party Clay and Quint throw to celebrate the adoption of their son, she captures what seems to be a murder in the building behind them. –e-book only (MLM). 3/3

1469. **Kendrick, Edward,** *Murder on Rainbow Lane,* JMS, 2016. (MM Amateur Sleuth) My name is Adam Moore, and I am not a happy camper at the moment. Someone is killing the residents on Rainbow Lane cul-de-sac. If that wasn't bad enough, they're trying to frame me for the murders. My only hope of proving my innocence? Detective Steve Jarrett ... if I can convince him I'm not the man he's looking for. Although he may be the man I've been looking for all my life. –e-book only (MLM). 3/3

1470. **Kendrick, Edward,** *Premonitions,* JMS, 2016. (MM Thriller) Artist Daniel Chase moves into the house he inherited from his grandfather – with the proviso he must live there or lose it. Soon after, he begins to get premonitions that something isn't right. Then he meets Griffin Pryce, a handsome man who lives off the grid. They become friends when Griffin agrees to become the subject for one of Daniel's paintings. However, Daniel's ex Ray arrives, wanting to partner with Daniel to turn the house into a fancy restaurant. When Daniel says no, Ray sends a man to threaten him if he doesn't sign the contract Ray has drawn up. Daniel refuses and things go from bad to worse. –e-book only (MLM). 3/3

1471. **Kendrick, Edward,** *Elevator Murders,* JMS, 2016. (MM Amateur Sleuth) When Tony Watkins discovers a dead man in the elevator of his apartment building, he has no idea there will be more murders. When the second body is found, he and his friends at the club put their heads together to try to figure out what's happening and who the killer might be. Kirk Logan is a man with problems. At twenty-nine, he still isn't out to his parents. On top of that, Tony thinks he's easy – which is true – and will have nothing to do with him, even though he wants to help Tony solve the murders. That is until he finally opens up to Tony about why he's the way he is. What Tony learns about Kirk, in addition to a third murder, changes everything. –e-book only (MLM). 3/3

1472. **Kendrick, Edward,** *The Hitchhiker Murders,* JMS, 2016. (MM Hard Boiled) When married private investigators Brent and Quinn Collins are hired to find Andrew, a young man who has disappeared after heading to Idaho Springs, little do they know they will become embroiled in murder. –e-book only (MLM). 3/3

1473. **Kendrick, Edward,** *Ghostly Investigations,* JMS, 2017. Ghostly Investigations #1 of 2. (MM Paranormal) Jon Watts heard stories about ghosts but never believed in them ... until he becomes one. Now, if he wants to move on, he has to solve his own murder. At least he'll have help from three new friends: Brody, an undercover cop who was killed five years earlier by an unknown assailant; Sage, a medium who can see and speak with ghosts; and Mike, the detective investigating Jon's murder, who doesn't know ghosts exist until Sage convinces him otherwise. –e-book only (MLM). 3/3

1474. **Kendrick, Edward,** *Searching for My Killer,* JMS, 2018. Ghostly Investigations #2 of 2. (MM Paranormal) My name is Tonio, and I'm a ghost. I want to, need to, find out who killed me so I can move on. The problem is, I have no idea how to do so. Or I didn't, until Brody and Jon showed up. They're ghosts, too, and they know Mike, a police detective, and Sage, a medium who can speak with the dead. With their help, and mine, will it be possible for Mike to find out who pushed me off the lighting bridge at the theater where I worked? At the same time, can I come to grips with the fact that, in death, I've lost David, an actor at the theater and the one man I ever loved? –e-book only (MLM). 3/3

1475. **Kendrick, Edward,** *The Agency,* JMS, 2018. (MM Hard Boiled) When runaway Kip Faulkner was seventeen, he witnessed two men commit a murder. Fear kept him from telling Sheriff Long the truth about what he'd seen. Guilt made him turn his life around. Eleven years later, he's the owner of a reputable private investigation agency in Denver. John Rigby looks like a typical biker, tattoos and all. But Kip discovers he's the antithesis of that stereotype when he hires John to work for his agency. When Kip learns about a recent killing exactly like the one he witnessed and recognizes one of the killers in a blurry photo on the news, he vows to find out how the two murders are connected ... and if there have been more. With John's help, can he learn the truth behind the murders while the two men fight their mutual attraction? Or will Kip become the next victim? –e-book only (MLM). 3/3

1476. **Kendrick, K. C.,** *Double Deuce,* Amber Allure, 2011. Amethyst #1 of 7. (MM Hard Boiled) Free spirited Ian Coulter works hard and plays harder. An ex-cop turned private investigator, Ian enjoys meeting new men and making new friends. A night out ends up with one man on the floor at his feet, and another asking for his help. Big trouble's brewing in little Amethyst Cove, and Ian's a step behind. He's quick to see Rick Mohr is the man holding the flare at the end a long, dark tunnel. –books 2, 4, and 7 were written by Christiane

France, available as an e-book only (MLM). 3/3

1477. **Kendrick, K. C.,** *Deuce of Diamonds,* Amber Quill, 2013. Amethyst #3 of 7. (MM Hard Boiled) Private investigator Ian Coulter has a knack for finding trouble even when he's minding his own business. Ian's in the midst of a routine weekly job for movie star client Saylor Blackwood when the man confides he thinks he has a fan turned stalker. Ian stays close to Saylor to observe the people around him and gets an unwelcome shock when FBI agent Rick Mohr contacts him. –e-book only (MLM). 3/3

1478. **Kendrick, K. C.,** *Ace, Deuce, Trey,* Amber Allure, 2014. Amethyst #5 of 7. (MM Hard Boiled) Ian Coulter has his hands full with a sexy office assistant, a favorite movie star client, and a drag queen determined to save the world one lost runaway at a time. He can juggle all of it because he and his lover, FBI agent Rick Mohr, are finally together. –e-book only (MLM). 3/3

1479. **Kendrick, K. C.,** *Circle of Steel,* Amber Quill, 2015. Amethyst #6 of 7. (MM Hard Boiled) Private investigator Ian Coulter and his FBI partner Rick Mohr work hard and play harder. Making their relationship a priority is a challenge they willingly embrace. Life is better together, and when their cases overlap, it also gets pretty interesting. –e-book only (MLM). 3/3

1480. **Kendrick, Edward,** *Wrong Side of the Law,* JMS, 2015. (MM Crime Drama) Undercover cop Dan Hudson is framed for blackmail and kicked off the NOPD force. Enraged about that, and the fact that his lover refuses to stand by him, Dan moves to Denver, where he becomes Dirk Steele. He finds a job working for the Powells, who are pawnbrokers ... and fences. When he proposes to them that he put together a team to steal on demand for the Powells' less than legitimate clients, a deal is struck, and the team is formed. The team consists of Maverick, a thief; Tripp, a street kid who shoplifts to survive; and Fey, another street kid who is an excellent pickpocket and petty thief. 3/3

1481. **Kendrick, Edward,** *A Deadly Homecoming,* JMS, 2016. (MM Journalism/Bibliomystery) When Spence Harden and Jeff, his writing partner and sometime lover, move into the house once owned by Spence's murdered parents, they have no idea what awaits them. Then the unthinkable happens. Jeff is killed, and Spence is framed for his murder. Crime reporter Gregg Rowe wants to help Spence clear his name. 3/3

1482. **Kendrick, Edward,** *Everyone has Secrets,* Createspace, 2018. (MM Crime Drama) My name is Brant Colton. I'm a blackmailer – a good one – and I make no apologies for my chosen career. One evening, at a very private club I belong to, I spotted a young man who piqued my interest. Why? Because he, Lorne Raynell, wasn't taking advantage of what the club had to offer. It took time, but I finally found out why. He was intent on finding out who murdered his brother. 3/3

1483. **Kendrick, Edward,** *Murderous Twins,* JMS, 2018. (MM Crime Drama) Blaine Ayers and Lloyd Thomas are identical twins – separated at birth, reunited by accident, and serial killers by choice. Two men, posing as one. –available as an e-book only (MM). 3/3

1484. **Keneally, Thomas,** *Victim on the Aurora,* Harcourt Brace Jovanovich, 1978. (Historical) In the waning years of the Edwardian era, a group of English gentlemen- adventurers led by Sir Eugene Stewart launched an expedition to reach the South Pole. More than sixty years later, Anthony Piers, the official artist of the New British South Polar Expedition, finally unveils the sobering conditions of their perilous journey: raging wind, bitter cold, fierce hunger, absolute darkness-and murder. –a journalist on the expedition had been murdered and the main character had to inform the expedition leader that the man was homosexual (MLM). 1/3

1485. **Kennedy, Jonathan,** *Patti DeVerre and the Case of the Missing Slingbacks,* Kindle, 2013. Caradog #1 of 2. (Soft Boiled) Times are hard for the South Wales Gay Detective Agency. Located above a Poundstretchers in Caerphilly and run by the well-meaning if daft Bear Caradog. Things start looking up when the striking Patte De Verre walks into his office wanting Bear to retrieve her Jimmy Choo's. What should be an easy job, turns into an adventure of colorful and memorable characters and events, climaxing at The Big Cheese Festival in Caerphilly. –available as an e-book only (MLM). 3/3

1486. **Kennedy, Jonathan,** *Bambi Bruschetta and the Case of the Cremated Canary,* Kindle, 2015. Caradog #2 of 2. (Soft Boiled) Murder, mystery and home baking as our hapless Welsh private investigator attempts to save the nations favorite songstress from a murder most fowl. –available as an e-book only (MLM). 3/3

1487. **Keogh, Theodora,** *The Double Door,* Creative Age Press, 1950. (Crime Drama) Candy de Tudelos, the lovely young daughter of a degenerate, self-styled Spanish aristocrat was cloistered from the realities of the world by her lonely existence in an imposing New York mansion. One day she ventured into the sinister house next-door, which her father had peopled with a corrupt and decadent group of associates. There she met an earthy young laborer, and in a brief and bitter love affair learned the meaning of the ugly secrets which had poisoned her life. –inspired by the Lonergan murder case (MM).1/3

1488. **Kerr, Philip,** *Pale Criminal,* Viking, 1990. Bernie Gunther #2 of 14. In the sweltering summer heat wave of 1938, the German people anxiously await the outcome of the Munich conference, wondering whether Hitler will plunge Europe into another war. Meanwhile, private investigator Bernie Gunther has taken on two cases involving blackmail. The first victim is a rich widow. The second is Bernie himself. –the hero seems to be anti-gay. The villains of the story are a gay couple working with Nazi Germany to rid the country of Jews (MLM). 1/3

1489. **Keswick, Jackie,** *The Power of Zero,* Createspace, 2018. Power of Zero #0 of 4. (Crime Drama) Twelve-year-old Jack Horwood has run from the pimp his mother sold him to, preferring to take his chances on the streets. A house with a cheerful, red door–and a classic convertible out front–prompts him into a spot of breaking and entering, and soon he has a warm, dry basement to squat in. Until the owner of the house, Jamaican hacker Rio Palmer, discovers his hideout. –expanded version of a previous short story (MLM). 3/3

1490. **Keswick, Jackie,** *Job Hunt,* Dreamspinner, 2016. Power of Zero #1 of 4. (MM Espionage) You don't greet your new boss dressed like an underage rent boy. But when Jack Horwood–ace hacker and ex-MI6 operative–opens the door to Gareth Flynn, he's too busy to worry over details like that. And anyway, his potential new boss is his former Commanding Officer – the same guy Jack has had a crush on since he was seventeen. So, he should understand, right? 3/3

1491. **Keswick, Jackie,** *Ghosts,* Dreamspinner, 2016. Power of Zero #2 of 4. (MM Espionage) Jack Horwood doesn't do families. Or Christmas. From the time his mother sold him to her pimp to the moment he walked out on the man he loved, Christmas has always been about change and painful choices. This year seems no different. Helping Daniel and Nico recover from their imprisonment and hunting down those responsible puts Jack in a frame of mind he doesn't want to inflict on anyone. Least of all Gareth and the tentative relationship they've started to rebuild. 3/3

1492. **Keswick, Jackie,** *House Hunt,* Dreamspinner, 2016. Power of Zero #3 of 4. (MM Espionage) Jack Horwood hates owing favors. But when a simple day out to treat Gareth to the best oysters in England leads to a discovery of drugs and counterfeit money–things that neither Jack nor Gareth have the jurisdiction to handle–he has to call in help. 3/3

1493. **Keswick, Jackie,** *Swings and Roundabouts,* Createspace, 2018. Power of Zero #4 of 4. (MM Espionage) Desperate for a relationship reset, Jack treats Gareth to a romantic getaway and Sweden's frigid peace gives them the break they both need. But Jack's a trouble magnet and the next dead body just a wild skidoo ride away. 3/3

1494. **Kidwell, Alex,** *Gumption and Gumshoes,* Dreamspinners, 2013. (MM Paranormal) August Adahy Mendez would rather be buried in the world of his detective novels or a good film noir movie than in real life. He's overweight, undermotivated, and stuck in a dead-end job. As a Chincha, he's part of a long line of chinchilla shifters, but the greatest accomplishment in his life so far has been moving an hour away from his close-knit herd. That all changes when August's grandfather leaves him enough cash to pursue his dream: becoming a detective himself. 3/3

1495. **Kienzle, William X (1928-2001),** *Deadline for a Critic,* Andrews, McMeel & Parker, 1987. Father Koesler #9 of 24. (Amateur Sleuth) It's curtains for Ridley Groendal. When the performing arts critic for the "Detroit Suburban Reporter" dies suddenly, insiders know he could have choked on his own rage. Having returned to Detroit from a vituperative career at the prestigious" New York Herald," Groendal was known to have destroyed more than a few reputations with his vicious criticism. Was his death an act of revenge? –the murdered man is gay and is lover is one of the suspects (MLM). 1/3

1496. **Kimberling, Nicole,** *Bellingham Mystery Series Volume One,* Blind Eye, 2015. Bellingham Mystery #1 of 2. (Journalism) This print volume collects the first three novellas, *Primal Red, Evergreen* (previously titled *Baby, It's Cold Outside*), and *Black Cat Ink*. Peter Fontaine just wants to break a juicy story and maybe win an award for his intrepid journalism. But all too soon his instinct for prying and his fantastical turn of mind conspire to draw him deep into murder and mystery. 3/3

1497. **Kimberling, Nicole,** *Bellingham Mystery Series Volume Two,* Blind Eye, 2018. Bellingham Mystery #2 of 2. (Journalism) Four years ago, Peter Fontaine made a name for himself as Bellingham, Washington's premiere investigative reporter. Since then he's got an award, a cat and good-looking artist to come home to every night. Nick Olson, Peter's long-suffering lover has a lot of reasons for wanting Peter to stop investigating the many and varied crimes committed in the City of Subdued Excitement. Peter's nasty habit of getting held at gunpoint by lunatics has Nick wondering if any story is worth losing the Peter for good. But Peter's thirst for knowledge must be satisfied. And whether it's at the Farmer's Market, the microbrewery or a mid-century meth motel, Peter will use his power of ultimate nosiness to uncover the town's long-kept secrets.

Contains the novellas, "One Man's Treasure," "Birds of a Feather," and "Pentimento Blues." 3/3

1498. **Kimberly, Alice (Cleo Coyle),** *The Ghost and Mrs. McClure,* Berkley, 2004. (Cozy) Penelope Thornton-McClure manages a Rhode Island bookshop rumored to be haunted. When a bestselling author drops dead signing books, the first clue of foul play comes from the store's full-time ghost - a PI murdered on the very spot more than fifty years ago. –gay secondary character (MLM). 1/3

1499. **King, Atticus,** *Pretense...of Innocence,* New Falcon, 1996. (Thriller) The complexities of life for Southern gay men, lives lived in pretense of innocence...when there was no guilt. Set in Shreveport, Louisiana, pictures the complications of life for Southern gay men born "lucky" enough to pass for straight" in areas where pretense can equal survival. It illustrates the varied manners in which they come to accept and define themselves, empowering others to be the judge in the process. 3/3

1500. **King, Frank,** *Down and Dirty,* Richard Marek, 1978. (Thriller) A gay NY police officer forced into retirement, and the bizarre murder mystery he becomes involved in (courtesy of Bookshop Baltimore for the description of the book they had listed online). –although the main character is gay, he is homophobic and not very likeable. King seems to be setting the character up to be the main character in a series of books that were never written (MLM). 3/3

1501. **King, Rufus,** *Murder by Latitude,* Novel Selections, 1930. Lt. Valcour #3 of 11. (Police Procedural) When the wireless operator on a luxury cruiser bound from Bermuda to Halifax is murdered, it's bad luck for the killer that Valcour happens to be on the passenger list. He probes into the pasts of his cruise mates–especially, a lovely and lethal man-eater–but the killer strikes again before Valcour arrives at a solution. –wireless operator and a fellow crew member seem to have been in a relationship (MLM). 1/3

1502. **King, G. Toby,** *The Boystown Murders,* Kindle, 2014. (Police Procedural) At his birthday party, Mitchell Davies is found dead, and all the guests seem to have motive to want him out of the way. –available as an e-book only. All of the G. Toby King titles are subtitled as Gay Murder Mysteries but there is little clue as to whether they're connected or not (MLM). 3/3

1503. **King, G. Toby,** *The Go-Go Boy Murders,* Kindle, 2015. (Police Procedural) At Miss Tillie's birthday party, the hunky party-goers, mostly go-go boys, are put into a state of shock when the handsome Marcus is found murdered with a knife stuck in his neck. Then two more murders take place, and two attempted murders. Deputy Sheriff Pete Lang comes to the house where the party is being held and starts an intense investigation. –available as an e-book only (MLM). 3/3

1504. **King, G. Toby,** *The Drag Queen Murders,* Independently Published, 2017. (Police Procedural) Leah Cummins wants to tell her new lover that she's really a man, but it doesn't go well when she does. And the next morning her body is found mutilated. 3/3

1505. **King, G. Toby,** *Murder Under Queer Circumstances,* Independently Published, 2017. (Police Procedural) At a housewarming party on the edge of the Shawnee National Forest, one of the hosts has a fatal accident while serving cocktails. The next morning, the second host is found with his throat slit, and one of the guests has apparently hanged himself in his room. The answer to why this has happened becomes the puzzle that a young deputy sheriff must unravel. 3/3

1506. **King, G. Toby,** *The Size-Queen Murders,* Independently Published, 2017. (Police Procedural) The owner of a famous gay club in Chicago's Boystown watches as a serial killer moves ever closer to her club, a man who murders both patrons and employees of the club, called the Kandy Bar. Eventually, attacks take place in the club itself, and the owner is herself one of the victims. A lengthy investigation ensues and in time the psychotic murderer is revealed–to the total surprise of everyone involved! 3/3

1507. **King, G. Toby,** *The Hollywood Beach Murders,* Independently Published, 2017. (Police Procedural) Young men enjoyed the gay-friendly beach called Hollywood Beach are being gruesomely murdered. It seems that innocent young men are being stalked and gruesomely murdered. But by whom? And why? 3/3

1508. **King, G. Toby,** *Gay Murder in the Alps,* Independently Published, 2017. (Police Procedural) An American is brought to his ancestors' castle in Austria to collect his inheritance, but within hours of arrival, he and his friends begin to experience murders. Their dream vacation in the Austrian Alps is going terribly wrong. And is there really a ghost roaming the castle halls? 3/3

1509. **King, G. Toby,** *Gym Bunnies–Gay Hunk Murders,* Independently Published, 2017. (Police Procedural) In one of Chicago's many gyms, gym bunnies are being targeted for murder. When the Gym Bunnies begin to realize that anyone could be next, they really start to worry. 3/3

1510. **King, G. Toby,** *The West Hollywood Murders,* Independently Published, 2017. (Police Procedural) Brett arrives in Los Angeles and makes his way to the area of West Hollywood, a famous gay mecca and playground of those living an alternative life-style. He rents a studio and meets Sol, a vivacious and handsome man, who is earning his living as a dancer and stripper in a club called the Whine Bar. When Brett visits the club, he meets Tony, and there is an immediate attraction. But before the two young men can begin a relationship, the whole club is disrupted when the body of one of the dancers is found in a room at the next-door hotel. The victim has been viciously stabbed to death. And that's just the beginning. 3/3

1511. **King, G. Toby,** *The Closet-Queen Murders,* Independently Published, 2017. (Police Procedural) A Russian billionaire and his handsome ballet dancer son move into their new penthouse in Chicago. They host a celebration party to congratulate the son on his leading role in the premiere of 'Coppelia'. That evening at the celebration the father is found dead, and soon two more unexplained murders take place. 3/3

1512. **Kirby, Madeline,** *Not a Werewolf,* Createspace, 2015. Jake and Boo #1 of 4. (MM Paranormal) When perpetual student Jake Hillebrand starts having strange dreams, no theory is too outlandish - even the possibility that he has become a werewolf. His best friend Don is no help, though – he doesn't even believe in werewolves! 3/3

1513. **Kirby, Madeline,** *Not a Mermaid,* Createspace, 2018. Jake and Boo #2 of 4. (MM Paranormal) It's July in Houston, and when heat waves and storm warnings finally give way to flooding rains, Jake Hillebrand's strange dreams take a sinister turn. When the flood waters recede, the body of a young woman is found on the banks of Buffalo Bayou - a young woman whose life overlaps with that of Detective Victoria Perez. 3/3

1514. **Kirby, Madeline,** *Not a Zombie,* Createspace, 2018. Jake and Boo #3 of 4. (MM Paranormal) Jake, Petreski, and the rest are back for another installment of caffeine, snark, and a touch of romance. It's the start of a new semester and familiar faces are popping up all over – most of them unwelcome. 3/3

1515. **Kirby, Madeline,** *Not an Elf,* Createspace, 2018. Jake and Boo #4 of 4. (MM Paranormal) It's Jake and Boo's first Christmas together, and they're heading to Waxahachie to spend it with Petreski's family. As if meeting your boyfriend's parents isn't nerve-wracking enough, there's also a mob of siblings, a town full of gossips, trouble with a holiday display, and someone's been sending poison pen letters to the local priest. –available as an e-book only (MLM). 3/3

1516. **Kitchin, C. H. G. (1895-1967),** *Death of my Aunt,* Hogarth Press, 1929. Warren #1 of 4. (Amateur Sleuth) Tricked into delivering a fatal dose of poison to his wealthy aunt, Malcolm Warren, a conservative stockbroker, must solve the mystery of her murder before he becomes the prime suspect. –Warren is mostly modeled after Kitchin who was gay (MLM). 1/3

1517. **Kitchin, C. H. B.,** *Crime at Christmas,* Hogart Press, 1934. Warren #2 of 4. (Amateur Sleuth) A Christmas party in Hampstead is rudely interrupted by a violent death. Can the murderer be one of the relatives and intimate friends celebrating the festive season in the great house? The stockbroker sleuth Malcolm Warren investigates. 1/3

1518. **Kitchin, C. H. B.,** *Death of his Uncle,* Hogarth Press, 1939. Warren #3 of 4. (Amateur Sleuth) Malcolm Warren, a young English stockbroker, is asked by a friend, Dick Findlay, to look into the disappearance of Findlay's uncle. 1/3

1519. **Kitchin, C. H. B.,** *The Cornish Fox,* Secker & Warburg, 1949. Warren #4 of 4. (Amateur Sleuth) The scene is Cornwall, and the characters are for the most part English settlers in a county which is still apt to look upon the Englishman as a foreigner. Their differing reactions to the post-war world and an alien environment, and the clashes between their personalities are admirably portrayed and form more than a mere background. 1/3

1520. **Kitteridge, Harrison,** *Before Holmes met Watson,* Uprise, 2016. John + Sherlock #1 of 2. (MM Dystopian Sherlock Holmes) What does it mean to be a detective with no cases to solve? Sherlock Holmes tries not to ponder this question as he distracts himself from his professional failings with bare-knuckle boxing at an underground fight club and vials of cocaine and morphine. John Watson spends his days in an operating theatre on an Army base in Afghanistan, doing his best to patch up the wounded and failing more often than he'd like. The dark, violent worlds in which both men choose to live complicate their romantic lives and cause them terrible suffering but set them on paths that are destined to cross. 3/3

1521. **Kitteridge, Harrison,** *Sherlock Holmes and the Adventure of the Paper Journal,* Uprise, 2016. John + Sherlock #2 of 2. (MM Dystopian Sherlock Holmes) Sherlock takes on a case involving a prolific blackmailer, and the lengths to which he goes to resolve the matter reveal a dark, incredibly manipulative side of him that leaves John doubting whether he ever knew his dear friend at all. The consequences of Sherlock's actions unfold with catastrophic results that threaten to destroy his relationship with John, which both men are coming to realize is deeply felt romantic love. 3/3

1522. **Knight, Geoffrey,** *The Cross of Sins,* Starbooks, 2008. Fathom's Five #1 of 5. (Thriller) Somewhere in the world is a statue so sinful that a secret sect of the Church wants it destroyed at any cost. Somewhere in the Turkish desert, in the streets of London, and in the depths of Venice, are the clues to find it. And, somewhere in the hearts of five sexy, daring, thrill-seeking gay men, is the courage and die-hard determination to unravel one of the greatest mysteries of all time. 3/3

1523. **Knight, Geoffrey,** *The Riddle of the Sands,* Cleis, 2009. Fathom's Five #2 of 5. (Thriller) The clock is ticking! Blackmailed by Jake's nemesis - the vengeful Pierre Perron - Professor Fathom's team of five horny gay adventurers is sent on a seemingly impossible mission to uncover the legendary Riddle of the Sands in order to save one of their own from a rare and deadly poison. But what is the Riddle of the Sands? Where are the long-lost clues and hidden maps that can lead to its whereabouts? Is it a myth, a mirage, or the greatest engineering feat in the history of ancient Egypt? From the icy plains of Siberia to the shadowy bathhouses of Cairo, from the scorching valley of the Nile to the heart of the Amazon jungle, readers join these hunks – treasure-hunter Jake, Brazilian biologist Eden, Texas cowboy Shane, art expert Luca, and quarterback Will – in a search that blends nonstop action and high-octane sex! 3/3

1524. **Knight, Geoffrey,** *The Curse of the Dragon God,* Cleis, 2011. Fathom's Five #3 of 5. (Thriller) China. A land of ancient wonders. A history of tradition, triumph and tyranny. As it casts a shadow across the entire globe, this once forbidden country awakens as the dominant force in a new world economy. Business empires will rise, deals will be made, lives will be lost as money changes hands, but one treasure will remain the most precious in all of China: a diamond known as the Eye of Fucanglong, the Dragon God of lost jewels and buried treasures. The diamond is flawless. It is priceless. It is cursed. And it is about to be stolen in the heist of the century. Can Professor Fathom's team of gay adventure-seekers find the diamond before this perfectly executed crime leads to a cataclysmic event of mass destruction? From the towers of Hong Kong to the diamond mines of Shandong; from the streets of San Francisco to the deserts of Dubai to the male strip clubs of Beijing; from China's mystical past, to the boardrooms and backrooms of a modern industrial giant, take the high road to China. 3/3

1525. **Knight, Geoffrey,** *The Dame of Notre Dame,* Geoffrey Knight, 2015. Fathom's Five #3.5 of 5. (Thriller) Within a centuries-old tapestry on display in the palatial French estate of Lawrence Vanderbilt is a map to one of the greatest treasures of all time–the sword of Joan of Arc. 3/3

1526. **Knight, Geoffrey,** *The Tomb of Heaven,* Geoffrey Knight, 2017. Fathom's Five #4 of 5. (Thriller) There is a man who changed the course of Russian history in his quest for the ultimate power. There is a hidden tomb that holds the secret to eternal life. There are five keys that can unlock the riddle to something every man desires–immortality. 3/3

1527. **Knight, Geoffrey,** *The Temple of Time,* Geoffrey Knight, 2018. Fathom's Five #5 of 5. (Thriller) There is a civilization that vanished without trace. There is a lost temple that can change time as we know it. There is a fragile fraternity that protects the most important secret in human history. And there is one man who will destroy everything and anyone to know the truth–his name is Caro Sholtez. 3/3

1528. **Knight, Geoffrey,** *Scott Sapphire and the Emerald Orchid,* Cleis, 2012. (MM Suspense) Meet Scott Sapphire–lover of French champagne, Belgian chocolate and dangerous men. He is suave. He is sexy. He is a man of the world–and a man that the world desperately wants to catch. For Scott Sapphire is the greatest jewel thief of our time. Dashing. Daring. And always neck-deep in trouble. But when Scott's latest heist lands him in possession of a map to a rare and precious orchid, it'll take more than bedroom eyes and a charming smile to stay one step ahead of one of the world's most powerful business tycoons, as well as keep the CIA off Scott's back and a handsome special agent out of his pants–or maybe not. From the Venice canals to the Amazon rainforest, from Rio de Janeiro to the casinos of Monte Carlo, comes a brand-new gay hero as irresistible as diamonds and pearls. Adventure has a new name! And that name is Scott Sapphire. 3/3

1529. **Knight, Geoffrey,** *Buck Baxter, Love Detective,* Wilde City, 2014. Buck Baxter #1 of 2. (MM Hard Boiled) Welcome to Wilde City, 1924–a crane on top of every skyscraper, a party in every club, a romance on every dance floor, a shooting every night, a broken heart on every street corner and a dirty secret behind every window with the curtain drawn. It's the kinda town that keeps Buck Baxter, private detective, in business. 3/3

1530. **Knight, Geoffrey,** *Buck Baxter and the Disappearing Divas,* Wilde City, 2015. Buck Baxter #2 of 2. (MM Hard Boiled) Something sinister is happening at the Maharaja Majestic Theater on Broadville Boulevard. The domineering actress, Dominique Darlington, has vanished without a trace, the opening night of the theater's new production of The Snake Charmer's Slave is now in jeopardy, and six suspects are about to have the pleasure of meeting Buck Baxter, Private Detective, as he investigates whether there's a killer on the loose... or a phantom at the opera? 3/3

1531. **Knight, Rob,** *Touching Evil,* Torquere, 2006. (MM Paranormal) Greg has a special talent he'd give anything to be rid of. After an accident many years ago that left him in a coma, Greg woke up to find that he could touch things and know what had happened to them. Too bad he can't control the talent enough to keep it from overwhelming him. He's lived with it long enough that it he can make it day by day, but when he starts being stalked, he has to depend on his friends to help him cope. The only good thing his gift has brought him is Artie, an overprotective cop with a psychotic cat and a great bedside manner. Artie is all about helping Greg cope, and about finding out who's threatening his friend. Through grisly gifts and terrifying attacks, Artie stays by Greg's side. Even ordering take-out can be an ordeal for Greg, and Artie is happy to run interference. Greg hasn't touched anyone without pain in years, but with Artie he finds he has someone to lean on, even as the stalker finds new ways to torment him. Can the two of them find a way to solve the mystery of Greg's tormenter before one of them gets hurt? 3/3

1532. **Konohara, Narise,** *Cold Sleep,* Digital Manga, 2006. Cold Sleep #1 of 3. (Yaoi Manga) After losing his memory in a serious car accident, Tohru Takahisa is taken in by Fujishima, an older man who claims to be his friend. But the taciturn Fujishima refuses to reveal anything about Tohru's past! Despite the gulf between them, a strange and awkward tenderness grows, even as they are held apart by the tragic events of Tohru's forgotten past! Dramatic, heart-wrenching romance and tragedy combine in a gripping story where the past and present are intricately entwined. 3/3

1533. **Konohara, Narise,** *Cold Light,* Digital Manga, 2010. Cold Sleep #2 of 3. (Yaoi Manga) The wound Fujishima suffered from protecting Tooru has healed and he's finally been released from the hospital. Their life together starts again once more. Tooru wants them to live together as lovers, but Fujishima refuses, saying "I have no intentions of loving you." Is Fujishima afraid of Tooru remembering something in particular if he regains his memories? The bonds of the past are finally becoming clearer... 3/3

1534. **Konohara, Narise,** *Cold Fever,* Digital Manga, 2011. Cold Sleep #3 of 3. (Yaoi Manga) Tohru lost his most of his memory in an accident. He can't remember anything that happened from the past six years. Struggles, but with time, he slowly recovers his memory. He feels as if he is a different person now, and he hates "the other guy" – the "himself" from six years ago... And thinking, Fujishima was his friend, felt like he was being watched over like a guardian angel but in the end, he's betrayed. Miserable and emotionally drained, Tohru is trying not to relive in the shadow of his past. He is trying to move on with his new life... but harder he tries, he finds himself being pulled in by Fujishima. 3/3

1535. **Kowalski, William,** *Crypt City,* Createspace, 2014. (Historical) The year is 1970. When U.S. Army Capt. Howard Starling is caught in the arms of another man, his commanding officer, Lt.-Col. Christopher Huygens, he's dismissed from the service in disgrace. With a background in intelligence, he tries in desperation to make a living as a private eye. His first client, Lorna Sutter, is a wealthy woman who wants to find a young girl with whom she grew up in an orphanage. As Howard investigates, not only does he discover that the orphanage was the epicenter of a series of horrific crimes, but his past as a Cold War intelligence officer is about to catch up to him in the form of a Soviet agent whom he had helped turn, and who has once again changed employers–this time, to a shadowy organization with a strange connection to his vanished lover. 3/3

1536. **Kramer, Gregg,** *The Pursemonger of Fugu: A Bathroom Mystery,* Cormorant, 1998. (Amateur Sleuth) Unbound from stiff-upperlip stagnation by sudden widowhood, Adelaide Simcoe has yielded to her creative impulses – and the pull of the volatile avant-garde fugu gallery. But at the opening of her first group show, art is displaced by horror as the performance art piece by the gallery's mercurial co-founder goes spectacularly and fatally wrong. –several secondary gay characters (MLM). 2/3

1537. **Kramer, Scott,** *Taking the Plunge,* Turquoise Morning, 2012. Jane Monterrey #1 of 5. (Modern Cozy) Jane "CK" Monterrey is an inexperienced Cincinnati private eye whose world is flipped when local millionaire George Halberran plunges to his death outside her office window. Hired by George's eccentric mother, Vucktoria, to investigate her son's death, Jane has no idea how messy things can get. With the help of sexy Officer Brad Hyatt, her nosy mother and all sorts of quirky new friends–from little numismatics to a monkey that dances to Michael Jackson's Thriller–Jane stumbles along trying to find out if George really was murdered without getting hurt herself. –friend of the main character, Ms. G, with male pronouns helps investigate (MLM). 1/3

1538. **Kramer, Scott,** *Trouble Comes in Pairs,* Turquoise Morning, 2014. Jane Monterrey #2 of 5. (Modern Cozy) A prized horse is missing and private investigator Jane "CK" Monterrey is on the case. CK hasn't had a big case in six months, when a millionaire plummeted to his death from her roof, so she certainly needs some action. Her new client is Shanel Richards, the sassy-mouthed part owner of the J&R Ranch, who hires CK to locate Abacus Starling, an expensive race horse. 1/3

1539. **Kramer, Scott,** *Kicking the Habit,* Createspace, 2017. Jane Monterrey #3 of 5. (Modern Cozy) Jane 'CK' Monterrey is visited by a Catholic priest, seeking her help in his sibling's murder. Reluctant at first, she feels pity for the priest who believes it is a catholic cover up. The next day the priest is struck by a car downtown. Jane becomes involved whether she likes it or not. -e-book only (MLM). 1/3

1540. **Kramer, Scott,** *Ruffling a Few Feathers,* Createspace, 2017. Jane Monterrey #4 of 5. (Modern Cozy) Buried in grief, Jane 'CK' Monterrey holds vigil over her comatose fiancé, Brad Hyatt. Jane's Mom is holding down the fort at the office and picks up a case. A penguin is stolen from the zoo. -e-book only (MLM). 1/3

1541. **Kramer, Scott,** *Chasing a Rhyme,* Createspace, 2018. Jane Monterrey #5 of 5. (Modern Cozy) Caught up in life, Jane Monterrey awaits the coming of her child and marriage to Brad Hyatt, her fiancé. But things get complicated when a serial killer terrorizing Cincinnati takes in interest in her. A package from the Phantom Poet turns her world sideways, involving her in a case that originally wasn't hers. To top that, her friend Gene, aka Ms. G, plans to move to New York, leaving her to fend for herself as tensions rise, clients get demanding, and the need to use the restroom becomes more frequent. 1/3

1542. **Krause, Krandall,** *Love's Last Chance,* Alyson, 2000. (MM Amateur Sleuth) Fate has strange and wonderful plans for wisecracking Nigel Adams and cynical, aristocratic Nicky Borja, who are accidentally thrown together in a Tuscany villa, where they have both fled to escape from life and its heartbreaks. But just as a fiery romance is kindled from oil and water, Nicky and Nigel discover that a friend they recently met, the publishing heiress Evelyn VanDeventer Iversen, has been drowned in a remote Arizona lake while camping with her new and much younger husband. Suddenly, the newly-in-love and eager-for-adventure pair find themselves in the deserts of Utah and Arizona on the trail of the truth in this delightfully poignant and funny blend of mystery and romance. 3/3

1543. **Kray, Selina,** *Fangs of Scavo,* Selina Kray, 2017. Stoker and Bash #1 of 2. (Historical Police Procedural) At Scotland Yard, DI Timothy Stoker is no better than a ghost. A master of arcane documents and niggling details who, unlike his celebrity-chasing colleagues, prefers hard work to headlines. But an invisible man is needed to unmask the city's newest amateur detective, Hieronymus Bash. A bon vivant long on flash and style but short on personal history, Bash just may be a Cheapside rogue in Savile Row finery. When the four fangs of the Demon Cats of Scavo–trophies that protect the hunters, who killed the two vicious beasts–disappear one by one, Stoker's forced to team with the very man he was sent to investigate to maintain his cover. 3/3

1544. **Kray, Selina,** *The Fruit of the Poisonous Tree,* Selina Kray, 2018. Stoker and Bash #2 of 2. (Historical Police Procedural) Finding lost poodles and retrieving stolen baubles is not how DI Tim Stoker envisioned his partnership with his lover, Hieronymus Bash. So, when the police commissioner's son goes missing, he's determined to help, no matter what secrets he has to keep, or from whom. 3/3

1545. **Krender, Ian James,** *Murder in Torbaydos,* Prizm, 2014. (Horror) What could possibly go wrong when buying an old Victorian property by the seaside to remodel and run as a hotel. Plenty when the ghostly inhabitants from past generations want their say... 3/3

1546. **Krier, L. M.,** *The First Time Ever,* Createspace, 2017. DI Darling #1 of 12. (Police Procedural) Ted Darling is a Specialist Firearms Officer, and a good one. With a promising career in front of him. Then he meets someone who could change everything but who can't live with his police role. His skills get him noticed and he's seconded to help with a big CID operation. It isn't long before he's facing his first murder case. –originally published as a prequel but is now listed as the first book in the series (MLM). 3/3

1547. **Krier, L. M.,** *Baby's Got Blue Eyes,* Createspace, 2015. DI Darling #2 of 12. (Police Procedural) Someone is dumping bodies on DI Ted Darling's patch and he's not happy. Ted's a good solid copper, in an old-fashioned way, with an excellent clear-up rate. He also happens to be gay and has his own unique way of dealing with any prejudice that brings him. But this killer seems to be running effortless rings round him and every promising lead just takes him up another blind alley. Then it starts to get personal... 3/3

1548. **Krier, L. M.,** *Two Little Boys,* Createspace, 2015. DI Darling #3 of 12. (Police Procedural) In his darkest and most complex case to date, DI Ted Darling has to confront demons from his own past when investigating the brutal murder of a young boy. 3/3

1549. **Krier, L. M.,** *When I'm Old and Gray,* Createspace, 2015. DI Darling #4 of 12. (Police Procedural) DI Ted Darling doesn't like coincidences. There are too many for comfort surrounding his latest case. They're spilling over into his private life, too, when some toxic family secrets are uncovered. A serial killer appears to be targeting vulnerable elderly people in care homes and despatching them in the most cynical way. Ted and his team are struggling to get a lead on who the killer really is. 3/3

1550. **Krier, L. M.,** *Shut Up and Drive,* Createspace, 2016. DI Darling #5 of 12. (Police Procedural) A serial sex attacker is spreading fear in Stockport and DI Ted Darling and his team are on the case. The man randomly targets young women and abducts them from busy supermarket car parks. He's armed with a knife and is clearly highly trained in how to handle it. 3/3

1551. **Krier, L. M.,** *Only the Lonely,* Createspace, 2016. DI Darling #6 of 12. (Police Procedural) Ted Darling is back and his boss has news for him. He'll be taking on more responsibility over an expanded area, with a bigger team. Before he even has chance to take stock, he's facing his first body in what could be the most cynical murder he's ever encountered. 3/3

1552. **Krier, L. M.,** *Wild Thing,* Createspace, 2016. DI Darling #7 of 12. (Police Procedural) Random, unrelated killings, seemingly without motives? Or the work of a single cold-blooded killer? And are the murders in any way connected to the shocking crimes which RSPCA officers are investigating in the same area? 3/3

1553. **Krier, L. M.,** *Walk on By,* Createspace, 2016. DI Darling #8 of 12. (Police Procedural) It's a big operation and a complex one. With the Big Boss out of action, Ted's in charge of one part of the enquiry, a robbery and brutal stabbing of a woman in a car park. But overseeing it all is a senior officer with a serious grudge against Ted. One who'd stop at nothing to take him down. Then another face from the past turns up, needing Ted's help. One whose presence can only mean trouble of a serious kind. 3/3

1554. **Krier, L. M.,** *Preacher Man,* Createspace, 2017. DI Darling #9 of 12. (Police Procedural) A teenager is found naked and wandering in a lane near Stockport. He can't answer any questions about the serious injuries he's sustained, only repeatedly recite a biblical passage. 3/3

1555. **Krier, L. M.,** *Cry for the Bad Man,* Createspace, 2018. DI Darling #10 of 12. (Police Procedural) 'Where does a wise man hide a pebble?' Home Office Pathologist Professor Nelson's question marks the beginning of Detective Chief Inspector Ted Darling's latest case. Not one he was expecting to get for him and his team. The tragic but seemingly straightforward suicide of a young man. 3/3

1556. **Krier, L. M.,** *Every Game You Play,* Createspace, 2018. DI Darling #11 of 12. (Police Procedural) Two missing women. One will die. The pressure's on for Ted Darling and his team. There's an inquiry into their last case, still unsolved. Then a woman disappears. The clock's ticking to find where she is and what's happened to her. A second missing person. A body. But whose? And why is Ted seeing similarities between the previous crime scene and the one from the last case? –*Where the Girls,* the twelfth book in the series is set to be released in 2019 (MLM). 3/3

1557. **Kreisler, Kurt,** *Shadows,* Blueboy, 1978. (Pulp) "Accidental sleuth Thaddeus (Thad) Martin, 35, M. D., a pediatrician, has an eerie adventure (Gunn)." 3/3

L

1558. **Lain, Tara,** *The Case of the Sexy Shakespearean,* Dreamspinner, 2018. Middlemark #1 of 2. (MM Bibliomystery) Dr. Llewellyn Lewis leads a double life, as both an awkward but distinguished history professor and the more flamboyant Ramon Rondell, infamous writer of sensational historical theories. It's Ramon who first sets eyes on a gorgeous young man dancing in a club, but Llewellyn who meets teaching assistant Blaise Arthur formally at an event held for wealthy socialite Anne de Vere, descendant of Edward de Vere, seventeenth Earl of Oxford-who some believe was the real Shakespeare. Anne wants Llewellyn to prove that claim, even though many have tried and failed. And she's willing to offer a hefty donation to the university if he succeeds. –*The Case of the Voracious Vintner* will be released in 2019 (MLM). 3/3

1559. **Lamb, Sebastian (Lyal H. Stevens 1927-1995),** *Brothers,* Blueboy, 1976. (Pulp) "Story about a misguided attempt at revenge (Gunn)." 3/3

1560. **Lamb, Sebastian,** *The Slasher,* Blueboy, 1977. (Pulp) "Police detective Todd Douglas is part of a team after a psychopath (Gunn)." 3/3

1561. **Lamb, Sebastian,** *Trapped Chicken,* Surree, 1978. (Pulp) "Police detective Malcolm (Gordy) Gordon rights everything (Gunn)." 3/3

1562. **Lambert, William J. III (b. 1942),** *Adonis,* Greenleaf, 1969. Adonis #1 of 3. (Pulp) "Private investigator Adonis Tyler, a Korean War veteran, transforms from a standard gumshoe to an adventure hero (Gunn)." 3/3

1563. **Lambert, William J. III,** *Adonis at Actum,* Phoenix, 1970. Adonis #2 of 3. (Pulp) Over the hills and through the primeval passes, the four of them fought their gory way to Actum, the site of the grave of Kutamehan II. Their goal – to find the beetle which, when crushed and eaten, provided thirty-six nonstop hours of sodomistic bliss! 3/3

1564. **Lambert, William J. III,** *Adonis at Bomasa,* Phoenix, 1970. Adonis #3 of 3. (Pulp) "The four, having escaped, split up–Louis being captured by the natives to serve as their god, Adonis finding his way back to meet Louis's cousin, Sebastian de Bouvier, and return with him in search of Louis (Gunn)." –conclusion to series had never been written (MM). 3/3

1565. **Lambert, William J. III**, *Valley of the Damned,* Greenleaf, 1971. (Pulp) There was another sound to pierce the darkness: a forlorn howling that echoed and re-echoed to chill the bones. Some said there was a wolf run mad in the valley. But there were those who knew better. There were those who knew this was something other than a four-legged wild dog accustomed to tamed flesh. This wolf walked on two legs among the very people in was destined to eventually kill. Maritu had returned to the valley. His spirit had been reincarnated. 3/3

1566. **Lambert, William J. III**, *Assignment: Grey Area,* American Art Enterprises, 1981. (Pulp) "Secret agent Peter Galveston, 36, Swiss-born, beds an Italian hustler in his search to discover the truth about the disappearance of three agents working in the Grey Area of international intrigue–one of whom, Taylor Pauls, was gay (Gunn)." 3/3

1567. **Lang, Raymond (William J. Lambert III)**, *Secret of the Phallic Stone,* Blueboy, 1977. (Pulp) "U. S. secret agent Peter Stort, pulled from his Russian assignment to return to the United States, finally catches on to what is happening (Gunn)." 3/3

1568. **Langley, J. L.**, *The Tin Star,* Loose Id, 2006. Ranch #1 of 3. (MM Mystery) When James Killian comes out to his father, he finds himself banished from his home and fired from his job. His savior comes in the unlikely form of Ethan Whitehall, his older brother's best friend. Ethan has always had a soft spot where Jamie Killian was concerned, and he will do whatever it takes to keep his new lover safe. –next two books are non-mysteries (MLM). 3/3

1569. **Langley, J. L.**, *Without Reservation,* Samhain, 2007. With or Without #1 of 4. (MM Paranormal) Chayton Winston is a veterinarian. He is also a werewolf. Much to his Native American parent's chagrin, he has always dreamed of a fair-haired, Caucasian mate. Keaton Reynolds wakes up, in wolf form, and finds himself with a mate. He's instantly attracted. When a power struggle in Keaton's pack threatens Keaton's life, the two men learn to depend on one another. 3/3

1570. **Langley, J. L.**, *With Caution,* Samhain, 2008. With or Without #2 of 4. A brother's vow. A lover's promise. Both could put them all at deadly risk. Remington Lassiter is trying his best to stay out of trouble while he learns the ropes of being a werewolf. When his little brother turns up covered in bruises, he is driven to finally bring their abusive father to justice. To do it, he must face a past he hides behind his cocky, trouble-making attitude. A past so dark it haunts him only in dreams. –the next two books are non-mysteries including the short stories (MLM). 3/3

1571. **Lansdale, Joe,** *Savage Season,* Bantam, 1990. Hap and Leonard #1 of 12. (Thriller) Here comes Trudy back into Hap's life, thirty-six but looking ten years younger, with long blonde hair and legs that begin under her chin, and the kind of walk that'll make a man run his car off the road. Here comes trouble, says Leonard, and he's right. She was always trouble, but she had this laugh when she was happy in bed that could win Hap over every time. Trudy has a proposition: an easy two hundred thousand dollars, tax-free. It's just a simple matter of digging it up... Hap Collins and Leonard Pine, white and black, straight and gay, are the unlikeliest duo in crime fiction. 2/3

1572. **Lansdale, Joe,** *Mucho Mojo,* Mysterious Press, 1994. Hap and Leonard #2 of 12. (Thriller) Inheriting one hundred thousand dollars and a small hiccup of a house in a dilapidated district is not so bad, and Uncle Chester made a nice gift of it to his nephew Leonard... though the clean-up is intensive, the floor is Rotten, and the neighbors are something from a nightmare. It is one thing to renovate a house to sell it. It is another to cut down the walls and risk discovering hidden skeletons... 2/3

1573. **Lansdale, Joe,** *Two-Bear Mambo,* Mysterious Press, 1995. Hap and Leonard #3 of 12. (Thriller) Florida Grange, Leonard's drop-dead gorgeous lawyer and Hap's former lover, has vanished in Klan-infested Grovetown while in pursuit of the real story behind the jailhouse death of a legendary bluesman's blackguard son. Fearing the worst, Hap and Leonard set out to do the kind of investigating the good ole boy cops can't - or won't - do. In Grovetown they encounter a redneck police chief, a sadistic Christmas tree grower, and townsfolk itchin' for a lynchin'. Add to this a dark night exhumation in a voodoo graveyard, a thunderstorm of Biblical proportions, and flat-out sudden murder. Hap and Leonard vow to face the hate and find Florida, even if Leonard has to put a hole in anyone who gets in the way. Besides, they've packed a lunch. 2/3

1574. **Lansdale, Joe,** *Bad Chili,* Mysterious Press, 1997. Hap and Leonard #4 of 12. (Thriller) Hap Collins has just returned home from a gig working on an offshore oil rig. With a new perspective on life, Hap wants to change the way he's living, and shoot the straight and narrow. That is until the man who stole Leonard Pine's boyfriend turns up headless in a ditch and Leonard gets fingered for the murder. Hap vows to clear Leonard's name, but things only get more complicated when Leonard's ex shows up dead. To the police it is just a matter of gay-biker infighting, but to Hap and Leonard murder is always serious business, and these hit a little too close to home. 2/3

1575. **Lansdale, Joe,** *Rumble Tumble,* Mysterious Press, 1998. Hap and Leonard #5 of 12. (Thriller) Bouncing at a local club by night and living by the grace of his best friend Leonard Pine and his good woman Brett Sawyer by day, Hap Collins is down but a long throw from out. And he'll need all his strength for the quick rescue of Brett's daughter Tillie – a drugged-out, trick-turning prodigal who doesn't care to be found. 2/3

1576. **Lansdale, Joe,** *Captains Outrageous,* Mysterious Press, 2001. Hap and Leonard #6 of 12. (Thriller) Hapless chicken-plant guard Hap Collins gets into trouble when he takes his best friend Leonard on a Caribbean cruise. The two find themselves abandoned in Mexico, saved from armed attackers by a geriatric fisherman and his lovely daughter, who's currently having to fend off a Mexican mobster who is also a practicing nudist... Trying for once to stay out of other people's business, Hap returns to East Texas but is overwhelmed when he learns of the senorita's murder. He then persuades Leonard to return with him to Mexico to even the score. –*Veil's Visit: A Taste for Hap and Leonard* published by Subterranean Press in 1999 featuring two short stories (MLM). 2/3

1577. **Lansdale, Joe,** *Vanilla Ride,* Knopf, 2009. Hap and Leonard #7 of 12. (Thriller) Hap is an East Texas smart mouth with a weakness for southern women. Leonard is a gay, black veteran pining for a lost love. They're not the makings of your typical dynamic duo, but never underestimate the power of a shared affinity for stirring up trouble and causing mayhem. When an old friend asks Leonard to rescue his daughter from an abusive, no-good drug dealer, he gladly agrees and, of course, invites Hap along for the fun. Even though the dealer may be lowly, he is on the bottom rung of the Dixie Mafia, and when Hap and Leonard come calling, the Mafia feels a little payback is in order. Cars crash, shotguns blast, and people die, but Hap and Leonard come out on top. Unfortunately for them, now they're facing not only jail time but also the legendary–and lethal–Vanilla Ride, who is still out to claim the price on their heads. Full of twists and turns, gunfire and gaffes, this hilarious, rip-roaring novel will have readers turning the pages faster than a Texas tornado. 2/3

1578. **Lansdale, Joe,** *Devil Red,* Knopf, 2011. Hap and Leonard #8 of 12. (Thriller) When their friend Marvin asks Hap and Leonard to look into a cold-case double homicide, they're more than happy to play private investigators: they like trouble, and they especially like getting paid to find it. It turns out that both of the victims were set to inherit serious money, and one of them ran with a vampire cult. The more closely Hap and Leonard look over the crime-scene photos, the more they see, including the image of a red devil's head painted on a tree. A little research turns up a slew of murders with that same fiendish signature. And if that's not enough, Leonard has taken to wearing a deerstalker cap ... Will this be the case that finally sends Hap over the edge? –the novellas *Hyenas, Dead Aim,* and *Briar Patch Boogie* were published by Subterranean in 2011, 2013, and 2016 (MLM). 2/3

1579. **Lansdale, Joe,** *Honky Tonk Samurai,* Mulholland, 2017. Hap and Leonard #9 of 12. (Thriller) Only Hap and Leonard would catch a cold case with hot cars, hot women, and ugly skinheads. The story starts simply enough when Hap, a former 60s activist and self-proclaimed white trash rebel, and Leonard, a tough black, gay Vietnam vet and Republican with an addiction to Dr. Pepper, are working a freelance surveillance job in East Texas. The uneventful stakeout is coming to an end when the pair witness a man abusing his dog. Leonard takes matters into his own fists, and now the bruised dog abuser wants to press charges. One week later, a woman named Lilly Buckner drops by their new PI office with a proposition: find her missing granddaughter, or she'll turn in a video of Leonard beating the dog abuser. The pair agrees to take on the cold case and soon discover that the used car dealership where her granddaughter worked is actually a front for a prostitution ring. What began as a missing-person case becomes one of blackmail and murder. –novellas *Hap and Leonard, Hap and Leonard Ride Again, Hoodoo Harry,* and *Coco Butternut* were published in 2016, 2016, 2017, and 2017 by Tachyon, Tachyon, Mysterious Press, and Subterranean (MLM). 2/3

1580. **Lansdale, Joe,** *Rusty Puppy,* Mulholland, 2017. Hap and Leonard #10 of 12. While Hap, a former 60s activist and self-proclaimed white trash rebel, is recovering from a life-threatening stab wound, Louise Elton comes into Hap and Leonard's PI office to tell him that the police have killed her son, Jamar. 2/3

1581. **Lansdale, Joe,** *Blood and Lemonade,* Tachyon, 2017. Hap and Leonard #11 of 12. (Thriller) Hap Collins is a complicated man. He looks like a good 'ol boy, but his politics don't match. After way too many jobs, Hap has discovered what he's best at: kicking ass. Vietnam veteran Leonard Pine is even more complicated: black, Republican, gay–and an occasional arsonist. As childhood friends and business associates, Hap and Leonard have a gift for the worst kind of trouble: East Texan trouble. –novella *Cold Cotton* was published by Crossroad Press in 2017 (MLM). 2/3

1582. **Lansdale, Joe,** *Jackrabbit Smile,* Mulholland Press, 2018. Hap and Leonard #12 of 12. (Thriller) Hap and Leonard are an unlikely pair - Hap, a self-proclaimed white trash rebel, and Leonard, a tough-as-nails black gay Vietnam vet and Republican - but they're the closest friend either of them has in the world. Hap is celebrating his wedding to his longtime girlfriend, when their backyard barbecue is interrupted by a couple of Pentecostal white supremacists. They're not too happy to see Leonard, and no one is happy to see them, but they have a problem and they want Hap and Leonard to solve it. –*The Elephant of Surprise* is to be released in 2019 (MLM). 2/3

1583. **Lansdowne, Ken,** *Secrets Don't Belong in Closets,* H Publishing, 2009. Bent Mysteries #1 of 8. (Bibliomystery Amateur Sleuth) A Queer Story of Hidden Lives, Lies, and Murder in 1986 New York City where JB tries to help his friend Len Matthews find out who killed the body he found in his bathtub one morning after a drinking blackout. Everyone in Len's building has a secret. Someone killed to keep theirs. 3/3

1584. **Lansdowne, Ken,** *A Murderous Ball of Fluff,* H Publishing, 2009. Bent Mysteries #2 of 8. (Bibliomystery Amateur Sleuth) A story of crossed phone lines, attempted murder, and transformation among the rich of 1986 New York. JB and Len are in rehearsals for his play to open Off-Broadway when one day they hear a plot to kill someone on JB's answering machine. They have no choice but to find the person and warn him. That search leads them to old friends, odd clubs, and an end to a budding relationship. 3/3

1585. **Lansdowne, Ken,** *The Fairy Dust Killer,* H Publishing, 2009. Bent Mysterious #3 of 8. (Bibliomystery Amateur Sleuth) Jeremy Bent and Len Matthews are back to find the serial killer who is terrorizing the gay men of Christopher Street in 1986 NY's Greenwich Village. 3/3

1586. **Lansdowne, Ken,** *Home Sweet Homo,* H Publishing, 2010. Bent Mysteries #4 of 8. (Bibliomystery Amateur Sleuth) JB travels back to his hometown in Kansas to aid a childhood friend who is being charged with the murder of a local cop. Meanwhile Len is on the road with a musical and has to solve the suspicious accident of one of his fellow cast members. 3/3

1587. **Lansdowne, Ken,** *Dance: Ten Murder: Maybe,* H Publishing, 2012. Bent Mysteries #5 of 8. (Bibliomystery Amateur Sleuth) Jeremy Bent (JB to everyone who knows him) investigates the death of the famous Broadway dancer, choreographer, and director Teddy Brewster. 3/3

1588. **Lansdowne, Ken,** *A Mystery, Wrapped in a Mystery, Surrounded by a Mystery,* H Publishing, 2013. Bent Mysteries #6 of 8. (Bibliomystery Amateur Sleuth) JB tries to help an amnesiac found wandering NYC's Greenwich Village with his murky and mysterious past, while also helping Len find a confessed hired killer in the AA rooms.

1589. **Lansdowne, Ken,** *The Art of Death,* H Publishing, 2014. Bent Mysteries #7 of 8. (Bibliomystery Amateur Sleuth) JB and Len are back for their seventh case. It is the year 1987. This time Len has grabbed a graffiti drawing from the subways and gets to meet the artist through a Hollywood starlet who knows both him & JB. There are art scams, forgeries, muggings, and murder as JB solves another crime in New York City. 3/3

1590. **Lansdowne, Ken,** *Bathhouse Bloodbath!,* H Publishing, 2016. Bent Mysteries #8 of 8. (Bibliomystery Amateur Sleuth) A night out at the baths for Len and JB ends up with them investigating the shooting death of the manager of the singer Dimity London, who is appearing at the tubs. 3/3

1591. **Lanyon, Josh (Dianne L. Browne),** *Snowball in Hell,* Aspen Mountain Press, 2007. Doyle and Spain #1 of 1. (MM Historical) Los Angeles, 1943. Reporter Nathan Doyle had his reasons to want Phil Arlen dead, but when he sees the man's body pulled from the La Brea tar pit, he knows he'll be the prime suspect. He also knows that his life won't stand up to intense police scrutiny, so he sets out to crack the case himself. –e-book only. (MLM). 3/3

1592. **Lanyon, Josh,** *Collected Novellas Vol. 1,* MLR, 2009. (MM Short Stories) In *Dangerous Ground* a casino robbery finds government agents Taylor and Will playing a game of cat-and-mouse with remorseless killers in the wilderness of California's High Sierras. *Snowball in Hell* introduces police detective Lt. Matthew Spain and reporter Nathan Doyle, men thrown together by murder. But, in post-WWII Los Angeles consequences of their attraction are serious, even for good guys. Writer Tim North assures his lover, homicide detective Jack Brady, that there's little danger in researching a sensational Hollywood murder committed decades before either of them was born. But, with *Cards on the Table*, Tim discovers that he's very, very wrong. This collection includes the bonus short story In Sunshine or In Shadow. 3/3

1593. **Lanyon, Josh,** *Collected Novellas Vol. 2,* MLR, 2009. (MM Short Stories) In *A Dark Wood* and *Ghost of a Chance* explore the terrors of houses haunted by something far worse than ghosts: the toxic product of guilt and shattered memory. British agent Mark Hardwicke is on the run from a mission gone horribly wrong, looking for shelter and care. But, in *I Spy Something Bloody* the only man who can offer that shelter and care is also the only man that Mark seems determined to push from his life. This collection includes the bonus short story *A Limited Engagement*, written for a collection whose sales support funding for marriage equality in the United States. 3/3

1594. **Lanyon, Josh,** *Committed to Memory,* MLR, 2009. Partners in Crime #5 of 5. (MM Short Stories) Two men: one with memories he can't escape, the other with memories he can't recapture – both trusting strangers who lie. Amnesiac Peter Killian, suspected art thief, can't understand why LAPD detective Michael Griffin takes his memory loss so personally. American expatriate Jack Stoyles, exiled in a distant Atlantic outpost, is suddenly in love with a stranger who kisses him – and then dies. With good reason Jack calls his place "Heartache Cafe." 3/3

1595. **Lanyon, Josh,** *The Dickens with Love,* Samhain, 2009. (MM Bibliomystery) Three years ago, a scandal cost antiquarian "book hunter" James Winter everything that mattered to him: his job, his lover and his self-respect. But now the rich and unscrupulous Mr. Stephanopoulos has a proposition. A previously unpublished Christmas book by Charles Dickens has turned up in the hands of an English chemistry professor by the name of Sedgwick Crisparkle. Mr. S. wants that book at any price, and he needs James to get it for him. There's just one catch. James can't tell the nutty professor who the buyer is. – e-book only (MLM). 3/3

1596. **Lanyon, Josh,** *Strange Fortune,* Blind Eye Books, 2009. (MM Adventure) Valentine Strange, late of his Majesty's 21st Benhali Lancers, needs money. Happily, the wealthy Holy Orders of Harappu are desperate to retrieve the diadem of the Goddess Purya from an ancient temple deep in the mountainous jungle–an area Strange knows well from his days quelling rebellions. The pay is too good, and the job seems too easy for Strange to refuse. But when Master Aleister Grimshaw, a dangerous witch from a traitorous lineage, joins the expedition, Strange begins to suspect that more is at stake than the retrieval of a mere relic. 3/3

1597. **Lanyon, Josh,** *The Mysterious,* MLR, 2010. (MM Short Stories) Newspaper man David Flynn knows a phony when he sees one, and he's convinced the Spiritualist Medium Julian Devereaux is as fake as a cigar store Indian. And he's absolutely right. But when Julian begins to see bloodstained visions of a serial killer, the only person he can turn to for help is the cynical Mr. Flynn (Lanyon). "The Wages of Sin" (Beecroft) Charles Latham, wastrel younger son of the Earl of Clitheroe, returns home drunk from the theatre to find his father gruesomely dead. He suspects murder. But when the Latham ghosts turn nasty, and Charles finds himself falling in love with the priest brought in to calm them, he has to unearth the skeleton in the family closet before it ends up killing them all. "Shadows in Time" (Baumbach) Trying to avoid ruin and disgrace, young naive Neal Clifton, wealthy heir to a sizable Boston family fortune faces the illicit and dangerous complication of his first affair with man–a scheming, unscrupulous man with influence and power that reaches beyond the grave. Neal vows to never give into his own unnatural desires again but finds his only hope for escape in the hands (and arms) of stoic silversmith, Peter Wade. 3/3

1598. **Lanyon, Josh,** *The Dark Farewell,* Samhain, 2010. (MM Journalism) It's the Roaring Twenties. Skirts are short, crime is rampant, and booze is in short supply. Prohibition has hit Little Egypt, where newspaperman David Flynn has come to do a follow-up story on the Herren Massacre. The massacre isn't the only news in town though. Spiritualist medium Julian Devereux claims to speak to the dead and he charges a pretty penny for it. 3/3

1599. **Lanyon, Josh,** *Lover and other Strangers,* Just Joshin, 2011. (MM Amateur Sleuth) Recovering from a near fatal accident, artist Finn Barret returns to Seal Island in Maine to rest and recuperate. But Seal Island is haunted with memories, some sweet, some sad; three years ago, Finn found his lover in the arms of Fitch, Finn's twin brother. Since that day, Finn has seen neither Conlan nor Fitch. In fact, no one has seen Fitch. –ebook only, originally appeared in the *Partners in Crime: The Art of Dying* anthology (MM). 3/3

1600. **Lanyon, Josh,** *The Darkling Thrush,* Just Joshin, 2012. (MM Bibliography Paranormal) Fed up with his desk duty in the Imperial Arcane Library, book hunter Colin Bliss accepts a private commission to find The Sword's Shadow, a legendary and dangerous witches' grimoire. But to find the book, Colin must travel to the remote Western Isles and solve a centuries' old murder. 3/3

1601. **Lanyon, Josh,** *Cards on the Table,* Just Joshin, 2012. (MM Mystery) Fifty years ago, a glamorous Hollywood party ended in murder – the only clue a bloody Tarot card. Timothy North is trying to find out what happened that long ago summer's night, but when a Tarot card turns up pinned to his front door, the only person Tim can turn to for help is his ex-lover, Detective Jack Brady. –e-book only and originally published in the "Partners in Crime" anthology (MLM). 3/3

1602. **Lanyon, Josh,** *Blood Red Butterfly,* Just Joshin, 2013. (MM Police Procedural) Despite falling in love with aloof manga artist Kai Tashiro, Homicide Detective Ryo Miller is determined to break the alibi Kai is supplying his murderous boyfriend–even if it means breaking Kai with it. –e-book only (MLM). 3/3

1603. **Lanyon, Josh,** *In Plain Sight,* Just Joshin, 2013. (MM Mystery) Nash didn't believe in love until it was too late. Now he's looking for reasons, for answers, for meaning. Sometimes the truth is right in front of you the whole time. –e-book only but was originally published in the print edition of the short stories collection, *In Sunshine* *or in Shadow* (MLM). 3/3

1604. **Lanyon, Josh,** *Stranger on the Shore,* Carina Press, 2014. (MM Journalism) Twenty years ago, young Brian Arlington, heir to Arlington fortune, was kidnapped. Though the ransom was paid, the boy was never seen again and is presumed dead. Pierce Mather, the family lawyer, now administers and controls the Arlington billions. He's none too happy, and more than a little suspicious, when investigative journalist Griffin Hadley shows up to write about the decades-old mystery. Griff shrugs off the coldly handsome Pierce's objections, but it might not be so easy to shrug off the objections of someone willing to do anything to keep the past buried. –e-book only unless you live in Italy (MLM). 3/3

1605. **Lanyon, Josh,** *Winter Kill,* Just Joshin, 2015. (MM Police Procedural) Clever and ambitious, Special Agent Adam Darling was on the fast track to promotion and success until his mishandling of a high profile operation left one person Now he's got a new partner, a new case, and a new chance to resurrect his career, hunting a legendary serial killer known as The Crow in a remote mountain resort in Oregon. Deputy Sheriff Robert Haskell may seem laid-back, but he's a tough and efficient cop – and he's none too thrilled to see feebs on his turf – but a butchered body in a Native American museum is out of his small-town department's league. –e-book only (MLM). 3/3

1606. **Lanyon, Josh,** *Murder between the Pages,* Just Joshin, 2016. (MM Bibliomystery) Felix Day, author of the Constantine Sphinx mysteries, and Leonard Fuller, author of the Inspector Fez mysteries, are bitter rivals and the best of enemies. Both happen to present when a notorious author of roman à clef is shot by an invisible assailant during a signing at historic Marlborough Bookstore. –e-book only (MLM). 3/3

1607. **Lanyon, Josh,** *Night Watch,* Just Joshin, 2016. Three years ago investigative reporter Parker Davidson barely survived a brutal attack by his psychopathic ex-boyfriend. It's given him a dim view of romance. –e-book only (MLM). 3/3

1608. **Lanyon, Josh,** *The Curse of the Blue Scarab,* Just Joshin, 2016. (Historical) Dr. Armiston, an irascible, confirmed bachelor who believes in medicine not mysticism, is certain the deaths are only tragic accidents. 3/3

1609. **Lanyon, Josh,** *The Dark Horse,* Loose Id, 2007. The Dark Horse #1 of 2. (MM Amateur Sleuth) Paul Hammond is dead. That's what tough and sexy LAPD Detective Daniel Moran tells his lover, Hollywood actor Sean Fairchild–and Sean wants to believe him, but what about those threatening postcards in Hammond's handwriting? The last thing Sean needs is someone doubting him. But then, what does Sean really know about his new boyfriend? Dan is a dark horse–and maybe Sean is betting too much on this relationship. He can't afford to take foolish chances. It not just Sean's career at stake or his relationship or even his sanity–it's his life. –e-book only (MLM). 3/3

1610. **Lanyon, Josh,** *The White Knight,* Loose Id, 2009. The Dark Horse #2 of 2. (MM Amateur Sleuth) Actor Sean Fairchild has a not-so-secret admirer: a psycho stalker who thinks taking out the sexy, shy young actor will leave the world a better place. His manager insists Sean needs protection, and Sean's beginning to think he's right. –e-book only (MLM). 3/3

1611. **Lanyon, Josh,** *I Spy Something Bloody,* Loose Id, 2008. I Spy #1 of 3. (MM Espionage) "Stephen, I'm in trouble ... " The voice on the phone was the last voice Dr. Stephen Thorpe expected to hear. But ex-lover Mark Hardwicke is injured and in trouble – and Stephen has always had a hard time saying no to this particular brand of trouble. –e-book only (MLM). 3/3

1612. **Lanyon, Josh,** *I Spy Something Wicked,* Just Joshin, 2011. I Spy #2 of 3. (MM Espionage) It's All Hallow's Eve and Mark Hardwicke's past has come back to haunt him. The Old Man needs Mark to go on one last mission to the wild, lonely hills of Afghanistan – a mission Mark knows he can't survive. Even if he does make it back, Stephen has made it very clear Mark is out of second chances. Should Mark place his lover and his own happiness before duty? –e-book only (MLM). 3/3

1613. **Lanyon, Josh,** *I Spy Something Christmas,* Just Joshin, 2012. I Spy #3 of 3. (MM Espionage) Nothing says Christmas like a bullet with your name on it. Mark is used to death and danger. Stephen will never be okay with violence – or Mark's attitude toward it. –e-book only (MLM). 3/3

1614. **Lanyon, Josh,** *The Ghost Wore Yellow Socks,* Loose Id, 2008. Ghost Wore Yellow Socks #1 of 2. (MM Amateur Sleuth) There's a dead body in Perry Foster's bathtub. A dead body in a very ugly sport's coat and matching socks. The dead man is a stranger to Perry, but that's not much of a comfort; how did a strange dead man get in a locked flat at the isolated Alton Estate in the wilds of the "Northeast Kingdom" of Vermont? Perry flees downstairs to get help and runs into "tall, dark and hostile" former navy SEAL Nick Reno. 3/3

1615. **Lanyon, Josh,** *The Ghost had an Early Check-Out,* Just Joshin, 2018. Ghost who Wore Yellow Socks #2 of 2. (MM Amateur Sleuth) To live and draw in L.A. Now living in Los Angeles with former navy SEAL

Nick Reno, artist Perry Foster comes to the rescue of elderly and eccentric Horace Daly, the legendary film star of such horror classics as Why Won't You Die, My Darling? Horace owns the famous, but now run-down, Hollywood hotel Angels Rest, rumored to be haunted. But as far as Perry can tell, the scariest thing about Angels Rest is the cast of crazy tenants–one of whom seems determined to bring down the final curtain on Horace–and anyone else who gets in the way. 3/3

1616. **Lanyon, Josh,** *Dangerous Ground,* Loose Id, 2008. Dangerous Ground #1 of 6. (MM Police Procedural) Special Agents for the Department of Diplomatic Security, Taylor MacAllister and Will Brandt have been partners and best friends for three years, but everything changed the night Taylor admitted the truth about his feelings for Will. And when Taylor was shot a few hours later, Will felt his reluctance to get involved was vindicated. –e-book only (MLM). 3/3

1617. **Lanyon, Josh,** *Old Poison,* Loose Id, 2009. Dangerous Ground #2 of 6. (MM Police Procedural) Happy Birthday, Taylor! Taylor has pretty well recovered from his shooting, but not everyone is happy to see him reach his next birthday. Does a cobra pickled in a bottle of wine means someone cares enough to send the very death – best? –e-book only (MLM). 3/3

1618. **Lanyon, Josh,** *Blood Heat,* Loose Id, 2010. Dangerous Ground #3 of 6. (MM Police Procedural) Special Agents for the Department of Diplomatic Security Taylor MacAllister and Will Brandt have been partners forever and lovers for three months, but their new relationship is threatened when Will is offered a plum two-year assignment in Paris. –e-book only (MLM). 3/3

1619. **Lanyon, Josh,** *Dead Run,* Loose Id, 2011. Dangerous Ground #4 of 6. (MM Police Procedural) For Special Agents of the Department of Diplomatic Security, Taylor MacAllister and Will Brandt, the strain of a long-distance relationship is beginning to tell after eleven months of separation. A romantic holiday could be just the thing to bridge the ever-growing distance, but when Taylor spots a terrorist from the 70s, long believed dead but very much alive, it's c'est la vie. –e-book only (MLM). 3/3

1620. **Lanyon, Josh,** *Kick Start,* Just Joshin, 2013. Dangerous Ground #5 of 6. (MM Police Procedural) Will is finally braced to bring Taylor home to meet the folks. Unfortunately, not every member of the Brandt clan loves Taylor the way Will does. Then again, not everyone loves the Brandts. In fact, someone has a score to settle – and too bad for any former DS agents who get in the way when the bullets start to fly. –e-book only. Book 6, *Blind Side,* will be released in

2019 by Just Joshin (MLM). 3/3

1621. **Lanyon, Josh,** *Fair Game,* Carina Press, 2010. All's Fair #1 of 3. (MM Amateur Sleuth) A crippling knee injury forced Elliot Mills to trade in his FBI badge for dusty chalkboards and bored college students. Now a history professor at Puget Sound university, the former agent has put his old life behind him–but it seems his old life isn't finished with him. –e-book only (MLM). 3/3

1622. **Lanyon, Josh,** *Fair Play,* Carina Press, 2014. All's Fair #2 of 3. (MM Amateur Sleuth) Fifty years ago, Roland Mills belonged to a violent activist group. Now, someone is willing to kill to prevent him from publishing his memoirs. –e-book only (MLM). 3/3

1623. **Lanyon, Josh,** *Fair Chance,* Carina Press, 2017. All's Fair #3 of 3. (MM Amateur Sleuth) Ex–FBI agent Elliot Mills thought he was done with the most brutal case of his career. The Sculptor, the serial killer he spent years hunting, is finally in jail. But Elliot's hope dies when he learns the murderer wasn't acting alone. Now everyone is at risk once again–thanks to a madman determined to finish his partner's gruesome mission. –e-book only (MLM). 3/3

1624. **Lanyon, Josh,** *Fatal Shadows,* Gay Men's Press, 2000. Adrien English #1 of 5. (MM Bibliomystery) One sunny morning Los Angeles bookseller and aspiring mystery author Adrien English opens his front door to murder. His old high school buddy (and employee) has been found stabbed to death in a back alley following a loud and very public argument with Adrien the previous evening. 3/3

1625. **Lanyon, Josh,** *Stranger Things have Happened: An Adrien English Write Your Own Damn Story,* MLR, 2013. Adrien English 1.5 of 5. (MM Bibliomystery) Book store assistant and all-around bad boy Robert Hersey has been murdered – and you are the #1 suspect! To clear your name and get your life back, you must figure out who killed your best friend and first love. –this is just *Fatal Shadows* in a choose your own adventure style book (MLM). 3/3

1626. **Lanyon, Josh,** *A Dangerous Thing,* Gay Men's Press, 2002. Adrien English #2 of 5. (MM Bibliomystery) Suffering from writer's block and frustrated with his tentative relationship with hot but closeted L.A.P.D. Homicide Detective Jake Riordan, gay bookseller and mystery writer Adrien English travels to northern California where he finds a body in his front drive. By the time the sheriffs arrive, the body has disappeared, and Adrien once again finds himself playing amateur sleuth. But when the game turns deadly, Adrien turns to Jake. Jake may be confused about some things but keeping his lover alive is not one of them–no matter what the cost. 3/3

1627. **Lanyon, Josh,** *The Hell You Say,* iUniverse, 2006. Adrien English #3 of 5. (MM Bibliomystery) After bookstore clerk Angus flees following terrifying death threats, owner Adrien must contend with a mysterious Satanic cult, a hot and handsome university professor, and his on-again/off-again relationship with closeted LAPD Homicide Detective Jake Riordan. 3/3

1628. **Lanyon, Josh,** *Death of a Pirate King,* MLR, 2008. Adrien English #4 of 5. (MM Bibliomystery) Gay bookseller and reluctant amateur sleuth Adrien English's writing career is suddenly taking off. His first novel Murder Will Out, has been optioned by notorious Hollywood actor Paul Kane. 3/3

1629. **Lanyon, Josh,** *The Dark Tide,* MLR, 2010. Adrien English #5 of 5. (MM Bibliomystery) As if recovering from heart surgery beneath the gaze of his over-protective family wasn't exasperating enough, someone keeps trying to break into Adrien English's bookstore. What is this determined midnight intruder searching for? 3/3

1630. **Lanyon, Josh,** *So this is Christmas,* Just Joshin, 2017. Adrien English #5.5 of 5. (MM Bibliomystery) Arriving home early after spending Christmas in jolly old England, sometimes amateur sleuth Adrien English discovers alarming developments at Cloak and Dagger Books–and an old acquaintance seeking help in finding his missing boyfriend. 3/3

1631. **Lanyon, Josh,** *Somebody Killed his Editor,* Samhain, 2010. Holmes and Moriarity #1 of 5. (MM Bibliomystery) For sixteen years reclusive mystery writer Christopher (Kit) Holmes enjoyed a very successful career, thanks to the popularity of elderly spinster sleuth, Miss Butterwith, and her ingenious cat, Mr. Pinkerton. But sales are down in everything, but chick lit, and Christopher's new editor doesn't like geriatric gumshoes. It's a pink, pink world for Mr. Holmes. 3/3

1632. **Lanyon, Josh,** *All She Wrote,* Samhain, 2011. Holmes and Moriarity #2 of 5. (MM Bibliomystery) A murderous fall down icy stairs is nearly the death of Anna Hitchcock, the much-beloved American Agatha Christie and Christopher Holmes's former mentor. Anna's plea for him to host her annual winter writing retreat touches all Kit's sore spots: traveling, teaching writing classes, and separation from his new lover, J.X. Moriarity. 3/3

1633. **Lanyon, Josh,** *The Boy with the Painful Tattoo,* Just Joshin, 2014. Holmes and Moriarity #3 of 5. (MM Bibliomystery) It's moving day at Chez Holmes. Somehow, against Kit's better instincts, he and J.X. are setting up house together. But while J.X. is off at a writing conference, Kit unpacks a crate that should contain either old books or new china. It doesn't. Within the mounds of green Styrofoam popcorn is a dead body. A very dead body. There goes the neighborhood. 3/3

1634. **Lanyon, Josh,** *In Other Words...Murder,* Just Joshin, 2018. Holmes and Moriarity #4 of 5. (MM Bibliomystery) Death reveals all secrets. Mystery author Christopher Holmes now comfortably married to sometimes rival, sometimes nemesis J.X. Moriarity, is starting a new career as a true crime writer when threatening anonymous notes start arriving. –*The 12.2-Per-Cent Solution,* the fifth book in the Holmes and Moriarity series is due out in 2020 (MLM). 3/3

1635. **Lanyon, Josh,** *This Rough Magic,* Loose Id, 2011. Shot in the Dark #1 of 2. (MM Bibliomystery Hard Boiled) Wealthy San Francisco playboy Brett Sheridan thinks he knows the score when he hires tough guy private eye Neil Patrick Rafferty to find a priceless stolen folio of Shakespeare's The Tempest. Brett's convinced his partner-in-crime sister is behind the theft – a theft that's liable to bring more scandal to their eccentric family, and cost Brett his marriage to society heiress Juliet Lennox. What Brett doesn't count on is the instant and powerful attraction that flares between him and Rafferty. –e-book only. The second book *Ill Met by Moonlight* was originally supposed to be published in 2014 but is still on-hold (MLM). 3/3

1636. **Lanyon, Josh,** *Mummy Dearest,* Samhain, 2011. XOXO Files #1 of 2. (MM Paranormal) The truth is out there. Way, way, way out there! –e-book only. The second book, *Bite Club,* has not been released yet (MLM). 3/3

1637. **Lanyon, Josh,** *In a Dark Wood,* Just Joshin, 2011. In a Dark Wood #1 of 2. (MM Thriller) In a dark, dark wood there was a dark, dark house... –e-book only. This novelette is also available in print in *Josh Lanyon Vol. 2* (MLM). 3/3

1638. **Lanyon, Josh,** *The Parting Glass,* Just Joshin, 2013. In a Dark Wood #2 of 2. (MM Thriller) Two and a half years ago, travel writer Timothy O'Shay let NYPD Detective Luke O'Brien talk him into hiking into the New Jersey Pine Barrens to face down a monster. –e-book only (MLM). 3/3

1639. **Lanyon, Josh,** *The Mermaid Murders,* Just Joshin, 2016. Art of Murder #1 of 3. (Police Procedural) Special Agent Jason West is seconded from the FBI Art Crime Team to temporarily partner with disgraced, legendary "manhunter" Sam Kennedy when it appears that Kennedy's most famous case, the capture and conviction of a serial killer known as The Huntsman, may actually have been a disastrous failure. 3/3

1640. **Lanyon, Josh,** *The Monet Murders,* Just Joshin, 2017. Art of Murder #2 of 3. (Police Procedural) The last thing Jason West, an ambitious young FBI Special Agent with the Art Crimes Team, wants–or needs–is his uncertain and unacknowledged romantic relationship with irascible legendary Behavioral Analysis Unit Chief Sam Kennedy. 3/3

1641. **Lanyon, Josh,** *The Magician Murders,* Just Joshin, 2018. Art of Murder #3 of 3. (Police procedural) Jason West, hot shot special agent with the FBI's Art Crime Team, is recuperating from a recent hit-and-run accident at the Wyoming home of BAU Chief Sam Kennedy when he's asked to aid in the investigation of a suspicious death in a National Forest. 3/3

1642. **Lardo, Vincent,** *China House,* Alyson, 1983. (Thriller) High on a hill near the New England town of Salem, an elegant Mansion stands deserted. Something happened there twenty years ago, something so horrible that those who remember keep it a secret. Now Scott Evans, haunted throughout his life by vague childhood memories of the house, has inherited the estate and its secrets. With the help of his handsome lover, Michael, Scott enlists the aid of Howard Roth, a psychologist who specializes in the supernatural, and his son, Ken, for a trip to Salem. They soon discover that in China House, anything can happen. –slight incest worship (MLM). 3/3

1643. **Lardo, Vincent,** *The Mask of Narcissus,* Alyson, 1987. (Police Procedural) As Mike Manning grieves over the heroic death of his lover, NY police officer Ken Farley, he gets a call from socialite Mildred Hamilton who confesses to killing her husband and his girlfriend. Drawn into a double murder on a snowy New Year's Eve takes Mike from a Fifth Avenue penthouse to a gay strip bar, a ride on a corporate jet and, finally, to two humpy preppies who do their best to change Mike's grief into unabashed passion. Many private lives go public before Mike uncovers THE MASK OF NARCISSUS to reveal the face of a murderer. 3/3

1644. **Larsen, Markus,** *Sex Club Murders and other Kinky Tales,* Nazca Plains, 2008 (Hard Boiled) New York Private Investigator rescues a kidnapped slave. –short story collection (MLM). 3/3

1645. **Lascarso, Laura,** *In the Pines,* Dreamspinner, 2018. Charlie Schiffer #1 of 1. (YA Mystery) After the disappearance of Eastview High's homecoming king, seventeen-year-old Charlie Schiffer must put his detective skills to work to help class heartthrob Dare Chalmers find his missing twin brother. From the gator-filled swamps of Paynes Prairie to the truck-stop strip club Café Risqué, there's no situation too dicey for this amateur sleuth when he's on the prowl for clues to this mystery. –e-book only (MLM). 3/3

1646. **Laskin, Steven,** *The Siegfried Contingency,* Steven Laskin, 2018. (Bibliomystery) When Carl Traeger, a quick-witted bookstore owner in 1970s Seattle, is bequeathed a well-hidden book by his aunt, he quickly learns he inherited much more than he bargained for. Carl's quiet life turns upside down when the German mob comes after him, willing to go to any lengths to get the book. –available as an e-book only (MLM). 3/3

1647. **Laurel, C. S.**, *B. Quick*, Five Star, 2005. Quick #1 of 3. (Amateur Sleuth) It was a night of triumphal activity for the Society for the Elimination of Good-Looking Blonds. By sheer chance, middle-aged literature professor Bill Yates interrupts a murderer in the act of dumping an unconscious young man into the local river. Bill surprises himself by rescuing the young man and unwittingly plunges into a maelstrom of murder, psychoanalysis and falling in love. 3/3

1648. **Laurel, C. S.**, *Quicksand*, Naked Reader, 2012. Quick #2 of 3. (Amateur Sleuth) When a dying man rings his doorbell, secrets from Professor William Yates's past rise up, which threaten his relationship with Brian Quick, his reputation and his life. Caught in the quicksand of his past, he has to solve the murder to get free. 3/3

1649. **Laurel, C. S.**, *Quick Change Artist*, Naked Reader, 2012. Quick #3 of 3. (Amateur Sleuth) Professor William Yates' gets more than he bargains for when he wakes up with a snake tattoo, a pierced tongue and an even bigger surprise. It turns out a serial rapist who answers his description EXCEPT for having those, has kidnapped him and made him match. Bill and Brian interview "ink artists" and various one night stands to find him. 3/3

1650. **Laurie, Paul**, *Night of the Sadist*, Parisian, 1971. (Journalism) Journalist Tom Maxon's investigation into his brother Bob's brutal murder takes him deep into the underworld of BDSM clubs and parties in this Agatha Christie-style mystery with a twist: Can Tom unmask the vicious killer before he strikes again? 3/3

1651. **Laurie, Paul**, *Man Eater*, Parisian, 1972. (Police Procedural) Jake Gold, a Vietnam veteran with PTSD, moved to Europe and reinvented himself as a United Nations Crime Control Commission agent; he investigates vicious offenses that cut across national borders. But pursuing the "man eater," a sadistic serial killer murdering gay men with a pair of steel teeth, forces Jake to face the personal demons that could get him killed. 3/3

1652. **Law, Janice**, *Fires of London*, Open Road Media, 2012. Francis Bacon #1 of 5. (Amateur Sleuth) A killer takes refuge in the blacked-out streets of wartime London, upending the world of one of Britain's greatest painters in this chilling and captivating reimagining of the life of Francis Bacon 3/3

1653. **Law, Janice**, *The Prisoner of the Riviera*, Open Road Media, 2013. Francis Bacon #2 of 5. (Amateur Sleuth) Peace has come to England

and the blackout is over, but the gloom has yet to lift from London. One night, leaving a gambling club where he has run up a considerable tab, the young painter Francis Bacon, accompanied by his lover, sees a man gunned down in the street. They do what they can to stanch the flow of blood, but the Frenchman dies in the hospital. Soon afterward, Bacon receives a strange offer from the club owner: He will erase Bacon's debts if the painter delivers a package to the dead man's widow, Madame Renard, on the Riviera. What gambler could resist a trip to Monte Carlo? –winner of the 26th LAMBDA Award for Best Gay Mystery (MM). 3/3

1654. **Law, Janice,** *Moon over Tangier,* Open Road Media, 2014. Francis Bacon #3 of 5. (Amateur Sleuth) In colonial Morocco, a painter navigates a conspiracy of forgery, corruption, and murder. For Francis, life with David grows more dangerous by the day. When sober, he is charming, but when he drinks, he is violent, slashing Francis's paintings and threatening to gut the painter, too. When David leaves London for Morocco, Francis cannot help but follow this man whom he loves but can no longer trust. In Tangier, they find a thriving community of expats who guzzle champagne while revolutionaries gather in the desert. But in Morocco's International Zone, death does not wait for rebellion. After Francis identifies a friend's Picasso as a fake, the police call him in to investigate the forger's demise. If he refuses, they will throw David in jail, where inmates and the DTs will kill him within the week. Between the bustle of the city and the emptiness of the desert, Francis finds that in Morocco, even the fakes can be worth killing for. 3/3

1655. **Law, Janice,** *Nights in Berlin,* Open Road Media, 2016. Francis Bacon #4 of 5. (Amateur Sleuth) Francis Bacon has never cared much for country living, so he is overjoyed when his father sends him to Berlin as punishment for his not-so-innocent flirtations with the other boys at school. With afternoons at the cinema, dinner at the Hotel Adlon, and nights at the most outrageous cabarets in Germany and in his uncle Lasting's bed he'll fit right in. 3/3

1656. **Law, Janice,** *Afternoons in Paris,* Open Road Media, 2017. Francis Bacon #5 of 5. (Amateur Sleuth) Francis Bacon was having a ball in Berlin–until his uncle disappeared, leaving Francis alone, broke, and wanted by the German police as well as the burgeoning Nazi party for a political murder he didn't commit. Luckily, for a young painter still learning his craft, there's no better place to find refuge than the cafes of Paris. In the City of Lights, Francis can perfect his French, complete his education, and–if he's lucky–escape with his life. 3/3

1657. **Laws, Jay B.,** *Steam,* Alyson, 1991. (Horror) A vaporous presence is slowly invading San Francisco. One by one, selected gay men are seduced by it–then they disappear, leaving only a ghoulish reminder of their existence. Can anyone stop this shapeless terror? 3/3

1658. **Laws, Jay B.,** *Unfinished,* Alyson, 1993. (Horror) They are the unfinished. Their lives were interrupted by an untimely death. Now their terrible predicaments chain them to this earth, jailing them until their stories are known. One man hears their cry, but if he isn't careful, he too may end up...unfinished. 3/3

1659. **Lear, James,** *Back Passage,* Cleis, 2006. Mitch Mitchell #1 of 3. (Modern Pulp) A seaside village, an English country house, a family of wealthy eccentrics and their equally peculiar servants, a determined detective – all the ingredients are here for a cozy Agatha Christie-style whodunit. But wait – Edward "Mitch" Mitchell is no Hercule Poirot. Mitch is a handsome, insatiable 22-year-old hunk who never lets a clue stand in the way of a steamy encounter, whether it's with the local constabulary, the house secretary, or his school chum and fellow athlete Boy Morgan, who becomes his Watson when they're not busy boffing each other. When Reg Walworth is found dead in a cabinet, Sir James Eagle has his servant Weeks immediately arrested as the killer. But Mitch's observant eye pegs more plausible possibilities: polysexual chauffeur Hibbert, queenly pervert Leonard Eagle, missing scion Rex, sadistic copper Kennington, even Sir James Eagle himself. Blackmail, police corruption, a dizzying network of spyholes and secret passages, watersports, and a nonstop queer orgy backstairs and everyplace else mark this hilariously hard-core mystery by a major new talent. 3/3

1660. **Lear, James,** *Secret Tunnel,* Cleis, 2008. Mitch Mitchell #2 of 3. (Modern Pulp) The Flying Scotsman, one of the world's legendary train journeys, has many attractions for Edward "Mitch" Mitchell, from the obliging porter to the mean guard to a troop of rough-and-ready soldiers in easily lifted kilts in the third-class carriage. But Mitch may not have time for them all before they arrive in London. When the train gets stuck in a tunnel, a dead body is found in the first-class toilet! Ever-ready Mitch decides to intervene and solve the crime. With his new Belgian sidekick Benoit, he pursues the killer through a crazy kaleidoscope of movie stars, drug dealers, royal scandals, and queens of every description. Can he finger the villain before the villain fingers him? What is the connection between Buckingham Palace and a bunch of backstreet pornographers? And what is the mystery of the secret tunnel? Mitch intends to go all the way to figure it all out. 3/3

1661. **Lear, James,** *Sticky End,* Cleis, 2010. Mitch Mitchell #3 of 3. (Modern Pulp) Mitch Mitchell needs a vacation, and he is determined to make the most of his trip to the Mediterranean island of Gozo.

Death never takes a break however, and at the behest of fellow doctor Bob Southern, Mitch soon finds himself investigating the demise of a young, gay lance corporal. The police have ruled it a suicide, but the young man's boyfriend claims it was murder. Suspecting an official cover-up of a queer scandal, Mitch gets to work on an investigation that leads him into a labyrinth of lies, false identities and secret sex. 3/3

1662. **Lear, James,** *The Hardest Thing,* Cleis, 2013. Dan Stagg #1 of 3. (Modern Pulp) Once a major in the US Marines, Dan Stagg fell foul of Don't Ask, Don't Tell and is now struggling to make sense of civilian life. In his late 30s, tall and muscular, Dan works as a bouncer at an East Village nightclub. When he's offered a fortune to protect the young male secretary of a powerful real estate developer, Dan takes off on a road trip with a hot blond companion who makes it clear that "protection" doesn't stop at the bedroom door. But Dan soon realizes that he's being used as a shield for a much more sinister operation and has to choose between easy money and the ideals that he once fought for. 3/3

1663. **Lear, James,** *Straight Up,* Cleis, 2015. Dan Stagg #2 of 3. (Modern Pulp) Who is trying to kill the members of an elite special ops team that worked off the radar in Iraq in the '90s? It's up to Dan Stagg to track down the survivors – the men with whom he stormed an undefended surveillance station, killing everyone inside. And now, many years later, the team is being targeted in what seems like a series of unrelated attacks. Dan teams up with his old comrade Al Benson, once a rising star of the USMC, now a respectable married civilian with a few secrets to hide. As they dig deeper into the secrets of the past, Dan discovers that Benson's looking for more than just answers. An explosive affair threatens everyone's future and connects Dan to a past he thought he'd left behind. 3/3

1664. **Lear, James,** *In the Ring,* Cleis, 2018. Dan Stagg #3 of 3. (Modern Pulp) Concealed identities, beautiful double agents, corruption, power, and passion. 3/3

1665. **Leaton, Simon,** *The Gay Detective,* Createspace, 2012. (Cozy) In the quiet market town of Wimborne, murder is afoot! But fear not, for out of the maelstrom of dirty deeds and gossip comes Wimborne's very own Private Detective Matt Powers, a young man with the weight of the world on his shoulders, determined to solve the case of his murdered friend and mentor. As the body count rises, could the murderer be his charming new neighbour and army medic Captain Jared Allmes? The Wimborne Detective Agency is open for business. 3/3

1666. **Leaton, Simon,** *Reapers at Albion Dawn,* Createspace, 2012.

(Hardboiled) Tomas Dark, a carefree Barber from a Southern English Fishing town and Marcus Rand, an American Detective from L.A. hold the key to preventing the return of an evil from the time of legend and Myth. What connection do they have with a serial killer dressed as a Reaper, an international businessman and the imminent arrival of the Albion Dawn and a world of magic and terror. 3/3

1667. **LeCarre, John,** *A Murder of Quality,* Walker, 1962. (Spy as an Amateur Sleuth) George Smiley was simply doing a favor for Miss Ailsa Brimley, and old friend and editor of a small newspaper. Miss Brimley had received a letter from a worried reader: "I'm not mad. And I know my husband is trying to kill me." But the letter had arrived too late: it's scribe, the wife of an assistant master at the distinguished Carne School, was already dead. –villain is gay but is sympathetic to a gay reader but not to the author or Smiley (MLM). 3/3

1668. **Lee, Will,** *Cobalt,* Vantage, 1999. (Paranormal) "San Francisco policeman Frank Lee, with Louisiana ties, comes to the aid of a straight private investigator Cobalt Bluesberg (Gunn)." 3/3

1669. **Legleitner, Robert**, *Golden Legend,* Write Words, 2002. Kydon Chronicles #1 of 5. (Espionage) German-born archaeologist Kydon Schmidt has a secret that would ruin him in the homophobic atmosphere of the 1940s. So, when the U.S. Government recruits him for a mission against Nazi artifact collectors, he is hardly in a position to refuse Filled with suspense and drama. –e-book only (MLM). 3/3

1670. **Legleitner, Robert,** *A Brief Madness,* Write Words, 2002. Kydon Chronicles #2 of 5. (Espionage) In WWII, Kydon Schmidt, a man with a secret, spies on Nazis and helps fugitives escape.... Kydon is seeking revenge on the men who shot his friend Val. If they want a spy, they'll get one! –e-book only (MLM). 3/3

1671. **Legleitner, Robert,** *Death in the Ruins,* Write Words, 2003. Kydon Chronicles #3 of 5. (Espionage) Sent to authenticate Roman antiquities at an English country estate, gay archeologist Kydon Schmidt assumes his task is tame stuff after spying for OSS and MI-6. But his post-WWII assignment soon turns to murder. In addition to the ruins of a 12th- century abbey, the estate has a missing host, some possibly stolen antiquities, and the odd dead body. And amid a fine collection of suspects, Kydon may have found the love of his life. –e-book only (MLM). 3/3

1672. **Legleitner, Robert,** *Tangled Web,* Write Words, 2003. Kydon Chronicles #4 of 5. (Espionage) Kydon Schmidt, our favorite gay hero, is back, and this time he's involved in a tangled web of espionage. –e-book only (MLM). 3/3

1673. **Legleitner, Robert,** *Wake the Dead,* Write Words, 2004. Kydon Chronicles #5 of 5. (Espionage) Dead men seem to be breaking out of their graves. Are they the walking dead? Or are these sightings connected to a posh spa run by a doctor rumored to have worked with Nazi medical experimentation? Reunited lovers Kydon Schmidt and Robin Wyngate track fleeing Nazi war criminals. –this is the only book in the series that is available in print (MLM). 3/3

1674. **Lennon, David,** *The Quarter Boys,* Blue Spike, 2010. Doucette and Jones #1 of 6. (Police Procedural) The day that a tourist is discovered murdered in a guest house in New Orleans' French Quarter, Joel Faulkner, an innocent 23-year-old from Mississippi, arrives in town hoping to start a new life. When he meets homicide detective Michel Doucette, he feels his life is finally coming together but soon he finds himself being drawn into a world of drugs and prostitution, and directly into the path of the killer. When Michel and his partner, Alexandra "Sassy" Jones, are given the case, Michel sees it as a chance for a fresh start. Little does he suspect that Joel's life depends on his finding the killer or foresee the personal sacrifices he'll have to make to succeed. 3/3

1675. **Lennon, David,** *Echoes,* Blue Spike, 2010. Doucette and Jones #2 of 6. (Police Procedural) When three young girls go missing, rookie police officer Sassy Jones is assigned to create a profile of the abductor. Seeing the case as an opportunity to establish herself professionally, she immerses herself in her work, but soon worries about her personal life lead her off-track. –won the twenty-third LAMBDA Award (MM). 3/3

1676. **Lennon, David,** *Second Chance,* Blue Spike, 2011. Doucette and Jones #3 of 6. (Hard Boiled) As former New Orleans homicide detectives Michel Doucette and Alexandra "Sassy" Jones try to get their fledgling private investigation agency off the ground, someone from their past reappears, seeking their help to untangle a business venture with two members of an organized crime family. When the head of the family hires Michel and Sassy to find his missing son, they soon find themselves caught up in an apparent turf war between aging kingpins and an emerging power. 3/3

1677. **Lennon, David,** *Blue's Bayou,* Blue Spike, 2011. Doucette and Jones #4 of 6. (Hard Boiled) When his cousin Verle is accused of murder, private investigator Michel Doucette heads to the small town of Bayou Proche to help prove Verle's innocence. In the process, he uncovers a blackmail plot against one of Verle's closest friends, and an apparent conspiracy to gain control of the mineral rights to Verle's land in the Atchafalaya Basin. He is also forced to finally confront painful memories from his own childhood. 3/3

1678. **Lennon, David,** *Reckoning,* Blue Spike, 2012. Doucette and Jones #5 of 6. (Hard Boiled) After two years of near-constant upheaval in their professional and personal lives, private investigators Michel Doucette and Alexandra "Sassy" Jones have finally found some peace. For Michel, in particular, everything is near-idyllic, as he and his boyfriend, Joel, build a life together and search for a new home for themselves and their dog, Blue. But when Michel receives a mysterious ransom note, things quickly change, and he and Sassy find themselves at the center of a police investigation. As old friends and enemies suddenly reappear, it becomes all too clear that the past isn't quite done with them yet. 3/3

1679. **Lennon, David,** *Fierce,* Blue Spike, 2013. Doucette and Jones #6 of 6. (Hard Boiled) Two years after the death of his boyfriend, private investigator Michel Doucette is still emotionally adrift. Estranged from his best friend and partner, Sassy Jones, he immerses himself in the familiar routines of work and caring for his dog. When a wealthy socialite hires him to find her missing son, though, Michel sees it not just as a chance to take Sassy's mind off problems of her own, but as an opportunity to mend their fractured relationship. What appears to be a simple missing person's case, however, soon turns deadly. –this is listed as the sixth and final mystery in the series but Lennon, in 2018, stated that he is working on the seventh book (MLM). 3/3

1680. **Lennon, David,** *Deadfall,* Blue Spike, 2014. (Thriller) Thirteen years after a serial killer stalked the streets and forests of a small Massachusetts town, the last near-victim returns hoping to rebuild his life after recovering from a coma. As Danny Tyler pieces together fragments of lost memory, however, he begins to realize that not only was his childhood very different than he thought at the time, but the wrong man might be in jail for the murders. 3/3

1681. **Lennon, David,** *Irish Black,* Blue Spike, 2016. (Police Procedural) As racial tension escalates in the wake of the court-ordered desegregation of the city's public schools, the already-on-edge neighborhood of South Boston is rocked by a series of seemingly gang-related killings. But when three children are murdered, police detective Tommy Doyle begins to wonder if something more sinister is at play. Are the killings all connected, and how could the killing of the children so closely mirror a nightmare from his own childhood? As the investigations continue, Doyle forms an uneasy alliance, but soon finds himself being pulled into a dark journey through his own psyche. 3/3

1682. **Leon, Donna,** *The Anonymous Venetian,* Macmillan, 1994. (Italian Police Procedural) Commissario Brunetti #3 of 28. Commissario Guido Brunetti's hopes for a refreshing family holiday in the mountains are once again dashed when a gruesome discovery is made in Marghera - a body so badly beaten the face is completely unrecognizable. Brunetti searches Venice for someone who can identify the corpse but is met with a wall of silence. He then receives a telephone call from a contact who promises some tantalizing information. And before night is out, Brunetti is confronting yet another appalling, and apparently senseless, death. –victim is a man dressed as a woman so Brunetti spends a lot of time in gay bars but as the book is from 1994 his opinions on gay men is dated and mostly negative. Leon and her publisher often list her books in the gay mystery section on Amazon but other than a lesbian couple who have appeared in two or three novels there is no gay content in these books (MLM). 1/3

1683. **Leonhard, Sam C.,** *Tainted Blood,* Dreamspinner, 2010. Tainted #1 of 2. (MM Paranormal) Gabriel Jordan lives a lonely life on the streets, taking the rare job that usually means spending hours in the cold, waiting for a chance to take a photograph of a cheating spouse. That's how he meets Dr. Aleksei Tennant-who he sees suspiciously jumping from a window of a woman's apartment. Tennant is eager to teach, and a fragile friendship develops amidst a series of murders. The killer has a grudge against the mixture of other races: he doesn't kill humans, only those of the hidden worlds who are producing children of tainted blood. 3/3

1684. **Leonhard, Sam C.,** *Tainted Soul,* Dreamspinner, 2011. Tainted #2 of 2. (MM Paranormal) Gabriel Jordan, part-time werewolf and full-time private investigator, should be living a happy life. Three years ago, he was a homeless thief; now he's got a loving partner and a job he enjoys, he lives in a nice house, and he doesn't have to worry about tomorrow. So why the sudden urge to cheat on Aleksei, the handsome and occasionally deceptive fae he loves? Why does Gabriel feel compelled to flee the life he's built for himself? 3/3

1685. **Leslie, Peter,** *The Gay Deceiver,* Macgibbon and Kee, 1967. (Espionage) "London-based secret agent David Charter is one of a number of spies at work in Cold War England in a comic *tour de force* (Gunn)." 3/3

1686. **Levay, Simon,** *Albrick's Gold,* Richard Kasak, 1997. (Thriller) Dr. Roger Cavendish, a leading researcher into the mysteries of sexuality and the mind, finds himself faced with a mystery straight out of his worst nightmares. Violence is on the rise at ultra-conservative Levitican University – and Cavendish becomes a reluctant gumshoe, busily involved in discovering what fuels this sudden rise in brutal crime. The truth seems to lie somewhere in the laboratory of Dr. Guy Albrick – and enigmatic scientist who claims to have developed a "cure" for homosexuality. Soon, Cavendish is in a race with time, struggling to unlock the secrets of Albrick's work as the wave of violence threatens to overtake him and all others in its path. –biotech thriller ex-gays vs. gays (MLM). 3/3

1687. **Leventhal, Stan,** *Faultlines: Stories of Suspense,* Banned Books, 1989. (Short Stories) San Francisco setting, something evil is beginning to fester, and the most that anyone can figure out is that it's connected to a small-time hood and a phony preacher. 3/3

1688. **Leventhal, Stan,** *The Black Marble Pool,* Amethyst, 1990. (Amateur Sleuth) There's a dead body at the bottom of a pool in the backyard of a guest house in Key West. Who is he? And what caused his untimely demise? –ReQueered Tales is republishing this title in 2019 (MLM) 3/3

1689. **Levey, Michael,** *Tempting Fate,* Hamish Hamilton, 1982. (Crime Drama) Precocious, brilliant, sophisticated and disturbing, Nicholas Gonville is a sixteen-year-old public schoolboy who appears to be cool and amused enough to cope with any experience. Desired by all who meet him, he leads a charmed life, lightly eluding the embraces of his over-fond schoolmaster and observing the antics of his elders with merciless wit. But when his godfather dies in mysterious circumstances Nicholas is forced to abandon his role of detached spectator: he is pitched into a threatening world of police investigations, and the murderer seems to be about to strike again... 3/3

1690. **Levine, Laura,** *This Pen for Hire,* Kensington, 2002. Jaine Austen #1 of 16. (Amateur Sleuth) Smarmy personals ads. Daring declarations of love. Writer-for-hire Jaine Austen has penned them all. But when one of the love connections she made is broken up by murder, Jaine finds herself freelancing free-of-charge–and uncovering more than she bargained for... –"Beverly Hills shoe salesman Lance Venable, with preternatural hearing, becomes useful to amateur sleuth Jaine Austen (Gunn)." 2/3

1691. **Levine, Laura,** *Last Writes,* Kensington, 2003. Jaine Austen #2 of 16. (Amateur Sleuth) Jaine still hasn't found a good man–or a way to keep all those sugary snacks from going straight to her hips. But– with a little help from her best friend Kandi–she's finally landed a gig as a sitcom writer! True, Muffy isn't going to win any Emmys, but for Jaine, being on staff sure beats writing boring brochures and bad resumes. Until the plot thickens–with murder. 2/3

1692. **Levine, Laura,** *Killer Blond,* Kensington, 2004. Jaine Austen #3 of 16. (Amateur Sleuth) When Beverly Hills socialite Sue Ellen Kingsley offers Jaine megabucks to ghostwrite a book of hostess tips, it's time to sharpen the #2s. So, what if Jaine has to take dictation from a rail-thin lady of leisure in a bubble bath? Pride doesn't feed the cat and the dubious side benefit of this particular job is an up-close, personal view of the amorous exploits of Hollywood's ladies-who-lunch. But everything short circuits when Jaine finds Sue Ellen floating face down in her tub, fried by her own blow dryer. 2/3

1693. **Levine, Laura,** *Shoes to Die For,* Kensington, 2005. Jaine Austen #4 of 16. (Amateur Sleuth) The indomitable sleuth Jaine Austen is out to find who murdered a well-heeled French shop owner. 2/3

1694. **Levine, Laura,** *The PMS Murder,* Kensington, 2006. Jaine Austen #5 of 16. (Amateur Sleuth) While trying on bathing suits in the communal dressing room at Loehmann's, freelance writer Jaine Austen makes a new friend–a wannabe actress named Pam–and gets a new job: sprucing up Pam's bare-bones resume. Their feeling of connection is mutual, so Pam invites Jaine to join The PMS Club–a women's support group that meets once a week over guacamole and margaritas. 2/3

1695. **Levine, Laura,** *Death by Pantyhose,* Kensington, 2007. Jaine Austen #6 of 16. (Amateur Sleuth) Freelance writer Jaine Austen has never been able to resist the siren call of an Eskimo Pie, just like she can't resist renewing her romance with Andrew, an old crush. With her bank account hitting new lows, she's also just agreed to write jokes for Dorcas, a stand-up comic who throws her pantyhose into the audience as a punch line. Not only is Dorcas's act a bomb, she is heckled by Vic, a gorgeous fellow comic. Naturally when Vic is murdered with Dorcas's pantyhose and that same Dorcas is standing over his dead body, the police arrest...Dorcas. They figure it's an open-and-shut case, although Jaine figures no killer can be that dumb. –*Candy Cane Murder* short story published in 2007 by Kensington (MLM). 2/3

1696. **Levine, Laura,** *Killing Bridezilla,* Kensington, 2008. Jaine Austen #7 of 16. (Amateur Sleuth) When writer-for-hire Jaine Austen signs on to script vows for the ultimate Bridezilla, "I do's" soon become "I wish I hadn't's"–and curtains for the bride spell a veil of woes for Jaine... Jaine's accepted her share of lame gigs to pay the bills, but rewriting Shakespeare's got to be an all-time low. The fiasco begins with a call from Jaine's high-school nemesis, uber rich uber witch Patti Devane. It seems Patti will soon be sashaying down the aisle with another former classmate from Hermosa High, and she'd like the exchange of vows to evoke Romeo and Juliet...except without the "downer" of an ending. 2/3

1697. **Levine, Laura,** *Killer Cruise,* Kensington, 2009. Jaine Austen #8 of 16. (Amateur Sleuth) The wordsmith and sleuth dives into her most dangerous case yet. 2/3

1698. **Levine, Laura,** *Death of a Trophy Wife,* Kensington, 2010. Jaine Austen #9 of 16. (Amateur Sleuth) Without a job or a date in sight, freelance writer Jaine Austen is equally out of luck in finance and romance. So, when her friend Lance offers to treat her to brunch at the Four Seasons, Jaine leaps at the invite. –*Gingerbread Cookie Murder* short story released in 2010 by Kensington (MLM). 2/3

1699. **Levine, Laura,** *Pampered to Death,* Kensington, 2011. Jaine Austen #10 of 16. (Amateur Sleuth) Jaine Austen is looking forward to an indulgent spa getaway - until she learns it's more about deprivation that relaxation. Between miniscule meals and a deadly brush with fame, surviving this vacation will be no piece of cake. 2/3

1700. **Levine, Laura,** *Death of a Neighborhood Witch,* Kensington, 2012. Jaine Austen #11 of 16. (Amateur Sleuth) When her faithful feline Prozac unwittingly scares to death a parakeet belonging to the neighborhood's resident curmudgeon, Jaine finds herself knee-deep in toil and trouble. The cantankerous Hollywood has-been once played the part of Cryptessa Muldoon, television's fourth most famous monster mom. Now a bitter, paranoid old dame, Cryptessa spends her days making enemies with everyone on the street, and accidental bird killer Jaine is no exception. So, when the ornery D-lister is murdered with her own Do Not Trespass sign on Halloween night, the neighborhood fills with relief–and possible culprits. –*Secret Santa* short story released in 2013 by Kensington (MLM). 2/3

1701. **Levine, Laura,** *Killing Cupid,* Kensington, 2013. Jaine Austen #12 of 16. (Amateur Sleuth) When Jaine lands a job writing web copy and brochures for matchmaker Joy Amoroso, she's excited for a chance to help the lovelorn–until she realizes Joy is a ruthless taskmaster who screams at her employees for the smallest infractions, pads her website with pictures of professional models posing as clients, and offers up convincing but empty promises of love. So, it's no surprise when the chiseling cupid turns up dead at a Valentine's Day mixer. Now, finding the culprit may prove harder than spotting that elusive caramel praline in a box of chocolates. 2/3

1702. **Levine, Laura,** *Death by Tiara,* Kensington, 2015. Jaine Austen #13 of 16. (Amateur Sleuth) Jaine has been hired by über-pushy stage mom Heather Van Sant to write lyrics for her daughter Taylor's song in the talent competition for the Miss Teen Queen America pageant. It's different from anything Jaine has done before, but if nothing else, she's looking forward to a free weekend in a swanky hotel and a chance to see what really goes on backstage at a beauty pageant. But the hotel is a dump, the cattiness is out of control, and Candace–the perfectly-coiffed, whip-cracking pageant director–is making even Jaine's life miserable. 2/3

1703. **Levine, Laura,** *Murder has Nine Lives,* Kensington, 2016. Jaine Austen #14 of 16. (Amateur Sleuth) The future is looking bright for freelance writer Jaine Austen. She's signed up for a new job, she's looking forward to a tropical vacation, and her cat Prozac is slated to star in a major commercial. But when the claws come out behind the scenes, Jaine worries that murder might be the only thing to meow about... 2/3

1704. **Levine, Laura,** *Death of a Bachelorette,* Kensington, 2017. Jaine Austen #15 of 16. (Amateur Sleuth) Jaine's life has been a royal pain since she started penning dialogue for Some Day My Prince Will Come–a cheesy dating show that features bachelorettes competing for the heart of Spencer Dalworth VII, But Jaine never expected murder to enter the script. When one of the finalists dies in a freak accident, it's clear someone wanted the woman out of the race for good–and the police won't allow a soul off the island until they seize the culprit. Terrified of existing another day without air conditioning and eager to return home, Jaine is throwing herself into the investigation. And she better pounce on clues quickly–or there won't be any survivors left. 2/3

1705. **Levine, Laura,** *Death of a Neighborhood Scrooge,* Kensington, 2018. Jaine Austen #16 of 16. (Amateur Sleuth) Scotty Parker is a former child star who once played Tiny Tim, but now he's grown up into the role of neighborhood Scrooge. Scotty thinks he can stage a comeback with the screenplay he's working on and Jaine's been reluctantly helping him edit it. So, when Scotty is bludgeoned with a frozen chocolate yule log and the police start making a list of suspects and checking it twice, Jaine's name is unfortunately included. 2/3

1706. **Levy, Owen,** *A Brother's Touch,* Pinnacle, 1982. (Amateur Sleuth) Cautionary Tale Angus had lost track of his younger brother through the years. He'd been too busy trying to clear the jungles of Vietnam out of his brain. And now Earl is dead, his body found on the Manhattan waterfront, in one of the West Village's notorious gay cruising areas. Recent photos of Earl before he died show a sweet, laughing face, surrounded by the feathery blond curls of a cherub. His diary reveals a life on the street, a needle in his arm, his body wracked with drugs paid for by men wanting love in return. Angus' grim journey into his brother's brief life leads him to a dark corner of society he never knew existed, and the dark corners of his own soul he wishes he could forget. 2/3

1707. **Lewis, Stephen,** *Cowboy Blues,* Alyson, 1985. (Hard Boiled) Gay detective Jake Lieberman gets an assignment to help a rodeo competitor find his missing younger lover. 3/3

1708. **Lilly, Greg,** *Fingering the Family Jewels,* Regal Crest, 2004. Derek Mason #1 of 2. (Amateur Sleuth) Derek Mason arrives in Charlotte, North Carolina for the funeral of his Aunt Walterene. He encounters the family who sent him away because he revealed he was gay. His mother and Uncle Vernon want him out of town because of Vernon's senate campaign. His sister and Aunt Ruby urge him to stay. His cousin Mark denies their past relationship. Derek uncovers mysteries in the death of a family gardener, possibly at the hands of a young Vernon. Secrets and lies unravel as Derek digs into the family history with the help of hunky reporter Daniel. 3/3

1709. **Lilly, Greg,** *Scalping the Red Rocks,* Cherokee McGee, 2010. Derek Mason #2 of 2. (Amateur Sleuth) Something's askew in the red rocks of Sedona, Arizona. The town's inhabitants are divided by urban growth. Some entrepreneurs try to make a quick buck by selling out the very aspect of the town that drew them: the awe-inspiring views and natural beauty. Spirited, passionate, and a bit mettlesome, Derek Mason helps his aunt Ruby find her place in the New Age haven, but instead they discover her real estate agent scalped in an empty condo. 3/3

1710. **Lindquist, Hakan,** *My Brother and his Brother,* Bruno Gmuder, 2011. (Crime Drama) Jonas, an 18-year old boy, throughout his teenage years he has been trying to get an image of Paul, the brother he never met, a brother who died at the age of 16, the year before Jonas himself was born. The story is told like a crime story, with loose ends, clues and cliff hangers. In his search for his brother, Jonas soon finds out that Paul had an intense love affair with another boy during the last year of his life. –translated from the Swedish by the author (MLM). 1/3

1711. **Linington, Elizabeth,** *Green Mask!,* Harper Collins, 1964. (Police Procedural) His head was bashed in, the body left to lie in the rear of the hole-in-the-wall restaurant he ran on Fountain Avenue. A copy of the county directory neatly tied with green ribbon lay on the body and tucked into the ribbon there was a note: THIS IS NUMBER ONE! GREENMASK. Number two was a woman. complete with county directory and neat green ribbon. Then there was number three, and suddenly number tour, slumped in a movie house on Sunset Boulevard, county directory, green ribbon. and the note on his lap. It looked like a series of psycho murders, but Sergeant Ivor Maddox of the Los Angeles Police Department had feeling he'd heard it all before, and then he had a hunch. –unsure of gay content (MLM). ?/3

1712. **Lipez, Richard, & Peter Stein,** *Grand Scam,* Dial Press, 1979. (Amateur Sleuth) What is the Pacific Ocean doing in Midland, Texas? And what has happened to the Alaskan crude that should be flowing through the newly inaugurated oil pipeline in place of the seawater and flotsam that are gushing from it? Oil company security officer Ernie Hoopes hopes to track down the conspirators behind the gigantic scam. –gay secondary character (MLM). 1/3

1713. **Litman, Robert,** *Treblinka Virus,* Ivy League, 1990. (Dystopian) Due, in part, to the nefarious activities of the Hivvies (a well-organized band of infected people, who are spreading the pestilence purposefully as a means of terrorism), the world's population is diminishing rapidly. 3/3

1714. **Llewellyn, A. J.,** *Fawnskin,* Amber Quill, 2010. Fawnskin #1 of 2. (MM Paranormal) When Rallus quits his FBI job and moves to the mountain town of Fawnskin, California, to get away from it all, he has no clue that rural life will mean falling in love with another mysterious newcomer. He falls hard and fast for Knox Baylor, who's taken an unusual job as a shommerin, a corpse watcher at a funeral home. For Knox, the job should be easy money, even if the hours are long... except that he falls asleep on the job and accidentally releases Mr. Harold Hoxheimer's angry spirit, or dybbuk, which starts creating unholy havoc in Fawnskin. 3/3

1715. **Llewellyn, A. J.,** *Frenzied,* Amber Quill, 2010. Fawnskin #2 of 2. (MM Paranormal) Ever since Knox fell asleep and released Harold Herxhiemer's spirit, the town of Fawnskin has never been the same, and probably never will again. 3/3

1716. **Lloyd, Jason,** *The Garden of Fibs and Sin,* Createspace, 2015. Filthy Fibbers #0 of 1. (MM Mystery) Daniel Patrick Darling II is gorgeous, rich, and conceited, with just the right amount of bitch. You may think he has it all; friends, money, power, but all those things won't help Danny when he mysteriously vanishes one night after hanging out with his best friends. Danny is loved by few, but unfortunately hated by many. Anyone could have been behind his disappearance. –supposedly a prequel for a series but no series yet exists (MLM). 3/3

1717. **Lloyd, John S.,** *Why did he Die?,* Spalding and Wallace, 2015. (Amateur Sleuth) After a long planned but delayed vacation to Hawaii and Hong Kong John Haffner's life is radically changed. On a whim he leaves a secure job as a CPA in Chicago to work for Lee Kwan in Hong Kong. He accidentally befriends devilishly handsome but reclusive Andrew Henley, who has a business relationship with the illusive Mr. Kwan. John and Andrew's friendship develops quickly but ends abruptly. 3/3

1718. **Lloyd, L. V.,** *Murder in 1975,* self-published, 2013. (Police Procedural) It's 1975 and a young girl has been brutally murdered. Chief Inspector William Harper is in charge of the case, but has he fallen in love with a murderer? Color TV has just gone on the market, writers use typewriters and gay lovers were actually committing a crime... –available as an e-book only through the Wattpad website. Marked as a first in a series but the sequel is not forthcoming (MLM). 3/3

1719. **Lloyd, L. V.,** *Rough Play and Other Stories,* Smashwords, 2013. (Police Procedural) A collection of gay short stories, sci-fi and romance. Includes "Rough Play," a novella in the Aurigan Space Saga series and "Love in 1975," a sequel to "Murder in 1975." –according to Goodreads this collection of short stories is no longer available (MM). 3/3

1720. **Logan, Margaret,** *A Killing in Venture Capital,* Walker, 1989. (Amateur Sleuth) After a deal between Dynagen, a biotechnology firm developing a cure for multiple sclerosis, and venture capitalist Drew Lispenard falls through, murder strikes aboard a Dynagen executive's boat, and Drew investigates. 2/3

1721. **Logan, Patricia,** *Silver Bullets,* Westburg, 2012. Silver #1 of 4. (MM Police Procedural) Sexy, selfish Michael Francis has hit rock bottom. His boyfriend has dumped him, stolen all his money and his career as a super model has come to a screeching halt. Tyler Winston, macho Texas lawman, has lost the only love he's ever had and the shocking memories of his long buried past have come back to haunt him. Set on a collision course, can these two broken men find common ground and begin to heal each other or will a ruthless killer part them forever? 3/3

1722. **Logan, Patricia,** *Silver Secrets,* Createspace, 2013. Silver #2 of 4. (MM Espionage) Rome Wilkins hopes to start his life free from covert operations and impending danger. As a black ops Navy SEAL, Rome is the best assassin the US government has at its disposal. When they call him in to help with mission after mission, it seems as though his best laid plans are slipping through his fingers. Thom Akecheta, a Native American born warrior in his own right and a Marine Corps veteran, works in the FBI's Houston office as a forensic scientist. His immediate attraction to the handsome and enigmatic Rome is complicated by his lust for Pepper Rawlings; his very beautiful, very young lab partner. He's wanted her for a very long time, and now, he wars with his attraction between the two. When the three become involved, none of them expect their country will once more call on their service and ultimately put all of their lives in terrible danger. –relationship becomes a MMF (MLM). 3/3

1723. **Logan, Patricia,** *Silver Ties,* Createspace, 2013. Silver #3 of 4. (MM Police Procedural) A serial killer is preying upon gay men in Los Angeles. Detective Cassidy Ryan of the LAPD is out to stop the monster before more mutilated corpses turn up. The victims have one thing in common and it leads back to an infamous online club called DOMZ.com. The website owner, Zachary Teak, is stunningly gorgeous and infuriatingly uncooperative. Having spent years in vice, investigating crimes fueled by pornography, Cassidy hates the Dom on sight. –A BDSM romance (MLM). 3/3

1724. **Logan, Patricia,** *Silver Linings,* Createspace, 2015. Silver #4 of 4. (MM Police Procedural) LAPD detective Cassidy Ryan has been living with his Dom, Zachary Teak, for more than two years. Having met when a serial killer targeted gay members of the online BDSM club owned by Zack, the men think they've put the past behind them... until another victim turns up. 3/3

1725. **Logan, Patricia,** *Death and Destruction,* Createspace, 2016. Death and Destruction #1 of 9. (MM Police Procedural) Forced to go into witness protection, ATF Special Agent Thayne Wolfe, is less than thrilled. The State's Attorney needs him to testify against one of the most ruthless and notorious arms dealers in the world. Expecting boredom and lots of daytime television, he instead ends up with a ridiculous new job, a stupid new name, and the world's most annoying shadow. Jarrett Evans, is nevertheless tasked with keeping Wolfe alive long enough to put Mills Lang and his crew away for the rest of their miserable lives. 3/3

1726. **Logan, Patricia,** *Flash and Bang,* Createspace, 2017. Death and Destruction #2 of 9. (MM Police Procedural) If running from a hit man wasn't scary enough, ATF agent Thayne Wolfe, has a new challenge in his life and this one may be even more dangerous than the last. He has to figure out how work with his reckless new partner, a handsome former Marine who seems to have a death wish. When their boss sends them to San Diego to investigate a fireworks accident, he figures Jarrett can't hurt anyone playing with sparklers, not even himself. The fact is, danger, intrigue and Jarrett's dubious past seem to follow the men wherever they go. From a Marine base at the Mexican border to an explosion in LA's Chinatown, they aren't prepared for a seriously pissed off militia, a smoking hot ex-lover, and more guys who want them dead. 3/3

1727. **Logan, Patricia,** *Slip and Slide,* Createspace, 2016. Death and Destruction #3 of 9. (MM Police Procedural) ATF special agents, Thayne Wolfe, and his partner, Jarrett Evans, have gotten into sticky situations in the past but nothing prepares them for the daunting task of being loaned out to a coal mine in West Virginia where Jarrett's grown up. Investigating a deadly mining explosion may be the end of them yet. 3/3

1728. **Logan, Patricia,** *Locked and Loaded,* Createspace, 2017. Death and Destruction #4 of 9. (MM Espionage) ATF agents Thayne Wolfe and Jarrett Evans are back and this time, they'll be facing a familiar foe. International arms dealer, Mills Lang, has acquired a stolen cache of tabun, a powerful nerve agent, to sell to the highest bidder. The last thing either Thayne or Jarrett wants to do is get involved with the psychopath again but duty calls. Jarrett is sent in undercover as an Iranian who's looking to trade cold hard cash to stop the deadly weapon's sale only to learn he has to bid against the world's nastiest scumbags. 3/3

1729. **Logan, Patricia,** *Point and Shoot,* Createspace, 2017. Death and Destruction #5 of 9. (MM Police Procedural) Thayne Wolfe and Jarrett Evans have been working together for nearly a year. Now, living together as well, their relationship has taken on a whole new meaning for both men. It seems that danger has always been a part of their lives in the ATF but when SAC Stanger sends them to a relatively routine crime scene, things quickly get complicated. Someone has been arming Los Angeles street gangs with automatic weapons missing their serial numbers. 3/3

1730. **Logan, Patricia,** *Thunder and Lightning,* Createspace, 2017. Death and Destruction #6 of 9. (MM Police Procedural) Jarrett Evans and Thayne Wolfe have been partnered in the ATF for nearly two years and their love and commitment to each other has grown over time. Now faced with one final challenge, the boys are headed to Arizona to help Thayne's mom, stumbling headfirst into a brand-new case. When a man is shot on Dot's sister's ranch, their informal investigation leads to the Native American reservation bordering the property. 3/3

1731. **Logan. Patricia,** *Body and Soul,* Createspace, 2017. Death and Destruction #7 of 9. (MM Police Procedural) More than ten years ago, a series of train bombings devastated railways throughout Europe. Strange poetry sent to local newspapers right before each bombing, confounded investigators at the time. In one of only a handful of failed covert missions, Jarrett had been sent into North Korea to take out the bomber. Now, as his wedding to Thayne approaches, an explosion in Southern California, threatens to ruin their plans for a very special day. 3/3

1732. **Logan, Patricia,** *Endings and Beginnings,* Createspace, 2018. Death and Destruction #8 of 9. (MM Police Procedural) Recently married ATF special agents Thayne Wolfe and Jarrett Evans are ready for some normalcy to return to their work in the ATF the way it has at home. FBI special agent Mac McCallahan and his partner, Lincoln Snow, have a new boss and are handed a dangerous case involving rogue military elites, as strong as an army. Someone has plans to take over control of the world's supply of palladium, crippling the US economy. ATF Special Agent Nicodemo Devecchio and FBI Special Agent Mac McCallahan are sent in undercover while Thayne and Jarrett are assigned to monitor things from the SCIF... as if Jarrett could easily just sit still and watch... as if. –*Spies and Allies* is set to be released in 2019 (MLM). 3/3

1733. **Logan, Patricia,** *Thin Blue,* Createspace, 2018. Thin Blue Line #1 of 2. (MM Police Procedural) Detective Pope Dades is a veteran police officer working in the Hollywood division, one of the busiest police precincts in the country. Dealing with drug dealers, hookers, and mentally ill suspects on a daily basis is his stock and trade. He once loved his job with the LAPD but three years ago, he put his trust in the wrong man and he's been paying the price ever since. Refusing to work with a partner after the first one nearly killed him, Pope is jaded, still hurting, and hanging onto the career he once adored by a thread. 3/3

1734. **Logan, Patricia,** *Order and Anarchy,* Createspace, 2018. Thin Blue Line #2 of 2. (MM Espionage) Homeland Security investigators Felix Jbarra and Pope Dades are about to work their first big case as partners. Someone is creating counterfeit government documents and selling them through a site similar to the old Silk Road which was shut down years ago. As they dive into the case with the help of their friends at the FBI and LAPD, Felix and Pope realize the Dark Web site is selling more than documents. It's selling death. –book 3, *Crime and Chaos* will be released in 2019 (MLM). 3/3

1735. **London, Clare,** *True Colors,* Dreamspinner, 2009. (MM Mystery) From the very first, Zeke Roswell and Miles Winter are like oil and water. After a tragic fire claimed his brother's life, Zeke's personal and professional life spiraled out of control, and now he has no choice but to sell his gallery to cover his debts. Enter successful entrepreneur Miles, who buys it and plans to make a commercial success out of Zeke's failure. Their initial hostility stands no chance against the strong passion that ambushes them. Zeke's talent and lust for life intoxicate Miles, and Zeke finds Miles' self-assurance and determination equally fascinating. But it's not until an unsolved mystery of violence and stolen sketches threatens to sabotage any chance at happiness. 3/3

1736. **London, Clare,** *72 Hours,* Dreamspinner, 2010. (MM Suspense) Tanner Mackay and Niall Sutherland were once far more than just fellow intelligence agents. But then a mission went horribly wrong and everything fell apart, sending Tanner into hiding and splitting the team and their affair wide apart. 3/3

1737. **Long, Charles Alan,** *God Killer,* Createspace, 2011. (Police Procedural) The first victim is hung in crucifixion position–a gash in his side and a wreath on his head. Homicide detectives Dylan Black and Vivienne Sheffield are baffled by strange words written in Scrabble tiles, the dead man's discarded glass eye, and wolf hair left at the scene. The victim's neighbor, a college student and mythology buff named Trevor McDaniel, is convinced the victim is not meant to represent Jesus, as the detectives first concluded, but rather an ancient Viking god who was killed by a monstrous, mythical wolf. 3/3

1738. **Long, J. S.**, *Mai Tais and Murder,* NineStar, 2017. Gabe Maxfield #1 of 3. (MM Court Drama) Gabe Maxfield never wanted to be a detective or a policeman or anything of the sort. The closest he wanted to come to the law was writing legal briefs and doing research for a big-shot law firm. Nice and safe, and without all the stress. No unanswered questions, just well-defined legal precedents. When he moves to Hawaii in the wake of a disastrous breakup and betrayal by an ex, a murder investigation is the last thing he expects to get wrapped up in, but he can't help himself when a dead body, a hunky cop, and his best friend get involved. 3/3

1739. **Long, J. S.**, *Tiki Torches and Treasure,* NineStar, 2017. Gabe Maxfield #2 of 3. (MM Hard Boiled) Gabe Maxfield has reached a comfortable point in his life. His past troubles in Seattle are all but forgotten, he co-owns his own business, Paradise Investigations, with his best friend Grace Park, and he's happy in his relationship with sexy cop–his neighbor–Maka Kekoa. Maybe the best part is, no one's pointed a gun at him in weeks. –*Palm Trees and Paparazzi,* the third book in the Gabe Maxfield series is set to be released in 2019 (MLM). 3/3

1740. **Long, J. S.**, *Matter of Duty,* NineStar, 2017. Hong Kong Nights #1 of 3. (MM Crime Drama) Noah Potter has come to Hong Kong to find his missing sister, Lianne, who disappeared after leaving him a voice mail pleading for his help. Unfortunately, the Hong Kong police are unwilling to help him, so Noah has to find her himself. Noah's search for his sister brings him across Wei Tseng, leader of the Dragons, a group of dedicated men and women willing to do whatever it takes to keep their district safe from the violence and triads that plague the rest of the city's underworld. 3/3

1741. **Long, J. S.**, *A Matter of Courage,* NineStar, 2017. Hong Kong Nights #2 of 3. (MM Crime Drama) Winston Chang has spent much of his young life admiring the Dragons who have kept his area safe and fought off the gangs that would bring violence to their area. Now that he's an adult, he wants nothing more than to join the Dragons and live up to those standards. The opportunity presents itself when his passion and knowledge of cars is just what the Dragons need. One of their own has been killed and his death seems linked to his involvement with the illegal racing scene known as the Dark Streets. Winston is needed to infiltrate the scene and find out who is responsible and why. 3/3

1742. **Long, J. S.**, *A Matter of Justice,* NineStar, 2018. Hong Kong Nights #3 of 3. (MM Crime Drama) The battle between the Dragons of the Eastern District and their bitter rivals, the Twisted Vipers, is reaching a dangerous point. The Anti-Gang Task Force is hard at work trying to bring down the Vipers. Tensions ratchet when Johnny Hwang guns down a prominent inspector on the task force, and Conroy Wong, Wei Tseng's second-in-command is a witness. Now, to keep him safe long enough to locate a second witness and put Hwang behind bars, Conroy is forced into close quarters with Allen Hong, a man who once fought side by side with the Dragons until he turned his back on them by joining the police, betraying them. 3/3

1743. **Long, W. S.**, *Love and Murder,* JMS, 2014. Love and Murder #1 of 2. (MM Court Drama) Jake Chandler is a struggling small-town Florida lawyer, and his life is falling apart. His ex-wife makes seeing his daughter difficult, his boyfriend Noah may be cheating on him, and his money woes are growing. Jake hopes that a new murder defense case will help with his money woes, but his ex-wife Elena is the prosecutor. It's bad enough she has to fight with him over custody of their daughter. Now she wants nothing more than to beat him in the courtroom, too. And then people around him start dying. 3/3

1744. **Long, W. S.**, *Love and Pain,* JMS, 2016. Love and Murder #2 of 2. (MM Court Drama) After their too-thrilling courtship that included capturing his former lover's killer, Jake Chandler has started a new life for himself with FBI agent Xavier. Living together is wonderful but moving to Washington D.C. has resulted in temporary jobs that don't last long. When Jake finally lucks out on a too-good-to-be-true position with a big law firm, Xavier suspects Jake's new boss is crooked. When a key witness is shot to death in front of Jake, they both begin to realize how high the stakes are. 3/3

1745. **Lopez, Dan**, *The Show House,* Unnamed Press, 2016. (Thriller) when news of a serial killer that targets gay men at nightclubs rocks the community, over-worked pharmacist Laila grows concerned for her handsome and arrogant younger half-brother, Alex. Sunshine leads to darkness as the calculating murderer's own life, hidden away in a show house, is spiraling out of control after falling for a would-be victim. 3/3

1746. **Lopez, Gerald**, *All Queers Must Die,* Smashwords, 2015. (MM Mystery) Maynard Shores, Florida is an exclusive beachfront town where the rich and beautiful come to live out their fantasies. Fun in the sun, and hot nights filled with passion are to be expected in a locale that caters to every sexual taste and preference. But danger lurks behind the shore's glittering facade. The price for indulging in one of the area's newest pleasures could be high–very high. A dangerous new designer drug has been introduced to the scene and partaking of it could be deadly. Its effects have already been profoundly felt by one newcomer to the area. –e-book only. Lopez also writes under the pseudonym of Antonio no last name (MLM). 3/3

1747. **Lopez, Gerald,** *Between Lights and Death,* Createspace, 2016. (Horror) Best friends Barry, Gary, and Terry are off on a Halloween adventure. But what starts off as a normal trip to a haunted house ends up as anything but a usual occurrence. As the horror becomes all too real, love blossoms between two old friends. But will they survive the night for love to bloom. –e-book only (MLM). 3/3

1748. **Lopez, Gerald,** *The Detective's Last Case,* Gerald Lopez, 2018. (Police Procedural) With retirement looming, the detective gets a call from someone he can't refuse. He takes on a final case in an idyllic seaside town where strange things are taking place. This includes a murder he's been hired to investigate. But add in a lover not seen for years, a couple of bizarre sisters, and some children in distress and the detective has his hands full. –e-book only (MLM). 3/3

1749. **Lopez, Gerald,** *Blue Light by Night,* Smashwords, 2013. Layton Shayne #1 of 4. (MM Paranormal) Detective, and ex-military man, Layton Shayne's newest case has taken him from his home out west into the dark and ominous swamplands of Louisiana. His client Leticia Carter has only told him that the case is simple and involves three siblings with the last name of Kennedy. Layton's job is to discover who should inherit the old family estate located in Shelby, a town so small it doesn't even show up on most maps. Immediately after he entered Shelby, the detective met some colorful and mysterious characters. It wasn't long before he discovered that there was an ancient supernatural element which held the citizens of the town in fear. –e-book only (MLM). 3/3

1750. **Lopez, Gerald,** *Green Eyes Cry, You Die,* Smashwords, 2014. Layton Shayne #2 of 4. (MM Paranormal) Gay Detective Layton Shayne is on the case again, this time with his lover Alex working alongside him. If he thought his last case involving a cult and the supernatural had prepared him for everything–he couldn't have been more wrong. This new case for Leticia Carter and her mysterious organization would take him and Alex from Louisiana to central Florida. They would be on the hunt for a mysterious green-eyed lady statue possessing supernatural powers and rumored to cry real emerald tears which bring death with them. –e-book only (MLM). 3/3

1751. **Lopez, Gerald,** *Black Hearts Dance,* Smashwords, 2015. Layton Shayne #3 of 4. (MM Paranormal) Detective Layton Shayne and his partner Alex are back and working on a new case. While out with friends, the two catch the eye of a mysterious older woman who hires Layton to investigate the hauntings on her estate, Carson Court. Not only is Layton intrigued… he also feels compelled to take the job. New surprises greet him and Alex at every corner as they meet the hunks and mysterious citizens living in and around Carson Court. Layton knows to listen to his instincts, but this time could that lead to trouble of a supernatural nature in a house with a dark past and secrets desperate to come out? –e-book only (MLM). 3/3

1752. **Lopez, Gerald,** *Gray Days, and Wicked Ways,* Smashwords, 2016. Layton Shayne #4 of 4. (MM Paranormal) It was supposed to be a vacation for Layton and Alex, but how could Layton not help the young son of a fellow Marine. The vacation turns explosive and the case Layton took on for a quarter gets complicated. Someone is out for blood and no one is safe. It's difficult for Detective Layton Shayne to know who to trust and the situation hits home further when some fellow Marines get involved. Old familiar faces show up as well with hidden agendas of their own. Miss Lucy makes an appearance along with Leticia Carter who has a surprising revelation or two of her own. When Forrest Hanson pays a visit, things heat up in an altogether different way for Alex and Layton. And what would Layton's life be without some supernatural elements thrown in for fun. –e-book only (MLM). 3/3

1753. **Lopez, Gerald,** *Miss Lucy and the Pussy Brigade,* Smashwords, 2014. Miss Lucy Case Files #1 of 1. (Espionage) Miss Lucy dreaded training new agents in the field, more than almost anything else she had to do for the organization. This mission had already started off badly due to the fact she was retraining agent Buck Taggerty–or 'the fool' as she liked to call him. The team was supposed to be working a simple retrieval case involving one little pussycat statue, but things went crazy to a slapstick comedy level. As serious as the case was, it would become legendary among the organization's members for its comedic qualities. -e-book only and although it states that it is part of a series, it is currently the only one so far (MLM). 2/3

1754. **Lopez, Gerald,** *Dead Men Tell Tales,* Createspace, 2014. New Eden #1 of 2. (MM Crime Drama) Mason Kincaid's life is about to change. He's adjusting to being alone a year after the death of his lover when a call from his wayward sister sends him out west to New Eden to bring not only her, but her twin sons and a stepson home. –e-book only (MLM). 3/3

1755. **Lopez, Gerald,** *City of Dead Men,* Createspace, 2018. New Eden #2 of 2. (MM Police Procedural) Things in the town of New Eden have been quiet, but that's about to change. Ken and Mason have been living happily together raising their two adopted sons. But police officer Ken's new case will affect those he loves, including Mason. New people have come to town–some good and others bad. Familiar characters face big changes in their lives even as others are fighting for survival. And everything leads to the mysterious city of dead men. –e-book only (MLM). 3/3

1756. **Lopez, Gerald,** *Lost Bitches,* Smashwords, 2015. Abel Kane #1 of 2. (Hard Boiled) Private detective Abel Kane is on the case. And he is willing and able to do what it takes to get the job done. What starts off as a seemingly simple dognapping case turns into much more when the mob, a pretty call girl, and several hunky men get involved. –e-book only (MLM). 3/3

1757. **Lopez, Gerald,** *Only the Young and Beautiful Need Apply,* Createspace, 2018. Abel Kane #2 of 2. (Hard Boiled) Abel Kane is on the case again. But when he goes undercover in a Bible school his personal demons from the past resurface. It's good religion versus bad with bizarre sexual situations thrown into the mix. Abel needs to figure out what exactly is going on at the school. And it's not easy when he's busy dealing with people who are either trying to kill him or bed him. –e-book only (MLM). 3/3

1758. **Lopez, Gerald,** *A Shared Darkness,* Createspace, 2017. Father Andrew #1 of 3. (Amateur Sleuth) The quiet town of Stratham, Florida has been shaken to its core. Explosive and deadly events have people scared. Father Andrew Madera is on the scene to help investigate. But he soon discovers the town has yet to come to grips with some dark secrets that have yet to see the light of day. With the help of his fellow priests and handsome, lusty-eyed Vincent Farragate, Father Andrew hopes to save the day. But can he solve the mystery in time, before another victim is claimed? –e-book only (MLM). 3/3

1759. **Lopez, Gerald,** *Crackpots, Crooks, and Cowboys,* Createspace, 2017. Father Andrew #2 of 3. (Amateur Sleuth) While trying to solve the mystery of his heart, Father Andrew has his hands full. It seems he's made an enemy who has it in for him. And this enemy's attacks are escalating. With the help of Officer Tate, Vincent, and others will Father Andrew be able to find the person behind the evil deeds inflicted on him before it's too late? –e-book only (MLM). 3/3

1760. **Lopez, Gerald,** *Andrew in Paradise,* Createspace, 2017. Father Andrew #3 of 3. (Amateur Sleuth) Life has certainly changed for Andrew Madera. Now it's taken yet another turn that finds him on an island paradise. But is this Eden all it seems or is there a snake hiding and waiting to strike? And what about Andrew's future with Vince? Meanwhile a new mystery has surfaced during the island's hedonistic gay festival. –e-book only (MLM). 3/3

1761. **Lord, Christopher,** *The Christmas Carol Murders,* Harrison Thurman, 2012. Dickens Junction #1 of 2. (Cozy) It's the holiday season in Dickens Junction, Oregon. Local bookstore owner, Simon Alastair, is getting ready for the community's annual celebration of Charles Dickens' well-known story. But when a mysterious stranger shows up in the Junction and is murdered hours later, Simon begins to suspect that his little community has been targeted for destruction by a shadowy organization. 3/3

1762. **Lord, Christopher,** *The Edwin Drood Murders,* Harrison Thurman, 2013. Dickens Junction #2 of 2. (Cozy) The Droodists have arrived in Dickens Junction. Local bookstore owner Simon Alastair has his hands full in his role as co-chair for the latest convention honoring Charles Dickens's uncompleted novel, The Mystery of Edwin Drood. A movie star, a pesky blogger, dueling scholars, a stage hypnotist, and an old family friend (among others) all have claims on Simon's time. In addition, some Droodists are clearly more–or less–than they appear, including a mysterious young man with the improbable name of Edwin Drood. –there had been attempts at publishing a third book in the series but after failing to find a publisher Lord retired from writing (MLM). 3/3

1763. **Lord, David Thomas,** *Bound in Blood,* Kensington, 2001. Jean-Luc #1 of 2. (Fantasy) By all appearances, Jean-Luc "Jack" Courbet has the perfect life. His art critiques appear regularly in The New York Times. His Greenwich Village apartment is filled with tasteful antiques. And his finely chiseled face and body make him an object of longing for the men he meets in clubs and bars – men who satisfy his dual need for pleasure and cruel pain. But beneath the glittering social whirl of Jack's elite lifestyle lies a deadly secret: he is a vampire, transformed a century ago in Paris by his powerful stepfather. 3/3

1764. **Lord, David Thomas,** *Bound in Flesh,* Kensington, 2006. Jean-Luc #2 of 2. (Fantasy) Vampire Jean-Luc Courbet is back with his lover and fellow vampire Claude Halloran and together they wreak havoc on cities across the world, leaving a trail of bodies in their wake. One of their victims, Mike O'Donald, is the only one who may be able to stop them and save the lives of countless victims. 3/3

1765. **Lore, Phillips,** *Murder behind Closed Doors,* Playboy, 1980. (Hard Boiled) Leo Roi #3 of 3. Leo Roi looks to the Chicago and Evanston gay community for clues as he investigates the murder of a wealthy advertising executive and two of his homosexual friends. –Lore is a pseudonym for Terrence Lore Smith (MLM). 1/3

1766. **Lorenz, Lynn,** *No Good Deed,* Amber Quill, 2010. (MM Police Procedural/Crime Drama) They say no good deed goes unpunished. Two men are about to find out if that old saying is true... Captain Daniel Chan works for the Riceland Police Department. It's a small town in Texas and he's the only Chinese American on the force. Mark's a man with a terrible past and he's in hiding from it and the man who tried to kill him so long ago. 3/3

1767. **Love, F. W.,** *Cop Coming Out,* Greenleaf, 1980. (Pulp) "Undercover policeman Frank Streicker, 25, spends more time having sex with adolescents than trying to uncover an alleged ring of homosexuals preying on underage runaways and resigns in a pulp pseudo-procedural (Gunn)." 3/3

1768. **Lovell, Ron,** *Danger in Unlikely Places,* Penman, 2015. Lorenzo Madrid #1 of 4. (Court Drama) Because of his involvement in breaking up a drug gang, Oregon attorney Lorenzo Madrid has become a marked man. The surviving members of that gang, led by Esteban Perez, want revenge. He also needs a break from his law practice where he specializes in helping migrants deal with the harshness of their lives. An invitation to teach an immigration law course at UCLA provides the perfect escape. He moves to Los Angeles and settles into a pleasant new life. Unfortunately, the ruthless bosses of the cartel track him down. After Lorenzo witnesses a shooting, where the bullet might have been meant for him, he is lured to an abandoned warehouse where Pantera reveals a secret from Lorenzo's past that has haunted them both for years. –the mc is not blantantly gay as there is very little reference to his sexual orientation however, in the third novel there is a brief mention of a past lover by the name of Thaddeus (MLM). 3/3

1769. **Lovell, Ron,** *A Dangerous Assignment,* Penman, 2016. Loranzo Madrid #2 of 4. (Court Drama) What starts as a simple review of actor contracts turns into much more. Before long, he is handling all aspects of production of a low budget movie to be filmed in Oregon. The location is an abandoned sanitarium on the Oregon Coast where he has to deal with a temperamental movie queen called by her fans The Queen of the Bs her drunken husband a stuntman, strange incidents on the set and murder. 3/3

1770. **Lovell, Ron,** *Danger by the Sea,* Penman, 2017. Lorenzo Madrid #3 of 4. (Court Drama) As he is setting up a law practice in a small-town Oregon, Lorenzo Madrid is faced with two vexing cases. In one, he must get a young politician out of a mental clinic where his unscrupulous stepmother had him committed so she can gain control of his family's timber company. In the other, an old flame of Lorenzo's good friend Tom Martindale asks for help in adopting an Ecuadorian orphan. The problem is, she has already taken him to the U.S. When she returns to that country, she is imprisoned. –another series, Tom Martindale mysteries, by Lovell is tied to this one but there are no avert gay references in those titles however there may be secondary or tertiary gay characters (MLM). 3/3

1771. **Lovell, Ron,** *Dangerous Decisiones,* Penman, 2018. Lorenzo Madrid #4 of 4. (Court Drama) Although Oregon Attorney Lorenzo Madrid was at first reluctant to take care of Tito, an orphan brought to this country illegally, he grows to love the little boy. That love turns into an obligation when the woman who took the boy leaves him in Lorenzo's care. After Maxine March goes to Ecuador to arrange for a formal adoption, things take a turn for the worse. she is arrested and put on trial for kidnapping. Despite having no knowledge of trying a case overseas, Lorenzo agrees to represent her. In doing so he is torn between wanting to help her and adopting Tito as his son. –this title sounds a lot like *Danger by the Sea and* may just be the same story with a different title (MLM). 3/3

1772. **Lowe, Barry,** *Gravy Train,* Loveyoudevine, 2011. (MM Short Stories) Kaden 'Buddy' Reznor is gorgeous, hung like an elephant, built like a brick shithouse, and the host of the world's top-rating television cooking program, The Six-Pack Chef. So why is someone trying to kill him? –collection of six short stories (MLM). 3/3

1773. **Lowell, Elizabeth,** *Night Diver,* William Morrow, 2014. (MF Suspense) After a family tragedy, Kate Donnelly left the Caribbean behind forever. But a series of bad management decisions has left her family's diving and marine recovery business drowning in red ink. Now her brother pleads with her to come back to the island nation of St Vincent. Without Kate's financial expertise, the iconic treasure-hunting enterprise started by her grandfather will go under. Unable to say no to the little family she has left, Kate heads back to the beautiful and terrifying ocean that still haunts her nightmares. –two of the divers are gay (MLM). 1/3

1774. **Lowndes, Marie Belloc,** *Lodger,* Scribner's Sons, 1913. (Suspense) Somewhere in London a madman was at large. And then one night there came a knock at the door of a quiet lodging house in the Marylebone Road. –This novel paints Jack the Ripper as a latent homosexual, was made into a film by Alfred Hitchcock and two others, all with gay men playing the role of Jack the Ripper (MLM). 1/3

1775. **Luckhart, Brenner,** *A Rotten Way to Die,* Blueboy, 1976. (Pulp) "Southwestern insurance claims investigator Lewis (Lew) Patton, 30, bisexual, checks out a death in a pulp whodunit (Gunn). –reprinted as *Body Embezzlers* by Numbers Illustrated Library in 1978 (MLM). 3/3

1776. **Lynley, E. M.,** *Rarer than Rubies,* Dreamspinner, 2011. Precious Gems #1 of 4. (MM Espionage Bibliomystery) When Trent Copeland runs into Reed Acton at a Bangkok airport, he thinks the handsome American is too good to be true. Why would someone like Reed be interested in a quiet, introverted gay-romance writer? Reed Acton has one mission and one mission only–he needs to get the map that was accidentally slipped into Trent's bag and keep the mobsters who want the priceless artifact from taking deadly revenge. –original e-book title was *Thief of Hearts: Tempted in Thailand* and was published the same year and same publisher (MLM). 3/3

1777. **Lynley, E. M.,** *Italian Ice,* Dreamspinner, 2012. Precious Gems #2 of 4. (MM Espionage Bibliomystery) Gay romance author Trent Copeland and former FBI agent Reed Action head to Italy for a Roman holiday. What should be a relaxing and romantic vacation is interrupted when Reed's not-so-former boss asks for his help with a case. Trent's shocked to discover in the six months they've been living together in LA, Reed hasn't been completely honest about his "retirement." 3/3

1778. **Lynley, E. M.,** *Jaded,* Dreamspinner, 2013. Precious Gems #3 of 4. (MM Espionage Bibliomystery) Gay-romance writer Trent Copeland finds his life in a rut while his boyfriend, Special Agent Reed Acton, is away on an undercover mission. After attending a special course at FBI headquarters in Quantico, Trent's eager for another challenge. He jumps at the opportunity for a trip to Japan to oversee appraisals of two art collections to be sold at the gallery he co-owns. But the trip isn't all cherry blossoms and Hello Kitty. When one of the collectors he meets–rumored to be the head of a Yakuza gang–turns up dead, Trent is accused of the murder and thrown in jail. 3/3

1779. **Lynley, E. M.,** *24-Karate Conspiracy,* Dreamspinner, 2015. Precious Gems #4 of 4. (MM Espionage Bibliomystery) Former Ranger turned FBI agent Reed Acton faces his biggest challenge yet: a Christmas visit from partner Trent Copeland's parents. He's less equipped to handle hugs and holidays than the Taliban or international art thieves. When he's assigned to track down a set of gold Babylonian artifacts looted from the Iraqi National Museum after the fall of Baghdad, things start to look up. 3/3

1780. **Lynn, David,** *Bull Nuts,* Greenleaf, 1968. (Pulp) "Private investigator Mick Bucher, sexually insatiable, does his part in a pulp whodunit (Gunn)." 3/3

1781. **Lynne, Carol**, *Cattle Valley volume 1*, Total-E-Bound, 2008. (MM Short Stories) "Play and No Work": A community built on tolerance, Cattle Valley is one of the few places in the country where the residents won't bat an eyelash at a threesome relationship. Nate, Rio and Ryan fit right in. But, with Ryan busy in his new job as town Sheriff, Rio and Nate are left to wonder how they're supposed to make a living. What use are a highly trained mercenary and a private detective in a peaceful community the size of Cattle Valley? "Cattle Valley Mistletoe": The Reverend Casey Sharp loves his church, his congregation and his community. Contractor Halden Kuckleman, loves his quiet life. After a childhood trauma, Hal gave up on love and God. He's fine working on the renovation as long as Reverend Sharp doesn't try to save him. When Casey offers to lend a hand however, he begins to wonder if the willowy minister will help or lead him straight into temptation. –two short stories collected in the single volume. Later books do not have a mystery element to them, only romance (MLM). 3/3

1782. **Lynne, Carol**, *Dracul's Blood,* Total-E-Bound, 2010. Dracul's Revenge #1 of 2. (Fantasy) When people begin turning up dead, drained of their blood, in New York City, it falls on Detective Bobby Marks to solve the crime. Enlisting the help of Professor Nikolay Radin to help with a strange cask found at a murder scene changes Bobby's life in ways he never imagines. A simple consultation turns into so much more when sparks fly between the two men, and Nik is unknowingly pulled into the dangerous world of a secret society. The Knights of Paiderastia have been around for thousands of years and refuse to sit by while an ordinary detective and a bookish professor try to take them down. In a battle against true evil, Bobby begins to wonder whether he can solve the crime and still manage to keep his new lover alive. 3/3

1783. **Lynne, Carol**, *Anarchy in Blood,* Total-E-Bound, 2010. Dracul's Revenge #2 of 2. (Fantasy) Washington, D.C. is rocked by the vicious murders of several young men. As the body count rises, tension builds. Who could be killing and draining their victims of blood? Soon whispers arise that the trail leads right to the most important man in America. Aaron Baker is President Douglas's right-hand man. 3/3

1784. **Lyons, Arthur**, *Hard Trade,* Holt, Rinehart, Winston, 1981. (Hard Boiled) Los Angeles detective Jacob Asch investigates an ordinary domestic case that becomes complicated with multiple murder against the backdrop of the California lifestyle. –gay men are both villains and heroes but not the main character in this gritty suspense story of political corruption (MLM). 1/3

M

1785. **MacBeth, George,** *The Samurai: An Entertainment,* Houghton Mifflin Harcourt, 1975. (Espionage) A provocative British Secret Service agent called Cadbury uses her sex the way James Bond uses a gun, with equally devastating results. –unsure of gay content (MLM). ?/3

1786. **MacDonald, John,** *Dress her in Indigo,* Lippencott, 1971. McGee #11 of 21. (Hard Boiled) A wealthy old man laid up in the hospital is desperate to understand the last months of his daughter's life before she was killed in a car crash in Mexico. It was puzzling. She'd cleaned out her considerable bank account, left Miami and hadn't been heard from again. Travis McGee ventures into the steep hills and strange backwoods of Oaxaca through a bizarre world of dropouts, drug freaks, and kinky rich people–and begins to suspect the beautiful girl's death was no accident.... –gay characters are side characters and two male rape scenes occur, one in prison and the other a drug addict who will do anything for drugs (MLM). 1/3

1787. **MacDonald, Philip,** *Something to Hide,* Crime Club/Doubleday, 1952. (Suspense) A collection of short stories and a 'Queen's Quorum' title: "The Green-and-Gold String" - "Something to Hide" - "The Wood-for-the-Trees" - "Malice Domestic" - "Love Lies Bleeding" and "The Fingers of Fear". –"Love Lies Bleeding" has a gay man arrested for killing a woman but is then released when two more people are killed (MLM). 1/3

1788. **MacDonald, Ross (Mark Millar),** *The Drowning Pool,* Knopf, 1950. Lew Archer #2 of 20. (Hard Boiled) When a millionaire matriarch is found floating face-down in the family pool, the prime suspects are her good-for-nothing son and his seductive teenage daughter. Lew Archer takes this case in the L.A. suburbs and encounters a moral wasteland of corporate greed and family hatred– and sufficient motive for a dozen murders. –character loosely based on W. H. Auden, "With his coltish sideways steps, and his Adam's apple bobbing like a soft egg caught in his throat, the poet-playwright is a pretentious and unappealing figure. His legs were pale and hairless above the drooping socks. His pale blond gaze seemed lashless... He was an aging Peter pan, glib, bland, and eccentric..." Marvell has none of Auden's genius or warmth (Tom Nolan, "Claude was doing all right: Homosexuality, Hard-Boiled Crime Fiction and the Evolution of Ross MacDonald", *Murder in the Closet*, edited by Curtis Evans, McFarland, 2017) (MLM). 1/3

1789. **MacDonald, Ross,** *The Barbarous Coast,* Knopf, 1956. Lew Archer #6 of 20. (Hard Boiled) Private investigator Lew Archer's pursuit of a girl who jackknifed too suddenly from high diving to high living leads him to an ex-fighter with an unexplained movie contract and a big-time gambler who died by his own knife. –Lance (Torres) Leonard, a former crooked boxer, current actor is the boyfriend of mobster Carl Stern (MLM). 1/3

1790. **MacDonald, Ross,** *The Zebra Striped Hearse,* Knopf, 1962. Lew Archer #10 of 20. (Hard Boiled) Strictly speaking, Lew Archer is only supposed to dig up the dirt on a rich man's suspicious soon-to-be son-in-law. But in no time at all Archer is following a trail of corpses from the citrus belt to Mazatlan. And then there is the zebra-striped hearse and its crew of beautiful, sunburned surfers, whose path seems to keep crossing the son-in-law's and Archer's. –American hotel-keeper in Mexico was probably gay (MLM). 1/3

1791. **Macer, T. P.,** *The Sorcerer's Web,* Wayward, 2000. (Fantasy)The Royal Family of Cardia has been viciously murdered and the country's borders are being attacked. Adam Pell is a ranger, defending the realm as he mourns the death of his cousin, the king. 3/3

1792. **Mackle, Elliott,** *Six-Day War,* Alyson, 2009. Captain Harding #1 of 3. (Military) Assigned to baby-sit a loose-cannon colonel at remote Wheelus Air Base, Libya, handsome, hard-charging Captain Joe Harding spends his off-duty time bedding an enlisted medic and a muscular major, then begins a nurturing friendship with the American ambassador's teenage son. The boy swiftly develops a crush on the man, feelings that Joe, a Southern gent with a strong moral sense, feels he cannot acknowledge or return. A clerk's murder, a flight-surgeon's drug abuse, a fist-fight in the officers' club bar, a straight roommate whose taste for leather gets him in trouble, the combat death of Joe's former lover, and participation in an all-male orgy witnessed by two very married but somewhat confused fighter jocks also occur. 3/3

1793. **Mackle, Elliott,** *Captain Harding and His Men,* Lethe, 2012. Captain Harding #2 of 3. (Military) When a C-130 bound for Southeast Asia explodes on takeoff at remote Wheelus Air Base, Libya, handsome, hard-charging Captain Joe Harding instinctively realizes that the cargo list - "medical supplies and radio tubes" - was faked. When Joe's newly-married workout buddy does a swan dive off a fifth story balcony in downtown Tripoli, Joe refuses to accept the semi-official verdict: suicidal depression. And when Joe's tennis partner, the son of the American ambassador, decides to celebrate his eighteenth birthday by appearing unannounced at Joe's BOQ door, the potential difficulties of their love-match must be addressed–seriously and without delay. 3/3

1794. **Mackle, Elliott,** *Welcome Home, Captain Harding,* Lethe, 2013. Captain Harding #3 of 3. (Military) Returning to California after eighteen terrifying months in Vietnam, Captain Joe Harding is assigned a trio of duties: assisting his fatherly former commander at base operations, spying on misbehaving bomber pilots and organizing an air show designed to counter the anti-war fever sweeping the state. Meanwhile, his much younger tennis partner has enrolled at Cal Berkeley, enmeshed himself in pacifist politics and resumed his role as Joe's lover. 3/3

1795. **Mackle, Elliott,** *It Takes Two,* Alyson, 2003. Caloosa Club #1 of 3. (Historical) February 1949. Fort Myers Florida. It started out to be such a nice day. But early morning gunfire at the Royal Plaza Motor Hotel changed all that. One white man is dead. One black man is dead. The widow of the white man has just crashed the investigation and is waving a gun around. 3/3

1796. **Mackle, Elliott,** *Only Make Believe,* Lethe, 2012. Caloosa Club #2 of 3. (Historical) It's amateur night at the ultra-private, members-only Caloosa Club on the Fort Myers, Florida, riverfront. Trouble begins when the fat lady sings. Her triumph is sweet. But, only hours later, the diva lies near death in a hotel room upstairs, the victim of a vicious beating. Hotel manager Dan Ewing and his sidekick, Lee County Detective Bud Wright, soon discover that this was no lady and that a variety of unsavory characters hoped to dance on the dead diva's grave. In Southwest Florida in January 1951, almost anyone who wanted to have a little illicit fun put his–or her–life on the line. 3/3

1797. **Mackle, Elliott,** *Sunset Island,* Lethe, 2014. Caloosa Club #3 of 3. (Historical) February 1950. Lee County, Florida. In the freewheeling, celebratory aftermath of World War II, survivors and veterans are starting new lives, resuming old ones, or just picking up the pieces. Former Navy officer Dan Ewing feels safer than any gay man might expect in a segregated, dry county where the Ku Klux Klan is still strong. Managing an ultra-private club-hotel in Ft. Myers with a mixed-race staff, untaxed alcohol, high-stakes card games and escorts of both sexes, he's been acting like he has nothing to lose: business is good, and his romantic life is better. Lee County Detective Bud Wright, a former Marine sergeant and Dan's secret lover, is outwardly strong and brave, but uneasy with the knowledge that, every time he and Dan get naked together, they're breaking laws he's sworn to uphold. 3/3

1798. **Maclean, Del,** *Bitter Legacy,* Blind Eye Books, 2016. (MM Police Procedural) Detective Sergeant James Henderson of London's Metropolitan Police Murder Investigation Team is no ordinary police officer. His remarkable gut instincts and relentless detective work have put him on a three-year fast track to becoming an inspector. When the murder of barrister Maria Curzon-Whyte lands in his lap, he finds himself drawn back into the insidious world of London's privileged elite where men like James's father possess wealth and power enough to hold the law in contempt. 3/3

1799. **Maclean, Del,** *Object of Desire,* Blind Eye Books, 2018. (MM Amateur Sleuth/Police Procedural) Tom Gray is one of the world's top models–an effortless object of desire. Self-contained, elusive and always in control, he's accustomed to living life entirely on his own terms. But when Tom comes under suspicion in the gory death of his employer, his world spirals into chaos. 3/3

1800. **Mains, Geoff,** *Gentle Warriors,* Knights Press, 1989. (Political/Crime Drama) In San Francisco, Gregg and a group of fellow gays, plot to assassinate the president, because of government inaction on the AIDS epidemic. 3/3

1801. **Maltese, William,** *A Slip to Die For,* Millivres Prowler, 2000. Stud Draqual #1 of 2. (Amateur Sleuth) Someone not only killed the author, who'd been an "underground" movie star, who'd been a model, who'd been a hustler, who'd been a cross-dresser ... but killed the borderline drunk, who'd been a TV-network executive and anchor-man for the national news. –main character is straight but is constantly looking at and thinking of men while he's with women (MLM). 1/3

1802. **Maltese, William,** *Thai Died,* Green Candy, 2003 Stud Daqual #2 of 2. (Amateur Sleuth) When a lingerie manufacturer goes to Thailand on business, he gets far more than he bargained for. While innocently shopping for silk and taking in the sights of Bangkok, Stud Draqual finds himself being stalked by a mercenary – one who's been implicated in the murder of a male prostitute. –listed as a gay mystery but again the main character has sex with lots of women while thinking of men (MLM). 1/3

1803. **Maltese, William,** *The Fag is Not for Burning,* Wildside Press, 2007. (Hard boiled) Seattle gay art gallery owner Horton Lendland is definitely dead, and it wasn't just a weenie roast! The suspects are legion: A hustler – two business partners – the best friend – the once-successful painter – the Catholic priest – sundry street urchins – the gay bar owner – the S&M crowd – the American Indian – the teacher accused of pederasty... 3/3

1804. **Maltese, William,** *The Gomorrha Conjurations,* Wildside Press,

2007. (Thriller) TAKE AN A-BOMB INTO MAHUD WADI? But wasn't that like carrying coals to Newcastle? Everyone knew the Arabs had almost completed an a-bomb of their very own, no matter what the U.N. Security Council and Nuclear Proliferation Committee might say. Except–"reliable sources" insisted that the Arab a-bomb wasn't quite finished. SODGIA, the U.S. government watchdog agency, wanted and expected the delivered bomb to explode in place, forever providing a warning to the Arabs and other third-world entities from joining the nuclear community. 3/3

1805. **Maltese, William,** *Incident at Aberlene,* Wildside Press, 2011. Spies and Lies #1 of 4. (Espionage) Welcome to the Grey Zone, and its nefarious and shadowy landscape that knows no international boundaries–whose every individual agent has special expertise, but no permanent ties or allegiances to any nationalities, countries, or governments. Freelance agents Roger Lenic, Terrence Flag, and Howard Cahn are among those in the Zone who have been hired to... bury the INCIDENT AT ABERLENE. 3/3

1806. **Maltese, William,** *Incident at Brimzinsky,* Wildside, 2011. Spies and Lies #2 of 4. (Espionage) Welcome to the Grey Zone, and its nefarious and shadowy landscape that knows no international boundaries–whose every individual agent has special expertise, but no permanent ties or allegiances to any nationalities, countries, or governments. Freelance agents Troy Candle, Gregory Ohm, and Johan Darnel are among those in the Zone who have been hired to... bury the INCIDENT AT BRIMZINSKY. –available as an e-book only (MLM). 3/3

1807. **Maltese, William,** *Incident at Christiva,* Wildside, 2016. Spies and Lies #3 of 4. (Espionage) On the Caribbean island state of Christiva, arms dealer Key Meyers and his go-between, Jack York, must help sort out the chaotic aftermath of the overthrow of the country's dictator by the beautiful revolutionary, Paloma Jola. –available as an e-book only (MLM). 3/3

1808. **Maltese, William,** *Incident at Dupunu,* Wildside, 2013. Spies and Lies #4 of 4. (Espionage) The assassination of the president of the African republic of Dupunu brings Grey Zone agents Denim Grady and Gena Mullen to help reestablish stability amidst the ensuing chaos. –available as an e-book only (MLM). 3/3

1809. **Maltese, William,** *Amaz'n Murder: A Cozy Mystery,* Wildside, 2013. (Cozy) Carolyne Santire, plant-hunter extraordinaire! Carolyne's search for the next major botanical find takes her to Brazil in South America, where she encounters political machinations, mayhem, and... murder. The suspect list is long–fellow scientists, Brazilian land barons, prospectors, a cuckolded video director, a rock star–

and, eventually, even her! During the shooting of an entertainment film in the Amazon jungle, amidst threats from a man-eating jaguar, cannibals, and a mysterious British kidnapper, Carolyne finds the prospect of ferreting out the real killer anything but a leisurely stroll in the park. Can she solve the mystery before the next murder occurs? 3/3

1810. **Mandon, Alex (pseudonym),** *Murder on the Champs-Elysees,* Avid, 2016. (French Historical Police Procedural) Paris 1900: When the most famous courtesan in Paris becomes the prime suspect in the death of a wealthy young man, Inspector Devré is reluctantly drawn into the opulent parlors and witty manners of high society. As the investigation unfolds, he must contend with a bloodthirsty press and the outrageous behavior of his suspect...as well as his own prejudices and unfulfilled needs. –the main character has secrets of his own and may be gay (MLM). 2/3

1811. **Maney, Mabel,** *Nancy Clue and the Hardly Boys in a Ghost in the Closet,* Cleis, 1995. (Parody) With their fearless crime-fighting, good manners, and manly fashion sense, the Hardly boys are the pride of Feyport, Illinois. Dark-haired, muscular Frank and his lovable kid brother Joe return from a gay trip to Europe to find that their parents – world-famous detective Fennel P. Hardly and his wife, Mrs. Hardly – have been kidnapped! Even worse, so have six poodles from the Lake Merrimen Dog Show! Pals Nancy Clue, Cherry Aimless, R.N., and Police Detective Jackie Jones help the Hardly boys track down the criminals – and in the meantime, pick up useful tips on fingerprinting, evidence retrieval, and the laundering of sporty twill slacks. 3/3

1812. **Mankell, Hanning,** *One Step Behind,* New Press, 2002. Kurt Wallander #7 of 10. (Swedish Crime) It is Midsummer's Eve. Three young friends meet in a wood to act out an elaborate masque. But unknown to them, they are being watched. With a bullet each, all three are murdered. Soon afterwards, one of Inspector Wallander's colleagues is found murdered. Is this the same killer, and what could the connection be? In this investigation, Wallander is always, tantalizingly, One Step Behind. –gay police officer killed prior to the start of the story (MLM). 1/3

1813. **Manly, D. J.,** *Severing,* Silver, 2011. Severing #1 of 3. (Fantasy) Billy doesn't remember much about how he was taken abruptly from life and sent to this lonely place where he watches the living but can't touch them. When his name is taken off the door of his office to be replaced by someone else's, he has to accept that he is really gone. 3/3

1814. **Manly, D. J.,** *Terrance,* Silver, 2012. Severing #2 of 3. (Fantasy)

Something wakes Terrance in the middle of the night, a voice that won't let him sleep. Alex, his lover, has accepted that Terrance can talk to the dead, but this time it's different; this time the voice is dead... dead serious. This time, the voice won't be denied. Terrance has been talking to the dead ever since he was a boy. The dead find Terrance when they have something to tell him, and now, something or someone is reaching out. But something else doesn't want Terrance to connect. It will torment him with images from his own past and try to distract him, even kill to keep Terrance from knowing the truth. In The Severing, Billy's ghost found Terrance and brought Alex into his life. 3/3

1815. **Manly, D. J.,** *Gabriel,* Silver, 2012. Severing #3 of 3. (Fantasy) Terrance and Alex are settling into their new house and Terrance's son Gabriel is living with them. As Gabriel's eighteenth birthday approaches, he falls in love and all hell is about to break loose... 3/3

1816. **Manly, D. J.,** *Blood Pond,* Silver, 2011. Blood Pond #1 of 2. (Fantasy) Ten years ago, August Greystone's adolescent brother was brutally murdered and dumped in Blood Pond. And the one person he is sure can identify the killer is on the run... 3/3

1817. **Manly, D. J.,** *Blood Pond Resurfacing,* Silver, 2011. Blood Pond #2 of 2. (Fantasy) When another head is found in Blood Pond, Detective August Greystone must try to keep his own head while searching for the killer. All this time, August and his lover Bruce Monkton have tried to put the past behind them and build a secure and happy future as a couple, only to be brutally reminded of the terrible circumstances that initially brought them together. 3/3

1818. **Mann, Alex,** *Big Foot,* Arena, 1979. (Pulp) "East Coast men's magazine writer Cort Wallen, 30, investigates a Sasquatch sighting in the northwestern Washington rain forest in a pulp mystery (Gunn)." 3/3

1819. **Mann, Alex von***, Slaves,* Prowler, 1997. (Espionage) The adventures of Jack Mallard in/on Zanzibar and his exploits with natives of the land. Muscled bodies and dominant men meet in secluded, exotic places where the pulse of primal surroundings urge hunky studs to ever more outrageous encounters. Nothing is taboo in a land where men are men and lust is set free. African passions drive men to make real rumbles in the jungle! –reprinted by William Maltese in 2007 by Wildside Press (MLM). 3/3

1820. **Mann, William J.,** *All American Boy,* Kensington, 2005. (Psychological) When a call from his estranged mother brings him home, actor Wally Day is forced to confront his dark past and his relationship with his family, which leads him on a powerful journey of self-discovery, self-acceptance, and salvation. 3/3

1821. **Mano, D. Keith,** *Topless,* Random House, 1991. (Comic moral tale) Episcopalian priest Mike Wilson's sister-in-law Ethel asks him to return to his native New York from a small Nebraska town when his brother Tony disappears. She wants Mike to take over Tony's restaurant, which turns out to be a seedy topless bar in Queens. The police have no idea where Tony is, or whether he is still alive. –a gay farm hand, a bunch of lesbians, and a toples dancer's niece has a doll with AIDS (MLM). 1/3

1822. **Manotti, Dominique,** *Rough Trade,* Arcadia, 2001. Daquin #1 of 4. (French Crime) One spring morning a Thai girl is found dead in a fashion workshop. A club is uncovered where people secretly get filmed having sex - including some very distinguished men. This is the seedy underworld of Paris. This tale takes the reader along dark paths of sinister events in Le Sentier, the heart of Paris's rag trade. –Daquin is bisexual in this dark and depressing story (MLM). 3/3

1823. **Manotti, Dominique,** *Dead Horsemeat,* Arcadia, 2006. Daquin #2 of 4. (French Crime) A group of school friends campaigned together at Rennes in 1968. In 1989, the paths of these former students cross each other as they start playing with fire, carried along by the euphoria born of power. Events begin to take off, with race horses dying under mysterious circumstances and huge quantities of cocaine appearing at Parisian parties. –the next two books in the series have yet to be translated into English (MLM). 3/3

1824. **Marcus, A. J.,** *Eagle's Blood,* DSP, 2014. Mountain Spirits #1 of 4. (MM Mystery) Brock Summers is a Colorado Parks and Wildlife Officer with a heart of gold. When he discovers a video of golden eagles being shot and learns of a nest in trouble, not even a blizzard can stop him from trekking up the mountain in an attempt to rescue them. 3/3

1825. **Marcus, A. J.,** *Grizzly Discovery,* DSP, 2015. Mountain Spirits #2 of 4. (MM Mystery) Landon Weir and Brock Summers are happily settling into their life as a couple, easily balancing Landon's work as an animal rehabber with Brock's career as a Colorado Parks and Wildlife Officer. When they find a bear shot and skinned, they set out to discover who's behind the heinous act. 3/3

1826. **Marcus, A. J.,** *Moose Fever,* DSP, 2016. Mountain Spirits #3 of 4. (MM Mystery) Colorado Parks and Wildlife Officer Brock Summers and his fiancé, wildlife rehabber Landon Weir, are preparing for their wedding when someone starts killing moose along a creek in the northern part of Teller County. As the moose casualties rise, human bodies turn up, and the case is taken over by the sheriff's office. When a Forestry Service Ranger is killed, the service joins the hunt. 3/3

1827. **Marcus, A. J.**, *Cougar Chaos,* DSP, 2016. Mountain Spirits #4 of 4. (MM Mystery) Parks and Wildlife Officer Brock Summers-Weir and his new husband, wildlife rehabber Landon Weir-Summers, are on their honeymoon high in the northern Colorado Rockies when they find an orphaned cougar cub. They quickly discover that there have been a number of cougars injured or killed in the area around Steamboat Springs. Although they are supposed to be on vacation, they work with local officials to try to find out what's happening to the big cats. 3/3

1828. **Mark, Julian (Vincent Lardo),** *Special Duty,* Hamilton House, 1975. (Pulp) "New York police detectives Kevin Bello, 26, and Joseph (Joe) Stokes, partners, examine the nature of love in a pulp procedural (Gunn)." –later republished as *Hard Training* by Mitch Stone in 1984 by Arena (MLM). 3/3

1829. **Markham, Philip,** *The Fair Cop,* Idol, 1999. (Historical Procedural) The second world war is over and in 1950s New York, that means dirty business. Hanson's a detective who's been dealt a lousy hand, but the Sullivan case is his big chance. How many junior detectives get handed blackmail, murder and perverted sex all in one day? 3/3

1830. **Maron, Margaret,** *One Coffee With,* Raven House, 1981. Sigrid Harald #1 of 9. (Police Procedural) A new series featuring NYPD homicide detective Sigrid Harald There was more than coffee in Professor Quinn's morning coffee. Someone in the art department office had slipped in a spoonful of poison. Among the suspects are a young secretary, an enraged Hungarian maintenance man, and a colleague who had an affair with Quin's wife. NYPD detective Sigrid Harald is called in to find the killer with an artistic temperament and an aptitude for death. –Roman Tramegra, a gay New York writer, is friends with the MC, however Roman is more portrayed as asexual than homosexual (MLM). 2/3

1831. **Maron, Margaret,** *Death of a Dragonfly,* Raven House, 1984. Sigrid Harald #2 of 9. (Police Procedural) Lt. Harald investigates the death of Julie Redmond, a beautiful but cold, self-centered and demanding woman. Sigrid digs into Julie Redmond's past, untangling a web of blackmail and murder and half a million dollars' worth of stolen gems, revealing a ruthless mastermind whose cruelty has finally caught up with her. 2/3

1832. **Maron, Margaret,** *Death in Blue Folders,* Raven House, 1985. Sigrid Harald #3 of 9. (Police Procedural) A bullet sends a prominent lawyer into permanent retirement amid a bonfire of blackmail papers, and Harald finds a filing cabinet brimming with suspects and motives. Wading through a flurry of forged documents, trust funds, and contested annuities, Harald searches for one missing file–the one marked M for murder. 2/3

1833. **Maron, Margaret,** *The Right Jack,* Raven House, 1987. Sigrid Harald #4 of 9. (Police Procedural) NYPD Homicide Detective Sigrid Harald's partner, Detective Tildon, should have been safe at his cribbage tournament in a posh Manhattan hotel but a bomb blast leaves him in intensive care. Sigrid is sent to investigate who the real target was. 2/3

1834. **Maron, Margaret,** *Baby Doll Games,* Raven House, 1988. Sigrid Harald #5 of 9. (Police Procedural) When a shadowy figure kills a dancer in a Greenwich Village theater before an audience of horrified children, NYPD detective Sigrid Harald is outraged and soon has a gut feeling that passion played a large part in the murder. With no physical evidence, she turns to special dolls used by therapists to help children talk about crimes they've witnessed. 2/3

1835. **Maron, Margaret,** *Corpus Christmas,* Raven House, 1989. Sigrid Harald #6 of 9. (Police Procedural) A relic of Manhattan's Gilded Age, the Erich Bruel House on Gramercy Park contained three floors of glorious art–and one Christmas corpse. Now it's up to Lieutenant Sigrid Harald to wrap up this homicide before the killer strikes again in this classic mystery by the author of Rituals of the Season. 2/3

1836. **Maron, Margaret,** *Past Imperfect,* Raven House, 1991. Sigrid Harald #7 of 9. (Police Procedural) A highly respected detective with the New York City Police Department, Harald is the daughter of a NYPD cop who was killed in the line of duty. Now as she looks into the fatal shooting of an off-duty police officer, Harald realizes that the case may provide a clue to the secret of her father's death. 2/3

1837. **Maron, Margaret,** *Fugitive Colors,* Raven House, 1995. Sigrid Harald #8 of 9. (Police Procedural) Losing a fellow officer in a shootout is enough to rattle Sigrid's cool, controlled demeanor. Discovering that her lover, famous artist Oscar Nauman, has also been killed devastates her. She withdraws from her colleagues, her police career, her life. But it is art she cannot escape: Oscar has left her his paintings worth millions, and galleries are clamoring to sell them. Sigrid begins to see through the vibrant surface of New York's art world to the interplay of revenge, greed, and power beneath. –a collection of short stories published in 2004 includes the short story "Suitable for Hanging" which has Roman in a mystery on his own. The novel *Three Day Town* is a cross between Maron's two series;

Sigrid Harald and Deborah Knott and is considered as 8.5 in the Harald series and 17 in the Knott series. I am unsure if Roman appears. It was published in 2011 by Grand Central Publishing (MLM). 2/3

1838. **Maron, Margaret,** *Take Out,* Grand Central Publishing, 2017. Sigrid Harald #9 of 9. (Police Procedural) NYPD Detective Sigrid Harald is still reeling from the untimely death of her lover, acclaimed painter Oscar Nauman, when she is called to investigate the poisoning of two homeless men in the West Village. As she examines the mysterious deaths, Sigrid uncovers a grim neighborhood scandal surrounding two influential women: one a haughty mafia widow, the other a retired opera prima donna, both with dark secrets they've kept under wraps for decades. Was the poison really meant for the homeless men or were they merely unintended victims as the decades-long feud between the two women comes to a head? – this is supposedly the last book Margaret Maron plans on writing as she announced her retirement with the release of this book (MLM). 2/3

1839. **Marrinan, Patrick,** *Scapegoat,* Robert Hale, 2009. (Crime Thriller) Public outrage at the brutal killing of a young man in the heart of "pink Dublin" provokes a high-profile murder investigation. As the circumstances of the killing unravel, the police suspect they are hunting a homophobic serial killer. When the investigation stalls, Detective Sergeant Pat O'Hara, a police officer with a dubious past, pursues a hunch and adopts unorthodox techniques in tracking down the killer. Mohamed Barouche, a doctor working in a Dublin hospital, emerges as his prime suspect, and he allegedly breaks down under interrogation and confesses. But have the police framed Dr. Barouche? Has the lawyer hired to defend him got a hidden agenda? –Police detective Noel Brannigan may be closeted (MLM). 3/3

1840. **Marsh, Ngaio,** *Enter a Murderer,* Bles, 1935. Roderick Alleyn #2 of 33. (Police Procedural) The script of the Unicorn Theatre's new play uncannily echoes a quarrel in the star's dressing room. And the stage drama gets all too real when charming Felix Gardener shoots his blustering rival, Arthur Surbonardier, dead – with a gun Arthur himself loaded with blanks. –Slide states that Ngaio may have been the most homophobic of the classic mystery writers. However, in *Enter a Murderer,* "effete" Alleyn spends a great deal of time with Nigel Bathgate where the two of them "refer to each other lovingly as "old tripe" and "sausage" and speak in the most outrageously camp fashion. At one-point Nigel falls asleep while watching a play and "woke up to Alleyn's hand on his knee" (Slide)." (MLM) 1/3

1841. **Marsh, Ngaio,** *Artists in Crime,* Furman, 1938. Roderick Alleyn #6 of 33. (Police Procedural) It was a bizarre pose for beautiful model Sonia Gluck–and her last. For in the draperies of her couch lay a fatal dagger, and behind her murder lies all the intrigue and acid-etched temperament of an artist's colony. Called in to investigate, Scotland Yard's Inspector Roderick Alleyn finds his own passions unexpectedly stirred by the feisty painter Agatha Troy. – In *Artists in Crime*, she describes a young man as an opium addict, who only has male friends, and compared with Oscar Wilde (MLM). 1/3

1842. **Marsh, Ngaio,** *Singing in the Shroud,* Little Brown, 1958. Roderick Alleyn #20 of 33. (Police Procedural) All aboard for murder. The Cape Farewell steams out to sea, carrying a serial strangler who says it with flowers and a little song. Behind, on a fogbound London dock, lies his latest lovely victim; and on board, working undercover to identify him before he strikes again, is Inspector Roderick Alleyn. –Slide states that this is the most homophobic of Marsh's books. One of the crew of the ship, "a queer little job" quips Alleyn, dresses as a Flamenco dancer and is killed by the serial strangler. He is described as a "sex monster," and his never identified homosexuality as "his own private, inexorable weakness." (MLM) 1/3

1843. **Marsh, Ngaio,** *Killer Dolphin,* Little Brown, 1966. Roderick Alleyn #24 of 33. (Police Procedural) At the newly restored Dolphin Theatre, murder takes center stage. The once-dilapidated Dolphin Theater, now restored to its former glory, is open again-and all of London is buzzing about its new play, The Glove, inspired by the discovery of a genuine Shakespearean glove. But on one unfortunate evening, the Dolphin opens its doors to the harshest critic of all: death. Now Inspector Roderick Alleyn must find out who stole the scene with a most murderous act. –Marsh has two young effeminate male actors living together in seemingly innocence (MLM). 1/3

1844. **Marsh, Ngaio,** *When in Rome,* Little, Brown, 1971. Roderick Alleyn #26 of 33. (Police Procedural) It was April in Rome and gathered together in the church of San Tommaso in Pallario was the kind of varied group of people that can only meet on a tour. It included a superannuated jetsetter and her junkie nephew, a bad-tempered, ultra-British major, a boisterous Baron and Baroness, and an extremely reticent best-selling author. They were there under the aegis of one Sebastian Mailer, who had promised them a most unconventional tour–a claim no one later disputed, after encountering murder, blackmail and drug-running. –a member of the tour is a drug user, who had been almost charged with manslaughter a few years earlier following "an accident resulting from high jinks at what was called a 'gay pad'" (MLM). 1/3

1845. **Marsh, Ngaio,** *Last Ditch,* Little Brown, 1977. Roderick Alleyn #29 of 33. (Police Procedural) Horseplay turns deadly... Young Ricky Alleyn has come to the picturesque fishing village of Deep Cove to write. Though the sleepy little town offers few diversions, Ricky manages to find the most distracting one of all: murder. For in a muddy ditch, he sees a dead equestrienne whose last leap was anything but an accident. And when Ricky himself disappears, the case becomes a horse of a different color for his father, Inspector Roderick Alleyn. –Roderick's son, Ricky, is accused by another young man of making a pass at him which causes Ricky to become sick with disgust (MLM). 1/3

1846. **Marston, Edward,** *The Queen's Head,* St. Martin's, 1988. Nicholas Bracewell #1 of 16. (Historical) 1587, and Mary, Queen of Scots, dies by the executioner's axe; her head, shorn of its auburn wig, rolling across the platform. Will her death end the ceaseless plotting against Mary's red-haired cousin, Elizabeth? –one of the actors is gay and constantly attempts to sleep with the young male apprentices who play the female roles and is stymied by the other men of the company. Very disappointing that the only gay character in the series is depicted as a pederast (MLM). 1/3

1847. **Marston, Edward,** *The Merry Devils,* St. Martin's, 1990. Nicholas Bracewell #2 of 16. (Historical) Bookholder Nicholas Bracewell, fresh from his triumph holding together his volatile players' company during a treasonous plot against Queen Elizabeth, is set to make the galleries of The Queen's Head ring with laughter with a new comedy, The Merry Devils. The lugubrious landlord is sure mischief will result. Nicholas sees only a harmless comedy that will not summon up real devils, but two actors adept at tumbling. How then, during the crucial scene, do three devils appear on stage, one looking disturbingly real? And what of the deviltry that follow? One imp, in fact, soon lies dead beneath the stage. 1/3

1848. **Marston, Edward,** *The Trip to Jerusalem,* St. Martin's, 1990. Nicolas Bracewell #3 of 16. (Historical) London is under siege by the Black Plague, closing its theaters and losing its frightened citizens to the countryside. Lord Westfield's Men decide upon the relative safety of the road and a tour of the North. Before they can pack up and depart, one player in the troupe is murdered. 1/3

1849. **Marston, Edward,** *The Nine Giants,* St. Martin's, 1991. Nicolas Bracewell #4 of 16. (Historical) The fiery star, Laurence Firethorn, is hot for a lady, wife of the Lord Mayor elect. A tryst at London's Nine Giants inn is arranged. Meanwhile, the lugubrious landlord of the actors' home base is laid even lower by a plot to take over ownership of the inn. A young apprentice actor is subjected to a horrible assault. And a waterman pulls a mangled corpse from the Thames. The drama comes to a climax at the annual Lord Mayor's show as his barge moves grandly down the river.... 1/3

1850. **Marston, Edward,** *The Mad Courtesan,* St. Martin's, 1992. Nicolas Bracewell #5 of 16. (Historical) Though the lusty star of Lord Westfield's Men, Laurence Firethorn, is always ripe for seducing women bewitched by his art, the vicious rivalry that disrupts the acting troupe erupts between two other players. Owen Elias is a surly, envious Welshman, while Sebastian Carrick is an amiable and attractive gentleman. Their onstage duels become ever more realistic, but it is an axe that splits open Sebastian's head one night in a Clerkenwell alley. 1/3

1851. **Marston, Edward,** *The Silent Woman,* St. Martin's, 1994. Nicolas Bracewell #6 of 16. (Historical) When a young woman is poisoned before she can deliver a message to Nicholas, he takes leave to pursue a mystery from his own childhood. 1/3

1852. **Marston, Edward,** *The Roaring Boy,* St. Martin's, 1995. Nicolas Bracewell #7 of 16. (Historical) Dame Fortune has abandoned Lord Westfield's men to calamity... One member of the popular London acting troupe has died. Their present production is a failure. Then an anonymous playwright hands company mainstay Nicholas Bracewell a chance for salvation: a new script that exposes a tragic miscarriage of justice in a murder case. 1/3

1853. **Marston, Edward,** *The Laughing Hangman,* St. Martin's, 1996. Nicolas Bracewell #8 of 16. (Historical) Jonas Applegarth is a brilliant but belligerent playwright. When his play, The Misfortunes of Marriage, is performed by Lord Westfield's Men, it causes an uproar. All of Applegarth's enemies attack the company. Nicholas Bracewell defends the playwright loyally, but alas, Applegarth is soon found hanged by the neck. 1/3

1854. **Marston, Edward,** *The Fair Maid of Bohemia,* St. Martin's, 1997. Nicolas Bracewell #9 of 16. (Historical) When Westfield's Men are invited to perform at the Imperial Court in Prague for the Holy Roman Emperor and King of Bohemia, Rudolph II, they believe it will be their crowning glory. But the brutal murder of an actor during the performance turns the journey into a nightmare. 1/3

1855. **Marston, Edward,** *The Wanton Angel,* St. Martin's, 1999. Nicolas Bracewell #10 of 16. (Historical) Westfield's Men are flying high after a performance of The Insatiate Duke. However, victory is bittersweet as they are soon faced with dissolution; were it not for one of the company's rising stars they have acquired a new benefactor. However, before they have the chance to unmask this guardian angel, one of the group is found brutally murdered. 1/3

1856. **Marston, Edward,** *The Devil's Apprentice,* St. Martin's Minotaur, 2001. Nicolas Bracewell #11 of 16. (Historical) London is in the grip of an icy winter and Westfield's Men are out of work. Invited to perform at a manor house in Essex, they accept willingly even though the offer comes with two conditions: they must perform an entirely new play and agree to take a new apprentice, Davy Stratton, into the company. Then a prominent audience member dies during the opening night performance, and Nicholas Bracewell has to confront the deadliest foe of all. 1/3

1857. **Marston, Edward,** *The Bawdy Basket,* St. Martin's Minotaur, 2002. Nicolas Bracewell #12 of 16. (Historical) Westfield's Men, the Elizabethan theater troupe at the heart of Edward Marston's intricate and popular series, are enjoying good fortune in their native London. Their talented playwright is at work on his next opus, set to open in a few short weeks, and the group's trusty stage manager and reliable problem-solver Nicholas Bracewell is looking forward to a productive and calm season. Unfortunately for Nicholas, his friendship with Frank Quilter, a young actor who's just joined the troupe, is about to cause him a lot of trouble. 1/3

1858. **Marston, Edward,** *The Vagabond Clown,* Minotaur, 2003. Nicolas Bracewell #13 of 16. (Historical) When unexpected disaster strikes Lord Westfield's Men during a packed performance, Nicholas Bracewell, the theater company's stage manager and all-around performer of miracles, must save the day once again. A melee caused by disguised men is brought under control, but before the troupe can lament their destroyed set Nick discovers a body in the stands with a knife sticking out of it's back. They soon realize they are out one theater and one clown: Barnaby Gill, always hilarious on the stage and hopelessly curmudgeonly off, has broken his leg. 1/3

1859. **Marston, Edward,** *The Counterfeit Crank,* Minotaur, 2004. Nicolas Bracewell #14 of 16. (Historical) Nicholas Bracewell finds his job with the London theater troupe Westfield's Men complicated by an ailing playwright, the disappearance of the group's costumes, a troublesome gambler, a pair of con artists, and murder. 1/3

1860. **Marston, Edward,** *The Malevolent Comedy,* St. Martin's Minotaur, 2005. Nicolas Bracewell #15 of 16. (Historical) The theaters of Elizabethan England can be a very dangerous environment. With dozens of troupes competing for the attentions of a fickle theater-going public, rival companies regularly resort to nefarious activities to thwart a competitor's success, tensions occasionally erupt into violence and, in some instances, the result is murder. 1/3

1861. **Marston, Edward,** *The Princess of Denmark,* St. Martin's Minotaur, 2006. Nicolas Bracewell #16 of 16. (Historical) Winter approaches and Westfield's Men are out of work. When their widowed patron decides to marry again, he chooses a Danish bride with vague associations to the royal family. Since the wedding will take place in Elsinore, the troupe is invited to perform as guests of King Christian IV. One of the plays they select is The Princess of Denmark--and it will prove a disastrous choice. 1/3

1862. **Martin, Evelyn,** *Kind Hearts,* Wayward, 2001. (MM Romance) Nick Ryan's life is an open book for anyone to read; on the other hand, Edward Ashton, his partner in the successful Burford's Detective Agency, is more of an enigma. Together they get results, but then a new case threatens to drag Ashton's past into the limelight. 3/3

1863. **Martin, Kenneth,** *Billy's Brother,* Heretic Books, 1989. (Amateur Sleuth) When Billy dies in mysterious circumstances, his brother comes to San Francisco to try and uncover the truth of his death and is immediately drawn into the network of AIDS sufferers and support groups that Billy had been a part of. Among them, he is sure is the clue to Billy's death will be found–but he is unprepared for the other revelations that his investigation reveals. 3/3

1864. **Martin, Sean,** *Triptych,* JA, 2006. (Psychological jeu d'esprit) "Vancouver writer Benjamin, in the course of writing a murder mystery, comes to accept the death of his lover when he realizes his fictional inspector Carruthers is his alter ego and that he wants to let him, and the butler leave together (Gunn)." 3/3

1865. **Martinez, Angel,** *Lime Gelatin and other Monsters,* Amber Allure, 2015. Offbeat Crimes #1 of 6. (MM Paranormal) Kyle Monroe's encounter with a strange gelatinous creature in an alley leaves him scarred and forever changed, revealing odd abilities he wishes he didn't have and earning him reassignment to a precinct where all the cops have defective paranormal abilities. –available as an e-book only (MLM). 3/3

1866. **Martinez, Angel,** *The Pill Bugs of Time,* Amber Quill, 2015. Offbeat Crimes #2 of 6. (MM Paranormal) Vikash Soren, the perfect police officer except for his odd paranormal ability, never seems to lose his temper. Always serene and competent, he's taken on the role of mediator in a squad room full of misfits. But on the inside, he's a mess. Unable to tell his police partner that he loves him, Vikash struggles silently, terrified of losing Kyle as a lover, partner and friend. -available as an e-book only. Short story *Hunter Green Pea Coat* (2017) which falls between books two and three is just two pages long and has no mystery plot and is only available as an e-book only (MLM). 3/3

1867. **Martinez, Angel,** *Skim Blood and Savage Verse,* Pride, 2017. Offbeat Crimes #3 of 6. (MM Paranormal) When a ferocious book attacks Carrington at his own birthday party, he believes it's an isolated incident. But similar books soon appear all over town, menacing innocent people with harsh bits of poetry and blank verse that deliver damaging physical blows. It's a frustrating case with too many variables and not enough answers, and the stakes go up with each attack. –available as an e-book only (MLM). 3/3

1868. **Martinez, Angel,** *Feral Dust Bunnies,* Pride, 2017. Offbeat Crimes #4 of 6. (MM Paranormal) Officer Alex Wolf responds to a lot of 'paranormal' calls that aren't. Exotic pet birds aren't monsters and unusual dog breeds aren't aliens. It's a good thing he likes the animal control officers, but he both yearns for and dreads those calls where he runs into ACO Jason Shen. Jason's scent is so delicious that Wolf has a difficult time humaning around him. –available as an e-book only (MLM). 3/3

1869. **Martinez, Angel,** *Jackalopes and Woofen-Poofs,* Pride, 2017. Offbeat Crimes #5 of 6. (MM Paranormal) All Animal Control Officer Jason Shen ever wanted was a quiet life of rescuing lost kittens and helping animals in need. Having a paranormal cop boyfriend guarantees an end to the quiet part. What at first seems a random encounter with jackalopes in the park might be more than chance and when State Paranormal sends a handsome, charming vampire to consult with the Seventy-Seventh, he finds his relationship with Alex on shaky ground. –available as an e-book only (MLM). 3/3

1870. **Martinez, Angel,** *All the World's an Undead Stage,* Pride, 2018. Offbeat Crimes #6 of 6. (MM Paranormal) Carrington Loveless III, skim-blood vampire and senior officer of Philly's paranormal police department, has long suspected that someone's targeting his squad. The increasingly bizarre and dangerous entities invading their city can't be a coincidence. So when a walking corpse spouting Oscar Wilde attacks one of his officers, Carrington's determined to uncover the evil mind behind it all. –available as an e-book only (MLM). 3/3

1871. **Massa, J. J.,** *Agency: Engel and Gustavo,* loveyoudevine, 2006. (MM Mystery) Ever wondered what happens at a bar after closing time? Ever looked at a hot bartender and wished he was looking your way? When the bar back shows up late one night for work, the dominant bartender has a good snarl, and notices that the kid is a natural sub. Then the bartender finds out why the kid was late, and he knows he's got a hot little bottom he can't let get away. Will their steamy encounter lead to something more? 3/3

1872. **Massa, J. J.,** *Agency: Zeki and Aaron,* loveyoudevine, 2006. (MM Espionage) Some men tip their bartenders heavily. Some men count on the benevolence of a personal secretary or mechanic. Aaron

Trimmer is ever on the lookout for a good gadget maker. In his line of work, an exploding button or a razor hidden in his Cross pen are the difference between life and death. Zeki al-Filastini is very good at his job, no matter where he's from. That's the only reason that Aaron has begun seeking him out when he's at headquarters. Looks and personality have nothing to do with it. 3/3

1873. **Massa, J. J.**, *Agency: Marek and Tyrone,* loveyoudevine, 2006. (MM Espionage) Marek Dublecek is a loner. He's satisfied with his life as an agent. He has an apartment, a bed, a kitchen, a couch. The Agency is his real home, though, and The Old Man is the closest thing he has to family. He doesn't have friends... Well, maybe one. The night cook in The Agency cafeteria who always gives him little treats. His name is Tyrone. He's nice enough... Tyrone Johnson may look big and mean and tough, but he wouldn't hurt a butterfly. He's always had a soft spot for stray dogs and lost causes. That skinny little white boy with the bad attitude - he's both. Something about him makes Tyrone feel good inside. He'll do anything for one of those rare half-smiles. Anything. 3/3

1874. **Massa, J. J.**, *Agency: Vanya and Lance,* loveyoudevine, 2007. (MM Espionage) Vanya Ambrozak, Doctor of Chemistry, and Lancelot Morgan, secret agent extraordinaire, couldn't be more different. Both men are in service to The Agency, however. They must both work together to fight terrorism throughout the world. Usually, the two men serve separately, only passing one another at occasional staff meetings. An assignment that required the use of both men's talents would have to be unusual to say the least. In fact, such an assignment would be unusual and dangerous. Lance is used to danger. Time and again he's used his body to aid his government. 3/3

1875. **Massa, J. J.**, *Knights and Cookies,* loveyoudevine, 2006. (MM Romance) Life was hard in the Ukraine. Dr. Vanko Elaschuk is happy to come to the land of chocolate chip cookies, Budweiser, and white knights. The opportunity for research and growth just wasn't available in his homeland. He might find opportunities he never even dreamed of. But the land of opportunity might not be as welcoming as he hoped... 3/3

1876. **Massa, J. J.**, *The Edge,* Linden Bay Romance, 2007. (MM Police Procedural) Detective Paytah has spent his entire life fighting to overcome ignorance and gain acceptance in a world too quick to judge. Always willing to take on any challenge, the tough-as-nails Native American has never shied away from the truth. Until he meets Tyler Baker, that is. Tyler represents everything that Paytah hates; the blond haired blue-eyed gay detective with a penchant for bending the rules was born with a silver spoon in his mouth and a champagne glass in his hand. When Paytah is assigned to work with Tyler he anticipates that the partnership will be difficult. After all, working high profile serial murder cases are always challenging. But as the case of the decade unravels, so does his ability to control his attraction and to deny his own needs. 3/3

1877. **Mason, Erica Gerald,** *Lala Thank You: Dark Homecoming,* self-published, 2018. (MM Mystery Short Stories) MURDER IS A DRAG... From the outside looking in, Lazarus Mercy has it all. He's a fan favorite on a reality tv show, his career as drag queen Lala Thankyou has never been better, and he's learned to hide his introversion from his adoring fans...until he's framed for a murder he didn't commit. OUT OF TOWN, OUT OF LUCK, UNDER SUSPICION... Desperate to prove his innocence, Lazarus turns to an old friend to help bring the true killer to justice. Knowing the police are on his tail, Lazarus must let his stage persona loan him the bravery he needs to solve the crime. --can Lazarus must fight his inner demons...while fighting for his life? –e-book only (MLM). 3/3

1878. **Massey, Sujata,** *The Salaryman's Wife,* HarperCollins, 2000. Rei Shimura #1 of 11. (Japanese Cozy) Japanese-American Rei Shimura is a 27-year-old English teacher living in one of Tokyo's seediest neighborhoods. She doesn't make much money, but she wouldn't go back home to California even if she had a free ticket (which, thanks to her parents, she does.) Her independence is threatened however, when a getaway to an ancient castle town is marred by murder. –best friend Richard Randall is gay but does not appear in every novel (MLM). 1/3

1879. **Massey, Sujata,** *The Flower Master,* HarperCollins, 1999. Rei Shimura #3 of 11. (Japanese Cozy) Rei Shimura is a half-American, half-Japanese antiques dealer who's all sleuth when it comes to crime. At her aunt's bidding, Rei signs up for a course in ikebana, the famous Japanese art of flower arranging. But before she's even finished her first lesson, one of her teachers is brutally murdered. It's up to Rei to catch the killer, even if it means revealing skeletons in her own family's closet. 1/3

1880. **Massey, Sujata,** *The Bride's Kimono,* Harper, 2001. Rei Shimura #5 of 11. (Japanese Cozy) Antiques dealer Rei Shimura has managed to snag one of the most lucrative and prestigious freelance jobs of her career: transporting a packet of exquisitely embroidered nineteenth-century kimonos from Tokyo to Washington, D.C., for an exhibit, and to give a lecture on them. 1/3

1881. **Massey, Sujata,** *The Typhoon Lover,* Harper, 2005. Rei Shimura #8 of 11. (Japanese Cozy) A young woman with a foothold in two cultures, Rei Shimura has gone wherever fortune and her unruly passions have led her throughout her chaotic twenties. Now, after the streamers for her thirtieth birthday celebration have been taken down, the Japanese-American antiques dealer and part-time sleuth finds herself with an assignment to find and authenticate an ancient Middle Eastern pitcher that disappeared from Iraq's national museum. 1/3

1882. **Massey, Sujata,** *The Kizuna Coast,* Ikat Press, 2014. Rei Shimura #11 of 11. (Japanese Cozy) It starts with an SOS from Rei's beloved elderly friend, the antiques dealer Mr. Ishida, who's trapped among thousands on the ravaged Tohoku coast. Rei rushes from Hawaii to blacked-out Tokyo, where she discovers Ishida Antiques may have been burglarized and its cuddly watchdog, Hachiko, needs a caregiver. 1/3

1883. **Mathur, Ashok,** *Once Upon an Elephant,* Arsenal Pulp, 1998. (Fantasy) When the police find unusual boy parts, a young man's head and an elephant's body, they assume a murder has been committed, and the case goes to trial. But the appearance of Vighnesvara, a manifestation of Ganesh with the body of a young man and the head of an elephant, in the courtroom of ultra-conservative Judge McEchern throws things into chaos. Around the world statues of Ganesh are drinking offered milk, and poor Judge McEchern has troubles enough with his carnival court: witnesses who testify in languages other than English, testimony from an accused who grows extra arms at will, and a murder victim, with the head of an elephant, who refuses to stay dead. 3/3

1884. **Maugham, Robin,** *The Man with Two Shadows,* Harper, 1958. (Espionage) Strange and frightening phenomenon of the mind known as dissociation of personality, but is also an enthralling story of adventure, love and intrigue in North Africa. The hero's appalling disability, as a result of a head wound during the war (WWII), adds immeasurably to the danger of his already hazardous work with MI-5. 1/3

1885. **Maugham, Robin,** *The Link,* McGraw Hill, 1969. (Historical) The bizarre and licentious life of James Steede unfolds within a stunning portrayal of Victorian society and among a group of colorful and vivid characters, moving from Public School and great estates in England to lurid bars and brothels of Mexico's West Coast, Australia's rugged gold fields and, finally, to Sessions Court at Westminster. 2/3

1886. **Maugham, Robin,** *The Wrong People,* Heinemann, 1970. (Historical) Tangier in the 1960s where an uptight Brit unzips his emotions. Is it love or lust? And can he escape from debauched countrymen who desire the object of his affection. 3/3

1887. **Mayer, Martin,** *A Voice that Fills the House,* Simon and Schuster, 1959. (Psychological) professional and personal lives of a small group of people in the music world, with all the drama that comes with it. –police inspector is gay and in a relationship with fellow officer who is African American (MLM). 3/3

1888. **Mayne, Xavier,** *Frat House Troopers,* Dreamspinner, 2012. Brandt and Donnelly Caper #1 of 6. (MM Police Procedural) State trooper Brandt's new assignment to infiltrate a sex-cam operation puts him in a very uncomfortable position, especially since he'll have to perform naked on camera for his audition. Fortunately, his partner and best friend, Donnelly, has his back–whether that means helping Brandt shop gay boutiques for sexy underwear or offering Jäger and encouragement while he researches porn. –the rest of the books are not murder mysteries (MLM). 3/3

1889. **Maxwell, B. L.,** *Ghost Hunted,* Createspace, 2018. Valley Ghost #1 of 2. (MM Paranormal) Jason Thomas had always been obsessed with the ghost stories he'd watched on television from the time he was a kid. He'd always dreamed of visiting those haunted places and playing amateur ghost hunters with his best friend Wade. As they grew older, Jason's fascination with ghosts grew as well, and he'd drag Wade along to different haunted houses or hotels, always hoping to see an actual ghost. The chance to spend a weekend alone in a famous haunted house was too much for Jason to resist, and almost too much for Wade to endure. He knew going to the deserted house was everything Jason had ever dreamed of, so Wade tried to put his fears aside. But when paranormal things start to happen, admitting to Jason how he feels suddenly isn't the scariest thing Wade will encounter. 3/3

1890. **Maxwell, B. L.,** *Ghost Haunted,* Createspace, 2018. Valley Ghost #2 of 2. (MM Paranormal) Wade Rivers finally has what he's always wanted, his best friend Jason Thomas as his boyfriend. Their first date, hopefully the first of many, starts out with a simple dinner, but Wade has a surprise in store for Jason. They end up at a haunted house exhibit for Halloween. Wade finds out that Jason loves investigating the paranormal, but he's not as enthused about the other attractions. When they meet up with a fellow paranormal researcher, Jimbo, their fun night gets more frightening with each room in the haunted house. 3/3

1891. **McBain, Ed,** *He Who Hesitates,* Delacorte, 1965. 87th Precinct #19 of 55. (Police Procedural) Outside the 87th Precinct a stranger stands in the falling snow. He knows he should go in and tell a policeman about what happened the night before, about Molly. Every second that he hesitates takes him one step farther away from the 87th Precinct station, as another second ticks away on an innocent woman's life. –a country boy is propositioned while sitting on a park bench (MLM). 1/3

1892. **McBain, Ed,** *The House that Jack Built,* Henry Holt, 1988. Matthew Hope #8 of 14. (Hard Boiled) When Ralph, a loving older brother upset by his brother's gay lifestyle, is accused of his murder and the evidence points to his guilt, Matthew Hope must work with a few fleeting but crucial clues to prove Ralph's innocence. –very negative depictions of homosexuality. AIDS is the house Jack built as one sexual encounter builds upon another (MLM). 2/3

1893. **McBride, Scott,** *Kentucky Stud,* Blueboy Library, 1976. (Pulp) "Jeremy Peters, 17, is first accused of stealing from and then murdering a Kentucky horse breeder (Gunn). 3/3

1894. **McBride, Scott,** *Lavender Triangle Murders,* Surree, 1978. (Pulp) "Los Angeles-based avenger Eric Braden, 20s, a camera business owner, is recruited to bring a Nazi to justice (Gunn)" 3/3

1895. **McCade, Cole,** *The Cardigans,* self-published, 2018. Criminal Intentions #1 of 6. (MM Police Procedural) When a string of young queer men turn up dead in grisly murders, all signs point to the ex-boyfriend–but what should be an open-and-shut case is fraught with tension when BPD homicide detective Malcolm Khalaji joins up with a partner he never wanted. Rigid, ice-cold, and a stickler for the rules, Seong-Jae Yoon is a watchful presence whose obstinacy and unpredictability constantly remind Malcolm why he prefers to work alone. Seong-Jae may be stunningly attractive, a man who moves like a graceful, lethal bird of prey...but he's as impossible to decipher as this case. And if Malcolm doesn't find the key to unravel both in time, another vulnerable young victim may end up dead. 3/3

1896. **McCade, Cole,** *Junk Shop Blues,* self-published, 2018. Criminal Intentions #2 of 6. (MM Police Procedural) A murdered night club mogul unlocks a web of infidelity and deceit. The most likely suspect? The daughter of the richest family in Baltimore, if only Detectives Malcolm Khalaji and Seong-Jae Yoon can piece the evidence together. The clues just aren't lining up–but Malcolm can't tell if he's missing a piece of the puzzle or completely missing the mark. The McAllister case still haunts him. So many dead. So many he couldn't save. It's throwing him off his game. And the only one who really understands is his strange, coldly aloof partner. A partner he can never see the same way, after a moment of intimacy that haunts him as much as the voices of the dead. 3/3

1897. **McCade, Cole,** *The Man with the Glass Eye,* self-published, 2018. Criminal Intentions #3 of 6. (MM Police Procedural) Multiple execution-style murders hint at a mob hit, but when Malcolm and

Seong-Jae follow the clues the last thing they expect is a host of very familiar–and very dead–faces. They say dead men tell no tales, but if Malcolm and Seong-Jae can't even trust the words of the living, they'll never catch a hit man dead set on burying every trace of an underworld secret...along with a few more bodies. But it's not just the cold bodies on their minds, when a little undercover work sends them to a nightclub once owned by none other than Marion Garvey. Forced to play at being lovers, neither man can ignore the distraction of the very warm body in his arms. To Malcolm, Seong-Jae remains as aloof as ever...but what's really smoldering under that icy mask? –e-book only (MLM). 3/3

1898. **McCade, Cole,** *Changing Faces,* self-published, 2018. Criminal Intentions #4 of 6. (MM Police Procedural) With Malcolm on forced bed rest and off duty, Detective Seong-Jae Yoon faces his first solo case since joining the BPD–and it's one that will challenge his morals, his sense of duty, and his insistence on adhering to the letter of the law, especially when his actions in the Bishop case leave him questioning his own integrity. When the supposedly accidental death of a husband and father points to foul play in the victim's family, how close will Seong-Jae look to determine if the ends justify the means...and will he be able to live with the choices he makes? Especially when his mind is as far from the case as possible, and lingering on Malcolm Khalaji, Malcolm's ex-wife, and Seong-Jae's own conflicted feelings? –e-book only (MLM). 3/3

1899. **McCade, Cole,** *It's Witchcraft,* self-published, 2018. Criminal Intentions #5 of 6. (MM Police Procedural) An eerie ritualistic murder sends Malcolm and Seong-Jae down a bizarre path of the occult to find a killer–but when it comes to witchcraft, the suspect's not the only one casting a spell. With Seong-Jae haunting his dreams, Malcolm is practically bewitched, his trust in Seong-Jae growing deeper and deeper as both men learn to rely on each other. But when the murder triggers memories from both Seong-Jae's and Malcolm's shadowed pasts, will the secrets they share bring them closer...or drive them further apart? –e-book only (MLM). 3/3

1900. **McCade, Cole,** *Where There's Smoke,* self-published, 2018. Criminal Intentions #6 of 6. (MM Police Procedural) They say where there's smoke, there's fire–but Malcolm and Seong-Jae have a lot of blood and no body in a case where the only witness to a murder may be the killer himself. Yet as they chase down a victim who may or may not exist in a crime that may or may not have happened, it's the sparks flying between them that threaten to ignite into dangerous flame...and by the time this case is over, their relationship may never be the same. One kiss, one case, one night may change everything... –the next seven chapters will be published in 2019 (MLM).

3/3

1901. **McCaffrey, Vincent,** *Hound,* Small Beer Press, 2009. Sullivan #1 of 2. (Bibliomystery-Amateur Sleuth) A bookhound, Henry Sullivan buys and sells books he finds at estate auctions and library sales around Boston and often from the relatives of the recently deceased. He's in his late thirties, single, and comfortably set in his ways. But when a woman from his past, Morgan Johnson, calls to ask him to look at her late husband's books, he is drawn into the dark machinations of a family whose mixed loyalties and secret history will have fatal results. –one suspect is gay, and the landlord's son is gay (MLM). 1/3

1902. **McCracken, James M.,** *Ellensburg,* Createspace, 2017. Andrews #1 of 2. (Amateur Sleuth) Harrison Andrews' roommate Thomas has gone missing while on a trip down the Oregon coast to San Diego. His attempts to get help from the police fail, so Harrison decides to look for his friend on his own. –later in 2017, this is republished under the pseudonym of A. M. Huff and the second book in this series is available under that name (MLM). 3/3

1903. **McCrea, Barry,** *The First Verse,* Carrol and Graf, 2005. (Psychological) When freshman Niall Lenihan moves to Trinity College, he dives into unfamiliar social scenes, quickly becoming fascinated by a reclusive pair of students [who are] literary mystics who let signs and symbols from books determine their actions. Reluctantly, they admit him to their private sessions, and what begins as an intriguing game for Niall becomes increasingly esoteric, dramatic, and addictive. 3/3

1904. **McDonald, Gregory,** *Flynn's In,* Mysterious Press, 1984. Flynn #3 of 4. (Police Procedural) When it comes to crime, Boston Police Inspector and part-time intelligence agent, Francis Xavier Flynn is no stranger to the bizarre, the perverse, or the ridiculous. But when he is suddenly summoned by Police Commissioner D'Esopo to a secret wilderness compound far outside of their jurisdiction, he is a little surprised to find himself the hostage of a secret club of the nation's most powerful and peculiar. Famous for his irreverent methods and razor-sharp intellect, Flynn is forced to conduct a clandestine murder investigation. But before one murder is even solved, membership at the Rod and Gun Club continues to drop. –one of the victims likes to wear dresses (MLM). 1/3

1905. **McGown, Jill,** *Murder Movie,* St. Martin's, 1990. (Police Procedural) Frank Derwent (F.D. to everyone in the business), the Hollywood hotshot, has come to western Scotland to shoot a movie. But what happens offscreen is much more interesting. Especially when Barbara, budding starlet and F.D's nineteen-year old mistress, is killed.

Not quite as sweet as she seemed, the wee lass knew how to blackmail like a pro. Although clever Detective Patterson is on call to lend the local bobby a hand, he can't prevent further loss of life. And Patterson begins to suspect that no one is safe from his past–no matter where he (or she) hides.... –a gay actor on set is set up on a date by the detective with the gay screenwriter (MLM). 1/3

1906. **McGown, Jill,** *The Murders of Mrs. Austin and Mrs. Beale,* St. Martin's, 1991. Lloyd and Hill #4 of 13. (Police Procedural) Newly promoted Detective Inspector Judy Hill and Detective Chief Inspector Lloyd investigate the complicated romantic lives of Mrs. Austin and Mrs. Beale, two women who were recently murdered. –one of the murderers is gay (MLM). 2/3

1907. **McIlvanney, Liam,** *The Quaker,* HarperCollins, 2018. Duncan McCormack #1 of 1. (Historical Crime Drama) Glasgow, 1969. In the grip of the worst winter for years, the city is brought to its knees by a killer whose name fills the streets with fear: The Quaker. He's taken his next victim – the third woman from the same nightclub – and dumped her in the street like rubbish. The police are left chasing a ghost, with no new leads and no hope of catching their prey. After six months, DI Duncan McCormack, a talented young detective from the Highlands, is ordered to join the investigation – with a view to shutting it down for good. –gay subtext (MLM). 1/3

1908. **McIlvanney, William,** *Laidlaw,* Pantheon, 1977. Jack Laidlaw #1 of 3. (Police Procedural) The unorthodox, complex, sardonically humorous, intriguing policeman Jack Laidlaw makes his debut in an engrossing tale of murder. In Glasgow, the city with the worst slums in Europe, a city of hard men, powerful villains, bitter victims and cynical policemen, Laidlaw uses unconventional methods. –young teenage boy rapes and kills his girlfriend before running to his male lover for help (MLM). 2/3

1909. **McKenna, Kendall,** *Brothers in Arms,* Silver, 2012. Recon Diaries #1 of 3. (MM Military) Jonah Carver is a Marine Staff Sergeant and veteran of both Iraq and Afghanistan. After one scorching night with his former Platoon Commander, Kellan Reynolds, Jonah lost touch with him and has regretted it ever since. When an investigation into government corruption and the murder of U.S. troops ends in the killing of a V.I.P. on Jonah's watch, the FBI arrive to take over and see the investigation through. 3/3

1910. **McKenna, Kendall,** *Fire for Effect,* MLR, 2013. Recon Diaries #2 of 3. (MM Military) Hired to investigate the denial of a Marine the Medal of Honor, Kellan Reynolds and Jonah Carver try to untangle a web of lies, deceit, and heroism. 3/3

1911. **Mckenna, Kendall,** *The Final Line,* MLR, 2013. Recon Diaries #3 of 3. (MM Military) Staff Sergeant Corey Yarwood is an instructor at the Basic Reconnaissance Course. His last deployment ended in horror, but he can't remember those events. Battling severe PTSD, Corey's drinking is growing out of control. Corey's lost memories are pivotal to a civilian murder, and a military investigation. 3/3

1912. **McKevett, G. A.**, *Just Desserts,* Kensington, 1995. Savannah Reid #1 of 24. (Cozy) Detective Sergeant Savannah Reid is in her element cruising for crime in Southern California. But when she's told she's too fat to stay on the force, Savannah opens up her own detective agency and soon finds herself investigating a murder. With suspects abounding, Savannah finds herself sifting through the nasty mess of sex, adultery and down-and-dirty politics. –a gay ex-FBI agent and his lover assist the main character with her investigations (MLM). 2/3

1913. **McKevett, G. A.**, *Bitter Sweets,* Kensington, 1996. Savannah Reid #2 of 24. (Cozy) Savannah Reid, that big, sexy, Southern-born sleuth with a black belt in karate has finally established herself as a P.I. in posh San Carmelita, California. All her Moonlight Magnolia Detective Agency needs now is enough business to pay the rent and put some serious sweets on the table. No sooner does Savannah complete her first case–finding the long-lost sister of a local real estate broker–than murder enters the picture. 2/3

1914. **McKevett, G. A.**, *Killer Calories,* Kensington, 1997. Savannah Reid #3 of 24. (Cozy) Savannah Reid is back to track down the killer of an actress-turned-health spa owner found dead in her own hot tub. Unmasking the murderer won't be easy, but Savannah knows the most delectable endings are always worth waiting for. 2/3

1915. **McKevett, G. A.**, *Cooked Goose,* Kensington, 1998. Savannah Reid #4 of 24. (Cozy) A sexy, Southern-born private detective Savannah Reid is back, keeping the streets of exclusive San Carmelita, California, safe while indulging both her passion for food and her appetite for solving crime. 2/3

1916. **McKevett, G. A.**, *Sugar and Spite,* Kensington, 2000. Savannah Reid #5 of 24. (Cozy) Private detective Savannah Reid returns to investigate the murder of the ex-wife of her ex-partner, Dirk Coulter, whose body has turned up in his trailer. 2/3

1917. **McKevett, G. A.**, *Sour Grapes,* Kensington, 2001. Savannah Reid #6 of 24. (Cozy) When it comes to sassy private detectives, no one's bigger than Savannah Reid. The feisty, full-figured, steel magnolia knows how to turn every investigation into a delicious romp, even when she's dealing with a bunch of waif-like beauty queen hopefuls who will kill to be crowned. Things finally seem to be calm and peaceful in Savannah's life, but before she can celebrate, her spoiled, egocentric baby sister, Atlanta, shows up on her doorstep. Atlanta's determined to become a star, and her first step is the Miss Gold Coast Beauty Pageant that's being held right in San Carmelita. But the competition becomes so fierce that someone is driven to murder. 2/3

1918. **McKevett, G. A.**, *Peaches and Screams*, Kensington, 2002. Savannah Reid #7 of 24. (Cozy) Private eye Savannah Reid returns to the Deep South for her sister Marietta's wedding, only to find her young brother Macon accused of killing the Honorable Judge Patterson - and that he is counting on her to prove his innocence. –gay ex-FBI agent and his lover may not appear in this mystery (MLM). 2/3

1919. **McKevett, G. A.**, *Death by Chocolate*, Kensington, 2003. Savannah Reid #8 of 24. (Cozy) Business has been a little slow at the Moonlight Magnolia Detective Agency, but full-figured P.I. Savannah Reid doesn't have time to drown her sorrows in a box of double-chocolate truffles. She's too busy watching the Gourmet Network–and drooling over the sinfully scrumptious confections that Lady Eleanor ("The Queen of Chocolate") whips up on-air. But someone isn't sweet on the Queen's charming chatter–and wants her to hang up her oh-so-quaint apron–for good... 2/3

1920. **McKevett, G. A.**, *Cereal Killer*, Kensington, 2004. Savannah Reid #9 of 24. (Cozy) In a world where stick-thin women adorn fashion magazines and silver screens, plus-sized private eye Savannah Reid is grateful for the wild success–and fabulous fashion tips–of full-figured model Cait Connor. When Cait is found dead after months of extreme dieting, everyone assumes the risky regimen did her in. But then a second full-figured model meets an untimely end, and it's time to weigh the facts...and search for suspects. 2/3

1921. **McKevett, G. A.**, *Murder a la Mode*, Kensington, 2005. Savannah Reid #10 of 24. (Cozy) Voluptuous P.I. Savannah Reid's culinary cravings come second only to her appetite for adventure. Of course, every girl needs a little down time, and Savannah adores curling up with a box of chocolates, a steaming Irish coffee, and an even steamier romance novel–preferably one with sexy Lance Roman on the cover. But when she meets her dream hunk in person, things take a decidedly nightmarish turn... 2/3

1922. **McKevett, G. A.**, *Corpse Suzette*, Kensington, 2006. Savannah Reid #11 of 24. (Cozy) Full-figured P.I. Savannah Reid, accompanying her assistant's cousin Abigail, who has won an extreme makeover, to a glamorous new luxury spa called Emerge, investigates the mysterious disappearance of a renowned plastic surgeon, a strange case

1923. **McKevett, G. A.**, *Fat Free and Fatal,* Kensington, 2007. Savannah Reid #12 of 24. (Cozy) Beloved P.I. Savannah Reid rubs elbows with the rich, famous, and deadly. 2/3

1924. **McKevett, G. A.**, *Poisoned Tarts,* Kensington, 2008. Savannah Reid #13 of 24. (Cozy) Halloween in Southern California just doesn't have the frosty bite Savannah's used to, although her latest job promises chills aplenty. The Skeleton Key Three, a celebutante clique so named by the media because of their super-skinny figures and fat trust funds, are in the spotlight again-but this time, it's for something more than partying. It seems the one member of the Three who was neither wealthy nor particularly svelte hasn't been heard from in days. Just when Savannah thinks she has the case all figured out, the vibe surrounding the Skeleton Key Three changes from vacuous and suspicious to downright murderous. Now Savannah will have to put her Halloween candy on the shelf until she's deserving of a reward. And that means finding a killer-fast-before more Hollywood money becomes buried treasure... 2/3

1925. **McKevett, G. A.**, *A Body to Die For,* Kensington, 2009. Savannah Reid #14 of 24. (Cozy) Beloved plus-sized P.I., Savannah Reid, finds herself thrown into the world of physical fitness and exercise when a weight loss queen becomes the prime suspect in a big murder case. 2/3

1926. **McKevett, G. A.**, *Wicked Cravings,* Kensington, 2010. Savannah Reid #15 of 24. (Cozy) Savannah Reid may have a few extra curves on her full-figured body, but that hasn't stopped her from becoming one of the most successful private investigators in California. Her latest case puts her hot on the trail of a shady weight lose therapist who has made a killing treating - and cheating - his overweight patients. –gay ex-FBI agent may not appear in this mystery (MLM). 2/3

1927. **McKevett, G. A.**, *A Decadent Way to Die,* Kensington, 2011. Savannah Reid #16 of 24. (Cozy) Plus-sized P.I. Savannah Reid prides herself on cracking even the toughest cases. But her latest investigation is leaving her hungry for answers as she tries to unmask the identity of a cunning, would-be killer. His prey? A famous octogenarian with a fortune in the bank and a target on her back. . 2/3

1928. **McKevett, G. A.**, *Buried in Buttercream,* Kensington, 2012. Savannah Reid #17 of 24. (Cozy) After a recent brush with death, plus-sized P.I. and bride-to-be Savannah Reid has decided to stop sweating the small stuff. But when an event planner comes in to arrange her wedding, she discovers that murder can ruin even the best laid plans. 2/3

1929. **McKevett, G. A.,** *Killer Honeymoon,* Kensington, 2013. Savannah Reid #18 of 24. (Cozy) Now that plus-sized P.I. Savannah Reid has finally walked down the aisle, she's ready for a romantic island getaway with new husband Dirk Coulter. The trip is supposed to be a blissful week of rum drinks and sunshine–but finding a dead body on the beach can be a real killjoy. Welcome to the honeymoon from hell... –gay ex-FBI agent may not appear in this mystery (MLM). 2/3

1930. **McKevett, G. A.,** *Killer Physique,* Kensington, 2014. Savannah Reid #19 of 24. (Cozy) Plus-sized P.I. Savannah Reid gets a taste of the high life when she attends a Hollywood premiere on the arm of husband Dirk Coulter. Savannah may be a newlywed, but even she gets weak in the knees when she meets celebrity athlete-turned-moviestar Jason Tyrone. So, imagine how she feels when the star's rock-hard body is found rock-hard dead... 2/3

1931. **McKevett, G. A.,** *Killer Gourmet,* Kensington, 2015. Savannah Reid #20 of 24. (Cozy) Plus-sized P.I. Savannah Reid and her pals at the Moonlight Magnolia Detective Agency know a thing or two about fine dining. But when murder shows up on the menu, it's time to go back to the kitchen... 2/3

1932. **McKevett, G. A.,** *Killer Reunion,* Kensington, 2016. Savannah Reid #21 of 24. (Cozy) If you think going home again is hard, try being a plus-sized PI with a troubled family legacy. But Savannah Reid is no shrinking violet. She's ready for her high school reunion, complete with mean girls, ex-beaus–and murder charges... 2/3

1933. **McKevett, G. A.,** *Every Body on Deck,* Kensington, 2017. Savannah Reid #22 of 24. (Cozy) Plus-sized P.I. Savannah Reid has no problem mixing business with pleasure especially if that means a free trip while on the job. But when a gruesome murder rocks the boat, Savannah may finally be in over her head... 2/3

1934. **McKevett, G. A.,** *Hide and Sneak,* Kensington, 2018. Savannah Reid #23 of 24. (Cozy) As one of nine siblings raised in the Deep South, plus-sized P.I. Savannah Reid has experienced her share of family drama. But shotgun weddings and snooty in-laws don't worry her nearly as much as a search for a missing mother and child–especially when it leads to murder ... –book 24 of the Savannah Reid cozy series, *Bitter Brew,* is set to be released in April of 2019 (MLM). 2/3

1935. **McKinley, Brooke,** *Shades of Gray,* Dreamspinner, 2009. (MM Police Procedural/Crime Drama) Miller Sutton, a by-the-book FBI agent, is starting to see some troubling shades of gray in his black-and-white world. He comes face-to-face with his doubts in the person of Danny Butler, a mid-level drug runner Miller hopes to use to catch a much larger fish: Roberto Hinestroza, a drug lord Miller has pursued for years. Danny has no interest in being a witness against his boss, both out of a sense of twisted loyalty and because he knows double-crossing Hinestroza is a sure death sentence. But he reluctantly agrees to cooperate, and as he suspects, it doesn't take long for Hinestroza to figure out the betrayal. 3/3

1936. **McKinney, T. D.,** *Portrait of a Kiss,* AmberQuill, 2008. Southern Beaus #1 of 4. (MM Fantasy) The painting's compelling blue eyes fascinate former police detective David Schaeffer. Those beautiful eyes, that gorgeous face, couldn't possibly belong to a killer. But according to all the evidence in this small, sleepy river town in Alabama, that's exactly who the man in the portrait is...or was. –the next three books in the series are only fantasy romance without a mystery component (MLM). 3/3

1937. **McKinney, T. D.,** *Kissing Sherlock Holmes,* AmberQuill, 2011. (MM Sherlock Holmes) Amidst the beauty of an English country party, the greatest detective the world has ever known searches for a traitor. Somewhere among the glittering nobility a sadist lurks, using blackmail to destroy lives and endanger a nation. Only Sherlock Holmes can save an innocent man and bring the traitor to justice. It's a search that could cement the greatest friendship of all time into something far deeper and stronger...if the hunt doesn't end Watson's life first. 3/3

1938. **McKittrick, Casy,** *Murder on the Faux Pas Island,* Lethe, 2015. (MM Speculative) The year is 1935 but this is an America where cross-dressing goes almost unremarked, often unnoticed, and gay relationships are mundane; gay marriage, a quotidian fact of life. Famed chef and female impersonator Pancetta Brulee of New Orleans has been hired to cater a gay engagement party for two prominent grooms at the infamous Faux Pas Island and the Robicheaux estate. Both family and island have a terrible past, and most Cajuns and Creoles avoid the place like the plague. Pancetta attends the weekend engagement party, only to be faced with the gory murder. 3/3

1939. **McMahan, Jeffrey,** *Somewhere in the Night: Eight Gay Tales of the Supernatural,* Alyson, 1989. (Fantasy) The realms of nightmare and reality converge in eight tales of suspense and the supernatural in this Lambda Literary Award-winning collection. Featuring a gruesome Halloween party, a vampire whose conscience bothers him, and a suburbanite with a killer lawn, these stories contain just the right amount of horror, humor, and eroticism. 3/3

1940. **McManus, Alan,** *Tricks of the Mind,* Createspace, 2014. Bruno Benedetti #1 of 1. (Psychological) In a quirky flat in the Westend of

Glasgow, during the tension preceding the second Gulf War, Bruno walks in on Justin exercising and gives in to his pleading to massage taut muscles. As Justin groans in pleasure, Bruno reads him a strange astrological dream, a dream which begins to echo eerily in various narratives of family and friends as the dream turns to nightmare. 3/3

1941. **McMurray, Kate,** *In Hot Pursuit,* Loose Id, 2010. (MM Mystery) Hard-working NYPD cop Noah Tobin didn't even want to go on vacation. But it's been a tough eighteen months since the death of his lover, so he's determined to make the most of it. On his first night in sunny Florida, a chance encounter with a handsome man in a bar bathroom jumpstarts something in Noah that's been dormant for all those months. Then the man disappears. 3/3

1942. **McNab, Claire,** *Cop Out,* Naiad Press, 1991. Carol Aston #4 of 17. (Police Procedural) Bryce Darcy has been brutally murdered. Charlotte Darcy, sister to the victim, has confessed. Open and shut case, Detective Inspector Carol Ashton is informed. Not so, argues Carol's aunt, friend to the Darcy family. She contends that Charlotte is mentally incompetent. Carol reopens the investigation. –closeted husband and father is killed at the beginning of the mystery (MLM). 2/3

1943. **McNab, Claire,** *Dead Certain,* Naiad Press, 1992. Carol Aston #5 of 17. (Police Procedural) Convinced that the recent death of young Australian opera star Collis Raeburn was not a suicide, as widely believed, Detective Inspector Carol Ashton opens up an investigation, an act that makes her unpopular with the victim's next-of-kin. –victim killed was gay and possibly spread HIV willingly to those he slept with (MLM). 2/3

1944. **McNease, Mark,** *Murder at the Pride Lodge,* Createspace, 2012. Kyle Callahan #1 of 5. (Suspense) Kyle and his partner Danny Durban head to Pride Lodge in the Pennsylvania countryside for a weekend of Halloween fun. Just as they arrive, Kyle's friend Teddy the lodge handyman is found dead at the bottom of the empty swimming pool. 3/3

1945. **McNease, Mark,** *Pride and Perilous,* Createspace, 2012. Kyle Callahan #2 of 5. (Suspense) Amateur photographer Kyle is about to have his first photo exhibit at the gallery, just as someone begins killing people connected to it. 3/3

1946. **McNease, Mark,** *Death by Pride,* Createspace, 2013. Kyle Callahan #3 of 5. (Suspense) It's Gay Pride weekend, the most festive weekend of the year in New York City. Hundreds of thousands of partygoers arrive to show the world how to have a good time. Stalking the party is the most successful serial killer the city has ever seen. 3/3

1947. **McNease, Mark,** *Death in the Headlights,* MadeMark, 2014. Kyle Callahan #4 of 5. (Suspense) Kyle Callahan and his partner Danny Durban head to rural New Jersey for a relaxing week with their dear friend, Detective Linda Sikorsky, recently retired and newly in love. Driving back from dinner with Linda and her fiancée Kirsten, they discover the body of Abigail Creek, run off the road on a bicycle wearing only her nightgown and slippers. Kyle and Linda quickly find themselves learning more than they want to know about the Creek family and the home they call CrossCreek Farm. In the words of Clara Presley's grandmother, "Whatever grows there, grows in the shadows." Come along as Linda and Kyle make their way into the shadows and enter the spider's web, determined to find out who in this family of spiders is the deadliest one. 3/3

1948. **McNease, Mark,** *Kill Switch,* MadeMark, 2015. Kyle Callahan #5 of 5. (Suspense) Putting an end to evil was the right thing to do, but it left Kyle in need of the services of psychotherapist Peter Benoit. Kyle decides the best way to re-engage with life is to do what he can't stop doing: solving murders. Joined once again by his friend Detective Linda Sikorsky, Kyle takes on his first cold case, the murder of a teenager three years ago. Corinne Copley was killed on a Manhattan side street for nothing more than her cell phone. Or was that really the reason? Come along as Kyle delves into the murky undercurrent of New York City politics, pursues a crime boss who kills as easily as she breathes, and seeks justice for the father of a murdered child. 3/3

1949. **McNease, Mark,** *Last Room at the Cliff's Edge,* MadeMark, 2016. (Police Procedural) Retired homicide detective Linda Sikorsky and her wife Kirsten McClellan head to Maine for a long weekend of rest, relaxation and rewrites as Kirsten finishes drafting her first novel. Bad weather alters their plans, forcing them to stop for the night at the Cliff's Edge, a motel known for secrecy and indiscretion. Something murderous goes bump in the night, sending the women on a search for justice when a young reporter's body is found dumped and violated on a back road. –sheriff of the small town is gay (MLM). 3/3

1950. **McNease, Mark,** *Murder at the Paisley Parrot,* Createspace, 2017. Marshall James #1 of 1. (Historical) The year was 1983. The bar was the Paisley Parrot, a gay, mob-run dive where people came to drink and few of them remembered the night before. Marshall loves his job as a bartender there. But one night, among the regulars, a killer arrives. Body by body, death by death, Marshall finds himself pulled into a web of murder, deceit and crime, with a psychopath waiting at the center of it all. Marshall falls for the cop who's investigating him, not knowing if their relationship will survive or even if he'll come out of this alive. Find out before last call come around, in Murder at the Paisley Parrot. –the book left off with the option of a sequel (MLM). 3/3

1951. **McNease, Mark,** *Black Cat White Paws,* Createspace, 2018. Maggie Dahl #1 of 2. (Amateur Sleuth) recently widowed Maggie Dahl finds herself faced with challenges on all fronts: life alone in a new town, running a business she and her husband had dreamed of and started together, and now pursuing a killer. Her sister Gerri moves from Philadelphia to Lambertville, New Jersey, to support her sister and start a new life of her own. Together the women search for a murderer, helped in critical ways by their neighbor's cat. –Maggie's son is gay, and the author is at work on a second Maggie Dahl title (MLM). 1/3

1952. **Medley, James,** *Huck and Billy,* Badboy, 1994. (Pulp) "New Orleans hustlers Billy, 19, the narrator, and Huck, 21, his lover act as decoys to catch a murderer and, as a result of their success, become policemen working as liaisons with the gay community in a crime story (Gunn)." 3/3

1953. **Medley, James,** *The Revolutionary and other stories,* Badboy, 1996. (Pulp) Billy, the son of the station chief of the American Embassy in Guatemala, is kidnapped and held for ransom. Frightened at first, Billy gradually develops an unimaginably close relationship with Juan, the revolutionary assigned to guard him. 3/3

1954. **Meeker, Lloyd,** *The Companion,* Createspace, 2014. (MM Mystery) Shepherd Bucknam hasn't had a lover in more than a decade and doesn't need one. As a Daka, he coaches men in the sacred art and mystery of sexual ecstasy all the time, and he loves his work. It's his calling. In fact, he's perfectly content–except for the terrors of his recurring nightmare and the ominous blood-red birthmarks on his neck. He's convinced that together they foretell his early and violent death. 3/3

1955. **Melville, James,** *The Chrysanthemum Chain,* St. Martin's, 1982. Tetsuo Otani #2 of 13. (Japanese Crime Fiction) The murder of respected foreign academic David Murrow, a leading light in Kobe's expatriate community, is clearly a case for Superintendent Otani and his team of detectives but also a source of anxiety for Andrew Walker, the innocent and well-meaning British Vice-Consul in Osaka, who has to learn – rapidly – the diplomatic niceties of a formal Japanese police investigation and also the intricacies and rituals of Japanese mourning ceremonies. Both Walker and Otani discover that following the Chrysanthemum Chain leads to the secret life of the victim, which both local criminal gangs and high-powered politicians are determined should stay secret. –victim killed was a gay man who sought to connect homosexual tourists and residents (MLM). 2/3

1956. **Mendez, Gene,** *A Twist of Faith,* Createspace, 2016. (Police Procedural) Matt Manser a San Francisco police department inspector is assigned to investigate the murder of a prominent biblical archaeologist. Matt doesn't know that his investigation will place him in the middle of an underground war between a group of progressive Christians called the Lulav, and a conservative Christian cooperative called the Order of the White Dove. 3/3

1957. **Mendicino, Tom,** *The Boys from 8th and Carpenter,* Kensington, 2015. (Contemporary Classic) S. Gagliano & Son has been a barber shop fixture in South Philly for decades. Frankie and Michael Gagliano's Italian immigrant father–Luigi to his customers, Papa to his sons–presides over the store, enlisting his children as soon as they're big enough to wield a broom. After their father's death, Frankie takes over the shop, transforming it to fit in with the gentrifying neighborhood. Michael becomes a successful prosecutor with a rising political career, still close to his big brother despite the differences between them. Then comes an unthinkable, impulsive act that will force Michael to choose between risking his comfortable life and keeping a sacred oath–made before he knew how powerful a promise can be. 2/3

1958. **Menon, David,** *The Wild Heart,* Trafford, 2008. (Espionage) Mark Earnshaw was bored with his life as a banking call center supervisor in the Salford Quays development just outside Manchester. Then he meets Ian Taylor, a builder working on a new block of flats going up at the end of Mark's street. They begin an intense relationship, but Ian is hiding the darkest of secrets from decades ago in Northern Ireland. As a volunteer for one of the loyalist paramilitaries he was forced into a deal with British intelligence in which his evidence sends his comrades to gaol and means he has to be moved to the UK mainland and given a new identity. 3/3

1959. **Meriwether, Sean,** *Men of Mystery: Homerotic Tales of Intrigue and Suspense,* Haworth, 2007. (Fantasy Short Stories) Men of Mystery presents 16 stories that abandon the sanitized version of homosexuality to drive down darker alleys searching for crimes of passion and hard sex that still carries a threat. You'll meet dirty cops who harass their suspects, shifty criminals who'll leave you aching for more, mob types who live with the constant threat of death ... even ghosts from beyond the grave who demand a whole new definition of pleasure. 3/3

1960. **Merrick, Gordon,** *The Good Life,* Alyson, 1997. (Crime Drama)

Perry Langham's eternal attraction to beautiful young men got in the way of his marriage to heiress Bettina Vernon – and love leads to murder. –published after Merrick's death and finished by Charles S. Hulse, this book is loosely based on the Lonergan murder case (MM). 3/3

1961. **Merrigan, Peter,** *Rider,* Lulu, 2012. Rider #1 of 3. (Suspense) Love. Betrayal. Revenge. When Kane Rider's partner is murdered, he has no time to grieve. He is quickly thrust into a world of secrets and lies, pursued by criminals for something he knows nothing about. He thought he had the perfect life, but all that changes the night Ryan Cassidy is stabbed to death. As Ryan's secrets slowly come to light, Kane must challenge what he thought to be the truth with what he knows could kill him. With nowhere to hide, and no one to turn to, he has only one choice - survive or die. 3/3

1962. **Merrigan, Peter,** *Lynch,* Createspace, 2017. Rider #2 of 3. (Suspense Short Stories) THE SURVIVORS: Eighteen months after their ordeal in London, Kane Rider and Margaret Bernhard are secured in witness protection and moving on with their lives. But Alberto Ramirez isn't about to let them off so easily. THE ASSASSIN: Ex-Spanish soldier turned hired-hitman Miguel Fernandez has a taste for blood. Employed by kingpin Ramirez, he's now on the trail of a man and woman who disappeared a year and a half ago. THE LAW: Interpol detective Ann Clark, responsible for getting Kane and Margaret into witness protection, is at a loose end. Suspended from the force for a careless mistake, but determined to protect her charges, the decisions she makes now will have consequences for them all. –book three in the series is supposed to have been released in 2018 (MLM). 3/3

1963. **Merritt, Rich,** *Code of Conduct,* Kensington, 2008. (MM Military) At thirty-three, Don Hawkins has spent the better part of his life, in every sense, as a U.S. Marine. Enlisting to escape an alcoholic father and stepmother, he became the unofficial leader of a group of gay servicemen and women, all compelled to guard their sexual identity as faithfully as they serve their country. But with newly inaugurated President Clinton's promise to lift the ban on gays in the military, Don is optimistic that a brighter era is dawning–and not just politically. Ten years now since his lover died in Beirut, Don is finally ready to love again, and falls headlong for Patrick, a handsome young helicopter pilot. As their relationship develops, Don lets his guard down–in potentially dangerous ways. Because forces are at work in the Naval Investigative Service, in Congress, and even in the bars and clubs that Don views as his turf, with a vicious agenda that will have unforeseen consequences... 3/3

1964. **Merrow, J. L.,** *Pressure Head,* Samhain, 2013. Plumber's Mate #1 of 5. (MM Paranormal) To most of the world, Tom Paretski is just a plumber with a cheeky attitude and a dodgy hip, souvenir of a schoolboy accident. The local police keep his number on file for a different reason–his sixth sense for finding hidden things. He's called in to help locate the body of a missing woman up on Nomansland Commons. 3/3

1965. **Merrow, J. L.**, *Relief Valve*, Samhain, 2014. Plumber's Mate #2 of 5. (MM Paranormal) The relationship between Tom Paretski, a cheeky plumber with a gift for finding hidden things, and PI Phil Morrison may only be a few weeks old, but already it's under attack. Tom's friends and family are convinced the former bully isn't good enough for him, and they're not shy about saying so. 3/3

1966. **Merrow, J. L.**, *Heat Trap*, Saimhain, 2015. Plumber's Mate #3 of 5. (MM Paranormal) It's been six months since plumber Tom Paretski was hit with a shocking revelation about his family. His lover, P.I. Phil Morrison, is pushing this as an ideal opportunity for Tom to try to develop his psychic talent for finding things. Tom would prefer to avoid the subject altogether, but just as he decides to bite the bullet, worse problems come crawling out of the woodwork. 3/3

1967. **Merrow, J. L.**, *Blow Down*, Samhain, 2016. Plumber's Mate #4 of 5. (MM Paranormal) The last thing newly engaged plumber Tom Paretski needs is to stumble over another dead body. He's got enough on his mind already as the reality of his impending marriage sinks in. Not only is his family situation complicated, but his heroism at a pub fire has made him a local celebrity, and now everyone knows about his psychic talents–and wants a piece of them. 3/3

1968. **Merrow, J. L.**, *Lock Nut*, Riptide, 2018. Plumber's Mate #5 of 5. (MM Paranormal) Tom Paretski, plumber with a talent for finding hidden things, and his private investigator fiancé Phil Morrison have been hired to locate a runaway husband, Jonathan Parrot. The job seems simple enough–until their quarry turns up dead in a canal, and a photofit of Tom's face is splashed all over the news, making him chief suspect. 3/3

1969. **Merrow, J. L.**, *To Love a Traitor*, Samhain, 2015. (MM Historical) When solicitor's clerk George Johnson moves into a rented London room in the winter of 1920, it's with a secret goal: to find out if his fellow lodger, Matthew Connaught, is the wartime traitor who cost George's adored older brother his life. 3/3

1970. **Michael, Sean**, *Tripwire*, Torquere, 2004. (MM Romance) Set in the steamy jungles of South America, Trip a merc for hire, just out for his next adrenaline rush. And his next paycheck. Bones is a doctor on the payroll of a major tree hugging organization, gone native and patching up the people who wander into his camp. Someone puts a price on Bones' head. Someone wants the man dead, someone they would never expect to pop up in a million years. Can they figure out why in time to save their skins? And can love overcome a merc's greed? 3/3

1971. **Michaels, Grant,** *A Body to Die For,* St. Martin's, 1990. Stan Kraychik #1 of 6. (Amateur Sleuth) Hot water is nothing new for Stan Kraychik, a smart-mouthed Boston hairdresser who gave up a career in psychology to "shrink 'em at the sink" instead. When a vacationing National Park ranger turns up dead in Boston, Stan is implicated in the murder, and must find the killer to clear his own name. With an eye for detail and a mettlesome spirit, Stan finds plenty of clues, but he also confronts the police lieutenant assigned to the case, a man with little tolerance for the world of fashion and style, or for Stan's cheeky attitude. With a sharp tongue as his best defense, a most unlikely detective uses even more unlikely techniques to close the loop and get the killer. –going to be republished by ReQueered Tales in 2019 (MLM). 3/3

1972. **Michaels, Grant,** *Love You to Death,* Sty. Martin's, 1992. Stan Kraychik #2 of 6. (Amateur Sleuth) Valentine's Day is fast approaching and everyone has a sweetheart, except Stan Kraychik, Boston's sassiest hairdresser. Ever hopeful of meeting Mr. Right, Stan attends a gala reception that culminates in a death by poisoning, and romantic problems take a back seat to murder. 3/3

1973. **Michaels, Grant,** *Dead on your Feet,* St. Martin's, 1993. Stan Kraychik #3 of 6. (Amateur Sleuth) The founder of a ballet company is discovered murdered and the conductor is the prime suspect. Seduced by the choreographer, a hairdresser sets out to prove the conductor's innocence. Among many suspects, including the lover, the hairdresser discovers life is more complex–and deadly–than art. 3/3

1974. **Michaels, Grant,** *Mask for a Diva,* St. Martin's, 1994. Stan Kraychik #4 of 6. (Amateur Sleuth) Stan Kraychik, Boston hair-dresser extraordinaire, has been hired as the wig master's assistant for the upcoming season of a local opera company. For the main event, Italian opera diva and aging soprano Marcella Ostinata will perform the lead. As the company heads unsteadily towards opening night, murder threatens the entire festival and Stan finds himself playing a crucial role in a deadly grand opera, performed without music, and with real weapons and killers. 3/3

1975. **Michaels, Grant,** *Time to Check Out,* St. Martin's, 1995. Stan Kraychik #5 of 6. (Amateur Sleuth) It's October in Key West, as quiet as the tropical island will ever be. Or so thinks Boston salon star Stan "The Widow" Kraychik, who has recently lost his lover. Stan is grief-stricken, but he's also grotesquely wealthy, thanks to a landmark cash settlement to a domestic partner, as well as his dead lover's life insurance. But instead of sanctuary in an off-season resort town, Stan finds himself in a fizzy, dizzy world that few tourists experience. The trouble starts when Stan is forced to change his guest-house. When he goes to settle his bill, the manager is on the floor of her office - dead by violence. Never one to mind his own business, Stan discovers that the victim was embroiled in a legal battle over the estate of a Key West millionaire. As he meddles further into the investigation, he encounters an exotic lineup of suspects reminiscent of a circus sideshow. They may be worthy foils for Stan's melancholy, but he must also identify the killer before he becomes the next victim. 3/3

1976. **Michaels, Grant**, *Dead as a Doornail*, Sy. Michael's, 1996. Stan Kraychik #6 of 6. (Amateur Sleuth) Newly wealthy ex-hairdresser Stan Kraychik buys the last unrenovated brownstone in Boston's fabulously chic South End only to have the renovations held up by a freak April snowstorm-and the murder of the young, attractive contractor. Because the victim bears some resemblance to Stan himself, the police think he might have been the intended target and want to leave town while they look for the killer. Instead Stan begins to snoop around on his own, discovering a web of secrets and jealousies that someone has killed to protect-and the contractor's murder is only the beginning. 3/3

1977. **Michaels, Kenneth**, *The Gay Detective: Nick and Norm in Chicago*, La Mancha Press, 2015. Nick and Norm #1 of 2. (Police Procedural) The premier of Nick Scott's TV talk show, The Gay Detective, appears to be a big hit until his first guest ends up murdered. Nick, also a gay detective with the Chicago Police Department, and his older, straight partner Detective Norm Malone hunt this heinous serial killer tagged The Reaper. This odd couple encounters both personal and professional conflict as this suspenseful noir thriller races to a surprise conclusion that leaves Nick and Norm battling for their lives. 3/3

1978. **Michaels, Kenneth**, *Only in Key West*, La Mancha Press, 2017. Nick and Norm #2 of 2. (Police Procedural) When vacationing Chicago detectives Nick and Norm witness a tragic accident involving a famous entertainer, the local police chief asks for their help. The duo's investigation uncovers crime and corruption in paradise as they come face-to-face with a ruthless killer. 3/3

1979. **Michaels, Ward**, *Murder Motel*, Wide-Wake, 1981. (Pulp) "Milwaukee-based psychic sleuth Denis Vernon, 20s, solves the crime in a pulp whodunit (Gunn)." 3/3

1980. **Michaels, Ward,** *Soaking up the Sun,* Adam's Gay Reader, 1984. (Pulp) "The cabdriver, Rob Zillman, who invites accidental sleuth Charles Major, to his home, is murdered. Major manages to solve a murder between countless bouts of sex and romance in a pulp whodunit (Gunn)." 3/3

1981. **Michaelsen, Jon,** *Pretty Boy Dead,* Wilde City Press, 2013. Kendall Parker #1 of 2. (Police Procedural) A murdered male stripper. A missing go-go dancer. A city councilman on the hook. Can Atlanta homicide detective Sergeant Kendall Parker solve the vicious crime while remaining safely hidden behind the closet door? –book two in the Kendall Parker series, *Deadwood Murders,* is set to be published late in 2019 (MLM). 3/3

1982. **Mickelbury, Penny,** *Night Songs,* Naiad Press, 1995. Mimi and Gianna #2 of 4. (Police Procedural) Someone is killing prostitutes – three to date – and no one seems to care in crime-weary Washington, except Police Lieutenant Gianna Maglione, head of the Hate Crimes unit and her lover Mimi Patterson, investigative journalist. – "Washington D. C. police detective Tim McCreedy, a "flaming queen" with a "weightlifter's body" goes behind the scene (Gunn)." 2/3

1983. **Miles, A. K. M.,** *Stone Canyon,* MLR, 2010. (MM Mystery) Rancher Micah Stone shows up at Private Detective Able Kenton's office with a letter from his late mother. Micah wants answers. Able has his own letter to show Micah. Together they set out to find who killed Micah's mother and why. Their first clue leads them to an attorney and the police. Micah and Able fall in love while going back and forth from the ranch to the city, from one crisis to another. The characters at the ranch keep things hopping with their own lives filled with comedy, tragedy, and love. They get their answer, but it comes hard. 3/3

1984. **Miles, A. K. M.,** *Cold Winters,* MLR, 2010. (MM Mystery) When Mason Davenport shows up in Sheriff Cole Winters' Deerville, Kentucky life in the sleepy rural town changes for everyone. Mason has come looking for Cole, but he didn't come alone. There are four men who followed him from Chicago and they want to kill him before he can tell what he saw. Cold Winters is filled with romance, fear, beatings, babies, good food, friends, gorgeous countryside, evil men, and some really good sex that turns into everlasting love. Old men with funny sayings, young men who need life lessons, get them, and sweet pretty women who provide good friendship. 3/3

1985. **Millar, Kenneth,** *The Dark Tunnel,* Dodd Mead, 1944. Chet Gordon #1 of 2. (Espionage) Doctor Robert Branch is a university professor, not a secret agent. But his best friend is dead, and Branch knows that it can't have been suicide. He is also certain that the murder has been arranged by a Nazi espionage group operating on campus. The only trouble is, no one will believe him. Branch knows that the Nazis will have him eliminated as soon as it is convenient. He's even narrowed his choice of executioner down to three: a psychotic homosexual, a respected educator-and the women he loves... –reprinted under the pseudonym Ross MacDonald in 1955 (MLM). 1/3

1986. **Millar, Marcus,** *Copsucker,* Greenleaf, 1970. (Pulp) "Policeman Rod Mann, 28, reassigned from a city's vice squad to an FBI unit, penetrates a hippy movement and, as a result, turns on to his sexuality and drops out of law enforcement in a pulp procedural (Gunn)." 3/3

1987. **Millar, Margaret,** *Wall of Eyes,* Random House, 1943. Inspector Sands #1 of 2. (Psychological Suspense) Since the accident that left her blind, Kelsey has become more difficult than ever. At least this is what Alice told the psychiatrist. Languishing in a house full of servants and unloving family, Kelsey has become bitter. She was driving the car that night. Geraldine did die, and Kelsey will never see again. But that was two long years ago. Time enough to heal. So why would Kelsey now want her life to end with a grain of morphine? –side gay character who talks in a high tenor (MLM). 1/3

1988. **Millar, Margaret,** *Spider Webs,* William Morrow, 1986. (Courtroom Drama) The murder trial of Cully Paul King, handsome black skipper of the yacht Bewitched, takes place in a California coastal town. Events prove King had strangled Madeline Pherson aboard the yacht, after hiring her as a cook. The prosecutor claims that the victim's jewel case, which can't be found, was King's motive for murder. The contents of the case mark one of the startling disclosures in the proceedings, most shedding merciless light on the people involved with the defendant. The judge, the opposing attorneys, the amorous court clerk–everyone has more at stake in the verdict than the defendant. All, for different reasons, want to control King's future. –defense attorney comes out during the trial (MLM). 1/3

1989. **Miller, Geoffrey,** *Black Glove,* Viking Press, 1981. (Hard Boiled) Terry Traven is an L. A. private eye who modeled himself after Philip Marlowe and thrived in the 1960s, becoming a minor celebrity for his hardboiled style and his skill at tracking down runaways. But now it's the 1980s, his minor fame has completely faded, and he's barely making a living. So, he jumps at the opportunity to find a wealthy, born-again industrialist's missing son who has been dabbling in drugs and punk rock. It's not just a chance to save the kid... but himself. Traven's search leads him into a bizarre, cocaine-drizzled world populated by kidnappers, drug dealers, talent agents, greedy entrepreneurs, religious zealots and desperate killers. – criminal fraternity targets gay men (MLM). 1/3

1990. **Miller, Terry,** *Standing By,* Gay Presses, 1984. (Suspense) Tom Gardner, a supreme jerk, working as an understudy of William Sheppard in a major revival of Noel Coward's *The Vortex,* believes William Sheppard despises and works to constantly humiliate him. 1/3

1991. **Mills, Carley,** *A Nearness of Evil,* Coward-McCann, 1961. (Crime Drama) Based closely to the Lonergan case, including the line, "if he's good enough for daddy he's good enough for me." 2/3

1992. **Miner, Valerie,** *Murder in the English Department,* St. Martin's, 1982. (Suspense) Assistant professor Nan Weaver, an outspoken feminist, is working toward tenure at Berkeley. Nan's blue-collar family left her with a legacy of endurance and hard work, and she is dedicated to her ideals and her students. But Nan's bold campaign against on-campus sexual harassment may be putting her career prospects in jeopardy. When an infamously chauvinistic male English professor turns up dead in his office, everyone suspects activist Nan. But she is innocent. And she knows who the murderer is. –best friend of main character is a closeted gay professor (MLM). 1/3

1993. **Mispiel, E. M.,** *Garnetville: A Gay Novel,* Createspace, 2012. Quinn and Dave #1 of 2. (MM Romance) Dave wants to know why his mentor, a gay teacher, was murdered. Quinn just wants to make sure he doesn't die in the process. Dave's obsessive search for justice stirs up trouble and drives more than one man over the edge. 3/3

1994. **Mispiel, E. M.,** *The Closed Mouth,* Createspace, 2013. Quinn and Dave #2 of 2. (MM Romance) Quinn and Dave are perfect for each other. Dave doesn't want a long-term relationship, and Quinn's relationships never last very long. Quinn and Dave have been together for a few months when they get involved in a murder investigation. Quinn's childhood friend, Hector, needs help, and he is going to get it whether he wants it or not. Quinn and Dave investigate his connection to a murder and why a witness is keeping silent. 3/3

1995. **Mitchell, Gladys,** *The Death-Cap Dancers,* St. Martin's, 1981. Mrs. Bradley #59 of 66. (British Cozy) While en route to visit relatives, Hermione Lestrange falls into company with three agreeable women who are spending their autumn holiday in a forest cabin. Out for a drive, the group discovers a battered bicycle by the side of the road, and closer inspection reveals the unfortunate owner, seemingly dead from head wounds, her body found in a nearby ravine. The police are contacted, but Hermione becomes concerned that suspicion may fall on herself and her new acquaintances, as the scene resembles a hastily covered-up automobile accident. Fearing the worst, she rings up her great-aunt and voices her fears. –two members of a dance group are a gay couple (MLM). 1/3

1996. **Mitchell, K. A.**, *Chasing Smoke,* Samhain, 2010. (MM Mystery) In the best of times, Daniel Gardner hates visiting his family. With his boyfriend pressuring him for a mortgage-serious commitment, Christmas in Easton, PA sounds, for once, like a welcome escape. His old house holds more than memories of a miserable adolescence, though. It has Trey Eriksson. At seventeen, Trey was taken in by the wealthy Gardner family after his father was jailed for his mother's murder. Trey is still looking for the real killer. Now new clues to the murder are resurfacing. 3/3

1997. **Mitchell, Kay,** *Lively Form of Death,* St. Martin's, 1991. Chief Inspector Morrissey #1 of 5. (Police Procedural) The gossips of a tranquil village on the outskirts of Malminster have a field day spreading the news that Helen Goddard's husband has been seduced by the local femme fatale, Marion Walsh. Then Marion's charwoman is poisoned by milk obviously intended for her employer, and suspicion naturally falls on Helen Goddard until Marion herself is brutally murdered and Chief Inspector Morrissey discovers that a lot of people wanted her dead. And then there are the missing children, too… As Morrissey digs deeper he begins to untangle a hideous web of perversion, envy and murder - and skeletons start to tumble out of some very influential cupboards indeed… –novel is not gay friendly (MLM). 1/3

1998. **Moll, Sarah Kay,** *Dark City,* Nine Star Press, 2018. (Hard Boiled) Jude has a tender heart. Yet he was born into a criminal empire and groomed from childhood to step into his father's violent footsteps. To survive, he created a second personality. Ras is everything Jude isn't–cruel, remorseless, and utterly without fear, as incapable of love as Jude is of malice. But when Ras meets a ruthless socialite, he begins to feel a strange stirring of emotion, a brush of Jude's passion against his own dark heart. Meanwhile, Jude finds himself with a knife in his hand, the evil in Ras's soul bleeding into his own. As the walls between them crumble, they could lose everything–their lovers, their family, and their hold on the dark city itself. Coming together could break them…or make them whole. 3/3

1999. **Monette, Paul,** *Taking Care of Mrs. Carroll,* Little Brown, 1978. (Caper) Two male lovers, a legendary movie goddess, an estate caretaker, a repressed prep-school teacher, and a polyestered Beverly Hills agent mount an incredible scam. Beth Carroll, a wealthy old lady cared for by her gay houseboy David and by Phidias, the overseer of the estate and her lover for fifty years, has died before signing her will which will protect her magnificent property from being sold to developers, Phidias enlists David's aid, and David calls in his old lover Rick and the latter's famous friend, the Dietrich-esque chanteuse Madeleine Cosquer, who in turn brings in her agent, Aldo, a hip L.A. queen. Together they develop an impossible plan to fulfill Mrs. Carroll's last wish. 3/3

2000. **Monette, Paul,** *The Gold Diggers,* Avon, 1979. (Caper) Perched on top of a hill in the oldest part of Bel Air, Crook House is the grand mansion that gilded Hollywood dreams are made of. It seemed like the perfect place for the exhausted and neurotic Rita to take time away from her life and catch up with her old friend Peter and his lover, Nick. What she didn't count on was her friends' emotional baggage, not to mention the suspicious tales of a buried treasure underneath the house. 3/3

2001. **Monette, Paul,** *The Long Shot,* Avon, 1981. (Caper) An unconventional cast of characters whose tangled lives play out against the backdrop of a Hollywood that is at once luminous and melancholy – a Hollywood where making it to the top can be far more harrowing than never making it at all. It was just a surreal one-night stand with a virtual stranger, a gypsy-eyed drifter with an inexplicably infectious passion for Thoreau. Yet for would-be screenwriter Greg Cannon, the fleeting encounter bears the promise of something even more elusive in this jaded town than coveted stardom. Then, Harry Dawes is found with his wrists slashed, naked in a hot tub with the body of Hollywood's hottest – and also closeted – actor. 3/3

2002. **Montague, Murray, (Jerry Murray)** *Damocles Conspiracy,* Blueboy, 1976. (Pulp) "FBI agents Phil Anzeloni, 22, Italian American, and Beech Waggoner, 22, are on joint assignment in Washington in a pulp action thriller (Gunn)." –reprinted *Sexual Espionage* by Paul Baxter in 1978 and published by Numbers (MLM). 3/3

2003. **Montague, Murray, (Jerry Murray)** *Security Risk,* Blueboy, 1976. (Pulp) "Department of Defense employee Randy Page, 32, does no real sleuthing to implicate a dishonest contractor for sabotage, bribes, and other illegalities in a pulp crime case (Gunn)." 3/3

2004. **Montague, Murray, (Jerry Murray)** *Acapulco Affair,* Blueboy, 1977. (Pulp) "U. S. Customs agent Drew Kendall, 35, while on assignment in Acapulco, deserts to the criminals, takes part in their drug haul, and comes out as a crossdresser in an action thriller (Gunn)." 3/3

2005. **Montalban, Manuel V,** *Southern Seas,* Pluto, 1986. (Spanish Crime) The body of Stuart Pedrell, a powerful businessman, is found in a Barcelona suburb. He had disappeared on his way to Polynesia in search of the visionary spirit of Paul Gauguin. Who better to find the killer of a dead dreamer than Pepe Carvalho, overweight bon viveur and ex-communist? The trail for Pedrell's killer unearths a world of disillusioned lefties, graphic sex and nouvelle cuisine - major ingredients of post-Franco Spain. A tautly-written mystery with an unforgettable - and highly unusual - protagonist. –black servant suspected of being a homosexual (MLM). 1/3

2006. **Moorcock, Michael,** *Cornelius Chronicles: Four Novels,* Phoenix, 1977. (Sci-Fi/Fantasy) Cornelius is an English assassin, physicist, rock star, and messiah to the Age of Science. –main character is bisexual (MLM). 3/3

2007. **Moorcock, Michael,** *The Lives and Times of Jerry Cornelius: Stories of the Comic Apocalypse,* Four Walls, 2002. (Sci-Fi/Fantasy) Jerry Cornelius – English assassin, physicist, rock star, messiah to the Age of Science – Cornelius is the ultimate postmodern antihero, more Borgesian than Asimovian. Three of the stories in this collection are here anthologized for the first time: "The Spencer Inheritance," which enmeshes Jerry with Princess Di; "Cheering for the Rockets," involving an attack on a Sudanese pharmaceutical plant; and "Firing the Cathedral," a novella based on 9/11 and its aftermath. 3/3

2008. **Moore, Christopher,** *His Lordship's Arsenal,* Freundlich Books, 1985. (Court Drama) Matthew Burlock is a brilliant, eccentric judge, faces with the facts of a bizarre ritual murder. In the run-down Delrose Hotel, two men are found half-eaten by flames: one tied to a cross, the other tied up on the bed, with African lioness masks laid next to him. The police say it is a homosexual murder, but Burlock disagrees. A strange connection between Burlock's exotic past and the murder is revealed. Somewhere in the family history of the international gun trade, his father's mysterious identity and his radical ex-girlfriend lies the answer to the bizarre puzzle. 1/3

2009. **Moore, Gary W.,** *Bearly Obsessed,* iUniverse, 2009. (Serial Amateur) Take a glimpse into a world that may be foreign to you, even though it takes place in Houston. Follow along with this tight-knit group of gay men and the year that will change their lives forever. But be forewarned, these big, burly, bear men aren't your garden-variety gays. They've been through tough times and their close bonds confirm this. However, nothing's prepared them for what happens early in the New Year when their lives are shattered by a gunman's bullet. –this novel is written in a serial, almost soap opera fashion (MLM). 3/3

2010. **Moore, Martin,** *Under Cover,* Blueboy, 1976. (Pulp) "Midwestern policeman Gary Brannon, 20s, a law student at night, centers the lives of others in a pulp mystery series (Gunn)." 3/3

2011. **Moore, Martin,** *To Dare to be Different,* Blueboy, 1977. (Pulp) "Gary has a small role in a political case in which John is defeated in his run for mayor but is appointed to the Human Rights Commission (Gunn)." 3/3

2012. **Moore, Martin,** *The Price of Pride,* Blueboy, 1977. (Pulp) "The mob returns to town, murders occur, and corruption spreads in the police department with the result that Gary is constantly harassed by his fellow officers (Gunn)." 3/3

2013. **Moore, Martin,** *Hot Cop's Buns,* Surree, 1978. (Pulp) "John's first lover, the bisexual and married Jonathan Madden, is murdered along with a hustler he has picked up, and his secret apartment is torn apart (Gunn)." 3/3

2014. **Moore, T. A.,** *Bone to Pick,* Dreamspinner, 2017. Digging up Bones #1 of 2. (MM Romance/Police Procedural) Cloister Witte is a man with a dark past and a cute dog. He's happy to talk about the dog all day, but after growing up in the shadow of a missing brother, a deadbeat dad, and a criminal stepfather, he'd rather leave the past back in Montana. These days he's a K-9 officer in the San Diego County Sheriff's Department and pays a tithe to his ghosts by doing what no one was able to do for his brother–find the missing and bring them home. This time the missing person is a ten-year-old boy who walked into the woods in the middle of the night and didn't come back. –*Skin and Bone* will be released in 2019 (MLM). 3/3

2015. **Moore, Tony,** *Pent-up Passion,* Surey, 1988. (Pulp) "Houston private investigator Ray Marlowe throws his body into finding out who at Christopher Matthew's all-male birthday party raped and beat a stripper into a coma, a crime Chris is accused of, in a pulp whodunit given more sex than to sleuthing (Gunn)." 3/3

2016. **Moore, Tony,** *Prisoner of Passion,* American Art Enterprises, 1989. (Pulp) "Private investigator Chance Michael (or Michaels depending on the page), 30s, uses sex to rescue Ted Durham and to take prisoner a Columbian drug lord and the American boss who kidnapped Ted and deliver them to federal agent Brad Mason in a pulp action thriller (Gunn)." 3/3

2017. **Montoya, Gregory,** *The Powder Room,* Self-Published, 2017. (Police Procedural) At first glance it didn't look like a crime scene to detective Lawrence Oliver "Lo" Faeth. It simply read as a terrible accident. One of San Francisco's aging gas lines blew and took a woman's life. Besides, Lo is dealing with his own loss. His brother vanished after Lo condemned him for dressing in drag. Now he spends his days haunted by his brother's mysterious fate. –victims are transgender women (MLM). 2/3

2018. **Morgan, Alex,** *Breathless,* loveyoudevine, 2009. Corey Shaw #1 of 4. (Paranormal) The body of a man is found as Provincetown prepares for Mates weekend, a popular leather gathering. Corey thinks a BDSM scene went past its extreme limit. He tours the town's dark dungeons, looking for a murderer preying on young men. Can Corey find him before becoming a victim to the ultimate BDSM fantasy of execution? –originally published as a short story called "Safe Word" in 2008 and is also listed as .5 in the Corey Shaw series (MLM). 3/3

2019. **Morgan, Alex,** *Murder at the Green Lantern,* loveyoudevine, 2010. Corey Shaw #2 of 4. (Paranormal) After a fetish party at a gay bar in Washington, DC, a young man is murdered and left nailed to a St. Andrew's Cross. Paranormal gay sleuth Corey Shaw thinks someone has passed a divine judgment on him and may be a signal to other gays in the city. The mystery leads him on a trail from Boston to the halls of the U.S. Capitol Building in DC. 3/3

2020. **Morgan, Alex,** *Invisible Curtain,* loveyoudevine, 2011. Corey Shaw #3 of 4. (Paranormal) Corey Shaw is torn between a vacation with his family, his burgeoning attraction to handsome dancer, Raul and solving the mystery behind a series of explosions that follow the ship from London across the Baltic Sea. Can he protect the ones he loves and identify the terrorist before an even greater tragedy occurs? Paranormal sleuth Corey Shaw is enjoying vacation with his family in the Baltic Sea when terrorists bomb restaurants hosting World Cup parties in London and Copenhagen. On each occasion the explosion coincides with the cruise ship leaving port. Although the United States isn't attacked directly, Corey and his colleagues are unavoidably drawn into the investigation with or without the blessing of international intelligence agencies. When a third bomb goes off in St. Petersburg, Russia, Corey is convinced the answer lies aboard his ship. He must use all his psionic abilities to protect his family, and his friends, and keep the world safe from this worrying upsurge in international terrorism. 3/3

2021. **Morgan, Alex,** *Legacy of Hephaestus,* Wilde City Press, 2015. Corey Shaw #4 of 4. (Paranormal) Paranormal sleuth Corey Shaw is wrapping up what's left of his European vacation by enjoying the beautiful men in Europe. During his visit, the largest yellow diamond in the world is stolen from a factory in Amsterdam. On his way home, an attempt is made on his life, and his house is broken into upon his arrival home in Boston. Just as Corey finds the "Lava Diamond", a professor from Boston College disappears while on sabbatical at Bergen University in Norway. 3/3

2022. **Muller, Marcia,** *Ask the Cards a Question,* St. Martin's, 1982. McCone #2 of 33. (Hardboiled) There's trouble in Sharon McCone's quiet San Francisco apartment building. Madame Anya, with her cards, her tame crow, and her candles, had predicted evil for Molly Antonio. Linnea Carraway, drinking heavily and careening crazily in the wake of a divorce, had argued with her. Now the sweet, elderly lady lies in her apartment. Linnea, last to see Molly alive, is the prime suspect and if Sharon means to clear her best friend, she has to find the murderer fast. Suddenly death is in the cards, threatening Sharon's oldest friendship, her professional credibility-and her life. –office worker and later manager Ted Smalley is a gay man written very well and some of the books discusses AIDS in a sympathetic way (MLM). 1/3

2023. **Muller, Marcia,** *The Cheshire Cat's Eye,* St. Martin's, 1983. McCone #3 of 33. (Hardboiled) Sharon McCone investigates the murder of her best friend in San Francisco, pursuing a single, valuable clue and becoming, herself, implicated in the murder. 1/3

2024. **Muller, Marcia,** *Games to Keep the Dark Away,* St. Martin's, 1984. McCone #4 of 33. (Hardboiled) Picture Salmon Bay: an isolated, run-down northern California village, home to an idle fleet of fishing boats, a deserted amusement park, and a handful of secretive, even hostile residents. When private investigator Sharon McCone arrives in search of one of the town's wayward daughters, the train leads to the thriving resort of Port San Marco. 1/3

2025. **Muller, Marcia,** *Leave a Message for Willie,* St. Martin's, 1984. McCone #5 of 33. (Hardboiled) Amid the shifting world of San Francisco flea markets, shady vendors sell junk, precious antiques, and stolen goods side by side. Somewhere in the mix, a priceless collection of sacred Torah scrolls is gathering dust - and attracting a group of fanatical killers. 1/3

2026. **Muller, Marcia, and Pronzini, Bill,** *Double,* St. Martin's, 1984. McCone #5.5 of 33. (Hardboiled) Sharon McCone has come home to her warm, troubled family, to San Diego and a convention of private detectives in a posh seaside hotel. For Sharon it's a chance to catch up with old friends–all except for the one who fell four stories from one of the hotel spires. Now, Sharon is determined to find out why her friend died. 1/3

2027. **Muller, Marcia,** *There's Nothing to be Afraid Of,* St. Martin's, 1985. McCone #6 of 33. (Hardboiled) The Globe Apartments, six stories of decaying brick and concrete, rises above San Francisco's volatile Tenderloin district. The seedy former hotel, once a haven for the city's down and out, now houses Vietnamese families striving to improve their lives. But private eye Sharon McCone believes that someone from the Tenderloin's shadowy underworld is determined to drive the newcomers out. The suspects range from the colorful to the dangerous: a poetry-loving drifter, a mean-spirited preacher, a flower seller with a deadly touch, an enterprising photographer, and a developer who'd like nothing better than to unload his worst investment - the Globe Hotel. 1/3

2028. **Muller, Marcia,** *There's Something in a Sunday,* Mysterious Press, 1989. McCone #8 of 33. (Hardboiled) It's a cold Sunday in San Francisco. Sharon McCone's alone on a routine surveillance job, following a man named Frank Wilkinson through the city's lush horticultural hot spots to the sere foothills of the Diablos. But when she returns to find her kindly old client in a pool of blood nothing she's learned explains it. 1/3

2029. **Muller, Marcia,** *The Shape of Dread,* Mysterious Press, 1989. McCone #9 of 33. (Hardboiled) Bobby Foster, car-hop at the chic Cafe Comedie, is going to the gas chamber. He's already confessed to the murder of Tracy Kostakos, the club's rising star. But two years after the crime, Tracy's body is still missing, and Bobby's confession is full of holes. 1/3

2030. **Muller, Marcia,** *Trophies and Dead Things,* Mysterious Press, 1990. McCone #10 of 33. (Hardboiled) When a former sixties radical is murdered during a string of random sniper attacks, the All Souls Legal Cooperative must settle his surprisingly large estate. Then private investigator Sharon McCone comes across a new will, made just days before he died, that disinherits his two children in favor of four unknown and unconnected parties. 1/3

2031. **Muller, Marcia,** *Where Echoes Live,* Mysterious Press, 1991. McCone #11 of 33. (Hardboiled) Responding to a former colleague's request for help, Sharon McCone travels to the high-desert town of Tufa Lake, California, to track down a commercial mining operation that could seriously damage the ecosystem ... and a killer bent on even deadlier destruction. 1/3

2032. **Muller, Marcia,** *Pennies on a Dead Woman's Eyes,* Mysterious Press, 1992. McCone #12 of 33. (Hardboiled) It looked like a lost cause. Convicted of a brutal society murder in 1956, Lis Benedict had served a long sentence and just been released from jail. Then in a last desperate attempt to clean the Benedict name, her daughter Judy convinced All Souls Legal Cooperative to take her mother's case before the Historical Tribunal. 1/3

2033. **Muller, Marcia,** *Wolf in the Shadows,* Mysterious Press, 1993. McCone 13 of 33. (Hardboiled) Successful in her investigative work for All Souls Legal Cooperative, happy with her newly renovated house, and feeling somewhat more secure in her relationship with the mysterious environmental activist, Hy Ripinsky, Sharon is shocked to find herself suddenly faced with a wrenching ultimatum. No longer a small, informal co-op, All Souls has grown. New legal partners, exasperated with Sharon's free-wheeling ways, want to kick her upstairs with a raise, perks, and a "career opportunity" that will chain her to a desk forever. Offered a take-it-or-leave-it deal, Sharon is in turmoil. And to make matters worse, Hy has disappeared. 1/3

2034. **Muller, Marcia,** *Till the Butchers Cut Him Down,* Mysterious Press, 1994. McCone #14 of 33. (Hardboiled) In the biggest professional move of her life, Sharon is cutting her umbilical cord of All Soul's Legal Cooperative and opening her own shop. But even before the phone lines are installed, McCone Investigations gets its first case - one that lifts Sharon off a roof in a helicopter and deposits her on a posh hideaway on the north California coast. 1/3

2035. **Muller, Marcia,** *A Wild and Lonely Place,* Mysterious Press, 1995. McCone #15 of 33. (Hardboiled) It's worth a $1 Million reward to Sharon McCone if she catches the man called the Diplo-bomber, who has set off bombs at consulates all over the U.S. Now he's in San Francisco–and that's McCone's turf. When he misses his latest target, the embassy of a small Arab emirate, McCone's on the spot–and soon discovers some disturbing things about this strange, forbidding embassy. One is the American woman kept a virtual prisoner there by her Arab mother-in-law. –short story *The McCone Files* published in 2011 by Crippen and Landru available as an e-book (MLM). 1/3

2036. **Muller, Marcia,** *The Broken Promise Land,* Mysterious Press, 1996. McCone #16 of 33. (Hardboiled) Someone is bent on getting revenge on Ricky Savage, Sharon McCone's brother-in-law and a two-time Grammy Award-winning country singer. The danger escalates as Sharon realizes that more than one person has been playing underhanded games–and that the music industry is truly a broken promise land. 1/3

2037. **Muller, Marcia,** *Both Ends of the Night,* Mysterious Press, 1997. McCone #17 of 33. (Hardboiled) McCone's flying instructor Matty asks for help when her lover goes missing. Then, during an airshow, Matty's plane suddenly crashes. Convinced this is not an accident, McCone follows a trail of leads, and confronts the man who ordered Matty's death. 1/3

2038. **Muller, Marcia,** *While Other People Sleep,* Mysterious Press, 1998. McCone #18 of 33. (Hardboiled) With her agency going great guns, Sharon McCone is known as one of the best detectives in the business...until her reputation is threatened by an impostor. The woman's resemblance to McCone is uncanny. Her knowledge of McCone's life is chilling. And with lover Hy Ripinsky away on business,

McCone is alone as the double insidiously sabotages McCone's career, invades her home, and leads her into a deadly game of cat and mouse through San Francisco's underworld. 1/3

2039. **Muller, Marcia,** *A Walk Through the Fire,* Mysterious Press, 1999. McCone #19 of 33. (Hardboiled) Accidents are plaguing a documentary film crew on breathtakingly beautiful Kauai. Can San Francisco P.I. Sharon McCone ferret out possible sabotage behind the scenes? The job sounds like a breeze – McCone envisions romantic, tropical nights with her lover, Hy Ripinsky. –short story *McCone and Friends* published in 1999 by Crippen and Landru is available as an e-book only (MLM). 1/3

2040. **Muller, Marcia,** *Listen to the Silence,* Mysterious Press, 2000. McCone #20 of 33. (Hardboiled) For PI Sharon McCone, when one door opens, another shuts. In the midst of celebrating a joyous wedding, she gets word that her father has died. The news leads her to the rituals of death: the scattering of ashes, the sharing of grief, the sorting of a loved one's belongings. But the last of these acts leads to a shocking discovery that will flip her life upside down. 1/3

2041. **Muller, Marcia,** *Dead Midnight,* Mysterious Press, 2002. McCone #21 of 33. (Hardboiled) Stretching flat across the water, the San Francisco-Oakland Bay Bridge is a popular spot...for jumpers. Roger Nagasawa, a brilliant employee at a popular Internet magazine, is its latest "suicide" and veteran P. I. Sharon McCone's new case. 1/3

2042. **Muller, Marcia,** *The Dangerous Hour,* Mysterious Press, 2004. McCone #22 of 33. (Hardboiled) Sharon McCone is back to investigate a personal betrayal by one of her operatives that has put her business and reputation on the line. The future's looking bright for Sharon McCone and the staff of McCone Investigations-until one of the firm's operatives, Julia Rafael, is arrested for major credit card fraud. 1/3

2043. **Muller, Marcia,** *Vanishing Point,* Mysterious Press, 2006. McCone #23 of 33. (Hardboiled) Sharon McCone is hired to investigate one of San Luis Obispo County's most puzzling cold cases. A generation ago, Laurel Greenwood, a housewife and artist, inexplicably vanished, leaving her young daughter alone. 1/3

2044. **Muller, Marcia,** *The Ever-Running Man,* Grand Central, 2007. McCone #24 of 33. (Hardboiled) Sharon McCone is hired by her husband's security firm to track down "the ever-running man," a shadowy figure who has been leaving explosive devices at their various offices. She doesn't have to search for long. 1/3

2045. **Muller, Marcia,** *Burn Out,* Grand Central, 2008. McCone #25 of 33. (Hardboiled) Traumatized by a recent life-or-death investigation,

Sharon McCone flees to her ranch in California's high desert country to contemplate her future. Deep depression shadows her days and nights, and a chance encounter with a troubled, highly secretive Native American woman begins to haunt her dreams. 1/3

2046. **Muller, Marcia,** *Locked In,* Grand Central, 2009. McCone #26 of 33. (Hardboiled) Shot in the head by an unknown assailant, San Francisco private eye Sharon McCone finds herself trapped by locked-in syndrome: almost total paralysis but an alert, conscious mind. Since the late-night attack occurred at her agency's offices, the natural conclusion was that it was connected to one of the firm's cases. 1/3

2047. **Muller, Marcia,** *Coming Back,* Grand Central, 2010. McCone #27 of 33. (Hardboiled) San Francisco private eye Sharon McCone struggles to regain control over her body after she was shot in the head and suffered from locking-in syndrome. But when Sharon's friend from physical therapy goes missing, she must call upon those closest to her to find out the truth behind the disappearance. 1/3

2048. **Muller, Marcia,** *City of Whispers,* Grand Central, 2011. McCone #28 of 33. (Hardboiled) Private eye Sharon McCone receives an e-mail asking for help from her emotionally disturbed half-brother Darcy Blackhawk. She replies ... but gets no response. As Sharon digs deeper, she discovers that Darcy sent his message from an Internet café in San Francisco, a city he's never been to before. Sensing that her brother is in terrible danger, Sharon begins a search for him throughout the city. –short story *Skeleton in the Closet* published by Grand Central in 2012 available as an e-book (MLM). 1/3

2049. **Muller, Marcia,** *Looking for Yesterday,* Grand Central, 2012. McCone #29 of 33. (Hardboiled) Three years ago, Caro Warrick was acquitted for the murder of her best friend Amelia Bettencourt, but the lingering doubts of everyone around Caro are affecting her life. Sharon McCone is confident that she can succeed where other detectives have failed. 1/3

2050. **Muller, Marcia,** *The Night Searchers,* Grand Central, 2014. McCone #30 of 33. (Hardboiled) When new clients Jay and Camilla Givens come to Sharon McCone with Camilla's stories of devil worshippers performing human sacrifices in San Francisco, the detective is skeptical, to say the least. –short stories *Merrill-Go-Round (*Speaking Volumes, 2014) and *Tell Me Who I Am (*Grand Central, 2016) are available as e-books (MLM). 1/3

2051. **Muller, Marcia,** *Someone Always Knows,* Grand Central, 2016. McCone #31 of 33. (Hardboiled) Finally settled into their new home after losing their house in a fire, and fully established in their new shared offices, private investigator Sharon McCone and her business partner husband Hy are starting to feel comfortable. That calm is shattered when Hy's former colleague Gage Renshaw–a shady troublemaker who they had presumed dead–reappears, and it's unclear what he wants from his prosperous former associate. 1/3

2052. **Muller, Marcia,** *The Color of Fear,* Grand Central, 2017. McCone #32 of 33. (Hardboiled) A knock on the door in the middle of the night. It can only be bad news, and it is: Sharon's father Elwood has been the victim of a vicious, racially-motivated attack. 1/3

2053. **Muller, Marcia,** *The Breakers,* Grand Central, 2018. McCone #33 of 33. (Hardboiled) On a foggy summer morning, private investigator Sharon McCone receives a call from her former neighbors, the Curleys. Their usually dependable daughter Chelle hasn't been answering their calls for weeks. Would Sharon check on her? 1/3

2054. **Munder, Laura,** *Therapy for Murder,* St. Martin's, 1984. (Thriller) The suspicious suicide of a patient prompts psychiatric social worker Sara Marks to uncover the motive, method, and perpetrator of what she is certain was murder. –good friend of the main character is gay, and the book treats gay people favorably, although the book itself can read like a psychiatric treatise (MLM). 1/3

2055. **Munger, Katy,** *Out of Time,* Avon, 1998. Casey Jones #2 of 6. (Cozy) Meet Casey Jones–an unlicensed, no-nonsense private detective who hides 160 pounds of muscle with an in-your-face femme fatale style. She's bold, she's bad and, most of all, she's nobody's fool. Underneath her wise-cracking, 100% Southern exterior, there beats a 14-karat heart with a definite spot for life's losers. With the brains to take on any challenge and the guts to impose her own brand of justice, Casey Jones has what it takes to be your best friend–or your very worst enemy. –Marcus Dupree is a desk clerk at the Durnham Police Department who unofficially retrieves information for Jones occasionally (MLM). 1/3

2056. **Munger, Katy,** *Money to Burn,* Avon, 1999. Casey Jones #3 of 6. (Cozy) Casey Jones is a take-no-prisoners female PI who wouldn't be caught dead whining over a lousy boyfriend or asking for help. She's too busy lifting weights, running off at the mouth and making doughnut runs for her overstuffed business partner, the larger-than-life Bobby D.–a 360 lb. lothario whose little black book is almost as big as his appetite. With a stretch in the Florida pen behind her and no official PI license, Casey comes from nothing and has nothing to lose. She lives full speed ahead, with a healthy respect for the screw-ups of others. 1/3

2057. **Munger, Katy,** *Bad to the Bone,* Avon, 2000. Casey Jones #4 of 6. (Cozy) Casey proves a sucker for the fragile blond who claims her estranged husband has disappeared with their child. But when Casey locates the fugitive spouse a little too easily, she begins to suspect that the lovely Tawny Bledsoe has played her for a fool. Especially when Casey gets stiffed on the fee, then finds herself embroiled in a murder case with Tawny's name written all over it. Bad check in hand and a bad taste in her mouth, Casey resolves to stop Tawny once and for all, but the battle quickly turns personal when Tawny proves more than a match for the irrepressible Casey. 1/3

2058. **Munger, Katy,** *Better off Dead,* Avon, 2001. Casey Jones #5 of 6. (Cozy) Helen McInnes, the victim of a horrible crime, barely escaped with her life. Traumatized by the experience, she can no longer set foot outside her home. Further devastated by her attacker's acquittal and the anonymous threats she begins to receive, Helen turns to Casey for help reclaiming her life. 1/3

2059. **Munger, Katy,** *Bad Moon on the Rise,* Createspace, 2012. Casey Jones #6 of 6. (Cozy) When a young basketball star and his drug-addicted mother disappear without a trace, the boy's ailing grandmother begs a reluctant Casey to find him before she dies. But even the normally unflappable Casey Jones is thrown for a loop when she discovers evidence of a murder in their wake and uncovers a shocking secret about the identity of the boy's father. 1/3

2060. **Murphy, Haughton (James Duffy),** *Murder Takes a Partner,* Simon and Schuster, 1987. Reuben and Cynthia Frost #2 of 8. (Hard Boiled) While striding down Fifth Avenue, reveling in the beauty of the city, Reuben Frost loses his footing–and is caught by a ballerina. Hailey Coles is a slip of a girl, but her firm grip keeps the retired lawyer from crashing down to earth. Soon, Frost will have a chance to return the favor. When the stage of the National Ballet is darkened by murder, only he can ensure that the show will go on. –choreographer that is killed is gay (MLM). 1/3

2061. **Murphy, Haughton,** *A Very Venetian Murder,* Simon and Schuster, 1992. Reuben and Cynthia Frost #7 of 8. (Hard Boiled) Venice in September provides the colorful setting for Gregg Baxter, the best and hottest American fashion designer since Halston, has arrived to host the Euro-party of the year: a dinner at the stunning Palazzo Labia to promote his stylish clothes and a new association with la marchesa Scamozzi, a local fabric designer. Baxter and his entourage are staying at the world-famous Hotel Cipriani, as are Reuben Frost, the distinguished retired Wall Street lawyer, and his wife, Cynthia, a retired ballerina. The Frosts, on their annual Venetian holiday, are inexorably drawn into the strange goings-on involving the celebrity designer, which climax with Baxter's murder in the deserted Calle dei Tredici Martiri (the Street of the Thirteen Martyrs) after a loud, argumentative meal with his staff and a gondola ride with a handsome young male prostitute. –Baxter, who is killed, is gay (MLM). 1/3

2062. **Murphy, Michael,** *It Should Have Been You,* Dreamspinner, 2013. (YA Fictional True Crime) After a hit-and-run driver kills David McCleary, his mother, Frieda McCleary, tells her younger son, Patrick, "It should have been you." While the McCleary family limps along for a while, it clearly died with David. In an effort to deal with her son's death, Frieda joins a fundamentalist church while her family watches her become a stranger. When she discovers Patrick is gay, she is convinced he is the reason David was taken from her. Patrick's father runs interference, but when he leaves town for work, she throws Patrick out onto the streets. 3/3

2063. **Musgrove, Eleanor,** *Submerge,* Manifold, 2016. (MM Thriller) Jamie Hill walks into his local LGBT+ nightclub, Submerge, intending to make friends and have a good time. When he meets comedian Addie Crewe and her girlfriend Gina Wilson, his night is already looking up – but it's the man Gina introduces him to who really catches his eye. Miles Bradford seems to be everything Jamie could want in a man: smart, funny, kind. Jamie can't take his eyes off him but Miles might not be as clean-cut as he appears. 3/3

2064. **Myers, John,** *Holy Family,* Alyson, 1992. (Gay Romance) David Harriman believes in minding his own business… until the handsome young heir who seduces him one night is found dead the next morning. – To his dismay, David is the prime suspect. With the help of a young hustler named Snake, David sets out to find the real killer. Meanwhile, he must deal with a troubled Catholic priest named Father Alexander and a deadly specter from the past. –two books; *Virgins of the Rosary* and *How Sweet the Sound* are sequels, but I have not been able to find any trace of them or if they've even been published (MLM). 3/3

2065. **Myers, Tamar,** *Larceny and Old Lace,* Avon, 1996. Den of Antiquity #1 of 16. (Cozy) As owner of the Den of Antiquity, recently divorced (but never bitter!) Abigail Timberlake is accustomed to delving into the past, searching for lost treasures, and navigating the cutthroat world of rival dealers at flea markets and auctions. Still, she never thought she'd be putting her expertise in mayhem and detection to other use – until crotchety "junque" dealer, Abby's aunt Eulonia Wiggins, was found murdered! –fellow antique store owners Rob and Bob are gay neighbors and provide assistance to the main character (MLM). 1/3

2066. **Myers, Tamar,** *Gilt by Association,* Avon, 1996. Den of Antiquity #2 of 16. (Cozy) Petite, indomitable North Carolinian Abigail Timberlake rose gloriously up from the ashes of divorce–parlaying her savvy about exquisite old things into a thriving antiques enterprise: The Den of Antiquity. Now she's a force to be reckoned with in Charlotte's close-knit world of mavens, eccentrics and cutthroat dealers. But a superb, gilt-edged 18th-century French armoire she purchased for a song at estate auction has just arrived along with something she didn't pay for: a dead body. 1/3

2067. **Myers, Tamar,** *Ming and I,* Avon, 1997. Den of Antiquity #3 of 16. (Cozy) North Carolina native Abigail Timberlake, owner of the Den of Antiquity, is quick to dismiss the seller of a hideous old vase–until the poor lady comes hurtling back through the shop window minutes later, the victim of a fatal hit-and-run. 1/3

2068. **Myers, Tamar,** *So Faux, So Good,* Avon, 1998. Den of Antiquity #4 of 16. (Cozy) Abigail Timberlake, owner of the Den of Antiquity, has never been happier. She is about to marry the man of her dreams and has just outbid all other Charlotte, North Carolina, antique dealers for an exquisite English tea service. Then Mama (who is running off to be a nun) stops by to deliver an early wedding present, and it rains on Abby's parade. The one-of-a-kind tea service Abby paid big bucks for has a twin. A frazzled Abby finds more trouble on her doorstep–literally–when a local auctioneer mysteriously collapses outside her shop and a press clipping of her engagement announcement turns up in the wallet of a dead man. (Obviously she won't be getting a wedding present from him.) 1/3

2069. **Myers, Tamar,** *Baroque and Desperate,* Avon, 1999. Den of Antiquity #5 of 16. (Cozy) Unflappable and resourceful, Abigail Timberlake, antique dealer and owner of Charlotte, North Carolina's Den of Antiquity, relies on her knowledge and savvy to authenticate the facts from the fakes when it comes to either curios or people. Her expertise makes Abby invaluable to exceptionally handsome Tradd Maxwell Burton, wealthy scion of the renowned Latham family. He needs her to determine the most priceless item in the Latham mansion and then split the proceeds of it with her. A treasure hunt in an antique-filled manor? All Abby can say is "let the games begin." 1/3

2070. **Myers, Tamar,** *Estate of Mind,* Avon, 1999. Den of Antiquity #6 of 16. (Cozy) When North Carolina antique dealer Abigail Timberlake makes a bid of $150.99 on a truly awful copy of Van Gogh's The Starry Night, she's just trying to win Mama's approval by supporting the church auction. Hopefully, she'll make her money back on the beautiful gold antique frame. Little does she expect she's bought herself a fortune...and a lot of trouble. 1/3

2071. **Myers, Tamar,** *A Penny Urned,* Avon, 2000. Den of Antiquity #7 of 16. (Cozy) All that remains of Lula Mae Wiggins-who drowned in a bathtub of cheap champagne on New Year's Eve-now sits in an alleged Etruscan urn in Savannah, Georgia. Further north, at the Den of Antiquity antique shop in Charlotte, North Carolina, plucky proprietor Abigail Timberlake is astonished to learn that she is the sole inheritor of the Wiggins estate. Late Aunt Lula Mae was, after all, as distant a relative as kin can get. 1/3

2072. **Myers, Tamar,** *Nightmare in Shining Armor,* Avon, 2001. Den of Antiquity #8 of 16. (Cozy) Den of Antiquity proprietress Abigail Timberlake's Halloween costume party is a roaring success–until an unexpected fire sends the panicked guests fleeing from Abby's emporium. One exiting reveler she is only too happy to see the back of is Tweetie "Little Bo Peep" Timberlake–unfaithful wife of Abby's faithless ex, Buford. But not long after the conflagration is brought under control, the former Mrs. T. discovers an unfamiliar suit of armor in her house. And stuffed inside is the heavily siliconed, no-longer-living body of the current Mrs. T. 1/3

2073. **Myers, Tamar,** *Splendor in the Glass,* Avon, 2002. Den of Antiquity #9 of 16. (Cozy) Antiques dealer Abby Timberlake Washburn is thrilled when the Mrs. Amelia Shadbar, doyenne of Charleston society, invites her to broker a pricey collection of Lalique glass sculpture. These treasures will certainly boost business at the Den of Antiquity, and maybe hoist Abby into the upper crust, which would please her class-conscious mom, Mozella, no end. Alas, Abby's fragile dream is soon shattered when Mrs. Shadbark meets a foul, untimely end. 1/3

2074. **Myers, Tamar,** *Tiles and Tribulations,* Avon, 2003. Den of Antiquity #10 of 16. (Cozy) Abigail Timberlake Washburn would rather be anywhere else on a muggy Charleston summer evening – even putting in extra hours at her antiques shop – than at a séance. But her best friend, "Calamity Jane," thinks a spirit – or "Apparition American," as ectoplasmically-correct Abby puts it – lurks in the eighteenth-century Georgian mansion, complete with priceless, seventeenth-century Portuguese kitchen tiles, that C.J. just bought as a fixer-upper. 1/3

2075. **Myers, Tamar,** *Statue of Limitations,* Avon, 2004. Den of Antiquity #11 of 16. (Cozy) Charleston antique shop owner Abigail Timberlake (a.k.a. Mrs. Greg Washburn) knows the importance of not mixing business and private life – that's why she has two names, for crying out loud. But when Mrs. Washburn's best friend, Wynell, begs for a part in Ms. Timberlake's new venture – redecorating a very upscale bed-and-breakfast – Abby breaks that cardinal rule and agrees. 1/3

2076. **Myers, Tamar,** *Monet Talks,* Avon, 2005. Den of Antiquity #12 of 16. (Cozy) Charleston antiques dealer Abigail Timberlake Washburn is thrilled by her recent estate auction purchase of a spectacular bejeweled birdcage from India, but not so much by its occupant, a mouthy mynah named Monet. Still, her customers at the Den of Antiquity seem charmed by the insufferable birdbrain, so Abby figures she's stuck with him. That is, until she finds a stuffed starling resting on his usual perch with a ransom note demanding a real Monet (the painted variety) in exchange for her purloined pet. 1/3

2077. **Myers, Tamar,** *Cane Mutiny,* Avon, 2006. Den of Antiquity #13 of 16. (Cozy) Abigail Timberlake Washburn understands the antiques game is a gamble–so she doesn't know what to expect when she wins the bidding for the contents of an old locker that has been sealed up for years. It's a delightful surprise when she discovers inside a collection of exquisite old walking sticks–and a not-so-delightful one when she pulls out a decrepit gym bag containing...a human skull! 1/3

2078. **Myers, Tamar,** *Death of a Rug Lord,* Avon, 2008. Den of Antiquity #14 of 16. (Cozy) Business isn't booming for antiques dealer Abigail Timberlake Washburn. A local rug store is luring away her customers with its rock-bottom prices. Eager to check out the competition, Abby is delighted to find a priceless Persian amid the cut-rate carpets–and shocked when Gwendolyn Spears, the store's beleaguered owner, begs her to take it home! Abby feels more than a little guilty about getting such a great deal ... especially when Gwendolyn is found dead the next morning. 1/3

2079. **Myers, Tamar,** *Poison Ivory,* Avon, 2009. Den of Antiquity #15 of 16. (Cozy) All antiques dealer Abigail Timberlake Washburn wanted was to find a perfect gift for her darling (if not altogether together) mama Mozella's birthday. She never expected her online purchase of an exquisite, seventeenth-century rosewood linen chest to place her in federal custody, accused of trafficking in illegal ivory! Then insult is heaped on her injury when she's forced to turn to her lawyer-snake ex, Buford, to spring her–since ex-cop /current hubby Greg's "good ol' boy" contacts don't happen to include any feds. 1/3

2080. **Myers, Tamar,** *The Glass is Always Greener,* Avon, 2011. Den of Antiquity #16 of 16. (Cozy) A real death at a fake wake gets Charleston, South Carolina antiques dealer Abigail Timberlake Washburn into serious hot water in this masterful cozy farewell from the author of *The Witchdoctor's Wife, The Headhunter's Daughter,* and the Magdelena Yoder mysteries. Collectables connoisseurs and Antiques Roadshow nuts won't want to miss a single minute of Abby's amateur sleuthing. 1/3

2081. **Myles, Jere,** *Murder on the Pier,* Southwest, 2008. Murder #1 of 3. (MM Cozy) Events etched against the Chicago skyline that will involve every echelon of the Chicago police department and make a talk show host a household name. A menagerie of characters that include a priest who belongs on the cover of GQ; a widowed matriarch with an estranged daughter, and an inveterate fundamentalist who personifies evil as he is determined to leave no stone unturned while seeking to destroy one of the most celebrated love stories. 3/3

2082. **Myles, Jere,** *Murder Behind Closed Doors,* Southwest, 2009. Murder #2 of 3. (MM Cozy) Jonathan Rose, a handsome black artist, has become a threat to several rather high-ranking officials in Chicago, and many want to see him dead. Naive and trusting, Jon Rose has no clue about this. Set in the 1990s, amidst 'Don't ask, don't tell.' 3/3

2083. **Myles, Jere,** *Murder on Michigan Avenue,* Fideli Publishing, 2012. Murder #3 of 3. (MM Cozy) Jon and Eileen, the police lieutenant who botched the investigation into Mieko's murder, and the priest who is as handsome as a model. They are all here and they're seeking justice. New characters like lawyer Geri Legg, the former NFL star who's gay, and an Agatha Christi matriarch sleuth add twists that keep you reading as Myles seamlessly interweaves them into the fabric of the story. 3/3

N

2084. **Nadel, Barbara,** *Passion for Killing,* Headline, 2007. Cetin Ikman #9 of 20. (Turkey Crime by English writer) A serial killer is stalking the streets of Istanbul, seemingly targeting gay men. A man is found dead in a hotel room, a single stab wound in his heart. Could he be a victim of the 'Peeper'? –A Turkish secret agent is bisexual and comes onto Suleyman but is refused (MLM). 1/3

2085. **Nava, Michael,** *The Little Death,* Alyson, 1986. Henry Rios #1 of 7. (Court Drama) Henry Rios meets Hugh Paris when Paris is arrested for drug possession and being high on PCP. A burnt-out public defender battling alcoholism, Rios has reached a crossroads in his life. While interviewing Paris in jail, Rios goes through the motions, but notices that Paris is far more polished and well-off than the usual drug suspects. Paris is mysteriously bailed out–but a few weeks later, he turns up on Rios's doorstep. Skittish and paranoid, he admits to using heroin and says he's afraid that his wealthy grandfather wants to murder him. –Michael Nava is one of the fathers of the gay mystery genre along with Joseph Hansen, Richard Stevenson, and John Morgan Wilson. (MLM). 3/3

2086. **Nava, Michael,** *Goldenboy,* Alyson, 1988. Henry Rios #2 of 7. (Court Drama) Henry Rios may have something few defense attorneys ever experience: a truly innocent client. It's a cause Henry Rios can't resist: defending a young gay man on trial for killing the coworker who threatened to out him. Jim Pears is charged with first-degree murder; Pears says he's innocent, but the evidence is damning. Pears was found covered in the victim's blood and with the murder weapon in his hand. But nothing about the People v. Jim Pears is what it seems. –*Goldenboy* was the first winner of the LAMBDA Award (MLM). 3/3

2087. **Nava, Michael,** *How Town,* Harper and Row, 1990. Henry Rios #3 of 7. (Court Drama) A controversial case brings lawyer Henry Rios back home to Oakland–and into the sights of a stone-cold killer. It's been almost a decade since Henry Rios has seen his sister, Elena. A troubled family history has left them both with unhappy memories. But his visit with his sister isn't the reunion he imagined. She's asking him to defend Paul Windsor, someone they had grown up with–who has a history of pedophilia and has just been charged with murder after his fingerprints were found at a crime scene. –won the third LAMBDA Award (MM). 3/3

2088. **Nava, Michael,** *Hidden Law,* HarperCollins, 1992. Henry Rios #4 of 7. (Court Drama) Henry Rios is back to his roots when he defends a Latino teenager accused of murder. State senator and mayoral hopeful Gus Peña has been gunned down in the parking lot of a restaurant in East Los Angeles. When Chicano teen and ex-gang member Michael Ruiz is arrested for the murder, Henry Rios takes the case. It's a tough road: Ruiz claims he did it and refuses to help Rios in his defense. But Rios finds inconsistencies in the kid's story, and is sure Ruiz is covering for the real killer. –won the fifth LAMBDA Award. Short story "Street People" appears in the anthology *Finale* edited by Michael Nava in 1989 (MLM). 3/3

2089. **Nava, Michael,** *The Death of Friends,* Putnam, 1996. Henry Rios #5 of 7. (Court Drama) When a judge leading a double life is murdered, Henry Rios comes to the controversial defense of the prime suspect. –won the ninth LAMBDA Award (MM). 3/3

2090. **Nava, Michael,** *The Burning Plain,* Putnam, 1997. Henry Rios #6 of 7. (Court Drama) Attorney Henry Rios fights for his freedom and his life when a homophobic serial killer targets gay men in Los Angeles. 3/3

2091. **Nava, Michael,** *Rag and Bone,* Putnam, 2001. Henry Rios #7 of 7. (Court Drama) The Latino lawyer faces his most daunting personal and professional challenges as he comes to terms with his past– and a cache of family secrets. –won the fourteenth LAMBDA Award (MLM). 3/3

2092. **Nava, Michael,** *Lay Your Sleeping Head,* Korima, 2016. Henry Rios Remake #1 of 1. (MM Court Drama) Henry Rios, a gifted and humane lawyer driven to drink by professional failure and personal demons, meets a charming junky struggling to stay clean. He tells Rios an improbable tale of long-ago murders in his wealthy family. Rios is skeptical, but the erotic spark between them ignites an obsessive affair that ends only when the man's body is discovered with a needle in his arm on the campus of a great California university. Rios refuses to believe his lover's death was an accidental overdose. His hunt for the killer takes him down San Francisco's mean streets and into Nob Hill mansions where he uncovers the secrets behind a legendary California fortune and the reason the man he loved had to die. –Nava uses much of *The Little Death* in this new version with many MM Romance influences (MLM). 3/3

2093. **Nava, Michael,** *Street People,* Korima, 2017. Henry Rios Remake #1.5 of 1. (Hard Boiled) Street People is the story of lives at the margin, about the throw-away people we see without seeing, and the real meaning of family. –fleshed out version of the short story of the same name with Rios playing a small part (MLM). 3/3

2094. **Nazario,** *Anarcoma,* Catalan, 1984. Anarcoma #1 of 2. (Graphic Novel) Anarcoma, streetwise transvestite and self-styled detective - Barbarella with a twist! –translated into English by David H. Rosenthal (MM). –book 2 has yet to be translated into English (MLM). 3/3

2095. **Neihart, Ben,** *Burning Girl,* Rob Weisbach Books, 2000. (Psychological) Drew Burke is twenty – a working-class college student in Baltimore. Seduced by the wealth that surrounds him, Drew finds himself drawn into a complex and sensually charged friendship with fellow student Bahar Richards and her brother, Jake. With Bahar, it's a soulmates' bond, with Jake, it's a romance born of a fierce sexual attraction. But a strange wall of mystery surrounds Jake, which Drew can't seem to penetrate. Then over an intimate long weekend at the Richards' family home, Jake confides to Drew that in high school he was wrongly accused of a grisly crime. The more details Drew learns, the more he suspects he hasn't heard the entire truth – from Jake or Bahar. Torn between brother and sister, whose versions of the story don't quite match, Drew becomes caught in a maze of half-lies and manipulations, as he tries to figure out who to trust and, ultimately, who to love. 3/3

2096. **Neilson, T.,** *The Glass House Murder,* JMS, 2014. (MM Historical Bibliomystery) Meet Lord Henry Carlisle: gentleman, wastrel, and mystery-novel lover. When his mother telephones him on a May evening to tell him they've just discovered a body in the glasshouse, Hal does what he loves to do: he goes to investigate. As it happens, the local constabulary, headed by an unusually well-spoken, well-educated fellow named Sayers, is already on the case, and Sayers is a bit of a mystery all on his own. 3/3

2097. **Nelson, Casey,** *Nothing Gold can Stay,* Alyson, 2000. (Hard Boiled) For Ray O'Brien, a summer in London as part of his graduate studies in theater was a chance of a lifetime. The presence of a handsome Argentinean fellow student, Eduardo, promises to make it truly extraordinary. It had to be too good to last. When a string of savage, sadistic murders culminates in the bludgeoning death of another student two doors away and a strong line of circumstantial evidence leads directly to Eduardo, Ray's dream summer is suddenly transformed into a desperate struggle to untangle a web of secrets that masks the killer's true identity. 3/3

2098. **Nevins, Francis,** *Publish and Perish,* Putnam's Sons, 1975. Mensing #1 of 4 (Hard Boiled) Was the fire that killed best-selling author Graham Dillaway an accident, or something more sinister? Is he a legal eagle or a private eye? That's the question Loren Mensing of Publish and Perish must decide when he begins to probe a case that releases a Pandora's box of horrors. Loren drew up a will for best-selling novelist Graham Dillaway and his equally successful wife, Hope Foxworth. When Dillaway and another writer die in a mysterious fire that guts the author's mountain cabin, the local newspaper suggests the deaths were not accident but murder. – Dillaway may have been gay and with a young lover when killed (MLM). 2/3

2099. **Nevins, Francis,** *The 120-Hour Clock,* Walker, 1986. Milo #1 of 2. (Revenge) Milo Turner, a high-living confidence man, has known but one real love in his life, a young woman he met first as a tawny-skinned child adopted by his mentor in crime. For a man who makes his living by deception, she is just about an ideal partner. But when posing as a lost heiress to a supermarket fortune proves her undoing, Milo sets out for vengeance, in a complex scheme inviting the killers to add him, a female artist, and her precocious young daughter to the death list. –main character seeks help from a gay man he assisted in protecting from a blackmail scheme (MLM). 1/3

2100. **Nichols, Beverley (John Beverley Nichols 1898-1983),** *The Moonflower,* Hutchinson, 1955. Horatio Green #2 of 5. (British Cozy) The case is about gardening and flowers, and the murder itself is committed in a greenhouse with one of the most baroque murder means which only a true gardening enthusiast would think of something so devilish (J. F. Norris). –Green seems obsessed with the gardener, "He might have sat for Praxiteles," exclaimed Green half aloud." The Nichols titles need to be read with a wink to the audience that there is subtle gay context. Republished in the United States as *The Moonflower Murder* (MLM). 1/3

2101. **Nichols, Beverley,** *Death to Slow Music,* Hutchinson, 1956. Horatio Green #3 of 5. (British Cozy) "Once again we enter the world of musicians; but also in the cast we find actors, theater producers, carnival workers, and a hidden clue… in this David and Jonathan [type] relationship traceable back to the Korean War (Norris)." 1/3

2102. **Nichols, Beverley,** *The Rich Die Hard,* Hutchinson, 1957. Horatio Green #4 of 5. (British Cozy) "Andrew Lloyd has exceptional tastes is art, music, and furnishings; his home is a veritable museum display… Lloyd also has an insatiable sexual appetite and indulges himself with a live-in mistress tolerated by his aloof wife Nancy, who is more interested in Andrew's intellect than his body… The mistress, Margot Larue, is found dead in a locked room from an apparently self-inflicted gunshot wound (Norris)." –the butler spends immense amounts of time valeting for Lloyd and there is also the young Lord Richard, who seems to develop a great rapport with the main character (MLM). 1/3

2103. **Nichols, Beverley,** *Murder by Request,* Hutchinson, 1960. Horatio Green #5 of 5. (British Cozy) "Mr. Green and his client Sir Owen Kent are staying at a spa resort. Kent is receiving threatening letters which promise that he will die within a specific date range of eight days. Green is given a list of the guests and staff at the spa in order to prepare for a job he thinks he is unsuited for–the prevention of Sir Owen's murder (Norris)." –the spa massage therapist is "aggressively" male except the curve of his lips "which were loose and curved in too delicate a bow for such rugged features (MLM). 1/3

2104. **Nickle, M. Daniel,** *The Dashing Mister R,* Createspace, 2010. (Thriller) A mysterious stranger with a secret, a voodoo queen, three dead crows, whispered messages from a dead priest, and a cold case murder all disturb the peace Sebastian Stephens sought in his New Orleans garden. These fragments of the life he left behind in New York now entice him to complete the puzzle and reclaim his life or lose it. There's just one catch. He has just three days...starting now. –main character is gay (MLM). 3/3

2105. **Nickle, M. Daniel,** *The Altered Boys Club,* Createspace, 2013. Stephens #2 of 2. (Journalism) Synchronicity. Not only does award-winning investigative journalist Sebastian Stephens believe in it, synchronicity guides his life. Stephens is teased throughout the day by the spirit of an Indian boy until a Native American apparition asks him to save her boy. Stephens suspects she must have something to do with the spirit-boy, but he doesn't comprehend his mission until he arrives in New York City. There at the invitation of his friend Detective Cliff Nolte, synchronicity points the way. Since their last collaboration, Nolte has been appointed head of a special task for investigating a suspected ring of pedophiles that includes a number of Catholic priests in Brooklyn. 3/3

2106. **Nielsen, N. J.,** *A Different Way of Seeing,* MLR, 2014. Lancaster #2 of 2. (MM Western) Andrew Golding is an ass or so everyone believes. With his momma's wrath following him, he turns to the police as well as his ex-brother in-law, Riley, seeking refuge on the Triple H. A murder at the ranch has everyone pulling together to find out the truth. Drew discovers there's more to Chase than meets the eye. –book one was a romance (MLM). 3/3

2107. **Nielson, T.,** *The Glass-House Murder,* JMS, 2014. (MM Historical) Meet Lord Henry Carlisle: gentleman, wastrel, and mystery-novel lover. When his mother telephones him on a May evening to tell him they've just discovered a body in the glass-house, Hal does what he loves to do: he goes to investigate. As it happens, the local constabulary, headed by an unusually well-spoken, well-educated fellow named Sayers, is already on the case, and Sayers is a bit of a mystery all on his own. 3/3

2108. **Nisbit, Jim,** *The Gourmet,* Pinnacle, 1981. Windrow #1 of 2. (Hard Boiled) "I've always wanted to skin a woman." The line was typed on a blank sheet of paper stuck in a typewriter. Next door San Francisco cops turned up one of the most gruesome sex murders in history. Ex-cop turned private eye, not much surprises Martin Windrow anymore. But this case proves it's in a class by itself, peeling back the genteel surface of suburbia to reveal the murky world where sex and violence merge into murder, where crime blends with illicit pleasures ... –later republished as *The Damned Don't Die* (MLM). ?/3

2109. **Noble, Elizabeth,** *Run for the Roses,* Dreamspinner, 2014. Circles #1 of 5. (MM Mystery) Wanting to end his pattern of choosing controlling and abusive men, Vladimir 'Val' Mihalic figures it's better to live alone than live in fear. Just when things are settling down–his biggest trouble recently is a Kentucky Derby hopeful that won't load into a starting gate–his best friend Janelle's violent ex-boyfriend kidnaps her. After she's seriously injured in a car wreck, Wyatt Harig, Janelle's estranged father, comes around to tend to his daughter. Despite Val's determination to avoid relationships, Wyatt interests him in ways that make his resolve waver. As complications and repercussions pile on in the aftermath of Janelle's kidnapping–including a gambling charge and a murder–Wyatt and Val must work together to seek answers. And the closer they get to each other; the more Val wants them to stay that way. –e-book only (MLM). 3/3

2110. **Noble, Elizabeth,** *A Barlow Lens,* Dreamspinner, 2015. Circles #2 of 5. (MM Mystery) While planning a future with his partner, Val, Wyatt's past refuses to be forgotten. Wyatt's old friend asks him to look into the mysterious death of her uncle in a fire back in 1927, when men were silent, tough, and did not love other men–except when they did. Working with Val, Wyatt digs up clues uncovering the truth behind the tragic school fire and the one responsible. The story of Tom and Philip slowly reveals itself, and Wyatt and Val realize nothing is as simple as they originally believed. As their trail heats up, an old enemy of Wyatt's decides he's waited long enough for revenge. If Wyatt can't tie everything together, history might repeat itself. –e-book only (MLM). 3/3

2111. **Noble, Elizabeth,** *Jewel Cave,* Dreamspinner, 2015. Circles #3 of 5. (MM Mystery) Through ten wonderful years Griff Diamond and Clint Bishop weathered good times and bad together. Lately they haven't spent as much time together as they'd like, and their physical relationship is suffering. Then Clint loses his job at the steel mill. Instead of worrying, he sees it as an opportunity to lean on his steady partner, start his writing career, and rekindle the passion they've lost. –e-book only (MLM). 3/3

2112. **Noble, Elizabeth,** *Gone Away,* Dreamspinner, 2016. Circles #4 of 5. (MM Mystery) Mason Arquette isn't one for mincing words. In fact, he often rubs people the wrong way–with the exception of Riece Burrell. Riece came with his own set of social issues, but he saw right through Mason's tough exterior, and they made a perfect couple. Or so Mason thought... until Riece abruptly ended their relationship without much explanation. –e-book only (MLM). 3/3

2113. **Noble, Elizabeth,** *Bait,* Dreamspinner, 2016. Circles #5 of 5. (MM Mystery) Tyler McCall has made mistakes. He was a teacher–before he fell for a student in his school. That misstep cost him his job and everything he'd worked for. He moved to the Black Hills of Wyoming to start his life over, and he's happy working at the Big Rock Inn near Devils Tower. –e-book only (MLM). 3/3

2114. **Nolan, Kip,** *Mulholland Meat,* Bruno Gmunder, 2015. (Modern Pulp) Hollywood, Thursday 24 September 1953 - the star-studded West Coast premiere of The Robe, the world's first Cinemascope epic, lights up Hollywood with searchlights and glamour. Far from the bright lights, in a run-down apartment in West Los Angeles, private investigator and studio fixer Rick Barker finds a victim of brutal murder. 3/3

2115. **Nolan, Nick,** *Strings Attached,* Booksurge, 2006. Bellana Beach #1 of 3. (YA) Closeted teenager Jeremy is sent to live with wealthy relatives after his mother enters rehab. Struggling to fit into the posh world of Ballena Beach, Jeremy joins the high school swim team, dates a popular girl, and begins to think he may have landed in paradise - until his great aunt Katharine starts to dictate his every move and a late-night phone call insinuates that his father's accidental death was not so accidental after all. 3/3

2116. **Nolan, Nick,** *Double Bind,* Booksurge, 2008. Bellana Beach #2 of 3. (YA) Jeremy, now in a committed relationship with fun-loving, hotheaded Carlo; Arthur, Jeremy's protector, confidant, and mentor; and Katharine, Jeremy's wealthy benefactress, still hiding a slew of secrets and hidden agendas. 3/3

2117. **Nolan, Nick,** *Wide Asleep,* Lake Union, 2014. Bellana Beach #3 of 3. (YA) Arthur Blauefee promised to stay away from Jeremy Tyler forever. But when he learns that his troubled, heartbroken ex-lover has been seduced and swindled out of his inheritance, Arthur is off to the rescue. 3/3

2118. **Nussbaum, Tom,** *The Boy in the Book,* iUniverse, 2004. (Fantasy) When a thirty-something retired Microsoft millionaire is confronted by a homeless teenager; their lives are dramatically changed. The unlikely pair finds itself in a relationship based on suspicion and distrust. However, an unexpected series of events quickly changes the dynamics of their relationship. Jon and Rick are thrown into a world of unraveled mysteries, exposed dark secrets, and sexual deceptions. To solve these mysteries, the two embark on an odyssey that catapults them from a Seattle bookstore to the back rooms of the gay porn industry and home again. Along the way they learn, to their surprise, that Jon's father, mother, and Rick's best friend, Jay, are all involved in the deceit and lies. 3/3

O

2119. **O'Brien, Kevin,** *Make them Cry,* Pinnacle, 2002. (Thriller) A clever serial killer is stalking the streets of Seattle. Searching for his next victim. Creating a monument of madness that will be built victim by victim...piece by piece...bone by bone...–the first victim of the serial killer is gay, and the main character comes out in the end (MLM). 3/3

2120. **O'Faolain, J. L.,** *Thirteenth Child,* Dreamspinner, 2011. Section 13 #1 of 4. (MM Fantasy) Immortal sidhe Tuulois MacColewyn is living rough. After nearly two centuries of life as one of Faerie Queen Titania's prized wolves and a handful of years as a Roaring Twenties mob boss's favorite enforcer, he's now exiled to New York, making rent doing dirty jobs for other fey outcasts. He used to consult on the occult for Detective James Corhagen at the NYPD, but since their highly combustible friendship burned itself out a year ago, Cole hasn't heard from him. All that changes when Corhagen summons Cole right out of his shower and into the middle of a crime scene. 3/3

2121. **O'Failain, J. L.,** *Thirteenth Pillar,* Dreamspinner, 2011. Section 13 #2 of 4. (MM Fantasy) Tuulois MacColewyn's simple life performing dirty jobs for fey hiding in New York City has died a quick death. Cole has a new place to live, a steady-paying job working for the NYPD, and trying to solve every supernatural crime in New York, including a series of grisly child murders and evidence that local fey are being enslaved. 3/3

2122. **O'Failain, J. L.,** *The Thirteenth Sigil,* Dreamspinner, 2012. Section 13 #3 of 4. (MM Fantasy) A break-in at a high-tech storage facility leaves no witnesses–alive or, Cole's specialty, dead–and just one missing canister. They do have their hands full: some mysterious force is cutting a swath through the city in search of that canister. If Cole and Joss figure that out, there's the disappearances of employees connected to a local children's television program to solve. Meanwhile, Internal Affairs is breathing down their necks. 3/3

2123. **O'Failain, J. L.,** *The Thirteenth Shard,* Dreamspinner, 2013. Section 13 #4 of 4. (MM Fantasy) When a powerful witch is murdered by mundane means–with the killer leaving behind clues reminiscent of an old mortal folktale–the NYPD calls in Tuulois MacColewyn and the rest of Section Thirteen. 3/3

2124. **O'Hagan, Joan,** *A Roman Death,* Putnam's Sons, 1988. (Historical) It is 45 BC, and Julius Caesar is at the height of his power. Quintus Fufidius agrees against his wife's instincts to the marriage of their daughter to the handsome, young Lucius Scaurus. It is an alliance which could heal old feuds and create a new dynasty. But before the wedding takes place one of the principals is murdered. Suspects are few, but Roman society is shocked when Quintus' wife is accused, not only of murder, but also of incest. The trial of Helvia, in which she is defended by Cicero, is a courtroom battle on the grand scale and accompanied by the political shenanigans which result in Caesar's assassination. –future son-in-law used to engage in same sex relations as a bottom, and there is a male rape scene (MLM). 1/3

2125. **Olshan, Joseph,** *Black Diamond Fall,* Polis, 2018. (Police Procedural) Luc Flanders has just finished playing a game of pond hockey with his college roommates when he realizes he has lost something precious and goes back to the ice to find it. He never returns, and the police department in Middlebury, Vermont are divided in their assessment of what may have happened to him. Some feel that Flanders left on his own accord and is deliberately out of touch. Others, including detectives Nick Jenkins and Helen Kennedy, suspect that harm may have come to him. 2/3

2126. **Olson, Derik,** *Male Room,* Surey, 1990. (Pulp) "Pennsylvania accidental sleuth Jeff Owen, 18, a college freshman "from a small town outside Columbus, Ohio," proves trustworthy in a pulp mystery that makes a nice break from murder cases (Gunn)." 3/3

2127. **Olson, Donald,** *The Secrets of Mabel Eastlake,* Knights, 1986. (Psychological) "Los Angeles would-be biographer Alex Klein, 33, discovers the truth about what ended a movie star's career (Gunn)." 3/3

2128. **O'Reilly, Patrick J.,** *Fatal Muse,* Publish Green, 2012. Malone #1 of 2. (Police Procedural) Hapless FBI agent Freddy Malone is leading a dull existence, both personally and professionally. A handsome bartender and an artistic, sadistic killer are about to change all that. With the help of his partner and straight best friend, Freddy shakes himself out of his monotony, but can he successfully navigate a budding romance and catch a serial killer before another victim meets a gruesome end? –available as an e-book only, although I was unable to find a copy of this anywhere (MLM). 3/3

2129. **O'Reilly, Patrick,** *Wretched Need,* Publish Green, 2015. Malone, #2 of 2. (Police Procedural) A spur of the moment visit to a friend from his last case leads him to a new and even more twisted killer, the likes of which he has never seen before. While he unofficially thinks about the case, the appearance of a Detroit Police Officer unsettles Freddy more than he expects. –available as an e-book only (MLM). 3/3

2130. **Orr, Clifford,** *The Dartmouth Murders,* Farrar and Rinehart, 1928. (Amateur Sleuth) The Dartmouth Murders: The Dartmouth Hall clock strikes a "cold, damp six" as student Ken Harris awakens to the ominous sound of muffled rhythmic raps against a dormitory window. Upon rising and looking out the window, Ken finds to his horror that the eerie noise is coming from the two bare feet of his roommate, Byron Coates, whose rain-slicked, pajama-clad body hangs suspended from a rope fire escape. Initially it is believed that Byron committed suicide, but soon it is established that the moody Dartmouth student was the victim of a foul play. –Harris seemed to have loved his deceased roommate (MLM). 1/3

2131. **Osborne, Stephen,** *Pale as Ghost,* Dreamspinner, 2011. Duncan Andrews #1 of 6. (Fantasy) Private detective Duncan Andrews's best friend Gina is a witch. His dog is a zombie. And his dead boyfriend, Robbie, is a ghost. So it's hardly any wonder that he uses his connection to the supernatural to help him solve cases. Good thing, too, because Duncan has his hands full. Janice Sanderson, the richest woman in Indianapolis, wants him to find her stripper daughter, Brenda, and another client is having some trouble with a specter haunting her family home. On top of that, Duncan has decided to add dating into the mix, though after Robbie's death, he's not sure he's ready. 3/3

2132. **Osborne, Stephen,** *Animal Instinct,* Dreamspinner, 2012. Duncan Andrews #2 of 6. (Fantasy) Duncan certainly has his work cut out for him with this case. Someone's been using the skull of a powerful wizard to control animals, and whoever it is, they're not out to set up a petting zoo. For Gina, the case hits close to home–she knows just how dangerous it is, since the wizard was her father. 3/3

2133. **Osborne, Stephen,** *The Scarlet Tide,* Dreamspinner, 2013. Duncan Andrews #3 of 6. (Fantasy) Duncan's latest case leads him to a rock band in Indianapolis called The Scarlet Tide. It doesn't take Duncan long to realize all of the band members are vampires. He sets out to destroy them but runs into trouble with the charismatic leader of the band, Dominic Hunt. Duncan ends up under Hunt's psychic control and is forced to examine his relationships with Robbie and Nick, as well as his attraction for Hunt. 3/3

2134. **Osborne, Stephen,** *Dead End,* Dreamspinner, 2014. Duncan Andrews #4 of 6. (Fantasy) Robbie's cousin, Jason, has a problem. The house he's living in is haunted by the ghost of serial killer Dr. Stanley Moore. Duncan thinks banishing the spirit will be an easy task, but when confronted, the ghost nearly kills Duncan. If that's not bad enough, a witch-hunting group called the Order of Cotton Mather have tracked Gina down and are bent on destroying her. And Robbie and Duncan's relationship may be nearing an end, as Robbie feels he's holding Duncan back from having a lover he can actually touch. 3/3

2135. **Osborne, Stephen,** *Under a Blood-Red Moon,* Dreamspinner, 2016. Duncan Andrews #5 of 6. (Fantasy) Private Detective Duncan Andrews is back, along with the usual gang: Robbie, Gina, Nick, and Daisy, the zombie bulldog! Duncan is trying to figure out how his boyfriend, Robbie, will fit in with the team now that he is no longer a ghost. That worry is soon set aside when Duncan accepts a new case to locate a missing young man named Graig Betz. Duncan soon learns Graig is part of a werewolf pack that is terrorizing Indianapolis. The pack is led by a witch, Ashley Campbell, an old rival of Gina's. Duncan and his team must try to rescue and cure Graig and stop the wolf pack from destroying an entire city. 3/3

2136. **Osborne, Stephen,** *Cold as the Clay,* Beaten Track, 2018. Duncan Andrews #6 of 6. (Fantasy) Private detective Duncan Andrews is used to dealing with things strange and bizarre. Luckily, he's got friends to back him up, including Gina, a witch, Robbie, his boyfriend, and Daisy, their zombie bulldog. A new case brings Duncan face-to-face with a demon named Asmodeus. If that wasn't enough, one of the original Gorgons wants revenge against Duncan for killing her sister. Duncan and his team must pull out all the stops if they're going to get through this alive. 3/3

2137. **O'Toole, Zachary,** *Busted,* Less than Three, 2011. (Psychological) Pulled over on a rainy night, Joe's bad day starts to look up when he realizes the cop pulling him over is none other than his lover, Alex. Until Alex pretends not to know him, and finally drags him into the station for driving under the influence–and getting too personal with a Detective. Furious, Joe demands to know what the hell is wrong with his lover. Only to discover that the Detective he kissed is actually named Chris, and claims no knowledge of Alex, despite the fact they could be twins. But before Joe can begin to sort out the mystery of Chris and Alex, the murders begin… 3/3

2138. **Outland, Orlando,** *Death Wore a Smart Little Outfit,* Berkley, 1997. Binky and Doan #1 of 3. (Cozy) Doan McCandler, San Francisco's best dressed detective, is a Sherlock Holmes in high heels. His stunning sidekick Binky is Watson with a waistline. Together, they make a killer ensemble of amateur sleuths so smart and sassy, readers will just die! 3/3

2139. **Outland, Orlando,** *Death Wore a Fabulous New Fragrance,* Berkley, 1998. Binky and Doan #2 of 3. (Cozy) Binky's killing time before our heroes' detective license comes through, and why not make a little champagne money working as a perfume spritzer at the launch of superstar Jeff Breeze's new cologne? But when Jeff drops dead from a whiff of his own fresh, woodsy scent, and all the evidence points at Doan's friend Kenny, persistent outer of closeted gay movie stars, it's time to put on their sleuthing hats and descend on Hollywood. The shopping's good, the men are hot, so what could possibly go wrong? 3/3

2140. **Outland, Orlando,** *Death Wore the Emperor's New Clothes,* Berkley, 1999. Binky and Doan #3 of 3. (Cozy) Binky and Doan are rich after solving their latest case, but what's a girl and a girlish guy to do when you've bought everything up to and including platinum vegetable peelers and time hangs heavy on the hands? Why, take jobs in New York City with an eccentric gay billionaire, just in time to defend him after he's accused of murdering right-wing media mogul Herbert Kildare! Throw in a couple of insane, possibly homicidal fashion designers and a motivational speaker who promises that "You Can Rationalize Anything," and our intrepid duo will have their hands full! 3/3

2141. **Owen, Chris,** *Sex, Lies and Celluloid,* Torquere, 2007. (MM Hard Boiled) Detective Shane Mullin is used to domestic investigations. So, when Janet Brint hires him to tail her husband, City Councilor Daniel, he doesn't think much of it. Everyone has something to hide, and Janet thinks Daniel's problem is drugs. It's not drug abuse that has Daniel hiding out, though. As Shane follows Daniel about, he realizes the politician is having lots of sex. Gay sex at that. Shane is fascinated with Daniel's case, wondering just what Janet hopes to gain by exposing Daniel's secrets. Shane is also fascinated with Daniel the man, so much so that attraction blooms, and he and Daniel begin an online friendship. One thing leads to another, and Shane finds himself leading his own double life, seeing Daniel while continuing to investigate him. With no good way out of his deception, Shane has a decision to make about what to tell Daniel, and Daniel himself has some tough choices about his life and whether or not to go public with his sexuality. Can Shane and Daniel work their way through their web of lies? 3/3

2142. **Owens, Timothy,** *Aaron Bradley, Closet Detective,* Dreamspinner, 2010. (MM Soft Boiled) Aaron Bradley is restless. Despite a privileged upbringing, at twenty-seven he still hasn't figured out who he is or what he wants to do with his life. Then his friend Joe, a successful public prosecutor, asks him for a favor that will change Aaron's life. While investigating Joe's enigmatic girlfriend Candice, Aaron meets Bo, an out-and-proud, easygoing waiter, causing unfamiliar and confusing emotions to flutter to life. Caught up in the middle of Candice's clandestine activities, with Bo gently nudging him out of the closet along the way, Aaron will have to review everything he thought he knew about himself as he tries to make sense of his feelings for Bo. 3/3

P

2143. **Packer, Vin, (Marijane Meaker)** *Scott Free,* Caroll and Graf, 2007. (Hard Boiled) Transgender insurance investigator Scotti House gets caught up in a kidnapping plot among the rich in the Hamptons. –not recommended as the main character is misgendered on the first page and the cover, with several transphobic events (MLM). 3/3

2144. **Paddie, Dennis,** *Ask the Fire,* Lethe, 2010. (Espionage) high tech culture of modern espionage and the highly politicized social culture of Washington, D.C., the capital of the world, with the secret of the Knights Templar, Freemasonry in the architecture of the D.C. streets. Add a dash of 60s hippiedom, and plenty of urban gay and post-gay culture, and readers will discover the birth of a new trans-mythological, but deeply spiritual, vision of the meaning of human life in the charged world of the 21st century. 3/3

2145. **Paretsky, Sara,** *Burn Marks,* Delacorte, 1990. V. I. Warshawski #6 of 21. (Hardboiled) Someone knocking on the door at 3 A.M. is never good news. For V.I. Warshawski, the bad news arrives in the form of her wacky, unwelcome aunt Elena. The fire that has just burned down a sleazy SRO hotel has brought Elena to V.I.'s doorstep. Uncovering an arsonist – and the secrets hidden behind Elena's boozy smile – will send V.I. into the seedy world of Chicago's homeless… into the Windy City's backroom deals and bedroom politics, where new schemers and old cronies team up to get V.I. off the case – by hook, by crook, or by homicide. –the gay yuppie neighbor and his laid-back boyfriend appear slightly (MLM). 1/3

2146. **Paretsky, Sara,** *Guardian Angel,* Delacorte, 1992. V. I. Warshawski #7 of 21. (Hardboiled) Racine Avenue is going upscale–bad news for hand-to-mouth residents like V I Warshawski. As tax bills skyrocket, newcomers' pressure old inhabitants into fixing up their homes or moving out. To the yuppies on the block the worst eyesore belongs to old Hattie Frizell, whose yard is "returning to native prairie, complete with hubcaps." Their block club wants her and her five dogs gone. –her gay, yuppie neighbor makes another appearance (MLM). 1/3

2147. **Paretsky, Sara,** *Brush Back,* G. P. Putnam's Sons, 2015. V. I. Warshawski #17 of 21. (Hardboiled) No one would accuse V. I. Warshawski of backing down from a fight, but there are a few she'd be happy to avoid. High on that list is tangling with Chicago political bosses. Yet that's precisely what she ends up doing when she responds to Frank Guzzo's plea for help. –one gay victim and two gay men who assist Warshawski in her investigation (MLM). 2/3

2148. **Parker, Eliot,** *Fragile Brilliance,* Roundfire, 2015. Ronan McCullough #1 of 2. (Police Procedural) When off-duty Charleston police sergeant Ronan McCullough responds to the assault of a college student outside a downtown sports bar, he is brutally attacked and nearly killed by the assailants. 3/3

2149. **Parker, Eliot,** *A Knife's Edge,* Headline Books, 2018. Ronan McCullough #2 of 2. (Police Procedural) Six months after a drug cartel infiltrated Charleston, Ronan McCullough continues to fight the drug war that plagues the city. His investigations are halted when the body of a mutual acquaintance, Sarah Gilmore, is found in the trunk of a burning car. 3/3

2150. **Parker, Elle,** *Like Coffee and Donuts,* Lyrical, 2010. Dino Martini #1 of 2. (MM Hard Boiled) Dino Martini is an old-school P.I. in a modern age. Sure, he may do most of his work on a computer, but he carries a gun, drives a convertible, and lives on the beach. Best friend and mechanic Seth Donnelly will back him in a fight, and there's not a lot more Dino could ask from life. 3/3

2151. **Parker, Elle,** *Like Pizza and Beer,* Lyrical, 2011. Dino Martini #2 of 2. (MM Hard Boiled) Dino is caught off guard when his ex shows up out of the blue asking for help. His current lover, Seth, is pushing him to find dirt on his sister's boyfriend. Juggling between two cases – and his boyfriend and ex – isn't easy, but what choice does he have? Working with his ex takes Dino on a trip down memory lane, raising a few doubts and stirring up Seth's jealousy. Now he must save his ex's restaurant and his relationship with Seth before it's too late. 3/3

2152. **Parker, John,** *Come Clean,* Writer's Club, 2002. (Thriller) A diabolical murder is committed by a serial killer who believes Hannibal Lecter would envy his techniques. PI Kevin J. Porter (an ex-Royal Canadian Mounted Police Chief Inspector) takes you on a breathless trail in and around Hollywood North in Vancouver, Canada, as he tries to bag the psycho murderer. The reader is usually a jump ahead of Kevin Porter-privy to his foibles and flaws-and Porter has a lot of secrets. He was a cop, but for mysterious reasons, now he's not. He was also married, but not anymore. Instead, he's left his family for an inter-generational relationship. His lover, Brent Barnes, serves up some of the only relief from the heart-thumping suspense that builds right up to the final moments of Come Clean.

Will Porter catch the killer before he kills again? 3/3

2153. **Parker, Robert,** *Paper Doll,* Putnam's Sons, 1993. Spenser #20 of 46. (Hard Boiled) She was a model wife and mother, bludgeoned with a hammer on the streets of Beacon Hill. Spenser's searching for a motive and a murderer–and finding more secrets than meet the eye... –many of Parker's characters appear in different series. In *Paper Doll* PI Spenser works with a young gay police detective Lee Farrell whose lover dies of AIDS (MLM). 2/3

2154. **Parker, Robert,** *Walking Shadow,* Putnam's, 1994. Spenser #21 of 46. (Hard Boiled) In a shabby waterfront town, an actor is shot dead onstage. Granted, the script left much to be desired. But there's more behind the scenes than an overzealous critic–and Spenser and Hawk are combing Port City's underworld to find it... –Lee makes a small appearance (MLM). 1/3

2155. **Parker, Robert,** *Thin Air,* Putnam's, 1995. Spenser #22 of 46. (Hard Boiled) Her name is Lisa St. Claire. Her husband's a cop. Her whereabouts are unknown. Spenser thought he could help a friend find his missing wife. Until he learned the nasty truth about Lisa St. Claire. For starters, it's not her real name... –Lee makes another small appearance (MLM). 1/3

2156. **Parker, Robert,** *Small Vices,* Putnam's 1997. Spenser #24 of 46. (Hard Boiled) Ellis Alves is no angel. But his lawyer says he was framed for the murder of college student Melissa Henderson...and asks Spenser for help. From Boston's back streets to Manhattan's elite, Spenser and Hawk search for suspects, including Melissa's rich-kid, tennis-star boyfriend. But when a man with a .22 puts Spenser in a coma, the hope for justice may die with him... –Lee acts as bodyguard for Spenser's female lover (MLM). 2/3

2157. **Parker, Robert,** *Sudden Mischief,* Putnam's, 1998. Spenser #25 of 46. (Hard Boiled) Susan Silverman's ex doesn't call himself "Silverman" anymore–he's changed his name to "Sterling." And that's not the only thing that's phony about him. A do-gooding charity fundraiser, he's been accused of sexual harassment by no less than four different women. And not long after Spenser starts investigating, Sterling is wanted for a bigger charge: murder...–Lee is more involved in this case as Spenser's overlaps a murder case Lee is working on (MLM). 2/3

2158. **Parker, Robert,** *Hush Money,* Putnam's, 1999. Spenser #26 of 46. (Hard Boiled) he burly Boston P.I. and his redoubtable cohort, Hawk, against local intellectual heavyweights. When Robinson Nevins, the son of Hawk's boyhood mentor, is denied tenure at the University, Hawk asks Spenser to investigate. It appears the denial is tied to the suicide of a young gay activist, Prentice Lamont. While intimations of an affair between Lamont and Nevins have long fed the campus rumor mill, no one's willing to talk, and as Spenser digs deeper he is nearly drowned in a multicultural swamp of politics: black, gay, academic, and feminist. –Lee assists briefly in this case involving blackmail and gay men (MLM). 2/3

2159. **Parker, Robert,** *Family Honor,* Putnam's, 1999. Sunny Randall #1 of 7. (Hard Boiled) Sunny Randall is a Boston P.I. and former cop, a college graduate, an aspiring painter, a divorcée, and the owner of a miniature bull terrier named Rosie. Hired by a wealthy family to locate their teenage daughter, Sunny is tested by the parents' preconceived notion of what a detective should be. With the help of underworld contacts, she tracks down the runaway Millicent, who has turned to prostitution, rescues her from a vicious pimp, and finds herself, at thirty-four, the unlikely custodian of a difficult teenager when the girl refuses to return to her family. –Gay Boston restaurateur and actor Spike provides backup for his friend Sunny Randall. Spike was created when one of Parker's gay sons, Daniel T., cameoed as Spike on the Lifestyle teleplays, *Spenser* (MM). 2/3

2160. **Parker, Robert,** *Perish Twice,* Putnam's, 2000. Sunny Randall #2 of 7. (Hard Boiled) Boston P.I. Sunny Randall, coming to the aid of three very different women in three very dangerous situations. One is for business. One is for a friend. One is for family. And all could be fatal... –Lee Farrell works at odds with the main character and Spike appears to help Sunny (MLM). 2/3

2161. **Parker, Robert,** *Shrink Rap,* Putnam's, 2002. Sunny Randall #3 of 7. (Hard Boiled) Sunny Randall is hired to protect a bestselling novelist from her ex-husband. He's not only a stalker...he's a shrink. And when Sunny becomes his patient, she discovers as much about herself as she does about the criminal mind... –Lee appears briefly, and Spike continues to help Sunny (MLM). 2/3

2162. **Parker, Robert,** *Melancholy Baby,* Putnam's, 2004. Sunny Randall #4 of 7. (Hard Boiled) When Sunny Randall helps a young woman locate her birth parents, she uncovers the dark truth about her own past. –Spike returns to assist Sunny (MM). 2/3

2163. **Parker, Robert,** *Blue Screen,* Putnam's, 2006. Sunny Randall #5 of 7. (Hard Boiled) Sunny Randall, the Boston P.I. with a personal life as tangled as that of her clients, is hired on as a bodyguard to an up-and-coming starlet and discovers some ugly truths behind her glossy façade. –Spike assists once more (MLM). 2/3

2164. **Parker, Robert,** *Spare Change,* Putnam's, 2007. Sunny Randall #6 of 7. (Hard Boiled) Boston P.I. Sunny Randall joins forces with the most important man in her life-her father-to crack a thirty-year-old case. –Lee is involved with a raid on a suspect's house and Spike helps Sunny investigate (MLM). 2/3

2165. **Parkes, Matthew,** *Camera Shy,* Wayward, 2002. (Espionage) Assigned to trap a political assassin, AFIS agent, Jack Ballam, is ordered to use Sydney's top male model, Tane Caton, as bait. At their first meeting, Ballam is instantly, dangerously attracted to the man. 3/3

2166. **Parris, Eugenia,** *The Tattoo Murders,* Createspace, 2015. (Police Procedural) Deputy Sheriff Pete Branson's latest case rocks the desert town of Del Sueno when he finds the victim beaten to death behind the infamous local watering hole, The End of the Line. Yet what at first glance appears to be a simple killing drags Pete into a web of intrigue...when he finds out that the murderer may be striking out against a specific group of people: ones who carry a special hidden tattoo! –gay characters are secondary characters (MLM). 2/3

2167. **Paterson, G. J.,** *Bird of Paradise,* Ex Caliban Books, 2013. (MM Police Procedural) Carys Sterling, the daughter of Leviathon's lead singer, Allyn Sterling, is kidnapped. Assigned to lead the investigation for the missing girl are Paul Taglia and Jeff Kincaid, partners for seven years with LAPD's Missing Persons Unit. 3/3

2168. **Patrick, Q (Richard Wilson Webb and Hugh Callingham Wheeler),** *The Grindle Nightmare,* Hartney, 1935. (Crime Drama) The quiet New England village of Grindle was the last place in the world where murder might be expected. Vultures, traditional heralds of death in the valley, had not roosted in Grindle Oak for more than a hundred years. But now they swarmed there, sinister omens of death to follow. For a murderer stalked the woods and fields of Grindle, a creature whose twisted mind took fiendish joy in killing. And soon the signs began to appear–a dead monkey, savagely eviscerated ... the mutilated body of a kitten... And then a man, drifting face down in the shallow waters of a pond, a man who had been killed slowly by dragging his body behind a moving car. –a novel based loosely on the Leopold-Loeb killers (MLM). 1/3

2169. **Patterson, Edward C.,** *Turning Idolator,* Createspace, 2008. (MM Mystery) Philip Flaxen, who strips past his jockstrap on the Internet for manluv.org, acquires a rare gift - a book that transforms his life. With it, he sparks with a famous author, whittles away at a new craft, swims with an odd circle of new acquaintants and is swept up in mayhem. Philip leaves the world of the Porn Nazi and enters the realm of crisp possibilities - great expectations and dark secrets that unravel over deep waters. 3/3

2170. **Patterson, Edward C.,** *The Sapphire Astonishment,* Createspace, 2014. Firestone #1 of 2. (Science Fiction) Nick Firestone was a five-year-old scamp, precocious and filled with the spirit of adventure. Now he's all grow'd up, as Simone DeFleurry would say, and itching for an occupation worthy of the scratch. It's 2025 in San Francisco (post-earthquake of 2020) and things have changed for the adventurer as he wakes up to the sparkle of a rare relic – a Chinese hat-pin called The Sapphire Astonishment. 2/3

2171. **Patterson, Edward C.,** *Old Friend Cane,* Createspace, 2016. Firestone #2 of 2. (Science Fiction) Nick Firestone & Company has a new challenge. It's 2027 in a post-USA San Francisco. The world is drenched in intrigue, eShirts, GovCoupies, and GlimmerGlass. Still, the old folk of Chinatown are trying to hold on to their dearest traditions. Then, in a mysterious incident, the Don of Chinatown is conked on the head and taken out of commission. It's up to our intrepid sleuths, Nick, Amy, John and Wiggins to find the culprit. After all, the victim is Amy and John's uncle, Tangy Win. 2/3

2172. **Patterson, James & Howard Roughan,** *Murder Games,* Little Brown, 2017. (Police Procedural/Amateur Sleuth) Dr. Dylan Reinhart wrote the book on criminal behavior. Literally–he's a renowned, bestselling Ivy League expert on the subject. When a copy of his book turns up at a gruesome murder scene–along with a threatening message from the killer–it looks like someone has been taking notes. – republished as *Instinct,* and the sequel, *Killer Instinct,* expected out in late 2019 (MLM). 3/3

2173. **Patton, Lee,** *Love and Genetic Weaponry: Beginner's Guide,* Alyson, 2009. (Political Intrigue) Ray O'Brien, a high school drama teacher, as he becomes involved with a one-woman activist organization, Lottie Weiss, and her quest to free a young revolutionary imprisoned for bombing a genetics laboratory. What's the real truth behind the lab's shady dealings? –this same character is used in Patton's other book, *Nothing Gold Can Stay,* published under the name Casey Nelson although this O'Brien is very much different than the previous character (MLM). 3/3

2174. **Paulding, Roger,** *Jazzed: Case of the Stubborn Trick,* Greg Jennings Ink, 2013. Starlight #1 of 2. (Amateur Sleuth) Suave, buttoned-down Alex Upchurch seems an odd match with his position as Assistant District Attorney of Galveston, a city some say is like the antique store on the north end that advertises "Mostly Junque, a Few Jewels." But when a dead John Doe is discovered naked in the bedroom of Alex's baronial mansion, District Attorney John Henry Davenport has to cover up the crime to save not only his able assistant but also to placate Alex's mother, Honey Upchurch, whose money bought John Henry's position. Figuring out who is dead and why proves almost as challenging as keeping that information from becoming known, especially when Alex is appointed to prosecute a former lover who knows all but tells nothing. Fortunately, Leon McAdoo, known as Miss Starlight because of a gossip column he (or she?) writes, is on hand to guide us through the maze of power, money, sex and corruption. –originally published as *Bought Off* which excluded materials thought to be unsavory (MLM). 3/3

2175. **Paulding, Roger,** *Midnight in the Garden of Lust,* Createspace, 2015. Starlight #2 of 2. (Amateur Sleuth) Miss Starlight assigns young Donny to a ranch for homeless boys, little realizing she had delivered him over to Reverend Robbins, who promised to make a popular singer out of Donny, but the man is plagued by devils. Will Starlight be able to rescue him before the reverend's henchmen make him an example of those who defy the reverend? 3/3

2176. **Payne, Simon,** *The Beat,* GMP, 1985. (Crime Drama) Friday night in a city park and a young man is found battered to death in a public toilet. The motive appears obvious: the place is a well-known gay haunt and a common target for local thugs. But this is not the simple case of queer bashing that it seems. Six strangers hold the answer; they alone know what really happened that evening - when the intended victims suddenly struck back. 3/3

2177. **Payseur, Jessica,** *Shell Shocked,* Createspace, 2016. Yolks on You #1 of 5. (MM Cozy) When Dominic agrees to join his boyfriend Alec and his kids for a weekend away at the annual Eggstravaganza in Mount Angus, Wisconsin, he's expecting a boring, if kitschy, experience. He isn't expecting to discover Alec is cheating on him, and he certainly isn't expecting an exploding cow to drop him in the middle of a deadly mystery. 3/3

2178. **Payseur, Jessica,** *Egg Whites and Blue,* JMS, 2016. Yolks on You #2 of 5. (MM Cozy) Kiko and Dom are still getting used to settling in with each other, a task made difficult by their conflicting schedules and habits. With Mount Angus' Knee High 4th of July Festival approaching, they anticipate spending some quality time together again, if only for a weekend. When Dom stumbles across a body with a pie server in its back, they find themselves drawn into another small-town mystery where the dark secrets of family recipes and a generous serving of danger could very well get them killed. 3/3

2179. **Payseur, Jessica,** *Deal with the Deviled Eggs,* Createspace, 2016. Yolks on You #3 of 5. (MM Cozy) After a chaos-filled summer, Kiko and Dom are ready to ease into a more laidback autumn and really put in some quality time together. Allowing Dom's ex roommate to crash with them, however, turns out to be a mistake when the guy won't leave. Just when the tension seems to be too much, a murder after a Halloween party reignites the spark between Kiko and Dom.

2180. **Payseur, Jessica,** *Egg the Halls,* Createspace, 2016. Yolks on You #4 of 5. (MM Cozy) With the horrors of Halloween behind them, Kiko and Dom turn their puzzle solving skills to surviving the holiday season. Dom hasn't had a proper Christmas in years, and Kiko's sister visiting makes him feel almost like family – until his brother, Devin, decides to show up and throw his disapproval into the mix. When the property damage escalates and Kiko begins receiving threatening letters, this harmless little problem turns deadlier than anyone thought. And if they can't get to the bottom of the family drama fast enough, Kiko might never be home for the holidays again. 3/3

2181. **Payseur, Jessica,** *Eggs and Kisses,* JMS, 2017. Yolks on You #5 of 5. (MM Cozy) Tensions are running high in Mount Angus as the entire town plans for the annual Be Mount Valentine Heartstival and all residents keep an eye out for the latest relationship drama. Kiko and Dom just want to enjoy life together, a task made difficult by nosy residents demanding to know when they're going to tie the knot. But before anyone's matchmaking schemes can get too far, Kiko's employee Chad finds a body rolled in a rug. 3/3

2182. **Pearce, Jeff,** *Buddha on the Road,* Gallivant, 2011. (Supernatural) Burma is known as "The Golden Land." And for Brin Harper, Burma means golden memories from a youth spent in an exotic country with his mother, an accomplished diplomat. But today Brin Harper is an NYPD homicide detective haunted by his mother's suicide, and his grief is slowly eroding his relationship with his journalist boyfriend, Richard. Now a set of vicious murders is about to dredge up secrets and bitter regrets from thousands of miles away and many years ago. The trail leads to a strange monk who doesn't behave at all like a holy man. Brin is faced with a range of suspects, including the American widower of dissident Marlar Swe, to his on-again, off-again lover, Aung, a quiet professor who has survived time in Burma's infamous Insein Prison. As the killer claims more victims, each murdered in a fashion inspired by Burmese culture, Brin must confront his own past and play a duel of wits with the monk, trying to decipher what his role is in the case. And there are more disturbing personal revelations waiting for him than just exposing a psychotic murderer... 3/3

2183. **Peck, Dale,** *Now its Time to Say Goodbye,* Farrar Straus Giroux, 1998. (Thriller) On the run from the AIDS epidemic – and in search of their own lost love – Colin Nieman and Justin Time abandon New York City for the tiny Kansas village of Galatea. Racially polarized and desperately poor, the town is dominated by Rosemary Krebs. a white matriarch determined to resurrect her lost Southern childhood, and Abraham Greeving, the black preacher who will do anything to stop her. 3/3

2184. **Pederson, David,** *Death Comes Darkly,* Bold Stroke Books, 2016. Barrington #1 of 3. (Historical) Can a detective and a policeman find love amidst murder? Heath Barrington is an attractive, clever, big city detective, confident, strong, and crazy about police officer Alan Keyes. Down-to-earth, noble, and naïve, Alan struggles with his desires for Heath versus 1940s America and his guilty conscience. 3/3

2185. **Pederson, David,** *Death Goes Overboard,* Bold Stroke Books, 2017. Barrington #2 of 3. (Historical) Gregor Slavinsky went overboard. Or did he? He was murdered. Or was he? It's up to Detective Heath Barrington and his partner, police officer Alan Keyes, to find out as they search for clues and a missing twenty-five thousand dollars aboard an old lake steamer and throughout 1947 Milwaukee, Wisconsin. 3/3

2186. **Pederson, David,** *Death Checks In,* Bold Stroke Books, 2018. Barrington #3 of 3. (Historical) All Detective Heath Barrington and his partner, Alan Keyes, want is to get away for a weekend of romance, but they find murder instead when a missing tie leads them to the body of the peculiar Victor Blount, and Heath can't resist the urge to investigate. Who killed Blount, and why? 3/3

2187. **Peffer, Randall,** *Killing Neptune's Daughter,* Intrigue, 2004. Cape Island #1 of 6. (Hard Boiled) When Noelle Werlin, wife of rock 'n' roll legend Butch Werlin, is found murdered, Butch becomes the prime suspect for the NYPD, but Noelle's childhood friends believe that her murderer is Billy Bagwell, a high school buddy of theirs. –Billy's sexuality is ambiguous (MLM). 1/3

2188. **Peffer, Randall,** *Provincetown Follie, Bangkok Blues,* Bleak House, 2006. Cape Island #2 of 6. (Hard Boiled) Tuki Aparecio did not kill her lover. She did not burn down the Painted Lady–at least, not with fire. Tuki lit up the stage nightly, with her hair in braids and her glorious costumes; glittering, smoldering, singing her heart out for an audience who loved her. She brought the house down with her performances. But she's innocent of murder, innocent of arson. How can Michael DeCastro possibly hope to defend this beautiful drag queen, who brings with her a whole pack of nasty little secrets, straight from Bangkok's notorious tenderloin district? She speaks in aphorisms, the wisdom of the Buddha combined with the lyrics of Whitney Houston. She is fascinating. And Michael can't let her go to jail. 1/3

2189. **Peffer, Randall,** *Old School Ties,* Bleak House, 2008. Cape Island #3 of 6. (Hard Boiled) Winter in a New England prep school brings term papers, wet snow, and the suicide of a young black student. Except Liberty Baker's friends are convinced she couldn't have taken her own life, and Liberty's faculty advisor, Awasha Patterson, believes them. –Tuki reappears to assist in the investigation (MLM). 1/3

2190. **Peffer, Randall,** *Bangkok Dragons, Cape Cod Tears,* Bleak House, 2009. Cape Island #4 of 6. (Hard Boiled) When Michael Decastro gets an email from Tuki his long-gone client, the lady of ten thousand mysteries he doesn't hesitate a moment. He heads to Bangkok to find what? He doesn't know. To face what dangers? He hasn't imagined. All he knows is that she's beckoned, and he can't resist her call. And now, face-to-face with Tuki and a ruby so beautiful it has its own name, Michael must make a choice: move forward, protect Tuki, get to the bottom of her entanglement with the nak lin and see that she's safe, or run back to his father's fishing boat, hiding from the ills of the world beneath a watch cap and a raincoat. –the next two books do not have gay characters or themes (MLM). 2/3

2191. **Pelham, Raydon,** *Shame,* Idol, 1998. (Pulp) Martyn Townsend is on holiday in L.A. when a beautiful young man approaches him in a gay club. But passion soon turns to intrigue as Martyn discovers that mysterious strangers are pursuing his new admirer. Martyn's quest to discover the truth about his lover takes him back to London and then on to the hedonistic, sun-kissed resort of Ibiza. And his body is often called into service to buy the secrets he needs from the many men he meets along the way. 3/3

2192. **Pepper, Peter (Lyal H. Stevens),** *Brass Cock,* Surrey, 1972. (Pulp) "Television news commentator Temple King saves Kirby Wilkes from being killed, but his actual sleuthing is minor in a pulp whodunit (Gunn)." 3/3

2193. **Pepper, Peter,** *Big Dick,* Surree, 1975. (Pulp) "Surrogate sleuth York McRoy, a city parks employee, plays an altruistic role in bringing to justice in a pulp suspense thriller (Gunn)." 3/3

2194. **Perkins, Gary,** *Closet Governor,* iUniverse, 2004. (Political) Closeted Lieutenant Governor George Vantage is sworn in as governor after the sudden resignation of the incumbent but soon finds himself threatened by an anonymous caller eager to expose the "faggot governor." Reporter Michael Harrington views the new governor as his ticket onto the front page of his newspaper. He knows firsthand that Vantage is gay, but he also senses that there is a bigger story. Jason Covington is a peeping tom who gets off watching the new governor sleep. His antics end when security cameras catch him spying on Vantage. 3/3

2195. **Perry, Max (Jerry Oster),** *Final Cut,* Fawcett, 1980. (Police Procedural) "New York *Village Voice* reporter Stephen Foner turns over files to police officer Joseph Sparks to help him unravel the plot behind the sabotage of a film about a serial killer at loose in Greenwich Village in a whodunit (Gunn)." –plot based partly on the filming of *Cruising* (MLM). 3/3

2196. **Perry, Meg (Rachel Owens),** *Cited to Death,* Createspace, 2012. Jamie Brodie #1 of 17. (Bibliomystery Cozy) Academic librarian Jamie Brodie hasn't seen old boyfriend Dan Christensen in years. When Jamie reads Dan's obituary in the paper, he's surprised. When he receives a letter from Dan, written just before his death, Jamie is shocked. Dan's letter suggests that Dan was in danger, lists two article citations from medical journals, and asks Jamie to look into the citations. When Jamie requests the articles, strange things begin to happen. His computer is hacked, his tires are slashed, he thinks someone might be following him - and he uncovers two more deaths. The coroner's report says that Dan died of natural causes - but did he? Is there something suspicious about the articles, or was Dan just paranoid? The closer Jamie gets to answering those questions, the more it seems that someone is trying to stop him... 3/3

2197. **Perry, Meg,** *Hoarded to Death,* Createspace, 2013. Jamie Brodie #2 of 17. (Bibliomystery Cozy) When Jamie Brodie agrees to help his ex-sister-in-law Jennifer clean her hoarded apartment, the last thing he expects to find in the hoard is a dead body – and what the dead man was clutching in his hand might be the answer to a thousand-year-old mystery. As Jamie and the police investigate, they uncover a hoard of secrets – but the biggest secret of all belongs to Jamie's boyfriend, Pete. Suddenly Jamie is searching for the answers to three questions: who killed the man in Jennifer's apartment? Is the paper in his hand real? And can Jamie's relationship with Pete survive? 3/3

2198. **Perry, Meg,** *Burdened to Death,* Createspace, 2013. Jamie Brodie #3 of 17. (Bibliomystery Cozy) A phone call in the middle of the night is never good news. When Pete Ferguson's phone rings, he learns that one of his childhood friends, Mark Jones, has committed suicide. Mark's family is shocked, and wonders if Mark was abused by the same priest at whose hands Pete suffered. Pete and Mark's family want answers, and they ask Jamie to find them. Pete is convinced the priest is connected to his friend's suicide. Jamie isn't so sure. When the evidence starts pulling them in different directions, will it tear them apart? 3/3

2199. **Perry, Meg,** *Researched to Death,* Createspace, 2014. Jamie Brodie #4 of 17. (Bibliomystery Cozy) Librarian Jamie Brodie is looking forward to a week of vacation in Oxford, England, his first trip back in seven years. Before he's even packed, though, a couple of complications arise. 3/3

2200. **Perry, Meg,** *Encountered to Death,* Createspace, 2014. Jamie Brodie #5 of 17. (Bibliomystery Cozy) It seems Jamie Brodie can't go anywhere any more without a body turning up. Jamie and his boyfriend Pete Ferguson are taking a week of vacation to visit Pete's brother Steve in Alamogordo, New Mexico. They arrive to find that Alamogordo has been invaded - by fans of a TV show called Alien Visitors. The host of the show, Dixon Gill, was found dead in the lobby of Steve's building. Gill's fans believe he was killed by the FBI because he was about to reveal the truth about the government's cover-up of alien visitations. Jamie and Pete know that's not true. But who did kill Gill? The director of his show? A competitor on the same network? An angry commenter on Gill's blog? A shadowy anti-government group? Or one of his ex-wives? The deeper Jamie probes into Gill's past, the more potential suspects he finds. The truth is out there - but can Jamie uncover it? 3/3

2201. **Perry, Meg,** *Psyched to Death,* Createspace, 2014. Jamie Brodie #6 of 17. (Bibliomystery Cozy) Who killed Matt Bendel? The police suspect his partner, Elliott Conklin, the assistant chair of the psychology department at Santa Monica College. Elliott was found with the body, covered in blood – and he doesn't have an alibi. Elliott wants Pete Ferguson to help clear his name. But Pete doesn't have time – he's had to take over one of Elliott's classes – and he thinks Elliott might be guilty. Jamie Brodie isn't so sure. Matt had a secret that may have gotten him killed. The investigation of that secret leads to someone from Jamie's past - and another death that will change Jamie forever. 3/3

2202. **Perry, Meg,** *Stacked to Death,* Createspace, 2014. Jamie Brodie #7 of 17. (Bibliomystery Cozy) Library work-study student Austin Sharp upset a lot of people. When Jamie Brodie finds Austin dead, strangled to death in the library stacks, the police have plenty of suspects. When another library work-study student is found strangled, the focus of the investigation shifts – both students were from the same hometown. Then a third student is found dead. A serial killer is on the loose, and the police send in detectives from the elite Homicide Special unit. 3/3

2203. **Perry, Meg,** *Stoned to Death,* Createspace, 2015. Jamie Brodie #8 of 17. (Bibliomystery Cozy) In 1915, farmer and amateur archaeologist Robert Thomson disappeared from Scotland's Orkney Islands with a priceless Stone Age artifact. A century later, his great-great-grandson, Pete Ferguson, is coming to Scotland with boyfriend Jamie Brodie to meet his distant cousins and investigate

Robert's disappearance. But the homophobia of the Thomson patriarch threatens to derail their quest - and a chance meeting in a pub in Oxford brings Pete and Jamie's relationship to a turning point. 3/3

2204. **Perry, Meg,** *Talked to Death,* Createspace, 2015. Jamie Brodie #9 of 17. (Bibliomystery Cozy) Librarians gone wild! It's a typical state library association conference - presentations, networking, receptions, drinking, strangers appearing in Pete and Jamie's room in the middle of the night... What's atypical is murder. A lot of people hated library director Hugo Creighton, most of them librarians. Can Jamie help the police solve Creighton's murder before the conference ends and the suspects go home? 3/3

2205. **Perry, Meg,** *Avenged to Death,* Createspace, 2015. Jamie Brodie #10 of 17. (Bibliomystery Cozy) Who is Randall Chesterson Barkley, and why has he named Jamie Brodie and his brothers in his will? The answer to that question leads Jamie to another answer: the story of what really happened to his mom. Then two murders throw Jamie, Kevin and Jeff into an investigation that uncovers more secrets from the past - and forces Jamie into a decision where there is no option for a happy ending. 3/3

2206. **Perry, Meg,** *Played to Death,* Createspace, 2015. Jamie Brodie #11 of 17. (Bibliomystery Cozy) Jamie Brodie and Pete Ferguson are attending the lavishly over-the-top wedding of an acquaintance of Pete's when Jamie spots a ghost from his past in the string quartet - Scott Deering, the last guy he dated before Pete. The murder at the wedding is shocking, but it's not Jamie's business - until a theft from the music library at UCLA sucks him into the investigation. All Jamie wants to do is finalize the plans for his own wedding to Pete, but first he has to join forces with Scott to track down a killer - and deal with another ghost that throws everyone's lives into turmoil. 3/3

2207. **Perry, Meg,** *Filmed to Death,* Createspace, 2016. Jamie Brodie #12 of 17. (Bibliomystery Cozy) Rafe Conroy, has-been actor, is filming the first episode of the TV show intended to be his big comeback. But Rafe's comeback is cut short when he's found dead in his swimming pool. It was murder, all right, but there are nearly too many suspects to count. Was it the network owner, a wealthy heiress who was sleeping with Rafe? Was it the jealous girlfriend? Was it the cast member who hated Rafe? Was it the scriptwriter who saw his masterpiece edited into schlock? Was it Rafe's drug dealer? Or was it the drug dealer's ex-wife – Abby Glenn, Kevin Brodie's ex-girlfriend – who just happened to discover the body? Because of Abby's involvement, Kevin can't work the case. It's up to Jon Eckhoff and Jamie Brodie to figure out who would benefit most from Rafe's death

– before the killer strikes again. 3/3

2208. **Perry, Meg,** *Trapped to Death,* Createspace, 2016. Jamie Brodie #13 of 17. (Bibliomystery Cozy) Autumn brings a fresh start in academia, but there are signs that Jamie Brodie's autumn quarter might bring trouble. First, his next-door neighbors unexpectedly drop off the grid. Several days later Jamie discovers - with the help of his dog - that something very bad has happened in the neighbors' house. When the victim is identified, Jamie briefly becomes a suspect - but something far more dangerous is lying in wait for Jamie. And he doesn't recognize it until it's too late. 3/3

2209. **Perry, Meg,** *Promoted to Death,* Createspace, 2017. Jamie Brodie #14 of 17. (Bibliomystery Cozy) Elaine Pareja didn't have any fans among her colleagues in the psychology department at Santa Monica College. When her promotion application is denied, and she is terminated, no one is sorry to see her go. When Elaine is reinstated for no apparent reason, it causes a revolt in the department. When she turns up dead, her colleagues turn into suspects. But Elaine was a keeper of secrets - other people's, and her own. Jamie Brodie and his friend, business librarian Sheila Meadows, join forces with the police to pick their way through the tangled web of Elaine's life, searching for the thread that led to her death. 3/3

2210. **Perry, Meg,** *Published to Death,* Createspace, 2017. Jamie Brodie #15 of 17. (Bibliomystery Cozy) Mercedes Moran is one of the stars of the self-publishing world, a romance author who's made millions by selling 99 cent romance novels through all of the e-book platforms. Her fan base is enormous - but Mercedes is a horrible person, and she's made plenty of enemies, too. The Association of Self-Publishing is holding its annual conference on UCLA's campus, and Mercedes is the keynote speaker. When Jamie Brodie and Kristen Beach attend the keynote at the encouragement of their supervisors, they get an earful from other conference-goers about Mercedes. But it's nothing to do with them. Until Mercedes turns up dead in the back of the exhibit hall. Kevin Brodie and Jon Eckhoff are on the case, and they enlist Jamie's and Kristen's help with navigating the world of self-published authors. But the case takes a turn for the weird when Kevin and Jon are joined by a lieutenant from Internal Affairs, who claims to be brushing up on his investigative skills - and who only speaks in clichés. Who killed Mercedes? Why is a desk jockey from Internal Affairs dogging Kevin and Jon's every step? And why do so many covers of male-male romance novels feature headless torsos?? –Perry pokes fun at herself and the genre she writes. A short story, "Dirty Laundry" is available via e-book only (MLM). 3/3

2211. **Perry, Meg,** *Cloistered to Death,* Createspace, 2018. Jamie Brodie

#16 of 17. (Bibliomystery Cozy) Jamie Brodie is on deadline. The proposal for his second book is due, and he desperately needs uninterrupted writing time. At the suggestion of patron, friend, and former monk Clinton Kenneally - and over the protests of Pete Ferguson, Jamie's husband - Jamie schedules a week-long writing retreat at a local monastery. But the monastery is not exactly what Jamie expected...which might explain the flicker of disquiet in Clinton's eyes. Meanwhile, Kevin Brodie and Jon Eckhoff are dealing with a dead drug dealer, doggie diarrhea, and a camera crew from the reality TV show Two Days to Solve. The camera loves Jon, and vice versa. Kevin's just trying to refrain from swearing on TV. But when the victim turns out to be someone from Kevin's past, the case gets a whole lot more interesting. And there's no way it'll be solved in two days. 3/3

2212. **Perry, Meg,** *Haunted to Death,* Createspace, 2018. Jamie Brodie #17 of 17. (Bibliomystery Cozy) Jamie Brodie and his entire family are on vacation in Scotland, staying at their ancestral home, Brodie Castle. The family's fun is interrupted by a threat of blackmail... then they fall under suspicion when the blackmailer turns up dead. Jamie, Pete, Kevin, and Kristen set out to clear the Brodie name. Along the way they encounter a ghostly sighting, a wild rumor, centuries-old curses, and a massive cover-up. Will they find the truth before the detectives from Police Scotland arrest the wrong man? –e-book only (MLM). 3/3

2213. **Phillips, Edward O.,** *Sunday's Child,* McClelland & Stewart, 1981. Chadwick #1 of 6. (Thriller) Disposing of a corpse is no easy task–particularly on New Year's Eve, and particularly for upstanding lawyer Geoffry Chadwick. For Chadwick brought home the wrong kind of stranger and, while defending himself, dispatched his visitor too well. –main character is gay (MLM). 3/3

2214. **Phillips, Edward O.,** *Buried on Sunday,* McClelland & Stewart, 1986. Chadwick #2 of 6. (Thriller) When Geoffrey Chadwick, a gay lawyer, and the other guests at a country house are taken captive by criminals on the run from the law, he reminisces about one of the other hostages, a former lover, now married. 3/3

2215. **Phillips, Edward O.,** *Sunday Best,* McClelland & Stewart, 1990. Chadwick #3 of 6. (Thriller) Geoffrey Chadwick is back and this time (the) reluctant hero and social observer is going to a wedding - or maybe not. Geoffrey's niece, Jennifer, is about to marry Douglas, son of a prominent - or at very least notorious - Montreal socialite, Lois Fullerton. Lois is a wealthy widow with an impressive list of discarded lovers and it looks like she's decided Geoffrey will be her next conquest. But after meeting Lois on several occasions, Chadwick discovers he is being followed. Soon a nasty knife wound - on the front tire of his car - and a nasty note thicken the plot. Has Lois masterminded a trap? Who is her suspicious, swarthy, and sexy chauffeur? And why is the bridegroom more interested in his future brother-in-law than his future bride? 3/3

2216. **Phillips, Edward O.**, *Working on Sunday*, McClelland & Stewart, 1998. Chadwick #4 of 6. (Thriller) Facing a bleak Christmas following the sudden death of his friend Patrick, Geoffry Chadwick is cheered to discover a kindred spirit in the recently widowed Elinor Richardson. Amid the sinister forces of consumerism, eggnog, his sister Mildred and social obligations, Geoffry is also having to deal with a voice from the past that threatens to make this Christmas his last. 3/3

2217. **Phillips, Edward O.**, *A Voyage on Sunday*, Riverbank, 2004. Chadwick #5 of 6. (Thriller) No act of kindness goes unpunished; Geoffrey Chadwick discovers this cynical truism has greater truth in it than not when he reluctantly agrees to work on an amateur production of Hedda Gabler to raise funds for the Westmount Library. Chadwick, a retired lawyer, embarks on a Caribbean cruise won in a raffle. His companion is an old school friend, Frank Wilkinson. The travelers are beset by flu, boring table mates, and a flamboyant quartet who make overtures to Geoffrey. A thwarted love affair further complicates the voyage, and Geoffrey returns to Montreal, resigned to the inevitable fact of growing old. 3/3

2218. **Phillips, Edward O.**, *A Month of Sundays*, Cormorant Books, 2012. Chadwick #6 of 6. (Thriller) At the age of seventy, Geoffry Chadwick's life is ready to begin again. To commemorate his wife Elinor's death, seventy-year-old retiree Geoffry Chadwick plans to hold a grand party in lieu of a memorial service. His decision indirectly triggers a chain of surprising events: a man named Harold visits from Toronto, claiming to be his son from a youthful fling. Also visiting is his childhood friend Larry, accompanied by a new lover, Desmond, who Geoffry immediately takes a liking to. As the day of the party approaches, events take a turn for the worse. 3/3

2219. **Phillips, Rick,** *The Cop on 69th Street,* Surrey, 1973. (Pulp) "Telephone installer Ben, though he saves Billy, 19, from the machinations of a psychotic title character, does no sleuthing to nail the rogue officer in a pulp suspense thriller (Gunn)." 3/3

2220. **Phoenix, Wolf,** *Irreversible Error,* Dreamspinner, 2010. Error #1 of 2. (MM Police Procedural) Asked by an old friend for help solving her son's mysterious death, cop Erik Steppenwolf plunges into Houston's night world of drag queens and hustlers. First, he enlists the aid of a flamboyant drag queen named Lola, who introduces him to street hustlers who may have clues to the murderer's identity.

During one of Lola's outrageous shows, a naughty but nice dancer named Red bursts onto the scene, stealing Steppenwolf's heart. As the commitment between Red and Steppenwolf grows, each piece of the murderous puzzle uncovered reveals a wild string of events that leads to a capital murder conviction... but also a nagging suspicion that there's a lot more to the story. When he and Red break up, there's no reason for Steppenwolf to stay in Houston, unless he makes up his mind not to let go of his search for the truth–or Red. 3/3

2221. **Phoenix, Wolf,** *Acts of Redemption,* Dreamspinner, 2010. Error #2 of 2. (MM Police Procedural) After a murder investigation gone tragically wrong, Detective Erik Steppenwolf is determined to track down the man who killed his lover and his friend's son. His quest sends him on an around-the-world trek to bring the culprit to justice, and he'll take on the Russian Mafia, disinterested law enforcement officers, and misinformed witnesses to get to the bottom of the mystery. 3/3

2222. **Picano, Felice,** *The Lure,* Delacorte, 1979. (Psychological) Noel Cummings's life is about to change irrevocably. After witnessing a brutal murder, Noel is recruited to assist the police by acting as the lure for a killer who has been targeting gay men. Undercover, Noel moves deeper and deeper into the dark side of Manhattan's gay life that stirs his own secret desires–until he forgets he is only playing a role. 3/3

2223. **Picano, Felice,** *The Book of Lies,* Little Brown, 1998. (Thriller) Bright, ambitious, and handsome, Ross Ohrenstedt is a high flier in the fashionable field of queer studies. He has just taken a prestigious university position in Los Angeles and has been appointed to oversee the collection of papers and works of a leading light of the gay literary salon known as the Purple Circle. Ross stumbles across a lost work by an unknown author and his quest to identify the mystery writer and achieve the glory of scholastic tenure unveils increasingly bizarre and unbalanced facts about a group of writers who in the 1970s and 1980s broke new ground in the creation of a gay literary sensibility. But the dark truth contained within The Book of Lies is even more startling. With biting wit and a lush sense of place and character, Felice Picano's daring novel is at once a stylish mystery, a comical roman A clef, and a wicked send-up of the new Ivory Tower. 3/3

2224. **Picano, Felice,** *Onyx,* Alyson, 2001. (Psychological) Three men. Two gay, one straight. Two searching for meaning in the face of loss, one searching for the heart of masculinity. What awakens between them will change their lives forever. The narrative-exploring six months in the life of Ray Henriques, a successful Manhattan record producer-unearths a sometimes jolting examination of how loss can awaken dormant desires and postponed dreams. Endings lead to beginnings, appearances do not match reality, and love can harden hearts as surely as it can expand them. 3/3

2225. **Pickens, Steve,** *Final Departure,* Bold Stroke Books, 2016. Finnigan #1 of 2. (Amateur Sleuth) Jake Finnigan is already having the worst day of his life when the corpse of notorious tabloid reporter Susan Crane is found locked in the trunk of her car on the ferry where he works. Worse still, though Crane is bound, gagged, and shot in the forehead, her death is ruled a suicide. 3/3

2226. **Pickens, Steve,** *Sinister Justice,* Bold Stroke Books, 2018. Finnigan #2 of 2. (Amateur Sleuth) Arrow Bay: a picturesque seaside city of parks, mountain trails, incredible views...and corpses. An unidentified vigilante, unhappy with plans to alter the idyllic character of Jake Finnigan's hometown, goes to extreme ends–in disturbingly creative and fatal ways–to express their displeasure. 3/3

2227. **Pierce, Max,** *The Master of Seacliff,* Haworth, 2007. (Gothic Romance) The year is 1899, and Andrew Wyndham is twenty years old - no longer a boy, but not yet the man he longs to become. Brought up by a harsh and stingy aunt and uncle in New York City after the death of his parents, young Andrew dreams of life as an artist in Paris. He has talent enough but lacks the resources to bring his dream to fruition. When a friend arranges for him to work as tutor to the son of a wealthy patron of the arts, Andrew sees a chance to make his dream come true and boards a train heading up the Atlantic coast. His destination is the estate called Seacliff, where he'll tutor his new charge and save his pay to make the life he dreams of possible. But danger lurks everywhere, and nothing is quite as easy as it seems. 3/3

2228. **Piercy, Rohase,** *My Dearest Holmes,* GMP, 1988. (Historical) Together Holmes and Watson face disturbing revelations as they investigate the case of the Queen Bee; and we finally learn what actually happened at the Reichenbach Falls and the real reasons which lay behind Holmes' faked death and subsequent return. 3/3

2229. **Pincus, Elizabeth,** *The Two-Bit Tango,* Spinster's Book Co., 1992. Fury #1 of 3. (Hard Boiled) When ex-private investigator Nell Fury is hired by Olive Jones to find her missing twin, she finds herself involved in a world of shady real estate deals, prostitution, pornography, and corrupt politicians. –gay crooked politician (MM). 1/3

2230. **Plakcy, Neil,** *Mahu,* Haworth, 2005. Mahu #1 of 10. (Police Procedural) Kimo Kanapa'aka's world turns upside down in Mahu. At 32, the hero of Māhū has reached the pinnacle of his profession, detective on the Honolulu Police Department's homicide squad, based at the Waikīkī station. But a difficult murder case, as well as turmoil in his personal life, is about to threaten everything he has worked for. 3/3

2231. **Plakcy, Neil,** *Mahu Surfer,* Alyson, 2007. Mahu #2 of 10. (Police Procedural) Mahu is a generally negative Hawaiian term for homosexual, and for police detective Kimo Kanapa'aka, being gay doesn't make for an easy life. Especially when you're publicly outed. Now, semi-retired, Kimo must go undercover and stop a brutal killer. Already three surfers have been shot dead, and Kimo must infiltrate the close-knit surfing community, knowing his only way back to active duty is to catch a killer he may know all too well. 3/3

2232. **Plakcy, Neil,** *Mahu Fire,* Alyson, 2008. Mahu #3 of 10. (Police Procedural) Evil moves to paradise, as openly gay police detective Kimo Kanapa'aka battles an extreme religious group that opposes the idea of same-sex marriage. It begins with a simple shooting, but the danger intensifies as Kimo strives to unmask a killer. 3/3

2233. **Plakcy, Neil,** *Mahu Vice,* Alyson, 2009. Mahu #4 of 10. (Police Procedural) Months have passed since Honolulu homicide detective Kimo Kanapa'aka walked away from the blaze at Wa'ahila State Park–and from his partner Mike. Now, Kimo and Mike must work together to solve an arson-homicide while attempting to mend their relationship. 3/3

2234. **Plakcy, Neil,** *Mahu Blood,* MLR, 2011. Mahu #5 of 10. (Police Procedural) Billions of dollars are at stake in a fight over who the land of the Aloha State really belongs to. Is it the United States– or the indigenous people of the islands, many of whom feel their sovereign kingdom was overthrown by American businessmen? At the same time, Kimo and his fire investigator partner, Mike Riccardi, deal with the stress of moving in together to create their own ohana –- a Hawaiian term which means family, as well as community. 3/3

2235. **Plakcy, Neil,** *Zero Break,* MLR, 2012. Mahu #6 of 10. (Police Procedural) Zero break refers to the deep-water location where waves first begin, often far offshore. For Honolulu homicide detective and surfer Kimo Kanapa'aka, it means his most dangerous case yet. A young mother is murdered in what appears to be a home invasion robbery, leaving behind a complex skein of family and business relationships, and Kimo and his detective partner Ray Donne must navigate deadly waters to uncover the true motive behind her death and bring her killer to justice. –*Mahu Men,* a collection of short stories that bring in an MM romance element of graphic sex scenes which are not included in his full-length novels (MLM). 3/3

2236. **Plakcy, Neil,** *Natural Predators,* MLR, 2013. Mahu #7 of 10. (Police Procedural) The beautiful tropical island of O'ahu is filled with predators, from high-flying owls to bottom-dwelling criminals. When the body of an island patrician is found in a warehouse fire, tracking his killers will bring openly gay Honolulu homicide detective Kimo Kanapa'aka into contact with many of those predators, natural and otherwise. Kimo and his detective partner Ray Donne dig deep into the history of Hawai'i as the islands were teetering on the brink of statehood in order to understand the victim, his killer, and their motives. Kimo and his partner, fire investigator Mike Riccardi, decide to become foster parents for a homeless teen who witnessed the crime, while preparing to become dads themselves. 3/3

2237. **Plakcy, Neil,** *Accidental Contact,* MLR, 2014. Mahu #8 of 10. (Police Procedural) From murderers to missing babies to a shaggy dog with an unusual appetite, openly gay Honolulu homicide detective Kimo Kanapa'aka has his hands full in this selection of ten short investigations in the Aloha State. Sun-drenched streets hide bodies in their shadows and clues lurk in the most unusual places, from a hearse to flowering hedge to a psychic who provides Kimo with an unexpected revelation. –another collection of short stories that fill in gaps throughout the series but is listed as the eighth book in the series (MLM). 3/3

2238. **Plakcy, Neil,** *Children of Noah,* MLR, 2015. Mahu #9 of 10. (Police Procedural) A few months after the birth of his twins, openly gay Honolulu homicide detective Kimo Kanapa'aka begins a temporary assignment to the FBI's Joint Terrorism Task Force. Kimo and his HPD partner Ray Donne are quickly thrown into an investigation into threatening letters sent to a U.S. Senator. Are these screeds about racial purity related to an escalating series of attacks against mixed-race couples and families on Oahu? –*Kimo and Mike* is a short story with no mystery involved, just an MM romance (MLM). 3/3

2239. **Plakcy, Neil,** *Ghost Ship,* MLR, 2016. Mahu #10 of 10. (Police Procedural) When a sailboat carrying four bodies washes up on the Leeward Coast of O'ahu, openly gay Honolulu homicide detective Kimo Kanapa'aka, on loan to the FBI, must discover what sent this young family and their deadly cargo on a dangerous trans-Pacific voyage. Leaving behind his partner and their infant twins, Kimo must work with his police cohort Ray Donne to unravel the forces that led this family to their deaths. 3/3

2240. **Plakcy, Neil,** *Three Wrong Turns in the Desert,* Loose Id, 2009. Have Body Will Guard #1 of 9. (MM Suspense) From the moment he sees handsome Liam McCullough showering naked behind a Tunisian bar, ESL teacher Aidan Greene wants to screw the sexy bodyguard. At first, though, a dead courier and beefy hired thugs get in the way. But Liam soon convinces him – with wiles and smiles and solid logic – to join him on a race across the desert for a rendezvous with a Tuareg tribe at a remote oasis. Then nothing can stop them from getting naked and getting it on. Together they explore the passion Liam hid from as a closeted Navy SEAL, and the love Aidan's missed after his long-term boyfriend kicked him to the curb. 3/3

2241. **Plakcy, Neil**, *Dancing with the Tide,* Loose Id, 2010. Have Body Will Guard #2 of 9. (MM Suspense) Someone wants to kill cute, sexy gay pop star Karif al-Fulan, and it's up to bodyguards Liam McCullough and Aidan Greene to keep him safe. But will Karif destroy the burgeoning love between Liam and Aidan with his intimate advances? Between passionate romps in a private villa on the resort island of Djerba, off the coast of Tunisia, Liam and Aidan must face down bombs, guns, and the pressure of their own testosterone. 3/3

2242. **Plakcy, Neil**, *Teach Me Tonight,* Loose Id, 2011. Have Body Will Guard #3 of 9. (MM Suspense) Bodyguards Aidan Greene and Liam McCullough are hired to protect a spoiled teenager attending an English-language institute. Liam worries that Aidan loves teaching too much to commit to their bodyguard business – but when things go wrong and Liam's sexy SEAL buddy Joey shows up to help out, career options become the least of their problems. 3/3

2243. **Plakcy, Neil**, *Olives for the Stranger,* Loose Id, 2012. Have Body Will Guard #4 of 9. (MM Suspense) As demonstrators and police spar in the streets of Tunis, bodyguards Aidan and Liam must protect Leila, a young girl whose mother has been taken into police custody. While the threats against her and her activist parents grow, hunky ex-SEAL Liam is stuck in the Tunisian countryside while teacher and novice bodyguard Aidan travels to France on his own with Leila. 3/3

2244. **Plakcy, Neil**, *Under the Waterfall,* Loose Id, 2013. Have Body Will Guard #5 of 9. (MM Suspense) As soon as they're settled in their new home on the French Riviera, Aidan and Liam are sent to the island of Corsica to protect a mining executive and his family. The disruption, and the discovery that the client's son is gay and in a touchy relationship, causes both bodyguards to question their skills and their commitment to each other. 3/3

2245. **Plakcy, Neil**, *The Noblest Vengeance,* Loose Id, 2014. Have Body Will Guard #6 of 9. (MM Suspense) Bodyguard partners Aidan and Liam are deeply in love, living as expatriates in Nice, France. When Aidan's distant cousins in Istanbul need protection from dangerous adversaries, he and Liam are on the the next plane to Turkey – but the real danger to their relationship may come from their very different ideas about family connections. Can their love withstand assassins with a deadly secret to keep hidden – and Liam's foul-mouthed mother? 3/3

2246. **Plakcy, Neil,** *Finding Freddie Venus,* Loose Id, 2015. Have Body Will Guard #7 of 9. (MM Suspense) Aidan and Liam's new client is former gay porn star Freddie Venus, who survived an epic slide and now lives a solitary life in a restored farmhouse outside Nice. He hires bodyguards when he begins to believe he is being stalked. 3/3

2247. **Plakcy, Neil,** *A Cold Wind,* Loose Id, 2016. Have Body Will Guard #8 of 9. (MM Suspense) Now that he's been forced out of the closet and moved to Monaco, retired Russian oligarch Slava Vishinev longs for a sexy new life. An assassination attempt forces him to hire bodyguards Aidan and Liam to protect him. But can they keep him alive long enough to engineer a romance between him and their sad, handsome neighbor, still pining for his late lover? 3/3

2248. **Plakcy, Neil,** *The Same Page,* Samwise, 2018. Have Body Will Guard #9 of 9. (MM Suspense) Aidan Greene and Liam McCullough feel like they've aged out of the bodyguard business–but a desperate call from former client Slava Vishinev draws them back. In a story ripped from the headlines, Slava's gay son Arseny has vanished in Chechnya, where homosexuals are persecuted and imprisoned. –e-book only (MLM). 3/3

2249. **Plakcy, Neil,** *The Next One Will Kill You,* Diversion Books, 2016. Angus Green #1 of 3. (Police Procedural) Angus wants more adventure than a boring accounting job, so after graduating with his master's degree he signs up with the FBI. He's assigned to the Miami field office, where the caseload includes smugglers, drug runners, and gangs, but he starts out stuck behind a desk, an accountant with a badge and gun. It's his first real case: a desperate chase to catch a gang of criminals with their tentacles in everything from medical fraud to drugs to jewel theft. With every corner in this case–from Fort Lauderdale's gay bars to the morgue–turning to mayhem, Angus quickly learns that the only way to face a challenge is to assume that he'll survive this one–it's the next one that will kill him. 3/3

2250. **Plakcy, Neil,** *Nobody Rides for Free,* Diversion Books, 2017. Angus Green #2 of 3. (Police Procedural) With less than a year of experience under his belt and only one big case behind him, FBI Special Agent Angus Green has joined the rarefied group of agents who have been wounded in the line of duty. Now, assigned to a desk job while he recovers, Angus wonders if he's chosen the right career. He's been following his late father's dream for a life of adventure and travel–and instead encountered danger, pain and heartbreak. But when he discovers that gay teens are being sexually abused by a pornographer in the same neighborhood where he lives, he has to step up and bring his intelligence, his determination, and his unique insights to save these young men. 3/3

2251. **Plakcy, Neil,** *Survival is a Dying Art,* Diversion, 2018. Angus Green #3 of 3. (Police Procedural) Fort Lauderdale retiree Frank Sena is working with pawn shop owner Jesse Venable to retrieve a painting stolen from Frank's uncle, a gay Venetian killed during the Holocaust. Angus volunteers to help Frank, and discovers Venable is the subject of a task force looking into smuggling immigrants out of war-torn countries in the Middle East. 3/3

2252. **Podojil, E. William,** *The Tenth Man,* Haworth, 2004. (Thriller) Jack Barillo is losing friends–the hard way. A cunning killer named Lucifer is savaging the beautiful young men from Jack's past, eliminating them with a surgeon's touch, one by one. From Lincoln Park in Chicago, to the spire mansions and tradesmen houses of Amsterdam, to the rounded hills and uncharted mountains of the Le Marche region in Italy, the manhunter ruthlessly stalks and destroys his prey with horrifying precision, and each victim brings him one step closer to Jack. The Tenth Man is a twisted mystery full of secrets and lies, a sexy, scary thriller that plays out across oceans, continents, and lifetimes. Haunted by a string of grisly murders to which he's somehow linked, Jack escapes to Europe with little to his name save the will to survive. With the help of a resourceful gay couple, a determined Chicago homicide detective and her well-connected husband, and a mysterious FBI agent, Jack builds a new life, finding success, wealth, and love. Everything but peace. Just as Jack starts to convince himself that he's imagined the decade-long nightmare, Lucifer strikes again. The Tenth Man is the dark tale of one man's need for revenge-and another's need to survive. 3/3

2253. **Poe, C. S.,** *The Mystery of Nevermore,* DSP, 2016. Snow and Winter #1 of 3. (MM Amateur Sleuth) It's Christmas, and all antique dealer Sebastian Snow wants is for his business to make money and to save his floundering relationship with closeted CSU detective, Neil Millett. When Snow's Antique Emporium is broken into and a heart is found under the floorboards, Sebastian can't let the mystery rest. –Poe has two short stories listed on her website for free that is not a mystery that follows book one (MLM). 3/3

2254. **Poe, C. S.,** *The Mystery of Curiosities,* DSP, 2017. Snow and Winter #2 of 3. (MM Amateur Sleuth) Life has been pretty great for Sebastian Snow. The Emporium is thriving and his relationship with

NYPD homicide detective, Calvin Winter, is everything he's ever wanted. With Valentine's Day around the corner, Sebastian's only cause for concern is whether Calvin should be taken on a romantic date. It's only when an unknown assailant smashes the Emporium's window and leaves a peculiar note behind, that all plans get pushed aside in favor of another mystery. –there is one short story available on the author's website that follows this novel that is not a mystery (MM). 3/3

2255. **Poe, C. S.**, *The Mystery of the Moving Image,* DSP, 2018. Snow and Winter #3 of 3. (MM Amateur Sleuth) It's summer in New York City, and antique shop owner Sebastian Snow is taking the next big step in his relationship with NYPD homicide detective, Calvin Winter: they're moving in together. What should have been a wonderful week of playing house and celebrating Calvin's birthday comes to an abrupt end when a mysterious package arrives at the Emporium. –one short story is available on the author's website that is not a mystery (MLM). 3/3

2256. **Poe, C. S.**, *Southernmost Murder,* DSP, 2018. (MM Amateur Sleuth) Aubrey Grant lives in the tropical paradise of Old Town, Key West, has a cute cottage, a sweet moped, and a great job managing the historical property of a former sea captain. With his soon-to-be-boyfriend, hotshot FBI agent Jun Tanaka, visiting for a little R&R, not even Aubrey's narcolepsy can put a damper on their vacation plans. 3/3

2257. **Porter, Darwin,** *Midnight in Savannah,* Georgia Literary Association, 2008. (Amateur Sleuth) Both Lavender Morgan ('At 72, the world's oldest courtesan') and Tipper Zelda ('an obese, fading chanteuse taunted as the black widow') purchase lust from sexually conflicted young men with drop-dead faces, chiseled bodies, and genetically gifted crotches. These women once relied on their physicality to steal the hearts and fortunes of the world's richest and most powerful men. Now, as they slide closer every day to joining the corpses of their former husbands, these once-beautiful women must depend, in a perverse twist of fate, on sexual outlaws for le petit mort. And to survive, the hustlers must idle their personal dreams while struggling to cajole what they need from a sexual liaison they detest. –based on the book, *Midnight in the Garden of Good and Evil*, from a southern perspective (MLM). 2/3

2258. **Post, George,** *No Escape,* Market Arcade, 1967. (Pulp) Mystery-thriller hetero-sexcapades. –heterosexuals being hunted by homosexuals (MLM). 3/3

2259. **Powell, Brad,** *The Shadow on the Sand,* XXX. 1971. (Pulp) California amnesia victim Xenophon (Fon) Dmitri, aka William P. (Skip)

Saunders, 22, bisexual, searches for his identity in San Francisco and the murderer who tried to kill him in order to assume that identity, bit his search is only part of a complex psychological thriller (Gunn)." 3/3

2260. **Powell, Mason,** *For the Love of the Green-Eyed Piano Player,* Xlibris, 2001. (Thriller) Michael Fowler is doing his best not to fall in love with Steve Lopes, a piano player with eyes as green as willow shoots and hair the color of polished chestnuts. Love is just not in the cards for an actor whose career is on the rise, and who has just landed the triple part in Shakespeare's ""Hamlet;"" the role that Shakespeare himself is likely to have played. 3/3

2261. **Preston, John,** *Sweet Dreams,* Alyson, 1984. Alex Kane #1 of 6. (Thriller) Someone was daring to mess with young gay men in Boston. Somebody thought they could make a quick buck by exploiting the problems of gay youth. Somebody had never heard of Alex Kane. –revised and expanded by Badboy in *The Mission of Alex Kane I: Sweet Dreams* in 1992 (MLM). 3/3

2262. **Preston, John,** *Golden Years,* Alyson, 1984. Alex Kane #2 of 6. (Thriller) Do dreams belong only to the young? Not in Alex Kane's world. When evil threatens the plans of a group of olden gay men, Kane's got the muscle to take it head on. Along the way, the gay superhero wins the support - and very specialized attentions - of a cowboy plucked right out of the Old West. But not far down the trail, Kane and the Cowboy have a surprise waiting for them in this action-packed tale of hard men and the stuff they're made of. –revised and expanded by Badboy in *The Mission of Alex Kane II: Golden Years* in 1992 (MLM). 3/3

2263. **Preston, John,** *Deadly Lies,* Alyson, 1985. Alex Kane #3 of 6. (Thriller) Politics is a dirty business, filled with dirty lies. The dirt becomes deadly in Minneapolis/St. Paul when rampant political smearing and corruption turn toward unscrupulous politician's easiest targets: gay men. Who better to clean things up than Alex Kane! – With his lover and sidekick Danny Fortelli, Alex comes to protect the dreams - and lives - of gay men imperiled by the lies and deceit that threaten to tear them apart. Together they can generate the heat needed to burn away the political trash in Minnesota - and anywhere else it endangers the dreams of gay men. –revised and expanded by Badboy in *The Mission of Alex Kane III: Deadly Lies* in 1993 (MLM). 3/3

2264. **Preston, John,** *Stolen Moments,* Alyson, 1985. Alex Kane #4 of 6. (Thriller) A malicious newspaper editor targets Houston's evolving gay community in a cynical power play. But he never counted on the resolve of Alex Kane – a proud and fearless man devoted to the defense of gay dreams and desires everywhere. –Alex and his lover Danny take the Texan head-on. –revised and enlarged by Badboy in *The Mission of Alex Kane IV: Stolen Moments* in 1993 (MLM). 3/3

2265. **Preston, John,** *Secret Dangers,* Alyson, 1986. Alex Kane #5 of 6. (Thriller) Nobody ever heard of Lichtburg until a hijacking there endangered hundreds of people – including a gay tourist group from North Dakota. That was only the first of many attacks on gay people planned by right-wing terrorists. It was time for Alex Kane. –revised and enlarged by Badboy in *The Mission of Alex Kane V: Secret Dangers* in 1993 (MLM). 3/3

2266. **Preston, John,** *Lethal Silence,* Alyson, 1987. Alex Kane #6 of 6. (Thriller) The Mission of Alex Kane thunders to a conclusion with Kane's most dangerous adventure yet. Chicago serves as the scene of the right-wing's most vicious – and deadly – plan, fueled by bigotry and facilitated by unholy political alliances. Alex and Danny head to the Windy City to take up battle with the mercenaries who would squash gay men underfoot. –revised and enlarged by Badboy in *The Mission of Alex Kane VI: Lethal Silence* in 1993 (MLM). 3/3

2267. **Price, Jim,** *The Surfer Stud Secrets,* Luminosity, 2018. (Modern Pulp) On the most glittering beach resort in Australia, Skipper Trent, a lusty young PI uncovers forbidden secrets. When he's engaged by macho Clay Garrison to uncover a plot that could trigger a decadent resort-wide sex scandal, he faces a personal dilemma. While he's a savvy operator driven by skill, his desire for success in the bedroom with Clay is blocked by a frustrating downer: Clay doesn't play! –PUBLISHER NOTE: A Gay Romance Private Detective Novel with M/M, M/M/M+, Voyeurism, and Orgies (MLM). 3/3

2268. **Price, Jordan Castillo,** *Art of Dying: Partners in Crime 4,* MLR, 2009. (MM Short Stories) Body Art by Jordan Castillo Price His lover has betrayed and swindled Ray Carlucci out of everything he valued, including a tattoo business. Hounded by creditors, weary of heart, he accepts the job of chauffeur and body man for the dying owner of a remote estate. The island, minus its wealthy summer colony, is colorless in winter and Ray thinks he understands why staff on the estate periodically desert. But, he's baffled by, then drawn to, Anton, the eccentric artist who haunts the forest, bringing strange life to bizarre and disquieting sculptures amidst the ice and trees. When the body of a man who once held Ray's job rises from the frosty earth, Ray wonders what part Anton's wildness has in the escalating violence. –two short stories, the other is written by Josh Lanyon and is not a mystery (MLM). 3/3

2269. **Price, Jordan Castillo,** *Among the Living,* JCP, 2016. Psycop #1 of

9. (MM Paranormal) Victor Bayne, the psychic half a PsyCop team, is a gay medium who's more concerned with flying under the radar than in making waves. He hooks up with handsome Jacob Marks, a non-psychic (or "Stiff") from an adjacent precinct at his ex-partner's retirement party and it seems like his dubious luck has taken a turn for the better. But then a serial killer surface who can change his appearance to match any witness' idea of the world's hottest guy. Solving murders is a snap when you can ask the victims whodunit, but this killer's not leaving any spirits behind. 3/3

2270. **Price, Jordan Castillo,** *Criss Cross,* JCP, 2016. Psycop #2 of 9. (MM Paranormal) The medications that Victor usually takes to control his abilities are threatening to destroy his liver, and his new meds aren't any more effective than sugar pills. Vic is also adjusting to a new PsyCop partner, a mild-mannered guy named Roger with all the personality of white bread. At least he's willing to spring for the Starbucks. Jacob's ex-boyfriend, Crash, is an empathic healer who might be able to help Victor pull his powers into balance, but he seems more interested in getting into Victor's pants than in providing any actual assistance. 3/3

2271. **Price, Jordan Castillo,** *Body and Soul,* JCP, 2017. Psycop #3 of 9. (MM Paranormal) Thanksgiving can't end too soon for Victor Bayne, who's finding Jacob's family hard to swallow. Luckily, he's called back to work to track down a high-profile missing person. 3/3

2272. **Price, Jordan Castillo,** *Secrets,* JCP, 2017. Psycop #4 of 9. (MM Paranormal) Victor Bayne's job as a PsyCop involves tracking down dead people and getting them to spill their guts about their final moments. It's never been fun, per se. But it's not usually this annoying. 3/3

2273. **Price, Jordan Castillo,** *Camp Hell,* JCP, 2009. Psycop #5 of 9. (MM Paranormal) Victor Bayne honed his dubious psychic skills at one of the first psych training facilities in the country, Heliotrope Station, otherwise known as Camp Hell to the psychics who've been guests behind its razor wire fence. Vic discovered that none of the people he remembers from Camp Hell can be found online, nor is there any mention of Heliotrope Station itself. Someone's gone through a lot of trouble to bury the past. But who? –this is the first full length novel prior to Price revising and enlarging the previous books which had originally been written as short novellas (MLM). 3/3

2274. **Price, Jordan Castillo,** *GhosTV,* JCP, 2011. Psycop #6 of 9. (MM Paranormal) For the past dozen years, Victor Bayne has solved numerous murders by interrogating witnesses only he can see-dead witnesses. But when his best friend Lisa goes missing from the sunny California campus of PsyTrain, the last thing he wants to find there is her spirit. 3/3

2275. **Price, Jordan Castillo,** *Spook Squad,* JCP, 2013. Psycop #7 of 9. (MM Paranormal) Everyone enjoys peace and tranquility, and Victor Bayne is no exception. He goes to great lengths to maintain a harmonious home with his partner, Jacob. Although the cannery is huge, it's grown difficult to avoid the elephant in the room...the elephant with the letters FPMP scrawled on its hide. Once Jacob surrendered his PsyCop badge, he infiltrated the Federal Psychic Monitoring Program. In his typical restrained fashion, he hasn't been sharing much about what he actually does behind its vigilantly guarded doors. And true to form, Vic hasn't asked. In fact, he would prefer not to think about the FPMP at all, since he's owed Director Dreyfuss an exorcism since their private flight to PsyTrain. While Vic has successfully avoided FPMP entanglement for several months, now his debt has finally come due. –book 8, *Skin after Skin* is not a mystery (MLM). 3/3

2276. **Price, Jordan Castillo,** *Agent Bayne,* JCP, 2018. Psycop #9 of 9. (MM Paranormal) After years of frustration as a PsyCop, Victor Bayne reports for duty at the Federal Psychic Monitoring Program. As a fledgling agent, he's ready to smoke out a few ghosts and be home each night in time for dinner. But is he prepared to add a professional dimension to his romantic partnership with Jacob Marks? 3/3

2277. **Prokosch, Frederic,** *The Missolonghi Manuscript,* Farrar, Straus & Giroux, 1968. (Historical) A fictional re-creation of poet Lord Byron. ?/3

2278. **Pronzini, Bill,** *Twospot,* Putnam's Sons, 1978. Unnamed Detective #5 of 41. (Hard Boiled) "Nameless" and Lieutenant Frank Hastings are on a harrowing case of murder and bizarre conspiracy surrounding an old California wine-making family. –one gay man killed, and some politically correct discussion is uttered by the protagonist (MM). 1/3

2279. **Pronzini, Bill,** *Deadfall,* St. Martin's, 1986. Unnamed Detective #15 of 41. (Hard Boiled) "Nameless Detective" returns in his most baffling–and harrowing–case to date. While staked out on a routine car repossession, Nameless all but witnesses the shooting of a San Francisco lawyer, Leonard Purcell. He arrives on the scene in time to hear Purcell's dying words, one of which is "deadfall." But Purcell dies in Nameless's arms before the cryptic word can be explained. –unfortunately, this novel plays off the bitchy stereotype of gay men with one man threatening to scratch out the eyes of "nameless" (MLM). 2/3

2280. **Pronzini, Bill,** *Shackles,* St. Martin's, 1988. Unnamed Detective #16 of 41. (Hard Boiled) Nameless is pursued by a ruthless and amoral parolee who plans a horrible, lingering death for his victim. At first chained to a wall with shackles, Nameless must somehow remove the emotional shackles that have closed upon his mind from lack of food. –a former prisoner who had been incarcerated by the nameless detective and had been raped in prison and he blames the nameless detective (MLM). 1/3

2281. **Puccia, Charles,** *Ice Cream Man,* Carduna, 2016. VB #1 of 3. (MM Crime Drama) Solving a marital problem can create bigger problems –ones that lead to murder. –available as an e-book and audiobook (MLM). 3/3

2282. **Puccia, Charles,** *Baseball Man,* Carduna, 2017. VB #2 of 3. (MM Hard Boiled) Vinnie bonds with SLIDER, a homeless man. They share a sense of justice, and similar teenage experiences: both belittled and disowned by families for being gay. They also join to help Vinnie's neighbors. Vinnie revives his P.I. skills to expose Grace's rapist, despite Grace's fear to reveal the man's identity. Slider believes the truth closer to home. Vinnie reveals more than the rapist -but a murder. –available as an e-book (MM). 3/3

2283. **Puccia, Charles,** *Outlier Man,* Carduna, 2017. VB #3 of 3. (MM Hard Boiled) A high school teacher is not your typical murder victim, and more than one suggests a connection that P.I. Vinnie Briggs intends to make. This could be a dangerous undertaking so Vinnie hires Rita Light, a fitness fanatic and martial arts champion, for protection. –available as an e-book (MLM). 3/3

Q

2284. **Queen, Ellery (Barnaby Ross),** *The Last Woman in his Life,* World, 1970. Queen #33 of 35. (Cozy) John Lovering Benedict had more than most men, most of all more women–including 3 ex-wives with little in common but their extraordinary physiques. For Ellery the question was which one of them had bashed in Benedict's skull with a hunk of iron statuary? The clues were many, but puzzling. All had been planted at the scene of the crime, but by whom, and for what purpose? And who was the last woman in John Benedict's life? –the last "woman" in Benedict's life was a transvestite which Queen confused with gay and the last two pages of the novel discuss how to spot a homosexual including checking for a library stocked with Tchaikovsky music, first editions by Gide, Henry James, Oscar Wilde, Rimbaud, and Walt Whitman, as well as busts of Socrates, Lawrence of Arabia, Julius Caesar, Frederick the Great, and Lord Kitchener (MLM). 1/3

2285. **Quest, Erica,** *Model Murder,* Crime Club/Doubleday, 1991. Detective Chief Inspector Kate Maddox #3 of 4. (Police Procedural) When beautiful model Corinne Saxon is found murdered Detective Chief Inspector Kate Maddox has to begin to unravel the complex life of the model to try and establish which of the men in her life may have committed the dreadful deed. The list of suspects is endless and includes Kate's friend Richard Gower, admiral Fortescue who owns the hotel Corinne managed Yves Labrosse, her deputy and Larkin, Fortescue's manservant. Or could it be the unidentified male, known only as Ram? –the antagonist proves to be gay, but his homosexuality is barely touched upon (MLM). 1/3

2286. **Quick, Donna,** *Hallowed Illusions,* iUniverse, 2006. (Supernatural) Phillip Collier is a gay man haunted by the woman in his dreams. She's beautiful, tempting, and self-assured in her effect on the opposite sex. Phillip's dreams are just the thing his grandfather, a retired Fundamentalist minister, has been praying for. It must be a sign from God and Pastor is ecstatic, even if the woman is only a figment of his grandson's imagination. Imagine Phillip's astonishment when he sees a sixty-year-old portrait of a woman named Audrey Russell who's a dead ringer for the woman in his dreams. But Phillip has a bigger problem than trying to make Pastor understand why he's not romantically interested in women. Not only is he trying to figure out what makes his grandmother panic with near hysteria when she sees Audrey's portrait, he's wondering why a band of gypsies has suddenly become so treacherous. When the bunch of gypsies is caught beating up Keven, Phillip's life partner, the Collier family uncovers a gypsy curse that is more than just a threat. Is the Collier family the target of evil gypsy lore that promises punishment for past transgressions and the lies of hallowed illusions? 3/3

2287. **Quinton, Chris,** *Game On, Game Over,* Silver, 2011. (MM Military) Game On – John Jones, alias Aidan Whittaker, is undercover in Tajikistan to broker a deal with tribal leaders, a mission complicated when two Americans arrive to document the Silk Road and one starts asking very awkward questions. The other, Scott Landon, is a different kind of trouble; young, gay and single-minded, he clearly wants John. Unwilling to jeopardize his operation John rejects Scott, despite being attracted to him, but then events spiral out of control; will this be the start of a new life for both of them – or is it Game Over? 3/3

2288. **Quinton, Chris,** *Sea Change,* Manifold, 2010. (MM Suspense) Injured on duty and no longer fit for active service, soon-to-be-ex-Coast Guard Bran Kaulana is drifting, filling his days helping out at the Wai Ola Rescue Center, one of Honolulu's wildlife charities. He's working with the new veterinary, Steve, a man drawn to O'ahu by his fascination with dolphins. As their friendship slowly deepens into love, the two men are caught up in the mystery of injured seals and dolphins, a ruthless gang of smugglers and a not-so-dormant undersea lava vent. –available as an e-book only (MLM). 3/3

2289. **Quinton, Chris,** *Fox Hunt,* Manifold, 2012. (MM Paranormal Bibliomystery) Robert Rees, full-time librarian, part-time art restorer, is called in to finish a commission when his father goes into hospital – a pair of Elizabethan portraits on oak panelling, Adam Courtney and Ann Darcy. Trouble is, there's more interest in the paintings than Rob ever bargained for; a lot of people want to get their hands on such priceless treasures, and they're not always particular about their methods. –available as an e-book only (MLM). 3/3

2290. **Quinton, Chris,** *Undercover Blues,* Manifold, 2014. (MM Historical) London, the 1930s: With the cooperation of a top-ranking scientist and his son, Tom Langton and Robert Darnley are sent in as bait for a gang that uses blackmail to steal industrial secrets at a time when Hitler's rise to power in Germany threatens Europe. The two men are friends, but they each have secrets of their own. 3/3

2291. **Quinton, Chris,** *Dark Waters,* Createspace, 2014. (MM Paranormal) Flein is a wanderer by instinct and need, roaming the known world as the fancy takes him. In the Highland village of Glenfinnan, women have been raped and brutally murdered. The killer is a waterhorse, a monstrous shapeshifter by all accounts. But when Flein meets Donnchadh, first in its equine form, then its man-shape, he knows the waterhorse is innocent. Flein is drawn to the shapeshifter, but he finds it difficult to acknowledge it's more than a monster. –historical mm mystery, *Fall Guy* is set to be released in 2019 by Manifold Press (MLM). 3/3

R

2292. **Raftery, Roger,** *The Pink Triangle,* University of Queensland, 1981. (Australian Hard Boiled) "Australian private investigator Duane Dooley, though he insists he is straight, has trouble relating to women, allows his gay client to fellate him, and doggedly pursues a case of a gay bashing resulting in death in a whodunit (Gunn)." – the first "gay" Australian mystery (MLM). 3/3

2293. **Rahula, Robert,** *Bathhouse Stories,* Alma-Gator Press, 2016. Dan Landes #1 of 4. (Mexican Police Procedural) In an unnamed and timeless Latin American country, the lives of six men and three police officers intertwine after a brutal murder in a gay bathhouse. Dan Landes, an expat L.A. cop, is recruited to hunt for a serial killer who preys on lonely men in the dark steam rooms. Dan is forced to use his friend Ricardo as bait for the killer. 3/3

2294. **Rahula, Robert,** *All the Yages in Reno,* Alma-Gator, 2016. Dan Landes #2 of 4. (Police Procedural) No one would suspect that Dan Landes, a former L.A. cop known for methodically building cases against criminals, was a former ayahuasca user. He thought he had buried his past when he retired to Panama ten years ago. But a brutal murder forces him to return to the states. Now, to save his soul, he has to prevent another murder. But to do that, he may need to drink the psychedelic potion again. 3/3

2295. **Rahula, Robert,** *Exigent Circumstances,* Alma-Gator, 2018. Dan Landes #3 of 4. (Police Procedural) Dan Landes is "ex" everything: expatriate, ex-detective, and exhausted. He has returned to Panama from a year of recuperation in the United States, ready to resume a quiet life of hunting ayahuasca plants in the mountains. But evil is coming to Panama – or rather, through Panama – as a sinister team of murderers seeks to smuggle the world's most lethal biological weapon into the United States through Central America. A dead body in a hotel room starts the investigation and returns from beyond the grave to force Dan to find the killers. 3/3

2296. **Rahula, Robert,** *Uninvited Guest,* Alma-Gator, 2018. Dan Landes #4 of 4. (Police Procedural) Magali - a young prostitute of Villa Rosario, Panama - has died. Her ex-lovers, including friends Ricardo and Dan Landes, attend her funeral, each harboring different memories of her. In fact, everyone harbors different memories of her, because no one really knew who she was. But her ghost comes back from the grave to prod ex-detective Dan Landes to uncover the truth about her death.

2297. **Ramsay, Diana,** *Four Steps to Death,* St. Martin's, 1990. (Hard Boiled) Fancy footwork is required of dance instructor Maggie Tramayne when she finds her friend Nina skewered with one of her own kitchen utensils, and she must sidestep both the police and the killer's next culinary surprise in order to survive. –a few gay characters are present and one that died decades prior (MLM). 1/3

2298. **Rand, Lou,** *The Gay Detective,* Saber, 1961. (Hard Boiled) Set in the fictional Bay City, a thinly disguised San Francisco circa 1960, The Gay Detective is a hardboiled camp novel centering around a baffling blackmail and murder ring. When the latest corpse turns up and police realize they are faced with still another dead end, they contact the Morely Agency, a detective outfit recently bequeathed to the late Mr. Morely's nephew. –this is the first gay mystery marketed as such (MLM). 3/3

2299. **Randolph, Allen,** *The Belgium Conundrum,* Createspace, 2010. (Thriller) Walter Thompson and his partner, the jet setting owners of an international auction house, which serves the collecting needs of the rich and powerful, are at the center of danger and intrigue. Through Thompson's ties to the secret Societe de Belgique, the outspoken, crusading, egalitarian battles right-wing conservatism and hypocrisy in American politics; becoming the catalyst for conspiracy, espionage and murder. When Thompson himself is targeted for death, his chief of security, Tom Sheppard, a former FBI agent, is determined to figure out who's behind the crimes and why. Sheppard's search for answers exposes an intertwined web of deceit, corruption and subterfuge-a journey through cosmopolitan New York, London and Washington, DC to the mainstream America of Virginia and northwestern Ohio. 3/3

2300. **Randler, Ted,** *The Guessing Game,* Palari, 2002. (Psychological) The Guessing Game" unravels the dual mysteries of Tommy Stone's troubled past and his present-day efforts to assist authorities in apprehending an elusive, cyber serial killer. Apparently seducing men by pandering to their erotic fantasies and then ritualistically displaying their corpses, the murderer is seemingly capable of transforming identities and even gender before disappearing without a trace. 3/3

2301. **Rankin, Ian,** *Knots and Crosses,* Crime Club/Doubleday, 1987. Inspector Rebus #1 of 22. (Police Procedural) Detective John Rebus: His city is being terrorized by a baffling series of murders…and he's tied to a maniac by an invisible knot of blood. Once John Rebus served in Britain's elite SAS. Now he's an Edinburgh cop who hides from his memories, misses promotions and ignores a series of crank letters. But as the ghoulish killings mount and the tabloid headlines scream, Rebus cannot stop the feverish shrieks from within his own mind. Because he isn't just one cop trying to catch a killer, he's the man who's got all the pieces to the puzzle... –gay antagonist is seeking revenge (MLM). 1/3

2302. **Rankin, Ian,** *Hide and Seek,* Barrie and Jenkins, 1991. Inspector Rebus #2 of 22. (Police Procedural) A junkie lies dead in an Edinburgh squat, spread eagle, cross-like on the floor, between two burned-down candles, a five-pointed star daubed on the wall above. –the investigation takes Rebus into the world of male prostitutes and "rent" boys (MLM). 2/3

2303. **Raphael, Lev,** *Let's Get Criminal,* St. Martin's, 1996. Nick Hoffman #1 of 9. (Cozy) When Perry Cross, an outsider, is hired to fill a new position at the State University of Michigan, fellow teacher Nick Hoffman finds the situation curious. But his curiosity changes obsession when he learns that his longtime lover, Stefan, shares a past with Cross. Now Cross has been murdered, and both Nick and Stefan are prime suspects. –being republished by ReQueered Tales in 2019 (MLM). 3/3

2304. **Raphael, Lev,** *The Edith Wharton Murders,* St. Martin's, 1997. Nick Hoffman #2 of 9. (Cozy) Chaos hits the State University of Michigan when two bitterly rival Edith Wharton societies are brought together for the same conference. Its reluctant organizer, Professor Nick Hoffman, is desperate to get tenure, and when there's a murder, his only chance of saving his academic career is finding the killer. 3/3

2305. **Raphael, Lev,** *The Death of a Constant Lover,* Walker, 1999. Nick Hoffman #3 of 9. (Cozy) Nick Hoffman's been warned by his chair at the State University of Michigan to avoid trouble if he has any hopes of getting tenure. But his presence at the scene of a murder that involves a favorite student immediately threatens his position at the university, and soon after, his life. 3/3

2306. **Raphael, Lev,** *Little Miss Evil,* Walker, 2000. Nick Hoffman #4 of 9. (Cozy) It appears that Nick Hoffman's career is finally moving in the right direction, and the celebrity that comes with solving murders has brought him more students than he can possibly handle. But things are never calm at the State University of Michigan: Nick's partner's career seems to be spiraling down and out of control; a new faculty member is causing a lot of nasty talk; and cryptic messages are showing up in Nick's mailbox. 3/3

2307. **Raphael, Lev,** *Burning Down the House,* Walker, 2001. Nick Hoffman #5 of 9. (Cozy) Heading into the Christmas season, SUM is being torn apart by bizarre attempts to make it more diverse while an autocratic new provost pushes for a White Studies program and Nick faces not only a tenure battle but conflicting requests for support in a battle for department chair. 3/3

2308. **Raphael, Lev,** *Tropic of Murder,* Perseverance, 2004. Nick Hoffman #6 of 9. (Cozy) Edith Wharton scholar and untenured English professor Nick Hoffman escapes academic madness to vacation with his partner, Stefan, at a Caribbean getaway but ends up face-to-face with murder. 3/3

2309. **Raphael, Lev,** *Hot Rocks,* Perseverance, 2007. Nick Hoffman #7 of 9. (Cozy) When Professor Nick Hoffman and his partner Stefan return from a Caribbean vacation, Nick decides it's time to get back in shape at Michigan Muscle, a luxurious health club near the State University of Michigan. But every palace has its intrigue, and when Nick finds a dead trainer in the steam room, he's drawn into a web of passion and privilege like nothing he's experienced before. The prime suspect because he discovered the body, his academic and personal lives take unanticipated turns, and he gets a real workout in the bittersweet denouement. 3/3

2310. **Raphael, Lev,** *Assault with a Deadly Lie,* Terrace Books, 2014. Nick Hoffman #8 of 9 (Suspense) Successful professor Nick Hoffman finds his secure, happy, college-town life changed forever after a nightmarish encounter with police. But even when that horrible night is over, life doesn't return to normal. Someone is clearly out to destroy him. Nick and his partner Stefan Borowski face an escalating series of threats that lead to a brutal and stunning confrontation. –Raphael takes a dark turn with this novel from the Nick Hoffman whodunit series with this suspenseful novel about the dangers of a militarized police. The ninth book, *State University of Murder,* expected to be released in 2019 (MLM). 3/3

2311. **Rathbone, Julian,** *Watching the Detectives,* Pantheon, 1983. Inspector Argand #3 of 3. (Political) Commissioner Jan Argand of Brabt, head of the internal investigation's unit of the police, uncovers a series of disturbing cases of police corruption unexpectedly interwoven with political dissent. –two young gay men accuse the police of assault and are then assaulted again to recant their statements (MLM). 2/3

2312. **Raven, Simon,** *The Feathers of Death,* Simon and Schuster, 1960. (Historical) When Lieutenant Alastair Lynch shoots young Drummer Malcolm Harley in the back for desertion in the face of an enemy attack, his action seems to be clearly justified by military precedent. But after a court martial is convened to examine the facts of the case, a different story emerges. A tale of passionate love, possessiveness, and jealousy between the two men, a brazen and scandalous relationship that ended in Harley's violent death. The tension builds as the truth about the two men's liaison and Lynch's decision to pull the trigger gradually emerges, leading to a shocking finale. 3/3

2313. **Redmann, J. M. (Jean),** *Death by the Riverside,* New Victoria, 1990. Knight #1 of 9. (Hard Boiled) Among the moss-covered trees and wrought-iron balustrades of southern Louisiana, Detective Michele Knight (Micky to her friends) takes on the seemingly simple job of shooting a few photos for a client, but the going gets rough as Micky finds herself slugging through thugs and slogging through swamps in an attempt to expose a dangerous drug ring. The trail leads to the Hundred Oaks Plantation, a transvestite named Eddie, a beautiful doctor named Cordelia, and memories Micky thought she had buried twenty years ago. –Knight's first case in the book is to take incriminating photos of a young man to prove he's gay so he'll be dropped from his grandfather's will, her client was the young man's cousin who Knight proves is a lesbian and is also dropped from the will. The book goes in another direction after this (MLM). 1/3

2314. **Redmann, J. M.,** *Deaths of Jocasta,* New Victoria, 1992. Knight #2 of 9. (Hard Boiled) Micky Knight had a pleasant evening to look forward to; she was running security at a party of beautiful lesbians and gay men. But a dead body ruins the affair. When more dead women are found, the police target Dr. Cordelia James as the killer - the same Cordelia who broke Micky's heart. As Micky works to expose the killer she tries to keep her heart hidden. 2/3

2315. **Redmann, J. M.,** *The Intersection of Law and Desire,* Norton, 1995. Knight #3 of 9. (Hard Boiled) A scared little girl and the extortion of a wealthy woman - two completely separate cases - both lead bayou-bred PI Micky Knight to a seedy bar in the Big Easy, where she finds a world of evil. –introduction of Knight's drag queen cousin who makes regular appearances throughout (MLM). 2/3

2316. **Redmann, J. M.,** *Lost Daughters,* Norton, 1998. Knight #4 of 9. (Hard Boiled) Micky takes on the case of a widowed mother looking for her daughter and a tough gay boy hunting for his biological mother. Together, they stir in Micky a desire to search for her own mother who abandoned her when she was just a young girl. 2/3

2317. **Redmann, J. M.,** *Death of a Dying Man,* Bold Stroke Books, 2009. Knight #5 of 9. (Hard Boiled) Micky Knight just had to get into a butch contest with the journalist partner of a famous doctor working with her lover, Cordelia James, to prove that the skills of a reporter are of no use to a P.I. Now she's stuck with a drop-dead gorgeous assistant and the case of a dying gay man looking for a child he might have fathered. –dying man is gay (MLM). 2/3

2318. **Redmann, J. M.**, *Water Mark,* Bold Stroke Books, 2010. Knight #6 of 9. (Hard Boiled) It's just one more body in one more destroyed house. In New Orleans, a few months after Katrina, there are thousands of destroyed houses and hundreds of bodies yet to be found. Can one more matter? It does to Micky Knight as she takes on the quixotic search to find out who the woman was and why she might have died there. But is Micky searching for justice or just doing anything to avoid confronting the ways Katrina destroyed everything that had tied her to New Orleans? In a city that doesn't even have working stop lights, there seems little need for a private investigator. Her friends are all struggling with their own disrupted lives, lost jobs, destroyed homes. And the woman Micky thought she'd be with forever, Cordelia James, hasn't returned. –a private detective is mentioned in this book that Gunn assumes is Chanse MacLeod from Greg Herren's books (MLM). 2/3

2319. **Redmann, J. M.**, *Ill Will,* Bold Stroke Books, 2012. Knight #7 of 9. (Hard Boiled) First, do no harm. But as New Orleans PI Micky Knight discovers, not every health care provider follows that dictum. She stumbles into a tangle of the true believers to the criminally callous, who use the suffering of others for their twisted ends. In a city slowly rebuilding after Katrina, one of the most devastated areas is health care, and the gaps in service are wide enough for the snake oil salesmen–and the snakes themselves–to crawl through. First, her investigation is driven by anger, but then it becomes personal as someone very close to Micky uses her cancer diagnosis to go where Micky cannot, into the heart of the evil where only the ill are allowed. 2/3

2320. **Redmann, J. M.**, *The Shoal of Time,* Bold Stroke Books, 2013. Knight #8 of 9. (Hard Boiled) Michele "Micky" Knight, a New Orleans PI, meets an out-of-town team of investigators who are working a human trafficking case. They want someone local to show them around. It sounds easy, and a woman with smiling green eyes is asking. But it stays easy only if Micky stops asking questions–and she's never been good at that. What starts out as a tourist tour of the underside of New Orleans turns into a risky game of cat and mouse, and twists even further as Micky is caught between the good guys and the bad guys, each willing to do whatever it takes–including getting rid of an inconvenient PI–to achieve their ends. –may or may not have gay male characters (MLM). ?/3

2321. **Redmann, J. M.**, *The Girl on the Edge of Summer,* Bold Stroke

Books, 2017. Knight #9 of 9. (Hard Boiled) Micky Knight reluctantly takes on two cases, one for money, one for pity. The first is a trawl though archives to solve a century old murder, for an arrogant grandson who thinks riches should absolve his family of any sins. The other, to answer a mother's anguish as she tries to understand her daughter's suicide. Micky sees no happy ending to either case; the dusty pages of history aren't going to give up their secrets after holding them for so long. –Scotty Bradley from Greg Herren's books makes an entrance and there seems to be another gay friend Ned who pops in (MLM). 2/3

2322. **Redondo, Dolores,** *All This I Will Give to You,* Editorial Planeta, 2016. (Thriller) When novelist Manuel Ortigosa learns that his husband, Álvaro, has been killed in a car crash, it comes as a devastating shock. It won't be the last. He's now arrived in Galicia. It's where Álvaro died. It's where the case has already been quickly closed as a tragic accident. It's also where Álvaro hid his secrets. –translated into English from Spanish in 2018 (MLM). 3/3

2323. **Reed, Rick R.,** *Penance,* Dell, 1993. (Psychological) Barely into their teens, without homes, they dwell in neon shadows, the violent eddies of urban America. They trade their innocence for money, abuse their hopes, and then a monster comes... 3/3

2324. **Reed, Rick R.,** *IM,* Quest, 2007. (Thriller) The Internet is the new meat market for gay men. Now a killer is turning the meat market into a meat wagon. One by one, he's killing them. Lurking in the digital underworld of Men4HookUpNow.com, he lures, seduces, and charms, reaching out through instant messages to the unwary. When the first body surfaces, openly gay Chicago Police Department detective Ed Comparetto is called in to investigate. At the scene, the young man who discovered the body tells him the story of how he found his friend. But did this witness play a bigger role in the murder than he's letting on? 3/3

2325. **Reed, Rick R.,** *Riding the El at Midnight,* Amber Quill, 2008. (MM Horror) When the gorgeous, fire-maned, and twisted Mark boards a nearly deserted el train, he is looking for love in all the wrong places. And finding Julio aboard that same northbound train is the answer to Mark's dreams. But are his dreams really nightmares? And what weird secrets does the mild-mannered Julio hide beneath his attractive and charming exterior? –available as an e-book only (MLM). 3/3

2326. **Reed, Rick R.,** *Bashed,* MLR, 2009. (MM Paranormal) When Donald and Mark left the Brig that October night, they had no idea their lives and love were about to be shattered by fag bashers, intent on pain, and armed with ridicule, fists, and an aluminum baseball bat.

3/3

2327. **Reed, Rick R.,** *Mute Witness,* MLR, 2009. (MM Psychological) Sean and Austin have the perfect life. Their new relationship is only made more joyous by weekend visits from Sean's eight-year-old son, Jason. And then their perfect world shatters. 3/3

2328. **Reed, Rick R.,** *Reckless,* Kindle, 2009. (MM Thriller) Paul wasn't looking for anything special that rainy autumn afternoon when he met Max in a Chicago Starbucks. But Max was–a simple, uncomplicated romp while his boyfriend was out of town on business. And Paul was only too happy to oblige. There was only one problem: Paul was HIV positive. And just a few weeks after his hot encounter with Max, a letter arrived for him, containing some legalese about HIV infection being a criminal act, with a few chilling words: "You infected me. You didn't tell me. You need to pay." –available as an e-book only (MLM). 3/3

2329. **Reed, Rick R.,** *A Demon Inside,* MLR, 2010. (MM Paranormal) Hunter Beaumont doesn't understand his grandmother's deathbed wish: "Destroy Beaumont House." He'd never even heard of the place. But after his grandmother passes and his first love betrays him, the family house in the Wisconsin woods looks like a tempting refuge. Going against his grandmother's wishes, Hunter flees to Beaumont House. But will the house be the sanctuary he had hoped for? Soon after moving in, Hunter realizes he may not be alone. And who--or what--he shares the house may plunge him into a nightmare from which he may never escape. Sparks fly when he meets his handsome neighbor, a caretaker for the estate next door, but is the man salvation...or is he the source of Hunter's terror? 3/3

2330. **Reed, Rick R.,** *Echoes,* Amber Quill, 2011. (MM Paranormal) Rick and Ernie have found the perfect loft apartment on Chicago's west side. But before they are even settled, Rick begins having strange "dreams" that seem all too real. A young man, emaciated, with sad brown eyes, appears to him, frightening and obsessing him. –available as an e-book only (MLM). 3/3

2331. **Reed, Rick R.,** *Dinner at the Blue Moon Cafe,* Amber Quill, 2010. (MM Paranormal) Amid an atmosphere of crippling fear, Thad Matthews finds his first true love working in an Italian restaurant called the Blue Moon Café. Sam Lupino is everything Thad has ever hoped for in a man: virile, sexy as hell, kind, and... he can cook! 3/3

2332. **Reed, Rick R.,** *Third Eye,* Dreamspinner, 2014. (MM Paranormal) Who knew that a summer thunderstorm and his lost little boy would conspire to change single dad Cayce D'Amico's life in an instant? With Luke missing, Cayce ventures into the woods near their house to find his son, only to have lightning strike a tree near him, sending a branch down on his head. When he awakens the next day in the hospital, he discovers he has been blessed or cursed–he isn't sure which–with psychic ability. Along with unfathomable glimpses into the lives of those around him, he's getting visions of a missing teenage girl. –paperback states second edition but all previous editions were only available as an e-book (MLM). 3/3

2333. **Reed, Rick R.,** *The Couple Next Door,* Dreamspinner, 2015. (MM Domestic Violence) Jeremy Booth leads a simple life, scraping by in the gay neighborhood of Seattle, never letting his lack of material things get him down. But the one thing he really wants someone to love seems elusive. Until the couple next door moves in and Jeremy sees the man of his dreams, Shane McCallister, pushed down the stairs by a brute named Cole. 3/3

2334. **Reed, Rick R.,** *Tricks,* Dreamspinner, 2015. (MM Thriller) Arliss is a gorgeous young dancer at Tricks, the hottest club in Chicago's Boystown. Sean is the classic nerd, out of place in Tricks, but nursing his wounds from a recent break-up. When the two spy each other, magic blooms. But this opposites-attract tale does not run smooth. What happens when Arliss is approached by one of the biggest porn producers in the business? Can he make his dreams of stardom come true without throwing away the only real love he's ever known? And will this question even matter if the mysterious producers realize their dark intentions? 3/3

2335. **Reed, Rick R.,** *Orientation,* Createspace, 2017. (MM Paranormal) Christmas, 1983: A young man, Robert, tends to his soul mate, Keith, who is dying from AIDS. Robert tries valiantly to make this a special Christmas for his lover but loses the fight late Christmas night. Christmas, 2007: Robert ventures out late Christmas night and finds a young girl about to fling herself into the unforgiving waters of Lake Michigan. He rescues her, and the two form a bond forged from an odd feeling they share of familiarity, and even love. Neither understands it, since Jess is a lesbian and Robert has never been attracted to women. But there's more ... Jess begins having strange dreams, reliving key moments she couldn't know about in Keith and Robert's life and courtship. Robert and Jess begin to wonder if their inexplicable feelings might be rooted in something much more mystical than a savior/victim relationship. As the two move toward and pull away from each other, Ethan, Robert's younger lover, plots the unthinkable. His crystal meth-addled mind becomes convinced there's only one way to save himself, and that is through Robert's destruction. 3/3

2336. **Reese, Vicki,** *No Tears for Darcy,* Dreamspinner, 2018. (MM Amateur Sleuth/Police procedural) Former forensic accountant Cameron has lost nearly everyone he's ever loved, and now his vintage clothing shop has been broken into and trashed. Pete Minchelli is on leave from his job in Philadelphia due to a gunshot wound, but he figures he can help an academy buddy with some light police work. 3/3

2337. **Reginald, Robert,** *More Whodunits,* Borgo, 2011. (Short Stories) Sixteen great reads for another night of crime and punishment! –William Maltese has a gay story in this collection (MLM). 1/3

2338. **Reid, Paul Raymond,** *Walt Whitman and the Phrenology of Murder,* Independently Published, 2018. (Historical Journalism) The journalist Eugene Lannon has not seen his friend and colleague, Walt Whitman, for some time. They meet up at Pfaff's, a local watering hole. Whitman is at a critical juncture as he contemplates expanding and revising Leaves of Grass. Lannon is ensnared in some sort of a relationship with his landlady. Eugene and Walt are soon caught up as participants and would-be detectives in a series of gruesome murders. 3/3

2339. **Rendell, Ruth (1930-2015),** *Murder Being Once Done,* Crime Club/Doubleday, 1972. Wexford #7 of 25. (British Police Procedural) It seems fitting that the final resting place of a girl's body should be in a graveyard. But this is no peaceful burial. This is a brutal murder scene. –a stereotypical gay man (a dress designer) is the one to give Wexford the vital clue to solve the crime (MLM) 1/3

2340. **Rendell, Ruth,** *Kissing the Gunner's Daughter,* Mysterious Press, 1992. Wexford #15 of 25. (British Police Procedural) The thirteenth of May is famously the unluckiest day of the year. Sergeant Caleb Martin of Kingsmarkham CID had no idea just how terminally unlucky it would prove, as he embarked upon his last day on earth... –a bank robbery is conducted by a gay man sick with AIDS (MLM). 1/3

2341. **Renfro, Derek,** *Bridge Water,* Createspace, 2013. Cooper #1 of 2. (MM Police Procedural) Forced to come out of the closet to prove his innocence in a brutal murder, Detective Derek Cooper is warned by the police chief not to get involved in the case. Consumed with guilt, Derek knows he must unravel the secrets of his own drunken actions on the night of the murder in order to help find the killer. 3/3

2342. **Renfro, Derek,** *Ambiguity,* Createspace, 2014. Cooper #2 of 2. (MM Police Procedural) In the wake of a senseless and horrific crime a city is torn apart and a nation is in shock. As investigators delve into the lives of the suspect and the victims they unravel an even darker mystery. A grieving community will struggle to deal with the consequences of the secrets that are revealed. Secrets that will leave no life untouched. 3/3

2343. **Renraw, J. L.,** *Murder is a Drag,* Createspace, 2013. Slade #1 of 3. (Police Procedural) A demented knife wielding maniac is on the loose and DCI Slade, his anchorman Sergeant Dobbs and a dedicated team of officers attempt to stop this maniac before more bloodied mayhem erupts. 3/3

2344. **Renraw, J. L.,** *Hung for a Penny - Hung for a Pound,* Createspace, 2015. Slade #2 of 3. (Police Procedural) Unfortunately, when the first body is found nothing will ever be the same again. Slade and his professional team of officers have to pit their wits against this new monster in their midst. 3/3

2345. **Renraw, J. L.,** *Deadly Connections,* Createspace, 2017. Slade #3 of 3. (Police Procedural) The safety of the South East Coast of England rests in DI Conrad's hands. But is he up to the job, will he be able to solve this new spate of crimes? 3/3

2346. **Reyne, Layla,** *Single Malt,* Carina Press, 2017. Agents Irish and Whiskey #1 of 4. (MM Police Procedural) Eight months after the car crash that changed everything, FBI agent Aidan Talley is back at work. New department, new case and a new partner. Smart, athletic and handsome, Jameson Walker is twelve years his junior. Even if Aidan was ready to move on–and he's not–Jamie is off-limits. Jamie's lusted after Aidan for three years, and the chance to work with San Francisco's top agent directly is too good to pass up. Aidan is prickly–to put it mildly–but a growing cyber threat soon proves Jamie's skills invaluable. –e-book only (MLM). 3/3

2347. **Reyne, Layla,** *Cask Strength,* Carina Press, 2017. Agents Irish and Whiskey #2 of 4. (MM Police Procedural) Going undercover on a new case gets them out of town and off the killer's radar. They're assigned to investigate an identity theft ring involving a college basketball team in Jamie's home state, where Jamie's past makes him perfect for the role of coach. But returning to the court brings more than old memories. –e-book only (MLM). 3/3

2348. **Reyne, Layla,** *Barrel Proof,* Carina Press, 2017. Agents Irish and Whiskey #3 of 4. (MM Police Procedural) FBI agents Aidan "Irish" Talley and Jameson "Whiskey" Walker can't get a moment's peace. Their hunt for the terrorist Renaud seems to be nearing an end, until a fire allows him to slip through their fingers–and puts Jamie's life in danger. When Jamie is nearly killed, Aidan learns how many forms loss can take. –e-book only (MLM). 3/3

2349. **Reyne, Layla,** *Tequila Sunrise,* Carina Press, 2017. Agents Irish and Whiskey #4 of 4. (MF Police Procedural) Former FBI agent Melissa "Mel" Cruz spent years skirting the line between life and death, knowing the next assignment might be her last. Back from overseas and eager to enjoy life outside the Bureau, she's ready to give Danny Talley a Christmas Eve he'll never forget. A proven asset in high stakes missions, Danny's known for having the skill and brains to get the job done. When the Talley Flag Ship is hijacked during the company holiday party, he'll do anything to save his family, his love, and everything they've all worked so hard to build. But their enemies have a secondary protocol–leave no survivors–and that plan is already in play. –this is a spin-off of the Irish and Whiskey series focused more on the straight couple, Mel and Danny. The short story which follows this novel is a romance only. This is only available as an e-book (MLM). 1/3

2350. **Reyne, Layla,** *Imperial Stout,* Carina Press, 2018. Trouble Brewing #1 of 3. (MM Suspense) It's a good thing assistant US attorney Dominic Price co-owns a brewery. He could use a cold one. Nic's star witness has just been kidnapped, his joint operation with the FBI is in jeopardy, his father's shady past is catching up with him and the hot new special agent in San Francisco is the kind of distraction best handled with a stiff drink. 3/3

2351. **Reyne, Layla,** *Craft Brew,* Carina Press, 2018. Trouble Brewing #2 of 3. (MM Suspense) Assistant US attorney Dominic Price is staring down the barrel of his father's debts. The bull's-eye on his back makes him a threat to everyone he cares about, so when his lover wants to go public with their relationship, he bolts. Not because he isn't in love–he can't stomach the thought of putting Cam in danger. –*Noble Hops*, the third book in the series is coming out in 2019 (MLM). 3/3

2352. **Rhodes, M. L.,** *Falling,* Amber Quill, 2007. (MM Paranormal) As the leader of an elite British group that hunts criminals of the magic world, Christian Wetherly comes to the U. S. undercover, posing as a British cop, to investigate a series of murders he suspects have been committed by a dark mage. He never expects, however, to find himself intensely attracted to the American police detective in charge of the case. Christian has long struggled with his hidden desires and hasn't admitted them to anyone. But Alec Anderson stirs something deep within him that's difficult to ignore. 3/3

2353. **Ricardo, Jack,** *Death with Dignity,* Banned Books, 1991. (Hard Boiled) Private investigator Jim Halden has joined his local chapter of Dignity, an organization of gay Catholic men and women. At Jim's second meeting, Deacon Pete, recently estranged from his wife and newly out of the closet, is found dead behind the altar–strangled. 3/3

2354. **Ricardo, Jack,** *The Night GAA Died,* St. Martin's, 1992. (Hard Boiled) Driven off the force after coming out of the closet, former

New York City police officer Archie Cain starts his life anew as a private investigator, probing the death of Gay Activists Alliance vice president. 3/3

2355. **Ricardo, Jack,** *Last Dance at Studio 54,* Createspace, 2012. (Historical) 1977. NYC. Paul's dope-addled mind confronts frightening forces as he wallows in the maw of Studio 54, where he meets Adam, another reforming addict. A powerful but rushed connection sparks between the two before they are forced apart. Paul is compelled to find out exactly who Adam was. Only after he returns to The Studio for the second time and confronts the menacing forces, does Paul Discover the truth. 3/3

2356. **Ricardo, Jack,** *Desperate Innocence,* Createspace, 2013. (Hard Boiled) Private investigator, Jim Holden, is hired to discover who killed a young boy outside a gay church. His journey takes him from Fort Lauderdale to Arizona to New York City. 3/3

2357. **Rice, Christopher,** *A Density of Souls,* Miramax, 2000. (Psychological) Five years ago, Meredith, Brandon, Greg, and Stephen quickly discover the fragile boundaries between friendship and betrayal as they enter high school and form new allegiances. Meredith, Brandon, and Greg gain popularity, while Stephen is viciously treated as an outcast. Then two violent deaths destroy the already delicate bonds of their friendship. 3/3

2358. **Rice, Christopher,** *Snow Garden,* Hyperion, 2001. (Thriller) It is more than just the late November weather that has cast a chill over the campus of Atherton University. When the wife of respected professor Eric Eberman is killed in a tragic accident, her secret student lover, Randall Stone, fears the professor tried to avert career suicide by committing homicide. Or do the dead woman's haunting last words point to an even more damning crime? –won the fifteenth LAMBDA Award (MLM). 3/3

2359. **Rice, Christopher,** *Light Before Day,* Miramax, 2005. (Thriller) Adam Murphy wants to be a serious journalist. Unfortunately, he spends his days writing copy about underwear and abs for a gay lifestyle magazine. When a troubled young porn star brings him a tip about a recently deceased marine's secret visit to an infamous pimp for underage boys, Adam is determined to break the story... until someone starts threatening his life. 3/3

2360. **Rice, Christopher,** *Blind Fall,* Miramax, 2008. (Thriller) Home from Iraq, John pays a visit to his former captain, only to discover the captain has been gruesomely murdered. John pursues a strange man he sees running from the scene, but he discovers that Alex Martin is not the murderer. Alex is, in fact, the former captain's secret male lover and the killer's intended next victim. 2/3

2361. **Rice, Christopher,** *The Moonlit Earth,* Miramax, 2010. (Thriller) When Megan and Cameron Reynolds's father walked out on their mother, they forged an unbreakable bond. If their father could not be there to take care of them, they would always be there to take care of each other. But life intervenes, and siblings go separate ways ... until something happens to reforge that bond. 1/3

2362. **Rice, Christopher,** *The Heaven's Rise,* Gallery Books, 2013. (Horror) It's been a decade since the Delongpre family vanished near Bayou Rabineaux, and still no one can explain the events of that dark and sweltering night. No one except Niquette Delongpre, the survivor who ran away from the mangled stretch of guardrail on Highway 22 where the impossible occurred...and kept on running. Who left behind her best friends, Ben and Anthem, to save them from her newfound capacity for destruction...and who alone knows the source of her very bizarre–and very deadly–abilities: an isolated strip of swampland called Elysium. –not sure of gay content, when I reached out to Mr. Rice to ask he only said that there is gay content (MLM). ?/3

2363. **Rice, Christopher,** *Man Catch,* MIRA, 2017. (Thriller) Kate and her boyfriend, Rick, are getting ready to go off to separate lives and colleges in less than a month, so they plan a three-day getaway to spend some time together. But Kate discovers her love has another life involving a secret account on a gay website, so she dumps him. What she doesn't realize is that the truth about what she learned will destroy her life forever. –available as an e-book only (MLM). 3/3

2364. **Rice, Christopher,** *Bone Music,* Thomas and Mercer, 2018. Burning Girl #1 of 2. (Thriller) Charlotte Rowe spent the first seven years of her life in the hands of the only parents she knew–a pair of serial killers who murdered her mother and tried to shape Charlotte in their own twisted image. If only the nightmare had ended when she was rescued. Instead, her real father exploited her tabloid-ready story for fame and profit–until Charlotte finally broke free from her ghoulish past and fled. Just when she thinks she has buried her personal hell forever, Charlotte is swept into a frightening new ordeal. Secretly dosed with an experimental drug, she's endowed with a shocking new power–but pursued by a treacherous corporation desperate to control her. –not sure of gay content, when I reached out to Mr. Rice to ask he only said that there is gay content. *Blood Echo*, the second book in the series is coming out in 2019 (MLM). ?/3

2365. **Richards, Hayden,** *One Night at the Astoria: The Friends and Adventures of Rocky Star,* Independently Published, 2018. (Crime Drama) Let me introduce to you to Rocky Star, Sam Rockwell to his friends, and his group of friends as they embark on an adventure leading them to that One Night at the Astoria. Meet James, who falls in love with a drug dealer... and Dean, who tries to make him leave... who is cousin to Tom... who is best friends with Mark... who happens to be the estranged twin of the dealer's boss. Then there is Fred who has to fly back to Paris... who is best friends with Pip who runs a gentleman's club where all the men dress as ladies. There is also Ben, who cannot stand James, but is more interested in Mark discovering more about his sexuality at The Institute of Gentleman. You'll also meet Mrs. Potts, the 95-year-old neighbor of Rocky who drives a Rolls Royce. Join the group for a bizarre week when James and Dean manage to get themselves in to a whole heap of trouble and drag their friends along with them. 3/3

2366. **Richardson, Bill,** *Waiting for Gertrude: A Graveyard Gothic,* Douglas and McIntyre, 2001. (Paranormal) In Paris's Pere-Lachaise cemetery lie the bones of many renowned departed. It is also home to a large number of stray cats. Now, what if by some strange twist of fate, the souls of the famous were reborn in the cats with their personalities intact? 1/3

2367. **Rico, Don,** *The Man From PANSY,* Lancer, 1967. Buzz #1 of 2. (Pulp) Buzz Cardigan - fantastically handsome, tough, brainy, deft, agile, and hip. Hip, among other things, to the gay underworld where only vice is natural and where the vicious enemy agents lurk to prey on weakness. –straight man pretending to be a gay man (MLM). 3/3

2368. **Rico, Don,** *Daisy Dilemma,* Lancer, 1967. Buzz #2 of 2. (Pulp) "A gay scientist invents a dangerous weapon and disappears (Gunn)." –Buzz again pretends to be gay (MM). 3/3

2369. **Ridout, James W,** *Plantation Secrets,* Pilot, 2000. Pilot #1 of 2 (Family Saga) "Washington DC lawyer Dennis Jensen, though he has only a minor role solves two mysteries involving his ex-lover (Gunn)." 2/3

2370. **Ridout, James W,** *The Man Pilot,* Pilot, 2004. Pilot #2 of 2. (Family Saga) The Man Pilot is a story of plantation life in the steamy Louisiana delta where love, sex, lies, and deceit live among the slender stalks of sugar cane deep in the Bayou land. 2/3

2371. **Riley, A. M.,** *The Elegant Corpse,* Loose Id, 2008. (MM BDSM Police Procedural) Detective Roger Corso is open about his sexual orientation. He's less forthcoming about his leather lifestyle. He thinks he's doing a pretty good job of keeping it covert, but then something happen that changes his mind. Someone delivers an elegantly clothed corpse to his home. His couch to be precise. And that corpse is carrying a leather flogger. Roger's taking that personally. –available as an e-book only (MLM). 3/3

2372. **Riley, A. M.**, *Amor En Retrograde*, Loose Id, 2008. Bill Turner #1 of 2. (MM Police Procedural) In the year since JD Ryan, Robert Lemos's life partner, packed his bags and moved out, Robert has been in a painful daze, anesthetizing himself with work. Then one rainy night, he gets a call that his ex has been beaten and shot in a parking lot outside a gay dance club. JD is in critical condition and the man who was with him is dead. –available as an e-book only (MLM). 3/3

2373. **Riley, A. M.**, *Death by Misfortune*, MLR, 2010. Bill Turner #2 of 2. (MM Police Procedural) After a glamorous studio party, "Psychic to the Stars" Sylvie Black is found murdered in her fortune telling booth, a blood-soaked tarot reading spread out before her. Shortly afterwards, the high-profile director who was about to produce Ms. Black's 'tell-all' Hollywood screenplay, is found murdered as well. Closeted Homicide detective, Bill Turner, and his partner, Kate Crandall, find themselves sorting through a cast of likely suspects, who all seem to have secrets worth killing for. They soon run up against the studio rumor mill, and Jeremy Reilly, a young studio AD determined to protect their prime suspect. 3/3

2374. **Riley, A. M.**, *Son of a Gun*, MLR, 2010. (MM Mystery) Politics, drugs and secrets from the past collide in the town of Boerne Texas and end in a chase across the Devil's Backbone. 3/3

2375. **Roberts, Buck**, *Crossover Spy*, Nazca Plains, 2011. Crossover #1 of 2. (Espionage) "U. S. undercover agents Cliff Bradshaw, Brad Aimes, and other agents and double-agents connected with an illegal Russian arms dealer actually do some spying between multiple bouts of sex in a pseudo-thriller (Gunn)." 3/3

2376. **Roberts, Buck**, *Crossover Spy II*, Nazca Plains, 2012. Crossover #2 of 2. (Espionage) Cliff Bradshaw, an American operative with Homeland Security & a former SEAL, is dispatched yet again to crush a weapons trafficking ring operating out of Moscow, thought to have been neutralized & headed by his nemesis, a Russian Mafia kingpin. Cliff's training for his job required him to pass as a gay man, a lifestyle that had been unfamiliar to him. 3/3

2377. **Roberts, John (Robert Tait)**, *Mardi Gras*, Round the Square, 1995. (Political) "Sydney accidental sleuths Jason, 21, a vacationing Queensland university student, and Chip, a restaurateur, are part of the cast of characters in a crime case (Gunn)." 2/3

2378. **Roberts, Les**, *Not Enough Horses*, St. Martin's, 1988. Saxon #2 of 6. (Hard Boiled) When a bit-actor named Bingham is blown into Act Five in a car-bombing, P.I. Saxon is convinced it is a case of misdirected anger. His investigation leads him into the plush, competitive world of network television, where one over-achieving executive will stop at nothing to ascend to the top. –Saxon investigates the death of a gay hustler (MLM). 2/3

2379. **Roberts, Willo Davis (1928-2004),** *The Devil Boy: A Story of Unholy Genius,* Signet, 1970. (Crime Drama) In Keathley Castle live an ambassador, an actress, a writer, a senator, and a brilliant small boy they all fear is capable of murder. ?/3

2380. **Robins, A. B.,** *Peter Pansy Private Eye: A Collection,* Independently Published, 2011. (Hard Boiled Short Stories) A collection of 11 interrelated short stories. In this collection of eleven adventures, you'll meet Pete, a Jamesbondian, Double-0-Seven-character, macho, wealthy, cultured and gay. 3/3

2381. **Robiscoe, James,** *The Fire Island Murder,* Tanner Long, 1995. (Thriller) I see Fire Island come into view, a long narrow strip of heavily wooded sand dunes, tranquil and serene. In a world of liars and lovers, crimes of passion are always tough to survive. Its summer and men are flocking to the island paradise. Nick Barrons, former school teacher and aspiring screenwriter, wants more than sex: he wants vengeance. A cold, clever killer is on the prowl, stalking the boardwalks, and Nick is caught in an artful web of agents, producers, and friends. Spiraling down a vortex of violence, deception and romance, he comes face-to-face with the dark underbelly of movie glamour in the form of Peter, the handsome film actor, who will do anything to get his own way. Until the murderer strikes again. 3/3

2382. **Rockenbeck, Laurie,** *Bound to Die,* Bane & Bodkin, 2017. (Police Procedural) When a prominent Seattle businessman is found hanging naked in a dominatrix's studio, lead Detective Court Pearson is pressured to find a fast, quiet solution to the man's death. Court's investigation uncovers secrets within his own department and raises the ghosts that linger from the suicide of his wife–all details he fights to keep quiet as a leaker goes public. To make matters worse, his new partner resents his fast rise through the ranks as Seattle's only transmale homicide detective, and his lead suspect begins to look like a target for murder. 2/3

2383. **Rockenbeck, Laurie,** *Cleansed by Fire,* Bane & Bodkin, 2018. (Hardboiled) A serial killer is terrorizing Seattle. Private investigator Karen Hunter agrees to locate a teen who has gone missing. His mother is frantic to find the son she kicked out for being gay before he becomes the killer's next victim. 2/3

2384. **Roeder, Mark,** *Outfield Menace,* iUniverse, 2005. Gay Youth #3 of 48. (YA) Outfield Menace is the tale of Kurt, a fifteen-year-old baseball player, and living in a small, 1950s, Indiana town. During a confrontation with Angel, the resident bad boy of Blackford High School, Kurt attacks Angel, earning the wrath of the most dangerous gang in town. When Angel finally corners Kurt, however, something happens that Kurt wouldn't have imagined in his wildest dreams. As the murder of a local boy is uncovered, suspicion is cast upon Angel, but Kurt has learned there's more to Angel than his bad boy image. Angel has a secret, however, that could get both Kurt and himself killed. 3/3

2385. **Roeder, Mark,** *Someone is Killing the Gay Boys of Verona,* Writer's Club, 2000. Gay Youth #23 of 48. (YA) Someone is killing the gay boys of Verona, Indiana, and only one gay youth stands in the way. He finds himself pitted against powerful foes but finds allies in places he did not expect. 3/3

2386. **Roeder, Mark,** *Keeper of Secrets,* Writer's Club, 2002. Gay Youth #24 of 48. (YA) Sixteen-year-old Avery is in trouble, yet again, but this time he's in over his head. On the run, Avery is faced with hardships and fear. He must become what he's always hated, just to survive. He discovers new reasons to hate, until fate brings him to Graymoor Mansion and he uncovers a disturbing connection to the past. Through the eyes of a boy, murdered more than a century before, Avery discovers that all is not as he thought. 3/3

2387. **Roeder, Mark,** *Masked Identity,* Writer's Club, 2004. Gay Youth #25 of 48. (YA) Masked Destiny is the story of Skye, a high school athlete determined to be the Alpha male. Skye's obsessed with his own body, his Abercrombie & Fitch wardrobe, and keeping those around him in their place. Try as he might, he's not quite able to ignore the world around him, or the plight of gay boys who cross his path. Too frightened of what others might think, Skye fails to intervene when he could have saved a boy with a single word. The resulting tragedy, wise words for a mysterious blond boy, and a unique opportunity combine to push Skye toward his destiny. 3/3

2388. **Roeder, Mark,** *Dead Het Boys,* Writer's Club, 2007. Gay Youth #31 of 48. (YA) Marshall's experiences with ghosts and the supernatural are legendary, but when a boy a hundred-years dead turns up in his bedroom with the cryptic message "Blackford Manor," Marshall realizes his adventures with the other side have only began. As more specters appear to Marshall, he begins to assemble the pieces of a puzzle that lead him to Graymoor Mansion and a set of crimes more heinous than those of modern-day serial killers. 3/3

2389. **Roehrig, Caleb,** *Last Seen Leaving,* Feiwel and Friends, 2016. (YA Mystery) Flynn's girlfriend, January, is missing. The cops are asking questions he can't answer, and her friends are telling stories that don't add up. All eyes are on Flynn–as January's boyfriend, he must know something. 3/3

2390. **Roehrig, Caleb,** *White Rabbit,* Feiwel and Friends, 2018. (YA Mystery) Rufus Holt is having the worst night of his life. It begins with the reappearance of his ex-boyfriend, Sebastian–the guy who stomped his heart out like a spent cigarette. Just as Rufus is getting ready to move on, Sebastian turns up out of the blue, saying they need to "talk." Things couldn't get much worse, right? –a third novel, *Death Prefers Blondes* is due out in January of 2019 (MLM). 3/3

2391. **Rogers, Alexis,** *Cost of Love,* Lavender, 1990. (MM Romance) Dave Kaffey's a Viet Nam vet and a Los Angeles police officer. He's also gay and secretly in love with his partner, the married, now-separated JC Grayson. Will Kaff and JC get together or will the ghosts of Kaff's past in Southeast Asia interfere? 3/3

2392. **Rogers, Gina, & Kyle Adams,** *A Gay Romance,* MLR, 2014. (MM Police Procedural) Where can a sexy alpha cop and the hottest man on the planet solve a murder, save a fabulous plant, fall in love and discover an endless supply of lube? Homosapia, of course, where absolutely anything gay is possible. 3/3

2393. **Roome, Annette,** *A Real Shot in the Arm,* Crowne, 1991. Chris Martin #1 of 4. (Journalism) Following a bitter divorce and separation from her son, Julia finds herself broken and alone. Soon, she starts receiving a series of anonymous and menacing letters urging her to find her missing son in Venice. Despite the danger involved, Julia has no choice but to follow the taunting messages. With her miserable days in La Rivière still looming over her, she ventures to Italy on a train. But she can't shake the feeling that the letters were written by someone she knows, someone playing an awful and dangerous game. Meanwhile, Julia meets a handsome stranger on the train, but does she dare fall for him? –gay character is treated as a stereotype and disappears quickly (MLM). 1/3

2394. **Rooney, John F.,** *Unprotected Love,* Senneff House, 2011. (Police Procedural) A serial killer is on the loose stalking and murdering young male hustlers and depositing their bodies at New York City riverside locations. The predator displays his prey by reverently laying out each body like the deceased in a casket and decorates them by placing wrapped condoms in their mouths. Lieutenant Denny Delaney, the celebrated detective who brought down the dreaded terrorist, Felix the Cat, heads the NYPD special ops squad investigating the homicides. Experts school him into the arcane world of johns and hustlers, and Denny gets to know and care for one hustler named Tim who alters his life. Denny's wife Monny runs a popular web blog and receives scary e-mails from someone who knows far too much about the serial-killer case and the Delaneys' private lives. –two gay police detectives assist the main character (MLM). 2/3

2395. **Roscoe, Patrick,** *The Lost Oasis,* McClelland and Stewart, 1995. (Thriller) A telephone call from a small B.C. town awakens Richard in Sevilla with the news that his father has disappeared. His passport has been discovered in the desert, and Richard feels compelled to look for him. This will not be the first time that his father - a charismatic yet detached presence - has occasioned a difficult journey. Greetings from the end of the world. Seven words on the back of a postcard. His father's last, from the Moroccan town where Richard begins his search. A search both backwards and forwards through time. A search that leads towards where a passport was discovered somewhere on the sand. Pulled gradually deeper into the charged atmosphere of this landscape, Richard is caught between his desire to return to his lover in Spain and the need to find out what happened to his father. 3/3

2396. **Roscoe, Patrick,** *The Indivisible Heart,* Bold Stroke Books, 2015. (Spanish Police Procedural) The discovery of a grotesquely mutilated body of a young man in Seville, Spain, sets off an investigation into an apparently psycho-sexual murder that has disturbing personal implications for chief detective Manuel Arroyo and Olivier Joaquin Ortega, the forensic pathologist handling the case. 3/3

2397. **Rose, A. J.,** *Power Exchange,* Createspace, 2013. Power Exchange #1 of 4. (BDSM Police Procedural) From the moment Detective Gavin DeGrassi steps into the world of BDSM to solve the brutal slaying of Dom George Kaiser, his course is not his own. Mesmerized by the context in which the victim lived, and the images of the lifestyle seared into his soul, Gavin must find a way to navigate these unknown waters. With his personal life in upheaval due to marital trouble, and his professional life uncertain with the assignment of a new partner, Gavin needs all the help he can get understanding the case. 3/3

2398. **Rose, A. J.,** *Safeword,* Createspace, 2013. Power Exchange #2 of 4. (BDSM Police Procedural) Everywhere Detective Gavin DeGrassi looks he's reminded of his attack by the Breath Play Killer. It's in the house he lives in with his partner and Dom, Ben Haverson. It's in the sympathetic yet pitying looks he receives from his fellow detectives when he returns to the force after a year-long hiatus. It's in the suffocating coddling of his entire family, and the relentless reporter demanding an exclusive of his ordeal. 3/3

2399. **Rose, A. J.,** *Consent,* Createspace, 2014. Power Exchange #3 of 4. (BDSM Thriller) Former detective Gavin DeGrassi likes his new life and his job as a university professor, molding the minds of the next generation of law enforcement. It keeps him in the field he loves, but out of the media and out of the danger he seems to draw. He's settled and happy with his partner and Dom, Ben Haverson. 3/3

2400. **Rose, A. J.,** *Restraint,* Createspace, 2018. Power Exchange #4 of 4. (BDSM Thriller) Who brings a Glock on a honeymoon? Not retired detective Gavin DeGrassi. When his husband Ben asks who he plans to shoot, Gavin has no answer. They're spending three weeks in Ben's family cabin near Seattle, not chasing down bad guys. Or are they? 3/3

2401. **Rosen, Rob,** *Sparkle: The Queerest Book You'll Ever Love,* AuthorHouse, 2001. (MM Mystery) learn how they came out, had their first sexual experiences, got pierced and then tattooed, became drag queens, adopted a nearly full-grown son, placed a personal ad, and grew up to become the best of friends. Along the way, find out how many people wanted Sparkle dead and discover how much fun the bars and back streets of San Francisco really are. 3/3

2402. **Rosen, Rob,** *Divas Las Vegas,* Cleis, 2009. (MM Romance) What happens when you find out that Grandma's vase mistakenly sold at a yard sale is worth tens of thousands of dollars–and somebody else is about to cash in on it on Antiques Roadshow? Of course, you hop on a plane with your best friend and race off to Las Vegas to get Grandma's vase back! 3/3

2403. **Rosen, Rob,** *Southern Fried,* MLR, 2011. (MM Mystery) the romantic misadventure of Trip Jackson and his stable boy, Zeb Jones, is about the love of family, the love of one's heritage, and the love between friends, both old and new. It's as antebellum as Tara ever was, but with a deliciously suspenseful and sexy twist. Because what our heroes are quick to discover is that not all is as it appears to be, and sometimes life can get turned upside down when you least expect it. Especially when lip-smacking romance, deep-dish humor, and a side of mystery fall on your plate, all, of course, served up southern-style. 3/3

2404. **Rosen, Rob,** *Mary, Queen of Scotch,* JMS, 2018. (MM Soft Boiled) Four five-star Yelp reviews do you little good when you're nailed inside a giant barrel of whiskey, which is where our intrepid private detective Barry finds himself while on the case to help his campy drag friends, all of whom have numerous secrets to hide. –available as an e-book only (MLM). 3/3

2405. **Rossiter, John,** *The Villains,* Walker, 1976. Roger Tallis #6 of 7. (Police Procedural) Exploring the effects of a vicious crime on the two police officers involved and the lengths a man will go to establish his own integrity and sense of justice when the offender is acquitted. –offender's bodyguard is a gay stereotype who carries nude photographs of men in his pocket (MLM). 1/3

2406. **Rossner, Judith,** *Looking for Mr. Goodbar,* Simon and Schuster, 1975. (Crime Drama) Theresa was a quietly satisfied young teacher by day. But when the sun went down, her life was an endless, faceless whirl of bars and beds and men she'd never seen before and wouldn't see again. If she couldn't find love, she took chances on men who were better than no men at all. And learned, with each new night and each new nightmare, that finding her man was only the beginning. ?/3

2407. **Round, Jeffrey,** *The P'Town Murders,* Haworth, 2007. Fairfax #1 of 3. (Police Procedural) In a place that's "to die for," no one expects to die for real. So, muses undercover detective Bradford Fairfax after an anonymous caller tells him that his ex-boyfriend, party boy Ross Pretty, has died from an accidental overdose of ecstasy in "the gayest place on earth": Provincetown, Massachusetts. Brad becomes convinced that Ross's death is no accident, and his intention to bury his former lover suddenly turns into a full-scale investigation. Brad quickly pins the murder on Ross's ex-employer, the malevolent Hayden Rosengarten, owner of a high-end sex resort catering to a rich and famous clientele for whom discretion is everything. But when Rosengarten also turns up dead, the list of suspects suddenly grows: Could it be Cinder Lindquist, the flamboyant female-impersonator? Or Johnny K., one of Rosengarten's merciless henchmen? What about Big Ruby, the lesbian cafe owner with a big heart, but an even bigger gun? And why does everyone in P-Town seem to be a Buddhist? On top of it all, Brad finds himself falling in love with Zach, a blue-haired twink from his past. 3/3

2408. **Round, Jeffrey,** *Death in Key West,* Cormorant, 2009. Fairfax #2 of 3. (Police Procedural) The rich really are different. Bradford Fairfax, special agent, has a romantic New Year's Eve in store for his boyfriend Zach: a stay at a luxury resort in Key West. But their plans are turned upside down when the pair run into an improbable heiress to one of the world's great fortunes? someone who is desperate to convince anyone that his father wants him dead. But how much of a grasp on reality can a drug-abusing mega-wealthy man who thinks he's Maria Callas really have? And who or what is this mysterious Baby that he pines for? Does the transvestite ghost, Rosie, hold the answers to these and other troubling questions? 3/3

2409. **Round, Jeffrey,** *Vanished in Vallarta,* Cormorant, 2011. Fairfax #3 of 3. (Police Procedural) On assignment in the famed Mexican resort town, gay caballero Bradford Fairfax discovers he has far more to worry about than sand fleas and la turista. When a sultry diva sends out a distress signal, Brad answers the call. But why won't his boss, the shadowy Grace, tell him why he's really in PV? When a fellow agent gets blown away passing on top-secret information, Brad has no idea where to turn. Suddenly everyone seems unusually suspicious. Or suspiciously unusual. And what's a boy to do when his former partner in espionage-a.k.a. Little Wing-returns from the dead looking sexier than any corpse should be allowed to look? Will Brad let the past disrupt his relationship with the erstwhile and eternally sexy, blue-haired Zachary Tyler or will he beat a hasty retreat and nurse his broken heart under a coconut palm, saying Adios muchacho! to an old flame once again? 3/3

2410. **Round, Jeffrey,** *Lake on the Mountain,* Dundurn, 2012. Dan Sharp #1 of 6. (Police Procedural) Dan Sharp, a gay father and missing persons investigator, accepts an invitation to a wedding on a yacht in Ontario's Prince Edward County. It seems just the thing to bring Dan closer to his noncommittal partner, Bill, a respected medical professional with a penchant for sleazy after-hours clubs, cheap drugs, and rough sex. But the event doesn't go exactly as planned. –Winner of the 25th LAMBDA Award for Best Gay Mystery (MLM). 3/3

2411. **Round, Jeffrey,** *Pumpkin Eater,* Dundurn, 2014. Dan Sharp #2 of 6. (Police Procedural) Following an anonymous tip, missing persons investigator Dan Sharp makes a grisly find in a burned-out slaughterhouse in Toronto's west end. Someone is targeting known sex offenders whose names and identities were released on the Internet. When an iconic rock star contacts Dan to keep from becoming the next victim, things take a curious turn. Dan's search for a killer takes him underground in Toronto's broken social scene – a secret world of misfits and guerrilla activists living off the grid – where he hopes to find the key to the murders. 3/3

2412. **Round, Jeffrey,** *The Jade Butterfly,* Dundurn, 2015. Dan Sharp #3 of 6. (Police Procedural) A seemingly casual encounter in a downtown bar sends missing persons investigator Dan Sharp in search of a woman presumed dead in the Tiananmen Square Massacre. Twenty years after her disappearance, her brother believes that a woman he glimpsed on the Internet is his sister, now living in Toronto. The closer Dan gets to finding her, however, the less sense things make. Just when he thinks he knows what's driving his client, an unexpected revelation forces him to choose between what he's been told and his gut instinct, which says things are not all they seem. 3/3

2413. **Round, Jeffrey,** *After the Horses,* Dundurn, 2015. Dan Sharp #4 of 6. (Police Procedural) Dan Sharp scours Toronto s seamy underbelly after the murder of a notorious nightspot owner and finds his own life on the line. 3/3

2414. **Round, Jeffrey,** *God Game,* Dundurn, 2018. Dan Sharp #5 of 6. (Police Procedural) When the husband of a Queen's Park aide runs off to escape his gambling debts, private investigator Dan Sharp is hired to track him down. As the city's political landscape verges on the bizarre – with a crack-using mayor and a major scandal looming – Dan finds himself pitted against a mysterious figure known for making or breaking the reputations of upcoming politicians. It's not until a body turns up on his doorstep that Dan realizes he's being punished for sticking his nose into dirty politics. It's left to him to catch the killer and prove his own innocence. 3/3

2415. **Round, Jeffrey,** *Shadow Puppet,* Dundurn, 2018. Dan Sharp #6 of 6. (Police Procedural) When a serial killer stalks downtown Toronto, Private Investigator Dan Sharp finds an unexpected link between the missing men that even the police are reluctant to investigate. A meeting with the chief of police confirms his suspicions but does nothing to resolve the problem. Obsessed with uncovering the truth, Dan enlists a small group of friends to delve into illicit goings-on in the local sex industry. It's only when the next man disappears, that Dan finds himself in a race against time to track down an elusive, manipulative killer who is a master of disguise. 3/3

2416. **Roux, Abigail,** *The Archer,* Dreamspinner, 2008. (MM Espionage) Rocked to the core by traitors and spies, the Organization made an unprecedented move in bringing together six highly trained men to track down one rogue wolf: The Archer. 3/3

2417. **Roux, Abigail,** *Stars and Stripes,* Riptide, 2012. Cut and Run #6 of 9. (MM Police Procedural) Special Agents Ty Grady and Zane Garrett have managed the impossible: a few months of peace and quiet. After nearly a year of personal and professional turmoil, they're living together conflict-free, work is going smoothly, and they're both happy, healthy, and home every night before dark. But anyone who knows them knows that can't possibly last. –first five books in the series were co-written with Madeleine Urban (MLM). 3/3

2418. **Roux, Abigail,** *Touch and Geux,* Riptide, 2013. Cut and Run #7 of 9. (MM Police Procedural) After having their faces plastered across the news during a high-profile case, FBI Special Agents Ty Grady and Zane Garrett have become more useful to the Bureau posing for photo ops than working undercover. Just as Zane is beginning to consider retirement a viable option, Ty receives a distress call from a friend, leading them to a city rife with echoes from the past. 3/3

2419. **Roux, Abigail,** *Ball and Chain,* Riptide, 2014. Cut and Run #8 of 9. (MM Police Procedural) Home from their unexpected deployment, the former members of Marine Force Recon Team Sidewinder rejoin their loved ones and try to pick up the pieces of the lives they were forced to leave behind. Ty Grady comes home to Zane Garrett, only to find that everything around him has changed–even the men he went to war with. 3/3

2420. **Roux, Abigail,** *Crash and Burn,* Riptide, 2015. Cut and Run #9 of 9. (MM Police Procedural) It's been five years since Special Agents Ty Grady and Zane Garrett first worked together to solve the Tri-State murders, and time has been both harsh and kind. Engaged now, they face the challenge of planning a deeply uncertain future together. 3/3

2421. **Roux, Abigail,** *Shock and Awe,* Riptide, 2013. Sidewinder #1 of 4. (MM Military) After barely surviving a shootout in New Orleans, Sidewinder medic Kelly Abbott has to suffer through a month of recovery before he can return home to Colorado. He's not surprised when fellow Sidewinder Nick O'Flaherty stays with him in New Orleans. Nor is he surprised when Nick travels home with him to help him get back on his feet–after all, years on the same Marine Force Recon team bonded the men in ways that only bleeding for a brother can. The past can come back to ruin their future. 3/3

2422. **Roux, Abigail,** *Cross and Crown,* Riptide, 2014. Sidewinder #2 of 4. (MM Military) When Nick O'Flaherty arrives at the scene of a double homicide to find he has a witness to the crime, he thinks it's his lucky day. But when he realizes his witness is suffering from amnesia and can't even remember his own name, Nick wishes he'd gone with his gut and put in for vacation time. 3/3

2423. **Roux, Abigail,** *Part and Parcel,* Riptide, 2015. Sidewinder #3 of 4. (MM Military) Nick O'Flaherty and Kelly Abbott had their happy ending in sight when a friend's call for help almost ended with them losing it to the blade of a knife. Now, in the aftermath of near-disaster, both men are trying to heal and move on. –fourth book, *Tried and True,* has not been given a release date yet (MLM). 3/3

2424. **Rowland, Laura Joh,** *The Ripper's Shadow,* Crooked Lane, 2017. Victorian Mystery #1 of 4. (Historical Amateur Sleuth) Miss Sarah Bain, a photographer in Whitechapel, is an independent woman with dark secrets. In the privacy of her studio, she supplements her meager income by taking illicit "boudoir photographs" of the town's local ladies of the night. But when two of her models are found gruesomely murdered within weeks of one another, Sarah begins to suspect it's more than mere coincidence. Teamed with a motley crew of friends–including a street urchin, a gay aristocrat, a Jewish butcher and his wife, and a beautiful young actress–Sarah delves into the crime of the century. 2/3

2425. **Rowland, Laura Joh,** *A Mortal Likeness,* Crooked Lane, 2018. Victorian Mystery #2 of 4. (Historical Amateur Sleuth) A photographer in Whitechapel, London, Sarah Bain is also a private detective- skilled at capturing others' dark secrets, and expert at keeping her own. When a wealthy banker, Sir Gerald Mariner, posts a handsome reward for finding his missing infant, all of London joins in, hoping to win that money for themselves. Usually discouraged by a saturated market, Sarah is instead curiously allured as she realizes the case hits much closer to home than she first thought. –the third book *The Hangman's Secret* is coming out in 2019 and *The Woman in the Veil* is set to be released in 2020 (MLM). 2/3

2426. **Royal, Priscilla,** *Wine of Violence,* Poisoned Press, 2003. Medieval #1 of 15. (Historical) It is late summer in the year 1270 and England is as weary as its aging king, Henry III. Although the Simon de Montfort rebellion is over, the smell of death still hangs like smoke over the land. Even in the small priory of Tyndal on the remote East Anglian coast, the monks and nuns of the Order of Fontevraud long for a return to tranquil routine. Their hopes are dashed, however, when the young and inexperienced Eleanor of Wynethorpe is appointed their new prioress over someone of their own choosing. Nor are Eleanor's own prayers for a peaceful transition answered. Only a day after her arrival, a brutally murdered monk is found in the cloister gardens, and Brother Thomas, a young priest with a troubled past, arrives to bring her a more personal grief. Now she must not only struggle to gain the respect of her terrified and resentful flock but also cope with violence, lust and greed in a place dedicated to love and peace. –Brother Thomas is gay and assists the main character in her investigations (MLM). 2/3

2427. **Royal, Priscilla,** *Tyrant of the Mind,* Poisoned Press, 2004. Medieval #2 of 15. (Historical) A nun and a monk defy death and dishonor at her family's Welsh fortress... In the winter of 1271, Death stalks the corridors of Wynethorpe Castle on the Welsh border. When the Grim Reaper touches the beloved grandson of the castle lord, Baron Adam sends for his daughter, Prioress Eleanor of Tyndal, and her sub-infirmarian, Sister Anne, to save the child with prayers and healing talents. Escorting them to the remote fortress is Brother Thomas, an unwilling monk fighting his private demons. 2/3

2428. **Royal, Priscilla,** *Sorrow without End,* Poisoned Press, 2006. Medieval #3 of 15. (Historical) As the autumn storms of 1271 ravage the East Anglian coast, Crowner Ralf finds the corpse of a brutally murdered soldier in the woods near Tyndal Priory. The dagger in the man's chest is engraved with a strange, cursive design, and the body is wrapped in a crusaders cloak. Was the murder the act of a member of the Assassin sect, or was the weapon meant to mislead him in finding the killer? Ralfs decision to take the corpse to the priory for advice may be reasonable, but he is soon caught up in a maelstrom of conflict, both personal and political. The priory is deeply divided over whether to purchase a relic. 1/3

2429. **Royal, Priscilla**, *Justice for the Damned,* Poisoned Press, 2007. Medieval #4 of 15. (Historical) It is May of 1272, and Prioress Eleanor, recovering from a near-fatal winter fever, returns to Amesbury Priory to visit her aunt in time for the Feast of Saint Melor. Although Eleanor hopes to regain her strength in the midst of pleasant childhood memories, Death reveals a most troublesome fondness for her company, thwarting her desire for peace. 2/3

2430. **Royal, Priscilla**, *Forsaken Soul,* Poisoned Press, 2008. Medieval #5 of 15. (Historical) The summer of 1273 is peaceful for most of England, but not for Prioress Eleanor of Tyndal Priory. Her friend, Crowner Ralf, is newly widowed with a baby. And her new anchoress is welcoming visitors to her window at night: one of them a man the prioress secretly loves. Now his loyalty to her as head of Tyndal Priory is suspect. Then Martin the Cooper is poisoned at the local inn. Martin had a wealth of enemies. 2/3

2431. **Royal, Priscilla**, *Chambers of Death,* Poisoned Press, 2009. Medieval #6 of 15. (Historical) When one of her company falls ill on a return journey to Tyndal, Prioress Eleanor accepts lodging at a nearby manor. The hospitality may be warm but the underlying passions among the steward's family are scorching. Master Stevyn's wife is having an affair with the groom while a local widow acts more like the lady of the manor than the lady herself. Stevyn's eldest son and spouse are obsessed with sin and heaven, while his youngest son, bound for the Church, unexpectedly returns with more interest in lute playing than the priesthood. It is no surprise when someone's throat is cut. 2/3

2432. **Royal, Priscilla**, *Valley of Dry Bones,* Poisoned Press, 2010. Medieval #7 of 15. (Historical) In the late summer of 1274, King Edward has finally been anointed England's ruler, and his queen contemplates a pilgrimage in gratitude for their safe return from Outremer, a journey that will include a stay at Tyndal Priory. Envoys are sent to confirm that everything will be suitable for the king's wife, and Prioress Eleanor nervously awaits them, knowing that regal visits bring along expense and honor. The cost is higher than expected, however, when Death arrives as the unexpected emissary. 2/3

2433. **Royal, Priscilla**, *Killing Season,* Poisoned Press, 2011. Medieval #8 of 15. (Historical) Baron Herbert's return from crusade should have been a joyous occasion. Instead, he grows increasingly morose, withdraws from his family, and refuses to share his wife's bed. When his sons begin to die in strange accidents, some ask whether Herbert harbors a dark sin for which God has cursed him. The baron suddenly sends for Sir Hugh of Wynethorpe, begging his friend to bring spiritual and secular healers but giving little explanation for the request. Worried about Herbert's descent into melancholy and the tragic deaths, Sir Hugh persuades his sister, Prioress Eleanor of Tyndal Priory, to accompany him as well as a respected physician, Master Gamel. Although he is pleased when the prioress brings her healer, Sister Anne, he is dismayed to find Brother Thomas included, a man he has reason to despise. 2/3

2434. **Royal, Priscilla,** *Sanctity of Hate,* Poisoned Press, 2012. Medieval #9 of 15. (Historical) Summer 1276 is peaceful at Tyndal Priory until a villager's corpse is found floating in the millpond. The murder victim was greatly disliked, yet no villager wants to see one of their own hanged for the deed. Fingers quickly point to a Jewish family forced to take shelter while relocating under the provisions of King Edward's Statute of the Jewry. Riots loom; threats mount. Eleanor and Ralf have little time to gather evidence before popular opinion rules the murder solved. But just who is really responsible for this crime? 2/3

2435. **Royal, Priscilla,** *Covenant with Hell,* Poisoned Press, 2013. Medieval #10 of 15. (Historical) n the Spring of 1277, Prioress Eleanor goes on a pilgrimage to a famous East Anglian shrine. There are rumors that King Edward may also visit the shrine soon to seek God's blessing for his invasion of Wales. Lurking in this sacred place, however, is an assassin hoping to murder a king. 2/3

2436. **Royal, Priscilla,** *Satan's Lullaby,* Poisoned Press, 2015. Medieval #11 of 15. (Historical) It is the autumn of 1278. The harvest is in. The air is crisp. Dusty summer breathes a last sigh before the dark seasons arrive. For Prioress Eleanor, dark times arrive early in Norfolk. The head of her order, Abbess Isabeau, has sent Father Etienne Davoir from its headquarters in France to inspect all aspects of Tyndal Priory from its morals to its roofs. Surely the Abbess would not have chosen her own brother for this rare and thorough investigation unless the cause was serious, and she had reason to fear intervention from Rome. 2/3

2437. **Royal, Priscilla,** *Land of Shadows,* Poisoned Press, 2016. Medieval #12 of 15. (Historical) A royal birth, a nobleman's death, a scarlet woman's murder... In March, 1279, Edward I takes a break from hammering the Welsh and bearing down on England's Jews to vacation in Gloucestershire. The royal party breaks the journey at Woodstock Manor. And there one life begins as Queen Eleanor labors to birth a new daughter, and one draws to an end when apoplexy fells Baron Adam Wynethorpe. 2/3

2438. **Royal, Priscilla,** *The Proud Sinner,* Poisoned Press, 2017. Medieval #13 of 15. (Historical) In the winter of 1282, snow and ice ravage East Anglia while Prioress Eleanor awaits the decision of her young maid, Gracia, found starving on the streets some years ago, whether to take vows or to leave Tyndal Priory to make her way in the world. 2/3

2439. **Royal, Priscilla,** *Wild Justice,* Poisoned Press, 2018. Medieval #14 of 15. (Historical) It is Spring 1282. England is at war again with Wales. As Baron Hugh of Wynethorpe, a veteran of fighting in Outremer, prepares to join his King's army, he begs his sister, Prioress Eleanor, a favor. On her journey home to Tyndal Prior in Norfolk, she is to carry a gift of rents from the Wynethorpe estates to Mynchen Buckland Priory. The charter for the grant and a private letter is to be given to the Hospitaller nuns' Prioress Amicia, and none other. Eleanor agrees - if Hugh is heading into the Welsh wilderness, then she, Eleanor, will do him this service as well as pray for his protection. –*The Twice-Hanged Man,* the fifteenth book in the Medieval series is to be released in 2019 (MLM). 2/3

2440. **Roynesdal, John,** *The Last Death,* Writer's Showcase, 2000. Carnegie #1 of 3. (Police Procedural) Baffled by seven brutal slayings on Kuhio Beach, Wai'kiki, detective Phillip Michael Carnegie, of the Special Division Detective Team, Honolulu Police Department, finally uncovers the perfect suspect. The only problem is no one believes him, neither his teammates, nor his close friend and confidant, sixty-year-old Juliana Smith. 3/3

2441. **Roynesdal, John,** *The Curse,* 1st Books, 2002. Carnegie #2 of 3. (Police Procedural) The theft of a priceless family document, a corpse that drives a car, a confessed killer who cannot be guilty, and a fifty-year-old hex challenge Phillip Michael Carnegie of the Honolulu Police Department in John A. Roynesdal? 3/3

2442. **Roynesdal, John,** *Living in Darkness,* Lulu, 2005. Carnegie #3 of 3. (Police Procedural) A young, gay man's life is changed while walking the slopes of Diamond Head. A father is searching for his gay son. Paul Noa and Nick Keone, two gay police detectives, are convinced that a brutal attack and three murders are hate crimes. The lives of these people, along with detectives Phillip Michael Carnegie and George Maikai'moku, intersect. 3/3

2443. **Rucka, Greg,** *A Gentleman's Game,* Bantam, 2004. Queen and Country #1 of 3. (Espionage) Tara Chace may be the most dangerous woman alive. She can seduce you into believing she's the woman of your dreams–or kill you with the icy efficiency of an executioner. As the new head of Special Operations for British Intelligence, she no longer has to court death in the field–she wants to. –gay intelligence officer is mainly sidelined in the series (MLM). 1/3

2444. **Rucka, Greg,** *Private Wars,* Bantam 2005. Queen and Country #2 of 3. (Espionage) Tara Chace was once the most dangerous woman alive. And now that the international spy network thinks she's as good as dead, she's even more dangerous than ever. 1/3

2445. **Rucka, Greg,** *The Last Run,* Bantam, 2010. Queen and Country #3 of 3. (Espionage) For nearly a decade Tara Chace has been Britain's top covert agent. But Chace is past her expiration date. Her body hurts. Her nerves are scrambled. She's ready for a desk job, the quiet role of mentor to a new generation of special operations officers. But before her replacement can be chosen, there's one last job for Queen and country ... and it may be the last thing she does. Ever. 1/3

2446. **Rupured, Michael,** *The Case of the Missing Drag Queen,* DSP, 2018. Luke Tanner #1 of 1. (Suspense) Broke, saddled with a mountain of debt, and dependent on his Aunt Callie's support, aspiring writer Luke Tanner has returned to Kentucky to put his life back together after a failed five-year relationship. 3/3

2447. **Russel, Jay,** *Booty Boys,* Idol, 1999. (Pulp) Hard-boiled, hard-bodied black British private eye Alton Davies can't believe his eyes or his luck when he finds muscular African-American gangsta rapper Banji-B lounging in his office early one morning. Alton's disbelief, and his excitement - mount as Banji-B asks him to track down a stolen video of a post-gig orgy in which his homeboy, the notorious laydeez man Karamel, plays a starring and revealingly man-pleasing role. 3/3

2448. **Russell, David,** *Last Dance,* Napoleon, 2012. Winston #2 of 2. (Court Drama) Winston Patrick was a successful lawyer who defended the downtrodden of Vancouver's criminal world. Dissatisfied with his career, he traded in the courtroom for the high school classroom. Winston is barely surviving his first year at a Vancouver high school when his students present a human rights issue. A student wants to bring his same-sex partner to the high school prom, but the school won't let him. Winston reluctantly leads his proteges on their first legal quest: suing the school. He never thought that fighting for a student's rights could have deadly consequences, but as the issue gains publicity, Winston discovers that their opponents will stop at nothing to make their point – not even murder. 2/3

2449. **Russell, R. J.,** *Scandal on Cleveland Street,* Kindle, 2015. Swinscow #1 of 2. (Historical) In 1889 a scandal broke that was to shake the

British establishment to its core. A teenage telegram delivery lad, Charles Swinscow, who worked for the Central Telegraph Office, was originally investigated with regards to monetary theft when he was found to have 18 shillings on him. It was a company ruling that telegram lads were not allowed to carry any of their own money. In order to prove his innocence, he had to justify where the 18 shillings came from. The story he gave to the investigating officers was to send shock waves out into Parliament, the aristocracy and even the Royal Family. –available as an e-book only (MLM). 3/3

2450. **Russell, R. J.,** *Letters of State,* Kindle, 2018. Swinscow #2 of 2. (Historical) After the dust has settled from the Cleveland Street Scandal Charlie Swinscow finds himself with no job, no home and very little in the way of prospects. An unexpected visit from his sister brings a letter that will lead him to a new life, complete with adventure, excitement and danger the likes of which he only ever read about in weekly Penny Dreadfuls. –available as an e-book only (MLM). 3/3

2451. **Russoli, Dominic,** *The Making of Men,* iUniverse, 2009. (Historical)It's September 1943, and Scotty Velner, the son of America's secretary of war enrolls at a prestigious college near Washington. He expects to spend most of his time studying. Instead, he enters a world of murder, sex, and espionage. Scotty's roommate, a handsome jock named David La Font, has Scotty confused and questioning his sexuality. When a close friend is murdered, Scotty finds that sharing a room with David is more than he could have ever expected. 3/3

2452. **Ryan, A. J.,** *Darcy Boys and the Case of the Secret Skull,* Burnaby, 2009. Darcy Bros #1 of 2. (MM Romance) Step-brothers Tommy and Dash Darcy have only just met, and already they're stuck together for the summer while their parents disappear on a honeymoon abroad. What else are two sexy, strapping lads to do but solve a murderous mystery on a college campus full of hot male virgins who are dropping dead at an alarming rate? 3/3

2453. **Ryan, A. J.,** *Darcy Boys and the Case of the He-Bot Hunks,* Eternal, 2010. Darcy Bros #2 of 2. (MM Mystery) When the handsome, hunky models of the all-American fashion label Abercumbie & Felch arrive at the lake for their latest shoot, Tommy is seduced by their world of glamor, glitz and glistening abs. But being an Abercumbie & Felch model involves much more than Tommy imagined. This time, he may have bitten off more than he could chew. Will Tommy live long enough to learn that beauty is indeed only skin deep? Will Dash make the dash to rescue Tommy in time? Will Dash's dear dead Daddy help save Tommy's lily-white ass-or will he just dish Dash the 'tude? 3/3

2454. **Ryan, Cassidy,** *Sleeping with the Past,* Torquere, 2007. (MM Police Procedural) Nathaniel is a cop, assigned to protect professor and well-known writer Asher Munro. Asher has been receiving threats, and as the situation gets worse and worse, Nathaniel and Asher have to spend a lot of time together, for Asher's protection. 3/3

2455. **Ryan, Garry,** *Queen's Park,* NeWest, 2004. Paul Lane #1 of 10. (Police Procedural) Detective Lane has a knack for discovering the whereabouts of missing persons. But the city's latest case has disappeared without a trace. After a brutal attack on his young nephew, ex-mayor Bob Swatsky has gone missing with 13 million dollars of tax-payers' money. Is he on the run with the cash, or is it something more sinister? A zany cast of characters, including a love doll, and a chain-smoking grandma with an oxygen tank, lead Detective Lane on a thrilling romp through the streets of Calgary. 3/3

2456. **Ryan, Garry,** *The Lucky Elephant Restaurant,* NeWest, 2006. Paul Lane #2 of 10. (Police Procedural) When the young daughter of popular radio talk show host Bobbie Reddie disappears along with Bobbie's ex-husband, Detectives Lane and Harper are on the case. Haunted by flashbacks from a previous missing child case, Lane once again takes to the streets of Calgary looking for answers. –won the nineteenth LAMBDA Award (MLM). 3/3

2457. **Ryan, Garry,** *A Hummingbird Dance,* NeWest, 2008. Paul Lane #3 of 10. (Police Procedural) When Ryan Dudley ventures out on horseback and his horse returns without him, Lane and Harper are summoned to unravel the mystery. Dudley's disappearance marks the first anniversary of a young boy's murder in the same neighborhood, and evidence indicates the two incidents are connected. When Dudley's roommate also goes missing and mysterious shootings start happening in the area, Harper and Lane are swept into a feud between neighbors, races, and land owners, all in search of a murderer on the loose for much too long. 3/3

2458. **Ryan, Garry,** *Smoked,* NeWest, 2010. Paul Lane #4 of 10. (Police Procedural) When Jennifer Towers is found dead in a graffiti-tagged dumpster, Detectives Lane and Harper must decipher the art to find its artist - and possibly the victim's killer. What begins as an unconventional murder investigation leads to the disturbing discovery of two abused children, whose father becomes a prime suspect in the case. In true Detective Lane form, Lane must protect the damaged youths while keeping his own family intact. With a surprising shift in tone, "Smoked" highlights the Detective Lane mystery series as one that reminds us of this generation's obligation to the children in its care. 3/3

2459. **Ryan, Garry,** *Malabarista,* NeWest, 2011. Paul Lane #5 of 10. (Police Procedural) Under investigation by the Calgary Police Department, Lane finds himself fighting for his career. Then, when an Eastern European war criminal winds up dead in the city, and his partner Arthur is diagnosed with cancer, Lane must contend with dangerous criminals, broken allegiances, pressure from his superiors, a determined bomber, and the very real fear of losing the person he cares for most of all. 3/3

2460. **Ryan, Garry,** *Foxed,* NeWest, 2013. Paul Lane #6 of 10. (Police Procedural) After a long series of professional and personal upheavals, Detective Lane begins his latest adventure happy, at peace, and enjoying life with his partner Arthur, their children Christine and Matt, and his able new partner, RCMP officer Keely Saliba. 3/3

2461. **Ryan, Garry,** *Glycerine,* NeWest, 2014. Paul Lane #7 of 10. (Police Procedural) Lane and Li's first case, an investigation into the death of a migrant worker, points them in the direction of Douglas Jones, the leader of a radical religious compound in northern Alberta, who has been suspected of bombing oil and gas pipelines. With the Calgary Stampede just days away, and anti-Muslim tension mounting in town in the wake of the "honor killing" of a young girl, Lane and Li must foil a potential terror attack. 3/3

2462. **Ryan, Garry,** *Indiana Pulcinella,* NeWest, 2013. Paul Lane #8 of 10. (Police Procedural) Detectives Lane and Li find themselves on the hunt yet again, this time following a pair of gruesome killers whose perfectly composed crime scenes match those of an inmate put away by Calgary Police years earlier. As more people come into the line of fire, Lane must team up with some unlikely new allies in order to crack the case. 3/3

2463. **Ryan, Garry,** *Matanzas,* NeWest, 2017. Paul Lane #9 of 10. (Police Procedural) His psyche still reeling from having to kill a criminal in the line of duty, Calgary's Detective Lane flies to Cuba to celebrate the wedding of his beloved niece. While there, though, he finds himself drafted by the local police into investigating the murder of a Canadian tourist. 3/3

2464. **Ryan, Garry,** *Sea of Cortez,* NeWest, 2018. Paul Lane #10 of 10. (Police Procedural) After a series of assassinations rocks Calgary's underworld, Detective Lane is conscripted along with his husband Arthur into working undercover to seek out links in the Mexico - Canada drug connection and stop the violence. 3/3

2465. **Ryan, Hank Phillippi,** *Prime Time,* Harlequin, 2007. McNally #1 of 4. (Journalism) In the cutthroat world of television journalism, seasoned reporter Charlotte McNally knows that she'd better pull out all the stops or kiss her job goodbye. But it's her life that might be on the line when she learns that an innocent-looking e-mail offer resulted in murder, mayhem and a multimillion-dollar fraud ring. All too soon her investigation leads her straight to Josh Gelston, who is a little too helpful and a lot too handsome. Charlie might have a nose for news, but men are a whole other matter. Now she has to decide whether she can trust Josh...before she ends up as the next lead story. –McNally's 30s African American producer is gay in this straight romance (MLM). 1/3

2466. **Ryan, Hank Phillippi,** *Face Time,* Harlequin, 2007. McNally #2 of 4. (Journalism) Veteran TV reporter Charlotte McNally fights for justice, journalism–and the battle against on-air aging. The good news: she's got explosive evidence to free an innocent woman from prison. The bad news: that makes Charlotte–and someone she loves–the real killer's next target. 1/3

2467. **Ryan, Hank Phillippi,** *Air Time,* Harlequin, 2009. McNally #3 of 4. (Journalism) When savvy TV reporter Charlotte McNally enters the glamorous world of high fashion, she soon discovers that when the purses are fake-the danger is real. And no one can be trusted! Now Charlotte can't tell the real from the fake as she goes undercover to bring the couture counterfeiters to justice-and in her struggle to answer an all-important, life-changing question from a certain handsome professor. The one thing Charlotte knows for sure is that the wrong choice could be the last decision she ever makes! 1/3

2468. **Ryan, Hank Phillippi,** *Drive Time,* Harlequin, 2010. McNally #4 of 4. (Journalism) Investigative reporter Charlotte McNally is an expert at keeping things confidential, but suddenly everyone has a secret–and it turns out it is possible to know too much. 1/3

2469. **Ryan, J. D.,** *Spy Games,* JMS, 2015. (MM Historical Espionage) Cold War ... Hot Spies. It's the 1960's. Unbeknownst to the world, a secret international organization is working behind the scenes for world peace. –available as an e-book only (MM). 3/3

2470. **Ryan, J. D.,** *Southern Fried Spies,* JMS, 2015. (MM Historical Espionage) Cold War, hot spies, y'all. Vincent and Kolya are back – in the Deep South. They must protect a brilliant chemist and his family while the man completes the new formula he's promised to sell to T.H.R.U.S.T. –available as an e-book only (MLM). 3/3

2471. **Ryecart, A. E.,** *Captive Hearts,* Createspace, 2018. Deviant Hearts #1 of 2. (MM Mystery) When Dashiell Slater uses his fists to stop a vicious assault, the last thing he expects is to be offered a job as reward for being a Good Samaritan. Out of work and short of cash, all he has to do is chauffeur Billy around. It's easy money so saying yes should be a no-brainer. And if the offer's not quite legal, so what? Dashiell's smart and savvy and knows how the world works. But there are strings attached, and Dashiell doesn't want to get entangled. He's ready to say no and walk away – until he sees the fear, despair and fathomless sadness in Billy's jade-green eyes. 3/3

2472. **Ryecart, A. E.**, *Radical Hearts,* Createspace, 2018. Deviant Hearts #2 of 2. (MM Mystery) Taking shelter from a storm in an off-beat, alternative bookshop, security consultant Lee Adams only wants to wait out the weather. Wary and cautious following the collapse of his long-term relationship, Lee's got no time and even less interest in having a man in his life. Or that's what he tells himself as he works long, exhausting days in a futile effort to deny his crushing loneliness. But when the flirty, dark-haired assistant invites him to a campaign meeting to save an old pub from being bulldozed out of existence, Lee finds himself saying yes when everything tells him he should be saying no. 3/3

S

2473. **St. Clair, Allen,** *Death on the Dock: A Lake Agate Mystery,* Self-Published, 2018. (Paranormal) At the Cabins at Lake Agate, Preston Owens (owner and operator) can't exactly tell people that Cabin 6 is haunted. Preston didn't buy the campgrounds three years prior to attract amateur ghost hunters, nor does he want to scare potential renters away before they even make a reservation. So... he keeps that quiet. Just like he keeps the secret that he can see dead people to himself. And life is good. –e-book only (MLM). 3/3

2474. **St. Clair, Roger,** *Caged,* Midwood, 1976. (Pulp) "Pittsburgh bookkeeper Dave, though he does not find the evidence to nail his lover's killer, manages to trick the man into admitting his guilt (Gunn)." 3/3

2475. **Sacher, Jerry,** *The Saint of San Francisco,* Dreamspinner, 2011. Saint of San Francisco #1 of 2. (MM Mystery) After finding himself still depressingly single on his thirty-second birthday, Jeremy Haniver accepts an invitation to move to San Francisco. Though he falls in love with the Castro and the city, it's not enough to cure him of his loneliness or the depression that dogs him. He almost throws his life away, but fate intervenes when Jeremy meets Mark Caparelli. 3/3

2476. **Sacher, Jerry,** *The Rosary and the Badge,* Dreamspinner, 2012. Saint of San Francisco #2 of 2. (MM Mystery) Jeremy Haniver has finally started his new life in San Francisco, where he has a job working in a Castro coffee shop and a boyfriend, police officer Mark Caparelli, to watch out for him. After solving the mystery surrounding the death of a young sailor, Jeremy and Mark are ready to lay off the adventure for a while. But trouble has a way of finding Jeremy no matter how hard Mark tries to keep him out of it. 3/3

2477. **Sanders, J. Aaron,** *Speakers of the Dead,* Plume, 2016. Walt Whitman #1 of 1. (Historical) The year is 1843; the place: New York City. Aurora reporter Walt Whitman arrives at the Tombs prison yard where his friend Lena Stowe is scheduled to hang for the murder of her husband, Abraham. Walt intends to present evidence on Lena's behalf, but Sheriff Harris turns him away. Lena drops to her death, and Walt vows to posthumously exonerate her. –winner of the 29th LAMBDA Award for Best Gay Mystery (MLM). 3/3

2478. **Sanders, J. B.,** *Glen and Tyler's Honeymoon Adventures,* Lulu,

2011. Glen and Tyler #1 of 5. (Caper) Tyler can't inherit unless he gets married ... and when Glen proposes, hijinks ensue. Follow the guys on their world-spanning adventure as they defeat mobsters, an evil step-mother, a rakish brother-in-law and pirates. No, really – pirates! Plus, there's an underground super-base. And hockey. Come for the romance, stay for the hockey. –two bisexual guys take the plunge after decades of friendship (MM). 3/3

2479. **Sanders, J. B.,** *Glen and Tyler's Scottish Troubles,* Lulu, 2012. Glen and Tyler #2 of 5. (Caper) In typical Hardy Boys–er, Glen & Tyler fashion, there are secret passages, irascible old men, caves, missing treasure, fine liquor and kilts. Ok, the kilts thing is new – but believe me, you'll like 'em. Although there isn't much hockey this time around, there is shinty. There's also some romantic anniversary thing, but really, stay for the shinty. 3/3

2480. **Sanders, J. B.,** *Glen and Tyler's Parish Double-Cross,* Self-Published, 2013. Glen and Tyler #3 of 5. (Caper) Glen and Tyler are young, in love, and the wealthiest human beings on the planet. But when Glen's brother calls from a jail in Paris, they're off to France to tangle with spies, neo-Nazis, evil world-spanning conspiracies and French gangsters. Plus, they have a romantic dinner, and find long-lost treasure. Really, it's a fun-filled non-stop romp. 3/3

2481. **Sanders, J. B.,** *Glen and Tyler's High Seas Hijinks,* Self-Published, 2015. Glen and Tyler #4 of 5. (Caper) Let's be honest. Glen & Tyler go on vacation the same way the US Navy deploys: with much fanfare and crowds throwing streamers. Despite the pirates, smugglers, and the usual criminal crowd, this tale has hot men, Chemin De Fer, and some nice beach scenes. Come for the pirates, stay for the tight swimsuits. Oh, and rum. Lots of rum. 3/3

2482. **Sanders, J. B.,** *Glen and Tyler's Saratoga Trunk,* Kindle, 2018. Glen and Tyler #5 of 5. (Caper) When they get all nostalgic and head back to their old college town, Glen & Tyler get pulled into a cozy murder mystery, with a side dish of international spy intrigue. –available as an e-book only (MLM). 3/3

2483. **Sanders, Lawrence,** *Seduction of Peter S.,* Putnam's Sons, 1983. (Crime Drama) An unemployed actor walks the edge between sexy and seamy where homicide, mayhem, and the mob carve up the profits from prostitution. –main character is straight but operates in a world of male prostitution, involving gay and bisexual friends (MLM). 2/3

2484. **Saros, Chris,** *Semblance,* DSP, 2018. (MM Mystery) Drake isn't looking for justice. He's not interested in doing what's right. He's after one thing and one thing only: revenge. That means taking down the Boredega drug cartel–and the shadowy, seemingly invincible man who heads it–even if he goes down with them. 3/3

2485. **Sashner, Andra,** *Dragonfly,* Less Than Three, 2010. (MM Espionage) Ghost is good at what he does, quietly and efficiently executing the missions assigned to him by his superiors at Rescue & Investigations Global. They might not be the sorts of jobs he can ever brag about, but he's damned good at them. That is, until a mission to assassinate nearly results in the death of the wrong man, and Ghost and his superiors realize that they have been deceived, and that a greater game is being played. 3/3

2486. **Satterwait, Walter,** *Wilde West,* St. Martin's, 1991. (Historical) Though a world-renowned dandy, Oscar Wilde is not too refined for Colorado. As he travels across America on the lecture circuit, the famously witty playwright has found much to love about the western states. Whiskey, saloons, and friendly conversation with notables like John "Doc" Holliday - Wilde loves it all. There is even, in every town his entourage visits, a sensational murder. 3/3

2487. **Savage, Lon,** *Knave of Diamonds,* Blueboy, 1977. (Pulp) "Police Detective Walker, 30, proves Nico Martinez, 23, is not a jewel thief after all (Gunn)." 3/3

2488. ominously appears on his farm, Gordianus knows he must unlock the secret of Catilina's Riddle before Rome tears herself apart. –won the sixth LAMBDA Award (MLM). 2/3

2489. **Saw, Richard (Kevin James),** *A Curious Series of Events,* Kindle, 2012. Holmes #1 of 10. (Contemporary Sherlock Holmes) A lawyer who investigates bank fraud and an obstetrics & gynecological surgeon have no intention of being caught up in a world of crime. But when a friend who's never taken a drug in his life dies of an overdose, John Watson can't help but be suspicious. His reluctant boyfriend, a hard-headed, high-living lawyer who responds only to his surname – Holmes – is convinced that it's just his partner being over-dramatic. –available as an e-book only (MLM). 3/3

2490. **Saw, Richard,** *The Adventure of the Missing Oscar,* Kindle, 2013. Holmes #2 of 10. (Contemporary Sherlock Holmes) Jeremy Burrell is a wealthy and successful interior designer with a big house in Notting Hill, a new young plaything to help him with the pasturing and plenty of friends who he met at his Summer holiday home in Mykonos. Back in London however, over dinner one of those 'friends' has stolen his prize possession - one of Edith Head's Oscars. –available as an e-book only (MLM). 3/3

2491. **Saw, Richard,** *The Case of the Disappearing Translator,* Kindle, 2013. Holmes #3 of 10. (Contemporary Sherlock Holmes) What do you do when you go to visit a friend on holidays and they're not there? They have no family and their work doesn't seem to care and you spoke to them yesterday and yet... they've disappeared? –available as an e-book only (MLM). 3/3

2492. **Saw, Richard,** *The Mystery of Families,* Kindle, 2013. Holmes #4 of 10. (Contemporary Sherlock Holmes) John Watson found it most fascinating when his newest patient turned out to be the surrogate for the soon-to-be-married uber-powerful talent agent Simon Pearson and the up-and-coming politician Vernon Laing. But when Simon's business partners start to worry that he's more interested in his husband-to-be's career and not the next big Hollywood actor desperate for some West-End credibility, they decide that there's only one person they can trust to investigate this discreetly. –available as an e-book only (MLM). 3/3

2493. **Saw, Richard,** *The Case of the Church Lane,* Kindle, 2013. Holmes #5 of 10. (Contemporary Sherlock Holmes) It's a shock to everyone who knows him when Holmes unexpectedly suggests to Watson that they buy a house in the country together. But if Holmes was thinking that life would be simpler in the Homes Counties, then he wasn't counting on the other occupants of properties on the Church Lane. 'The Gang' - as they call themselves - seem overly involved in each other's lives and fascinated by the prospect of the arrival of Holmes and Watson into their midst shaking their lives. –available as an e-book only (MLM). 3/3

2494. **Saw, Richard,** *The Case of the Fallen Tycoon,* Kindle, 2013. Holmes #6 of 10. (Contemporary Sherlock Holmes) Patrick O'Brien is about to give new meaning to the phrase 'gay business tycoon'. He's turned his small bar business into an internationally renowned design and licensing agency and now he's going public with the intention of turning his brand and the ideas everyone else is going to give him, into a multi-million-dollar media empire. The fact that he's a nasty individual who no one in his right mind would trust, hasn't stopped his empire growing. That is, until he falls to his death from a second story window... just minutes after his husband Toby Gibbs sold the vast portion of their shares to the mysterious Maxima Hedge Fund. –available as an e-book only (MLM). 3/3

2495. **Saw, Richard,** *The Case of the Private Members' Club,* Kindle, 2013. Holmes #7 of 10. (Contemporary Sherlock Holmes) Already the toast of Tel-Aviv and Paris, entrepreneur Estaban Masci is about to open a Private Members' club in London. But someone seems determined to run him out of town and it seems they'll stop at nothing to ruin the launch party. When key members of staff leave, when suppliers stop deliveries and when One Direction cancels their appearance, he has no choice but to get the police involved. And they in turn know there is only one man in town who can track down the blackmailer. –available as an e-book only (MLM). 3/3

2496. **Saw, Richard,** *The Past that Haunts Us,* Kindle, 2014. Holmes #8 of 10. (Contemporary Sherlock Holmes) When the news came out that the high-performing hedge fund Mike & Laura Sudbury had created 10 years ago was in fact a Ponzi scheme, everyone had a lot to say - especially as it only came to light because Mike and Laura were found crushed to death by their garage door. –available as an e-book only (MM). 3/3

2497. **Saw, Richard,** *Encounter at Bowerman's Nose,* Kindle, 2014. Holmes #9 of 10. (Contemporary Sherlock Holmes) As Watson regales him with the tale of his teenage years, Holmes is fascinated by an event at the absent Dr Martin's flat. Though tenants have been evicted for shooting a porn film there, Holmes is suspicious that their filming interest actually lies in an apartment across the courtyard. But who is the mystery person that Detective Garrigues is so determined to keep Holmes from? –available as an e-book only (MLM). 3/3

2498. **Saw, Richard,** *The Vanity of Men,* Kindle, 2016. Holmes #10 of 10. (Contemporary Sherlock Holmes) There had been an assault on a man in a gay club in Lambeth with little clue as to who or why. Except that there had been another one with vaguely similar characteristics in Tower Hamlets. And another in Westminster. This was just the sort of case that Holmes could help them with, but he refused to budge from his declaration that their association was at an end. When Pomfrett's forceful attempt at reconciliation are met with defiance, his loyal associate Inspector Garrigues offered to try another route. John Watson. –available as an e-book only (MLM). 3/3

2499. **Saylor, Steven,** Roma Sub Rosa series, St. Martin's, 1991-2018. (Historical) Gordianus the Finder is a private investigator working around 56 b.c. in Ancient Rome. This series is rich with history and historical figures. Gordianus even counts Cicero as his friend and mentor. –Gordianus has a bisexual son who is involved with Julius Caesar and bisexuality and homosexuality is seen as normal. *Catalina's Riddle* won the sixth LAMBDA Award for Best Gay Mystery (MLM). 2/3

2500. **Schneider, James,** *In the Shadow of Silver Lake,* Wayward, 2011. (Thriller) In 1966, sixteen-year-old Rob Elliott's father is the headmaster of Tidewater Academy, a private school for wayward boys in Rehoboth Beach, Delaware. When he hires effeminate art teacher Bradley Baldwin on a moment's notice, it takes no time at all for Baldwin, Rob, and his cousin Carlo to become close friends. Rumors soon begin circulating that Baldwin is having an affair with fellow teacher Jeff Robinson. Even Robinson's wife suspects the affair, but before the truth can be found, both Robinson and Carlo are killed, rapidly followed by the mysterious death of Mrs. Robinson. 3/3

2501. **Scofield, Jamie,** *Brushback,* Dancing Fools, 2009. (MM Mystery) It couldn't be simpler. All Evan Austin needed to do was find R.J. Gibson before his eighteenth birthday and the kid would inherit a huge trust fund. Everybody would go home happy: R.J. would be set for life, the mom would appease her guilt, and maybe Evan would finally be able to put a tragic case from his past behind him. 3/3

2502. **Scholefield, Alan,** *Dirty Weekend,* St. Martin's, 1990. Macrae and Silver #1 of 6. (Police Procedural) An Easter weekend in cold, misty London. A man is found stabbed to death. Most of the inhabitants are spending a quiet few days with family and friends. But under Hungerford Bridge, where the homeless sleep, the body of a well-known television personality is found murdered. –the murdered man had a penchant for picking up young homeless and destitute teenage boys for sex, "frank and explicit in its commentary on racial stereotypes and the plight of the homeless young in contemporary London (Slide) (MLM). 2/3

2503. **Scholes, Joe,** *Malefactor,* Createspace, 2016. Gifford #1 of 2. (MM Hard Boiled) Private investigator Ren Gifford is hired by an eccentric billionaire to locate Glen Moreland, an employee who has disappeared. Everything about the case is strange, from the initial meeting with the client to the constant meddling by the client's front man. Glen had deliberately gone off the grid to avoid dire consequences he knew he would face when his employment contract ended. 3/3

2504. **Scholes, Joe,** *Transgressor,* Connie Suttle, 2017. Gifford #2 of 2. (MM Hard Boiled) Six months after successfully out-maneuvering the Malefactor, private investigator Ren Gifford is sucked back into M's vortex of evil manipulation. Despite the Malefactor's promise to leave Ren and company alone, he ultimately refuses to accept defeat. As a result, Ren and Terry, with Russ, Alex and Glen, find themselves in another battle of wits to survive. 3/3

2505. **Schriebman, Steven,** *Blood in the Hairspray,* Authorhouse, 2002. (Modern Cozy) A hard-bitten Mafia wife suddenly drops dead at the Beauty Shop, sending hotshot hairdresser Damian Shtup's tony Manhattan life into a tailspin. 3/3

2506. **Scoppetone, Sandra,** *Everything You Have is Mine,* Little Brown, 1991. Lauren Laurano #1 of 5. (Hard Boiled) Lauren Laurano, lesbian PI in New York City, gets obsessed by her cases. Lovely, shy Lake Huron refuses to talk about her rape, then is killed. As Lauren moves closer to the truth, her own life is endangered, and she discovers a family's past can't always stay buried. –brother is gay and has AIDS (MLM). 1/3

2507. **Scoppetone, Sandra,** *I'll be Leaving You Always,* Little Brown, 1993. Lauren Laurano #2 of 5. (Hard Boiled) The murder of Lauren's friend, Megan, in her jewelry store, sends the amateur sleuth on a personal search for the killer and forces her to come to terms with the death of the first person to accept Lauren's homosexuality. –introduction of Rick and William, a gay couple who live upstairs and have many difficulties with their relationship throughout the series. There is also a gay couple who run a business down the street from the victim (MLM). 2/3

2508. **Scoppetone, Sandra,** *My Sweet Untraceable You,* Little Brown, 1994. Lauren Laurano #3 of 5. (Hard Boiled) Hip, computer literate, and chocoholic, Lauren Laurano breaks the P.I. stereotype. And her new case breaks records for perplexity. Boston Blackie hires Lauren to find out what really happened to his mother, who reportedly died almost forty years before. What appears to be simply a case of a hurt inner child and a cold trail turns into a complex exploration of the dark secrets that haunt families and small towns. 2/3

2509. **Scoppetone, Sandra,** *Let's Face the Music and Die,* Little Brown, 1996. Lauren Laurano #4 of 5. (Hard Boiled) Witty, hip, pretty, and gay, Lauren Laurano isn't your typical private detective. She shares an apartment with Kip, her longtime lover, in New York's Greenwich Village, where they are surrounded by a close-knit group of friends. But Lauren and Kip's relationship has hit a rough patch, and when Kip goes out of town for a month-long conference, Lauren's life gets complicated by a new case, a new love interest, and a menace from her past. –Rick and William do not appear in book five, *Gonna Take a Homicidal Journey* (MLM). 2/3

2510. **Scott, D. Travers,** *One of these is Not Like the Others,* Suspect Thoughts, 2005. (Futuristic) Set in a reality one step removed from our own, this book is a darkly comic tale of masculine identity and relationships. What is a man, father, brother, son, lover? As four identical brothers seek the answers to these questions, they find the truth to be a quality as shifting as fog on the Oregon coast or sand in a Texas dust storm. –one of the brothers is gay, and one is closeted, won the 18th LAMBDA Award for Best Gay Mystery (MLM). 2/3

2511. **Scott, Geoffrey,** *Stealing Homer,* Prospective Press, 2018. (Amateur Sleuth) A widowed college professor adapting to a new life, a young man struggling with his future and his sexual orientation, a small Maine seaport seething with petty intrigues, and a newly found–and newly stolen–Winslow Homer painting. Stealing Homer is an art-flavored mystery that traces the connections and interconnections between people and the compelling, tragic, and humorous lives they lead. 3/3

2512. **Scott, Jack,** *The Poor Old Lady's Dead,* Harper and Row, 1976. Ralf Asher #1 of 10. (Police Procedural) Detective Inspector Rosher suspects foul play when an elderly nursing-home resident breaks her neck in a down-the-stairs plummet. This is the third questionable accident in less than a year, and Rosher is determined to wrap up the case and get the credit, even if it means convicting the wrong man! –not gay but male body worship (MLM). 1/3

2513. **Scott, Jack,** *Gospel Lamb,* Harper and Row, 1980. Ralf Asher #4 of 10. (Police Procedural) The local police were worried, and they had every reason to be. The fairground, during the pop festival, would be full of young people, girls and lads, some who'd brought their camping gear and the young people were everywhere, surround the three big open-air stages. The young audience was listening to the music, making love, basking in the sun, half nude, going on a few smoking trips...Just the sort of gathering that would attract The Avenger, a strange religious creature who enjoyed his deadly vengeance. The gathering had attracted, too, Donny Marks, a homosexual con man, and the not at all nice lover he'd picked up in jail. Fortunately, Detective Sgt Rosher was around... –things do not go well for Donny (MLM). 2/3

2514. **Scott, Melissa,** *The Armor of Light,* Baen, 1988. (Fantasy) The heavy summer air of 1595 is full of portents for Elizabeth, England's Queen, and James VI, King of Scotland. A coven of witches secretly controlled by the Wizard Earl of Bothwell has summoned a storm to sink the ship that bears James' bride to Scotland. Though the ship made port, the success of their summoning has emboldened them; the coven is now launching wizardly attacks on the King himself – and James is terrified. –Christopher Marlowe works as a spy (MLM). 2/3

2515. **Scott, Melissa,** *Point of Hopes,* Tor, 1995. Astreiant #1 of 5. (Fantasy Police Procedural) The royal city of Astreiant, the capital of the Kingdom of Chenedolle, is bracing itself for the influx of people, money, and trouble that invariably accompanies the Midsummer Fair. For Nicolas Rathe, the wiry, street-smart pointsman with a strong sense of justice, the fair means more work: keeping the peace, preventing the pickpockets from getting too bold, and tracking down runaway youths and apprentices. –Rathe is bisexual (MLM). 3/3

2516. **Scott, Melissa,** *Point of Knives,* Lethe, 2012. Astreiant #2 of 5. (Fantasy Police Procedural) The events of Midsummer have hardly been forgotten by the Fall Balance, and Nicolas Rathe can hardly complain that they've done any harm to his reputation, or to the reputation of the Points in general. However, it has meant that he's more in demand as an investigator, and the increased recognition and workload has made it hard to pursue friendship, or anything more, with Philip Eslingen, his comrade in the rescue of the stolen children. 3/3

2517. **Scott, Melissa,** *Point of Dreams,* Tor, 2001. Astreiant #3 of 5. (Fantasy Police Procedural) The city of Astreiant has gone crazy with enthusiasm for a new play, The Drowned Island, a lurid farrago of melodrama and innuendo. Pointsman Nicolas Rathe is not amused, however, at a real dead body on stage and must investigate. A string of murders follows, perhaps related to the politically important masque that is to play on that same stage. 3/3

2518. **Scott, Melissa,** *Fairs' Point,* Lethe, 2014. Astreiant #4 of 5. (Fantasy Police Procedural) During Dog Moon, the chief entertainment in the great city of Astreiant, for nobles and commons alike, is the basket-terrier races at New Fair. This year, with spectacularly bad timing, the massive and suspicious bankruptcy of a young nobleman has convulsed the city, leading to suicides, widespread loss of employment, and inconvenient new laws around the universal practice of betting on the races. As well, a rash of mysterious burglaries seems to suggest a magistical conspiracy. 3/3

2519. **Scott, Melissa,** *Point of Sighs,* Lethe, 2018. Astreiant #5 of 5. (Fantasy Police Procedural) Autumn downpours soak the city of Astreiant and cast a gloomy pall over its streets, while storms at sea have delayed merchant ships bearing important cargoes from distant lands. For Philip Eslingen, whose stars are bad for water, the season adds damp misery to the complications of organizing the new and controversial City Guard. 3/3

2520. **Scott, Melissa,** *Death by Silver,* Lethe, 2013. Julian and Ned #1 of 2. (MM Fantasy Historical) His practice newly established, metaphysician Ned Mathey can't afford to turn away any clients. But the latest Londoner to seek Ned's magical aid gives him pause: Mr Edgar Nevett, an arrogant banker, is the father of the bully who made Ned's life hell at boarding school. Nevertheless, Ned accepts the commission to ensure the Nevett family silver bears no ancient or modern curses, and then prepares to banish the Nevett family to unpleasant memory again. Until Edgar Nevett is killed by an enchanted silver candlestick–one of the pieces Ned declared magically harmless. –winner of the 26th LAMBDA Award for Science Fiction/Fantasy/Horror (MLM). 3/3

2521. **Scott, Melissa,** *A Death at the Dionysus Club,* Lethe, 2014. Julian and Ned #2 of 2. (MM Fantasy Historical) Metaphysician Ned

Mathey and private detective Julian Lynes again challenge magical and murderous threats in a Victorian London not quite the city in our history books. Mathey is recruited by Scotland Yard to assist the new Metaphysical Crimes Squad in the case of a literally heartless corpse. Mathey soon discovers that the magic used to rob the man of his heart and life does not conform to the laws of modern metaphysics and then a second victim turns up.

2522. **Scott, Michael,** *The Killer Queens,* Greenleaf, 1968. (Pulp) "Congolese undercover agent and mercenary Michael Cosgrave teams up with his bisexual married lover, Donald Watson, 20s, in a pulp action thriller (Gunn)." –this Michael Scott is different than the following Michael Scott (MLM). 3/3

2523. **Scott, Michael,** *Gay Exorcist,* Midwood, 1976. (Pulp) "San Francisco psychic sleuth Arthur (Darsie) Fleming, a defrocked Catholic priest, an exorcist, and avenger Paolo (Paul) Bottione, 18, a former hustler, work as a team to rid the city of evil in a pulp supernatural thriller (Gunn)." 3/3

2524. **Scott, Michael,** *Gay Psycho,* Midwood, 1976. (Pulp) "Toronto police detective Marc Diederich, 30s, closeted, investigates a serial slasher, but not all is what it seems (Gunn)." 3/3

2525. **Scott, Michael,** *Private Passions,* Midwood, 1976. (Pulp) "Police detective Frank McCormick, 30s, comes to the end of a relationship in a pulp action thriller [about] a teenage hustler is murdered, genitally mutilated, and his body thrown into a dumpster (Gunn)." 3/3

2526. **Scott, Michael,** *Chicken in Trouble,* Surree, 1978. (Pulp) "Mark Hamilton is engaged in a variety of illicit activities, backing the making of pornographic videos involving teenage players, providing teenage boys for Asian sex slavery rings, and running a hustler service that regularly supplies boys to various public figures... [The three detectives] move into an undercover operation to get the evidence to put him away (Gunn)." –Gunn notes that several pages are lifted directly from Scott's other novel *Private Passions*, listed above (MLM). 3/3

2527. **Scott, Michael,** *Hot Fire Fighter,* American Art Enterprises, 1988. (Pulp) "Rookie fireman Richard DiLorenzo suspects a fellow fireman of trying to kill him, but Captain James C. Jackson proves his suspicions are groundless (Gunn)." 3/3

2528. **Scott, Phillip,** *One Dead Diva,* Black Wattle, 1995. Marc and Paul #1 of 3. (Modern Cozy) Paul, a 50-ish opera queen with a habit of breaking everything he touches and Marc, a young, ditzy dancer and circuit boy, are an odd pairing as friends. As detectives, however, they are one small step from disaster. Why these two feel the need to investigate the death of Jennifer Burke, a rising opera star is almost a bigger mystery than whether the diva actually was pushed off a cliff. 3/3

2529. **Scott, Phillip,** *Gay Resort Murder Shock,* Penguin Australia, 1998. Marc and Paul #2 of 3. (Modern Cozy) Marc, a 50-ish opera queen, and his young, ditsy dancer friend Paul find themselves working at a gay resort off the coast of Queensland, run by Newton Heath, a friend of Marc's. All goes as expected as Marc continues to drop whatever he hasn't already forgotten, and Paul madly chases the guests, but when Newton is murdered our boys have a new mystery on their hands! 3/3

2530. **Scott, Phillip,** *Get Over It!,* Penguin Australia, 2000. Marc and Paul #3 of 3. (Modern Cozy) Against the backdrop of state elections, Phillip Scott's likable but unlikely amateur sleuths from down under, Marc and Paul, find themselves investigating a series of bizarre murders. But the investigation is hampered when Paul finds unexpected fame on television, and Marc must cope with a sexy new neighbor and a weepy ex-boyfriend. –renamed *Mardi Gras Murders* when published by Alyson in 2005 (MLM). 3/3

2531. **Scrivens, Matthew,** *Sole Survivor,* JMS, 2012. (MM Thriller) Two men want Adam Huntington. One wants to love him, the other wants to kill him. –available as an e-book only (MLM). 3/3

2532. **Seaton, George,** *A Circle of Magic,* iUniverse, 2005. (Fantasy) In 1943 Henry Stanley Clark died at the Roosevelt Hotel in New Orleans, Louisiana. Even though the New Orleans coroners determined that a brain aneurysm killed Henry, his widow, Maybelle Merriweather-Clark, was convinced otherwise. Until her death in 1984, Maybelle believed that Henry had been murdered. Maybelle's mastery of powerful black magic and voodoo, and her ability to conjure the spirits of the dead, are not enough to confirm her belief. –Michael Merriweather, nephew of Maybelle, is gay and investigates his uncle's death (MLM). 3/3

2533. **Seaton, George,** *Whispers of Old Winds,* Dreamspinner, 2015. (MM Paranormal) Sheriff Sam Daly, a veteran of Iraq and Afghanistan, and his husband, Michael Bellomo, have made a life for themselves in sparsely populated Pine County in the Colorado mountains. Sam oversees the small sheriff's department, and Michael sells his paintings and tourist items out of his shop, Needful Things. From the beginning, Sam has known Michael possessed gifts: the ability to see and hear things Sam cannot. 3/3

2534. **Seaton, George,** *Listening to the Dead,* Lethe, 2017. (Paranormal Police Procedural) Jack Dolan has spent almost thirty years solving homicides in Denver, his uncanny ability to speak to the dead learned from his aged mentor whom other cops refer to as Old Grim because of his incredible solve rate. 3/3

2535. **Serah, Tonne,** *Drop...Dead: The DJ Murders,* Haworth, 2007. (Modern Cozy) Dropping was no big deal for Joey De Vera. Everyone at Klub Galaxy took "party favors." They were circuit boys and they lived the fast-lane life of sex, drugs, designer jeans, and disco dancing. That is, until the night the DJ dropped dead, and the trail of clues led Joey across dance floors on both sides of the Pacific. 3/3

2536. **Severino, Thomas Paul,** *Seed Blood,* Pollywong Pond, 2018. Kayne Sorenson #1 of 3. (Psychological) In the Paradise of South Florida, a killer stalks, murders and stages victims to create a night world of torture, blood and death. Kayne Sorenson, Ph.D. pursues a murder whose rampage of complicated behavior patterns and dark turns of the psyche terrorize the communities of Ft. Lauderdale. -available as an e-book only (MLM). 3/3

2537. **Severino, Thomas Paul,** *Tribal Blood,* Pollywong Pond, 2018. Kayne Sorenson #2 of 3. (Psychological) In the snowy Aerie Valley of Aspen, Colorado, asking too many questions can result in abduction and death. Greed and vengeance trigger a chain of events fraught with monstrous corruption and violent struggles in the snowbound communities where Indigenous and Non-Native people share a landscape of natural wonder and exorbitant riches. – available as an e-book only (MLM). 3/3

2538. **Severino, Thomas Paul,** *Stage Blood,* Pollywong Pond, 2018. Kayne Sorenson #3 of 3. (Psychological) Amid the imperial vestiges of old Europe, Kayne Sorensen, Nick Sechi and Rebecca Quinto, face a brutal oligarch who sits at the center of a spider web of international intrigue, terror and murder controlling the forces of change on a continent rich in history and centuries of diversity. –available as an e-book only (MM). 3/3

2539. **Shade, Mike,** *Witness,* Torquere, 2007. (BDSM Mystery) Gary starts out as a murder suspect when a woman is killed, and he ends up wearing a good bit of her blood. The fact that Gary writes horror novels doesn't help his case one bit. Neither does his story of the big, monstrous man that actually did the killing, who stopped by on the way from the scene and gave him a hug. 3/3

2540. **Shade, Mike,** *Security,* Torquere, 2009. (MM Suspense) Ken and Bay are rich young men who like to party, make love together, and party some more. They also happen to be twins. Estranged from their father since their mother died when they were small children, they've learned to rely only on each other and not depend on anyone else. When their father hires a pair of bodyguards, Rick and

Simon, to watch their every move, they think it's just a bid on his part to keep them under his thumb, and Ken and Bay do their best to get rid of their babysitters. Then an all too real explosion rocks the mansion, and their bodyguards split the twins up, running in a different direction to keep them safe. 3/3

2541. **Sharon, Michael (Ed Wood Jr.)**, *A Half World,* Pad Library, 1967. (Erotica) A half world to many people some never know which half is theirs. ?/3

2542. **Shaw, Howard,** *Death of a Don,* Scribner's Sons, 1981. (Police Procedural) Inspector Barnaby is called to staid, old Beaufort College to investigate the murders of two dons and soon discovers that everyone had reason to hate at least one of the victims. –typical of British novels that take place in men only spaces such as a boy's school, there is one closeted teacher (MLM). 1/3

2543. **Shayne, Derek Taylor,** *Dark Star of Dambala,* Lulu, 2006. Solantro #1 of 4. (Supernatural) From the opulence of a Miami mansion, to the steamy jungles of the Dominican Republic, young Latino overnight billionaire, Tony Solantro, and his life-mate, full-blooded Blackfoot, Michael Taylor, embark on a laugh filled adventure. 3/3

2544. **Shayne, Derek Taylor,** *Wings over Hollywood,* Lulu, 2006. Solantro #2 of 4. (Supernatural) "While making a film in Mexico, the two men come up against a mad scientist, flying Chupacabras, and another huge cast of characters (Gunn)." 3/3

2545. **Shayne, Derek Taylor,** *The Star Shadow Effect,* Lulu, 2006. Solantro #3 of 4. (Supernatural) "Ned Pruitt wants the missing part of a flying saucer, a part that Tony's adopted father took form a crash site (Gunn)." 3/3

2546. **Shayne, Derek Taylor,** *Monte Carlo After Midnight,* Lulu, 2007. Solantro #4 of 4. (Supernatural) "A mysterious figure, "le Fantome de Monte Carlo," seizes its victims, leaving behind a synthetic diamond with a dark flaw that connects it to a Zimbabwe cult of soul snatchers (Gunn)." 3/3

2547. **Sheldon, Ben,** *Dragula,* AuthorHouse, 2005. (Paranormal Police Procedural) DRAGULA, a vampire often in drag, frequents the gay establishments of San Francisco and the Bay Area, in search of blood victims. He proves to be an elusive flying bat for S.F.P.D and Oakland police, across the Bay. Search is complicated when a homophobic Oakland officer is assigned to investigate alongside a gay San Francisco counterpart. 3/3

2548. **Sheldon, Ben,** *Rendezvous in Baghdad,* iUniverse, 2012. (Thriller) As throngs of humanity pack Rome's St. Peter's Square, all await the news from the Sistine Chapel as to who will be the next Pope. But no one is more anxious than Iraqi American Sami Yusuf, for he and one of the papal candidates share a well-kept secret. When it is finally announced that Cardinal Paul Rogan has been elected Pope, Sami knows the one thing about Father Rogan that no one in the crowd does-he is a humble shepherd who molests his unsuspecting sheep. 2/3

2549. **Shelton, Rod,** *Bokassa's Last Apostle,* Paradise Press, 2012. (Paranormal Adventure) Can Everton Jones discover how his father stole Emperor Bokassa's diamonds before Bokassa's followers - the Apostles - get there first? Everton and his friends romp all over the gay scene in London to find out, fight a demon and run into a street war. 3/3

2550. **Shepperd, Simon,** "Big Black Dildo," *Noirotica: Anthology of Erotic Crime Stories,* edited by Thomas S. Roche, Rhinocerous, 1996. (Pulp) A collection of darkly sexy tales, taking place at the crossroads of the crime and erotic genres. "A male prostitute is strangled, and a distinctive dildo stuffed down his throat in a brother room locked from inside, and another prostitute is gunned down (Gunn)." 3/3

2551. **Sheppard, Simon,** *The Dirty Boy's Club: The Soap Opera Murders,* Lethe, 2012. (Modern Pulp) When three hunky young newcomers to San Francisco are hired by a mysterious unseen boss to fulfill the fantasies of horny men, they get more–much more–than they bargained for. Their erotic adventures take them from a gangbang in a sleazy motel to a leather-clad day at a fetishists' fair, from a houseful of naked Marines to a Halloween orgy at an A-gay's mansion. 3/3

2552. **Sherman, Scott,** *First You Fall,* Alyson, 2008. Kevin Connor #1 of 3. (Amateur Sleuth) When his friend's death is ruled a suicide, Kevin Connor–a hustler by trade, sleuth by default–sets out to prove a case of murder. It doesn't help matters that the victim's grown children, who disapproved of their father's gay lifestyle, are only concerned about their inheritance. But they are not Kevin's only problem. His high-strung mother has moved in with him–and she knows nothing about his questionable ... job. –won the twenty-first LAMBDA Award (MLM). 3/3

2553. **Sherman, Scott,** *Second You Sin,* Kensington, 2011. Kevin Connor #2 of 3. (Amateur Sleuth) Someone is killing New York City's hottest male prostitutes, and it's up to full-time call boy, part-time sleuth Kevin Connor to find out who. With his spectacular boy-next-door looks, quick wit, and ability to role-play even the most outrageous scenarios, Kevin is facing his most challenging position yet–to stop a ruthless killer. 3/3

2554. **Sherman, Scott**, *Third You Die*, Kensington, 2012. Kevin Connor #3 of 3. (Amateur Sleuth) Finally settling down with his hunky cop boyfriend, former callboy Kevin Connor is giving up the "oldest profession" for a new career: producing his mom's TV talk show, "Sophie's Voice." But when their latest guest–gay porn sensation Brent Havens–ends up floating in the East River after vowing to blow the lid off the adult film industry, Kevin returns to the world of high-stakes sex to find out: Who killed the twink who had everything? 3/3

2555. **Sherwood, John**, *The Sunflower Plot*, Scribner's Sons, 1990. Celia Grant #7 of 11. (Cozy) Celia Grant, the diminutive, white-haired heroine is facing financial ruin because a new commercial garden center is taking business away from Archerscroft, her nursery. –the antagonist is gay (MLM). 1/3

2556. **Sherwood, Kate**, *Long Shadows*, Riptide, 2017. Common Law #1 of 4. (MM Police Procedural) LA cop Jericho Crewe got the hell out of Mosely, Montana, when he was seventeen. Fifteen years later, he's back, and everything is just as messed up as when he left. He planned a quick visit to deal with his injured father, but of course things are never that simple. Family complications, police complications, social complications–and, as always, Wade Granger complications. 3/3

2557. **Sherwood, Kate**, *Embers*, Riptide, 2017. Common Law #2 of 4. (MM Police Procedural) Small town–big problems. Jericho Crewe is back in Mosely, Montana, trying to deal with police corruption, interfering feds, his newly discovered family members, and, of course, Wade Granger. 3/3

2558. **Sherwood, Kate**, *Darkness*, Riptide, 2017. Common Law #3 of 4. (MM Police Procedural) A murdered prostitute. An obvious suspect. Clear evidence. For once, Jericho Crewe has a straightforward crime to investigate, and Wade Granger isn't involved. 3/3

2559. **Sherwood, Kate**, *Home Fires*, Riptide, 2017. Common Law #4 of 4. (MM Police Procedural) Trouble comes to Mosely, Montana, from the outside world. When the residents of Mosely are left on their own, they can make things work. Sure, there's always been a militia operating up in the hills, but they were small-scale–just survivalists doing their thing–until organizers came in from out of state. Now Jericho Crewe and the rest of the sheriff's department are facing down a heavily armed band of fanatics, and the feds are busy elsewhere. 3/3

2560. **Sievwright, Ashley**, *The Shallow End*, Clouds of Magellan, 2008. (MM Mystery) On a cloudless afternoon, a man dives into a crowded swimming pool and disappears. Is it murder, abduction, a staged disappearance, aliens, or the ghost of Anna Nicole Smith? 3/3

2561. **Silbert, Leslie,** *The Intelligencer,* Atria, 2004. (Historical) London, 1593: It is three weeks before the murder of Christopher Marlowe, playwright and spy in Queen Elizabeth I's secret service – a crime that remains unsolved to this day. Marlowe is hoping to find his missing muse as he sets off on a new intelligence assignment...and closes in on the secret that will seal his fate. New York City, present day: Renaissance scholar turned private eye Kate Morgan investigates a shocking heist and murder involving a mysterious, antique manuscript recently unearthed in central London. What secret lurks in those yellowed, ciphered pages...and how, centuries later, could it drive someone to kill? 2/3

2562. **Sillyman, William Lee,** *The Greek Affair,* Createspace, 2017. Cantrell #1 of 3. (YA) David is a young man when he escapes a powerful, yet abusive father, simply because he is gay. He runs away, changes his identity and builds his own life as far from his home as possible. After becoming a survivor of a severe beating, it is discovered to have been a murder attempt upon his life. A police detective is assigned his case. Upon investigating deeper into David's past, further attempts are made upon not only David's life, but the detective's life as well. 3/3

2563. **Sillyman, William Lee,** *The Missing One,* Createspace, 2017. Cantrell #2 of 3. (Police Procedural) A cold case that has taken over forty years to solve. David and Jonathan, the gay investor/criminal psychologist and the police detective, join forces to help solve crimes that have fallen through the cracks. More twists and turns than a roller-coaster and reaches beyond the bounds of the Los Angeles area. For over forty years, young gay men have disappeared, and their cases gone cold. 3/3

2564. **Sillyman, William Lee,** *The Lost Ones,* Createspace, 2017. Cantrell #3 of 3. (Police Procedural) David and Jonathan work on cold cases and help to bring, "The Lost Ones" home. 3/3

2565. **Simard, Samantha,** *Stitches,* Samantha Simard, 2018. (Thriller) Stitches follows Jim Wolfe, a PTSD-riddled Army Ranger turned private investigator. Between his questionable relationship with a Romanian restaurateur's son and investigating the disappearance of a famous musician's daughter with his partner, Scarlett Vaughn, Wolfe has a lot on his plate. When a string of grisly murders centering on college students grab the city of Boston by the throat, Wolfe finds himself entangled in more than one mystery. While Wolfe and his partner attempt to unravel the threads connecting the killings to their missing rock n' roll heiress, Sebastian Codreanu discovers how deeply his father is tied to the recent crime spree, and the Mass Art Murderer plots his masterpiece. Everything is not what it first appears to be, and everyone has a secret. –very little gay content and most of that is suggestive (MLM). 1/3

2566. **Simmons, D. N.**, *Desires Unleashed,* AuthorHouse, 2004. Knights of the Darkness #1 of 6. (MM Paranormal) When a grisly decapitated corpse pops up on a Chicago Street, drained of blood, the highly-trained, government-funded special police force assigned two of their best detectives to the case. S.U.I.T. Detectives Warren Davis and Matthew Eric delve deep into their investigation to discover just who or what is leaving mutilated bodies in public places. They soon realize that the killer or killers is one step ahead of them and if they are going to stop the menace before another innocent human is viciously attack, they are going to need help. 3/3

2567. **Simmons, D. N.**, *Guilty Innocent,* AuthorHouse, 2005. Knights of the Darkness #2 of 6. (MM Paranormal) Darian, the gorgeous, charismatic and charming master vampire of Chicago is framed for a crime he didn't commit, but why? His lover, Xavier, Natasha and a few others must travel halfway across the world to find out who and why before time runs out and all hell breaks loose! 3/3

2568. **Simmons, D. N.**, *The Royal Flush,* AuthorHouse, 2006. Knights of the Darkness #3 of 6. (MM Paranormal) The coven, Pack and Pride must join forces to stop a group of big game hunters by any means necessary! 3/3

2569. **Simmons, D. N.**, *Hostile Territory,* BookSurge, 2008. Knights of the Darkness #4 of 6. (MM Paranormal) A single orchestrated attack initiates a hunt unlike Darian and his friends have ever encountered. 3/3

2570. **Simmons, D. N.**, *The Lion's Den,* Rushmore, 2012. Knights of the Darkness #5 of 6. (MM Paranormal) Darian, Elise and Xander have been through very rough times in the past, but nothing has prepared them for the menace that is causing all kinds of havoc in their territory this time around. Chicago is at the mercy, or lack thereof, of a ruthless gang of supernaturals who seem to take extreme pleasure in other people's pain. In this game of cat and mouse, there's no way to tell who's the predator and who's the prey. 3/3

2571. **Simmons, D. N.**, *Unholy Alliance,* Rushmore, 2012. Knights of the Darkness #6 of 6. (MM Paranormal) Picking up the chaos from where The Lion's Den left off, Unholy Alliance unleashes a whole new threat to everyone's existence. It's the calm before the storm and once the storm hits, you'll have to pray and hope you survive. New alliances will be formed that will reshape the world with the blood of the innocent. There will be nowhere to hide, there will be no sanctuary. 3/3

2572. **Simmons, Steven,** *Body Blows,* Dutton, 1986. (Crime Drama) Living in the fast lane of contemporary California life, Cal Lynch, a young bisexual making a living as a hustler while struggling to become a successful actor, finds himself caught in a nightmarish web of murder and intrigue. 3/3

2573. **Simms, Chris,** *Shifting Skin,* Orion, 2006. DI Spicer #2 of 8. (Police Procedural) The Butcher of Belle Vue' has struck again. Like the others, the third victim has been partially skinned and dumped on waste ground, her muscles, tendons and ligaments exposed to view. Only this time her face has also been removed. Whoever the killer is, it appears he has a good knowledge of surgery. –DI Spicer's gay partner, Rick Saville, plays a stabilizing force (MLM). 2/3

2574. **Simms, Chris,** *Savage Moon,* Orion, 2008. DI Spicer #3 of 8. (Police Procedural) The body of a woman with her throat ripped out is found on Saddleworth Moor, near Manchester. She is discovered in an area where numerous sightings of a mysterious big black cat have been made. When analysis shows the hairs caught under her nails are those of a panther, it's assumed the animal has killed its first human victim. 2/3

2575. **Simms, Chris,** *Hell's Fire,* Orion, 2008. DI Spicer #4 of 8. (Police Procedural) A charred corpse and Satanic paraphernalia are found on the blackened alter of a torched church in Manchester. The killer is prepared to commit unspeakable acts of evil in homage to his god. Jon Spicer is in hot pursuit. 2/3

2576. **Simms, Chris,** *The Edge,* Orion, 2009. DI Spicer #5 of 8. (Police Procedural) It is a savage blow to DI John Spicer when he receives a phone-call saying that the body of his wild younger brother has been found chopped-up on the moor. 2/3

2577. **Simms, Chris,** *Cut Adrift,* Orion, 2011. DI Spicer #6 of 8. (Police Procedural) DI Jon Spicer's investigation into the vicious slaying of a Russian asylum-seeker grinds to a halt when the man's identity turns out to be false. It seems the only truth to his story was the fact he was found drifting off the British coast in a small boat. 2/3

2578. **Simms, Chris,** *Sleeping Dogs: Secrets can be Deadly,* Createspace, 2014. DI Spicer #7 of 8. (Police Procedural) Out walking with his family in the local park, Jon Spicer's life is shattered forever. The dog – aggressive and huge - appears from nowhere. At first, Jon assumes the attack was random. 2/3

2579. **Simms, Chris,** *Death Games: Will Your Next Move be Your Last?,* Createspace, 2017. DI Spicer #8 of 8. (Police Procedural) Manchester: an injured survivor from a motorway pile-up flees the scene, leaving behind evidence that a terror attack is being planned. 2/3

2580. **Simonson, Sheila,** *Larkspur,* St. Martin's, 1990. (MF Police Procedural) Lark Dailey faces a weekend at the mountain lodge of her mother's mentor, poet Dai Llewellyn, without enthusiasm, but Lark's detective-lover Jay finds the proximity of a notorious pot-farm interesting. The setting, a remote Sierra lake, is idyllic, perfect for canoeing and windsurfing, not to mention fireworks. Neither Lark nor Jay expects the Fourth of July to end in murder. –the two victims are gay (MLM). 1/3

2581. **Simpson, John,** *Murder Most Gay,* Dreamspinner, 2008. Pat St. James #1 of 5. (MM Police Procedural) A serial killer is targeting gay men, preying on them in popular bars and parks. Assigned to the case, rookie cop Pat St. James feels all too close to the victims. He's gay and firmly in the closet at work. The fact that he's sent undercover as a gay man is a stroke of irony. 3/3

2582. **Simpson, John,** *Task Force,* Dreamspinner, 2008. Pat St. James #2 of 5. (MM Police Procedural) Promoted to his own patrol beat after solving a series of anti-gay murders, Prince George County police officer Patrick St. James is happily deepening his relationship with his new lover, Dean, when more young, gay men start turning up dead. He and fellow officer Hank Capstone, now in a relationship of his own with a cute clerk from the local Seven-Eleven, face being outed by a blackmailer as they begin their investigation into the murders. –short story *Four Grooms and a Queen* released as an e-book in 2009 (MLM). 3/3

2583. **Simpson, John,** *The Rent Boy Murders,* Dreamspinner, 2011. Pat St. James #3 of 5. (MM Police Procedural) While Hank and Pat are very happy with their home lives and their husbands, the police work has become more perilous and unpleasant. Though Hank and Shawn, along with Pat and Dean, enjoy a weekend at Gay Pride in New York City, they know their investigation into the brutal murders of rent boys will be waiting when they return home. 3/3

2584. **Simpson, John,** *Murder on a Queen,* Dreamspinner, 2012. Pat St. James #4 of 5. (MM Police Procedural) It's trouble in paradise for homicide detectives Pat St. James and Hank Capstone. After four years as Pat's partner, Hank wants to move on from Homicide. Sensing the friendship might be about to implode, Pat's and Hank's husbands book the four of them a vacation on the gay-friendly cruise liner Queen Mary II. 3/3

2585. **Simpson, John,** *Rolling Thunder,* Dreamspinner, 2013. Pat St. James #5 of 5. (MM Police Procedural) Budget cuts shuffle the decks of the Prince George's County Police Department. Separated after years as partners, Hank Capstone and Patrick St. James find themselves having to make a new start. Assigned as a training officer, Hank takes on the tough task of showing hot, fit young rookie Jessie Morgan the ropes. 3/3

2586. **Sims, Elizabeth,** *The Actress,* St. Martin's Minotaur, 2008. Farmer #1 of 3. (Legal Drama) Aspiring actress and single mother Rita Farmer has gone from struggling to find work to downright desperate. If she doesn't land a paying job soon-horror movie, soap commercial, anything-she's afraid her ex-husband will use her dire financial straits to take away Petey, her cherished four-year-old son. While she's charming the crowd at story time at the L.A. public library, a celebrity defense attorney approaches her with an unusual job offer: So long as she's discreet, Rita can rake in a thousand dollars a day preparing his client for her appearance in court. –gay best friend and surrogate father to her son (MLM). 2/3

2587. **Sims, Elizabeth,** *The Extra,* St. Martin's Minotaur, 2009. Farmer #2 of 3. (Legal Drama) Rita Farmer knows what it feels like to be flat broke. Even now, when studying to be a lawyer, Rita is so far in debt that she has to scrounge for acting jobs to keep herself and her son afloat. Decked out in police uniform as an extra on a low-budget movie shoot, she wanders into a rough part of town and is pulled into a vicious assault. 2/3

2588. **Sims, Elizabeth,** *On Location,* Minotaur, 2010. Farmer #3 of 3. (Legal Drama) Rita Farmer knows exactly how hard it is to break into the movie business. Acting was the big dream that brought her out to L.A. in the first place. And while she never made the red carpet, that big dream did turn into a modest profession that kept her and her son afloat. So, from time to time she'll lend her talents as a favor. 2/3

2589. **Singer, Loren,** *The Parallax View,* Doubleday, 1970. (Political Intrigue) After the assassination of President Kennedy, a number of people involved in the investigation either "committed suicide," were killed in "accidents," or disappeared. –one journalist killed is gay, author is not kind to gay men (MLM). 1/3

2590. **Singer, P. D.,** *Fall Down the Mountain,* Dreamspinner, 2012. Mountain #3 of 5. (MM Mystery) Every night ski patrol Mark McAvoy relives the avalanche that took a life on his watch. Was the avalanche a tragic accident or cold-blooded murder? His role in the inquiry leaves Mark in trouble at work, at the mercy of the law, and with too much time on his hands. –the first two books in the series are romances (MLM). 3/3

2591. **Singer, P. D.,** *Blood on the Mountain,* Dreamspinner, 2012. Mountain #4 of 5. (MM Mystery) Jake Landon thinks a second ranger season in the Colorado Rockies with Kurt Carlson is close enough to heaven, and a national forest is big enough to be his closet. Jake may have no choices left after they stumble on armed men guarding a beautiful but deadly crop that doesn't belong among the pines and spruces. Angry men with guns are only one danger in the Colorado wilderness. –book five is a romance (MLM). 3/3

2592. **Singer, Shelley,** *Free Draw,* St. Martin's, 1984. Jake Samson #2 of 6. (Hardboiled) Unafraid, unlicensed, and, in this case, unpaid, unofficial Bay Area P.I. Jake Samson and his carpenter sidekick Rosie set out to clear a friend of a murder charge. The victim is found stabbed to death in a damp redwood canyon in woodsy, wealthy Marin County, outside San Francisco. –victim's son is gay. Author treated gay and lesbian people as people and not stereotypes (MLM). 1/3

2593. **Singer, Shelley,** *Full House,* St. Martin's, 1986. Jake Samson #4 of 6. (Hardboiled) An ark in the middle of suburban Oakland was interesting but not strange by California standards. Even one built by peaceful cultists preparing for the coming flood. Until sometime private eye Jake Samson is hired to find Noah, their leader, who has disappeared with a lovely devotee and a quarter million in cash. –MC has to visit Russian River, a gay resort, in a part of his investigation (MLM). 1/3

2594. **Sklepowich, Edward,** *Farewell to the Flesh,* William Morrow, 1991. Urbino McIntyre Mystery #2 of 9. (Italian Hardboiled) Each year, Carnevale transforms Venice into a wonderland of color and spectacle. From the Piazza San Marco to the Grand Canal, costumed celebrants cavort with wild abandon. Anything can happen... even murder. –victim killed in a high gay cruising area in Venice (MLM). 1/3

2595. **Smith, Amberly,** *Rinse and Repeat,* Dreamspinner, 2011. (MM Mystery) After reliving the same day sixty-two times, Repeater Peat Harris is about to give up on his latest case: saving Jake Schwinn. In the past, Peat has solved some seriously twisted crimes, caught the bad guys, and kept an emotional distance. But this time, his heart's involved, a definite must-never-do on Repeats, and he can't just walk away–even if that means putting himself into the bullet's path. 3/3

2596. **Smith, Dennis,** *Glitter and Ash,* E. P. Dutton, 1980. (Espionage) Insurance fraud, hot women, and even hotter fires. –incredibly offensive novel towards gay men; "fags" and "faggots" is the only terms used to describe gay men (MLM). 2/3

2597. **Smith, Julie,** *New Orleans Mourning,* St. Martin's, 1990. Skip Langdon #1 of 10. (Police Procedural) It's Mardi Gras in New Orleans, and civic leader and socialite Chauncy St. Amant has been crowned Rex, King of Carnival. But his day of glory comes to an abrupt and bloody end when a parade-goer dressed as Dolly Parton guns him down. Is the killer his aimless, promiscuous daughter Marcelle? Homosexual, mistreated son Henry? Helpless, alcoholic wife Bitty? Or some unknown player? Turns out the king had enemies... –Jimmy Dee, the gay landlord plays a part throughout the series (MLM). 2/3

2598. **Smith, Julie,** *Axeman's Blues,* St. Martin's, 1991. Skip Langdon #2 of 10. (Police Procedural) What's the perfect killing field for a murderer? A place where he (or maybe she) can learn your secrets from your own mouth and then make friends over coffee. A supposedly "safe" place where anonymity is the norm. The horror who calls himself The Axeman has figured it out and claimed his territory–he's cherry-picking his victims in the 12-Step programs of New Orleans. 2/3

2599. **Smith, Julie,** *Jazz Funeral,* Fawcett Columbine, 1993. Skip Langdon #3 of 10. (Police Procedural) Smack in the middle of the summer, Skip finds herself investigating the stabbing death of the universally beloved producer of the New Orleans Jazz and Heritage Festival. Then the victim's sixteen-year-old sister disappears, and Skip suspects that if the young woman isn't herself the murderer, she's in mortal danger from the person who is. 2/3

2600. **Smith, Julie,** *New Orleans Beat,* Ballantine, 1994. Skip Langdon #4 of 10. (Police Procedural) A computer genius dies after an apparent fall from a ladder, but the computer nuts with whom he associated believe his death was no accident. Now Skip is delving into the past to solve two murders. –renamed *Death Before Facebook* in 2013 (MLM). 2/3

2601. **Smith, Julie,** *House of Blues,* Ballantine, 1995. Skip Langdon #5 of 10. (Police Procedural) After prominent New Orleans restaurateur Arthur Hebert is murdered in his beautiful Garden District home, three family members suspiciously vanish: Hebert's daughter, who was soon to have taken over the management of his restaurant, his ex-addict son-in-law, and his small granddaughter–all missing without a trace. A kidnapping gone wrong? Homicide Detective Skip Langdon thinks it's possible, but why should the kidnappers have taken three hostages when one would have been enough? 2/3

2602. **Smith, Julie,** *The Kindness of Strangers,* Fawcett Columbine, 1996. Skip Langdon #6 of 10. (Police Procedural) The upcoming mayoral election pits the usual thugs and vipers against a Errol Jacomine, a liberal-minded, civic-spirited preacher. The trouble is, in Skip's opinion, Jacomine is a psychopath and dangerous as hell. 2/3

26003. **Smith, Julie,** *Crescent City Kill,* Fawcett Columbine/Ballantine, 1997. Skip Langdon #7 of 10. (Police Procedural) Who or what is The Jury? To her horror, NOPD detective Skip Langdon discovers it is a new, national, fast-growing, and very volatile organization headquartered in New Orleans. Its mission: to execute those who have "escaped" prosecution. What's more, Skip perceives that behind this deadly, clandestine group lies the evil brilliance of her old adversary, charismatic con man and cold-blooded killer Errol Jacomine. –renamed *Crescent City Connection* in 2012 (MLM). 2/3

2604. **Smith, Julie,** *82 Desire,* Fawcett Columbine/Ballantine, 1998. Skip Langdon #8 of 10. (Police Procedural) Councilwoman Bebe Fortier has misplaced her equally prominent husband. Across town, part-time detective-poet Talba Wallis has a simple wish–to find out what Russell Fortier's disappearance has to do with her. But the private investigator who hired Talba to spy on Fortier can't help her out. He's lying in his office with a bullet in his chest. At first, Police Detective Skip Langdon thinks it's just a small case with some big names–until she senses something huge starting to unfold. 2/3

2605. **Smith, Julie,** *Mean Woman Blues,* Forge, 2003. Skip Langdon #9 of 10. (Police Procedural) The nemesis of Skip Langdon, New Orleans police detective, is Errol Jacomine. This evangelical preacher has been leader of his own frenzied army of converts, has run for mayor of New Orleans, and now wants to become president of the United States. His campaign methods are rabble-rousing, theft, kidnapping, and multiple murder. –in 2004 this title was renamed *Boneyard Blues* when published by Robert Hale but all subsequent titles revert back to *Mean Woman Blues* (MLM). 2/3

2606. **Smith, Julie,** *Murder on Magazine,* Booksbnimble, 2018. Skip Langdon #10 of 10. (Police Procedural) A serial killer is using Airbnb units to stage his murders, but a teenage runaway has escaped his grasp and now she's in the wind, believing she's killed him. Meanwhile the real killer stalks the city – and her. 2/3

2607. **Smith, Mark Haskell,** *Blown,* Grove Press Black Cat, 2018. (Crime Drama) Bryan LeBlanc worked his way up into a plum position on Wall Street as the boy genius of the foreign exchange desk. Surrounded by acolytes of the free market, the true believers, the U.S. Marines of capitalism–"the few, the proud, the completely full of themselves"–Bryan soon realizes that being honest at a dishonest job is not the path to success. He decides to give Wall Street a taste of its own medicine and hatches an intricate plan to disappear permanently with just enough misappropriated money–and sailing classes–to spend his golden years cruising the Caribbean. 3/3

2608. **Smith, Mel,** *Nasty: Erotic Stories,* Alyson, 2005. (MM Short Stories) Heavy-duty raunch from the oversexed and pleasingly filth. 3/3

2609. **Smith, Rosamond (Joyce Carol Oates),** *Nemesis,* E. P. Dutton, 1990. (Psychological Thriller) Shy piano teacher Maggie Blackburn has selflessly devoted her life and career to her students at the Forest Park Conservatory of Music in an affluent Connecticut suburb. Then a rape shakes the school's refined grounds. The violated young student, Brendan Bauer, is a timid ex-seminarian. 2/3

2610. **Smith, Rupert,** *Service Wash,* Serpent's Tail, 2006. (Caper) Paul Mackrell would like to be writing sensitive prose fiction but when he's offered an incredible fee to ghost the memoirs of TV's most famous soap star, he can't refuse. Star of the long-running soap New Town, Eileen Weathers has played Maggie Parrott, manageress of the Clean Queen Launderette, for 30 years. 3/3

2611. **Soehnlein, K. M.,** *You Can Say You Knew Me When,* Kensington, 2005. (Psychological) Charming underachiever Jamie Garner is living a sexy slacker's life in San Francisco during the dot-com boom-avoiding his stalled career as a radio producer, barely holding on to his relationship, but surrounded by fun-loving friends. And then Jamie gets the call he's always dreaded: Teddy, the father who never accepted him, has died. 3/3

2612. **Soesbe, Douglas,** *Children in a Burning House,* Knights Press, 1987. (Crime Drama) Television and screenwriter Norris Manning shoots actor/hustler Christopher Danner. Explanations of the killing, depicting Manning as an innocent in Hollywood, caring for those around him and infatuated with an aging female Hollywood legend (Slide). 3/3

2613. **Soles, Caro,** *The Tangled Boy,* Baskerville, 2002. (Thriller) The murder of Jordan King shocks the small town. Cory was there. 3/3

2614. **Soles, Caro,** *The Danger Dance,* Haworth, 2007. (MM Science Fiction) Two members of the Merculian National Dance Company are ordered by the dreaded Praetan to leave their tranquil existence to go undercover aboard the starship Wellington to discover who is passing secrets about fleet movements and weaponry to the enemies in the Troia. 3/3

2615. **Soles, Caro,** *Drag Queen in the Court of Death,* Haworth, 2007. (MM Mystery) While cleaning out his dead ex-lover Ronnie's apartment, staid history professor Michael Dunn-Barten makes a grisly discovery, a mummified corpse in a trunk. Suddenly Michael must travel back 25 years to find answers by revisiting everybody who knew Ronnie. 3/3

2616. **Somer, Mehmet Murat,** *The Prophet Murders,* Serpent's Tail, 2008. Turkish Delight #1 of 7. (Turkish Crime Drama) Something's gone seriously wrong in Istanbul - a killer is on the loose, and transvestites are being murdered, the modus operandi becoming increasingly bizarre with each death. Our protagonist - fellow transvestite, nightclub owner and glamour puss extraordinaire downs her lipstick and ups the ante in the search for the religious nut. 3/3

2617. **Somer, Mehmet Murat,** *The Kiss Murder,* Serpent's Tail, 2009. Turkish Delight #2 of 7. (Turkish Crime Drama) When Buse, one of the "girls"at her club, fears someone is after private letters from a former lover, she comes to her boss for help. The next day Buse is dead and our girl must find the murderers before they find her. 3/3

2618. **Somer, Mehmet Murat,** *The Gigolo Murder,* Serpent's Tail, 2009. Turkish Delight #3 of 7. (Turkish Crime Drama) Software programmer by day and drag-queen club owner by night, our girl is back again, just jilted and feeling so blue she's violet until she meets the hunky, married lawyer, Haluk Perkedem. When their conversation is interrupted by a phone call delivering news that his brother-in-law has been arrested for the murder of a notorious gigolo, she decides to put her sleuthing instincts and Thai kickboxing skills to work unraveling the crime. 3/3

2619. **Somer, Mehmet Murat,** *The Serenity Murders,* Penguin, 2012. Turkish Delight #4 of 7. (Turkish Crime Drama) Oh, no! Burçak Veral–kickboxing transvestite, nightclub owner, Audrey Hepburn lookalike, and amateur sleuth–has finally been invited to strut her stuff on a local television show. But during her appearance, an angry viewer calls in vowing to kill off everyone close to Burçak. 3/3

2620. **Somer, Mehmet Murat,** *The Wig Murders,* Serpent's Tail, 2012. Turkish Delight #5 of 7. (Turkish Crime Drama) When the man wants to be a woman, when we want men, our hero wearing robes, master and internet master; from classical music, from plant herbs, from handsome men. And life has always made him do complicated murders. While he was rescuing him, he was helped by his sharp distractions as well as his buddies: The cheerleader, who made drag sov in a hotel, the uncompromising boss Hasan heard about his sexual identity, and the other girls come with the Altimermerli Gonul to the bastard; Siloz Pamir. –the next two books in the series have not yet been translated from Turkish (MLM). 3/3

2621. **Somerville, Ann,** *Somatesthesia,* Samhain, 2011. (MM Paranormal) Devlin Grace's experience with child exploitation cases lands him a new assignment with the Special Crimes Investigators unit of the Federal Justice Agency, plus a new partner who could make the job tougher than expected. Connor Hutchens possesses incredible, scientifically enhanced senses...and zero social skills. Word on the street is that his last partner left under a cloud–and it was Connor's fault. 3/3

2622. **Sommer, Sam,** *Jacob's Diary: Sleeping with the Past,* Bold Stroke Books, 2013. (Thriller) David Jacobs is your average, everyday gay Joe. He has a good job, the two best neighbors that anyone could ask for, and a precocious twelve-year-old son. Nothing out of the ordinary has ever happened to David. That is until the day he is nearly killed by a phantom truck, saved by a handsome stranger, and receives a bizarre FAX at his office that propels him, his son, his neighbors, and the attractive stranger who saved his life into the most fascinating and disturbing adventure of a lifetime. 3/3

2623. **South, M. K.,** *Of Our Own Device,* South Publishing, 2018. (Historical) Summer of 1985. Jack Smith is a rookie CIA case officer posted at the American Embassy in Moscow. Despite his gregarious nature, Jack is a lonely man: not only is he a reluctant spy, he is also gay. 3/3

2624. **Southerton, Peter,** *Finding Richard,* Exposure, 2005. (Hardboiled) A husband has gone missing in Rome so Richard Bradley, a private investigator, has been retained to find him. Richard discovers fraud, a failing business and the apparent suicide of a colleague but tracing the absent man's contacts leads him into the seedy gay worlds of London and Rome. After Richard gets caught up in a murder enquiry he begins to succumb to the charms of the promiscuous homosexual Clifford. Whether or not he finds his man he learns much more than he expected. 3/3

2625. **Spano, Mark,** *Midland Club,* Thunderfoot, 2016. (Historical) 1950s. A knotted tale of corruption, lies and murder in a midwestern town. Only one man is willing to reveal the truth–at the risk of his own life. –main character solves a murder of a waiter of a gay club (MLM). 3/3

2626. **Speart, Jessica,** *Gator Aide,* Avon, 1997. Rachel Porter #1 of 10. (Cozy) A failed New York actress, Rachel Porter figured that any new career would be an improvement–until she became a wildlife agent and found herself stuck in the steamy Louisiana bayous, chasing poachers and fending off mosquitoes the size of Central Park pigeons. –Terri Tune, a female impersonator, assists Porter (MLM).

2/3

2627. **Speart, Jessica,** *Bird Brained,* Avon, 1999. Rachel Porter #2 of 10. (Cozy) Tangling with shifty animal smugglers is all part of the job for U.S. Fish and Wildlife Agent Rachel Porter. On a hot tip, Rachel investigates the compound of an alleged exotic bird smuggler, but inside she finds her prey lying in a puddle of his own blood. Setting out to find the birds and the murderer, Rachel discovers a crazy goose chase, in which she might end up a sitting duck. 2/3

2628. **Speart, Jessica,** *Black Delta Night,* Avon, 2001. Rachel Porter #5 of 10. (Cozy) "It's called Delta Gold – caviar from the endangered Mississippi River paddlefish that rivals the world-renowned beluga. And now that greed has all but decimated a billion-dollar Caspian Sea industry, the Russian mafia is casting its lethal line into the land of Elvis" Tennessee is the purgatory where the U.S. Fish and Wildlife Service has consigned Rachel Porter for making trouble. 2/3

2629. **Speart, Jessica,** *Blue Twilight,* Avon, 2004. Rachel Porter #8 of 10. (Cozy) Something precious and beautiful is being ruthlessly destroyed. And those who champion the small, fragile, threatened lives are endangered themselves. An agent for the U.S. Fish and Wildlife Service, Rachel Porter has been assigned to the northern California wilds, where a biologist recently vanished while searching for a rare blue butterfly believed extinct – a hunt that may well have led him to his death. 2/3

2630. **Speart, Jessica,** *Unsafe Harbor,* Avon, 2006. Rachel Porter #10 of 10. (Cozy) U.S. Fish and Wildlife Service agent Rachel Porter's devotion to endangered creatures has carried her to many remote, exotic places. Now she's in Port Elizabeth, New Jersey, trying to help stop the import of illegal flora and fauna. This is a different jungle–dark, dangerous, and filled with predators–a fact that's driven home when a body is discovered just steps from Rachel's post. 2/3

2631. **Speed, Andrea,** *Prey,* Dreamspinner, 2010. Infected #1 of 10. (MM Paranormal) The murder of a former cop draws Roan into an odd case where an unidentifiable species of cat appears to be showing an unusual level of intelligence. He juggles that with trying to find a missing teenage boy, who, unbeknownst to his parents, was "cat" obsessed. And when someone is brutally murdering infecteds, Eli Winters, leader of the Church of the Divine Transformation, hires Roan to find the killer before he closes in on Eli. 3/3

2632. **Speed, Andrea,** *Bloodlines,* Dreamspinner, 2010. Infected #2 of 10. (MM Paranormal) The newly married Roan is struggling to balance his work with his home life as he grows increasingly distracted by his husband Paris's declining health. One case with strong emotions attached takes up most of his time: finding the murderer of a missing little rich girl. It's a family with secrets so toxic they'd rather no one investigate, and there's no shortage of suspects. But despite the dangers and obstructions involved, Roan won't stop... until he loses something infinitely precious as well. 3/3

2633. **Speed, Andrea,** *Life After Death,* Dreamspinner, 2011. Infected #3 of 10. (MM Paranormal) But when your heart is gone, it's easy to fall into a black hole and never crawl out. Roan has been lost and alone for more than a year, and his best friends think a new case might be just the motivation he needs. Roan forces himself back into the game and discovers a dead man who might not be all that dead, a street hustler that wants to hustle him, and a dominatrix who is well prepared to take Roan's orders. As Roan claws his way out of the darkness by diving back into his work, he finds himself in a race against time in the adrenaline-pumping realization that nothing helps a person want to live like helping someone else survive. 3/3

2634. **Speed, Andrea,** *Freefall,* Dreamspinner, 2011. Infected #4 of 10. (MM Paranormal) Conceived bearing the lion strain of the virus, Roan is the only fully functioning virus child in the country–maybe in the world. But that doesn't mean he's okay. He's still struggling with the death of his husband and the guilt of finding new love; his old enemy, the Church of the Divine Transformation, is becoming increasingly hostile; and he's taken on a tragic cold case involving a long-missing boy. 3/3

2635. **Speed, Andrea,** *Shift,* Dreamspinner, 2012. Infected #5 of 10. (MM Paranormal) Between his mutating virus and his rocky relationship with his artist boyfriend, Dylan, Roan has enough problems to solve without taking on other people's, but that's the nature of his work. Someone has to look into the case of the murdered trans woman, and if the perp is the dirty cop Roan suspects it is, the police are not the right people for the job. 3/3

2636. **Speed, Andrea,** *Lesser Evils,* Dreamspinner, 2012. Infected #6 of 10. (MM Paranormal) Until recently, Roan was ahead of the curve when it came to rein in the lion that lives inside him. Now his control is slipping at the worst possible times. A new drug has hit the streets–one that triggers unscheduled changes in infected users. Street hustler Holden Krause gets attacked by one of his clients, then is surprised to find himself involved in an unwanted, unexpected relationship. And a serial killer begins targeting infecteds in their cat form–something that's 100 percent legal. 3/3

2637. **Speed, Andrea,** *Undertow,* Dreamspinner, 2013. Infected #7 of

10. (MM Paranormal) Now Roan is locked in a coma as the struggle between his human and werecat sides reaches a new extreme. All Dylan can do is sit, wait, and think. Meanwhile, Roan's assistant, Holden, wants to shed his old street life and his relationship with Scott, but he can't seem to do either. Holden doesn't want a relationship with Scott but finds himself drawn to him all the same, even if he can never fully reveal his past. 3/3

2638. **Speed, Andrea,** *Epitaph,* DSP, 2014. Infected #8 of 10. (MM Paranormal) Tiger strain infections start showing up all over Seattle, much to Roan's dismay, and worse yet, they may have a personal connection. Meanwhile, Roan gets hired to look into the puzzling death of Dee's former lover. Then the FBI wants him to investigate a new apocalypse cult of infecteds pushing for a violent revolution against normals. All around Roan, events are spiraling out of control. Just when his singular abilities are needed most, Roan develops new symptoms that might signify dire consequences if he doesn't stop shifting at will. Roan finds himself at a crossroads and must make a difficult decision about his future. 3/3

2639. **Speed, Andrea,** *Holden,* DSP, 2016. Infected #9 of 10/Mean Streets #1 of 2. (MM Paranormal) With his friend lion shifter Roan McKichan no longer in the picture, former sex worker Holden Krause is now working as a detective investigating cases in Seattle. When he receives a request to investigate a rather unusual case for Big Mike, a local drug dealer, he ignores the potential hazards in working for such a client and takes it on. 3/3

2640. **Speed, Andrea,** *Throwaways,* DSP, 2018. Infected #10 of 10/Mean Streets #2 of 2. (MM Paranormal) Former prostitute and street kid turned private detective Holden Krause is asked to look into the murder of Burn, a black-market dealer, who turns up dead near the infamous homeless encampment known as the Jungle. It's a place Holden is familiar with–and his memories of it aren't entirely bad. The settlement has been taken over by sinister people, but Holden isn't afraid to take them on. A big part of his PI gig is cover for his more dangerous vigilante crusade: exacting justice for the people the system ignores, the throwaways–people just like the ones living in the Jungle. 3/3

2641. **Spencer-Fleming, Julia,** *In the Bleak Midwinter,* Minotaur, 2002. Rev. Clare #1 of 9. (Cozy) Clare Fergusson, St. Alban's new priest, fits like a square peg in the conservative Episcopal parish at Millers Kill, New York. She is not just a "lady," she's a tough ex-Army chopper pilot, and nobody's fool. Then a newborn infant left at the church door brings her together with the town's police chief, Russ Van Alstyne, who's also ex-Army and a cynical good shepherd for the stray sheep of his hometown. –coroner is gay and is a constant in the series (MLM). 1/3

2642. **Spencer-Fleming, Julia,** *A Fountain Filled with Blood,* Minotaur, 2003. Rev. Clare #2 of 9. (Cozy) The Episcopal priest and former Army Air Force chopper pilot proved to her flock and to police chief Russ Van Alstyne that she could cope with the unexpected, even when it was as dire as murder. –police investigate gay bashings (MM). 2/3

2643. **Spencer-Fleming, Julia,** *Out of the Deep I Cry,* Minotaur, 2004. Rev. Clare #3 of 9. (Cozy) On April 1, 1930, Jonathan Ketchem's wife Jane walked from her house to the police department to ask for help in finding her husband. The men, worn out from a night of chasing bootleggers, did what they could. But no one ever saw Jonathan Ketchem again. 1/3

2644. **Spencer-Fleming, Julia,** *To Darkness and to Death,* Minotaur, 2005. Rev. Clare #4 of 9. (Cozy) Millicent van der Hoeven has decided to sell her family's Adirondack estate to a nature conservancy. But on the day of the land transfer, her brother frantically calls the police. Millie has disappeared in the cold November forest... 1/3

2645. **Spencer-Fleming, Julia,** *All Mortal Flesh,* Minotaur, 2006. Rev. Clare #5 of 9. (Cozy) Russ Van Alstyne figures his wife kicking him out of their house is nobody's business but his own. Until a neighbor pays a friendly visit to Linda Van Alstyne and finds the woman's body, gruesomely butchered, on the kitchen floor. To the state police, it's an open-and-shut case of a disaffected husband, silencing first his wife, then the murder investigation he controls. To the townspeople, it's proof that the whispered gossip about the police chief and the priest was true. To the powers-that-be in the church hierarchy, it's a chance to control their wayward cleric once and for all. 1/3

2646. **Spencer-Fleming, Julia,** *I Shall not Want,* Minotaur, 2008. Rev. Clare #6 of 9. (Cozy) When a Mexican farmhand stumbles over a Latino man killed with a single shot to the back of his head, Clare is sucked into the investigation through her involvement in the migrant community. The discovery of two more bodies executed in the same way ignites fears that a serial killer is loose in the close-knit community. –short story *Letters to a Soldier,* takes place between books six and seven but is not a mystery (MLM). 1/3

2647. **Spencer-Fleming, Julia,** *One was a Soldier,* Minotaur, 2011. Rev. Clare #7 of 9. (Cozy) On a warm September evening in the Millers Kill community center, five veterans sit down in rickety chairs to try to make sense of their experiences in Iraq. What they will find is murder, conspiracy, and the unbreakable ties that bind them to one another and their small Adirondack town. 1/3

2648. **Spencer-Fleming, Julia,** *Through the Evil Days,* Minotaur, 2013. Clare #8 of 9. (Cozy) On a frigid January night, Chief of Police Russ Van Alstyne and Reverend Clare Fergusson are called to the scene of a raging fire, that quickly becomes a double homicide and kidnapping. –ninth book *Hid from Our Eyes,* has not yet been published and no release date has been announced (MLM). 1/3

2649. **Spindler, Christine,** *The Rhythm of Revenge,* Avid, 1999. Inspector Frederick Terry #1 of 3. (Police Procedural) Tap dancer Jessica Warner disappears the night before her show's premier, leaving behind a jealous husband, an obsessive former lover, and a trail of secrets and misunderstandings. DI Rick Terry is assigned to the case – and the race against time to save Jessica. 3/3

2650. **Spindler, Christine,** *The Pangs of Prophecy,* Createspace, 2004. Inspector Frederick Terry #2 of 3. (Police Procedural) Visions of lethal accidents and violent deaths govern April Stevenson's life, and both she and her mother go to extremes to prevent them from coming true. After a scandal that destroys her reputation, April moves to London to start a new life. Right on the first day in her new job, she has a vision that Stella, one of her colleagues, is going to be strangled. It is the first time she has seen a murder. Shocked and shaken, she informs the police. Inspector Terry believes her and unearths a vital secret buried in Stella's past, but a lethal chain of events has already been set in motion, and it seems that - once more - April's mother is involved. –originally published as a short story in the anthology of *Blood, Threat, and Fears* published in 2001 by Avid and is now available as an e-book (MLM). 3/3

2651. **Spindler, Christine,** *Faces of Fear,* Avid, 2001. Inspector Frederick Terry #3 of 3. (Police Procedural) You attract what you fear - or something far worse... Inspector Terry is drawn into a world of phobias and perversions as a highly intelligent, dangerously devious killer who calls himself Shadoe starts to single out the clients of renowned psychologist Dr. Joy Canova, torturing them to death with their own phobias. Patricia Miles, Joy's newest client, suffers from an intense fear of butterflies. Stranded in a pointless marriage and unaware of the dark secrets held by the people closest to her, she seeks the thrill of an affair and falls for Lionel Croft. What she doesn't know: he's one of Joy's former lovers and the main suspect in the case. Then Patricia's husband is found beaten to death - his mouth full of exotic butterflies. Is Patricia the next on Shadoe's list? 3/3

2652. **Stacey, Susannah,** *A Knife at the Opera,* Summit Books, 1988. Superintendent Bone #2 of 8. (Police Procedural) Backstage at the

Turnbridge Wells girls' school production of The Beggar's Opera, all was bedlam. Miss Claire Fairlie, the pretty English teacher, was found with a knife plunged into her back. The Superintendent was in the audience, and as he dug deeper in the case, he discovered there was a lot more to Miss Fairlie than met the eye. -two of the secondary characters are a gay couple who refuse to be stereotyped (MLM). 1/3

2653. **Stanley, Stephen,** *Midcoast Murder,* Booklocker, 2009. Jesse Ashworth #1 of 9. (Modern Cozy) High school English teacher Jesse Ashworth is in the midst of a mid-life crisis. Should he take early retirement or continue teaching? When his best friend, Rhonda Shepard, retires and moves to the coast of Maine to open a gift shop, Jesse offers to help her set up her business. 3/3

2654. **Stanley, Stephen,** *Murder in the Choir Room,* Stonefield, 2010. Jesse Ashworth #2 of 9. (Modern Cozy) Retired teacher Jesse Ashworth has been looking forward to a quiet retirement in the small town of Bath, Maine but for Jesse, retirement has been anything but quiet. After church trustee Jack Riley is found murdered in the choir room of All Saints Church, Jesse and his companion Police Chief Tim Mallory, begin a search for the killer. Soon it becomes apparent that almost everyone Jack knew had a motive for murder. 3/3

2655. **Stanley, Stephen,** *Big Boys' Detective Agency,* Stonefield, 2010. Jesse Ashworth #3 of 9. (Soft Boiled PI) (When retired teacher Jesse Ashworth and former police chief Tim Mallory buy the Bigg- Boyce Security Company in Bath Maine, interesting cases begin to cross their desks. Known locally as the "Big Boys' Detective Agency" Tim and Jesse begin new careers as private detectives. 3/3

2656. **Stanley, Stephen,** *Murder on St. Royal,* Stonefield, 2011. Jesse Ashworth #4 of 9. (Soft Boiled PI) Jesse Ashworth is attending cooking school in Montreal when the head chef of the school is found murdered in Mt Royal park. Jesse is inadvertently dragged into the investigation when he becomes a potential witness to the crime. 3/3

2657. **Stanley, Stephen,** *Dead Santa!,* Stonefield, 2012. Jesse Ashworth #5 of 9. (Soft Boiled PI) The Christmas season gets off to a rocky start in the sleepy coastal town of Bath, Maine, when a local shopkeeper finds a body dressed as Santa Claus in the doorway of the shop. 3/3

2658. **Stanley, Stephen,** *Cruising for Murder,* Stonefield, 2014. Jesse Ashworth #6 of 9. (Soft Boiled PI) It's Jesse's birthday, and as he says it's a" big birthday" and he's not taking it well; in fact, he has announced that anyone who mentions a certain number is in danger of being bitch-slapped. His partner Tim Mallory has just the perfect birthday gift to cheer Jesse up, a Caribbean cruise. 3/3

2659. **Stanley, Stephen,** *Trailer Trash,* Stonefield, 2016. Jesse Ashworth #7 of 9. (Soft Boiled PI) It's springtime in Bath, Maine and detective Jesse Ashworth is happy to say good bye to the long winter. When Jesse's partner Tim Mallory shows up with a new motorhome, Jesse looks forward to some travel time. Instead of the freedom of the road, Jesse and Tim become involved with three new cases. Tim and Jesse are happy to have the help of former Montreal police officer Hugh Cartier as they search for answers to the three mysteries. 3/3

2660. **Stanley, Stephen,** *Missing!,* Stonefield, 2017. Jesse Ashworth #8 of 9. (Soft Boiled PI) It's autumn in the sleepy Maine town of Bath and life seems perfect. At least that's what retired school teacher turned detective Jesse Ashworth thinks until his world is turned upside down. After celebrating the richness of autumn with a cookout for friends and family, Jesse's partner Tim Mallory goes missing. 3/3

2661. **Stanley, Stephen,** *Hawaiian Holiday,* Independent, 2018. Jesse Ashworth #9 of 9. (Soft Boiled PI) It's winter and retired teacher turned investigator Jesse Ashworth heads to Honolulu to recover from chemotherapy treatments. Jesse is pulled into a murder investigation when the sister of the murder victim hires Jesse to find the truth behind her brother's death. 3/3

2662. **Stanley, Stephen,** *Murder at the Windsor Club,* Stonefield, 2012. Jeremy Dance #1 of 5. (Historical Hard Boiled) The wealthy families of Boston's Beacon Hill like to keep their affairs private. When art objects disappear, when family members go missing, or when bodies turn up in unexpected places, they all turn to Jeremy Dance for damage control 3/3

2663. **Stanley, Stephen,** *Up in Flames,* Createspace, 2013. Jeremy Dance #2 of 5. (Historical Hard Boiled) In the sweltering summer of 1936, investigator Jeremy Dance is looking forward to spending some time at his mountain retreat in New Hampshire's White Mountains. Little does Jeremy realize that when he takes on a case for the lovely Nora Wilde that before the end of summer, Jeremy will find himself standing in a depression breadline, singing on a Vaudeville stage, and searching for an arsonist at the summer resort of Bar Harbor. 3/3

2664. **Stanley, Stephen,** *Murder and Misbehavior,* Createspace, 2015. Jeremy Dance #3 of 5. (Historical Hard Boiled) Jeremy Dance is young, rich and tough as nails. It's the autumn of 1938 and Europe is on the brink of war when the brother of Jeremy Dance's cook disappears in Berlin. 3/3

2665. **Stanley, Stephen,** *Wind in the Sails,* Createspace, 2016. Jeremy Dance #4 of 5. (Historical Hard Boiled) Jeremy Dance is young, rich, and tough. It's the summer of 1939 and the United States is far from the turmoil of Europe, yet Jeremy Dance Restorations has plenty of cases to investigate. "I restore things;" says Jeremy. "Sometimes it's missing objects, sometimes it's missing persons, and sometimes it's missing clues in a case of murder. I restore reputations and peace of mind to my clients, and my services don't come cheap." 3/3

2666. **Stanley, Stephen,** *Death Insurance,* Createspace, 2017. Jeremy Dance #5 of 5. (Historical Hard Boiled) It's the late 1930s as the depression is ending the war in Europe is building. "Restoration" agent Jeremy Dance must investigate the death of his former classmate. What at first appears to be an accidental drowning turns out to be a cold-blooded murder. 3/3

2667. **Stanley, Stephen,** *All the Way Dead,* Stonefield, 2013. Luke Littlefield #1 of 5. (Cozy) Former underwear model Danny Black has produced several bestselling crime novels, but there is only one problem. Danny Black doesn't exist. Danny Black is, in reality, anthropology professor Luke Littlefield. 3/3

2668. **Stanley, Stephen,** *A Grave Location,* Stonefield, 2014. Luke Littlefield #2 of 5. (Cozy) It's the end of the school term for anthropology professor Luke Littlefield and he's looking forward to summer and sharing a field experience with his graduate interns. When Luke's old college professor calls with a forensic project, Luke and his interns head to Maine with the task of identifying grave sites at the old Brookfield Asylum. 3/3

2669. **Stanley, Stephen,** *Pottery and Poets,* Createspace, 2015. Luke Littlefield #3 of 5. (Cozy) Anthropology professor and former model Luke Littlefield is spending his summer teaching an introductory course at Cranmore College and consulting on an archeological dig on New England's Cape Cod. The discovery of a centuries old murder in Provincetown is overshadowed by a series of murders in West Hollywood by an alleged religious terrorist group called The Followers. 3/3

2670. **Stanley, Stephen,** *Murder on Shaker Hill,* Createspace, 2016. Luke Littlefield #4 of 5. (Cozy) When anthropology professor Luke Littlefield receives an anonymous grant to run a summer enrichment course at an old Shaker Village in Maine, he jumps at the chance. Things are going along smoothly until a visitor is found dead. Luke and his partner Bryan are pulled into a mystery that seems to have no solution. 3/3

2671. **Stanley, Stephen,** *Road Kill,* Createspace, 2018. Luke Littlefield #5 of 5. (Cozy) Anthropology professor and former male model

Luke Littlefield has the unfortunate luck to witness a situation that later turns out to be a murder. As a witness, Luke finds himself involved with the investigation when he is deputized by Mary Brooks, the medical examiner. 3/3

2672. **Stanton, Mary,** *Defending Angels,* Berkley, 2008. Beaufort #1 of 5. (Paranormal Legal Thriller) With a long list of ethereal clients who need her help, Savannah lawyer Brianna Winston Beaufort's career choice is beginning to haunt her. –legal secretary Ronald Parchese assists Beaufort with her investigations (MLM). 1/3

2673. **Stanton, Mary,** *Angel's Advocates,* Berkley, 2009. Beaufort #2 of 5. (Paranormal Legal Thriller) Money's been tight ever since Bree Winston Beaufort inherited Savannah's haunted law firm Beaufort & Company along with its less-than-angelic staff. But she's finally going to tackle a case that pays the bills representing a spoiled girl who stole someone's Girl Scout cookie money. 1/3

2674. **Stanton, Mary,** *Avenging Angels,* Berkley, 2010. Beaufort #3 of 5. (Paranormal Legal Thriller) Law school hasn't prepared Bree to appeal cases for the dead. After inheriting her great-uncle's haunted law firm, she must now represent ex-banker O'Rourke, who supposedly killed himself after losing a fortune. 1/3

2675. **Stanton, Mary,** *Angel's Verdict,* Berkley, 2011. Beaufort #4 of 5. (Paranormal Legal Thriller) Celestial advocate Brianna Winston-Beaufort is eager to set aside handling appeals for condemned souls and get back to practicing law in the land of the living. Three months after taking over the family practice Bree jumps at the opportunity to work for an earthly client. –Parchese may or may not appear (MLM). 1/3

2676. **Stanton, Mary,** *Angel Condemned,* Berkley, 2011. Beaufort #5 of 5. (Paranormal Legal Thriller) Representing her Aunt Cissy's fiancé, museum curator Prosper White, in a case of fraud, attorney and celestial advocate Brianna Winston- Beaufort hopes to settle the matter out of court. But when Prosper is murdered and Cissy's arrested for the crime, Bree will have to solve the mystery of the Cross of Justinian-an artifact of interest in both Prosper's lawsuit and Bree's celestial case-to clear her aunt's name. –Parchese may or may not appear (MLM). 1/3

2677. **Starling, Boris,** *Visibility,* HarperCollins, 2006. (Police Procedural) It's the height of the Cold War, and as the Great Fog rolls in over London, a man meets his death in the icy shallows of the Long Water. Some say he was just drunk, wandering through Hyde Park. But for Scotland Yard's new detective, Herbert Smith, the body will lead to a far more interesting trail when it's discovered that the young victim's death was no accident. –an intelligence officer misleads

Smith about his real relationship with the deceased (MLM). "The author has some peculiar ideas about the effects of anal intercourse (Gunn)." 1/3

2678. **Stephens, Mick,** *Danny Malone's Way,* Encounter, 1978. (Pulp) "Denver, Colorado, private investigator Danny Malone, 20s, a Vietnam military police veteran, former Hollywood stuntman, who will take only gays for clients, is confronted with a variant of a locked-room puzzle (Gunn)." 3/3

2679. **Stephens, Mick,** *Shooting Schedule,* Encounter, 1978. Jerry Scott #1 of 4. (Pulp) "Los Angeles private investigator Jerry Scott, 30s, a Vietnam military police veteran… investigation leads him to the owner of the illegal casino at which closeted film actor Brett Taylor won a huge sum of money (Gunn)." –also listed under the authors Mick Stevens or Ray Sharp (MLM). 3/3

2680. **Stephens, Mick,** *Gay, Hot, & Deadly,* Wilmington, 1978. Jerry Scott #2 of 4. (Pulp) "A model disappears, and his roommate is found dead with an ice pick driven through his eye (Gunn)." –author listed as Ray Sharp (MLM). 3/3

2681. **Stephens, Mick,** *Sado Murder,* Surree, 1978. Jerry Scott #3 of 4. (Pulp) "Mac Walzak's car is blown up; then the movie studio head is murdered and one of his stars wounded (Gunn)." –author listed as Mick Stevens. Reprinted as *"S" and "M"* by Stu Chadwick published by Arena in 1985 (MLM). 3/3

2682. **Stephens, Mick,** *Teen Slave Ring,* Surree, 1979. Jerry Scott #4 of 4. (Pulp) "When an actor's life is threatened, he hires Jerry for protection (Gunn)." –author listed as Mick Stevens (MLM). 3/3

2683. **Stevens, Cassie,** *Tangled Web,* AmberQuill, 2009. (MM Suspense) Given their occupation as archaeologists, Rick Ramone and Val Lancaster were destined to meet. The two men even knew the date and time–until someone else's agenda pushed them together sooner than they'd anticipated. All Rick and Val want–besides each other– is to research ancient civilizations, not trek through the dirty, dense, and dangerous Central American rainforest on a rescue mission that weaves suspicion with every step. 3/3

2684. **Stevens, Jack,** *Fellowship of Iron,* Idol, 2000. (Pulp) Mike's a professional bodybuilder. Richard's an up-and-coming journalist. They're very much in love. But their world is torn apart and their lives put in danger when Mike's former lover and bodybuilding mentor is found dead, and they learn for the first time of the Fellowship of Iron. Suddenly the two young men are caught up in a vicious game of revenge, lies and betrayal that threatens to destroy their relationship as they are plunged into a world of dangerous men, sweat and pumping muscles. 3/3

2685. **Stevens, Nigel,** *Amendment 2 Murder,* Tanner Long, 1993. (Political) "Boulder private investigator Zachary (Zach) Scott, 29, fights for the rights of all Colorado gays in a political whodunit (Gunn)." 3/3

2686. **Stevenson, Jane,** *London Bridges,* Cape, 2000. (Legal Drama) Set in 1990s London and crafted with a very modern spin. Its plot centers on a treasure lost in the Blitz and newly discovered by an unscrupulous lawyer, who is tempted by greed into a series of crimes leading to murder. A highly contemporary cast of characters assembles to confound him, including a charming and flamboyant gay classicist in hot pursuit of a sixth-century homoerotic poem he hopes will revive his flagging career, a young Indian lawyer fighting British prejudices of race and class, and a very nice dog named Alice. 2/3

2687. **Stevenson, Richard (Richard Lipez b. 1938),** *Death Trick,* St. Martin's, 1981. Donald Strachey #1 of 15. (Hard Boiled) A young man has been brutally murdered. The gay son of a wealthy family has disappeared. Now it's up to private dick Don Strachey to get to the bottom of this mess–even if he has to cruise every gay bar in the city to do it. Don Strachey isn't exactly the most sought-after private eye in Albany, New York. 3/3

2688. **Stevenson, Richard,** *On the Other Hand, Death,* St. Martin's, 1984. Donald Strachey #2 of 15. (Hard Boiled) When the giant Millpond Company finds its plans for a mega-shopping mall stymied by the refusal of an elderly lesbian couple to sell their home, the ladies are subjected to ugly vandalism and frightening death threats. The powerful director of Millpond in turn hires Don Strachey, Albany's only gay detective, to protect the ladies, find the culprits, and clear the corporate name. 3/3

2689. **Stevenson, Richard,** *Ice Blues,* St. Martin's, 1986. Donald Strachey #3 of 15. (Hard Boiled) Shocked to discover the body of the grandson of the godfather of Albany's political machine in his car, P.I. Donald Strachey knows he is in for trouble. But when he learns that the murder victim left a $2.5 million legacy with instructions that it be used to destroy that machine, along with a personal letter to Strachey asking for his help, his suspicions are confirmed. Faced with power-brokers at all levels, Albany's only gay P.I. tries to fulfill the dead man's mission-with his own survival at stake. 3/3

2690. **Stevenson, Richard,** *Third Man Out,* St. Martin's, 1992. Donald Strachey #4 of 15. (Hard Boiled) After an attempt is made on his life, Queer Nation activist John Rutka asks tough-as-nails gay private detective Don Strachey to provide him with protection. Why does someone want to kill him? The activist's efforts at outing closeted gay homophobes have earned him a multitude of enraged enemies who would just as soon see him dead. After Strachey refuses to help, the man's body is found savagely murdered in apparent retribution for his deeds. 3/3

2691. **Stevenson, Richard,** *Shock to the System,* St. Martin's, 1995. Donald Strachey #5 of 15. (Hard Boiled) Donald Strachey is asked to investigate the suspicious death of Paul Haig by three different people-Haig's homophobic mother, his ex-lover, and the psychiatrist hired to "cure" him of his homosexuality. Just as he gets started, however, all three remove him from the case, leaving Strachey with a brutal murderer that now everyone wants left alone. 3/3

2692. **Stevenson, Richard,** *Chain of Fools,* St. Martin's, 1996. Donald Strachey #6 of 15. (Hard Boiled) Private Investigator Donald Strachey is asked to look into the events surrounding the months-old murder of Eric Osborne. His death, originally believed to be a random attack, takes on new significance when Janet Osborne, Eric's sister, survives an attempt on her life. 3/3

2693. **Stevenson, Richard,** *Strachey's Folly,* St. Martin's, 1998. Donald Strachey #7 of 15. (Hard Boiled) In Washington, D.C. to view the AIDS quilt, gay P.I. Donald Strachey, his lover Timmy, and a friend discover a panel for an ex-lover of their friend. The trouble is that the ex-lover isn't dead. When their friend barely survives a vicious attack, Strachey concludes that someone has a deadly secret – one that he or she will kill to protect. 3/3

2694. **Stevenson, Richard,** *Tongue Tied,* St. Martin's, 2003. Donald Strachey #8 of 15. (Hard Boiled) Under normal circumstances, PI Donald Strachey wouldn't take a job from right-wing radio "shock jock" J-Bird. But Strachey not only needs the money, he's also intrigued that the death threats against the radio DJ are being made in the name of a radical gay rights group that has been defunct for over twenty years. 3/3

2695. **Stevenson, Richard,** *Death Vows,* MLR, 2008. Donald Strachey #9 of 15. (Hard Boiled) Gay marriage in Massachusetts is a fine institution, except when it leads to murder. 3/3

2696. **Stevenson, Richard,** *The 38 Million Dollar Smile,* MLR, 2009. Donald Strachey #10 of 15. (Hard Boiled) Gadfly scion of Albany old money Gary Griswold goes missing in Thailand, and his ex-wife wants him found - with his 38 million dollars. 3/3

2697. **Stevenson, Richard,** *Cockeyed,* MLR, 2010. Donald Strachey #11 of 15. (Hard Boiled) "When Hunny 'You go, girl!' Van Horn, Albany's flaming-est flamer, wins the state lottery's first billion-dollar payout, it's PI Don Strachey who's brought in to deal with the skeletons, some of them violent, that come crashing out of Hunny's non-closet.

3/3

2698. **Stevenson, Richard,** *Red, White, Black, and Blue,* MLR, 2011. Donald Strachey #12 of 15. (Hard Boiled) In an election year, Don finds himself in the unlikely role of political operative. Rumors about the Tea Party's opportunistic gubernatorial candidate, Kenyon Louderbush, paint him as an unfaithful, callous exploiter of young men... young men that he puts into the hospital...or perhaps the morgue. –won the twenty-fourth LAMBDA Award (MLM). 3/3

2699. **Stevenson, Richard,** *The Last Thing I Saw,* MLR, 2012. Donald Strachey #13 of 15. (Hard Boiled) Eddie Wenske has gone missing. A popular investigative reporter renowned for both his gay-coming-out memoir and a frightening book on drug cartels, Wenske vanishes while investigating a gay media conglomerate with a controversial owner and dodgy business practices. 3/3

2700. **Stevenson, Richard,** *Why Stop at Vengeance,* MLR, 2015. Donald Strachey #14 of 15. (Hard Boiled) A young African living in Albany is bent on avenging the death of his former lover back in Uganda at the hands of a gay-hating mob. 3/3

2701. **Stevenson, Richard,** *WWW.DropDead,* MLR, 2016. Donald Strachey #15 of 15. (Hard Boiled) KickAssQueer is a gay website thousands go to for news, gossip, and as a forum to exchange often heated opinions about GLBT life in America. When one of KAQ's editors is savagely murdered, it's PI Don Strachey's job to uncover whether one of the site's many harsh critics, gay or straight, is responsible for this young man's death. –Stevenson has confirmed that he will be releasing the sixteenth book in the Donald Strachey series sometime in 2019 (MLM). 3/3

2702. **Steward, Samuel,** *Parisian Lives,* St. Martin's, 1984. (Psychological) John McAndrews narrates the strange interconnections between Sir Arthur Lyly's career as a painter and his increasingly dangerous and desperate loves- for a Chicago gangster, a disturbed British sailor, a young Parisian tough, and a Spanish peasant boy. 3/3

2703. **Steward, Samuel,** *Murder is Murder is Murder,* Alyson, 1985. Gertrude Stein and Alice B. Toklas Mystery #1 of 2. (Soft Boiled) "Chicago-based amateur sleuth John McAndrews, a professor of English in France on visits, is willing to use his mind and his genitals to help his adored master sleuths Gertrude Stein (1874-1946) and Alice B. Toklas (1877-1967) ... solve the murder of their gardener's father in Bilignin, 1937-1938 (Gunn)." –Steward uses John McAndrews in all of his books, but they are mostly unrelated except for the two Stein and Toklas mysteries (MLM). 3/3

2704. **Steward, Samuel,** *The Caravaggio Shawl,* Alyson, 1989. Gertrude

Stein and Alice B. Toklas Mystery #2 of 2. (Soft Boiled) A trio of sleuths: the intellectually bold Stein, the detail-oriented Toklas and gay writer John McAndrews, their legman, whose experience in the secret world of homosexual Paris yields critical clues. The three do not operate as Holmes and Watson but rather as a tripartite Holmesian mind, each contributing a unique perspective that assists in unraveling the puzzle. 3/3

2705. **Stewart, J. I. M.,** *Mungo's Dream,* Norton, 1973. (Family Drama) Mungo Lockhart goes up to Oxford and find himself sharing a room with the Honourable Ian Cardower, who is heir to a rich title and estate. Unimpressed by rank or riches, Mungo is nonetheless wary in his exchanges with Cardower, and this is reciprocated. However, the two do become good friends and Cardower takes Mungo on visits to his parents' home, to visit the head of the family, Lord Audlearn at Bamberton Court – a stately home in the grand style – and then to Mallachie, the true family seat, where the eldest son Lord Brightmony lives in splendid isolation, save for his companion; Leonard Sedley, sometime novelist. –no obvious gay men but Mungo and Cardower take a nude swim together; "Their naked bodies were cold, slippery, hard to get ahold on… The notion that that had been comporting themselves like the nude gentlemen in *Women in Love* amused them vastly." (MLM). 1/3

2706. **Stimson, Jim,** *Double Exposure,* Scribner's Sons, 1965. (Crime Drama) "An unemployed film director searches for the missing daughter of a studio owner and becomes involved in pornographic filmmaking and gay parties (Slide)." –this was meant to be the start of a series featuring Stoney Winston (MLM). 2/3

2707. **Stine, Scott,** *Pandemonium: A Miltonian Murder,* iUniverse, 2017. (Amateur Sleuth) It is 1984, and Brad Morton is a twenty-three-year-old college student who is still devastated by his brother's suicide. For four years, he has done his best to not think of Byron or his untimely death. All he needs to graduate from Brown University is to complete a thesis on Paradise Lost. But first, he needs to find out why his brother died. 2/3

2708. **Stoddard, Jeffrey Lynn,** *The House on Capitol Hill,* P. D., 2007. (Horror) The large stately mansion stood majestic and proud upon Capitol Hill, overlooking Seattle in a way that seemed almost to proclaim its dominance of the entire city. But behind those innocent walls lurked a very dark shadow of its past, and the new owners; Tommy and Geoffrey, were to be the next victims of a frightening journey that may well lead to the undoing of their relationship - if not their very lives. 3/3

2709. **Stoddard, Jeffrey Lynn,** *Face Your Fears,* P. D., 2008. (Horror) Are you ready to face your fears? That is the question being posed to all who respond to a newspaper ad requesting participants who think themselves brave enough to spend one night in a reputedly haunted castle in Scotland. Five people are eventually chosen for this task. Once locked inside the confines of the 11th century castle the five are forced to face fears far worse than any could have anticipated. 3/3

2710. **Stoddard, Jeffrey Lynn,** *The Haunted-The Hunted,* Smashwords, 2009. (Horror) Elija Morales and his partner of 3 1/2 years, Lobo Sanchez, have just moved into their new home. Strangely, recent unexplained events would seem to indicate that Elijah and Lobo are not the only ones occupying the home. In fact, they are soon to discover that whatever is haunting their 100-year-old house has plans for Elija far greater and more horrifying than any he could ever have imagined. 3/3

2711. **Stoddard, Jeffrey Lynn,** *The Eye of the Storm,* Smashwords, 2009. (Horror) Dante Dre, a single gay man, awakens one morning to find his simple world suddenly turned upside down with the discovery of a dead man in his bed. The blood on his hands proves Dante to be the murderer, but why can't he remember having done it? Outside forces combine to complicate matters even more forcing Dante to not only figure out his part in the crime but to survive the night of terror. –available as an e-book only (MLM). 3/3

2712. **Stoddard, Jeffrey Lynn,** *Neighbor,* Smashwords, 2010. (Horror) James Ferguson has moved into a new house, he has just met Kyle, a prospective lover, and all is looking great. Threatening James' happiness, though, is Deputy Neuberg who suspects James of having a hand in the disappearances of James' three neighbors. Making matters worse is the neighboring house, itself, which appears to be haunted by something within that seems to be luring James inside. 3/3

2713. **Stokoe, Matthew,** *High Life,* Akashic, 2002. (Crime Drama) Jack had gone to Hollywood with one ambition: to become famous, a star, exactly how he didn't care. He just wanted to be like the people whose lives he followed in gossip magazines...Instead he found a world seedier than anything he could have imagined, a world of whores and deceit, snuff shows, incest, drugs-and despair. –main character works as a hustler of men and women (MLM). 3/3

2714. **Stone, Ethan,** *In the Flesh,* Dreamspinner, 2010. Flesh #1 of 4. (MM Mystery) Reno Detective Cristian Flesh is an out and unashamed cop, but his slutty ways might be his downfall. Cristian lives by a strict set of personal rules, preferring hook-ups and anonymous encounters to committed relationships. His guidelines work for him... until one of his tricks is murdered and he becomes the prime suspect. 3/3

2715. **Stone, Christopher,** *Coming and Going,* MLR, 2016. St. James #1 of 3. (Metaphysical) For gay, metaphysical sleuth Dr. Minnow Saint James, the workplace spans time, space, dimensions, and the entirety of the vast, incomprehensible affair that is God's Creation. –available as an e-book only (MLM). 3/3

2716. **Stone, Christopher,** *Shaking the Holiday Blues,* MLR, 2015. St. James #2 of 3. (Metaphysical) As a last resort, a gay married ex-sailor turns to a Past Life Regression therapist to help him heal his chronic holiday blues. –available as an e-book only (MLM). 3/3

2717. **Stone, Christopher,** *The Coming of Beth,* MLR, 2018. St. James #3 of 3. (Metaphysical) It's the Summer of 2016, and Dr. Minnow Saint James's world is turned upside down by Beth, a disembodied book author who is channeling her book, On How to Be Human, through a psychic development teacher Minn has come to know. What's more, America's premier past life regression therapist is working with a Retro patient who is being harassed and haunted by a ghost. –available as an e-book only (MLM). 3/3

2718. **Stone, Ethan,** *Flesh and Blood,* Dreamspinner, 2011. Flesh #2 of 4. (MM Mystery) When a local man is attacked, and the suspect is a hustler, Cristian knows there's more to the case than meets the eye. His investigation will lead him into a maze of lies, deceit, and underage prostitution. But that's only the beginning as people start disappearing and turning up dead. 3/3

2719. **Stone, Ethan,** *Blood and Tears,* Dreamspinner, 2011. Flesh #3 of 4. (MM Mystery) The last thing Gabe Vargas wants to do after nearly dying is to leave his young son. But that's exactly what FBI Agent Drew Bradley is asking him to do. According to Drew, the only way to protect Gabe and find his wife's killer is to fake Gabe's death. 3/3

2720. **Stone, Ethan,** *Closing Ranks,* DSP, 2015. Flesh #4 of 4. (MM Police Procedural) Internal Affairs investigator Jeremy Ranklin is looking into corruption within the Reno Police Department when he's ordered to examine the suspicious death of the Chief of Police. The assignment partners Jeremy with Detective Cristian Flesh. Though they spar at first, Jeremy earns Cristian's trust, and they work well together. 3/3

2721. **Stone, Ethan,** *Compromised,* Totally Bound, 2013. Uniformity #1 of 3. (MM Mystery) Correctional Officer Daniel 'Kash' Kashaveroff is single, gay and working at a maximum-security prison. Not the best job to be out. Gun shy from a past relationship, he wants to fall in love again but doesn't expect it to happen anytime soon. Working with Zane Davis turns Kash's life upside down. They go from colleagues to friends to being in a relationship but it's anything but perfect. 3/3

2722. **Stone, Ethan,** *Damaged,* Totally Bound, 2014. Uniformity #2 of 3. (MM Mystery) Correctional Officer Zane Davis assumed the worst thing he had to worry about working at a maximum-security prison were the inmates but his co-workers could be just as dangerous. 3/3

2723. **Stone, Ethan,** *Recruited,* Totally Bound, 2014. Uniformity #3 of 3. (MM Mystery) Inmate Dylan Hoss never thought he'd fall for a man in prison. He also didn't think life on the outside would be more dangerous than inside. 3/3

2724. **Stone, Ethan,** *Bartender PI,* Silver Publishing, 2012. (MM Mystery) When hockey star Linc Carpenter is banned from playing his beloved sport, he starts over slinging drinks in Tampa. He's inept as a bartender, so when the opportunity arises to train as a private investigator he takes it. He's not very good at that either, but he still manages to get hired to follow fashion mogul Quentin Faulkner. 3/3

2725. **Stone, Ethan,** *Subject 13,* Silver Publishing, 2014. (MM Mystery) Luke Kincaid's life is exploding all around him. First his lover leaves him to marry a woman, then childhood nightmares return with a vengeance. 3/3

2726. **Stone, Hampton (Aaron Marc Stein),** *The Murder that Wouldn't Stay Solved,* Simon and Schuster, 1951. Gibby Gibson #4 of 18. (Legal Drama) "It happened in a dingy hotel. "You know the kind of hotel. it's sordid and cheap and dismal, and you hear noise through the walls all night. But you can check in at any hour - with or without baggage - and no questions asked. It's strictly private ... until a little item like murder gives it top spot on the police blotter. Like on the night the older man takes a room with a young boy - and is found beaten to death in the morning... (1st Wrappers Books listing of book for sale on their website)" –middle aged man who was murdered most likely picked up a male hustler (MLM). 2/3

2727. **Stone, Ethan,** *Hacked Up,* Silver Publishing, 2017. (MM Police Procedural) Seattle is being plagued by a string of gruesome murders. For Detective Peter Tao, it's a career-making case, but he's struggling to find a lead. How is the killer choosing his victims? What is he trying to prove? 3/3

2728. **Stone, Jack,** *The Running Man,* Blueboy, 1976. (Pulp) "New York courier Phil Evans, 30s... discovers the packages he is carrying contain jewels and government secrets (Gunn). 3/3

2729. **Stone, Jack,** *The Coke Runners,* Blueboy, 1977. (Pulp) "New York-based narcotics agent Phil Carter, though he realizes his profession is probably a meaningless game, finds satisfaction from doing a good job (Gunn)." 3/3

2730. **Stone, Jack,** *The Mystery of Toomey's Island,* Blueboy, 1977. (Pulp) "New York-based amateur sleuth Nate Drew, 20s, a construction worker, feels compelled to start an investigation that New York police special officer Ed Foley concludes (Gunn). 3/3

2731. **Stone, Jack,** *Bang the Bikers,* Blueboy, 1978. (Pulp) "Cyclist Elmer and his four comrades do not follow up on their hunches about what is going on with a bicycle tour, while Andy and Luke, members of a local rescue squad, are at the showdown with the gangsters (Gunn). 3/3

2732. **Stone, Jack,** *Hot Bodies,* Surree, 1978. (Pulp) "Florida ranch manager Daniel (Dan) Gurney, 28, faces a puzzle (Gunn)." –later published as *Gusher Coming* by Surree under the name Jack Groner (MM). 3/3

2733. **Stone, Jack,** *Semi Rough,* Numbers, 1978. (Pulp) "New York policemen Tige Nelson and Gregory (Gork) McCulloh are partners... [who] assume the identities of Connecticut playboys, and Tige becomes his sex slave in order to infiltrate the [mob] and get the goods... before a planned heist (Gunn)." 3/3

2734. **Stovall, S. A.,** *Vice City,* DSP, 2017. Vice #1 of 2. (Crime Drama) After twenty years as an enforcer for the Vice family mob, Nicholas Pierce shouldn't bat an eye at seeing a guy get worked over and tossed in the river. But there's something about the suspected police mole, Miles, that has Pierce second-guessing himself. The kid is just trying to look out for his brother any way he knows how, and the altruistic motive sparks an uncharacteristic act of mercy that involves Pierce taking Miles under his wing. 3/3

2735. **Stovall, S. A.,** *Vice Enforcer,* DSP, 2018. Vice #2 of 2. (Crime Drama) Eight months ago, Nicholas Pierce, ex-mob enforcer, faked his death and assumed a new identity to escape sadistic mob boss Jeremy Vice. With no contacts outside the underworld, Pierce finds work with a washed-up PI. It's an easy enough gig–until investigating a human trafficking ring drags him back to his old stomping grounds. 3/3

2736. **Strange, Liz,** *Missing Daughter, Shattered Family,* MLR, 2011. Lloyd #1 of 4. (MM Hardboiled) When a brutal homophobic attack ended David Lloyd's career as a police officer, his life was changed forever. Five years later David is running his own private detective agency, where a missing person's case comes to his attention. Digging into the circumstances of her disappearance forces David to realize he has not dealt with what happened to him, and that he can no longer deal with his long-time partner's fear of being honest about their relationship. 3/3

2737. **Strange, Liz,** *A Fresh Set of Eyes,* MLR, 2012. Lloyd #2 of 4. (MM Hardboiled) A mother turns to David to help free her son and another young man from prison, where they have spent the last ten years for a double murder many feel they did not commit. The police investigation was spotty, the evidence non-existent, and yet someone had to pay for the vicious assault on two young brothers. 3/3

2738. **Strange, Liz,** *Destination Unknown,* MLR, 2014. Lloyd #3 of 4. (MM Hardboiled) Tracking down the whereabouts of a girl last seen on a cruise ship takes David Lloyd far from the streets of Toronto and thrusts him into the seedy world of human trafficking. 3/3

2739. **Strange, Liz,** *Behind Closed Doors,* MLR, 2014. Lloyd #4 of 4. (MM Hardboiled) Ivan Holmes' life is picture perfect to the public eye, but behind closed doors lies a web of deceit and exploitation. 3/3

2740. **Straub, Peter,** *Koko,* E. P. Dutton, 1988. Underhill #1 of 5. (Horror) KOKO. Only four men knew what it meant. Now they must stop it. They are Vietnam vets a doctor, a lawyer, a working stiff, and a writer. Very different from each other, they are nonetheless linked by a shared history and a single shattering secret. –novelist Tim Underhill, during Vietnam, had a slew of teenage male lovers. The first three books are a trilogy and the last two are standalones with Underhill detecting. Although Underhill is gay his sexuality is rarely discussed or mentioned (MLM). 1/3

2741. **Straub, Peter,** *Mystery,* E. P. Dutton, 1990. Underhill #2 of 5. (Horror) After a tragic accident which he barely survives, Tom Pasmore develops an obsession with death–an obsession which leads him to investigate two murders–one in the past and one in the present. And during his investigation, Pasmore learns more than anyone needs–or deserves–to know! 1/3

2742. **Straub, Peter,** *The Throat,* E. P. Dutton, 1993. Underhill #3 of 5. (Horror) Underhill has been summoned by his childhood friend John Ransom to his home town of Millhaven, the site of old horrors now plagued by new demons. After decades of silence, it appears that the Blue Rose killer has struck again - brutally murdering Ransom's wife. –last book in the Blue Rose trilogy (MLM). 1/3

2743. **Straub, Peter,** *Lost Boy, Lost Girl,* Random House, 2003. Underhill #4 of 5. (Horror) Nancy Underhill commits suicide for no apparent reason. A week later, her son – fifteen-year-old Mark – vanishes. The boy's uncle, novelist Timothy Underhill, searches his hometown of

Millhaven for clues that might help unravel this horrible dual mystery. 1/3

2744. **Straub, Peter,** *In the Night Room,* Random House, 2004. Underhill #5 of 5. (Horror) Willy Patrick, the respected author of the award-winning young-adult novel In the Night Room, thinks she is losing her mind-again. One day, she is drawn helplessly into the parking lot of a warehouse. She knows somehow that her daughter, Holly, is being held in the building, and she has an overwhelming need to rescue her. But what Willy knows is impossible, for her daughter is dead. 1/3

2745. **Streete, Phillip,** *Naked Danger,* Hamilton House, 1975. (Pulp) "Policeman Kelley McWilliams, Irish-American, and FBI agent Curtis (Curt) Hardy work together... [with] Royal Canadian Mounted Policeman Jason Mills, [who] was on an undercover mission looking into pirated phonograph records (Gunn)." –reprinted as *Kelley's Naked Danger* by Mitch Stone in 1985 by Arena Press (MLM). 3/3

2746. **Stuart, Chad (William J. Lambert III),** *Joint Hunger,* Greenleaf, 1973. (Pulp) "International Narcotics Control agent Tad Wilcox fails to stop a shipment of heroin from Greece and falls in love with the charismatic drug lord in an undercover case (Gunn)." 3/3

2747. **Stuart, Chad,** *E-Mission,* Hamilton House, 1974. (Pulp) "Feigned CIA Agent Brad Winslow, an oilman, dramatically portrays the double nature of secret agents. CIA Agent Ty Hamilton is assigned the mission to use a Swiss oil exploration outfit as a cover to discover whether the country of San Marco has atomic missile capacity to strike at the United States. After Ty is killed, Brad assumes his identity upon meeting Ty's unknown contact (Gunn)." –reprinted as *Ty's Mission* by Mitch Stone in 1984 by Arena (MM) 3/3

2748. **Stuart, Chad,** *A Presidential Affair,* Hamilton House, 1975. (Pulp) "The presidential yacht is blown up, killing the president and his lover. After months of investigation, agents are no closer to discovering how the explosion occurred or who caused it. "Tambili" security agent Peter Coque, 30s, of Dutch descent, and his former lover, Greg Hanstler, 25, are assigned the case (Gunn)." –reprinted as *The President's Men* by Scott Weyburn in 1985 by Arena (MLM). 3/3

2749. **Stuart, Chad,** *Gusher Comin,* Surrey, 1977. (Pulp) "Oil rig foreman Cort Portland tries to convince the institutional psychiatrist that he understands what happened to Platforms A and B off the Washington Coast (Gunn). 3/3

2750. **Stukas, David,** *Someone Killed his Boyfriend,* Kensington, 2001. Robert, Michael, and Monette #1 of 4. (Modern Cozy) It's tough being fabulously wealthy Michael Stark's closest pal, particularly when you're an underpaid copywriter for feminine hygiene products, with a lousy apartment, and no lover of your own. 3/3

2751. **Stukas, David,** *Going Down for the Count,* Kensington, 2002. Robert, Michael, and Monette #2 of 4. (Modern Cozy) Blindsided by the fabulously wealthy Count Siegfried Von Schmidt, Robert, longing for old-fashioned romance, finds his dreams shattered when the Count is murdered, forcing Robert, along with his friend Michael and their lesbian sidekick Manette, to wade through Berber, Prada, and a wealth of suspect. 3/3

2752. **Stukas, David,** *Wearing Black to the White Party,* Kensington, 2003. Robert, Michael, and Monette #3 of 4. (Modern Cozy) The trio are off to Palm Springs, where a rivalry between the world-famous White Party and the upstart Red Party is sizzling, turning the hottest circuit in town into a festival of murder. 3/3

2753. **Stukas, David,** *Biceps of Death,* Kensington, 2004. Robert, Michael, and Monette #4 of 4. (Modern Cozy) It ain't easy being pretty, and in Chelsea it ain't easy NOT being pretty. That's why Robert is putting himself through a gruelling work-out regime under his roommate Michael's tutelage. It takes Robert by complete surprise, though, when bodybuilding hunk Flex, gives him a cheeky kiss in the locker room and disappears off promising him more to follow. The next morning, however, Flex is found dead - murdered by the person the papers have dubbed the bodybuilder serial killer. 3/3

2754. **Sublett, Jesse,** *Tough Baby,* Viking, 1990. Fender #2 of 3. (Crime Drama) Martin Fender is a veteran Austin musician who moonlights as a skip tracer and problem solver. In this second novel in the series, Martin returns to Austin numb and homesick after a hard tour and is sucked into a spiral of payola, blackmail, perversion and violence, tied to a crooked and demented record label owner and a thrift shop operator in the underworld of the Austin music scene. Dangerous women and desperate musicians and hustlers conspire, clash and create music, mayhem and violence. –villain is a gay man that likes to pay young men to let him hurt them (MLM). 1/3

2755. **Sudler, H. L.,** *Summerville,* Archer, 2014. Summerville #1 of 2. (Serialized Police Procedural) It's summertime in Rehoboth Beach, Delaware, and everything is beautiful. The town, the weather, the ocean, the people. For four months this seaside community becomes a playground for vacationers seeking to soak up all the fun the town has to offer. But this summer will be different, when devastating secrets threaten to destroy a family and nearly everyone they will come to know. A fugitive murderer, a wayward socialite, a deceptive med student, and a destructive sociopath all set the stage for a combustive summer. 3/3

2756. **Sudler, H. L.,** *Return to Summerville,* Archer, 2017. Summerville #2 of 2. (Serialized Police Procedural) Summertime comes once again to the gorgeous seaside resort of Rehoboth Beach, and with it comes beautiful people, enchanting weather, and seductive days filled with sex, sunbathing, and relaxation. But for some, the promise of pleasure comes with memories of last summer. 3/3

2757. **Suede, Damon,** *Pent Up,* Dreamspinner, 2015. (MM Suspense) Ruben Oso moves to Manhattan to start his life over as a low-rent bodyguard and stumbles into a gig in a swanky Park Avenue penthouse. What begins as executive protection turns personal working for a debonair zillionaire who makes Ruben question everything about himself. Watching over financial hotshot Andy Bauer puts Ruben in an impossible position. He knows zero about shady trading and his cocky boss lives barricaded in a glass tower with wall-to-wall secrets and hot-and-cold-running paranoia. 3/3

2758. **Sullivan, Colleen Baxter,** *Yolk,* Triplicity, 2014. Garwood #1 of 2. (Hard Boiled) Adam Garwood did not realize that when Jillian Lambert walked into his detective agency, his life would never be the same. Not only was Jillian trying to uncover a cold case from twenty years prior, but she was also looking for her twin sister, Devon, whose disappearance was the focus of this case. Adam would soon learn that his probing would uncover a hidden mystery surrounding the Centaur Theatre and its cast of actors, this also leading to frightening details about the Montreal mafia. Should he leave well enough alone? 3/3

2759. **Sullivan, Colleen Baxter,** *Gritty,* Waldorf, 2017. Garwood #2 of 2. (Hard Boiled) Garwood would soon be captivated by this homeless man living on the streets of Montreal. What power did he have and why did Adam take him on with no retainer or promise of future payment? Much against the advice of his partner and friends, he delves into and uncovers the corruption, cover ups and payoffs involving top executives working for one of Canada s largest pharmaceutical companies. 3/3

2760. **Sullivan, Kyle Michael,** *Rape in Holding Cell 6,* KMSCB, 2009. (Modern Pulp) When Antony met Collier, his life became perfect... until "Collie" was wrongfully arrested and brutally murdered in the city's jail, sending Antony's world into chaos. Then a chance comment led him to believe Collie's death was not a "tragic incident that no one have been prevented," but was actually part of a vicious conspiracy. –*Rape in Holding Cell 6* was originally printed in two volumes by Nazca Press in 2009 and 2010, this edition combines the two (MLM). 3/3

2761. **Swatling, David,** *Calvin's Head,* Bold Stroke Books, 2014. (MM Crime Drama) Life in Amsterdam isn't all windmills and tulips when you're homeless. Jason Dekker lives in a jeep with his dog, Calvin, on the outskirts of the city. A thesis on Van Gogh brought him to the Netherlands, and the love of Dutch artist Willy Hart convinced him to stay. But Willy is gone, and Dekker is on the brink of a total meltdown. On a summer morning in the park, Calvin sniffs out the victim of a grisly murder. 3/3

2762. **Sylvre, Lou,** *Loving Luki Vasquez,* Dreamspinner, 2011.Vásquez & James #1 of 5. (MM Mystery) Reclusive weaver Sonny Bly James controls every color and shape in his tapestries, but he can't control the pattern of his life–a random encounter with Luki Vásquez, ex-ATF agent and all-around badass, makes that perfectly clear. The mutual attraction is immediate, but love-shy Sonny has retreated from life, and Luki wears his visible and not-so-visible scars like armor. Neither can bare his soul with ease. 3/3

2763. **Sylvre, Lou,** *Delsyn's Blues,* Dreamspinner, 2012. Vásquez & James #2 of 5. (MM Mystery) Sonny James and Luki Vasquez are living proof that the course of love never runs smoothly. Ambushed by grief, Sonny listens to a voice singing the blues from beyond the grave. While revisiting the sorrows and failings of his past, in the here and now he puts up a wall against love. Just when Luki chips through that barricade, the couple becomes the target of a new threat from outside: an escalating and unexplainable rash of break-ins and assaults. 3/3

2764. **Sylvre, Lou,** *Finding Jackie,* Dreamspinner, 2013. Vásquez & James #3 of 5. (MM Mystery) Luki Vasquez and Sonny Bly James finally have their Hawaiian wedding, and it's perfect, almost. But their three-phase honeymoon is riddled with strife. Luki's status as a working badass spells discord for the newlyweds. A former informant from Luki's days with ATFE brings a troubling message (or is it a warning?) from a Mob hit man. 3/3

2765. **Sylvre, Lou,** *Saving Sonny James,* Dreamspinner, 2013. Vásquez & James #4 of 5. (MM Mystery) Luki Vasquez and his still newlywed husband are back home after pulling off a harrowing desert rescue of their teenage nephew Jackie. But the events of the last couple of years have begun to catch up with Luki–loving Sonny James and letting Sonny love him back has left gaps in his emotional armor. In the gunfight that secured Jackie's rescue, Luki's bullet killed a young guard, an innocent boy in Luki's mind. In the grip of PTSD, memories, flashbacks, and nightmares consume him, and he falls into deep, almost vegetative depression. 3/3

2766. **Sylvre, Lou,** *Because of Jade,* Dreamspinner, 2014. Vásquez & James #5 of 5. (MM Mystery) Luki Vasquez receives the news he's still cancer free after five years, and he wants to celebrate with his whole family. He and his husband, Sonny James, take a road trip south, intending to gather at the home of his nephew Josh, Josh's wife Ruthie, and Jade–a little girl who was still in the womb when she and her mother helped Luki beat lung cancer. Halfway to their destination, Luki learns Josh and Ruthie have met a tragic death. 3/3

2767. **Symons, Julian,** *Bogue's Fortune,* Harper and Row, 1956. (Bibliomystery Cozy) To research a new detective story, Charles Applegate takes a post in a progressive school of misfits, set deep in the English countryside. The game turns serious when a fellow teacher is murdered, and a weird variety of criminals seem convinced that Charles has something they want. –creepy older man with a much younger male lover, in the vein of *The Maltese Falcon* (MLM). 1/3

2768. **Symons, Julian,** *The Name of Annabel Lee,* Viking, 1983. (British Cozy) A quiet college professor takes a knight errant's quest for a vanished vision. Unlucky in love and estranged from his father, Dudley Potter's only wish is to immerse himself in his favorite seventeenth-century poet and to continue teaching at Graham, the small college outside New York that is so thankfully far from his unhappy youth in his native England. But a girl named Annabel Lee changes all that, a girl who comes to him mysteriously, transforms his life magically, and is then gone. –an acquaintance of Potter's discusses his revulsion in homosexuality (MLM). 1/3

2769. **Symons, Julian,** *Death's Darkest Face,* Viking, 1990. (Fictional True Crime) Decades after the fact, Geoffrey Elder calls on Julian Symons to clear the name of his father, accused not only of a playboy poet's murder but of having an affair with the man's lover. An ingenious mystery follows, weaving together flashbacks from the 1930s with Geoffrey's passionate desire to avenge his father. –according to Anthony Slide, Symons had very confused opinions on homosexuals. In one part of the book he bad mouths gay men, then in another discusses whether or not the main character is gay. (MLM). 1/3

T

2770. **Tabard, Jameson,** *The Scottish Bitch,* Beating Windward Press, 2016. (Crime Drama) Scottish drag queen, Latrine Dion does whatever it takes to win the title of Grand Dame. Latrine needs the title of Grand Dame to establish herself in the U.S. Drag World. Her husband Peyton wants the $100,000 prize money to jump-start their American Dream. 3/3

2771. **Tait, Robert,** *Trashtown,* Black Wattle, 1997. (Australian Thriller) At thirty, Andrew feels he's experienced everything life on Oxford Street can offer. It's time for a break. He heads north to visit his mother and grandfather in a small isolated coastal town. But instead of simplicity and tranquility, he finds a community in upheaval. A spate of shocking vandalism has unsettled everyone; there's religious revivalism, Hansonite politics, and homosexuality of a more dangerous, closeted kind. 3/3

2772. **Talbot, Julia,** *Manners and Means,* Torquere, 2007. (MM Fantasy) A combination of high fantasy with an old-fashioned house mystery, using a lush setting and a tight whodunit to sweep the reader right along with young Mistral, an account manager on the grand estate of Lord Gregori, as he attempts to catch a killer. 3/3

2773. **Talbot, Julia,** *An Itch to Scratch,* Torquere, 2008. Bloodrose #1 of 6. (MM Fantasy) Deke has a terrible itch to scratch. He's a werewolf looking for a safe place to get his addiction on; Deke loves to feed vampires. When he finds himself at Bloodrose, an exclusive club that caters to supernatural creatures, Deke thinks he might be at the right place, somewhere he can find a kindred spirit. –e-book only. The vampire who sponsors Deke as a member of Bloodrose is a private detective (MLM). 3/3

2774. **Talbot, Julia,** *The Werewolf Code: The Moon,* Torquere, 2008. Bloodrose #2 of 6. (MM Fantasy) Kasey and Deke make a pretty good living as private detectives, even for a werewolf and a vampire. They know they have trouble when a tall blonde shows up, asking them to keep tabs on her cheating husband. Kasey knows the woman is lying, but they have no idea what they're getting themselves into. -e-book only (MLM). 3/3

2775. **Talbot, Julia,** *Belling the Cat,* Torquere, 2008. Bloodrose #3 of 6. (MM Fantasy) Vampire Jonny runs Bloodrose, a club that pairs up supernatural creatures for the optimum sexual experience. Too bad he can't find anyone he wants to start a relationship with, even with all of the amazing creatures coming through his doors. Then cat burglar Luc shows up, intent on stealing something he needs very badly, and Jonny knows his luck has changed. –the first three stories have been collected into a physical book, *Codes and Roses* published by Torquere in 2009 (MLM). 3/3

2776. **Talbot, Julia,** *Lean on Me,* Torquere, 2011. Bloodrose #4 of 6. (MM Fantasy) Aiden has a special, and sometimes downright annoying talent. He doesn't mind being psychic, but it is a pain in the butt when it starts to affect his sex life. He thinks he might have found the answer in a club called the Bloodrose, a place where guys like him can find some companionship. –e-book only and only 40 pages (MLM). 3/3

2777. **Talbot, Julia,** *Incomparable,* Torquere, 2013. Bloodrose #5 of 6. (MM Fantasy BDSM) Nikolas is a performer at paranormal the nightclub Bloodrose. When it comes to bottoming on stage, he's incomparable. When it concerns dating co-workers, Nikolas is on way shakier ground. –e-book only and only 36 pages. Very little mystery if any (MLM). 3/3

2778. **Talbot, Julia,** *Emerald Eyes,* Torquere, 2015. Bloodrose #6 of 6. (MM Fantasy BDSM) When Jonny, the owner of club Bloodrose finds out his shifter mate Luc has a twin brother, he decides Yves needs protection from the bad guys who have tried to kill Luc. He sends Reuben, a werewolf security agent, to keep Yves safe from the killers. And from Yves himself. –e-book only and only 84 pages (MLM). 3/3

2779. **Tapply, William,** *Marine Corpse,* Scribner's Sons, 1986. Brady Coyne #4 of 28. (Legal Thriller) The man is found on the icy streets of Boston, vomit in his beard, alcohol in his system, and ice in his veins. The police assume he is just another in the dozens of derelicts whom the urban winter claims each year, but Brady Coyne knows better. Attorney to New England's upper crust, he was the dead man's lawyer, and he knows that Stuart Carver was no bum: He was a senator's nephew. –dead man is gay, and the main character investigates the man's significant other and friends (MLM). 1/3

2780. **Taylor, Rigby,** *Dome of Death,* Createspace, 2015. (Thriller) When the director of a prestigious new Art Gallery in Queensland falls to his death from the central dome, Peter reluctantly takes over the job. After rescuing a stranger from a typhoon-enraged sea, an investigation of an art swindle puts them both in great danger. After a horrifying ordeal Peter manages to escape, only to discover that he and Jon, are wanted for murder. 3/3

2781. **Taylor, W. L.,** *Death in a Fair Place,* Createspace, 2013. Bill Felkin #1 of 5. (Police Procedural) An idyllic, prestigious private school. Wealth, privilege and entitlement. Festering resentments. 3/3

2782. **Taylor, W. L.,** *Dread in a Fair Place,* Createspace, 2014. Bill Felkin #2 of 5. (Police Procedural) Menace has returned to the idyllic, prestigious Pemberly Oaks School. There's an unseen threat on the loose. Detective Bill Felkin must find the villain before it's too late. 3/3

2783. **Taylor, W. L.,** *Deceit in a Fair Place,* Createspace, 2015. Bill Felkin #3 of 5. (Police Procedural) Death comes again to Creighton Manor, that pristine and exclusive suburb of San Francisco. The skilled and accomplished Julian Wilkes is the surgeon everyone loves to loathe. He's tried his best to mask his tangled background until one September when his efforts begin to unravel. 3/3

2784. **Taylor, W. L.,** *Greed in a Fair Place,* Createspace, 2017. Bill Felkin #4 of 5. (Police Procedural) Summer's arrived and all appears serene in Creighton Manor, the pricey and exclusive suburb north of San Francisco. The Pemberly Oaks School is closed for the summer. Its hard-working staff members are taking well-deserved vacations, although one has decided to unwind a bit too much, with disastrous consequences. –available as an e-book only. Book five, *Betrayal in a Fair Place,* will be released in 2019 (MLM). 3/3

2785. **Telfer, Daniel,** *The Corrupters,* Frederick Muller, 1964. (Psychological) Mesa City could be any town, anywhere. Its inhabitants follow an organised, unremarkable life. Then one day the body of a young girl is found placed on a pyre and reduced to charred bone and flesh; but not far enough to conceal the fact that she was pregnant. Was it the talented seventeen-year-old Keith Newall, to whom this girl became sister and friend? Is it guilt which drives him into an illicit relationship with his own sex, or is he seeking a desperate revenge? Perhaps Milo Cable is guilty. He is wealthy, middle-aged, a connoisseur of youthful flesh, a virtuoso in the field of aberrant delights, a dilettante in Dionysian rites ... Or was it Arthur Benedict or Frank Cane, men of substance and responsibility, but whose wives call them corrupters? 1/3

2786. **Tey, Josephine,** *To Love and Be Wise,* Peter Davies, 1950. Inspector Grant #4 of 6. (Police Procedural) When a young strikingly handsome photographer mysteriously disappears, it's up to Inspector Alan Grant to discover whether he accidentally drowned, committed suicide, or met his death at the hands of one of his many female admirers. –throughout the series Grant is drawn to attractive men and has constant internal debates as to his fears that he may be "different." In *To Love and Be Wise,* there is a transgender theme mixed in to the plot (MLM). 2/3

2787. **Tey, Josephine,** *The Singing Sands,* Peter Davies, 1952. Inspector Grant #6 of 6. (Police Procedural) On sick leave from Scotland Yard, Inspector Alan Grant is planning a quiet holiday with an old school chum to recover from overwork and mental fatigue. Traveling on the night train to Scotland, however, Grant stumbles upon a dead man and a cryptic poem about 'the stones that walk' and 'the singing sand, ' which send him off on a fascinating search into the verse's meaning and the identity of the deceased. –Grant debates with himself as to why he's investigating and finds it's because he's drawn to the beauty of the deceased man (MLM). 1/3

2788. **Thibodeau, Perley,** *Lulu's Back in Town,* Tales of the Mystery, 2010. Lulu #1 of 5. (Amateur Sleuth) A professional female impersonator returns from New York City to his/her hometown of Bangor, Maine to play a club date and solves the two-year-old murder of the local Fundamentalist Minister's young gay son. 3/3

2789. **Thibodeau, Perley,** *The Stalker Pressed Send,* Tales of the Mystery, 2010. Lulu #2 of 5. (Amateur Sleuth) New York City Female Impersonator again returns to her small home city of Bangor, Maine to play another club date. Aware that she'll come into full contact with the dangerous psychopathic computer troll whom she met and ignored forty-two years previously, and who has now been stalking her relentlessly for years all over the world wide web, she puts her life in further danger as she again renews old friendships and investigates the case of a missing young local male high school basketball player. 3/3

2790. **Thibodeau, Perley,** *Murder by Wrote,* Tales of the Mystery, 2011. Lulu #3 of 5. (Amateur Sleuth) LuLu is a part of investigating the systematic killings of authors by the very same means they used to do away with the victims of their various murder/mystery novels that have now topped the New York Times Best Seller lists. 3/3

2791. **Thibodeau, Perley,** *Politics of Murder,* Createspace, 2015. Lulu #4 of 5. (Amateur Sleuth) LuLu left her hometown of Bangor, Maine to get away from politics. But she very soon finds out New York City Politics Mean-Might-Money-Murder. The ongoing turmoil of LuLu's personal emotions now finds her facing death. And, her very best longtime friend Randy could well turn out to become her eventual mad killer. 3/3

2792. **Thibodeau, Perley,** *A Murderous Revenge,* Self-Published, 2016. Lulu #5 of 5. (Amateur Sleuth) LuLu again gets caught up in a dangerous homicide investigation. As she tells her friends: 'Every time I plan to do something, murder gets in the way." –available as an e-book only (MLM). 3/3

2793. **Thomas, Aaron,** *Beefcake Boys,* Greenleaf, 1967. (Pulp) "New York-based newspaper journalist Steven Randall, 32, at the request of U. S. Customs, takes an undercover assignment... Heroin is getting from Algeria to the United States. Steve follows the trail from Algiers to Rome to Paris. Bedding suspects (and fellow agents), he cracks the case, but throughout the escapades, he remembers the man he left behind (Gunn)." 3/3

2794. **Thomas, A. J.,** *A Casual Weekend Thing,* Dreamspinner, 2013. Least Likely Partnership #1 of 3. (MM Suspense) Doug Heavy Runner left the life of an openly gay Miami police officer and returned to his home on the Salish-Kootenai Indian Reservation when his mother got sick. In the two years since she passed, he's carved out an empty life as a small-town deputy, relying on out-of-town one-night stands to keep him sane. Then he meets Detective Christopher Hayes. then an arsonist destroys the house Christopher inherited from his brother, and Christopher and Doug discover they are the primary suspects. 3/3

2795. **Thomas, A. J.,** *Holding out for a Fairy Tale,* Dreamspinner, 2014. Least Likely Partnership #2 of 3. (MM Suspense) When his vicious cousin Alejandro makes a violent late-night visit, San Diego homicide detective Ray Delgado gets a brutal reminder of why he left his family behind. Alejandro wants Ray to find his sister, Sophia, who disappeared from the UC San Diego campus, before the FBI digs too deep into his business. 3/3

2796. **Thomas, A. J.,** *The Intersection of Purgatory and Paradise,* Dreamspinner, 2015. Least Likely Partnership #3 of 3. (MM Suspense) Life in small-town Montana has become hell for former San Diego homicide detective Christopher Hayes. No one will hire him, he has made the seething racism his lover Doug Heavy Runner faces at work worse by adding homophobia to the mix, and his most recent jog through town ends when two gay-bashing teenagers hit him in the head with a rock. When the mutilated body of one of the boys who assaulted Christopher is found in Doug's garage, Christopher and Doug return from a vacation in San Diego and uncover a tangle of secrets, lies, and tragedy lurking beneath Elkin's small-town facade. 3/3

2797. **Thomas, A. J.,** *Pins and Needles,* Dreamspinner, 2017. (MM Mystery) After a devastating accident and a long stay in the hospital, the last thing petroleum engineer Sean Wilkinson wants to deal with is the settlement the oil company tries to force on him. He'll never be able to work in his field again, his education is all but useless, and his surgeons are pessimistic about whether he'll ever walk again.

2798. **Thomas, Josh,** *Murder at Willow Slough or The Caregiver,* Writer's Club, 2001. (Police Procedural) Jamie Foster has a lot going for him–he's young, blond and handsome, with an exciting career as a journalist. Then his life falls apart. Kent Kessler is a winner, too, a good-looking athlete and the youngest sergeant in state police history. Assigned to investigate a Gay murder, he comes up clueless. He teams with Jamie to track down the killer, and soon confronts a mind-boggling conspiracy. 3/3

2799. **Thomas, Lee,** *Stained,* Wildside, 2004. (Horror) A madman. A secret, generations old. Another missing boy. They called the sadistic killer The River Rat, and he'd struck again. In a desperate search for his neighbor's son, Ted Lewis came face to face with the killer and survived, but his life was irrevocably altered. The residents of Marchand, Louisiana believed they were safe. 3/3

2800. **Thomas, Lee,** *The Dust of Wonderland,* Alyson, 2007. (Horror) A panicked call from his ex-wife summons Ken Nicholson back to New Orleans, where his son has been attacked and left for dead. While his child's life hangs in the balance, Ken endures visions connected to a terrifying time from his past. As a teenager, he witnessed the brutal deaths of several young men, an act orchestrated by his benefactor, Travis Brugier. 3/3

2801. **Thomas, Lee,** *The German,* Lethe, 2011. (Historical Police Procedural) 1944 - Barnard, Texas. At the height of World War II, a killer preys on the young men of a quiet Texas town. The murders are calculated, vicious, and they are just beginning. Sheriff Tom Rabbit and his men are baffled and the community he serves is terrified of the monster lurking their streets. 3/3

2802. **Thomas, Lee,** *Butcher's Road,* Lethe, 2014. (Historical Crime Drama) 1932: Fortune and celebrity are years behind Butch Cardinal. Once a world-class wrestler, Cardinal now serves as hired muscle for a second-rate Chicago mobster. While collecting a parcel from a gangland lowlife, Cardinal witnesses the man's murder. Though wounded, he escapes the killers and flees into the night carrying the package. 3/3

2803. **Thomas, Lee,** *Down on your Knees,* Lethe, 2016. (Paranormal Crime Drama) Denny "The Bull" Doyle steps out of prison only to find a low-level gangster is attempting to take over his organization. Brendan Newton is a newbie to the gang, who's spent too much time in front of the television, building a grand fantasy about the machinations of the underworld. He's naive and weak, but he may be the only chance Doyle has. The Bull's associates are being murdered in violent and bizarre ways, and the next target is his beloved, though wholly sociopathic, brother, Jordie. 3/3

2804. **Thomas, Lee,** *Distortion,* Lethe, 2018. (Thriller) Mick Harris is disillusioned and disconnected from the world. Having come out after his glory days as the songwriter/bass player for metal act, Palace, he's all but given up on his dream of having a meaningful relationship, of leading a "normal," life. When a stranger calls to inform him that an old flame has died, leaving Mick's daughter alone in a hostile small Southern town, he sees an opportunity to build a meaningful connection with the girl. Of course, she is resistant to meeting her father. In fact, she hates him for having been absent her entire life, but the people close to her are dying horribly. 3/3

2805. **Thomas, Rupert,** *Street Life,* Idol, 2000. (Crime Drama) Ben is 18 and tired of living in the suburbs. As there's little sexual adventure to be found there, he decides to run away from both A-levels and his comfortable home - to a new life in London. When the friend he'd hoped to stay with is away, Ben is forced to spend the night on the streets, cold and afraid. 3/3

2806. **Thomas-Cook, L.,** *In Your Eyes,* Pywacket, 2013. (Police Procedural) Detectives Sonny Santini and Jay Jamison are undercover cops working the dangerous area of Oakland City during the 1980s. Professional partners, Sonny and Jay protect a secret about the true meaning of their relationship from others who are narrow minded. Their secret world seems to be working until Sonny is involved in a near fatal accident. 3/3

2807. **Thompson, Joyce,** *How to Greet Strangers,* Lethe, 2013. (Thriller) Archer Barron is rebuilding his life after hiding from it for years. Once he had grand expectations-graduating law school, donning drag to express his feminine aspects, and the love of a devoted boyfriend-but fate became cruel. HIV-positive cruel. And a growing involvement with an Oakland Santeria priestess who promised a cure in return for devotion and a lot of cash. His lover died. 3/3

2808. **Thompson, Will Kane,** *Patriots,* Self-Published, 2017. (Political Thriller) They came to this paradise of a college campus to find freedom, themselves, their future, sex, love, fun, God, intellectual discovery, their creative core ... but instead find their world being torn apart again by political divisiveness, extremism, rage. 3/3

2809. **Thomson, June,** *Not One of Us,* Harper and Row, 1971. Inspector Rudd #1 of 20. (Police Procedural) The townspeople decided that John Smith was an odd one. Although young and educated, he chose to live alone in a falling-down cottage, and he'd see no one, except his dog. This just wasn't normal. When Meyrick, a tractor driver, found the dead body of a young girl in a field, he immediately contacted Inspector Finch. And then Meyrick remembered that the day before he'd seen a man and his dog walking across the fields. –the name of the detective in England is Inspector Finch but was renamed in American copies beginning with book two in the series as Inspector Rudd to avoid confusion with Margaret Erskine's Detective Finch. The suspect, the man who was "not one of us" is told to have homosexual tendencies and is ultimately burned out of his home by torch wielding villagers (MLM). 1/3

2810. **Thomson, Rupert,** *The Five Gates of Hell,* Knopf, 1991. (Coming-of-Age Thriller) There was a sailor's graveyard in Moon Beach. This was where the funeral business first started. Rumor had it that the witch's fingers used to reach out and sink ships. But there hadn't been a wreck for years, and all the funeral parlors had moved downtown. 1/3

2811. **Thornton, Marshall,** *Boystown Prequels,* Createspace, 2017. Boystown #0 of 12. (Hard Boiled) "Little Boy Dead": Former Chicago police officer turned private investigator, Nick Nowak is haunted by a traumatic break-up and his abrupt departure from the department after being gay-bashed. It's fall 1979 and Nick has just received his P.I. license but has no clients. Short on funds, he takes a temporary job as a driver for Film Fest Chicago. In a very short time, Nick deals with stalking fans, a crowd of protesters, and a critic's stolen wallet that leads to murder. "Little Boy Afraid": It's winter 1980, private investigator Nick Nowak gets one of his first jobs working for an openly-gay senate candidate. Allan Grimley has been receiving death threats, a lot of them, and it's Nick's job to keep him alive until the election. As he protects Grimley from increasing dangers, his friendship with bartender, Ross deepens. –two short stories that were originally published as e-books; *Little Boy Dead* was released in 2012 and *Little Boy Afraid* was released in 2017 (MLM). ` 3/3

2812. **Thornton, Marshall,** *Boystown: Three Nick Nowak Mysteries,* Torquere, 2011. Boystown #1 of 12. (Hard Boiled) Haunted by his abrupt departure from the Chicago Police Department and the end of his relationship with librarian Daniel Laverty, Nick Nowak is a beat cop-turned-dogged private investigator. Nick works through three cases: a seemingly simple missing persons search, an arson investigation, and a suicide that turns out to be anything but. 3/3

2813. **Thornton, Marshall,** *Boystown: Three More Nick Nowak Mysteries,* Torquere, 2011. Boystown #2 of 12. (Hard Boiled) He's asked to help a young man who murdered his stepfather but refuses to assist in his own defense, hired to find the murderer of a dead porno star, and, in a case that traps him between the two men he loves, must search for a serial killer's only living victim. 3/3

2814. **Thornton, Marshall,** *Boystown: Two Nick Nowak Novellas,* Torquere, 2011. Boystown #3 of 12. (Hard Boiled) Nick Nowak works two challenging cases and grapples with an even more challenging personal life. In Little Boy Boom, Nick's car explodes when a thief attempts to steal it. Realizing the bomb was meant for him, Nick sets out to discover who wants him dead only to find that the list of possible suspects is longer than he'd like. When he begins to run out of suspects he wonders if the bomb was truly meant for him. Little Boy Tenor finds Nick investigating the murderer of a church choir's star tenor, while at the same time his friend Ross asks him to discover the truth behind his lover, Earl Silver's mysterious death. 3/3

2815. **Thornton, Marshall,** *Boystown: A Time for Secrets,* MLR, 2012. Boystown #4 of 12. (Hard Boiled) It's late summer 1982 and private detective Nick Nowak is asked to find a retired gentleman's long-lost lover. Instead, he finds himself embroiled in a decades old murder connected to the man who wants to be Chicago's next mayor. Meanwhile, an ambitious young reporter develops a friendship with Nick's lover Bert, making Nick wonder exactly where their relationship may be heading. –this is the first full length Boystown mystery (MLM). 3/3

2816. **Thornton, Marshall,** *Boystown: Murder Books,* MLR, 2013. Boystown #5 of 12. (Hard Boiled) It's fall 1982 and Chicago is gripped by panic after five people die from poisoned Tylenol capsules. Amid the chaos, the Bughouse Slasher takes his eighth victim, this time striking close to private investigator Nick Nowak. With the Chicago Police Department stretched to its limit, Nick takes matters into his own hands. But what will he do with the Bughouse Slasher once he finds him. 3/3

2817. **Thornton, Marshall,** *Boystown: From the Ashes,* MLR, 2014. Boystown #6 of 12. (Hard Boiled) It's winter 1984. Private Investigator Nick Nowak has allowed his life to fall to pieces: He's stopped taking cases, given up his apartment and taken a job as a bartender at a sleazy joint tucked under the El. All he wants to do is stay hidden and lick his wounds after the death of his lover, Detective Bert Harker. But when the least likely person in the world shows up at the bar and asks him to take a new case, he finds himself investigating the very unsuspicious death of a priest. Nick is convinced he's wasting his time until the clues begin to add up to something entirely unsuspected. 3/3

2818. **Thornton, Marshall,** *Boystown: Bloodlines,* Kenmore, 2015. Boystown #7 of 12. (Hard Boiled) Private Investigator Nick Nowak finds himself simultaneously working two cases for his new client, law firm Cooke, Babcock and Lackerby. A suburban dentist has been convicted of murdering her adulterous husband. Nick is asked to interview witnesses for the penalty phase of the trial–and possibly find the dead man's mistress. At the same time, he's deeply involved in protecting Outfit underboss Jimmy English from a task force out to prosecute him for a crime he may not have committed. While juggling these cases Nick slowly begins to rebuild his personal life. –winner of the 28th LAMBDA Award for Best Gay Mystery (MLM). 3/3

2819. **Thornton, Marshall,** *Boystown: The Lies that Bind,* Kenmore, 2016. Boystown #8 of 12. (Hard Boiled) Private investigator Nick Nowak is pulled into the troubled world of freelance journalist, and all-around pain-in-the-ass, Christian Baylor. When Christian can't stop lying about the corpse in his bathroom things slip slowly out of control. Meanwhile, Nick's relationship with former priest Joseph Biernecki takes an unexpected turn and the Federal case against Jimmy English proceeds toward trial. 3/3

2820. **Thornton, Marshall,** *Boystown: Lucky Days,* Kenmore, 2017. Boystown #9 of 12. (Hard Boiled) A young man wakes up covered in blood and no memory of the previous night. When hypnotism doesn't help, he turns to private investigator Nick Nowak. Meanwhile, the trial of Outfit kingpin Jimmy English begins. Quickly the case begins to unravel when an important witness goes missing and Nick must put his other cases, and his home life, on hold while he goes to Las Vegas to find him. 3/3

2821. **Thornton, Marshall,** *Boystown: Gift's Given,* Kenmore, 2017. Boystown #10 of 12. (Hard Boiled) It's Christmas 1984, and Nick is busy juggling a couple of cases with his hectic personal life. Sugar Pilson has decided to marry and has asked him to check up on her fiancé. Meanwhile, he's hired to investigate a shady financial planner at Peterson-Palmer. When the two cases begin to have too much in common, Nick searches for the link. Only to find out that he himself might be the link. 3/3

2822. **Thornton, Marshall,** *Boystown: Heart's Desire,* Kenmore, 2018. Boystown #11 of 12. (Hard Boiled) It's February 1985. Nick struggles to recover from a gunshot wound, while taking on the case of a woman with a mental illness, who may or may not have witnessed a murder. As he attempts to determine exactly what the woman saw and how much danger she may be in, he juggles the approaching DeCarlo trial, an ill Mrs. Harker, and the sexually precocious Terry. Valentine's Day with boyfriend Joseph produces some big changes in their relationship. Life is evolving, but there's no guarantee it's for the better. –book twelve of the Boystown series, *Broken Cord,* will be released in 2019 (MLM). 3/3

2823. **Thornton, Marshall,** *Desert Run,* Wordpress, 2014. (Crime Drama) Palm Springs, 1973. Don Harris is a piano player on the run after killing a Chicago mobster's son in a bar fight. On the lam, he meets a pretty blonde girl in town for a convention. He lets down his guard and spends the night with her only to discover she's the younger sister of his best friend all grown-up. Foolishly, she tips her brother off to Don's location, and he's on the run again, hoping to find a safe place to land. 3/3

2824. **Thornton, Marshall,** *Full Release,* Wordpress, 2014. (Crime Drama) Studio accountant, Matt Latowski orders an erotic massage on the one-year anniversary of a bad break-up but is surprised when the masseur calls him a couple weeks later to ask him out on a date. Unable to say no to a freebie, Matt begins a journey that eventually leads to his becoming a murder suspect. 3/3

2825. **Thornton, Marshall,** *Night Drop,* Kenmore, 2017. Pinx Video #1 of 4. (Modern Cozy) It's 1992 and Los Angeles is burning. Noah Valentine, the owner of Pinx Video in Silver Lake, notices the fires have taken their toll on fellow shopkeeper Guy Peterson's camera shop. After the riots end, he decides to stop by Guy's to pick up his overdue videos, only to find Guy's family dividing up his belongings. He died in the camera store fire–or did he? Noah and his charmingly meddlesome downstairs neighbors begin to suspect something else might have happened to Guy Peterson. –won the thirtieth LAMBDA Award (MLM). 3/3

2826. **Thornton, Marshall,** *Hidden Treasures,* Kenmore, 2018. Pinx Video #2 of 4. (Modern Cozy) It's about a dress. A valuable blue sequined dress worn by a famed actress in a film from the 1940s. For some reason everyone thinks video store owner Noah Valentine has it. Which might not be a big deal except that it's connected to the murder of a prominent Hollywood costumer. 3/3

2827. **Thornton, Marshall,** *Late Fees,* Kenmore, 2018. Pinx Video #3 of 4. (Modern Cozy) It's Thanksgiving, 1992 and Noah Valentine is late picking his mother up from the airport. When he arrives, he discovers that she's made a friend on the flight whose also waiting for her son. When women's son doesn't show up, they eventually take the woman home for breakfast with neighbor's Marc and Louis. Soon after, they learn that the woman's son has overdosed–or has he? Noah and his motley crew investigate over the holiday weekend; which includes a fabulous dinner, a chat with a male stripper, a tiny little burglary and some help from Detective Tall, Dark, and Delicious. –won the thirty-first LAMBDA Award (MM). –the fourth book, *Rewind,* is set to be released in 2019 (MLM). 3/3

2828. **Tierney, Ronald,** *Eclipse of the Heart,* St. Martin's, 1993. (Political

Thriller) Zachary Grayson, a middle-aged, gay writer, seems passionless, until a life-changing odyssey to Puerto Vallarta, Mexico, reveals a surprising answer to an innocent question. 3/3

2829. **Tillman, Lynne,** *Cast in Doubt,* Poseidon, 1992. (Amateur Sleuth) It seemed a simple case: a young American woman vanishes on the ancient island of Crete. But when crime writer Horace decides to investigate Helen's quiet life, the facts he uncovers reveal much more. 3/3

2830. **Topol, Carolyn LeVine,** *Waves of Fortune,* Dreamspinner, 2010. (MM Mystery) Jim Barton, a former hustler trying to escape a painful past, meets Greg Abel at a private Caribbean island resort. Despite significant differences in their ages and family backgrounds-Greg is heir to a technology fortune-sexual attraction draws them to one another and they become lovers. 3/3

2831. **Torr, Dominic,** *Diplomatic Cover,* Harcourt Brace, 1966. (Espionage) Set in Paris during the Cold War. Action and suspense as the Americans try to learn more about Russian intentions and the Russians seek to find out how much the Americans know in the run-up to the Cuban missile crisis. –bisexual diplomat in Paris has an affair with male artist which comes to the attention of a Russian spy (MLM). 1/3

2832. **Tortuga, B. A.,** *Old Town New,* Torquere, 2005. (MM Mystery) Danny is a teacher in small town Colorado, trying to live down his wild teenage years and living his life the only way he knows how; one day at a time. He's had a tough time of it, but Danny figures he's managed to become respectable, or at least less than notorious. 3/3

2833. **Tortuga, B. A.,** *Long Black Cadillac,* Torquere, 2007. (MM Paranormal) Vance is a vampire hunter on a mission. When the Colonel sends him to clear out a bloodsucker living in the Louisiana swamps, Vance figures it's all in a day's work. The problem is that Clay is no ordinary vampire. Clay and Vance have a connection that Vance has never felt before. He knows he should be fighting Clay off, but all he wants to do is give in to the feelings Clay inspires. 3/3

2834. **Townsend, Larry ('Bud' Bernhard 1930-2008),** *The Long Leather Cord,* Greenleaf, 1971. (Pulp) "Chuck's father seems to have more money than he should, he often disappears at night , and his closet contains several weapons, in addition to leather gear and S&M equipment (Gunn)." –there is an incestual relationship between father and son however, there was a second edition published by Badboy in 1994 in which the incest is censored out and the father is instead the step-father (MLM). 3/3

2835. **Townsend, Larry,** *Run No More,* L. T., 1972. Run #2 of 2. (Pulp)

The further adventures of the leather clad narrator as he travels every sexual byway available to the S/M male. As he works his way toward more elite circles, Wayne begins to make discoveries that shock even him. –republished by Badboy in 1993. The first book in this series, *Run Little Leather Boy,* is not a mystery (MLM). 3/3

2836. **Townsend, Larry,** *Chains,* L. T., 1974. (Pulp) "Salesman and leather designer Paul makes a few attempts to discover who is blackmailing embezzler Michael Chism (Gunn)." –republished by Badboy in 1994 (MLM). 3/3

2837. **Townsend, Larry,** *Master's Counterpoints,* Alyson, 1991. Bruce MacLeod #1 of 2. (Pulp) A handsome actor is kidnapped, tortured, and raped. As his therapist helps him investigate, they find adventure, S/M sex ... and a father-son partnership that's gone too far. 3/3

2838. **Townsend, Larry,** *One for the Master, Two for the Fool,* Alyson, 1992. Bruce MacLeod #2 of 2. (Pulp) A wealthy Beverly Hills couple is found dead, strangled with garrotes in their mansion. Bruce MacLeod investigates in this tale filled with passion, intrigue, and mystery. 3/3

2839. **Townsend, Larry,** *The Case of the Severed Head,* Nzcap, 1994. (Crime Drama) During the riots that followed the unpopular verdicts in the Rodney King trial, a group of skinhead punks preys on the Gay Community of West Hollywood. In the course of this they unwittingly set in motion a series of events that places them in the role of the hunted. They rape and nearly kill a young man who is more than capable of seeking a just revenge. 3/3

2840. **Townsend, Larry,** *A Contagious Evil: Mind of a Serial Killer,* L. T., 1998. (Psychological Thriller) "The Highway Stalker, Alfred Kleinhauser, though sentenced to death for his last serial killing, has refused to confess. He agrees to let Southwestern journalist Hal Mallory, 24, interview him while Hal's friend Ralph Humphries, 22, stands duty as prison guard (Gunn)." 3/3

2841. **Townsend, Peggy,** *See Her Run,* Thomas and Mercer, 2018. (Journalism) A former reporter for the Los Angeles Times, Aloa Snow knows what it means to be down and out. Once highly respected, she's now blackballed, in debt, and dealing with the echoes of an eating disorder. Until she gets one more shot to prove that she has what it takes–with a story some would die for... 1/3

2842. **Tracey, Chris,** *The Cherry Blossom Murders,* Kindle, 2017. (Amateur Sleuth) When Peter accepts a new and exciting job as a gay host in Tokyo's glamorously seedy Cherry Blossom Bar the last thing he expects is to be implicated in a series of gruesome murders. Drawing on all his derring-do and self-confidence Peter launches himself on a path to find the killer and clear his name while finding love and self-knowledge on the way. –available as an e-book only (MLM). 3/3

2843. **Travis, Aaron (Steven Saylor),** "Crown of Thorns," in *Flesh Fables,* Fire Island, 1990. (Pulp S&M) Set in Istanbul at the height of the Cold War, a young American intelligence officer's erotic submission to a brutal Turkish stevedore. 3/3

2844. **Travis, Aaron,** "Adventures of a Ragged Youth," *Exposed: An Anthology of Erotic Stories,* Badboy, 1993. (Pulp) "Jack Martin is sent by Moriarty to seduce and murder Sherlock Holmes (Gunn)." 3/3

2845. **Travis, Aaron,** *Big Shots,* Badboy, 1993. (Pulp) Two fierce tales in one electrifying volume. In "Beirut", the story of ultimate military power and erotic subjugation; "Kip", Travis' hyper-sexed and sinister take on film noir. 3/3

2846. **Travis, Don,** *The Zozobra Incident,* Martin Brown, 2012. BJ Vinson #1 of 5. (MM Hard Boiled) B J Vinson, a former Albuquerque police detective turned confidential investigator, hesitates when ex-lover and now prominent attorney Del Dahlman appeals to him for help in recovering some incriminating photographs of him and the hustler who broke up their relationship. 3/3

2847. **Travis, Don,** *The Bisti Business,* Martin Brown, 2012. BJ Vinson #2 of 5. (MM Hard Boiled) When a phone call from a Napa Valley wine mogul sends B.J. Vinson all over northern New Mexico in pursuit of an orange Porsche Boxster in the possession of his client's son, Lando Alfano, and Lando's gay lover, Dana Norville, the hunt for a classic car suddenly becomes a frantic race against time to find two missing young men being shadowed by a mysterious stranger. 3/3

2848. **Travis, Don,** *The City of Rocks,* DSP, 2017. BJ Vinson #3 of 5. (MM Hard Boiled) Confidential Investigator B.J. Vinson thinks it's a bad joke when Del asks him to look into the theft of a duck… a duck insured for $250,000. It ceases to be a funny when the young thief dies in a suspicious truck wreck. 3/3

2849. **Travis, Don,** *The Lovely Pines,* DSP, 2018. BJ Vinson #4 of 5. (MM Hard Boiled) When Ariel Gonda's winery, the Lovely Pines, suffers a break-in, the police write the incident off as a prank since nothing was taken. But Ariel knows something is wrong–small clues are beginning to add up–and he turns to private investigator BJ Vinson for help. –book five, *Abaddon's Locusts,* is to be released in 2019 by DSP (MLM). 3/3

2850. **Traynor, Fredryk,** *Bless the Thugz and the Li'l Chil'rins,* GLB, 2004. (Crime Drama) a gay gangsta paperback by a former denizen of the streets. This novel starts in the streets of San Francisco and ends up, via the ladder of successful rappers and gangster operations, in a castle in the Berkeley Hills, but in so doing it traces the lives of unforgettable characters and depicts especially the intense love between two men caught in traps, sometimes of their own making, but certainly mostly traps of the everyday societal morass of black urban life. 3/3

2851. **Tresswell, Jude,** *Badge of Loyalty,* Rowanvale, 2018. County Durham Quad #1 of 3. (MM Police Procedural) Mike Angells is an openly gay CID inspector based in North East England. There are three men in his life: Raith Balan, Phil Roberts and Ross Whitburn. Mike is particularly close to Ross. Following a routine but significant investigation into thefts of farm machinery, Mike investigates the suspicious death of a footballer. The suspect's father threatens to expose a crime Ross committed many years earlier, unless Mike withholds evidence that would incriminate his son. 3/3

2852. **Tresswell, Jude,** *Polyamory on Trial,* Rowanvale, 2018. County Durham Quad #2 of 3. (MM Police Procedural) A young Syrian needing treatment at Warbridge Hospital is seen by Phil Roberts, one quarter of a gay, polyamorous quad living in North East England. Phil is troubled. Is his patient in the UK legally? Who has caused his injuries? Is trafficking involved? As the foursome struggle to find out, hampered by the fact that Mike is no longer a detective, cracks begin to appear in their relationship. –third book *Ace in the Picture* is to be released in March of 2019 (MLM). 3/3

2853. **Trevanian (Rodney Whitaker),** *Eiger Sanction,* Crown, 1972. Hemlock #1 of 2. (Espionage) Jonathan Hemlock, Professor of Art, world-renowned mountain climber and freelance assassin for the CII. Hemlock is sent to Switzerland on a mission to climb the notorious Eiger peak of the Alps, whose north face has meant death to many climbers. Hemlock's target: one of his three fellow climbers. The only problem is, CII can't tell him which one... –former partner of Hemlock is gay (MLM). 1/3

2854. **Trevino, Orlando,** *The Unspoken Word,* iUniverse, 2004. (MM Police Procedural) For a successful actor privacy is non-excitant but yet Carter Anzur has always managed to keep one secret safely tucked away from preying eyes. When one of his most devoted fans stumbles across his closet, Carter's peaceful world is quickly turned inside out as he and his closest friends frantically search to find the one person that could ruin Carter's career. 3/3

2855. **Trigoboff, Joseph,** *Bone Orchard,* Walker, 1990. Yablonsky #1 of 2.

(Police Procedural) When two brutal murders are made to appear to be sex-drug-related crimes, Yablonsky doesn't buy it. The victims were male strippers who turn out to be connected in strange ways to many rich and influential men and women in the city, most notably high-level diplomats from Latin America. –villain is gay, but author writes positively of gay men (MLM). 1/3

2856. **Tripp, Miles,** *Some Predators are Male,* St. Martin's, 1985. John Samson #8 of 15. (Hard Boiled) Neil Pensom lived alone and had no close relationships. He was careful not to make enemies and yet someone seemed intent on driving him insane by creating bizarre situations around him. He knew he needed help to fight his unknown persecutor but was unsure whether to go to the police, a lawyer or a private detective. In the end he chose a detective, John Samson. –main character states that although he lived with his mother all his life that does not make him gay, yet he exhibits many of the stereotypes of a homosexual man (MLM). 1/3

2857. **Tripp, Miles,** *Cords of Vanity,* St. Martin's, 1989. John Samson #11 of 15. (Hard Boiled) Mrs. Huntingdon-Winstanley, an eccentric dowager, hires detective John Sampson to find out what her young husband is doing on his frequent trips to France. –Mrs. Huntington-Winstanley wants to know about the relationship between her husband and their handsome valet but she turns out to also be a transvestite (MLM). 2/3

2858. **Trott, Tom,** *You Can't Make Old Friends,* Createspace, 2016. Brighton's #1 PI #1 of 3. (Hard Boiled) Blacklisted by the police. Being sued by a client. And broke. Things can't get any worse for Brighton's No.1 Private Detective, Joe Grabarz. That's when his best friend's body washes up on the beach. Could it really have been ten years? What happened? How could his life have ended like this? He needs answers. But with the city in the grips of organized crime, and struggling to deal with an influx of legal highs, who cares about just another dead drug dealer? Joe, that's who. After all, you can't make old friends. 3/3

2859. **Trott, Tom,** *Choose Your Parents Wisely,* Createspace, 2017. Brighton's #1 PI #2 of 3. (Hard Boiled) One missing girl and the whole city goes crazy. It's been three days, and now everyone in Brighton is looking for her. There is an army of police searching, her picture is on every front page, and the public can't get enough of it. Gangs of good citizens are going door to door, turning their neighbors' houses upside down, but still no one can find her. –the third book, *It Never Goes Away* will be released in 2019 (MLM). 3/3

2860. **Truluck, Bob,** *Street Level,* Minotaur, 2000. Duncan Sloan #1 of 2. (Hard Boiled) When we meet private detective Duncan Sloan, he's just handed back a five thousand-dollar check meant as advance payment on a job. The wealthy prospective client wants Sloan to find a woman with an eyeball tattooed on her bottom. All he knows is the tattoo, that she's very young, white and probably somewhere in or near Orlando, Florida, Sloan's hometown. Thanks, but no thanks. Isaac Pike is the only son of a top-ranked tycoon. He is also gay. Because he genuinely wants to be a father, he has deposited sperm with a reputable clinic while he searches for a suitable mother. But a paroled convict working at the clinic steals the sperm, impregnates a teenager with it, and blackmails Pike - send money or we abort the child. 3/3

2861. **Truscott IV, Lucian,** *Dress Gray,* Doubleday, 1978. (Military/Politics) When the naked corpse of a young West Point cadet, David Hand, is found floating in a nearby lake, the academy's official statement is startlingly at odds with what Ray Slaight, his platoon leader, knows to be true. –the victim was gay and is about the search for his lover/killer (MLM). 2/3

2862. **Turnbull, Peter,** *Big Money,* St. Martin's, 1984. P Division #4 of 10. (Police Procedural) –divorced Sussock's son is gay but we don't see him (MLM). 1/3

2863. **Turnbull, Peter,** *Two Way Cut,* St. Martin's, 1988. P Division #5 of 10. (Police Procedural) The officers of Glasgow's P Division go back into action when PC Phil Hamilton stumbles upon a corpse, in a police procedural. –Sassock goes to his ex-wife's home to find his son decked out in jewelry and smelling of perfume with another young guy who has his arms wrapped around his son's waist (MLM). 1/3

2864. **Turnbull, Peter,** *Condition Purple,* St. Martin's, 1989. P Division #6 of 10. (Police Procedural) The young woman who was found at 10pm with the knife still in her throat triggers off Glasgow's P Division's latest investigation. She was a heroin addict and had the words 'I belong to Dino' tattooed on her groin. They were the only clues. –Sassock goes to his ex-wife's house to find his son with his jersey tucked into his pants. Also, a gay couple move in next door to him which only reminds him of his son's sexuality (MLM). 1/3

U

2865. **Underwood, Michael (John Michael Evelyn)**, *Crime upon Crime,* St. Martin's, 1981. A small-time blackmailer takes on a powerful judge, who is a victim of his own weaknesses: gambling, drink, and certain sins of the flesh. –the judge is being blackmailed for having sex with a male prostitute (MLM). 1/3

2866. **Unsworth, Cathi,** *Weirdo,* Serpent's Tail, 2012. (Hard Boiled) In 1984, 15-year-old Norfolk schoolgirl Corrine Woodrow was sentenced indefinitely for the ritualistic murder of a schoolfriend. With rumours of Satanism surrounding her, Corrine became a notorious hate figure. But 20 years later, re-examination of the forensic evidence suggests that the 'Wicked Witch of the East' didn't commit her crime alone. –gay secondary character (MLM). 1/3

2867. **Urban, Madeleine, and Abigail Roux,** *Cut and Run,* Dreamspinner, 2008. Cut and Run #1 of 9. (MM Police Procedural) A series of murders in New York City has stymied the police and FBI alike, and they suspect the culprit is a single killer sending an indecipherable message. But when the two federal agents assigned to the investigation are taken out, the FBI takes a more personal interest in the case. 3/3

2868. **Urban, Madeleine, and Abigail Roux,** *Sticks and Stones,* Dreamspinner, 2010. Cut and Run #2 of 9. (MM Police Procedural) Six months after nearly losing their lives to a serial killer in New York City, FBI Special Agents Ty Grady and Zane Garrett are suffering through something almost as frightening: the monotony of desk duty. 3/3

2869. **Urban, Madeleine, and Abigail Roux,** *Fish and Chips,* 2010. Cut and Run #3 of 9. (MM Police Procedural) Special Agents Ty Grady and Zane Garrett are back on the job, settled into a personal and professional relationship built on fierce protectiveness and blistering passion. Now they're assigned to impersonate two members of an international smuggling ring-an out-and-proud married couple-on a Christmas cruise in the Caribbean. 3/3

2870. **Urban, Madeleine, and Abigail Roux,** *Divide and Conquer,* Dreamspinner, 2011. Cut and Run #4 of 9. (MM Police Procedural) Baltimore, Maryland, is a city in alarming distress. Rising violence is fanning the flames of public outrage, and all law enforcement agencies, including the FBI, are catching blame. 3/3

2871. **Urban, Madeleine, and Abigail Roux,** *Armed and Dangerous,* Dreamspinner, 2012. Cut and Run #5 of 9. (MM Police Procedural) Left alone in Baltimore after his unpredictable lover bails, Special Agent Zane Garrett takes his frustration out on everything in his path until he is ordered to Chicago to backup an undercover operative. –last four books in the series was solo written by Abigail Roux (MLM). 3/3

V

2872. **Valentine, Deborah,** *A Collector of Photographs,* Bantam, 1989. Katherine Craig and Kevin Bryce #1 of 3. (Hard Boiled) San Francisco artist Roxanne Gautier's startling paintings of male prostitutes set off shock waves throughout the art world, but it is her wealthy stockbroker husband who is most disturbed of all. When her beautiful young model washes up dead on the rocks below the Golden Gate Bridge, he asks ex-policeman Kevin Bryce to discreetly probe the source of her inspiration. –Angelo Grey, a San Francisco police officer aids Bryce in solving the murder (MLM). 2/3

2873. **Van Adler, T.C.,** *St. Agatha's Beast,* Alyson, 1999. Pavlic and Brocard #1 of 2. (Hard Boiled) For the monks of San Redempto, a decaying monastery in Rome, the rewards of embezzlement and the indulgence of their carnal appetites are distraction enough to prevent them from noticing that someone has been plundering the monastery of its treasure. –Pavlic is transgender female (MLM). 3/3

2874. **Van Adler, T. C.,** *The Evil that Boys Do,* Alyson, 2003. Pavlic and Brocard #2 of 2. (Hard Boiled) "A missing painting and corruption in a Pennsylvania prison (Gunn)." 3/3

2875. **Vanden, Dirk,** *All of Me (Can You Take All of Me?),* Rosedog, 2010. (Suspense) On his sixtieth birthday, Sacramento Real Estate Broker Rick Vernor receives in the mail, along with birthday cards and advertisements, a note accusing him of being "an abomination in the sight of God" who is next in line to die for his sins for writing "dirty books" forty years ago. Rick soon learns that at least two other Gay men have received similar threats from the same killer, but no one has any idea who the murderer might be. 3/3

2876. **Vaughan, Stephanie,** *Off World,* Torquere, 2007. Off World #1 of 4. (MM Science Fiction) Sarhaan and his band of elite soldiers don't know what to make of Caleb when his little spaceship turns up on their viewscreen. Believing that he might be a Republican spy, they bring the junior diplomat onto their stolen spaceship and question him. Sarhaan is immediately attracted to the young aristocrat, despite his doubts about Caleb's motives, and his feeling that giving into his feelings would be a very bad idea. Caleb is no spy. –next three books develop new characters and include no mystery elements (MLM). 3/3

2877. **Vieira, Michael,** *Green with Envy,* Booklocker, 2006. (Modern Cozy) Steve Armstrong, his lover, and their best friend Katherine Bishop get involved in helping the police solve the murder of a neighbor. 3/3

2878. **Vieira, Michael,** *Red with Rage,* Booklocker, 2011. (Amateur Sleuth) The courage and willingness of a group of disfranchised inhabitants of Atlanta, Georgia helps a bigoted police force catch a serial killer of young, gay men. –possibly a sequel to *Green with Envy* (MLM). 3/3

2879. **Vine, Barbara (Ruth Rendell),** *The House of Stairs,* Shaye Areheart, 1989. (Thriller) Lizzie hasn't seen her old friend, Bell, for some fourteen years, but when she spots her from a taxi in a London street she jumps out and pursues her despite 'all the terrible things' that passed between them. As Lizzie reveals those events, little by little, the women rekindle their friendship, with terrifying results. –main character comments on what it must be like to be in a gay relationship (MLM). 1/3

2880. **Vine, Barbara,** *Gallowglass,* Harmony, 1990. (Thriller) When Sandor snatched little Joe from the path of a London Tube train, he was quick to make clear the terms of the rescue. 'I saved your life,' he told the homeless youngster, 'so your life belongs to me now'. Sandor began to tell him a fairy-tale: an ageing prince, a kidnapped princess chained by one ankle, a missed rendezvous. But what did this mysterious story have to do with Sandor's preparations? Joe had only understood his own role: he was a gallowglass, the servant of a Chief. –sadomasochistic non-sexual relationship (MLM). 1/3

2881. **Vine, Barbara,** *King Solomon's Carpet,* Viking, 1991. (Thriller) Tom Murray is a promising musician reduced to illegal busking in Underground stations and a sad little love affair with his accompanist Alice, who left her husband and newborn baby, taking only her violin. Together with Jasper Darne, another dropout from his family who likes to ride on the tops of Underground carriages, and Jed Lowrie, a Safeguard volunteer who's left behind his own family to live for his hunting hawk Abelard, they live in a failed schoolhouse–whose bell tolled for the only time in memory when the headmaster hanged himself from its rope.–a young man in the novel has AIDS and is living with his partner (MLM). 1/3

2882. **Vine, Barbara,** *No Night is Too Long,* Viking, 1994. (Thriller) Tim thought he'd gotten away with it. For months after the murder off the Alaskan coast he'd heard not a word. No policeman at his door asking questions. Nothing. And then the letters began. At first they seemed almost innocuous accounts of historical events. But a common theme emerged quickly. It was particularly germane to Tim, and it related directly to murder. 1/3

2883. **Virga, Vincent,** *Gaywyck*, Avon, 1980. (Historical Gothic) a world as authentic as anything penned by DuMaurier, retaining the creaking ancestral mansion and mysterious and brooding master of the manor, while replacing the traditional damsel in distress with the young and handsome Robert Whyte. 3/3

2884. **Voinov, Aleksandr,** *First Blood,* Dreamspinner, 2010. GORGON #2 of 2. (BDSM Military) On their last assignment, GORGON agents Chris Gibson and his partner John Soong protected Russian mob lawyer Andrei Voronin rather than killing him. They covered Andrei's tracks, forged a shaky relationship, and their international intelligence and paramilitary group staged Andrei's death and took him into the fold. Nikita Kazakov, a Russian cop who had used Andrei as a source and promised him protection, plots to avenge his protege. He soon tracks down Chris-the "killer"-only to find a man he desires, and Chris is just as intrigued. 3/3

W

2885. **Waites, Martyn,** *The Mercy Seat,* Pocket, 2006. Joe Donovan #1 of 4. (Crime Drama) A research scientist has gone missing. An ace newspaper reporter has disappeared; so, has a minidisc, along with its incriminating evidence. And a teenage hustler is on the run. In his pursuer, the Hammer, a skin-headed professional killer with a blue sapphire tooth and a taste for death metal, "the principle of evil" has indeed been "made flesh." –straight teenager/former rent-boy assists Donovan (MM). 1/3

2886. **Waites, Martyn,** *Bone Machine,* Pocket, 2007. Joe Donovan #2 of 4. (Crime Drama) The body is discovered in an abandoned burial ground: a young woman, blond, ritualistically mutilated, apparently. Her eyes and mouth have been crudely sewn shut. 1/3

2887. **Waites, Martyn,** *White Riot,* Pocket, 2008. Joe Donovan #3 of 4. (Crime Drama) When the savagely beaten body of a Muslim student is found, blame falls on the far-right National Unity Party - but for once they appear to be innocent. And, haunted by his violent past, Trevor Whitman has been receiving death threats over the murder of a policeman years ago. Joe Donovan is called in to investigate. 1/3

2888. **Waites, Martyn,** *Speak No Evil,* Pocket, 2009. Joe Donovan #4 of 4. (Crime Drama) Anne Marie Smeaton is back in the hometown she hasn't seen for forty years, trying to live a normal life with her partner and teenage son. But that's impossible for Anne Marie. Because forty years ago, when she was eleven, she killed a little boy. 1/3

2889. **Wald, Noreen,** *Ghostwriter,* Berkley, 1999. Ghost Writer #1 of 5. (Cozy) Manhattan ghostwriter Jake O'Hara races against time to find the serial killer targeting ghostwriters, before she can become the next victim. –republished as *Ghostwriter Anonymous* in 2006. Gay friend, Tom, assists O'Hara (MLM) 2/3

2890. **Wald, Noreen,** *Death Comes for the Critic,* Berkley, 2000. Ghost Writer #2 of 5. (Cozy) Richard Peter, an acerbic book critic that Americans love to hate, is literally stabbed in the back. His co-author, ghostwriter Jake O'Hara, is left ghosting for the dead and chasing down clues to a murder that hasn't seen its final chapter. 2/3

2891. **Wald, Noreen,** *Death Never Takes a Holiday,* Berkley, 2000. Ghost Writer #3 of 5. (Cozy) The Crime Writers' Conference kicks off on St. Patrick's Day in New York. But when green beer leaves two writers permanently green around the gills, ghostwriter Jake O'Hara must rewrite the murderer's plot. 2/3

2892. **Wald, Noreen,** *Remembrances of Murders Past,* Berkley, 2001. Ghost Writer #4 of 5. (Cozy) When ghostwriter Jake O'Hara's mother witnesses the murder of a parish priest, she becomes the killer's prime target. Now it's up to Jake to solve the crime-and keep her mother out of harm's way. 2/3

2893. **Wald, Noreen,** *Enter Dying,* Berkley, 2002. Ghost Writer #5 of 5. (Cozy) Miss Jake O'Hara has just joined the behind-the-scenes cast of a Broadway musical as a writer. But in this production, the star is about to fall-to her death. –Tom has a bigger role in this book (MM). 2/3

2894. **Walker, Gerald,** *Cruising,* Stein and Day, 1970. (Police Procedural) an undercover cop looking for a homosexual serial killer in the world of sadomasochism leather gay bars in Greenwich Village, New York. While undercover, he develops feelings for his gay neighbor at the same time he is in a relationship with his girlfriend. 3/3

2895. **Walker, Max,** *A Hard Call,* Self-Published, 2018. Stonewall #1 of 3. (MM Hard Boiled) Zane Holden hasn't had the easiest go of things. His childhood was rough, and adulthood hasn't been a walk in the park either. The only good thing in his life would be Stonewall Investigations, an investigative company he found to work primarily with the LGBTQ community. Things were ok, and Zane was finally healing from a personal tragedy, but the reemergence of a serial killer turns his world upside down. –e-book only (MLM). 3/3

2896. **Walker, Max,** *A Lethal Love,* Self-Published, 2018. Stonewall #2 of 3. (MM Hard Boiled) Alejandro Santos is a sharp as nails detective who's been struck with a spell of boring cases. He's left unstimulated and unhappy. That is until Griffin walks in through the doors of Stonewall Investigations and suddenly everything changes. –e-book only (MLM). 3/3

2897. **Walker, Max,** *A Tangled Web,* Self-Published, 2018. Stonewall #3 of 3. (MM Hard Boiled) Liam Wolfe isn't having the best of days. He's being falsely accused of things he'd never even think of doing and is now facing the loss of his career because of it. He has an idea of who's behind the attempt at assassinating his character but can't put the pieces together by himself. –e-book only. Book 4, *Deck the Halls,* is not a mystery (MLM) 3/3

2898. **Walker, N. R.,** *Cronin's Key,* Createspace, 2015. Cronin #1 of 4.

(MM Paranormal) NYPD Detective Alec MacAidan has always been good with weird. After all, his life has been a string of the unexplainable. But when an injured man gives him cryptic clues, then turns to dust in front of him, Alec's view on weird is changed forever. Cronin, a vampire Elder, has spent the last thousand years waiting for Alec. He'd been told his fated one would be a man wielding a shield, but he didn't expect him to be human, and he certainly didn't expect that shield to be a police badge. 3/3

2899. **Walker, N. R.**, *Cronin's Key II*, Createspace, 2015. Cronin #2 of 4. (MM Paranormal) Alec's blood is special, though its true purpose still eludes them. And given Alec's inability to be changed into a vampire, Cronin is free to drink from him at will. But the ramifications of drinking such powerful blood starts a ripple effect. This time their investigations lead them to the borders of China and Mongolia–but it's not what lies in the pits beneath that worries Alec. 3/3

2900. **Walker, N. R.**, *Cronin's Key III*, Createspace, 2015. Cronin #3 of 4. (MM Paranormal) Twelve months after his change, Alec MacAidan is still getting used to his many vampire talents. While most vampires would give anything to have more than one supernatural power, Alec craves nothing more than peace and time alone with Cronin. But when Alec meets entities from outside this realm, he's left powerless in their presence. Zoan are half-lycan, half-dragon creatures that have slipped through time and reality, seemingly undetected by man and vampire. Or have they? They bear an uncanny resemblance to gargoyles, leaving Alec's view on all things weird to get a whole lot weirder. –the fourth book, *Cronin's Key IV: Kennard's Story* is to be released in 2019 (MLM). 3/3

2901. **Walsh, Haley (Jeri Westerson),** *Foxe Tail,* MLR, 2010. Skyler Foxe #1 of 7. (MM Amateur Sleuth) Gay teacher Skyler Foxe thought teaching English Lit was murder. Wait till he falls into the real thing. 3/3

2902. **Walsh, Haley,** *Foxe Hunt,* MLR, 2011. Skyler Foxe #2 of 7. (MM Amateur Sleuth) High school English teacher Skyler Foxe finally hooks up with gorgeous assistant football coach Keith Fletcher. 3/3

2903. **Walsh, Haley,** *Out-Foxed,* MLR, 2012. Skyler Foxe #3 of 7. (MM Amateur Sleuth) Skyler breaks it off with Keith, a teacher is murdered, and a student might be involved through some twisted football initiation; Just another week at James Polk High. –the first three books form a trilogy each with its own mystery but also a larger overreaching mystery that encompasses all three books. The next four are standalone mysteries (MM). 3/3

2904. **Walsh, Haley,** *Foxe Fire,* MLR, 2014. Skyler Foxe #4 of 7. (MM Amateur Sleuth) Can out-and-proud high school teacher Skyler Foxe find the Redlands firebug before he falls prey to a killer? 3/3

2905. **Walsh, Haley,** *Desert Foxe,* MLR, 2014. Skyler Foxe #5 of 7. (MM Amateur Sleuth) Skyler and his friends go to Palm Springs for the annual White Party and find murder! 3/3

2906. **Walsh, Haley,** *Crazy Like a Foxe,* Foxe Press, 2016. Skyler Foxe #6 of 7. (MM Amateur Sleuth) High school English teacher Skyler Foxe swears he's done being an amateur sleuth. Instead, he'd rather concentrate on his career as a teacher and on his hot boyfriend and head football coach Keith Fletcher, who is busy with football practice and an interesting new player that puts Keith in the spotlight for a change. 3/3

2907. **Walsh, Haley,** *Stone Cold Foxe,* Createspace, 2017. Skyler Foxe #7 of 7. (MM Amateur Sleuth) Is it wedding bells for confirmed bachelor Skyler Foxe? The rocky road to marriage keeps the high school English teacher on edge, yet his football-coach-fiancé, Keith Fletcher, seems far too cool by half. Still, as the nuptials draw near, strange things seem to be plaguing Skyler. –an eighth book, *Foxe in the Hen House*, had been planned for a 2018 release but Walsh cancelled the series as sales dropped (MLM). 3/3

2908. **Walton, Jo,** *Farthing,* Tor, 2006. Small Change #1 of 3. (Science Fiction) One summer weekend in 1949 – but not our 1949 – the well-connected "Farthing set", a group of upper-crust English families, enjoy a country retreat. Lucy is a minor daughter in one of those families; her parents were both leading figures in the group that overthrew Churchill and negotiated peace with Herr Hitler eight years before. –London police inspector must keep his sexuality a secret in fascist England (MLM). 3/3

2909. **Walton, Jo,** *Ha'Penny,* Tor, 2007. Small Change #2 of 3. (Science Fiction) In 1949, eight years after the "Peace with Honor" was negotiated between Great Britain and Nazi Germany by the Farthing Set, England has completed its slide into fascist dictatorship. Then a bomb explodes in a London suburb. 3/3

2910. **Walton, Jo,** *Half a Crown,* Tor, 2008. Small Change #3 of 3. (Science Fiction) In 1941, the European war ended in the Farthing Peace, a rapprochement between Britain and Nazi Germany. The balls and banquets of Britain's upper class never faltered, while British ships ferried "undesirables" across the Channel to board the cattle cars headed east. 3/3

2911. **Wambaugh, Joseph,** *The Choirboys,* Delacorte, 1975. (Thriller) Partners in the Los Angeles Police Department, they're haunted by terrifying dark secrets of the night watch–shared predawn drink and sex sessions they call choir practice. Each wears his cynicism like a bulletproof jockstrap–each has his horror story, his bad dream, his night shriek. He is afraid of his friends–he is afraid of himself. 2/3

2912. **Ward, Donald,** *Death Takes the Stage,* St. Martin's, 1988. (Modern Cozy) Hollywood agent Jake Weissman has problems: his clients don't get many parts; his new secretary, a sexy illegal alien with a very large boyfriend tries to seduce and reform him; and a client he's almost forgotten, would-be actor Bobbie Lang, is murdered in a particularly nasty way. 3/3

2913. **Warren, J.,** *Remains,* Lethe, 2017. (Suspense) Kendall is drawn back to his hometown of Placerville, when the remains of a long-missing boy are finally found, a boy Kendall had shared a complicated history. No matter how much Kendall tries to resist the underside of the mystery behind Randy McPherson's disappearance, he must confront the lies that he has built his life upon. 3/3

2914. **Warren, Patricia Nell,** *Harlan's Race,* Wildcat, 1994. Harlan #2 of 2. (Psychological) After his young athlete lover is struck down on the Olympic track in Montreal, coach Harlan Brown is forced to enter the race of his life. To survive the hate and violence that threaten his chosen family: Betsy, valiant lesbian mother; Vince, angry activist seeking revenge; Chino, Vietnam vet with a wounded heart; and the secret child of Billy Sive. –sequel to *The Front Runner* (MLM). 3/3

2915. **Warwick, K. C.,** *Prove a Villain,* Cheyenne, 2010. (MM Historical) Having returned to Elizabethan London after an absence of two years, Hugh Seaton is happy to resume his old job as tailor to the company of actors known as Strange's Men. He is less content when he finds himself looking for a murderer, and hiding his former lover, playwright Christopher Marlowe, who is suspected of stabbing one of the players to death. 3/3

2916. **Watson, J. (Larry Townsend),** *The Sexual Adventures of Sherlock Holmes,* Traveller's Companion, 1971. (Pulp) To the rest of the world we were a pair of bachelor gentlemen sharing quarters. Between us, once the door at 221B Baker Street was closed against the world, we shared such moments of blissful contentment I doubt anyone outside ourselves could have understood or believed. 3/3

2917. **Weesner, Theodore,** *The True Detective,* Summit, 1987. (Hard Boiled) In the sleepy confines of Portsmouth, New Hampshire, Gil Dulac, a small-town investigator, broods over a deteriorating city he's grown to adopt as his own; a once proud city that's been infested with a sexual pathology that–in its breadth of depravity–is breaking out like a pandemic. –villain is a pedophile who attempts to have relationships with men but finds he cannot get over his lust for boys (MLM). 2/3

2918. **Webb, Donald,** *Death Came Calling,* Bold Stroke Books, 2014. Katsuro Tanaka #1 of 3. (MM Hard Boiled) When Katsuro Tanaka starts digging into the mysterious death of a prominent California lawyer, bodies begin piling up. Even though it has been two years since Tanaka left the police force, after the brutal slaughter of his spouse, Patrick, he still feels responsible for Patrick's death, and suffers from bouts of depression and anxiety. 3/3

2919. **Webb, Donald,** *The Grim Reaper's Calling Card,* Bold Stroke Books, 2016. Katsuro Tanaka #2 of 3. (MM Hard Boiled) Two months ago, Anne Bradley, a young California nurse, disappeared and the case has gone cold. Hired by her father, private investigator Katsuro Tanaka must pick up the pieces of the tragedy that occurred on that fateful day. 3/3

2920. **Webb, Donald,** *With Callous Indifference,* MLR, 2018. Katsuro Tanaka #3 of 3. (MM Hard Boiled) One year ago, Nigel Nash, a twenty-four-year-old musician is murdered, and his body is dumped beside the Madres Creek. 3/3

2921. **Webb, T. A.,** *Working it,* A Bear on Bear, 2013. City Knight #1 of 5. (MM Crime Drama) Marcus works the streets of Atlanta, determined to keep it a safe place. An ex-cop, he buried his heart years ago. Ben works the same streets, selling himself to pay for college. The victim of a horrible crime, he decided to Just. Not. Care. –fifty-page short story is available as an e-book only (MLM). 3/3

2922. **Webb, T. A.,** *Knightmare,* A Bear on Bear, 2013. City Knight #2 of 5. (MM Police Procedural) Marcus Prater has already lost one man to senseless violence. He won't lose another. Calling in all his resources, former blue knights on the Atlanta Police Department, and his own experience as a Vice cop, Marcus desperately searches for the new man in his life, college student and rent boy Ben Danvers. –available as an e-book only (MLM). 3/3

2923. **Webb, T. A.,** *Starry Knight,* A Bear on Bear, 2013. City Knight #3 of 5. (MM Police Procedural) Marcus Prater has spent the last two years of his life existing, ignoring his friends and family because remembering hurts too much. Benjamin Danvers, running from ghosts of his own, has separated himself emotionally from the world. Neither man needs anyone. –available as an e-book only (MLM). 3/3

2924. **Webb, T. A.,** *Knights Out,* A Bear on Bear, 2013. City Knight #4 of 5. (MM Hard Boiled) When Marcus is asked to investigate the disappearance of a young man close to Benjamin, that prompts him to begin the search for his brother too. What he finds changes everything. –available as an e-book only (MLM). 3/3

2925. **Webb, T. A.,** *Darkest Knight,* A Bear on Bear, 2013. City Knight #5 of 5. (MM Hard Boiled) Reunited with his estranged brother, Frankie, and closer than ever to his chosen family–the brothers of his heart–Marcus Prater and his lover Benjamin Danvers should be busy planning their first holiday season together. Not looking for the murderer of a too-young-to-die rent boy. –available as an e-book only (MLM). 3/3

2926. **Weisman, John,** *Evidence,* Viking, 1980. (Hard Boiled) Drugs, flesh peddling, and terrifying emptiness, an investigative reporter is driven to get his story, get it first, and stop at nothing. –main character is investigating the death of his friend, who was bisexual and very involved in the gay scene in Detroit (MLM). 2/3

2927. **Wells, K. C.,** *Truth will Out,* Dreamspinner, 2018. (Amateur Sleuth) Jonathon de Mountford's visit to Merrychurch village to stay with his uncle Dominic gets off to a bad start when Dominic fails to appear at the railway station. But when Jonathon finds him dead in his study, apparently as the result of a fall, everything changes. For one thing, Jonathon is the next in line to inherit the manor house. For another, he's not so sure it was an accident, and with the help of Mike Tattersall, the owner of the village pub, Jonathon sets out to prove his theory. 3/3

2928. **Welles, Paul O'M,** *Project Lambda,* Ashley, 1979. (Thriller) "Senator Chester Markowski, a closeted bisexual, devises a plan to purge all American gays under the guise of a Deviant Rehabilitation Act. Gays are drafted and dispatched to Marine camps in the west, where they are secretly experimented on and exterminated. Massachusetts Guardian editor Tony Abracan hires Boston reporter Tip Benjamin to go to Colorado to document what is happening. Tip's lover, George Taylor, is then kidnapped by the Marines (Gunn)." 3/3

2929. **Welsh, Louise,** *The Cutting Room,* Canongate, 2002. (Crime Drama) When Rilke, a dissolute and promiscuous auctioneer, comes across a collection of highly disturbing photographs during a house clearance he feels compelled to unearth more about the deceased owner who coveted them. 3/3

2930. **Welsh, Louise,** *Tamburlaine Must Die,* Canongate, 2004. (Historical Espionage) London, 1593. A city on edge. Under threat from plague and war, strangers are unwelcome, suspicion is wholesale, severed heads grin from the spikes on Tower Bridge. Playwright, poet, and spy Christopher Marlowe walks the city's mean streets with just three days to find the murderous Tamburlaine, a killer escaped from the pages of his most violent play. 3/3

2931. **West, Samuel,** *Hard-Headed Dick,* Surree, 1975. (Pulp) "New York con artist Gary Proctor, 23, the narrator, a former hustler, aids his bed mate, NYPD inspector Kevin O'Hara, to discover who stabbed blackmailing Hugo Brant to death in which much is not what it seems (Gunn)." 3/3

2932. **Wheat, Carolyn,** *Dead Man's Thoughts,* St. Martin's, 1983. Cass Jameson #1 of 6. (Amateur Sleuth) When Jameson's lover and colleague, Nathan Wasserstein, is murdered and the main suspect is a street hustler, Cass must face two possibilities–either the cops have the wrong man, or she never really knew Nathan at all. –deceased may have been living a secret life (MLM). 2/3

2933. **Wheeler, Sullivan,** *Billionaire's Row,* Dreamspinner, 2010. (MM Police Procedural) Detective Michael Weiss has enough to deal with. Between being part of a dysfunctional police department and having a vain and demanding lover who Michael suspects is only using him for personal gain, it's all Michael can do to keep himself sane. When the body of Craig Davies, a wealthy defense lawyer, is found on former television star Sam Christiansen's front lawn, Michael knows that everyone-his bosses, his partner at the police department, and Brian, his lover-will be looking to him for solutions. 3/3

2934. **White, Chester,** *Missing Male,* Megcorp, 1984. (Pulp) "Private Investigator Dick Long, the narrator, maintains a viable code of honor throughout a comedy, one of the better pulps from the 1980s. Hal Brewster is kidnapped from Dick's apartment. Dick has encountered the youth while informing his stepmother that her husband, whom she hired Dick to investigate, is seeing other men, not women. Dick searches for Hal with the help of an attractive young puppy, Ozzie, whom he meets in a bar (Gunn)." 3/3

2935. **White, Michael,** *Descent,* No Publisher, 2010. (Historical) On a cold February night in 1909, the nephew of President Theodore Roosevelt tumbled out of a window at Harvard and fell five stories to his death. "An accident," swore the coroner; "a horrible tragedy," stated the family; "a sobering loss," announced the College - and everyone agreed. Everyone that is, except a certain Henry Wadsworth, reporter on the Harvard Crimson, and Groton chum of the corpse now lying in the Cambridge morgue. 3/3

2936. **White, Michael Scott,** *The Drag Queen Murders,* Kindle, 2013. (Hard Boiled) A detective is hired to find a missing person. A body is found in Rock Creek Park in Washington D.C. When a second body is found, the media becomes interested as does the political world of Washington. The victims all happen to be drag queens and the detective hired to solve the murders, Sean Casey, is a former SEAL who happens to be gay. –available as an e-book only (MLM). 3/3

2937. **White, Teri,** *Triangle,* Ace Charter, 1982. (Crime Drama) Three men drawn inexorably together – by fear, by need; they form the Triangle. – Mac: He's a small-time gambler, a big time loser, a hood on the fringes of the Mob. He's also Johnny's keeper. – Simon: A San Francisco cop, he has sworn to avenge the murder of his partner, His search takes him across the country and back again, until he steps into hell in a Los Angeles hallway. –Simon forms a homoerotic bond with Griffith (MLM). 3/3

2938. **White, Teri,** *Bleeding Hearts,* Mysterious Press, 1984. Blue Maguire and Spaceman Kowalski #1 of 2. (Crime Drama) On the night he escapes the asylum, Tom does not take his medication. He slips out of bed soon after lights out, pockets a knife, and goes looking for a guard. At knifepoint, he takes the man's clothes, cuts his throat, and walks out of the institution a free man. His brother is waiting outside the gate. –incestual lovers/killers (MLM). 2/3

2939. **White, Teri,** *Outlaw Blues,* Mystery Scene, 1992. (Pulp) "California police detective "Evan Gibson," working undercover, forms a partnership with Roger, a former convict, to steal $2 million in a homoerotic caper (Gunn)." 3/3

2940. **Wilcox, Collin,** *Aftershock,* Random House, 1975. Lt. Hastings #6 of 20. (Police Procedural) A twisted teenage boy, James Biggs, stalks Lt. Frank Hastings's sweetheart, but the chief tells Hastings his fellow officers can handle young pervert. As a distraction, Hastings moves on to another homicide, an open and shut case. –the stalker is bisexual and the homicide of a dowager who has a gay son. Lt. Hastings books take place in San Francisco and may include more examples of gay men in this series (MLM). 1/3

2941. **Wilde, Vincent,** *Combat Zone,* Cleis Press, 2017. Cody Harper #1 of 2. (Amateur Sleuth) A serial killer haunts the seamy side of Boston's infamous sex district–The Combat Zone–as gay cross-dressing sleuth Cody Harper fights to save the life of his best friend. It's a thrill ride loaded with sex, betrayal, and murder. 3/3

2942. **Wilde, Vincent,** *An Absent God,* Cleis Press, 2017. Cody Harper #2 of 2. (MM Mystery) Rodney Jessup, the pious presidential candidate from THE COMBAT ZONE, asks Cody Harper for help. Someone is threatening Jessup's life and it's up to Cody to find the perpetrator. 3/3

2943. **Wilder, David (L. Butler),** *Everybody's Andy,* Gay Parisian, 1971. (Pulp) "San Francisco call boys Andrew (Andy) Fairchild, 23, and David (Davy) Douglas join forces after their lovers, Bits Thornton and Bert Evans, disappear at an orgy hosted by Bill Burns with male prostitutes supplied by Dan Matthews (Gunn)." 3/3

2944. **Wilhelm, Lambert (William J. Lambert III),** *Meat,* Arena, 1978.

(Pulp) "Reporter Monty Darnel, 22, and FBI agent Sean Bjorn work independently and without knowledge of each other in a pulp crime story. Danner Myles, along with his son and his lover, is operating a lucrative scam at the Russell Packing plant. A rogue FBI agent is ignorant of Sean's role but gains information to blow Monty's cover. Slowly Monty accepts he is gay (Gunn)." –reprinted as *Hard Packer* by Arena in 1982 (MLM). 3/3

2945. **Williams, Allan P.,** *Murder at the Colossus,* iUniverse, 2004. (Hard Boiled) Agatha-Christie style puzzle is brought into the twenty-first century with a bi-sexual detective who not only has to solve the mystery but fend off suspects–male and female–who seem determined to have sex with him. 3/3

2946. **Williams, Chuck,** *The Bonds of Death,* Nazca Plains, 2006. Morgan #1 of 3. (MM Psychological) A story about a gay leather family which happens to include a Episcopalian Priest. The conflict begins during a horrendous confession. Should he break the confessional and save lives? Or, should he contact the police. 3/3

2947. **Williams, Chuck,** *Broken Silence,* Nazca Plains, 2006. Morgan #2 of 3. (MM Psychological) Bringing another priest into the leather family. Circumstances develop that both priests have their faith tested against their commitment to their gay leather family. 3/3

2948. **Williams, Chuck,** *The Master's House,* Nazca Plains, 2006. Morgan #3 of 3. (MM Psychological) Initially a priest learned of a secret in the confessional which cannot be revealed. The story has many strange and unexpected twists and is mostly about love and leather family. 3/3

2949. **Williams, David,** *Treasure Preserved,* St. Martin's, 1983. Mark Treasure #6 of 17. (British Cozy) The fate of the 19th-century Round House could wreck the multi-million-pound development in a south coast resort. A dozen interested parties are in favor of knocking it down. They include an Arab oil sheikh, a sexy English Literature drop-out from Sussex University, the head of a construction company, and a romantic novelist. And where does Canon Tring's languorous young wife fit in to all this? –romantic novelist is gay, and Williams (author) is patronizing towards the gay character (MM). 1/3

2950. **Williams, J. X. (Victor J. Banis),** *Good-bye My Lover,* Greenleaf, 1966. (Pulp) "Los Angeles–based accidental sleuth Dennis Eastman, 20, a U. S. Sailor on leave, comes to understand himself. Dennis's lover, Lincoln Gardner, is murdered before he arrives. The police investigation seemingly going nowhere (even though Dennis suspects the Beverly Hills police detective is closeted), Dennis decides to track down the mysterious Jeff whom Linc was supposed to have met at a gay bar the evening he was shot (Gunn)." –This was the first American novel with a gay amateur sleuth and it holds up well. Later edition revised by Banis as *Goodbye, My Lover* in 2007 by Borgo Press (MLM). 3/3

2951. **Williams, J. X. (Edward D. Wood Jr., 1924-1978),** *Parisian Passions,* Greenleaf, 1966. (Pulp) "Texas erotic dancer Lorraine (Lorry) Peters, an ex-Marine, MTF transsexual, flies to Paris to help Texas sheriff Buck Rhodes and Paris inspector Henri Goulet trap a serial killer and ends the case in a three-way with the two straight men (Gunn)." –J. X. Williams is a pen name owned by Greenleaf and used by several authors (MLM). 3/3

2952. **Williams, Walter,** *Two Spirits: Story of Life with the Navajo,* Maple Shade, 2006. (MM Historical) Set in the Civil War era of the 1860s, this novel tells the story of a feckless Virginian who finds himself captivated by a Two-Spirit male highly respected among the Navajo. It is a story of tragedy, oppression, and discrimination, but also an enlightening story of love, discovery, and beauty. 3/3

2953. **Williamson, Hugh Ross (1901-1978),** *A Wicked Pack of Cards,* Michael Joseph, 1961. (Psychological) A young schoolmaster, on a motoring holiday, is attracted by an inn-sign of the Four Kings, representing the heads of the Tarot kings. He discovers that the sign-painter was found dead on the moors near the inn shortly after he had finished it. Although no one has challenged the verdict of 'Death by Misadventure,' there is an air of suspicion in the neighborhood and he finds himself drawn into a personal investigation as to whether the death was in fact accident, suicide or murder. 3/3

2954. **Wilson, Colin,** *Ritual in the Dark,* Granada, 1960. Sorme #1 of 3. (Crime Drama) A wave of sickening deaths hits the streets of modern London. Young women, mainly prostitutes, are found strangled and mutilated. The police are baffled, the press outraged - not since Jack the Ripper has such a sinister brand of violent murders been unleashed. Is the culprit a homicidal maniac or a cold-blooded, calculating killer wreaking a personal vendetta on a corrupt and callous society? –a reverse Jack the Ripper where the young killer is attracted to men that he can't have therefore he kills women. Author is fairly sympathetic of homosexuals for 1960 (MLM). 2/3

2955. **Wilson, Colin,** *The Glass Cage,* Random House, 1966. (Thriller) A series of brutal and bizarre murders has London on edge. Near the dismembered corpse of each victim, the killer has scrawled cryptic quotations from the eighteenth-century mystic poet William Blake. Baffled, the police enlist the aid of Damon Reade, a brilliant but reclusive Blake scholar, who reluctantly agrees to help. –murderer is gay and is tortured by the memory of his father's fixation on Blake and his mother's promiscuity (MLM). 1/3

2956. **Wilson, John Morgan,** *Simple Justice,* Doubleday, 1996. Justice #1 of 8. (Journalist) Following the death of his lover and a scandal involving his Pulitzer Prize-winning article, crime reporter Benjamin Justice has fallen into a hazy, alcoholic reclusiveness, hiding out in the West Hollywood neighborhood known as the Norma Triangle. He is called back to the world of the living by an unexpected, and unwelcome, visit from Harry Brofsky, his former boss. 3/3

2957. **Wilson, John Morgan,** *Revision of Justice,* Doubleday, 1997. Justice #2 of 8. (Journalist) There's a Hollywood one never gets to see on Oscar night, the Hollywood of wannabes, has-beens, and never-weres. It's this hidden Hollywood that Benjamin Justice finds when he accompanies Alexandra Templeton to an open house at the home of the well-known teacher of screenwriting Gordon Cantwell. 3/3

2958. **Wilson, John Morgan,** *Justice at Risk,* Doubleday, 1999. Justice #3 of 8. (Journalist) Benjamin Justice knows a reporter is nothing without credibility. He learned the hard way when a Pulitzer was snatched from his grasp. It's been a long, hard climb to find even a fraction of the work he once had. But his fortunes are about to change: Justice has been offered the opportunity to script a documentary for public television. –won the twelfth LAMBDA Award (MLM). 3/3

2959. **Wilson, John Morgan,** *The Limits of Justice,* Doubleday, 2000. Justice #4 of 8. (Journalist) Ex-reporter Benjamin Justice is trying to come to terms with his HIV status, no job, and no hope. Then the daughter of a onetime Hollywood hunk offers him a job to ghostwrite a payback book after a sleazy bio links the actor to a shadowy world of sinister perversion and blood-chilling crimes. When she's found dead with a needle in her arm, Justice goes looking for the truth. –won the thirteenth LAMBDA Award (MLM). 3/3

2960. **Wilson, John Morgan,** *Blind Eye,* St. Martin's, 2003. Justice #5 of 8. (Journalist) Benjamin Justice, a disgraced journalist in his mid-forties, is slowly putting his life back together. Under contract to write his tumultuous life story, Justice is trying to put all the elements of his life into perspective for the first time. When trying to locate his childhood priest, however, he runs into a bureaucratic stone wall. –won the sixteenth LAMBDA Award (MLM). 3/3

2961. **Wilson, John Morgan,** *Moth and Flame,* St. Martin's, 2004. Justice #6 of 8. (Journalist) Benjamin Justice used to be one of Los Angeles's most respected journalists, but a scandal over invented sources cost him the Pulitzer, his job and his reputation. With his life in ruins, he's spent much of the past decade slowly piecing it back together. Now he's under contract to write his biography, but the writing is going slowly and he's in need of a job to tide him over financially. So, when Bruce Bibby, a freelance writer, is murdered during an apparent burglary, Bibby's uncompleted assignment for the city of West Hollywood is a much-needed opportunity for Justice. 3/3

2962. **Wilson, John Morgan,** *Rhapsody in Blood,* St. Martin's, 2006. Justice #7 of 8. (Journalist) Disgraced journalist Benjamin Justice, at loose ends between jobs, takes a short vacation with a friend, Los Angeles Times reporter Alexandra Templeton, to a movie set at a faded resort hotel in the California desert. The film being shot is about a star's death in the 1950's and the lynching of a local black man for the murder–the last lynching in California. 3/3

2963. **Wilson, John Morgan,** *Spider Season,* St. Martin's, 2008. Justice #8 of 8. (Journalist) Justice has finally published a memoir revealing the truth behind the events that cost him so much and made him permanently radioactive in the journalism community. And this book may be his last chance to turn things around, to make a living writing as he'd always wanted. But his memoir brings out more than the truth - it brings out long-forgotten, long hidden ghosts from his past. And Justice finds himself, and everyone/everything he holds dear under attack. 3/3

2964. **Wilson, Jon,** *Cheap as Beasts,* Bold Stroke Books, 2015. Declan Colette #1 of 2. (Historical) Like most soldiers, Declan Colette lost his fair share in the war–in his case a sailor, drowned off Iwo Jima. Since then he's been scratching out a living as a cut-rate PI, drinking too much, and flirting with danger. Then a girl arranges to consult him, only to be murdered en route, and the cops tag Colette as their prime suspect. 3/3

2966. **Wilson, Jon,** *Every Unworthy Thing,* Bold Stroke Books, 2015. Declan Colette #2 of 2. (Historical) Gay PI Declan Colette finds himself in the middle of a gang war between resurgent Japanese mobsters and the black gangsters who expanded operations during World War II. Complicating matters is crime boss Max Harrold. 3/3

2966. **Wilson, Mikel,** *Murder on the Lake of Fire,* Acorn, 2017. Mourning Dove #1 of 2. (Police Procedural) At twenty-three and with a notorious case under his belt, Emory Rome has already garnered fame as a talented special agent for the Tennessee Bureau of Investigation. His career is leapfrogging over his colleagues, but the jumping stops when he's assigned a case he fought to avoid - an eerie murder in the Smoky Mountain hometown he had abandoned. 3/3

2967. **Wilson, Mikel,** *Death Opens a Window,* Acorn, 2018. Mourning Dove #2 of 2. (Police Procedural) Emory must unravel the inexplicable death of a federal employee in a Knoxville high-rise. But while the reticent investigator is mired in a deep pool of suspects – from an old mountain witch to the powerful Tennessee Valley Authority – he misses a greater danger creeping from the shadows. 3/3

2968. **Wilson, Tony,** *Follow the Queen,* Lulu, 2005. (Hard Boiled) ""Rosewood," California, private investigator Alexander (Alex) DeVane, 30s, seeks to avenge his new lover's death in a whodunit set in 1991. Quentin Phillips, who was accused but not indicted for two hit-and-run deaths seventeen years previously, is murdered. Terry Davis is similarly killed (Gunn)." –sequel *Secrets of the Night* has yet to be published (MLM). 3/3

2969. **Wiltshire, John,** *Love is a Stranger,* MLR, 2014. More Heat than the Sun #1 of 8. (MM Military) Ex-SAS soldier Ben Rider falls in love with his enigmatic married boss Sir Nikolas Mikkelsen, but Nikolas is living a lie. A lie so profound that when the shadows are lifted, Ben realizes he's in love with a very dangerous stranger. 3/3

2970. **Wiltshire, John,** *Conscious Decisions of the Heart,* MLR, 2014. More Heat than the Sun #2 of 8. (MM Military) Nikolas's dark past calls to him, inexorably dragging him back into its seductive embrace. While he goes on an errand of mercy to Russia, Ben travels to Denmark to learn Nikolas's language. Convinced Russia's vastness will swallow Nikolas, Ben doesn't see the enemy much closer to home. 3/3

2971. **Wiltshire, John,** *The Bridge of Silver Wings,* MLR, 2014. More Heat than the Sun #3 of 8. (MM Military) Ben discovers the truth of the old adage 'be careful what you wish for'. Nikolas has exorcised his demons, but when they end up stranded in Russia, the monster inside needs to be let loose. Siberia in winter isn't a place for good men. There is nothing Nikolas won't do to keep Ben alive. 3/3

2972. **Wiltshire, John,** *This Other Country,* MLR, 2014. More Heat than the Sun #4 of 8. (MM Military) Nikolas Mikkelsen could make a very long list of unpleasant things he's endured in his life. Then order it from 'nearly killed me' to 'extremely horrific and don't want to do again'. And what did it say about his forty-five years that being hit by a tsunami would be a considerable way down this list? But nothing, not torture, imprisonment, nor starvation has prepared him for what he now has to endure for Ben Rider's sake-attendance on a residential, gay therapy course. 3/3

2973. **Wiltshire, John,** *The Bruise-Black Sky,* MLR, 2016. More Heat than the Sun #5 of 8. (MM Military) Ben usually overlooks Nikolas's occasionally jarring dissonance. Not this time. A deep rift, a terrible lie, separates them. Eleven thousand miles from Nikolas, in New Zealand, it's bitter winter as Ben films the tragic story of a post-apocalyptic gladiator, a victim of his own personal darkness. 3/3

2974. **Wiltshire, John,** *Death's Ink-Black Shadow,* MLR, 2015. More Heat than the Sun #6 of 8. (MM Military) It takes a certain kind of courage to live as if favored by the gods, ignoring the ever-present ghosts of your past–or perhaps not bravery, but arrogance. And maybe not even that. Ben genuinely believes that the past is behind them–that they deserve to enjoy the life they have created. So, it's not hubris that leads him to overlook the signs that Nikolas does not share his faith, it's love. 3/3

2975. **Wiltshire, John,** *Enduring Night,* MLR, 2015. More Heat than the Sun #7 of 8. (MM Military) You'd have thought that Ben and Nikolas would have learnt that their romantic holidays inevitably end up as disasters. A short break on the polar ice sees them trapped in a nightmare of murder and deceit. 3/3

2976. **Wiltshire, John,** *His Fateful Heap of Days,* MLR, 2016. More Heat than the Sun #8 of 8. (MM Military) Only a few months from his fiftieth year, Nikolas is feeling a distinct wobble in his formidable certainties. Aleksey Primakov appears to have become irrelevant. All he needs, therefore, is to be dragged into an adventure with Devon's answer to the three musketeers. 3/3

2977. **Windhauser, Brad,** *Regret,* Star Publishing, 2007. (Police Procedural) The bodies of gay men are turning up all over Philadelphia. Detective John Thompson is determined to find out who is behind this string of murders before it is too late. 3/3

2978. **Winer, Jeanne,** *Her Kind of Case,* Bancroft, 2018. (Legal Drama) Lee Isaacs, a female defense attorney on the cusp of turning 60, who, out of curiosity, determination, and desire for a big, even impossible, professional challenge, chooses to take on a tough murder case in which a largely uncooperative young man is accused of helping kill a gay gang member. –lots of gay and bisexual men make up secondary characters (MM). 3/3

2979. **Witt, L. A. & Aleksandr Voinov,** *Hostile Ground,* Riptide, 2014. (MM Police Procedural) After the deaths of three undercover cops investigating a drug ring in a seedy strip club in Seattle, Detective Mahir Hussain has been sent to finish the job. He joins the club's security team in the hopes of finding enough evidence to bust the operation before the men in charge find a reason to put him in a shallow grave. 3/3

2980. **Witt, L. A.,** *If the Seas Catch Fire,* N. P., 2016. (MM Crime Drama)

Sergei Andronikov was a child when the Mafia wiped out his family, leaving him with nothing but a hunger for revenge. Years later, through ruthless strategy and tireless patience, he's a contract killer working for the three families ruling Cape Swan... and he's nearly in position to bring them all down from the inside. 3/3

2981. **Wood, Edward (1924-1978)**, *Black Lace Drag*, Raven, 1963. Glen/Glenda #1 of 2. (Crime Drama) A transvestite assassin with a fur-fetish, on the run from both police and the mob, buys a rundown travelling carnival and goes into hiding with a small-town hooker while his twin personalities - Glen and Glenda - continually vie for psychological supremacy. –republished as *Killer in Drag* in 1965 and then *The Twilight Land* in 1967 (MLM). 3/3

2982. **Wood, Edward,** *Death of a Transvestite,* Pad, 1967. Glen/Glenda #2 of 2. (Crime Drama) Hero/heroine Glen Marker sits on Death Row and offers to tell his life story in all its sordid detail in exchange for his last wish: to die in drag! –republished as *Let Me Die in Drag* in 1969 by Selected Adult Library as "Woodrow Edwards (MLM)." 3/3

2983. **Wood, Nick,** *Light Out,* Gay Men's Press, 2003. (Police Procedural) When farmer Rick and his veterinarian lover Jonny receive a phone call to say that Sarah, Rick's UN employee sister, has disappeared between boarding a flight in Manchester and its arrival in Bangkok, they little realize that they will become involved with abduction and assassinations, underworld mobsters and fanatical terrorists; and an ambiguous British agent, Andy. 3/3

2984. **Woodall, James,** *Murder at Queen Street,* Createspace, 2018. Piccadilly #1 of 2. (Historical Soft Boiled) Elderly landlady Mrs. Beck is appalled to discover the gentlemen detectives in flat #4 are more than just business partners. But when a man is murdered in the building, she is forced to ask for their help. –70-page novella available as an e-book only (MM). 3/3

2985. **Woodall, James,** *Deep End,* Createspace, 2018. Piccadilly #2 of 2. (Historical Soft Boiled) When a body is found in London's most celebrated Turkish bathhouse, the detectives must hunt down a killer targeting gay men. But the investigation puts strain on their relationship when Theodore reconnects with an old flame. –102-page novella available as an e-book only (MLM). 3/3

2986. **Woods, Sara (Lana Hutton Bowen-Judd 1922 - 1986),** *Nor Live so Long,* St. Martin's, 1986. Antony Maitland #47 of 48. (Legal Drama) The one thing Antony Maitland needed was a holiday in the lovely village of Burton Cecil. The last thing the barrister-sleuth needed was murder. Especially when the victim was an innocent young girl, gruesomely strangled! –murderer is gay, *Nor Live so*

Long was the first of two books to be published posthumously (MLM). 2/3

2987. **Woodward, Antony,** *The Mendacity Games,* Createspace, 2015. Bourgh #1 of 2. (Psychological) Christopher Bourgh is a shark in a very small pond. On the surface he's the perfect student, straight As and a promising career as an artist. Essentially orphaned by his mother, Callinghurst boarding school has become his home. With a magnetic personality, distracting good looks and a brilliant talent Chris is the shining star in the eyes of his headteacher. Only Chris isn't quite all he seems. 3/3

2988. **Woodward, Antony,** *The Killing Games,* Createspace, 2018. Bourgh #2 of 2. (Psychological) Christopher Bourgh is being hunted by hitmen but he has no idea who's sent them. As if that wasn't enough he's about to start college. Now a stranger in a strange land Chris is about to learn that those wicked games he'd played back in England are about to come circling right back to him. 3/3

2989. **Woodward, I. E.,** *Rubber Baby Buggy Bumpers,* iUniverse, 2010. Rendezvous #1 of 2. (Comic Thriller) The Rendezvous, the city's biggest gay brothel, is under attack, and poor Logan and his misfit band of detectives must track down the culprit before the whole place blows up. 3/3

2990. **Woodward, I. E.,** *Peck of Pickled Peppers,* iUniverse, 2012. Rendezvous #2 of 2. (Comic Thriller) Timothy Evans-Barnes is three and lives with his fathers in an apartment above their bar and grill, The Pickled Pepper. His grandfather, Miss Jason, runs The Rendezvous, the most successful gay brothel and restaurant in the state. His great-grandfather prefers to be called Mom and wears daffodil aprons and bright yellow earrings; he manages a homeless shelter for that well-known Stripper-for-God, the Reverend Margie Bartholomew. 3/3

2991. **Woody, Michelle,** *The Scarecrow's Kiss,* iUniverse, 2004. (Fantasy) In 1980, serial killer Joseph Parrish was killed in a raid by local authorities and his bizarre world uncovered. Now, Russell Kenyon has come to do a segment on Parrish for his show, Spooky History, hoping the report will be his show's saving grace. With a new victim missing, talk of Parrish's curse has spread through town. 3/3

2992. **Woody, Michelle,** *Merrick the Art Thief,* JMS, 2018. (MM Crime Drama) Brilliant art thief Merrick Davidson can steal anything, except Grant Silvan's heart. Wyatt Silvan, Grant's father and Merrick's employer, is after the famous seven Xanderclied paintings, which all contain clues to a treasure. Together, they hunt the paintings from art galleries to private collections, from city to city, dodging bullets and escaping from life threatening attacks. –available as an e-book only (MLM). 3/3

2993. **Woolrich, Cornell,** *Manhattan Love Song,* Godwin, 1932. (Noir) Blow past unhappily married narrator Wade's melodramatic first encounter with mobbed-up party girl Bernice Pascal on the pre-Depression Manhattan streets, and the story soon settles into a snappy Jazz Age essay of the many crimes lonely, deluded hearts willingly commit. Although Wade's sardonic jibes and cocky narcissism feel downright contemporary as he obsessively pursues his dangerous dame. –main character robs a gay man (MLM). 1/3

2994. **Worrall, Lisa,** *Laurel Heights 1,* Silver, 2012. Laurel #1 of 2. (MM Police Procedural) Detectives Scott Turner and Will Harrison are sent undercover after an apparent murder/suicide in Laurel Heights, an exclusive gay housing community. Will the two closeted officers be able to hide their attraction while each believing the other is straight? And is there a killer amongst them waiting to claim his next victim? 3/3

2995. **Worrall, Lisa,** *Laurel Heights 2,* Createspace, 2014. Laurel #2 of 2. (MM Police Procedural) Will and Scott are now out and proud and living together in Scott's tiny house. So, everything is perfect, right? Wrong... A sadistic serial killer is at large, torturing his way through the gay community, but Will and Scott have no leads. 3/3

2996. **Wright, B. K.,** *Son of a Boss,* Beau to Beau, 2011. (MM Crime Drama/Police Procedural) "FBI agent Rick Mason, 30s, and Jeff Giaconi, son of a mafia head, fall in love and have lots of unsafe sex before they bring Jeff's father down (Gunn)." 3/3

2997. **Wright, Eric,** *Smoke Detector,* Scribner's, 1984. Salter #2 of 11. (Police Procedural) Inspector Charlie Salter investigates the death of an antiques dealer who died in a fire caused by arson. –antique owner's assistant is gay (MLM). 1/3

2998. **Wright, Helen S.,** *Matter of Oaths,* Popular Library, 1990. (Science Fiction) Commander Rallya of patrol ship Bhattya thought she had a talent for making enemies–until she met Rafe. For no crime on his record, the young officer had been identity wiped, and his innumerable, now-forgotten enemies were still tracking him across the galaxy. 3/3

2999. **Wyatt, Stephen,** *Big Dipper,* Endeavour, 2012. (Court Drama) Julian Bryant. A successful, well-off lawyer. Nice flat, plenty of money, and a wide circle of friends. Gay, but discreet. A man with everything. But Julian's life is about to turn into Big Dipper: a terrifying roller-coaster ride from which there is no escape. 3/3

3000. **Wynne, S. C.,** *Shadow's Edge,* Wynne, 2017. Psychic Detective #1 of 2. (MM Paranormal) Liam Baker can see things. Dead people like to visit him and tell them how they were wronged. Some might call it a gift, other's a curse. But either way this ability makes him useful to Los Angeles homicide detective Kimball Thompson. 3/3

3001. **Wynne, S. C.**, *Shadow's Return,* Wynne, 2018. Psychic Detective #2 of 2. (MM Paranormal) Psychic Liam Baker and Detective Kimball Thompson have embarked on a romantic relationship after battling the deadly and powerful psychic, Steven Pine months ago. They ended his brutal killing spree of young male prostitutes, and he's safely in jail. 3/3

3002. **Wynne, S. C.**, *Strange Medicine,* Wynne/Wynne, 2018. (Police Procedural) Maxwell Thornton isn't really a people person, but that never mattered to him because he'd lived for his career. After losing a patient during a routine hysterectomy, he's shaken and afraid to pick up the scalpel again. He resigns his position in the city and takes a job as sole GP in the isolated town of Rainy Dale, Texas, population 1001. When one of his most annoying patients ends up dead and floating in Maxwell's pool, he has some explaining to do to the local sheriff. 3/3

Y

3003. **Yaffe, James,** *Nothing but the Night,* Bantam, 1959. (Psychological) The explosive story of two young men driven by abnormal passions to the crime that shocked the nation. One afternoon it happened. On a deserted country road, two seventeen-year-olds of highly respected families commit one of the most gruesome and terrible crimes ever conceived. When the truth came to light, no one was more shocked or surprised than those who had known them all their lives. 3/3

3004. **Yates, Bart,** *Leave Myself Behind,* Kensington, 2003. (MM YA) Noah York is a closeted gay teenager with a foul mouth, a critical disposition, and plenty of material for his tirades. After his father dies, Noah's mother, a temperamental poet, takes a teaching job in a small New Hampshire town, far from Chicago and the only world Noah has known. The crumbling house they try to renovate quickly reveals dark secrets, via dusty Mason jars they discover interred between walls. 3/3

Z

3005. **Z., Cari, and L. A. Witt,** *Risky Behavior,* Riptide, 2017. Bad Behavior #1 of 4. (MM Police Procedural) It's day one of Darren Corliss's career as a detective, and not only has he been assigned a notoriously difficult partner, but the guy might also be a pill-popping dirty cop. Internal Affairs needs proof, and Darren gets to be their eyes and ears whether he wants to or not. 3/3

3006. **Z., Cari, and L. A. Witt,** *Suspicious Behavior,* Riptide, 2017. Bad Behavior #2 of 4. (MM Police Procedural) Detective Darren Corliss is hanging by a thread. In between recovering from a near-fatal wound and returning to work at a hostile precinct, he's struggling to help care for his ailing brother. His partner and boyfriend, Detective Andreas Ruffner, wants to help, but doesn't know how. And with his own family crises brewing, Andreas is spread almost as thin as Darren. 3/3

3007. **Z., Cari, and L. A. Witt,** *Reckless Behavior,* Riptide, 2018. Bad Behavior #3 of 4. (MM Police Procedural) After too many years of putting his job first, Detective Andreas Ruffner is getting his priorities straight. He's ready to spend some quality time with his adult kids, not to mention come clean about some things he should've told them a long time ago. And introduce them to his partner and boyfriend, Darren Corliss. –e-book novella *Romantic Behavior* is the final chapter in this series, and it does not have any mystery but is just the wedding of the two main characters (MLM). 3/3

3008. **Z., Cari, and L. A. Witt,** *Double or Nothing,* Createspace, 2018. (Crime Drama/Police Procedural) Leotrim Nicolosi was born into a world of crime and bloodshed. When that bloodshed hits too close to home, taking down Leo's boyfriend–the son of a notorious mob boss–Leo is determined to destroy the Grimaldi family. He's got evidence that will send every last Grimaldi to prison, he's got the family's wealth in an electronic chokehold, and he's got a vendetta that can only be settled with the blood of the man who killed his lover. Rich Cody joined the U.S. Marshals to hunt down bad guys, not babysit witnesses. Orders are orders, though, and now he's protecting a hacker with ties to the Albanian and Sicilian mobs. It's just another exciting day in WITSEC. When a routine transfer to a safehouse goes horribly wrong, Rich and Leo narrowly escape with their lives. With the Marshals compromised and Leo being framed for murder, he and Rich are on the run from criminals and law enforcement alike. –may be the first book in a new series (MLM). 3/3

3009. **Zachary, Drew,** *Once Upon a Veterinarian,* Torquere, 2008. (MM Mystery) Ben has a good life. Partner in a thriving veterinarian clinic with his best friend Stacey, he has a great dog, a favorite Chinese take-out place and a great DVD collection. The only thing he doesn't have is a special someone to share his life with. When Ben has a number of poisoned animals come through his clinic, he calls in the police, suspecting that these aren't random tragedies, but deliberate killings. 3/3

3010. **Zachary, Drew,** *Eye Spy: Compilation,* Torquere, 2009. Eye Spy #1-3 of 4. (MM Paranormal) Private eye DB has a pretty unusual partner. Jesse's been in his office a lot longer than he has, hanging around like ghosts have to. They do pretty well together, playing chess and solving cases, which Jesse figures is better than an eternity popping in and out of walls. Three different cases keep DB and Jesse jumping in this compilation. –compilation of Eye Spy series 1-3 (MLM). 3/3

3011. **Zachary, Drew,** *Mother May I,* Torquere, 2010. Eye Spy #4 of 4. (MM Paranormal) Their latest client, Duke, is a bit of a jerk, but he's got plenty of money to burn, along with a bad case of being haunted by his deceased mother. DB and Jesse soon discover that the old lady is trying to protect her money rather than her son, and she isn't going to go gently into the light and what lies beyond for the dead. –a Christmas short story follows book 4 but is more Dickens than mystery (MLM). 3/3

3012. **Zachary, Logan,** *Big Bad Wolf,* Bold Stroke Books, 2013. Paavo Wolf #1 of 2. (Amateur Sleuth) Paavo Wolfe owns We're Wolfe's Books, the place to go for Lake Superior's horror book and movie aficionados. His best friend, Stacey, own Lotions and Potions next door. When a wolf attacks two of Stacey's employees, against all reason, they begin to suspect that one of the victims is turning into a werewolf. 3/3

3013. **Zachary, Logan,** *Gingerdead Man,* Bold Stroke Books, 2015. Paavo Wolf #2 of 2. (Amateur Sleuth) Paavo Wolfe sells horror, but he isn't prepared for what he finds in the baker's oven. A body burns at his feet, and his ex, Detective Joe DeCarlo, is on the case. Joe is getting unwanted help investigating the crime from Paavo and his best friend, Stacey. While Paavo and Joe's relationship is getting better, going undercover in the bathhouse isn't going to help Paavo mend their issues. 3/3

3014. **Zady, Steven,** *Pretty Boys Must Die,* Midwood, 1973. (Pulp) "New York police detective Raymond Maddox, though a husband and father, comes across as sexually ambiguous in a pulp whodunit (Gunn)." 3/3

3015. **Zarimba, Lance,** *Vacation Therapy,* MLR, 2011. (MM Mystery) Welcome to Club Fred Taylor's best friend, Molly planned his perfect vacation. Checking into an all-male resort, he and Sergio discover a dead body, which disappears. As Taylor stumbles over it again, the problems have only started in this tropical paradise. Taylor befriends the hottest male porn star, an angry drag queen, and a mystery novelist, whose new novel is paralleling Taylor's trip. 3/3

3016. **Zatti, Anthony,** *Going Forward,* iUniverse, 2002. Camping in the Backyard #2 of 2. (MM Amateur Sleuth) One of Michael's associates is brutally murdered outside the Naval Air Station. Michael and Jonathan do some sleuthing on their own to find his killer. Danger is closer than they realize. Theresa, pregnant with Jonathan's baby, promises to give Jonathan full custody of the child when it is born for a monetary settlement. 3/3

3017. **Zavo,** *Derrick Steele: Private Dick the Case of the Hollywood Hustlers,* Bold Stroke Books, 2012. Steele #2 of 2. (Hard Boiled/Modern Pulp) Derrick Steele, a hard-drinking, lusty private detective working for Steele Investigations, is being framed for the murder of a hustler in downtown Los Angeles. Despite Derrick's efforts to solve the crime and clear his name, the body count continues to rise. It quickly becomes apparent that Derrick is facing the most dangerous adversary of his career. 3/3

3018. **Zavo,** *The Case of the Rising Star,* Bold Stroke Books, 2013. Steele #2 of 2. (Hard Boiled/Modern Pulp) A young and famous movie star is receiving death threats, and Derrick is on the case. Without warning, Warren O'Malley, Derrick's long-forgotten half-brother, arrives in Los Angeles, bringing with him his two formidable younger brothers. 3/3

3019. **Zebrun, Gary,** *Someone you Know,* Alyson, 2004. (Journalist) Newspaper columnist Daniel Caruso has a wife he loves deeply, a daughter who means everything to him, and a secret that could destroy them. At a conference in Seattle, he meets and spends a passionate night with Stephen Hart, a handsome firefighter. Awakening alone and deeply conflicted, Daniel flies home to Providence, R.I., but on a layover in Chicago he receives a bizarre and frightening message indicating that someone knows of his deception. 3/3

3020. **Zimmerman, R. D. (Robert Alexander),** *Closet,* Dell, 1995. Todd Mills #1 of 5. (Journalist) It began with a brutal attack in a posh Minneapolis neighborhood. And from the first killing to the next, Todd Mills was at the center of the story. The son of Polish immigrants, Todd had changed his name and risen to the top of his field as a TV news reporter, winning two Emmy Awards along the way. Then his world came crashing down. Suddenly, the double life he'd hidden for so long was brutally uncovered: he was the secret lover of the first man to die. –won the eighth LAMBDA Award (MLM). 3/3

3021. **Zimmerman, R. D.**, *Tribe,* Dell, 1996. Todd Mills #2 of 5. (Journalist) Now he's out, warily beginning a romance with police detective Steve Rawlins, when an old friend, an ex-girlfriend, calls for help. The son she gave up for adoption years before has found her–and left his baby. Now she and the baby are being stalked by a cult of zealots who will stop at nothing to reclaim the child. But as Todd steps into the firing range of The Congregation, he's forced to face the nightmare of his own buried past, as murderous secrets return to kill again. 3/3

3022. **Zimmerman, R. D.**, *Hostage,* Dell, 1997. Todd Mills #3 of 5. (Journalist) Coup turns to chaos, and grief to despair, when Todd's interview ends with the Congressman abducted by gun-wielding kidnappers–and a tragic discovery puts an unsuspecting Rawlins on the trail of the abductors, a trio of unlikely domestic terrorists in the final stages of AIDS, willing to risk what's left of their lives to give violent expression to their desperate AIDS rage. 3/3

3023. **Zimmerman, R. D.**, *Outburst,* Delacorte, 1998. Todd Mills #4 of 5. (Journalist) Against his instincts, Todd is lured to the Stone Arch Bridge by an anonymous phone call with promises of a hot blackmail story. Under pressure, and in need of a scoop, Minneapolis television's most well-known (and only) openly gay reporter soon finds that his visit to the bridge does deliver a sensational exclusive, but not the one he is expecting: Todd arrives to see a man murdered, leaving him as the sole witness to the crime. –won the eleventh LAMBDA Award (MLM). 3/3

3024. **Zimmerman, R. D.**, *Innuendo,* Delacorte, 1999. Todd Mills #5 of 5. (Journalist) Tim Chase walked across the room and flashed Todd Mills his megawatt smile. Stunned, Todd almost forgot the ugliness swirling around them both. For Chase, Hollywood's hottest star, it's the rumors that claim he is gay–and that his high-profile marriage is a sham. For Todd, an award-winning TV reporter, it's a murder case that has put his relationship with policeman Steve Rawlins in jeopardy and spread a deadly chill through Minneapolis's gay world. 3/3

3025. **Zito, Chuck,** *Habit for Death,* Midnight Ink, 2006. Nicky D'Amico #1 of 2. (Modern Cozy) Escaping the heat and heartbreak of New York City for a summer in rural Pennsylvania sounded like the perfect plan to Nicky D'Amico. Little did he know that what began as a heavenly idea would turn out to be a hell of a job! Each year the nuns of rural St. Gilbert's College hire a city slicker to help with their summer theater festival. As the stage manager, Nicky has a lot to handle–a truly awful musical script, bickering school staff, a huge crush on the cute guy in the chorus but things are about to get a whole lot worse. 3/3

3026. **Zito, Chuck,** *Ice in his Veins,* Midnight Ink, 2007. Nicky D'Amico #2 of 2. (Modern Cozy) Nicky D'Amico moves back to New York to get his life in order. The good Company's all-male production of "A Midsummer Night's Dream" is a little unorthodox, but he's thrilled about working with some of his old college friends. This midwinter production of "Dream" soon becomes a nightmare when one of the actors is found dead behind the theater. 3/3

3027. **Zubro, Mark,** *A Simple Suburban Murder,* St. Martin's, 1989. Tom and Scott #1 of 14. (Modern Cozy) When a gay high school teacher starts investigating a colleague's murder, he finds beneath the calm veneer of his Midwestern suburb a seamy underbelly of gambling, prostitution, and child abuse. –won the 2nd LAMBDA Award (MLM). 3/3

3028. **Zubro, Mark,** *Why isn't Becky Twitchell Dead?,* St. Martin's, 1990. Tom and Scott #2 of 14. (Modern Cozy) One would think teaching would be a quiet profession. But not in Chicago, thinks high school teacher Tom Mason when he hears that one of his students has been accused of killing his girlfriend. As a friend of the boy's family, Tom is asked to help clear him, and the more he probes, the more it seems that something sinister is going on in the usually quiet suburbs of Chicago. 3/3

3029. **Zubro, Mark,** *The Only Good Priest,* St. Martin's, 1991. Tom and Scott #3 of 14. (Modern Cozy) Father Sebastian, the only good priest everybody knows, is dead. Pastor of a parish outside Chicago, Father Sebastian was also involved in the gay community through his work with Faith, the gay Catholic organization the diocese is trying to drive out of the church. 3/3

3030. **Zubro, Mark,** *The Principal Cause of Death,* St. Martin's, 1992. Tom and Scott #4 of 14. (Modern Cozy) When schoolteacher Tom Mason is accused of killing the high school principal, Tom and his lover, Scott Carpenter, set out to catch the murderer and prove Tom's innocence. –two short stories; "Next Year Kankakee" appears in the anthology *Cat Crimes III* published by Fine in 1993 and "Never on Santa" published in *Santa Clues* in 1993 by Signet take place between books four and five (MLM). 3/3

3031. **Zubro, Mark,** *An Echo of Death,* St. Martin's, 1994. Tom and Scott

#5 of 14. (Modern Cozy) When high school teacher Tom Mason and his lover, professional baseball player Scott Carpenter, return home after a night out to discover a corpse in their apartment, they are trapped in the middle of a deadly game of hide-and-seek. 3/3

3032. **Zubro, Mark,** *Rust on the Razor,* St. Martin's, 1996. Tom and Scott #6 of 14. (Modern Cozy) After he publicly comes out, baseball player Scott Carpenter is besieged by the media, dropped from his endorsements, and sidelined by an injury. Life couldn't get much worse for Scott and his lover, high school teacher Tom Mason. But, of course, it does. Scott's father has a heart attack, and Tom and Scott rush to his side in rural Georgia. When the local sheriff is found murdered, the townspeople would like nothing better than to pin the killing on Tom. –short story "Tea for Two" appears in the anthology *Homicide Hosts Presents* published in 1996 by Wright Way (MLM). 3/3

3033. **Zubro, Mark,** *Are You Nuts?,* St. Martin's, 1998. Tom and Scott #7 of 14. (Modern Cozy) After a difficult summer, the last thing that gay high school teacher Tom Mason needs in the new school year is turmoil. But a conservative parents' group, "worried" about gay teachers corrupting the students, is attempting to take over the local PTA. And it soon gets worse–one of the ringleaders of the parents' group is murdered in the high school after a very contentious PTA meetings, and Tom's best friend is arrested for the crime. 3/3

3034. **Zubro, Mark,** *One Dead Drag Queen,* St. Martin's, 2000. Tom and Scott #8 of 14. (Modern Cozy) A series of three bombs destroy a local health clinic, killing many and injuring many others including high school teacher and clinic volunteer Tom Mason. While Tom is hospitalized, his lover, professional baseball player Scott Carpenter, begins to believe that Tom may have been the intended victim of the bombing - the third bomb was wired to Tom's truck and Scott is receiving threatening letters saying that he's next. 3/3

3035. **Zubro, Mark,** *Here Comes the Corpse,* St. Martin's, 2002. Tom and Scott #9 of 14. (Modern Cozy) Chicago area high school teacher Tom Mason and his lover, professional baseball player Scott Carpenter have had a taxing year. After publicly coming out, Scott and Tom have had to deal with a firestorm of publicity, a major loss of privacy, a great outpouring of support and an equal number of cranks. Now, finally, they are going to do something that they've always wanted - get married in a service before their family and close friends. Despite the potential problems of such of an event, the ceremony comes off with nary a hitch. Tom happens to stumble over an ex-boyfriend from many years ago in the bathroom. Unfortunately, what he stumbles across is actually the corpse of the murdered ex-boyfriend and in addition to casting something of a pall across the proceedings, it puts Tom in the awkward position of being the prime suspect in the murder. 3/3

3036. **Zubro, Mark,** *File Under Dead,* St. Martin's, 2004. Tom and Scott #10 of 14. (Modern Cozy) After years of avoiding volunteer organizations, Chicago high school teacher Tom Mason is finally guilted into volunteering a few hours a week at a local gay services clinic. Since he finds the bitter in-fighting at the organization to be intolerable, and the head of the clinic to be downright poisonous, Tom does his hours on early Saturday morning before anyone else arrives and avoids most of the office politics. But his quiet Saturday goes quickly awry when two gay teens, in a particularly difficult situation, seek him out for counseling early to avoid being seen by anyone else. After they leave, Tom decides to tidy up the cramped, disordered office and file some of the teetering piles that are practically everywhere. Filing turns out to be a surprisingly gruesome task, however, when in one of the filing cabinet drawers Tom finds the severed head of the director of the clinic. 3/3

3037. **Zubro, Mark,** *Everyone's Dead but Us,* St. Martin's, 2006. Tom and Scott #11 of 14. (Modern Cozy) Tom Mason, former Chicago area high school teacher, recently made a public splash by marrying his long-term lover, former professional baseball player Scott Carpenter. After the hoopla surrounding Scott's public coming out and, of course, the marriage, the couple are in dire need of a quiet vacation – somewhere far from the fans, the paparazzi and the general noise of Chicago. Escaping to the privately-held Aegean island of Korkasi – a resort with twenty-two separate villas for those desiring, and who can afford, absolute privacy. But first a building storm traps them – and the others – on the island, cutting them off entirely from the outside world. 3/3

3038. **Zurbo, Mark,** *Schooled in Murder,* St. Martin's, 2008. Tom and Scott #12 of 14. (Modern Cozy) Tom Mason, Chicago area high school teacher, has been teaching at Grover Cleveland High School for a while - long enough to loathe the faculty meetings and long enough to know that as bad as they are, they aren't fatal. Usually. Having had all he can take of the endless bickering, picking and factional disputes, he sneaks out of the meeting for a short break only to find the meeting over when he returns, the usual suspects having departed to the four winds. Having decided that this was a sign of his good fortune, he decides to see if the stockroom actually has the supplies he needs. What he finds there however is a trysting couple in the dark (one married, the other not) and, once the light is turned on, a dead body in the corner. 3/3

3039. **Zubro, Mark,** *Another Dead Republican,* MLR, 2012. Tom and

Scott #13 of 14. (Modern Cozy) Another Dead Republican is a mystery of familial destruction set in a world of violent intrigue and deadly ambition. A ringing phone in the middle of the night set Tom Mason and his lover, baseball player, Scott Carpenter on the trail of a vicious killer in a suburban enclave. Tom's brother-in-law has been murdered. 3/3

3040. **Zubro, Mark**, *A Conspiracy of Fear,* MLR, 2014. Tom and Scott #14 of 14. (Modern Cozy) When an elderly gay man with a lifetime of fear and pain behind him approaches Tom Mason with an intriguing story, Tom has no idea that he and his husband Scott Carpenter will be plunged into an anti-gay conspiracy and a maelstrom of death. They race against time and a deadly killer who may have both of them in his cross-hairs. 3/3

3041. **Zubro, Mark**, *Sorry Now?,* St. Martin's, 1991. Paul Turner #1 of 12. (Police Procedural) While in Chicago, right-wing televangelist Bruce Mucklewrath is attacked, and his daughter killed. Sensing a potential time bomb, and with Mucklewrath creating great pressure, the police brass assigns the case to Detective Paul Turner whom they trust with sensitive matters. During their investigation, Turner and his partner discover that other right-wing bigots have been suffering odd attacks, and they begin to suspect a conspiracy of vengeance, perhaps even from the gay community. 3/3

3042. **Zubro, Mark**, *Political Poison,* St. Martin's, 1993. Paul Turner #2 of 12. (Police Procedural) Did someone in Chicago hate a city alderman enough to kill him? Chicago police detective Paul Turner is assigned the case and discovers that jealous professors and old-guard politicians have guilty secrets to protect. And Turner is not your ordinary cop. He's a widower who happens to be gay and trying to raise his two teen-aged sons. –short story "Mrs. Talucci's Dinner" appeared in the anthology *Murder for Mother* in 1994 by Signet (MLM). 3/3

3043. **Zubro, Mark**, *Another Dead Teenager,* St. Martin's, 1995. Paul Turner #3 of 12. (Police Procedural) When two suburban high-school students are found murdered–both boys who were well respected and liked, with solid family lives and no apparent enemies–Detected Paul Turner is assigned the case. However, as a gay father with two teenage sons and a new lover in his life, Paul Turner has trouble bringing his full attention to bear on the case. But as details slowly emerge, he begins to suspect that he is investigating something deadlier and horrifying than a pair of senseless killings, something that could threaten the lives of the people he holds most dear. 3/3

3044. **Zubro, Mark**, *The Truth can get you Killed,* St. Martin's, 1997. Paul

Turner #4 of 12. (Police Procedural) The last thing that Chicago Police Detective Paul Turner wants to do on New Year's Day is investigate a murder. But when the body is that of a conservative, homophobic judge and it is found outside a popular gay nightclub, the task takes on a new urgency for him. Now Turner must unravel the threads connecting the unlikely victim to his unsuspected murder scene-and look for answers in the most unusual places. 3/3

3045. **Zubro, Mark,** *Drop Dead,* St. Martin's, 1999. Paul Turner #5 of 12. (Police Procedural) When male supermodel Cullom Furyk plummets to his death from the top of a major downtown hotel, gay Chicago Police Detective Paul Turner and his partner, Detective Buck Fenwick, are called to find out what actually happened. One witness claims that Furyk was pushed to his death, and someone involved in Furyk's tumultuous personal or professional life may have played a role in the mysterious incident. Will Turner and Fenwick be able to determine the killer before someone gets away with murder? 3/3

3046. **Zubro, Mark,** *Sex and Murder.com,* St. Martin's, 2001. Paul Turner #6 of 12. (Police Procedural) Craig Lenzati, the rich and powerful CEO of Chicago's answer to Microsoft, is found brutally murdered with stab wounds all over his body. The murder is reported anonymously, and a quick and quiet resolution to the case is demanded by City Hall. 3/3

3047. **Zubro, Mark,** *Dead Egotistical Morons,* St. Martin's, 2003. Paul Turner #7 of 12. (Police Procedural) Boys4U is the world's most popular singing group - at least among teenage girls - and they have closed out their sold-out world tour with a series of shows in Chicago's brand-new arena. The premier group of the inexplicably popular "boy band" trend, they've just finished their very last concert of the tour. While hundreds of tour members, well-wishers, label executives, and various hangers on wait to celebrate another wildly successful tour, the lead singer is found murdered - shot in the back of the head at close range - in the shower of the backstage dressing area. 3/3

3048. **Zubro, Mark,** *Nerds who Kill,* St. Martin's, 2005. Paul Turner #8 of 12. (Police Procedural) [Paul's] life couldn't possibly get more complex and problematic: there's a Science Fiction and Media convention in Chicago this weekend - one of the world's largest such gathering - and his sons are both attending. In full costume. And Paul Turner, like any good father, is going with them. If the prospect of that weren't bad enough, one of the convention's guests - one of the field's most successful fantasy writers - is found murdered, mostly likely by the broadsword found rammed through the corpse's chest. 3/3

3049. **Zubro, Mark,** *Hook, Line, and Homicide,* St. Martin's, 2007. Paul Turner #9 of 12. (Police Procedural) All Chicago police Detective Paul Turner is hoping for on his annual retreat from the city and his job is a little peace and quiet. This time he's headed to the Canadian Great North Woods for a couple of weeks with family and friends – his two teenage sons, his lover Ben, neighborhood pals, and his long-term police partner, Detective Buck Fenwick, along with his wife. But hopes of tranquility are soon crushed when Turner intervenes in a scuffle between a group of First Nations teens and a local bully and his cohorts. In the days following the incident, Turner and company find themselves the object of a series of attacks, break-ins, and sabotage of their equipment. Unable to get the attention of the local police, the events continue to escalate, culminating in the local bully's dead body being found floating in the water near the dock of their houseboat. 3/3

3050. **Zubro, Mark,** *Black and Blue and Pretty Dead Too,* MLR, 2011. Paul Turner #10 of 12. (Police Procedural) A brutal Chicago cop is found murdered at a gay leather festival. Turner, plus his police department partner, Buck Fenwick are assigned the case. Through a rising tide of danger, they need to find the truth among police corruption and cover ups. Some top cops and A-list leather queens are among those whose lies and fears drive the web of desperation and deceit that Turner and his partner must unravel. 3/3

3051. **Zubro, Mark,** *Pawn of Satan,* MLR, 2013. Paul Turner #11 of 12. (Police Procedural) A dead bishop - scandal in the church. Amid concerns about his sons, detective Paul Turner's new case involves a dead Catholic bishop in Chicago. The intrigue and scandal swirling around the bishop while he was alive are nothing compared to the danger and deception that follow his murder. 3/3

3052. **Zubro, Mark,** *Ring of Silence,* MLR, 2017. Paul Turner #12 of 12. (Police Procedural) Paul Turner, gay police detective, would do the right thing and put a stop to a Chicago cop shooting an unarmed teenager. But that is only the beginning of the intrigue, danger, and death that surrounds them in a ring of silence as they try to solve a mystery and do the right thing for themselves, their families, their colleagues, the community, and the rule of law. 3/3

3053. **Zubro, Mark,** *Alien Quest,* MLR, 2013. Alien Danger #1 of 3. (MM Science Fiction) Chicago waiter Mike Carlson stumbles into intergalactic intrigue and romance as he becomes involved with Joe, an alien cop, who lands on Earth in pursuit of a dangerous mad scientist bent on taking over our corner of the universe. 3/3

3054. **Zubro, Mark,** *Alien Home,* MLR, 2014. Alien Danger #2 of 3. (MM Science Fiction) True love trying to survive against galactic dangers.

Through a maelstrom of intergalactic intrigue, cosmic danger, and terran peril, Mike Carlson, intrepid waiter madly in love with a man from another planet, must navigate between extremes of familial joy and hate balanced against the intrigues and wiles on Earth and out among the vast stars of the universe. 3/3

3055. **Zubro, Mark,** *Alien Victory,* MLR, 2015. Alien Danger #3 of 3. (MM Science Fiction) Mike from Earth, and Joe from Hrrrm an unlikely pair to have fallen in love. Together they struggle to build a world safe for gay people and keep the dangers and prejudices of the world at bay. All leading to the final titanic battle between prejudice and all that is good and kind. 3/3

3056. **Zubro, Mark,** *Safe,* MLR, 2014. Roger and Steve #1 of 3. (MM YA Mystery) Roger Cook is in the middle of his senior year when Kyle Davis, the most picked on kid in his high school commits suicide. Roger agrees to write an article on Kyle for the school newspaper. As he gathers information, Roger realizes the dead boy was gay and may have been murdered. Gay himself, Roger wants to find out the truth, but this leads him to danger and the possibility of love. Roger opens himself to even greater risk while trying to make those around him safe. 3/3

3057. **Zubro, Mark,** *Hope,* MLR, 2015. Roger and Steve #2 of 3. (MM YA Mystery) Roger Cook and Steve Koemer have been dating. Their world is turned upside down when Steve's father and mother find out he's gay and throw him out of the house. Then the ugliness and fear begin to build. Steve's father is murdered. The Church he was pastor of was in financial trouble, but the man was also involved in a plot against the two boys. A plot which was designed to destroy their relationship, and which continues even after his death. The boys must race to find out who the killer is and who is plotting against them. When the whole world seems against them, they have the hope of their love to sustain them. 3/3

3058. **Zubro, Mark,** *Always,* MLR, 2018. Roger and Steve #3 of 3. (MM YA Mystery) Roger and Steve are off to the prom and a night out together. While watching the stars traverse the desert sky, they stumble upon a horrific crime and are soon involved in danger and intrigue. The lives of openly gay high school students can be a whole lot better than they used to be, and a whole lot worse. They must uncover who is out to get them before they themselves become victims. 3/3

3059. **Zubro, Mark,** *Dying to Play,* MLR, 2015. Mike King #1 of 2. (Hard Boiled) Gay PI Mike King is called upon to investigate what is happening to a minor league baseball team. He follows the trail of drugs, death, and destruction through the deadly dangers he finds in the rural community. Through the lives of the hot studs involved in baseball, he has to navigate to find the truth about what is happening to them and their dreams. 3/3

3060. **Zubro, Mark,** *Dying for a Thrill,* MLR, 2016. Mike King #2 of 2. (Hard Boiled) Detective Mike King finds himself investigating international intrigue while the worst blizzard in Chicago history rages outside. A group of gay computer hackers desperately asks for his help and protection. As Mike King and his cohorts deal with the usual apocalyptic folderol of spies, plots, and fear, they have to blast their way, or trudge their way through building mountains of snow. A dead body, no one can find, plots against various characters and governments and individuals around the world become centered on a group of gay self-proclaimed Robin Hoods. It's up to Mike King to sort it out before the world caves in on them or himself. 3/3

3061. **Zubro, Mark,** *Gentle,* MLR, 2016. Shane and Corey #1 of 1. (MM YA Mystery) Shane Semereau wants to be left alone to read his books and carve his wood sculptures in the warm desert. His life is a swarm of confusion and violence, but he wants to be a force in making the world a gentle place. He grasps at those dreams. Cory Garcia is a bundle of electric energy who lashes out at everyone and everything but loves to let his mind go in the world of dance. Amidst great danger and looming violence, they find each other and unite against all that is arrayed against them at every turn. –Zubro states that he is working on the next book in the series (MLM). 3/3

The Man with the Watches:

Brief history:

The oldest example of a gay character I found was in the short story series, *Round the Fire Stories* by Arthur Conan Doyle which were written to be read around the fireplace some late wintery night, at least as far as Doyle is concerned, "This would be an ideal atmosphere for such stories...however, if they have the good fortune to give pleasure to any one, at any time or place, their author will be very pleased." The stories included in the collection are "concerned with the grotesque and with the terrible." I am unsure which *The Man with the Watches* falls under unless terrible describes the sad loss of life and the situation which caused it as there doesn't seem to be any grotesque aspect. I would hate for the story to be construed as grotesque simply for the gay relationship or the cross dressing. The debate over whether or not Sherlock Holmes was gay and had an attachment to Watson can be and probably will be argued over for as long as the characters are popular enough to be debated over. However, the two characters in this story obviously have feelings for each other as Sparrow MacCoy states towards the end, "You loved your brother, I've no doubt; but you didn't love him a cent more than I loved him, though you'll say that I took a queer way to show it." Edward was described as "young, short, smooth cheeked, and delicately featured," and took to dressing in drag to pull off criminal stunts or to avoid detection by the police. The main character, James, derides his brother for wearing drag and after Edward removes the women's clothing James throws it off the train and states that "'you'll never make a Mary Jane of yourself while I can help it." Mary Jane being an effeminate male homosexual in the late 19th, early 20th century slang. There is no ambiguity. Edward and Sparrow are a gay couple and although they're criminals their relationship is not discussed in a derisive manner.

THE MAN WITH THE WATCHES

by Arthur Conan Doyle*

THERE ARE MANY WHO WILL still bear in mind the singular circumstances which, under the heading of the Rugby Mystery, filled many columns of the daily Press in the spring of the year 1892. Coming as it did at a period of exceptional dullness, it attracted perhaps rather more attention than it deserved, but it offered to the public that mixture of the whimsical and the tragic which is most stimulating to the popular imagination. Interest dropped, however, when, after weeks of fruitless investigation, it was found that no final explanation of the facts was forthcoming, and the tragedy seemed from that time to the present to have finally taken its place in the dark catalogue of inexplicable and unexpiated crimes. A recent communication (the authenticity of which appears to be above question) has, however, thrown some new and clear light upon the matter. Before laying it before the public it would be as well, perhaps, that I should refresh their memories as to the singular facts upon which this commentary is founded. These facts were briefly as follows:

At five o'clock on the evening of the 18th of March in the year already mentioned a train left Euston Station for Manchester. It was a rainy, squally day, which grew wilder as it progressed, so it was by no means the weather in which anyone would travel who was not driven to do so by necessity. The train, however, is a favorite one among Manchester businessmen who are returning from town, for it does the journey in four hours and twenty minutes, with only three stoppages upon the way. In spite of the inclement evening it was, therefore, fairly well filled upon the occasion of which I speak. The guard of the train was a tried servant of the company — a man who had worked for twenty-two years without blemish or complaint. His name was John Palmer.

The station clock was upon the stroke of five, and the guard was about to give the customary signal to the engine-driver when he observed two belated passengers hurrying down the platform. The one was an exceptionally tall man, dressed in a long black overcoat with astrakhan collar and cuffs. I have already said that the evening was an inclement one, and the tall traveler had the high, warm collar turned up to protect his throat against the bitter March wind. He appeared, as far as the guard could judge by so hurried an inspection, to be a man between fifty and sixty years of age, who had retained a good deal of the vigor and activity of his youth. In one hand he carried a brown leather Gladstone bag. His companion was a lady, tall and erect, walking with a vigorous step which out-paced the gentleman beside her. She wore a long, fawn colored dust-cloak, a black, close-fitting toque, and a dark veil which concealed the greater part of her face. The two might very well have passed as father and daughter. They walked swiftly down the line of carriages, glancing in at the windows, until the guard, John Palmer, overtook them.

"Now, then, sir, look sharp, the train is going," said he.

"First-class," the man answered.

The guard turned the handle of the nearest door. In the carriage, which he had opened, there sat a small man with a cigar in his mouth. His appearance seems to have impressed itself upon the guard's memory, for he was prepared, afterward, to describe or to identify him. He was a man of thirty-four or thirty-five years of age, dressed in some gray material, sharp-nosed, alert, with a ruddy, weather-beaten face, and a small, closely cropped black beard. He glanced up as the door was opened. The tall man paused with his foot upon the step.

"This is a smoking compartment. The lady dislikes smoke," said he, looking round at the guard.

"All right! Here you are, sir!" said John Palmer. He slammed the door of the smoking carriage, opened that of the next one, which was empty, and thrust the two travelers in. At the same moment he sounded his whistle and the wheels of the train began to move. The man with the cigar was at the window of his carriage, and said something to the guard as he rolled past him, but the words were lost in the bustle of the departure. Palmer stepped into the guard's van, as it came up to him, and thought no more of the incident.

Twelve minutes after its departure the train reached Willesden Junction, where it stopped for a very short interval. An examination of the tickets has made it certain that no one either joined or left it at this time, and no passenger was seen to alight upon the platform. At 5:14 the journey to Manchester was resumed, and Rugby was reached at 6:50, the express being five minutes late.

At Rugby the attention of the station officials was drawn to the fact that the door of one of the first-class carriages was open. An examination of that compartment, and of its neighbor, disclosed a remarkable state of affairs,

The smoking carriage in which the short, red-faced man with the black beard had been seen was now empty. Save for a half-smoked cigar, there was no trace whatever of its recent occupant. The door of this carriage was fastened. In the next compartment, to which attention had been originally drawn, there was no sign either of the gentleman with the astrakhan collar or of the young lady who accompanied him. All three passengers had disappeared. On the other hand, there was found upon the floor of this carriage — the one in which the tall traveler and the lady had been ——— a young man, fashionably dressed and of elegant appearance. He lay with his knees drawn up, and his head resting against the further door, an elbow upon either seat. A bullet had penetrated his heart and his death must have been instantaneous. No one had seen such a man enter the train, and no railway ticket was found in his pocket, neither were there any markings upon his linen, nor papers nor personal property which might help to identify him. Who he was, whence he had come, and how he had met his end were each as great a mystery as what had occurred to the three people who had started an hour and a half before from Willesden in those two compartments.

I have said that there was no personal property which might help to identify him, but it is true that there was one peculiarity about this unknown young man which was much commented upon at the time. In his pockets were found no fewer than six valuable gold watches, three in the various pockets of his waistcoat, one in his ticket-pocket, one in his breast-pocket, and one small one in a leather strap and fastened round his left wrist. The obvious explanation that the man was a pick-pocket, and that this was his plunder, was discounted by the fact that all six were of American make, and of a type which is rare in England. Three of them bore the mark of the Rochester Watch making Company; one was by Mason, of Elmira; one was unmarked; and the small one, which was highly jeweled and ornamented, was from Tiffany, of New York. The other contents of his pocket consisted of an ivory knife with a corkscrew by Rodgers, of Sheffield; a small circular mirror, one inch in diameter; a re-admission slip to the Lyceum theater; a silver box full of vesta matches, and a brown leather cigar-case containing two cheroots — also two pounds fourteen shillings in money. It was clear, then, that whatever motives may have led to his death, robbery was not among them. As already mentioned, there were no markings upon the man's linen, which appeared to be new, and no tailor's name upon his coat. In appearance he was young, short, smooth cheeked, and delicately featured. One of his front teeth was conspicuously stopped with gold.

On the discovery of the tragedy an examination was instantly made of the tickets of all passengers, and the number of the passengers themselves was counted. It was found that only three tickets were unaccounted for, corresponding to the three travelers who were missing. The express was then allowed to proceed, but a new guard was sent with it, and John Palmer was detained as a witness at Rugby. The carriage which included the two compartments in question was uncoupled and side-tracked. Then, on the arrival of Inspector Vane, of Scotland Yard, and of Mr. Henderson, a detective in the service of the railway company, an exhaustive inquiry was made into all the circumstances.

That crime had been committed was certain. The bullet, which appeared to have come from a small pistol or revolver, had been fired from some little distance, as there was no scorching of the clothes. No weapon was found in the compartment (which finally disposed of the theory of suicide), nor was there any sign of the brown leather bag which the guard had seen in the hand of the tall gentleman. A lady's parasol was found upon the rack, but no other trace was to be seen of the travelers in either of the sections. Apart from the crime, the question of how or why three passengers (one of them a lady) could get out of the train, and one other get in during the unbroken run between Willesden and Rugby, was one which excited the utmost curiosity among the general public, and gave rise to much speculation in the London Press.

John Palmer, the guard, was able at the inquest to give some evidence which threw a little light upon the matter. There was a spot between Tring and Cheddington, according to his statement, where, on account of some repairs to the line, the train had for a few minutes slowed down to a pace not exceeding eight or ten miles an hour. At that place it might be possible for a man, or even for an exceptionally active woman, to have left the train without serious injury. It was true that a gang of platelayers was there, and that they had seen nothing, but it was their custom to stand in the middle between the metals, and the open carriage door was upon the far side, so that it was conceivable that someone might have alighted unseen, as the darkness would by that time be drawing in. A steep embankment would instantly screen anyone who sprang from the observation of the navvies.

The guard also deposed that there was a good deal of movement upon the platform at Willesden Junction, and that though it was certain that no one had either joined or left the train there, it was still quite possible that some of the passengers might have changed unseen from one compartment to another. It was by no means uncommon for a gentleman to finish his cigar in a smoking carriage and then to change to a clearer atmosphere. Supposing that the man with the black beard had done so at Willesden (and the half-smoked cigar upon the floor seemed to favor the supposition), he would naturally go into the nearest section, which would bring him into the company of the two other actors in this drama. Thus the first stage of the affair might be surmised without any great breach of probability. But what the second stage had been, or how the final one had been arrived at, neither the guard nor the experienced detective officers could suggest.

A careful examination of the line between Willesden and Rugby resulted in one discovery which might or might not have a bearing upon the tragedy. Near Tring, at the very place where the train slowed down, there was found at the bottom of the embankment a small pocket Testament, very shabby and worn. It was printed by the Bible Society of London, and bore an inscription: "From John to Alice. Jan. 13th, 1856," upon the fly-leaf. Underneath was written: "James, July 4th, 1859," and beneath that again: "Edward, Nov. 1st, 1869," all the entries being in the same handwriting. This was the only clew, if it could be called a clew, which the police obtained, and the coroner's verdict of "Murder by a person or persons unknown" was the unsatisfactory ending of a singular case. Advertisements, rewards and inquiries proved equally fruitless, and nothing could be found which was solid enough to form the basis for a profitable investigation.

It would be a mistake, however, to suppose that no theories were formed to account for the facts. On the contrary, the Press, both in England and in America, teemed with suggestions and suppositions, most of which were obviously absurd. The fact that the watches were of American make, and some peculiarities in connection with the gold stopping of his front tooth, appeared to indicate that the deceased was a citizen of the United States, though his linen, clothes, and boots were undoubtedly of British manufacture. It was surmised, by some, that he was concealed under the seat, and that, being discovered, he was for some reason, possibly because he had overheard their guilty secrets, put to death by his fellow passengers. When coupled with generalities as to the ferocity and cunning of anarchical and other secret societies, this theory sounded as plausible as any.

The fact that he should be without a ticket would be consistent with the idea of concealment, and it was well known that women played a prominent part in the Nihilistic propaganda. On the other hand, it was clear from the guard's statement, that the man must have been hidden there *before* the others arrived, and how unlikely the coincidence that conspirators should stray exactly into the very compartment in which a spy was already concealed! Besides, this explanation ignored the man in the smoking carriage, and gave no reason at all for his simultaneous disappearance. The police had little difficulty in showing that such a theory would not cover the facts, but they were unprepared in the absence of evidence to advance any alternative explanation.

There was a letter in the *Daily Gazette,* over the signature of a well-known criminal investigator, which gave rise to considerable discussion at the time. He had formed a hypothesis which had at least ingenuity to recommend it, and I cannot do better than append it in his own words.

"Whatever may be the truth," said he, "it must depend upon some bizarre and rare combination of events, so we need have no hesitation in postulating such events in our explanation. In the absence of data we must abandon the analytic or scientific method of investigation, and must approach it in the synthetic fashion. In a word, instead of taking known events and deducing from them what has occurred, we must build up a fanciful explanation if it will only be consistent with known events. We can then test this explanation by any fresh facts which may arise. If they all fit into their places, the probability is that we are upon the right track, and with each fresh fact this probability increases in a geometrical progression until the evidence becomes final and convincing.

"Now, there is one most remarkable and suggestive fact which has not met with the attention which it deserves. There is a local train running through Harrow and King's Langley, which is timed in such a way that the express must have overtaken it at or about the period when it eased down its speed to eight miles an hour on account of the repairs of the line. The two trains would at that time be traveling in the same direction at a similar rate of speed and upon parallel lines. It is within everyone's experience how, under such circumstances, the occupant of each carriage can see very plainly the passengers in the other carriages opposite to him. The lamps of the express had been lit at Willesden, so that each compartment was brightly illuminated, and most visible to an observer from outside.

"Now, the sequence of events as I reconstruct them would be after this fashion. This young man with the abnormal number of watches was alone in the carriage of the slow train. His ticket, with his papers and gloves and other things, was we will suppose, on the seat beside him. He was probably an American, and also probably a man of weak intellect. The excessive wearing of jewelry is an early symptom in some forms of mania.

"As he sat watching the carriages of the express which were (on account of the state of the line) going at the same pace as himself, he suddenly saw some people in it whom he knew. We will suppose for the sake of our theory that these people were a woman whom he loved and a man whom he hated — and who in return hated him. The young man was excitable and impulsive. He opened the door of his carriage, stepped from the footboard of the local train to the footboard of the express, opened the other door, and made his way into the presence of these two people. The feat (on the supposition that the trains were going at the same pace) is by no means so perilous as it might appear.

"Having now got our young man without his ticket into the carriage in which the elder man and the young woman are traveling, it is not difficult to imagine that a violent scene ensued. It is possible that the pair were also Americans, which is the more probable as the man carried a weapon — an unusual thing in England. If our supposition of incipient mania is correct, the young man is likely to have assaulted the other. As the upshot of the quarrel the elder man shot the intruder, and then made his escape from the carriage, taking the young lady with him. We will suppose that all this happened very rapidly, and that the train was still going at so slow a pace that it was not difficult for them to leave it. A woman might leave a train going at eight miles an hour. As a matter of fact, we know that this woman did do so.

"And now we have to fit in the man in the smoking carriage. Presuming that we have, up to this point, reconstructed the tragedy correctly, we shall find nothing in this other man to cause us to reconsider our conclusions. According to my theory, this man saw the young fellow cross from one train to the other, saw him open the door, heard the pistol-shot, saw the two fugitives spring out on to the line, realized that murder had been done, and sprang out himself in pursuit. Why he has never been heard of since — whether he met his own death in the pursuit, or whether, as is more likely, he was made to realize that it was not a case for his interference - is a detail which we have at present no means of explaining. I acknowledge that there are some difficulties in the way. At first sight, it might seem improbable that at such a moment a murderer would burden himself in his flight with a brown leather bag. My answer is that he was well aware that if the bag were found his identity would be established. It was absolutely necessary for him to take it with him. My theory stands or falls upon one point, and I call upon the railway company to make strict inquiry as to whether a ticket was found unclaimed in the local train through Harrow and King's Langley upon the 18th of March. If such a ticket were found my case is proved. If not, my theory may still be the correct one, for it is conceivable either that he traveled without a ticket or that his ticket was lost."

To this elaborate and plausible hypothesis the answer of the police and of the company was, first, that no such ticket was found; secondly, that the slow train would never run parallel to the express; and, thirdly, that the local train had been stationary in King's Langley Station when the express, going at fifty miles an hour, had flashed past it. So perished the only satisfying explanation, and five years have elapsed without supplying a new one. Now, at last, there comes a statement which covers all the facts, and which must be regarded as authentic. It took the shape of a letter dated from New York, and addressed to the same criminal investigator whose theory I have quoted. It is given here in extenso, with the exception of the two opening paragraphs, which are personal in their nature:

"You'll excuse me if I'm not very free with names. There's less reason now than there was five years ago when mother was still living. But for all that, I had rather cover up our tracks all I can. But I owe you an explanation, for if your idea of it was wrong, it was a mighty ingenious one all the same. I'll have to go back a little so as you may understand all about it.

"My people came from Bucks, England, and emigrated to the States in the early fifties. They settled in Rochester, in the State of New York, where my father ran a large dry goods store. There were only two sons: myself, James, and my brother, Edward. I was ten years older than my brother, and after my father died, I sort of took the place of a father to him, as an elder brother would. He was a bright, spirited boy, and just one of the most beautiful creatures that ever lived. But there was always a soft spot in him, and it was like mold in cheese, for it spread and spread, and nothing that you could do would stop it. Mother saw it just as clearly as I did, but she went on spoiling him all the same, for he had such a way with him that you could refuse him nothing. I did all I could to hold him in, and he hated me for my pains.

"At last he fairly got his head, and nothing that we could do would stop him. He got off into New York, and went rapidly from bad to worse. At first he was only fast, and then he was criminal; and then, at the end of a year or two, he was one of the most notorious young crooks in the city. He had formed a friendship with Sparrow MacCoy, who was at the head of his profession as a bunco-steerer, green goodsman, and general rascal. They took to card-sharping, and frequented some of the best hotels in New York. My brother was an excellent actor (he might have made an honest name for himself if he had chosen), and he would take the parts of a young Englishman of title, of a simple lad from the West, or of a college undergraduate, whichever suited Sparrow MacCoy's purpose. And then one day he dressed himself as a girl, and he carried it off so well, and made himself such a valuable decoy, that it was their favorite game afterward. They had made it right with Tammany and with the police, so it seemed as if nothing could ever stop them, for those were in the days before the Lexow Commission, and if you only had a pull, you could do pretty nearly everything you wanted.

"And nothing would have stopped them if they had only stuck to cards and New York, but they must needs come up Rochester way, and forge a name upon a check. It was my brother that did it, though everyone knew that it was under the influence of Sparrow

MacCoy. I bought up that check, and a pretty sum it cost me. Then I went to my brother, laid it before him on the table, and swore to him that I would prosecute if he did not clear out of the country. At first he simply laughed. I could not prosecute, he said, without breaking our mother's heart, and he knew that I would not do that. I made him understand, however, that our mother's heart was being broken in any case, and that I had set firm on the point that I would rather see him in a Rochester jail than in a New York hotel. So at last he gave in, and he made me a solemn promise that he would see Sparrow MacCoy no more, that he would go to Europe, and that he would turn his hand to any honest trade that I helped him to get. I took him down right away to an old family friend, Joe Willson, who is an exporter of American watches and clocks, and I got him to give Edward an agency in London, with a small salary and a 15 per cent. commission on all business. His manner and appearance were so good that he won the old man over at once, and within a week he was sent off to London with a case full of samples.

"It seemed to me that this business of the check had really given my brother a fright, and that there was some chance of his settling down into an honest line of life. My mother had spoken with him, and what she said had touched him, for she had always been the best of mothers to him, and he had been the great sorrow of her life. But I knew that this man Sparrow MacCoy had a great influence over Edward, and my chance of keeping the lad straight lay, in breaking the connection between them. I had a friend in the New York detective force, and through him I kept a watch upon MacCoy. When within a fortnight of my brother's sailing I heard that MacCoy had taken a berth in the *Etruria*, I was as certain as if he had told me that he was going over to England for the purpose of coaxing Edward back again into the ways that he had left. In an instant I had resolved to go also, and to put my influence against MacCoy's. I knew it was a losing fight, but I thought, and my mother thought, that it was my duty. We passed the last night together in prayer for my success, and she gave me her own Testament that my father had given her on the day of their marriage in the Old Country, so that I might always wear it next my heart.

"I was a fellow-traveler, on the steamship, with Sparrow Mac-Coy, and at least I had the satisfaction of spoiling his little game for the voyage. The very first night I went into the smoking-room, and found him at the head of a card table, with half-a-dozen young fellows who were carrying their full purses and their empty skulls over to Europe. He was settling down for his harvest, and a rich one it would have been. But I soon changed all that.

"'Gentlemen,' said I, 'are you aware whom you are playing with?'

"'What's that to you? You mind your own business!' said he, with an oath.

"'Who is it, anyway?' asked one of the dudes.

"'He's Sparrow MacCoy, the most notorious card sharper in the States.'

"Up he jumped with a bottle in his hand, but he remembered that he was under the flag of the effete Old Country, where law and order run, and Tammany has no pull. Jail and the gallows wait for violence and murder, and there's no slipping out by the back door on board an ocean liner.

"'Prove your words, you —!' said he.

"'I will!' said I. 'If you will turn up your right shirt sleeve to the shoulder, I will either prove my words or I will eat them.'

"He turned white and said not a word. You see, I knew something of his ways, and I was aware that part of the mechanism which he and all such sharpers use consists of an elastic down the arm with a clip just above the wrist. It is by means of this clip that they withdraw from their hands the cards which they do not want, while they substitute other cards from another hiding-place. I reckoned on it being there, and it was. He cursed me, slunk out of the saloon, and was hardly seen again during the voyage. For once, at any rate, I got level with Mister Sparrow MacCoy.

"But he soon had his revenge upon me, for when it came to influencing my brother he outweighed me every time. Edward had kept himself straight in London for the first few weeks, and had done some business with his American watches, until this villain came across his path once more. I did my best, but the best was little enough. The next thing I heard there had been a scandal at one of the Northumberland Avenue hotels: a traveler had been fleeced of a large sum by two confederate card-sharpers, and the matter was in the hands of Scotland Yard. The first I learned of it was in the evening paper, and I was at once certain that my brother and MacCoy were back at their old games. I hurried at once to Edward's lodgings. They told me that he and a tall gentleman (whom I recognized as MacCoy) had gone off together, and that he had left the lodgings and taken his things with him. The landlady had heard them give several directions to the cabman, ending with Euston Station, and she had accidentally overheard the tall gentleman saying something about Manchester. She believed that that was their destination.

"A glance at the time-table showed me that the most likely train was at five, though there was another at 4:35 which they might have caught. I had only time to get the later one, but found no sign of them either at the depot or in the train. They must have gone on by the earlier one, so I determined to follow them to Manchester and search for them in the hotels there. One last appeal to my brother by all that he owed to my mother might even now be the salvation of him. My nerves were overstrung, and I lit a cigar to steady them. At that moment, just as the train was moving off, the door of my compartment was flung open, and there were MacCoy and my brother on the platform.

"They were both disguised, and with good reason, for they knew that the London police were after them. MacCoy had a great astrakhan collar drawn up, so that only his eyes and nose were showing. My brother was dressed like a woman, with a black veil half down his face, but of course it did not deceive me for an instant, nor would it have done so even if I had not known that he had often used such a dress before. I started up, and as I did so MacCoy recognized me. He said something, the conductor slammed the door, and they were shown into the next compartment. I tried to stop the train so as to follow them, but the wheels were already moving, and it was too late.

"When we stopped at Willesden, I instantly changed my carriage. It appears that I was not seen to do so, which is not surprising, as the station was crowded with people. MacCoy, of course, was expecting me, and he had spent the time between Euston and Willesden in saying all he could to harden my brother's heart and set him against me. That is what I fancy, for I had never found him so impossible to soften or to move. I tried this way and I tried that; I pictured his future in an English jail; I described the sorrow of his mother when I came back with the news; I said everything to touch his heart, but all to no purpose. He sat there with a fixed sneer upon his handsome face, while every now and then Sparrow MacCoy would throw in a taunt at me or some word of encouragement to hold my brother to his resolutions.

"Why don't you run a Sunday-school?' he would say to me, and then, in the same breath: "He thinks you have no will of your own. He thinks you are just the baby brother and that he can lead you where he likes. He's only just finding out that you are a man as well as he."

"It was those words of his which set me talking bitterly. We had left Willesden, you understand, for all this took some time. My temper got the better of me, and for the first time in my life I let my brother see the rough side of me. Perhaps it would have been better had I done so earlier and more often.

"A man!' said I. "Well, I'm glad to have your friend's assurance of it, for no one would suspect it to see you like a boarding-school missy. I don't suppose in all this country there is a more contemptible-looking creature than you are as you sit there with that Dolly pinafore upon you.' He colored up at that, for he was a vain man, and he winced from ridicule.

"It's only a dust-cloak," said he, and he slipped it off. "One has to throw the coppers off one's scent, and I had no other way to do it.' He took his toque off with the veil attached, and he put both it and the cloak into his brown bag.

"Anyway, I don't need to wear it until the conductor comes round,' said he.

"Nor then, either,' said I, and taking the bag I slung it with all my force out of the window.

"Now,' said I, 'you'll never make a Mary Jane of yourself while I can help it. If nothing but that disguise stands between you and a jail, then to jail you shall go.'

"That was the way to manage him. I felt my advantage at once. His supple nature was one which yielded to roughness far more readily than to entreaty. He flushed with shame, and his eyes filled with tears. But MacCoy saw my advantage also, and was determined that I should not pursue it.

"He's my pard, and you shall not bully him,' he cried.

"He's my brother, and you shall not ruin him,' said I. "I believe a spell of prison is the very best way of keeping you apart, and you shall have it, or it will be no fault of mine.'

"Oh, you would squeal, would you?' he cried, and in an instant he whipped out his revolver. I sprang for his hand, but saw that I was too late, and jumped aside. At the same instant he fired, and the bullet which would have struck me passed through the heart of my unfortunate brother.

"He dropped without a groan upon the floor of the compartment, and MacCoy and I, equally horrified, knelt at each side of him, trying to bring back some signs of life. MacCoy still held the loaded revolver in his hand, but his anger against me and my resentment toward him had both for the moment been swallowed up in this sudden tragedy. It was he who first realized the situation. The train was for some reason going very slowly at the moment and he saw his opportunity for escape. In an instant he had the door open, but I was as quick as he, and jumping upon him the two of us fell off the foot-board and rolled in each other's arms down a steep embankment. At the bottom I struck my head against a stone, and I remembered nothing more. When I came to myself I was lying among some low bushes, not far from the railroad track, and somebody was bathing my head with a wet handkerchief. It was Sparrow MacCoy.

"I guess I couldn't leave you,' said he. "I didn't want to have the blood of two of you on my hands in one day. You loved your brother, I've no doubt; but you didn't love him a cent more than I loved him, though you'll say that I took a queer way to show it. Anyhow, it seems a mighty empty world now that he is gone, and I don't care a continental whether you give me over to the hangman or not.'

"He had turned his ankle in the fall, and there we sat, he with his useless foot, and I with my throbbing head, and we talked and talked until gradually my bitterness began to soften and to turn into something like sympathy. What was the use of revenging his death upon a man who was as much stricken by that death as I was? And then, as my wits gradually returned, I began to realize also that I could do nothing against MacCoy which would not recoil upon my mother and myself. How could we convict him without a full account of my brother's career being made public — the very thing which of all others we wished to avoid? It was really as much our interest as his to cover the matter up, and from being an avenger of crime I found myself changed to a conspirator against Justice. The place in which we found ourselves was one of those pheasant preserves which are so common in the Old Country, and as we groped our way through it I found myself consulting the slayer of my brother as to how far it would be possible to hush it up.

"I soon realized from what he said that unless there were some papers of which we knew nothing in my brother's pockets, there was really no possible means by which the police could identify him or learn how he had got there. His ticket was in MacCoy's pocket, and so was the ticket for some baggage which they had left at the depot. Like most Americans, he had found it cheaper and easier to buy an outfit in London than to bring one from New York, so that all his linen and clothes were new and unmarked. The bag, containing the dust cloak, which I had thrown out of the window, may have fallen among some bramble patch where it is still concealed, or may have been carried off by some tramp, or may have come into the possession of the police, who kept the incident to themselves. Anyhow, I have seen nothing about it in the London papers. As to the watches, they were a selection from those which had been entrusted to him for business purposes. It may have been for the same business purposes that he was taking them to Manchester, but — well, it's too late to enter into that.

"I don't blame the police for being at fault. I don't see how it could have been otherwise. There was just one little clew that they might have followed up but it was a small one. I mean that small circular mirror which was found in my brother's pocket. It isn't a very common thing for a young man to carry about with him, is it? But a gambler might have told you what such a mirror may mean to a card-sharper. If you sit back a little from the table, and lay the mirror, face upward, upon your lap, you can see, as you deal, every card that you give to your adversary. It is not hard to say whether you see a man or raise him when you know his cards as well as your own. It was as much a part of a sharper's outfit as the elastic clip upon Sparrow MacCoy's arm. Taking that, in connection with the recent frauds at the hotels, the police might have got hold of one end of the string.

"I don't think there is much more for me to explain. We got to a village called Amersham that night in the character of two gentlemen upon a walking tour, and afterward we made our way quietly to London, whence MacCoy went on to Cairo and I returned to New York. My mother died six months afterward, and I am glad to say that to the day of her death she never knew what happened. She was always under the delusion that Edward was earning an honest living in London, and I never had the heart to tell her the truth. He never wrote; but, then, he never did write at any time, so that made no difference. His name was the last upon her lips.

"There's just one other thing that I have to ask you, sir, and I should take it as a kind return for all this explanation, if you could do it for me. You remember that Testament that was picked up. I always carried it in my inside pocket, and it must have come out in my fall. I value it very highly, for it was the family book with my birth and my brother's marked by my father in the beginning of it. I wish you would apply at the proper place and have it sent to me. It can be of no possible value to anyone else. If you address it to X, Bassano's Library, Broadway, New York, it is sure to come to hand."

*Doyle, Arthur Conan, *Round the Fire Stories*, New York: McClure Company, 1908.

References:

Emkay, Hunter. "Elements of the Psychological Thriller, Mystery, Suspense and/or Crime Fiction Genres." hunterswritings.com, 12 Oct. 2012, hunterswritings.com/2012/10/12/elements-of-the-psychological-thriller-mystery-suspense-andor-crime-fiction-genres/.

Evans, Curtis, ed. *Murder in the Closet: Essays on Queer Clues in Crime Fiction Before Stonewall.* Jefferson, NC: McFarland & Company, 2017.

Gunn, Drewey Wayne. *The Gay Male Sleuth in Print and Film: A History and Annotated Bibliography.* Lanham, MD: The Scarecrow Press, 2013.

Kahn, Joseph P. "A life story with more twists than anything husband Robert Parker could have concocted." Bullets and Beer, Fandom Books, 2 May 1996, bulletsandbeer.fandom.com/wiki/A_life_story_with_more_twists_than_anything_husband_Robert_Parker_could_have_concocted.

Mason, Michael. "Then and Now, 1976." Times Literary Supplement, The Times, 25 Oct. 2012, www.the-tls.co.uk/articles/public/then-and-now-1976-raymond-chandler/.

Penzler, Otto. *Bibliomysteries: An Annotated Bibliography of First Editions of Mystery Fiction Set in the World of Books, 1849-2000.* New York: Mysterious Press, 2014.

Roger, Stephen D. "Cozy to Caper: A Guide to Mystery Genres." Critiqueville: The Guided Online Critique Group, edited by Moira Allen, Writing World, 2002, www.writing-world.com/mystery/genres.shtml.

Slide, Anthony. *Gay and Lesbian Characters and Themes in Mystery Novels: A Critical Guide to over 500 Works in English.* Jefferson, NC: McFarland & Co., 1993.

Steinbach, Christine. "Profile: barbara nadel & cetin ikmen / mehmet süleyman." More and More...Murder, 2 May 2019, www.moreandmoremurder.de/profile-barbara-nadel-cetin-ikmen-mehmet-suleyman/.

Young, Ian. *The Male Homosexual in Literature: A Bibliography.* Meuchen, NJ: The Scarecrow Press, 1982.

MATT LUBBERS-MOORE

One of the founders of ReQueered Tales, Matt served as a judge for the Lambda Literary Award for Best Gay Mystery twice. Matt is over educated with three associate degrees, a bachelor's in History and a minor in Human Rights, as well as working on his second master's degree in History after finishing his first in Library and Information Science in 2019. He lives in a converted creamery in Grand Rapids, Michigan with his farmer and truck driving husband, Doug. Other than ReQueered Tales, Matt works at a bookstore, a comic book store, an academic library. His traveling bookstore appears at comic cons, book fairs, gay pride events, and flea markets. He is also kept busy as one of the administrators of the Gay Mystery-Suspense-Thriller Facebook page. He has four hobbies: collecting gay mysteries, collecting Dr. Doom comics, going to used bookstores and pizza restaurants usually one right after the other, and traveling the country via train.

About ReQueered Tales

In the heady days of the late 1960s, when young people in many western countries were in the streets protesting for a new, more inclusive world, some of us were in libraries, coffee shops, communes, retreats, bedrooms and dens plotting something even more startling: literature—high brow and pulp—for an explicitly gay audience. Specifically, we were craving to see our gay lives—in the closet, in the open, in bars, in dire straits and in love—reflected in mystery stories, romance, paranormal and more. Hercule Poirot, that engaging effete Belgian creation of Agatha Christie might have been gay ... Sherlock Holmes, to all intents and purposes, was one woman shy of gay ... but where were the *genuine gay sleuths*, where the reader need not read between the lines?

Beginning with Victor J Banis's "Man from C.A.M.P." pulps in the mid-60s—riotous romps spoofing the craze for James Bond spies—readers were suddenly being offered George Baxt's Pharoah Love, a black gay New York City detective, and a real turning point in Joseph Hansen's gay California insurance investigator, Dave Brandstetter, whose world weary Raymond Chandleresque adventures sold strongly and have never been out of print.

Over the next three decades, gay storytelling grew strongly in niche and mainstream publishing ventures. Even with the huge public crisis—as AIDS descended on the gay community beginning in the early 1980s—gay fiction flourished. Stonewall Inn, Alyson Publications, and others nurtured authors and readers ... until mainstream success seemed to come to a halt. While Lambda Literary Foundation had started to recognize work in annual awards about 1990, mainstream publishers began to have cold feet. And then, with the rise of ebooks in the new millennium which enabled a new self-publishing industry ... there was both an avalanche of new talent coming to market and burying of print authors who did not cross the divide.

The result?

Perhaps forty years of gay fiction—and notably gay and lesbian mystery, detective and suspense fiction—has been teetering on the brink of obscurity. Orphaned works, orphaned authors, many living and some having passed away—with no one to make the case for their creations to be returned to print (and e-print!).

Until now. That is the mission of *ReQueered Tales*: to bring back to circulation this treasure trove of fantastic fiction which, for one reason or another, has fallen by the wayside. In an era of ebooks, everything of value ought to be accessible. For a new generation of readers, these mystery tales are full of insights into the gay world of the 1960s, '70s, '80s and '90s. And for those of us who lived through the period, they are a delightful reminder of our youth and reflect some of our own struggles in growing up gay in those heady times.

We are honored, here at *ReQueered Tales*, to be custodians shepherding back into circulation some of the best gay and lesbian fiction writing and hope to bring many volumes to the public, in modestly priced, accessible editions, worldwide, over the coming months and years.

So please join us on this adventure of discovery and rediscovery of the rich talents of writers of recent years as the PIs, cops and amateur sleuths battle forces of evil with fierceness, humor and sometimes a pinch of love.

The ReQueered Tales Team

Justene Adamec • Alexander Inglis • Matt Lubbers-Moore

More from ReQueered Tales

The Male Homosexual In Literature
A Bibliography
Ian Young

Ian Young's bibliography has served as a basic guide to English-language works of fiction, drama, poetry and autobiography concerned with male homosexuality or having male homosexual characters. Entries include titles published through 1980. Works of primary importance (those in which homosexuality is a major aspect or which are otherwise of particular relevance) are marked with an asterisk for the convenience of researchers and collectors. Works are identified by author, title, place of publication, publisher, and date. For easy reference, entries are numbered and a title index is provided at the end of the main text. Five highly-acclaimed essays on gay literature by Ian Young, Graham Jackson and Dr. Rictor Norton, including essay on gay publishing, round out the listings. A title index of gay anthologies completes the work.

"Ian Young's 1982 *The Male Homosexual in Literature: A Bibliography* is an outstanding work of careful research and dedication." – Michael Bronski in *Pulp Friction*

This edition is reset, but identical to, the classic and definitive 2nd edition, available the first time as an ebook and in print for the first time in decades.

The Male Homosexual In Literature
A Bibliography Supplement
Ian Young

The present supplement includes titles overlooked in the Bibliography Second Edition, plus works written before the 1981 cut-off date but published later, including works published for the first time in book form such as the original text of Oscar Wilde's *The Picture of Dorian Gray*, posthumous works (the diaries of Christopher Isherwood and Joe Orton), unexpurgated editions (James Jones' *From Here to Eternity*), and newly translated classics (e.g. Marcilio Ficino's *Alcibiades the Schoolboy*; the letters of Marcus Aurelius; John Henry Mackay's novel *Fenny Skaller*). The current study should be regarded not as a separate work but rather as a second, supplementary volume containing additional material. The two volumes together constitute a preliminary guide to classic (i.e. pre-1980's, pre-AIDS) gay and bisexual male literature.

A ReQueered Tales Original Publication.

Like People in History
Felice Picano

Solid, cautious Roger Sansarc and flamboyant, mercurial Alistair Dodge are second cousins who become lifelong friends when they first meet as nine-year-old boys in 1954. Their lives constantly intersect at crucial moments in their personal histories as each discovers his own unique – and uniquely gay – identity. Their complex, tumultuous, and madcap relationship endures against 40 years of history and their involvement with the handsome model, poet, and decorated Vietnam vet Matt Loguidice, whom they both love. Picano chronicles and celebrates gay life and subculture over the last half of the twentieth century: from the legendary 1969 gathering at Woodstock to the legendary parties at Fire Island Pines in the 1970s, from Malibu Beach in its palmiest surfer days to San Francisco during its gayest era, from the cities and jungles of South Vietnam during the war to Manhattan's Greenwich Village and Upper East Side during the 1990s AIDS war.

In a book that could have been written only by one who lived it and survived to tell, Picano weaves a powerful saga of four decades in the lives of two men and their lovers, relatives, friends, and enemies. Tragic, comic, sexy, and romantic, filled with varied and colorful characters, *Like People in History* is both extraordinarily moving and supremely entertaining.

Winner of the Ferro-Grumley Award for Best Gay Novel in 1995, this 25th Anniversary edition for 2020 features a new foreword by Richard Burnett and an afterword by the author.

The Family of Max Desir
Robert Ferro

It was a family dealing with old values, acceptance and death. Max Desir loved his Italian roots and hearing his mother, Marie, recount tales of the old country. And he loved his American family, his father John a successful self-made businessman in New Jersey. As he came of age, Max discovered something else he loved – men – and met the love of his life in Italy. Now, at age 40, the family is split: Marie and his siblings accept Max and Nick as a stable, long-term couple but his father John does not. When a needlepoint family tree is to be hung at Christmas, it's too much for John. Then the spectre of death enters as Marie rapidly declines with brain cancer. Loyalties divided, acceptance of family is re-examined.

In this beautiful, haunting tale, told in Robert Ferro's clear, impassioned narrative, he created a classic. "An honest, eloquent and entirely original novel ... at once realistic and mythological, intensely personal and public ... a triumph," opined Edmund White.

Originally published in 1983, this new edition includes a 2019 foreword by fellow author and friend Felice Picano.

Mountain Climbing in Sheridan Square
Stan Leventhal

A series of discrete episodes among friends provide snapshots of one gay man's life. There are parties, concerts, dinners with everyday life – and death – interwoven in the rich story-telling. An actress, a painter, a set designer, a writer – all sweating and surviving in Manhattan, all scoring their first successes. Part autobiography and part documentary, artfully written, it details the lives of these creative people. Young and professional, they know there is more to life than money. There is trust and the sort of love that trades in deeds of kindness.

Leventhal's debut novel was welcomed warmly garnering a Lambda Literary Awards Finalist in 1988, this new edition features a 2020 foreword by Christopher Bram.

Steam
Jay B. Laws

San Francisco was once a city of music and laughter, of parties and bathhouses, when days held promise and nights, romance. But now something sinister haunts its streets and alleyways, something that crept in with the fog to seek a cruel revenge... Flint, owner of a once thriving bathhouse, ravaged by a disease that has no cure, gives himself over to the evil lurking in the steam. Dying men get tickets that say Admit One, hoping for release, only to be dragged into the maelstrom. David, a writer of gay porn, finds himself writing another kind of story. Eddie disappears from his hospital bed, leaving slime and mold. Meanwhile, Bobby is searching for his lover, lost in the same horror.

In this new edition, Jay's brother Gary D. Laws quotes extensively from the author. Set at the height of the AIDS crisis, it is an allegory which chronicles the early days of the epidemic including the glittery discos of the seventies and an ominous abandoned gay bathhouse. Noted author Hal Bodner adds his voice and further context into a 1980s that suddenly turned dark and dangerous.

This classic gay horror suspense tale was first published in 1991. It was nominated for Best First Novel by the Lambda Literary Awards.

Mysteries from ReQueered Tales

Body to Dye For
Grant Michaels

A Stan Kraychik Mystery, Book 1 – Stan "Vannos" Kraychik isn't your everyday Boston hairdresser. Co-owner of Snips Salon with best bud (and occasional nemesis) Nicole, thought this day was an ordinary one. A delivery van backed into the salon's rear driveway and accidentally spilled gallons of conditioner, leaving Stan (and hunky Roger) embracing in a gooey mess trying to staunch the flow, with little success as they slid and slipped with Nicole watching on with rolling eyes. Later Roger is found murdered.

Grant Michaels' zany series of adventures starring Stan Kraychik garnered multiple Lambda Literary Awards including a 1991 nomination for Best Gay Mystery. For this 2019 edition, Carl Mesrobian reminisces about his brother Grant in an exclusive foreword, and Neil S. Plakcy provides an introduction of appreciation.

Let's Get Criminal
Lev Raphael

A Nick Hoffman / Academic Mystery, Book 1 – Nick Hoffman has everything he has ever wanted: a good teaching job, a nice house, and a solid relationship with his lover, Stefan Borowski, a brilliant novelist at the State University of Michigan. But when Perry Cross shows up, Nick's peace of mind is shattered. Not only does he have to share his office with the nefarious Perry, who managed to weasel his way into a tenured position without the right qualifications, he also discovers that Perry played a destructive role in Stefan's past. When Perry turns up dead, Nick wonders if Stefan might be involved, while the campus police force is wondering the same about Nick.

Originally published in 1996, this first book in the Nick Hoffman series is now back in print. This new edition contains a 2019 foreword by the author.

Sunday's Child
Edward O. Phillips

A Geoffry Chadwick Misadventure, Book 1 – Lawyer Geoffry Chadwick is 50, Canadian, single, gay and, after a brief struggle with a hustler who tries to shake him down, a murderer. Herein lies the device for this macabre, funny, first novel. Although Geoffry must dispose of the body – which he does by dropping off sections of it around town at night – the trauma of the murder affords him the opportunity to reminisce and ruminate: on the recent termination of his affair with a history teacher; on the not-so-recent deaths of his wife and daughter; on the alcoholism of his mother; on growing old; on being gay. The visit of a nephew and the New Year's festivities only serve to intensify his thoughts. Although Chadwick is abrasively disdainful early on, he is fascinating when he loosens up. Phillips keeps the reader hopping with throwaway quotations from Donne and scatological references and puns.

First published in 1981, and a Books in Canada First Novel nominee, this new edition contains a 2019 foreword by Alexander Inglis.

FreeForm
Jack Dickson

A Jas Anderson Thriller, Book 1 – A tough gay thriller set in the criminal underworld of Glasgow, Scotland. In the derelict inner-city of Glasgow's Dennistoun, *FreeForm* introduces a tough gay cop, Detective-Sergeant Jas Anderson. A violent anti-hero, suspended from duty for assault, Jas is the natural suspect when his lover is found brutally murdered. Now on the run and struggling to clear his name, Jas uncovers Leigh's involvement in a blackmail ring, and even his lover's identity becomes confused. Film-noir in inspiration, vividly characterised, and authentically exposing the raw nerves of Thatcherite Britain, *FreeForm* is pure suspense to it's final pulse-pounding closing pages.

Originally published in 1998, this new edition includes a 2019 foreword by Clive King.

In The Game
Nikki Baker

When businesswoman Virginia Kelly meets her old college chum Bev Johnson for drinks late one night, Bev confides that her lover, Kelsey, is seeing another woman. Ginny had picked up that gossip months ago, but she is shocked when the next morning's papers report that Kelsey was found murdered behind the very bar where Ginny and Bev had met. Worried that her friend could be implicated, Ginny decides to track down Kelsey's killer and contacts a lawyer, Susan Coogan. Susan takes an immediate, intense liking to Ginny, complicating Ginny's relationship with her live-in lover. Meanwhile Ginny's inquiries heat up when she learns the Feds suspected Kelsey of embezzling from her employer.

Nikki Baker is the first African-American author in the lesbian mystery genre and her protagonist, Virginia Kelly is the first African-American lesbian detective in the genre. Interwoven into the narrative are observations on the intersectionality of being a woman, an African-American, and a lesbian in a "man's" world of finance and life in general.

First published to acclaim in 1991, this new edition features a 2020 foreword by the author.

If you enjoyed this book,
please help spread the word
by posting a short,
constructive review at
your favorite social media site
or e-book retailer.

We thank you, greatly,
for your support.

And don't be shy! Contact us!

For more information about current and future releases, please contact us:

E-mail: *requeeredtales@gmail.com*
Facebook (Like us!): www.facebook.com/ReQueeredTales/
Twitter: @ReQueered
Instagram: www.instagram.com/requeered
Web: www.ReQueeredTales.com
Blog: www.ReQueeredTales.com/blog
Mailing list (Subscribe for latest news): http://bit.ly/RQTJoin

www.ingramcontent.com/pod-product-compliance
Lightning Source LLC
Chambersburg PA
CBHW030314100526
44592CB00010B/422